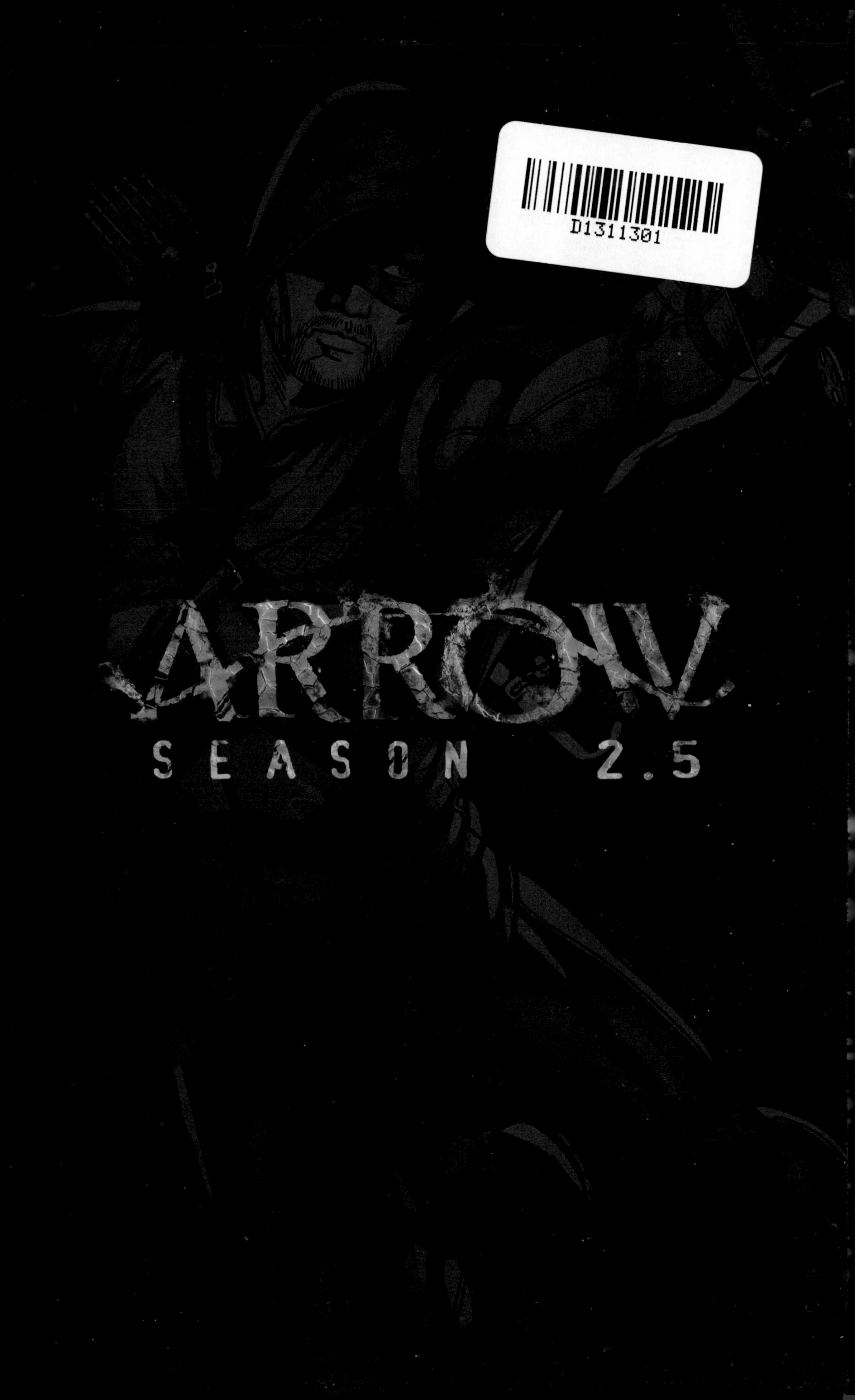
ARROW
SEASON 2.5

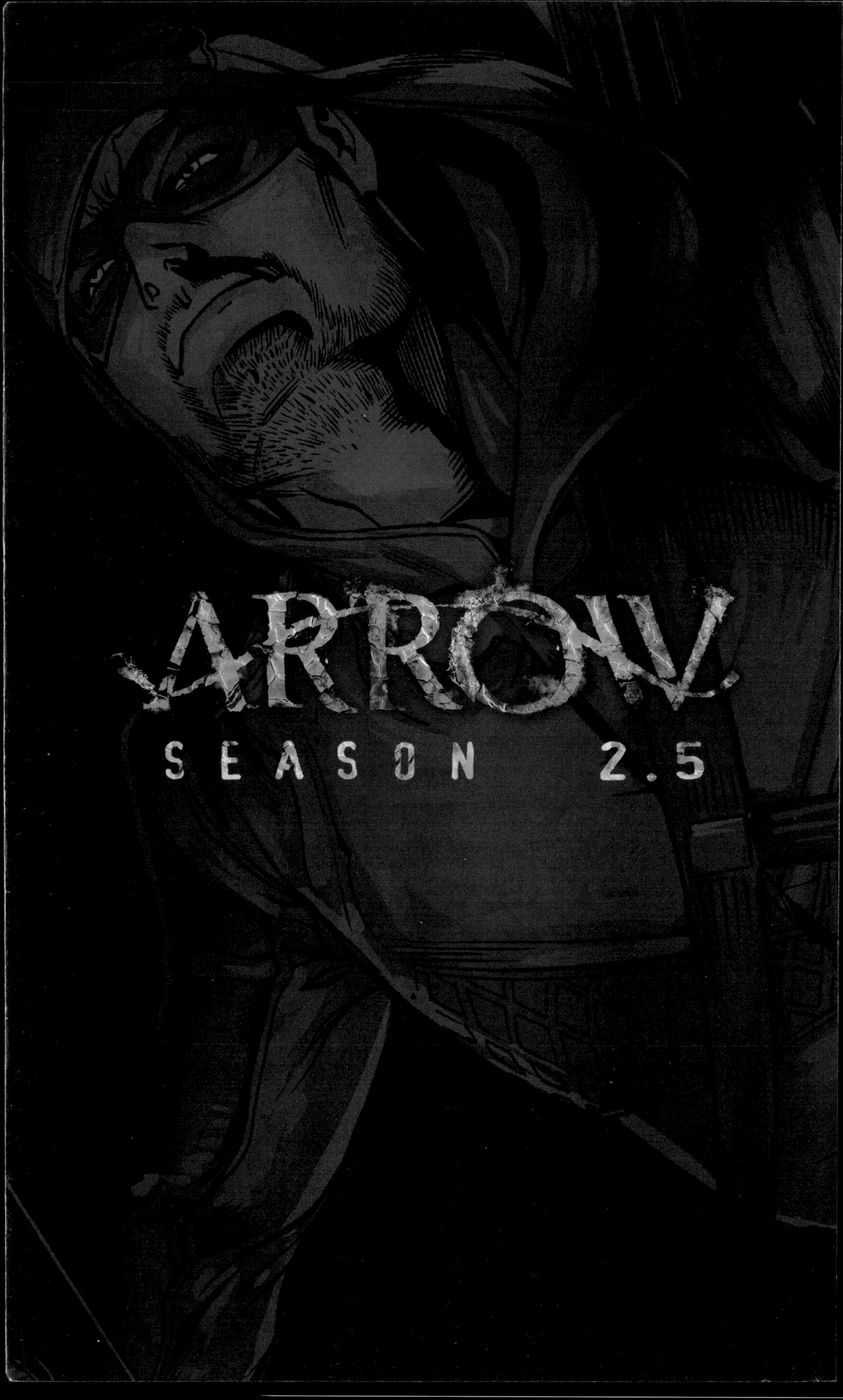
ARROW
SEASON 2.5

BOOK 1
BLOOD
Script: Marc Guggenheim
Brian Ford Sullivan
Keto Shimizu
Art: Joe Bennett
Craig Yeung
Jack Jadson
Neil Edwards
Beni Lobel
Angel Hernandez
Elena Casagrande
Rod Reis

BOOK 2
SUICIDE SQUAD:
CRISIS IN KAHNDAQ
Script: Keto Shimizu
& Marc Guggenheim
Art: Szymon Kudranski

BOOK 3
GREEN
Script: Marc Guggenheim
& Brian Ford Sullivan
Pencils: Joe Bennett
Inks: Craig Yeung

Colors by Jim Charalampidis
Letters by Deron Bennett

ALEX ANTONE Editor–Original Series BRITTANY HOLZHERR Assistant Editor–Original Series JEB WOODARD Group Editor LIZ ERICKSON Editor DAMIAN RYLAND Publication Design

BOB HARRAS Senior VP – Editor-in-Chief, DC Comics

DIANE NELSON President DAN DIDIO and JIM LEE Co-Publishers GEOFF JOHNS Chief Creative Officer AMIT DESAI Senior VP – Marketing & Global Franchise Management NAIRI GARDINER Senior VP – Finance
SAM ADES VP – Digital Marketing BOBBIE CHASE VP – Talent Development MARK CHIARELLO Senior VP – Art, Design & Collected Editions JOHN CUNNINGHAM VP – Content Strategy ANNE DEPIES VP – Strategy Planning & Reporting
DON FALLETTI VP – Manufacturing Operations LAWRENCE GANEM VP – Editorial Administration & Talent Relations ALISON GILL Senior VP – Manufacturing & Operations HANK KANALZ Senior VP – Editorial Strategy & Administration
JAY KOGAN VP – Legal Affairs DEREK MADDALENA Senior VP – Sales & Business Development DAN MIRON VP – Sales Planning & Trade Development NICK NAPOLITANO VP – Manufacturing Administration
CAROL ROEDER VP – Marketing EDDIE SCANNELL VP – Mass Account & Digital Sales SUSAN SHEPPARD VP – Business Affairs COURTNEY SIMMONS Senior VP – Publicity & Communications JIM (SKI) SOKOLOWSKI VP – Comic Book Specialty & Newsstand Sales

ARROW SEASON 2.5

Published by DC Comics. Compilation Copyright © 2015 DC Comics. All Rights Reserved.

DC Comics, 4000 Warner Blvd., Burbank, CA 91522
A Warner Bros. Entertainment Company.
Printed by RR Donnelley, Owensville, MO, USA. 8/28/15. First Printing.
ISBN: 978-1-4012-5748-4

Library of Congress Cataloging-in-Publication Data

Guggenheim, Marc.
Arrow season 2.5 / Marc Guggenheim, writer ; Joe Bennett and Craig Yeung, artists.
pages cm
ISBN 978-1-4012-5748-4 (paperback)
1. Graphic novels. I. Bennett, Joe, 1968- illustrator. II. Yeung, Craig, illustrator. III. Title.
PN6728.G725G86 2015
741.5'973—dc23
2015014142

INTRODUCTION
by *ARROW* Executive Producer, MARC GUGGENHEIM

Twenty-three episodes of television per season.

You'd think that would be enough.

The truth is, however, that the amazingly talented *Arrow* writing staff—upon whose coattails I comfortably ride—generates much more story for Oliver and his merry band than we can comfortably fit into the roughly sixteen hours (sans commercials) that make up a season of television.

Moreover, crime in Starling City does not take a vacation even when the writers do. Team Arrow does not become frozen in amber at the conclusion of whatever season-ending calamity the city might face. Life goes on for our characters even after the season finale fades to its end title card.

This is that story.

To be specific and fair, this is the story of what happened to the characters of *Arrow* between Seasons Two and Three. (Hence our insanely imaginative title, "Season 2.5.") If for some reason you watched Season One but missed Season Two (for shame! for shame!) I doubt you'll be muchly confused. Now, if for some reason you've never seen any episode of *Arrow* ever and bought this book anyway—which, I imagine is wholly possible, because we put a shirtless Stephen Amell on the cover—I still think you'll be able to follow along.

That said, if you've watched *Arrow* Season Three in its semi-entirety, I think that's where this book really shines. Ever since the first *Arrow* tie-in comic that Andrew Kreisberg, Geoff Johns and I wrote in advance of San Diego Comic-Con 2012, we have operated under the rule that these comic book adventures of Team Arrow are—to use the geek parlance—"canon." These stories "really happened" within the universe of our show. As such, I—aided and abetted by my cowriters, Keto Shimizu and Brian Ford Sullivan—was able to use this series to answer some questions that we didn't have the screen time to answer in Season Three: How and why did Roy Harper receive his Arsenal uniform? The answers lie herein. Why did Malcolm Merlyn target Sara Lance for death? Our second arc—"Green"— holds the answer. How did Oliver realize that he had romantic feelings for Felicity? You're about to find out. Is Felicity ever going to get that bottle of Lafite Rothschild 1982 Oliver promised her waaaay back in Episode 11? Believe it or not, I got asked that question a lot on Twitter... #stopaskingme

I don't have enough space here to document all the points of connection between this graphic novel and the television series, but believe me when I tell you that they are manifold. Better yet, don't believe me and read for yourself.

But before you dive in—if I haven't already lost you—I'd like to use this space to thank a few critical people who made this collection of stories possible. I've already mentioned Keto and Brian—members of the *Arrow* writing staff, both. Keto masterminded the Suicide Squad story, which buffers the two *Arrow* story arcs. Brian saved my bacon multiple times when my obligations to the live-action incarnation of *Arrow* threatened to put this book behind schedule.

The gorgeousness that is this book's art comes to you courtesy of the amazingly talented Joe Bennett, Chris Yeung, Jim Charalampdis and Szymon Kudranski. These stories were originally published as biweekly digital comics over the course of an entire year. I cannot overstate how rare it is for any comic to hit such a schedule without a single missed day. That's all due to the talent and hard work of these fine gentlemen...

...and one other: Alex Antone. Our editor extraordinaire, who somehow managed to get seven clocks to chime all at once.

Finally, I want to give thanks to someone who made a thankless—but nevertheless critical—contribution to this project. Fidelity to the looks, costumes, logos, and props of the show was critical to this endeavor, and it would not have been possible without someone pulling copious reference materials from *Arrow's* 69 episodes. That sucker person was my gracious assistant, Nolan Dunbar.

This is to say nothing of the hundreds of hard-working men and women who work tirelessly and without fail to produce *Arrow* week in and week out. This book is dedicated to them.

Best,

MARC GUGGENHEIM
Burbank, California
July 2015

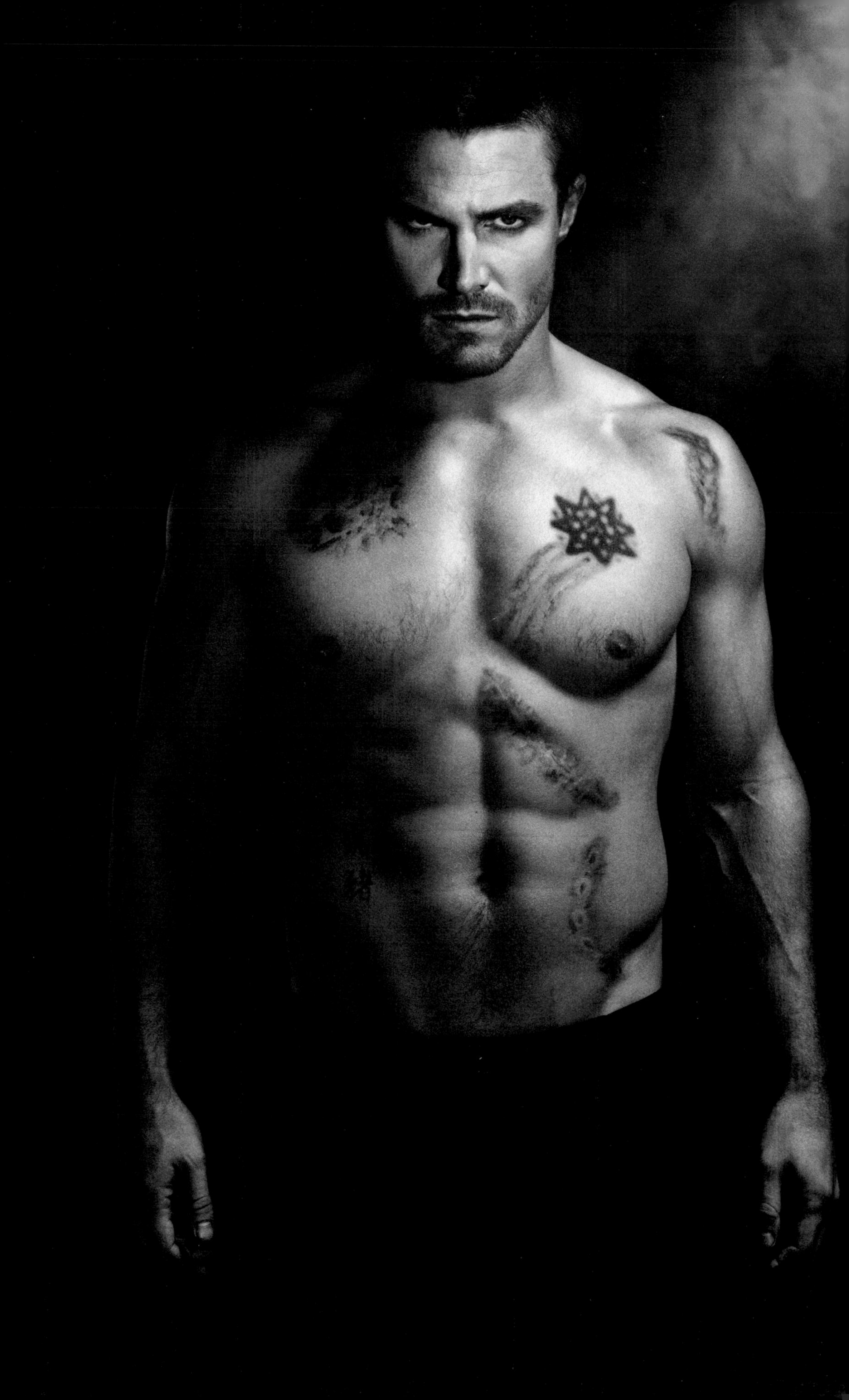

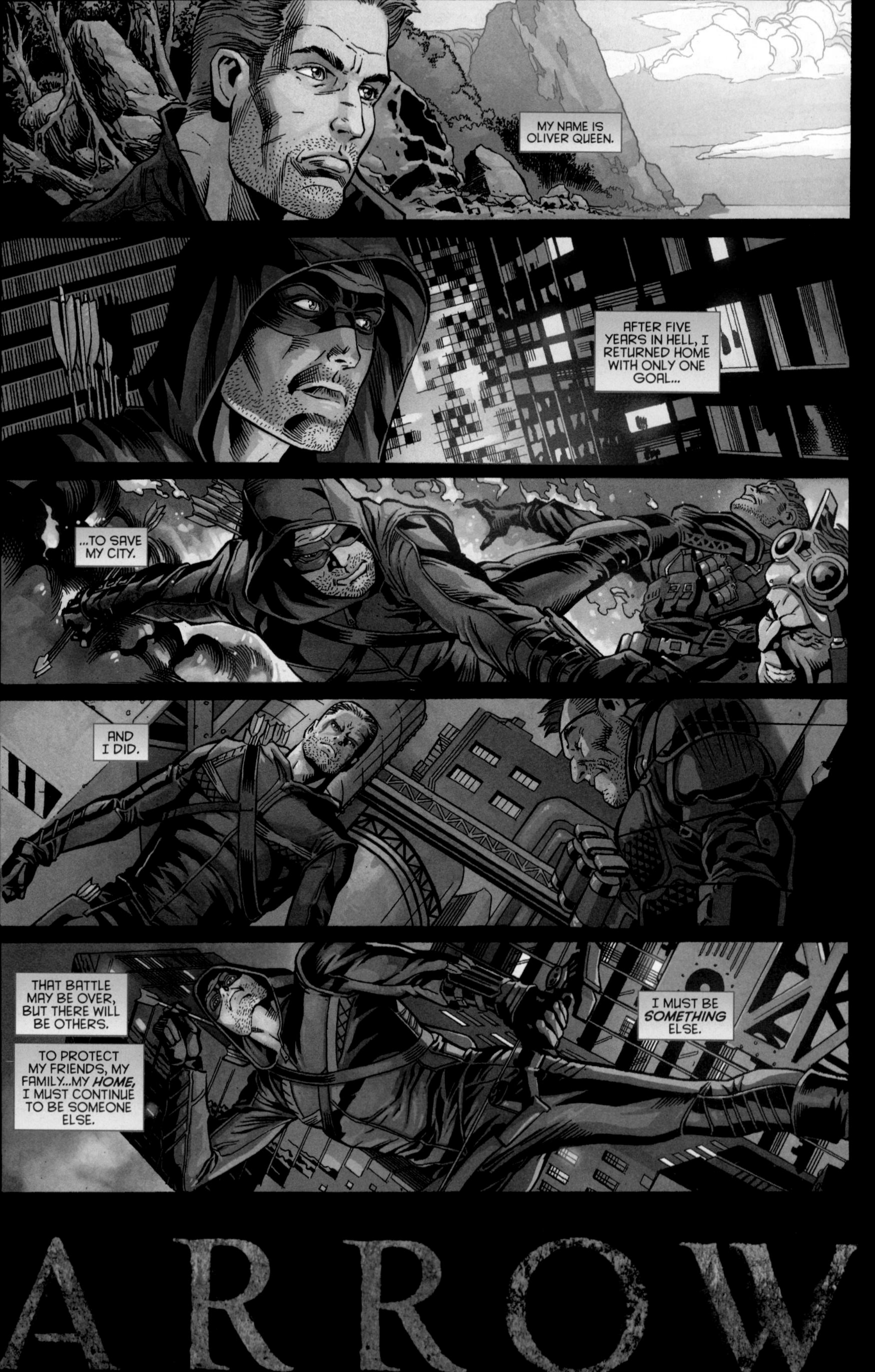
MY NAME IS OLIVER QUEEN.
AFTER FIVE YEARS IN HELL, I RETURNED HOME WITH ONLY ONE GOAL...
...TO SAVE MY CITY.
AND I DID.
THAT BATTLE MAY BE OVER, BUT THERE WILL BE OTHERS.
TO PROTECT MY FRIENDS, MY FAMILY...MY *HOME,* I MUST CONTINUE TO BE SOMEONE ELSE.
I MUST BE *SOMETHING* ELSE.
ARROW

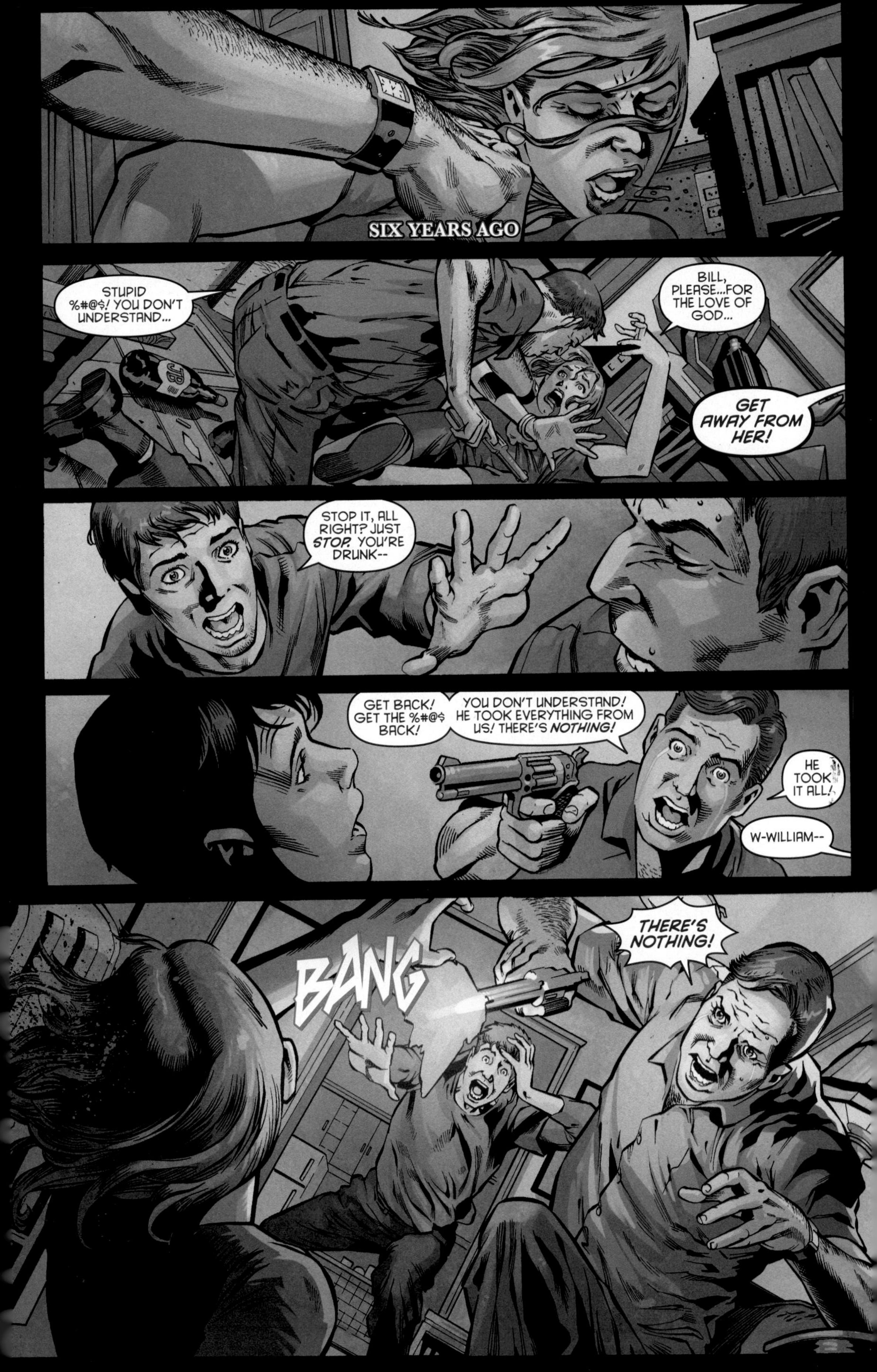
SIX YEARS AGO
STUPID %#@$! YOU DON'T UNDERSTAND...
BILL, PLEASE...FOR THE LOVE OF GOD...
GET AWAY FROM HER!
STOP IT, ALL RIGHT? JUST STOP. YOU'RE DRUNK--
GET BACK! GET THE %#@$ BACK!
YOU DON'T UNDERSTAND! HE TOOK EVERYTHING FROM US! THERE'S NOTHING!
HE TOOK IT ALL!
W-WILLIAM--
THERE'S NOTHING!
BANG

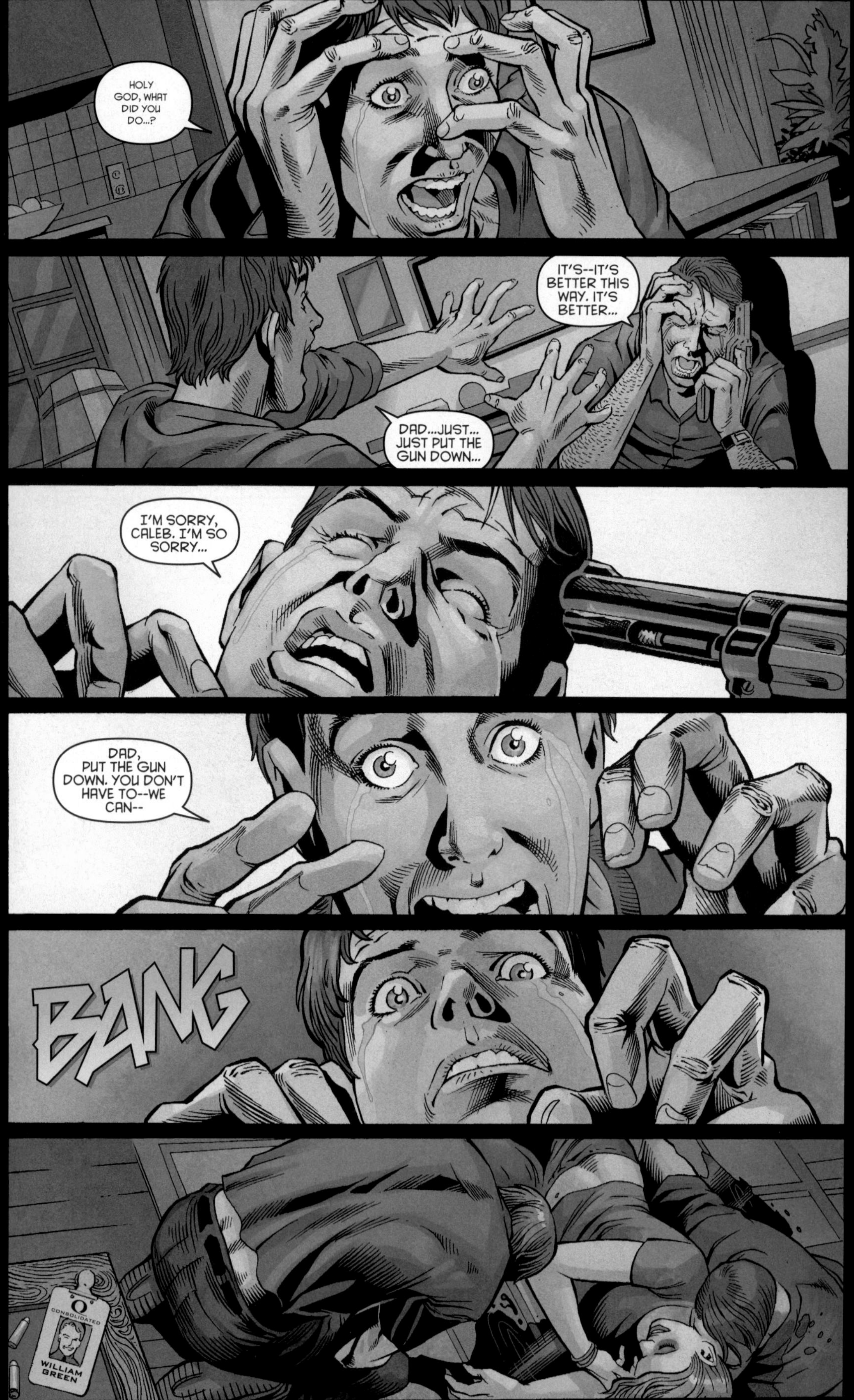
HOLY GOD, WHAT DID YOU DO...?
IT'S--IT'S BETTER THIS WAY. IT'S BETTER...
DAD...JUST... JUST PUT THE GUN DOWN...
I'M SORRY, CALEB. I'M SO SORRY...
DAD, PUT THE GUN DOWN. YOU DON'T HAVE TO--WE CAN--
BANG
CONSOLIDATED
WILLIAM GREEN

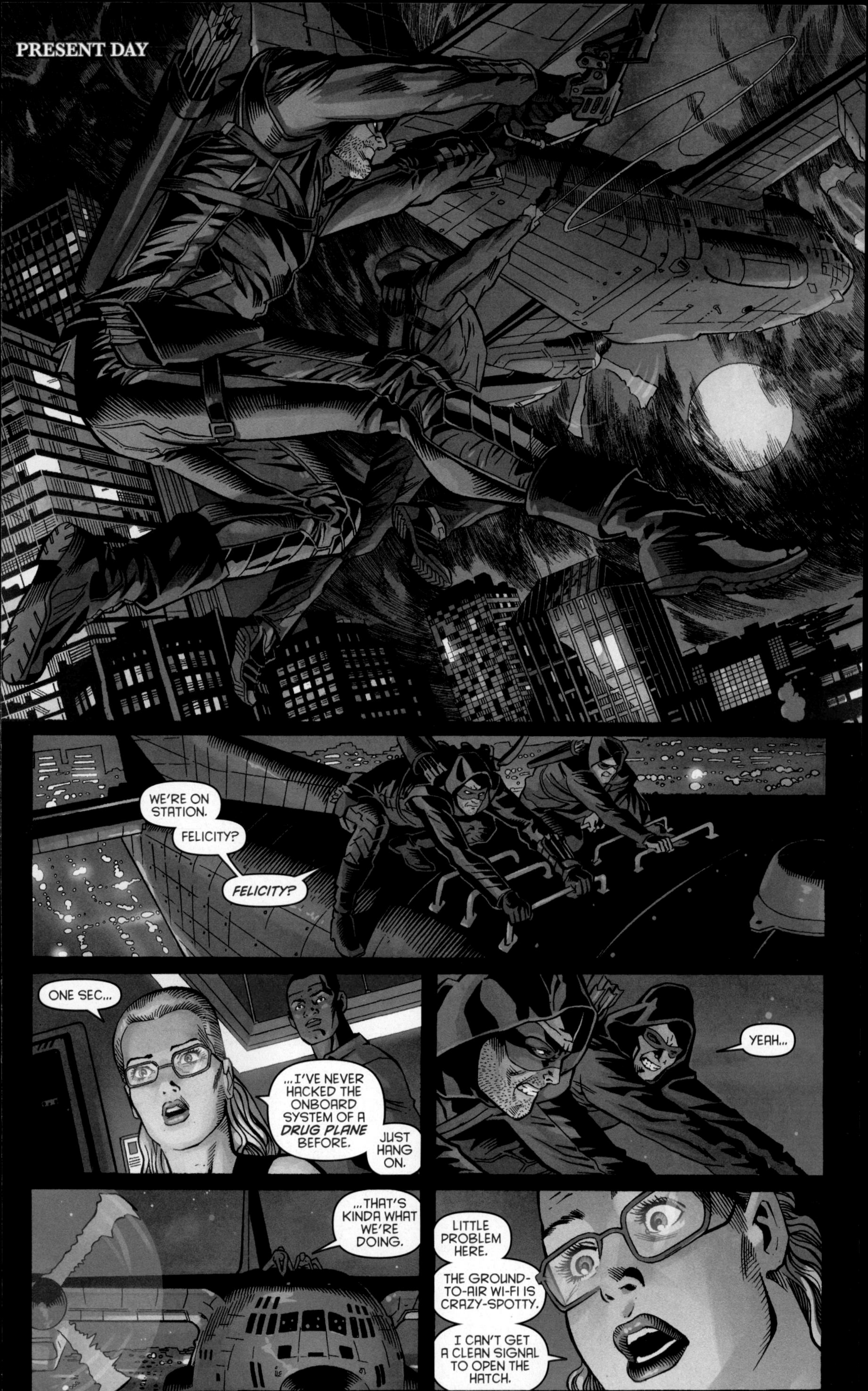
PRESENT DAY
WE'RE ON STATION.
FELICITY?
FELICITY?
ONE SEC...
...I'VE NEVER HACKED THE ONBOARD SYSTEM OF A *DRUG PLANE* BEFORE.
JUST HANG ON.
YEAH...
...THAT'S KINDA WHAT WE'RE DOING.
LITTLE PROBLEM HERE.
THE GROUND-TO-AIR WI-FI IS CRAZY-SPOTTY.
I CAN'T GET A CLEAN SIGNAL TO OPEN THE HATCH.

GO TO PLAN B, OLIVER.

WHAT'S PLAN B?

HOLD TIGHT.

SHUK

I *HATE* PLAN B...

YOU READY?

TO STOP HANGING ON TO THE OUTSIDE OF A PLANE GOING 100 MILES AN HOUR? LET'S SAY, "YES."

ON THREE. ONE...TWO...

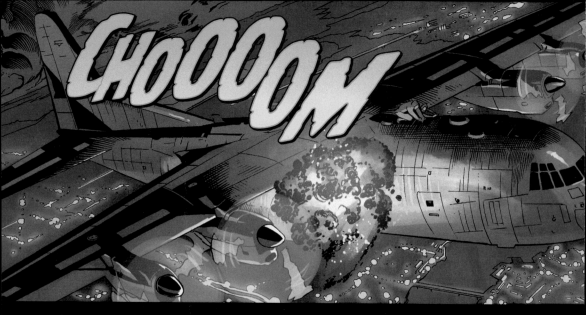

CHOOOOM

THREE!

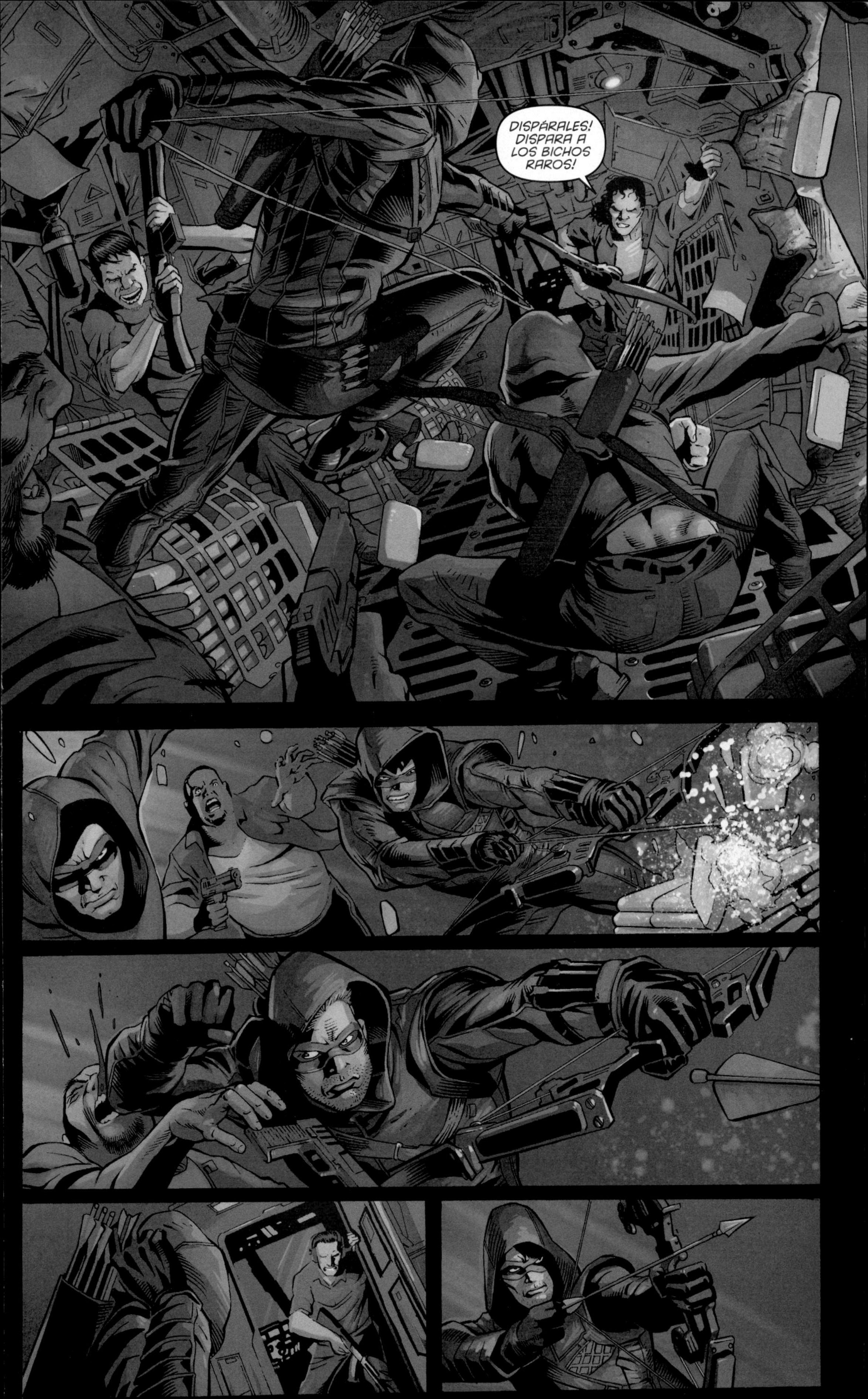
DISPÁRALES! DISPARA A LOS BICHOS RAROS!

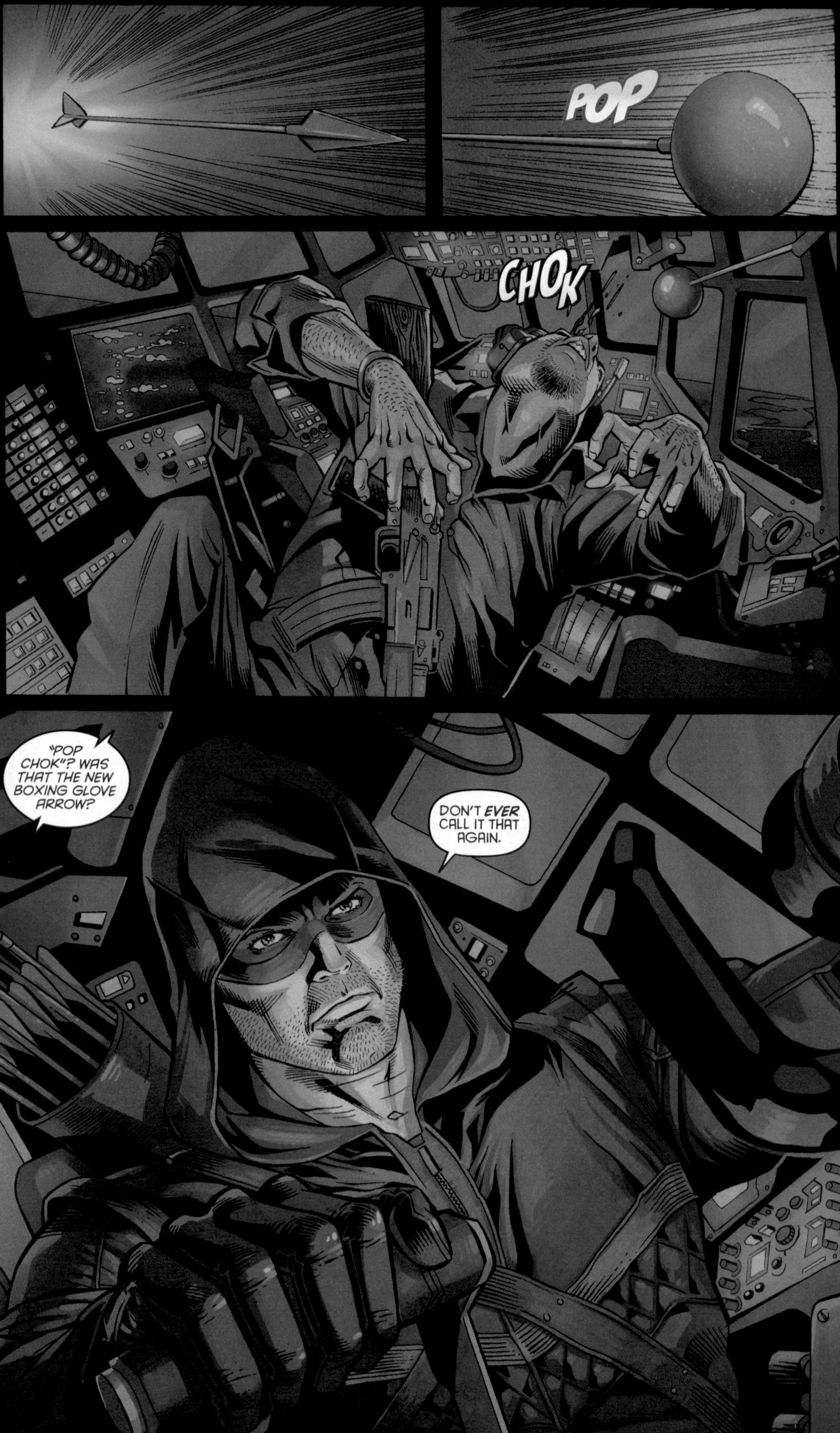
POP
CHOK
"POP CHOK"? WAS THAT THE NEW BOXING GLOVE ARROW?
DON'T EVER CALL IT THAT AGAIN.

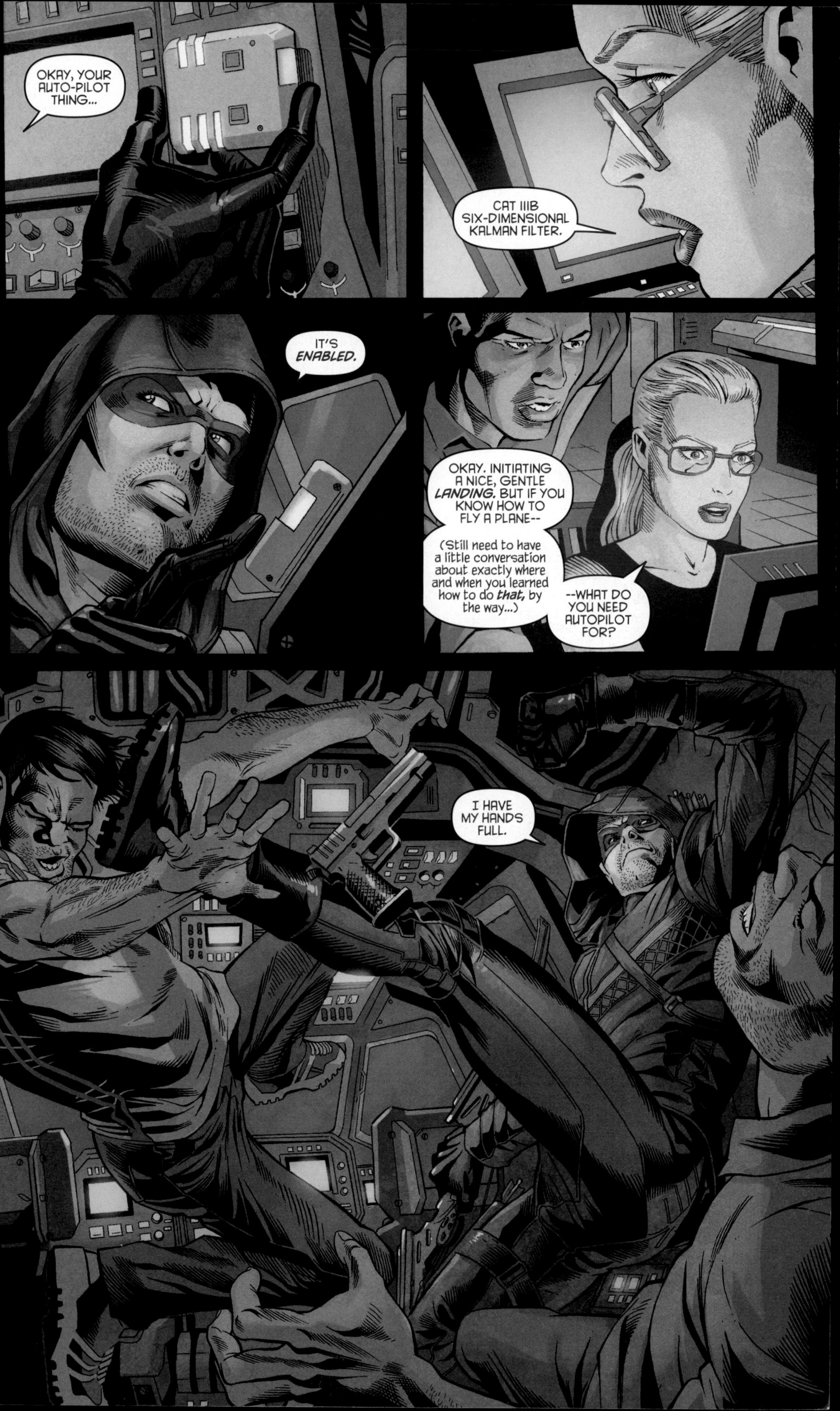
OKAY, YOUR AUTO-PILOT THING...
CAT IIIB SIX-DIMENSIONAL KALMAN FILTER.
IT'S *ENABLED.*
OKAY. INITIATING A NICE, GENTLE *LANDING.* BUT IF YOU KNOW HOW TO FLY A PLANE--
(Still need to have a little conversation about exactly where and when you learned how to do *that,* by the way...)
--WHAT DO YOU NEED AUTOPILOT FOR?
I HAVE MY HANDS FULL.

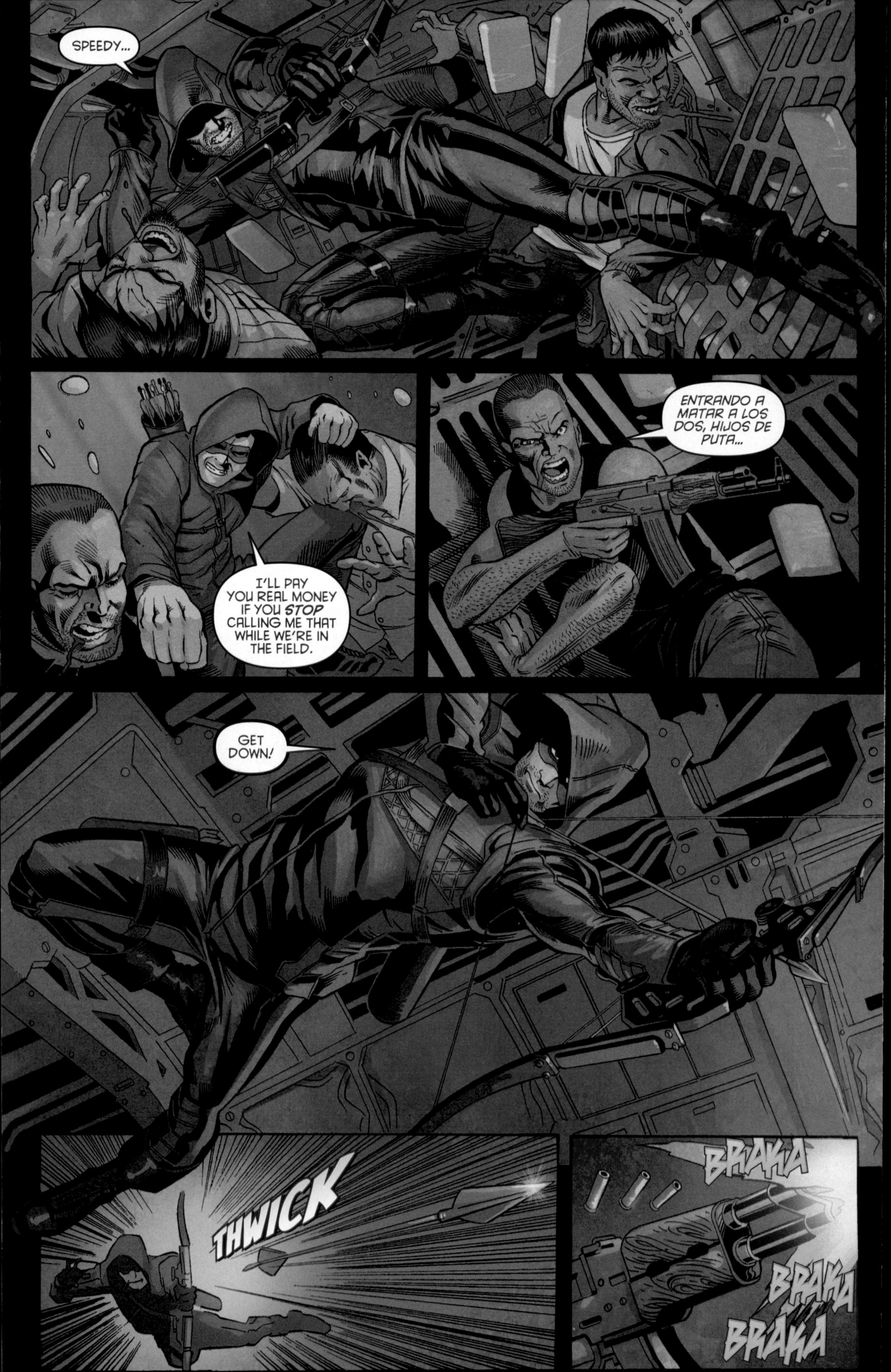
SPEEDY...
I'LL PAY YOU REAL MONEY IF YOU STOP CALLING ME THAT WHILE WE'RE IN THE FIELD.
ENTRANDO A MATAR A LOS DOS, HIJOS DE PUTA...
GET DOWN!
THWICK
BRAKA
BRAKA
BRAKA

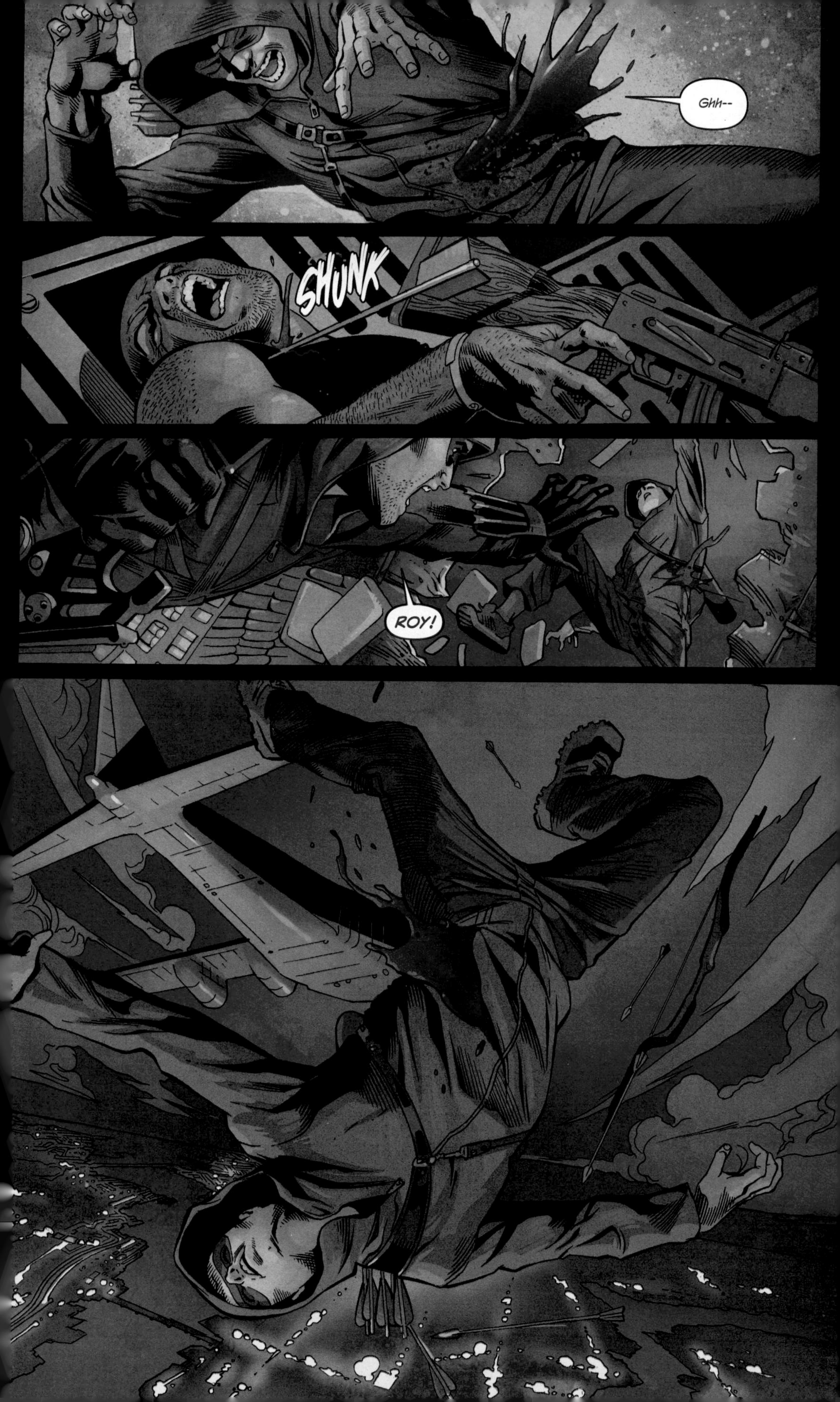
Ghh--
SHUNK
ROY!

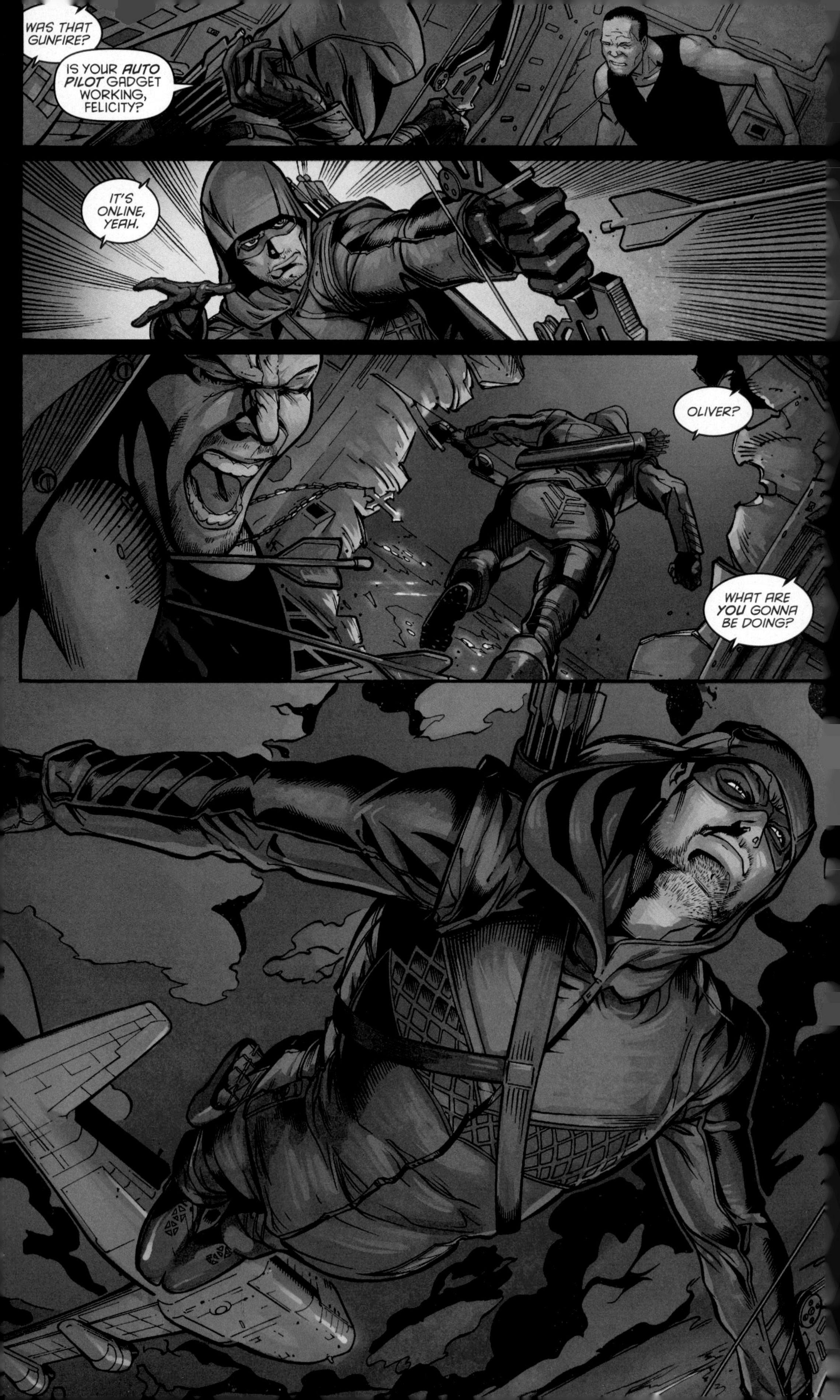
WAS THAT GUNFIRE?
IS YOUR AUTO PILOT GADGET WORKING, FELICITY?
IT'S ONLINE, YEAH.
OLIVER?
WHAT ARE YOU GONNA BE DOING?

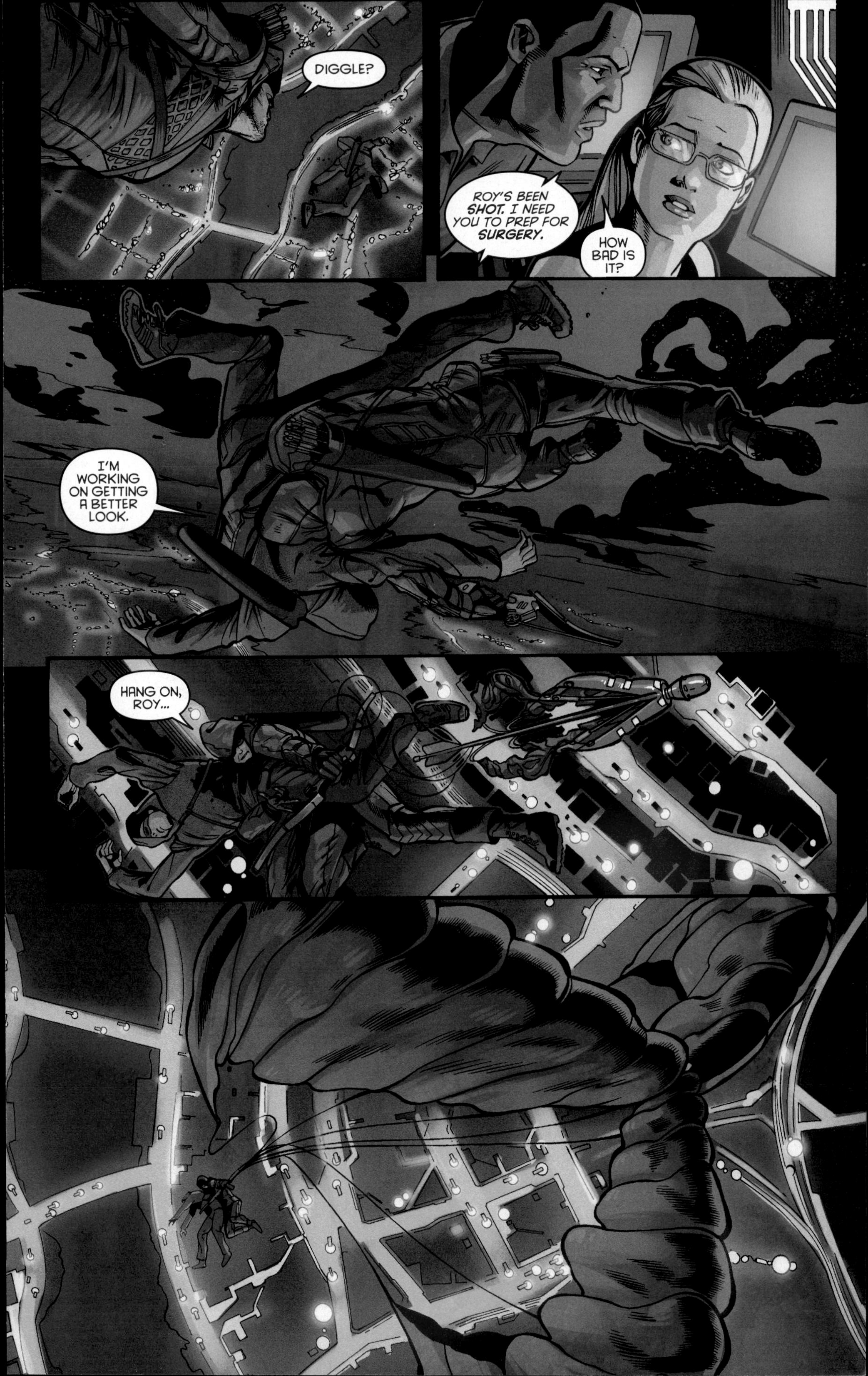
DIGGLE?
ROY'S BEEN SHOT. I NEED YOU TO PREP FOR SURGERY.
HOW BAD IS IT?
I'M WORKING ON GETTING A BETTER LOOK.
HANG ON, ROY...

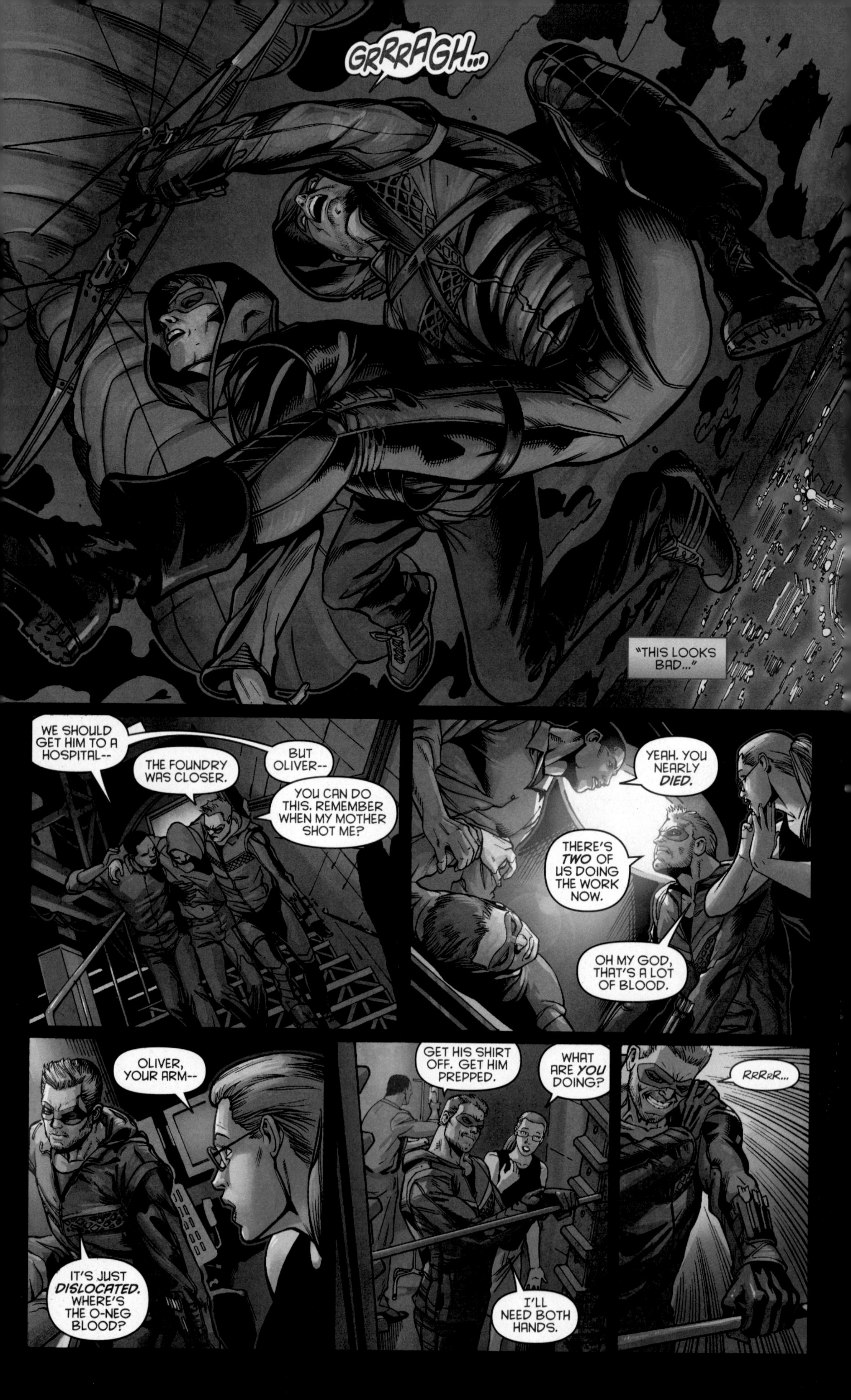
GRRRAGH...
"THIS LOOKS BAD..."
WE SHOULD GET HIM TO A HOSPITAL--
THE FOUNDRY WAS CLOSER.
BUT OLIVER--
YOU CAN DO THIS. REMEMBER WHEN MY MOTHER SHOT ME?
YEAH. YOU NEARLY DIED.
THERE'S TWO OF US DOING THE WORK NOW.
OH MY GOD, THAT'S A LOT OF BLOOD.
OLIVER, YOUR ARM--
IT'S JUST DISLOCATED. WHERE'S THE O-NEG BLOOD?
GET HIS SHIRT OFF. GET HIM PREPPED.
WHAT ARE YOU DOING?
I'LL NEED BOTH HANDS.
RRRRR...

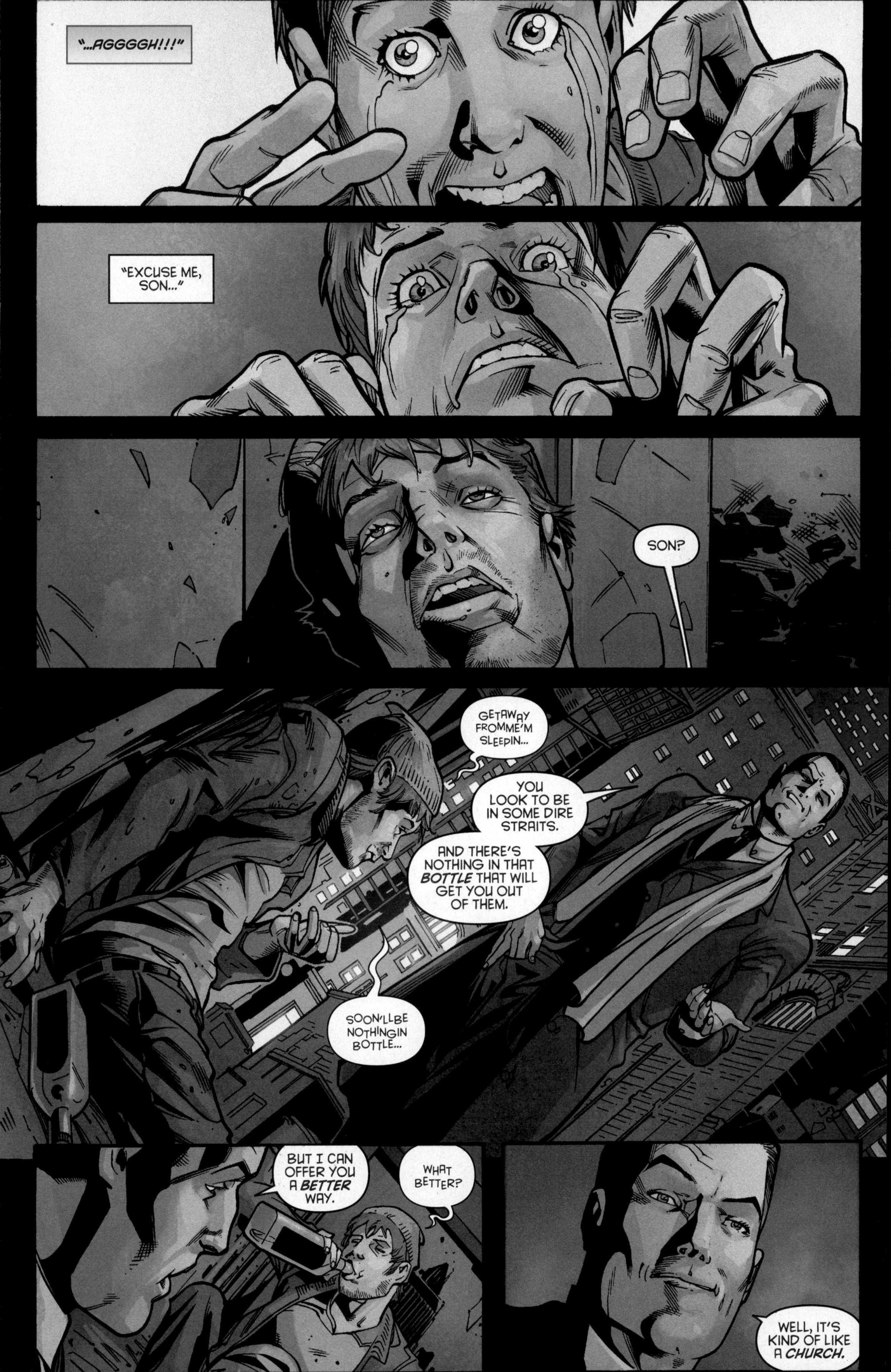
"...AGGGGH!!!"
"EXCUSE ME, SON..."
SON?
GETAWAY FROMME'M SLEEPIN...
YOU LOOK TO BE IN SOME DIRE STRAITS.
AND THERE'S NOTHING IN THAT BOTTLE THAT WILL GET YOU OUT OF THEM.
SOON'LLBE NOTHINGIN BOTTLE...
BUT I CAN OFFER YOU A BETTER WAY.
WHAT BETTER?
WELL, IT'S KIND OF LIKE A CHURCH.

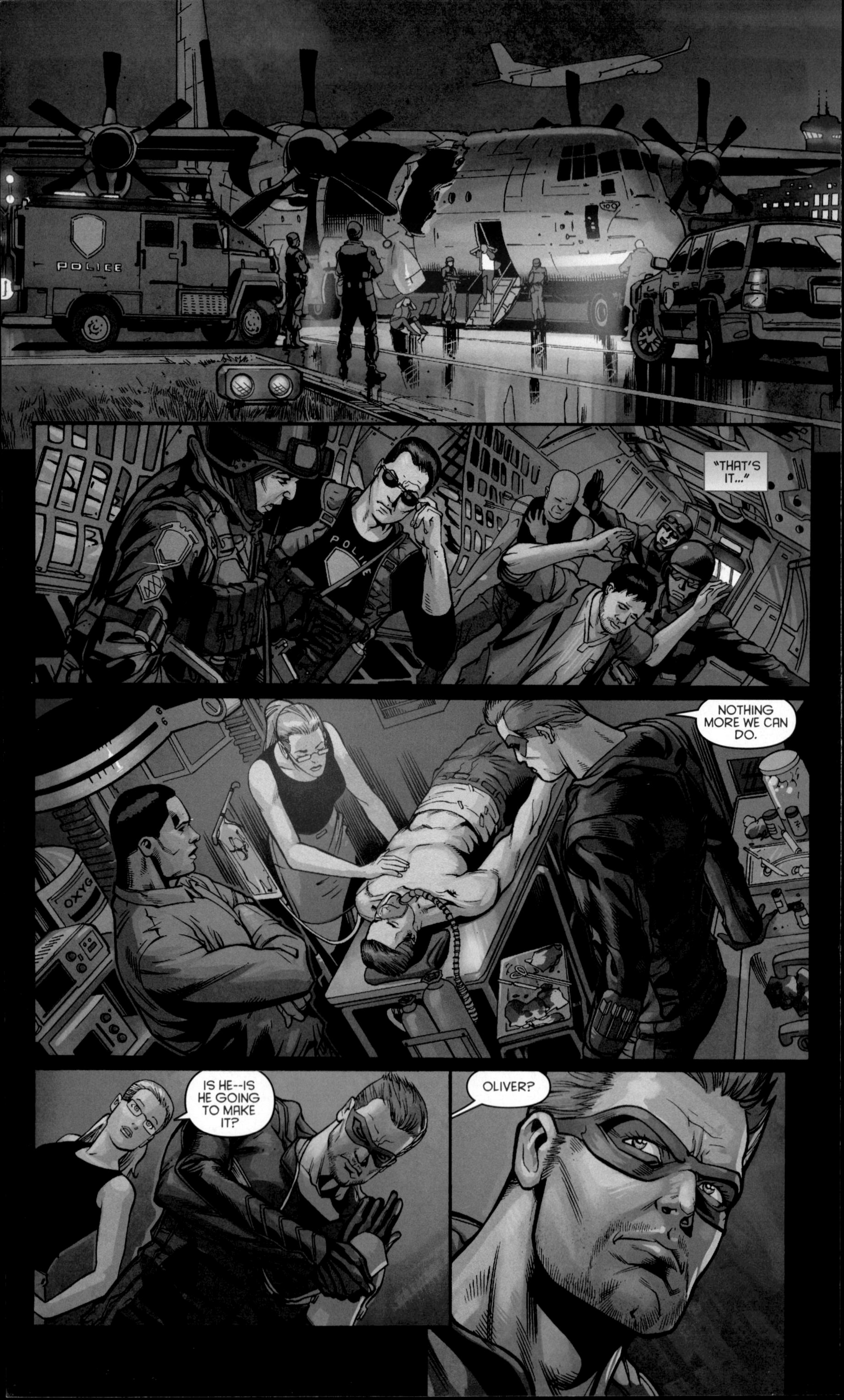
POLICE
POLICE
"THAT'S IT..."
NOTHING MORE WE CAN DO.
OXYG
IS HE--IS HE GOING TO MAKE IT?
OLIVER?

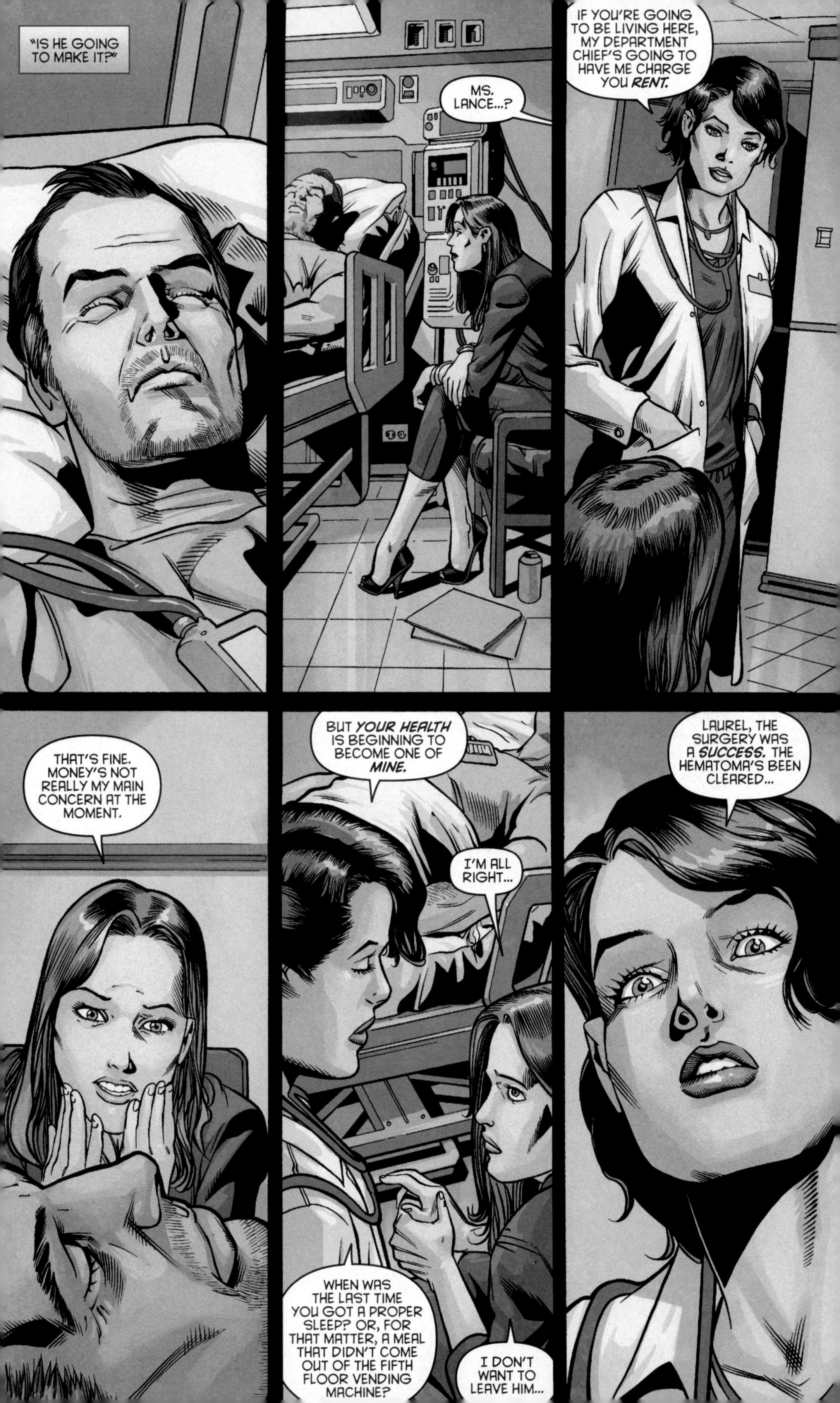

"IS HE GOING TO MAKE IT?"
MS. LANCE...?
IF YOU'RE GOING TO BE LIVING HERE, MY DEPARTMENT CHIEF'S GOING TO HAVE ME CHARGE YOU *RENT.*
THAT'S FINE. MONEY'S NOT REALLY MY MAIN CONCERN AT THE MOMENT.
BUT *YOUR HEALTH* IS BEGINNING TO BECOME ONE OF *MINE.*
I'M ALL RIGHT...
WHEN WAS THE LAST TIME YOU GOT A PROPER SLEEP? OR, FOR THAT MATTER, A MEAL THAT DIDN'T COME OUT OF THE FIFTH FLOOR VENDING MACHINE?
I DON'T WANT TO LEAVE HIM...
LAUREL, THE SURGERY WAS A *SUCCESS.* THE HEMATOMA'S BEEN CLEARED...

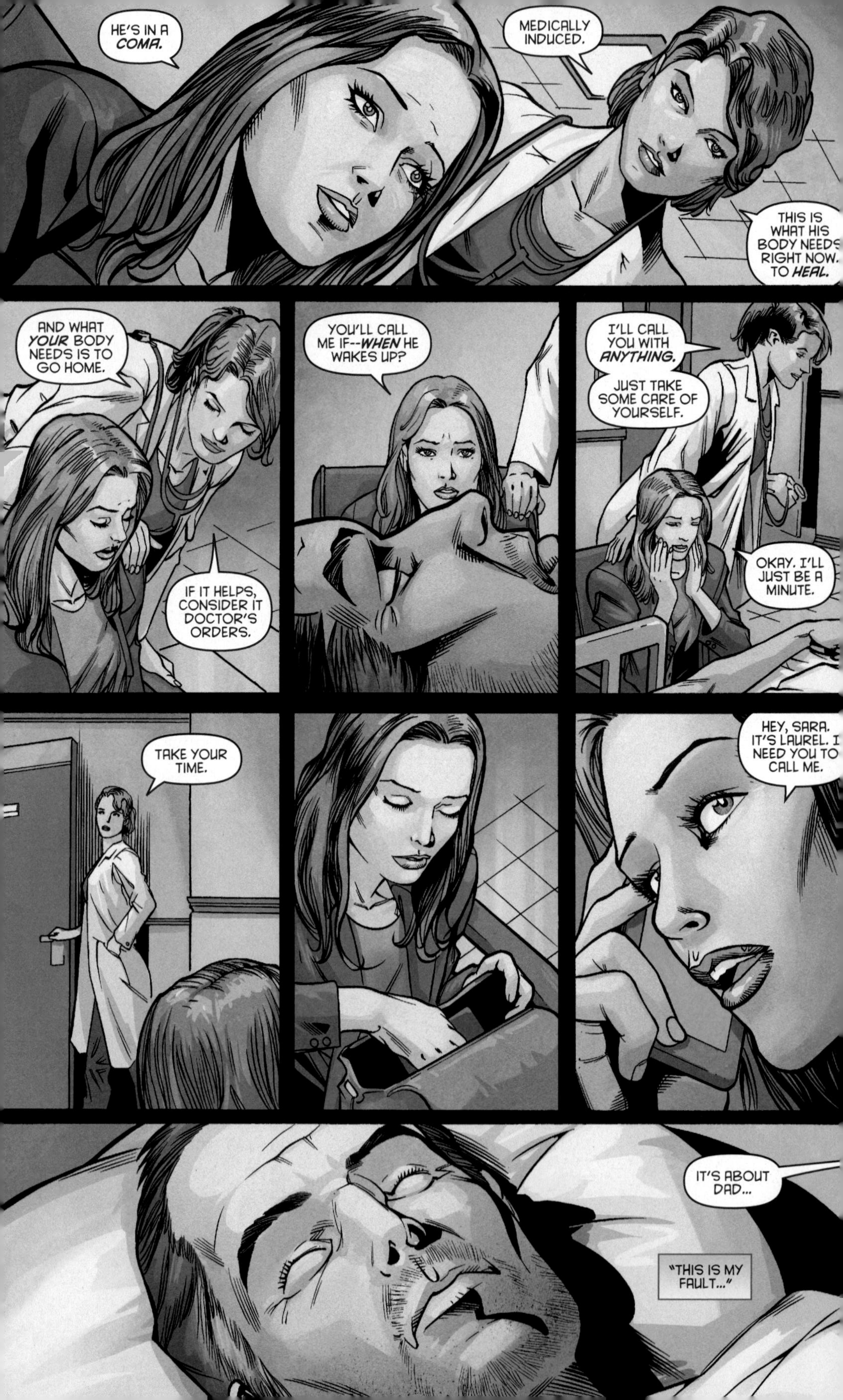
HE'S IN A COMA.
MEDICALLY INDUCED.
THIS IS WHAT HIS BODY NEEDS RIGHT NOW. TO HEAL.
AND WHAT YOUR BODY NEEDS IS TO GO HOME.
IF IT HELPS, CONSIDER IT DOCTOR'S ORDERS.
YOU'LL CALL ME IF--WHEN HE WAKES UP?
I'LL CALL YOU WITH ANYTHING.
JUST TAKE SOME CARE OF YOURSELF.
OKAY. I'LL JUST BE A MINUTE.
TAKE YOUR TIME.
HEY, SARA. IT'S LAUREL. I NEED YOU TO CALL ME.
IT'S ABOUT DAD...
"THIS IS MY FAULT..."

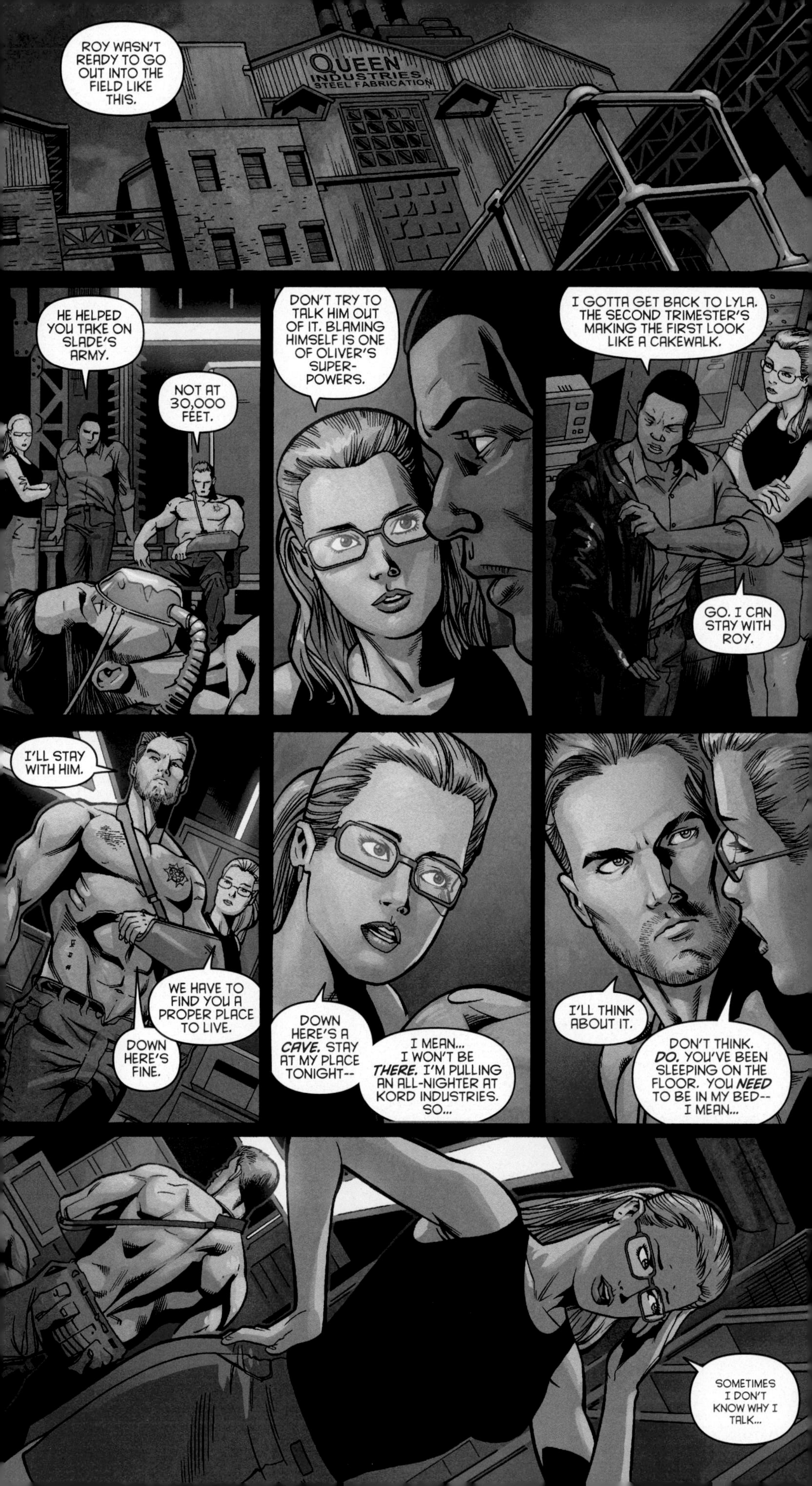
ROY WASN'T READY TO GO OUT INTO THE FIELD LIKE THIS.
QUEEN INDUSTRIES STEEL FABRICATION
HE HELPED YOU TAKE ON SLADE'S ARMY.
NOT AT 30,000 FEET.
DON'T TRY TO TALK HIM OUT OF IT. BLAMING HIMSELF IS ONE OF OLIVER'S SUPER-POWERS.
I GOTTA GET BACK TO LYLA. THE SECOND TRIMESTER'S MAKING THE FIRST LOOK LIKE A CAKEWALK.
GO. I CAN STAY WITH ROY.
I'LL STAY WITH HIM.
WE HAVE TO FIND YOU A PROPER PLACE TO LIVE.
DOWN HERE'S FINE.
DOWN HERE'S A *CAVE.* STAY AT MY PLACE TONIGHT--
I MEAN... I WON'T BE *THERE.* I'M PULLING AN ALL-NIGHTER AT KORD INDUSTRIES. SO...
I'LL THINK ABOUT IT.
DON'T THINK. *DO.* YOU'VE BEEN SLEEPING ON THE FLOOR. YOU *NEED* TO BE IN MY BED-- I MEAN...
SOMETIMES I DON'T KNOW WHY I TALK...

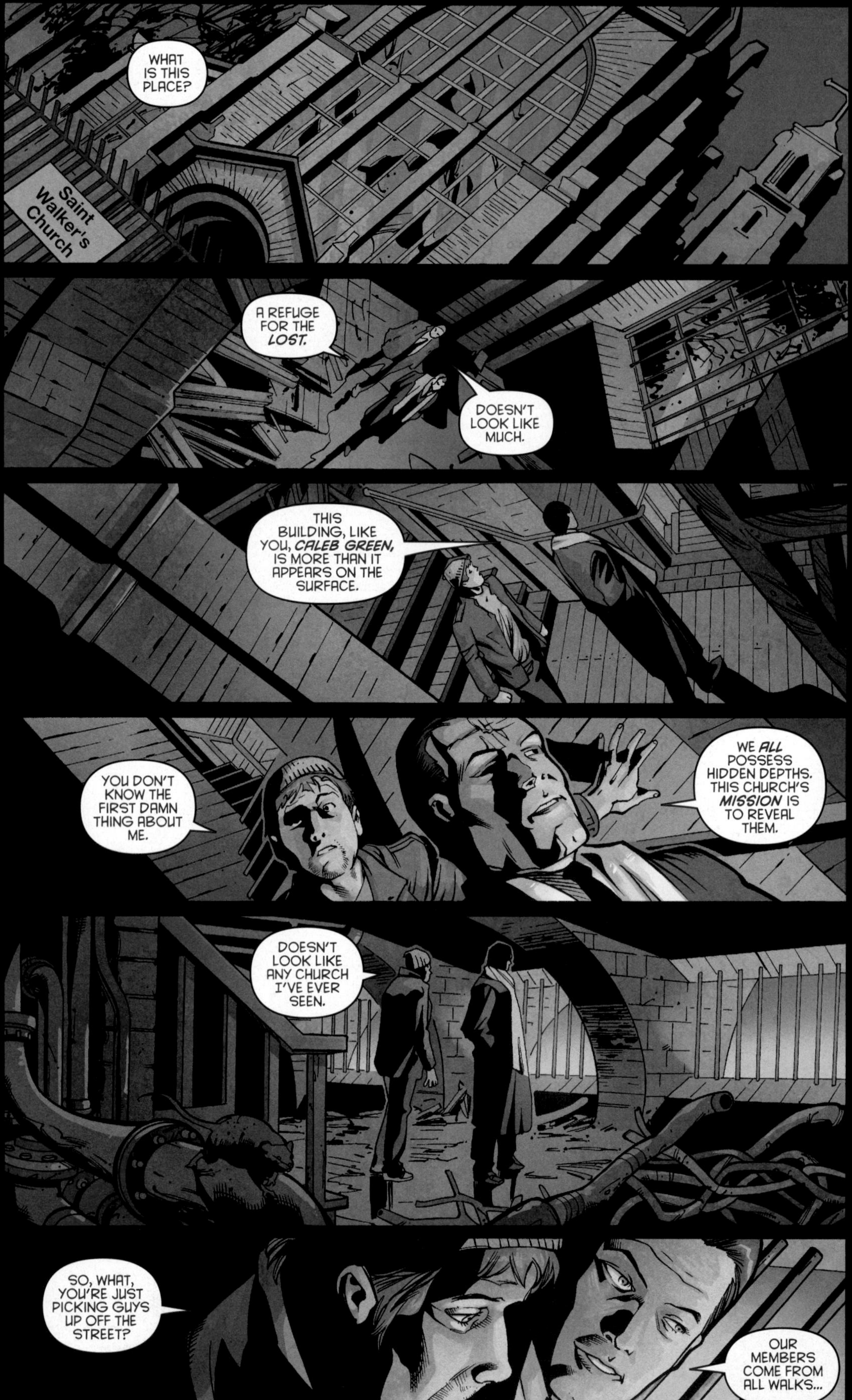
WHAT IS THIS PLACE?
Saint Walker's Church
A REFUGE FOR THE *LOST.*
DOESN'T LOOK LIKE MUCH.
THIS BUILDING, LIKE YOU, *CALEB GREEN,* IS MORE THAN IT APPEARS ON THE SURFACE.
YOU DON'T KNOW THE FIRST DAMN THING ABOUT ME.
WE *ALL* POSSESS HIDDEN DEPTHS. THIS CHURCH'S *MISSION* IS TO REVEAL THEM.
DOESN'T LOOK LIKE ANY CHURCH I'VE EVER SEEN.
SO, WHAT, YOU'RE JUST PICKING GUYS UP OFF THE STREET?
OUR MEMBERS COME FROM ALL WALKS...

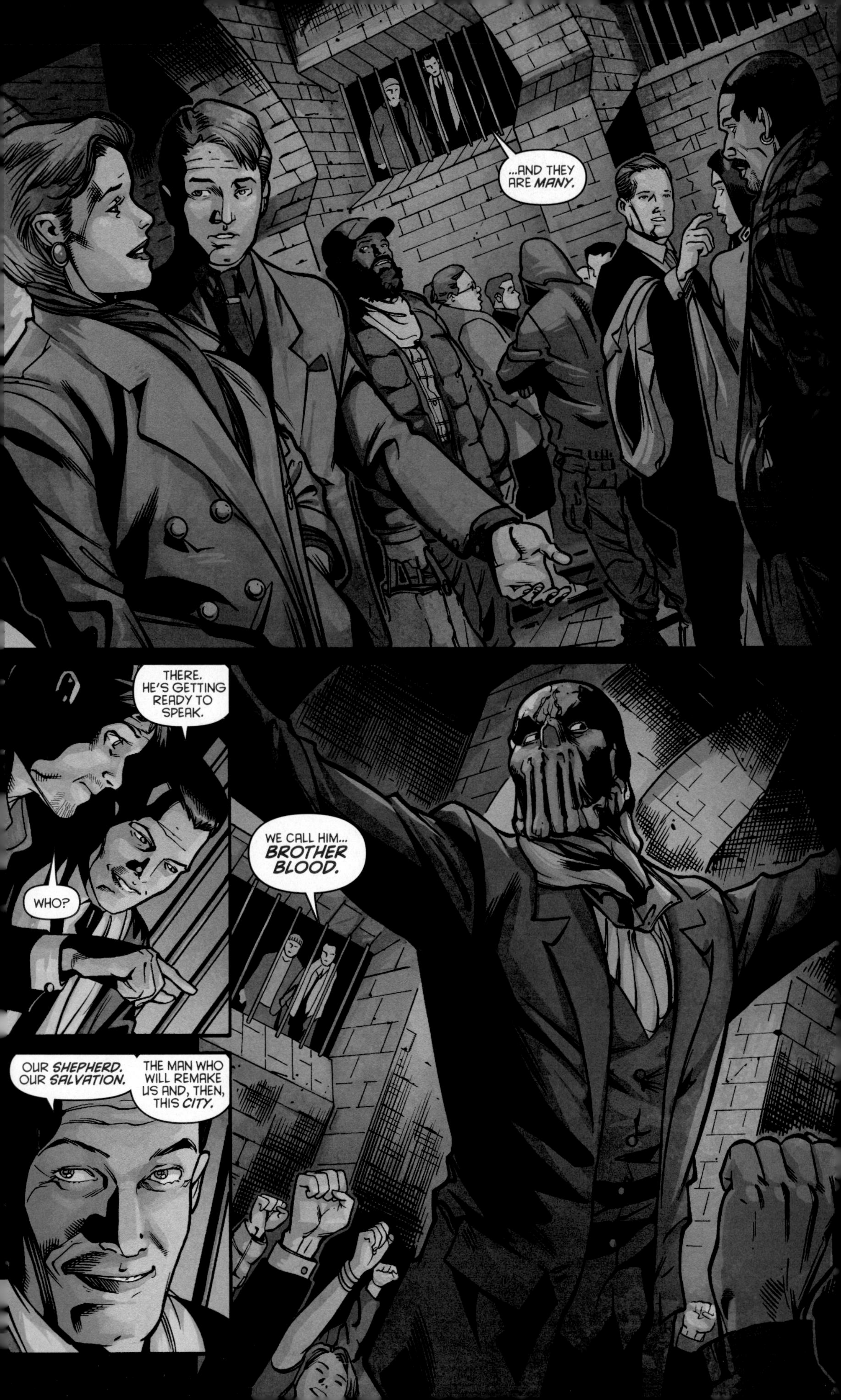
...AND THEY ARE MANY.
THERE. HE'S GETTING READY TO SPEAK.
WHO?
WE CALL HIM... BROTHER BLOOD.
OUR SHEPHERD. OUR SALVATION.
THE MAN WHO WILL REMAKE US AND, THEN, THIS CITY.

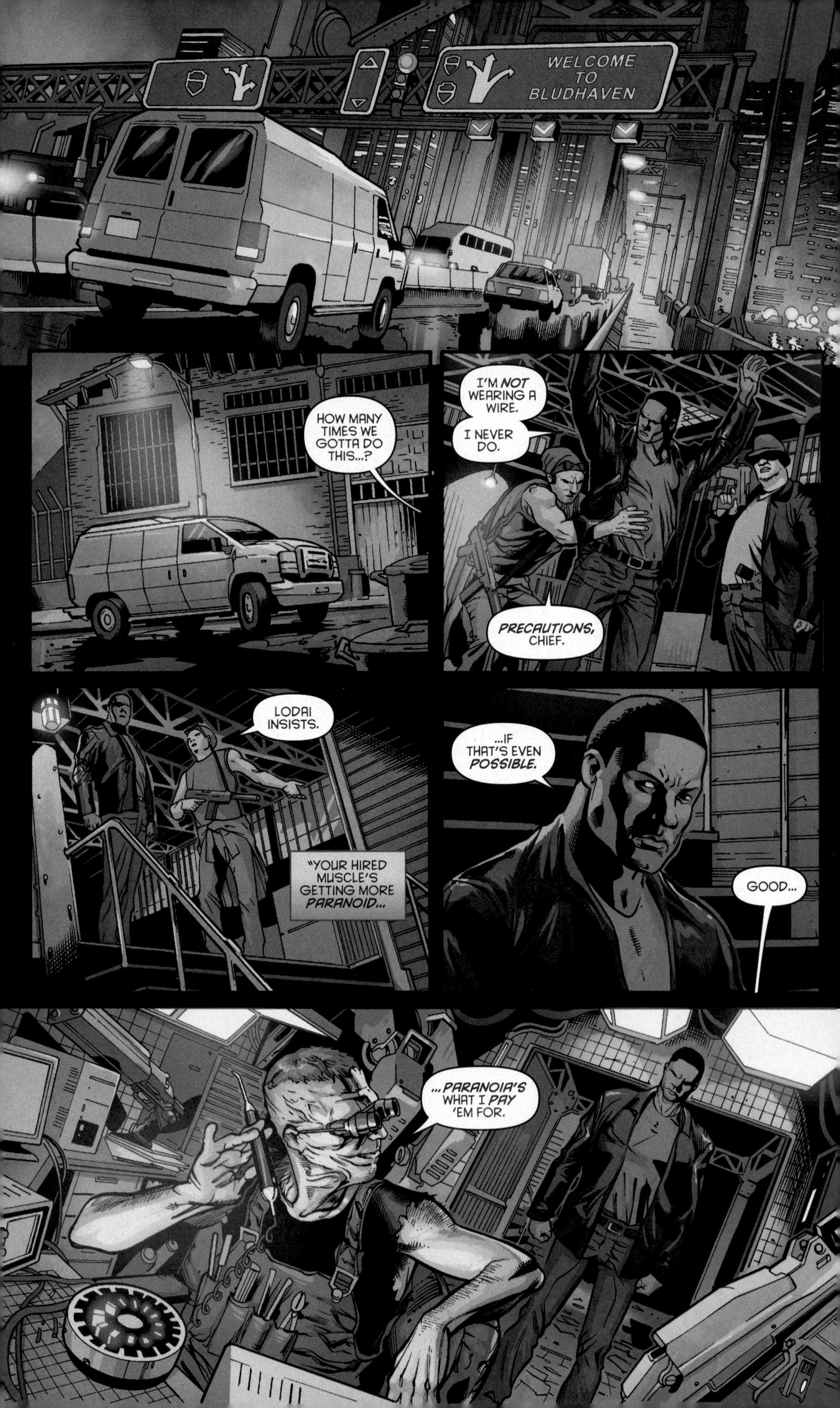
WELCOME TO BLÜDHAVEN
HOW MANY TIMES WE GOTTA DO THIS...?
I'M NOT WEARING A WIRE.
I NEVER DO.
PRECAUTIONS, CHIEF.
LODAI INSISTS.
"YOUR HIRED MUSCLE'S GETTING MORE PARANOID...
...IF THAT'S EVEN POSSIBLE.
GOOD...
...PARANOIA'S WHAT I PAY 'EM FOR.

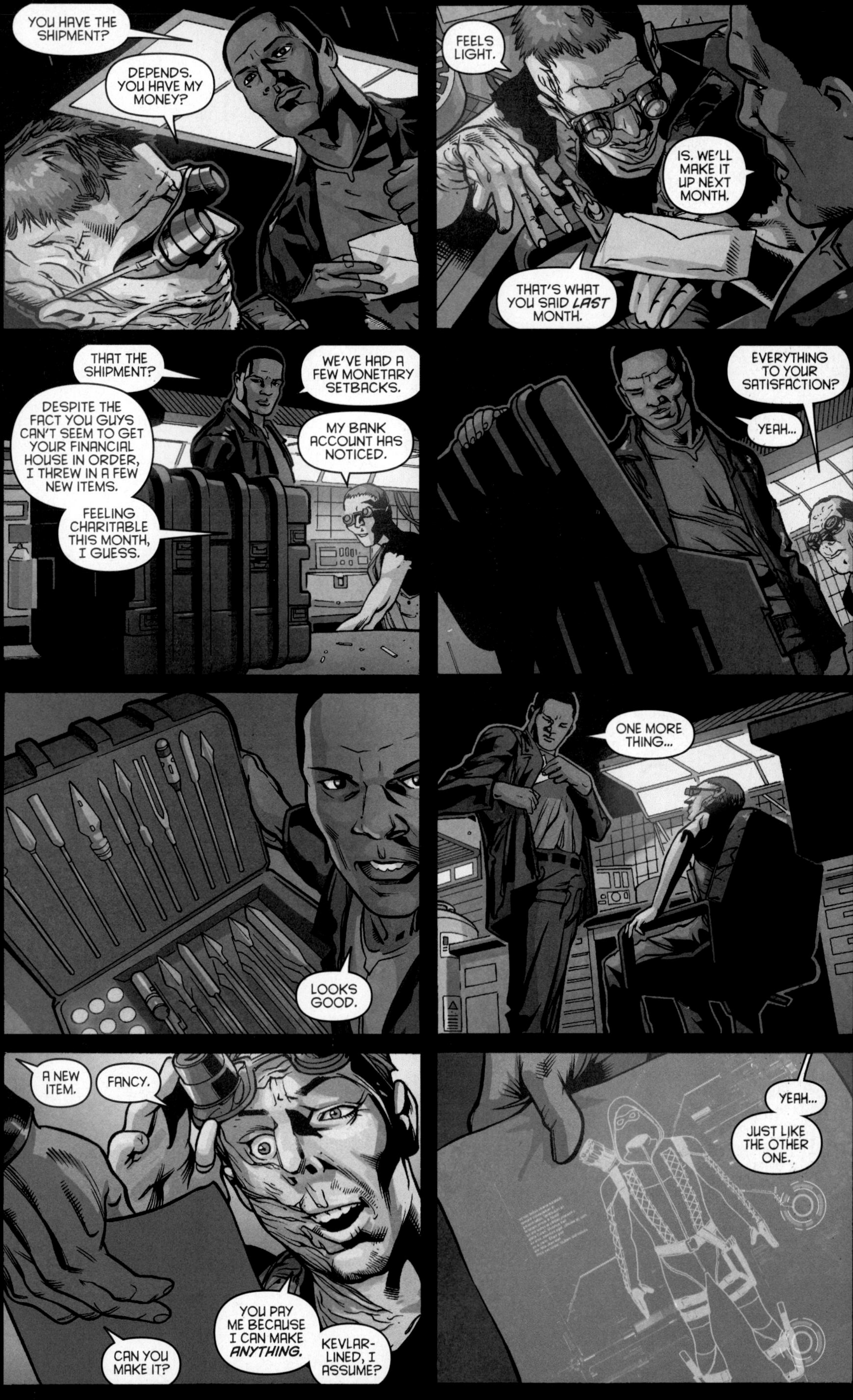

YOU HAVE THE SHIPMENT?
DEPENDS. YOU HAVE MY MONEY?
FEELS LIGHT.
IS. WE'LL MAKE IT UP NEXT MONTH.
THAT'S WHAT YOU SAID LAST MONTH.
THAT THE SHIPMENT?
WE'VE HAD A FEW MONETARY SETBACKS.
DESPITE THE FACT YOU GUYS CAN'T SEEM TO GET YOUR FINANCIAL HOUSE IN ORDER, I THREW IN A FEW NEW ITEMS.
MY BANK ACCOUNT HAS NOTICED.
FEELING CHARITABLE THIS MONTH, I GUESS.
EVERYTHING TO YOUR SATISFACTION?
YEAH...
LOOKS GOOD.
ONE MORE THING...
A NEW ITEM.
FANCY.
CAN YOU MAKE IT?
YOU PAY ME BECAUSE I CAN MAKE ANYTHING.
KEVLAR-LINED, I ASSUME?
YEAH...
JUST LIKE THE OTHER ONE.

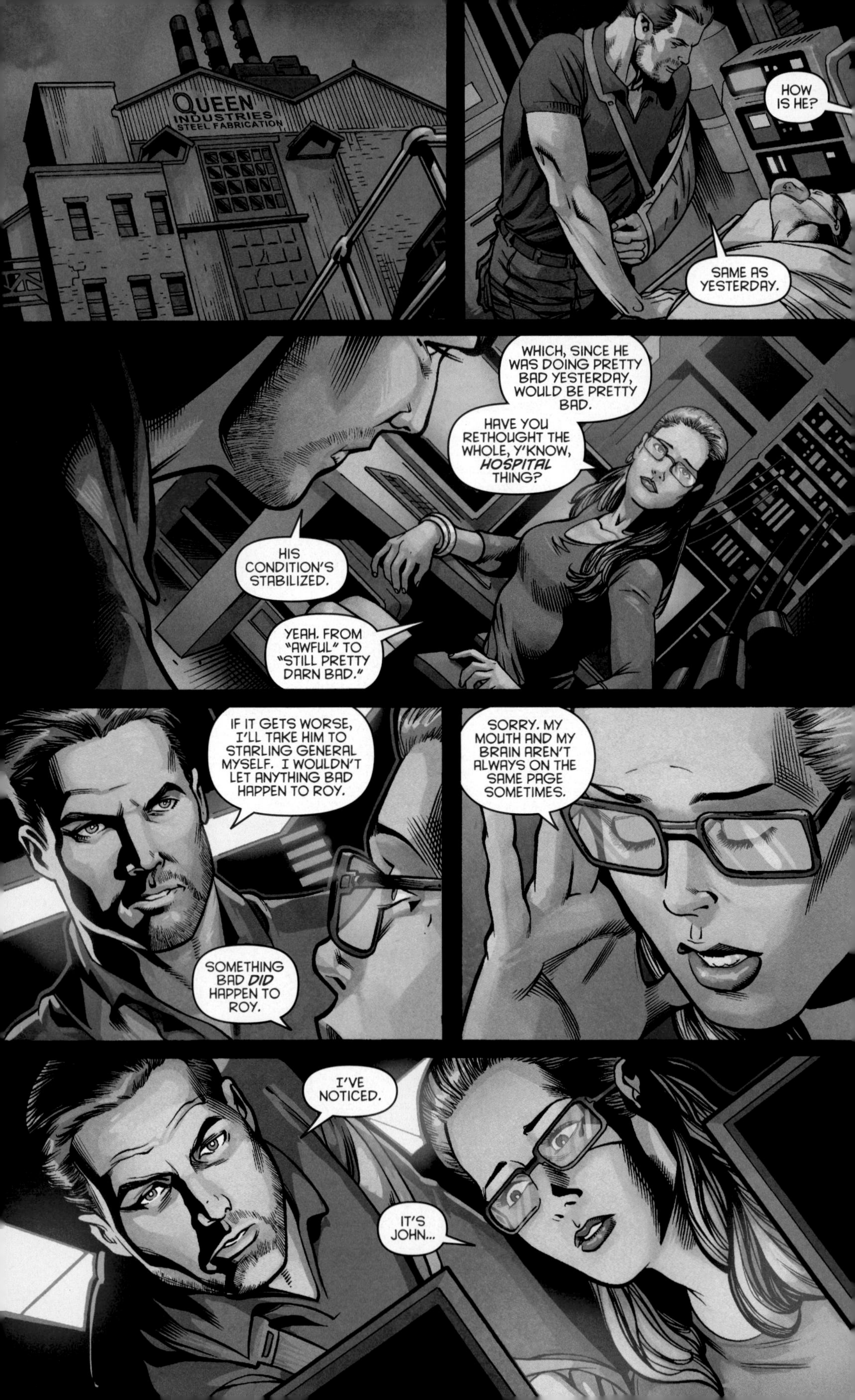
QUEEN INDUSTRIES STEEL FABRICATION
HOW IS HE?
SAME AS YESTERDAY.
WHICH, SINCE HE WAS DOING PRETTY BAD YESTERDAY, WOULD BE PRETTY BAD.
HAVE YOU RETHOUGHT THE WHOLE, Y'KNOW, *HOSPITAL* THING?
HIS CONDITION'S STABILIZED.
YEAH. FROM "AWFUL" TO "STILL PRETTY DARN BAD."
IF IT GETS WORSE, I'LL TAKE HIM TO STARLING GENERAL MYSELF. I WOULDN'T LET ANYTHING BAD HAPPEN TO ROY.
SOMETHING BAD *DID* HAPPEN TO ROY.
SORRY. MY MOUTH AND MY BRAIN AREN'T ALWAYS ON THE SAME PAGE SOMETIMES.
I'VE NOTICED.
IT'S JOHN...

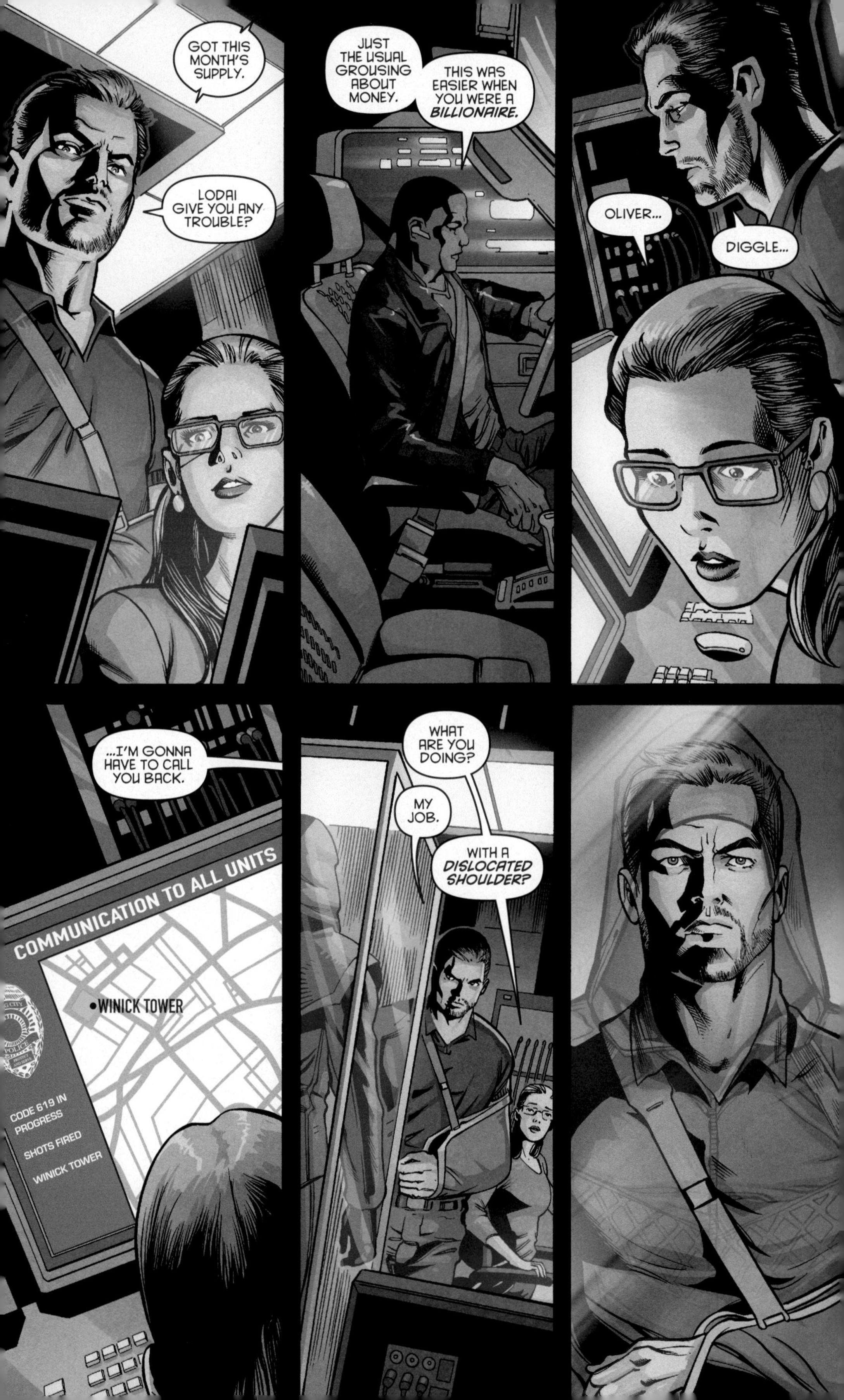
GOT THIS MONTH'S SUPPLY.
LODAI GIVE YOU ANY TROUBLE?
JUST THE USUAL GROUSING ABOUT MONEY.
THIS WAS EASIER WHEN YOU WERE A *BILLIONAIRE.*
OLIVER...
DIGGLE...
...I'M GONNA HAVE TO CALL YOU BACK.
COMMUNICATION TO ALL UNITS
WINICK TOWER
CODE 619 IN PROGRESS
SHOTS FIRED
WINICK TOWER
WHAT ARE YOU DOING?
MY JOB.
WITH A *DISLOCATED SHOULDER?*

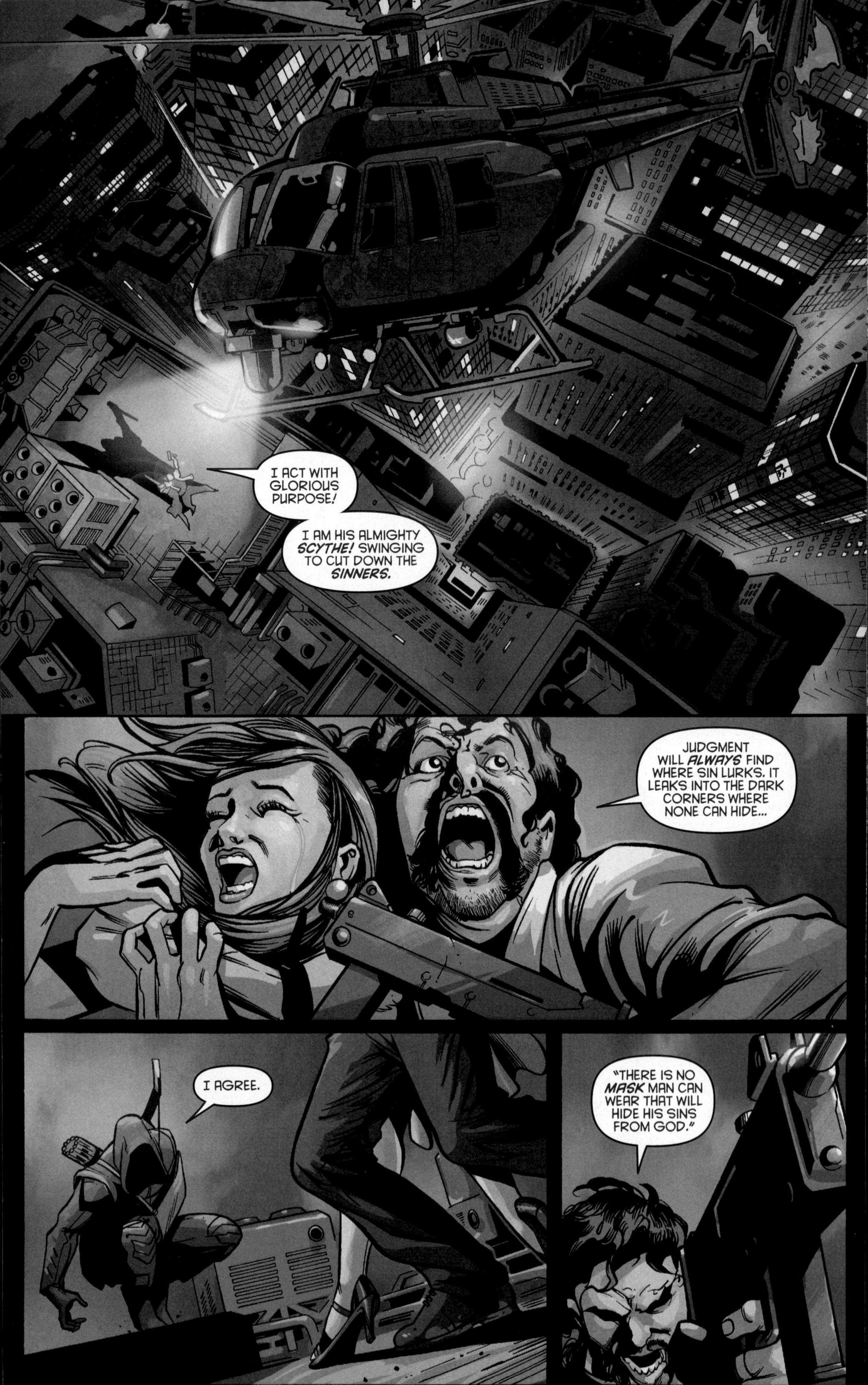
I ACT WITH GLORIOUS PURPOSE!
I AM HIS ALMIGHTY SCYTHE! SWINGING TO CUT DOWN THE SINNERS.
JUDGMENT WILL ALWAYS FIND WHERE SIN LURKS. IT LEAKS INTO THE DARK CORNERS WHERE NONE CAN HIDE...
I AGREE.
"THERE IS NO MASK MAN CAN WEAR THAT WILL HIDE HIS SINS FROM GOD."

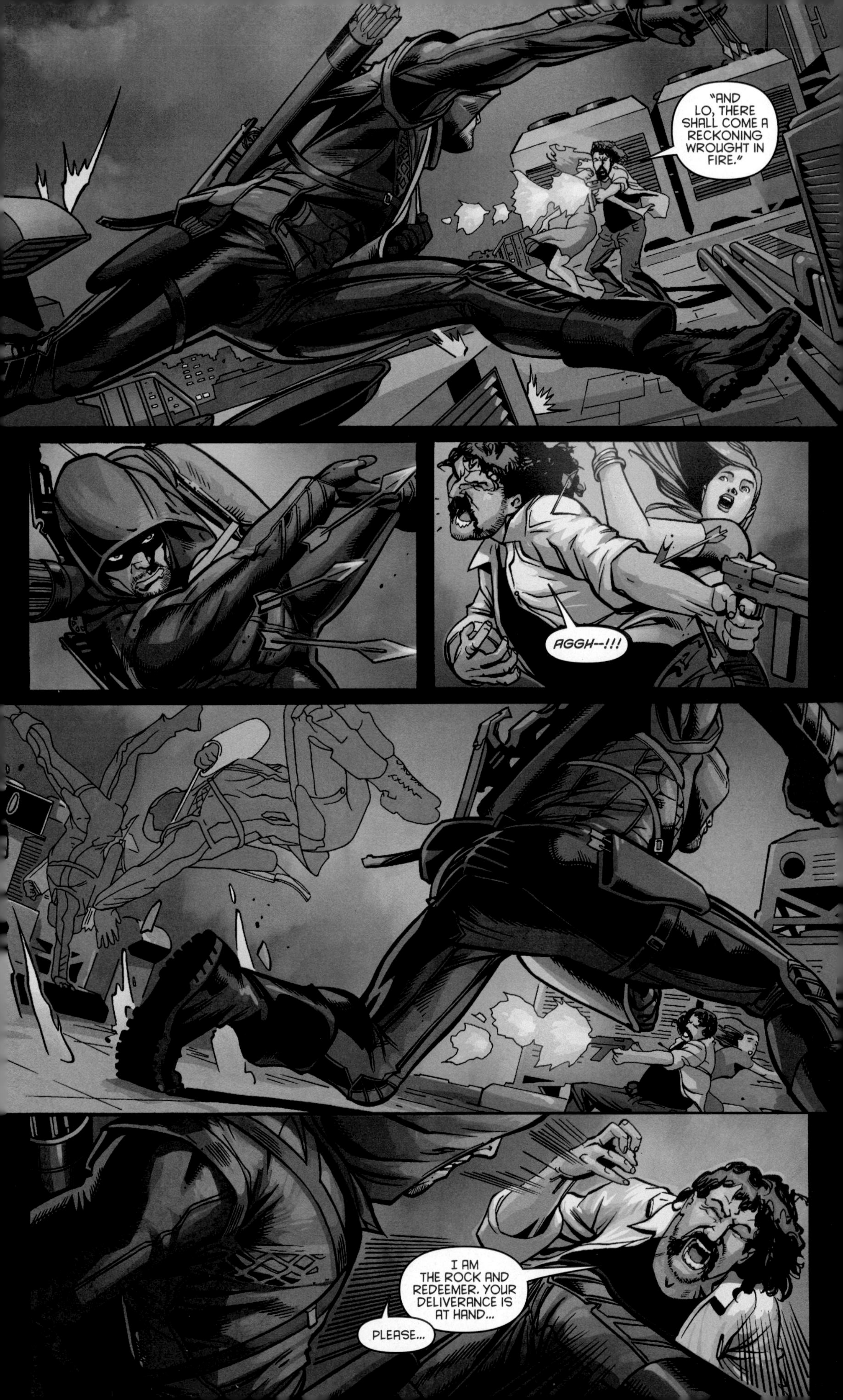
"AND LO, THERE SHALL COME A RECKONING WROUGHT IN FIRE."
AGGH--!!!
I AM THE ROCK AND REDEEMER. YOUR DELIVERANCE IS AT HAND...
PLEASE...

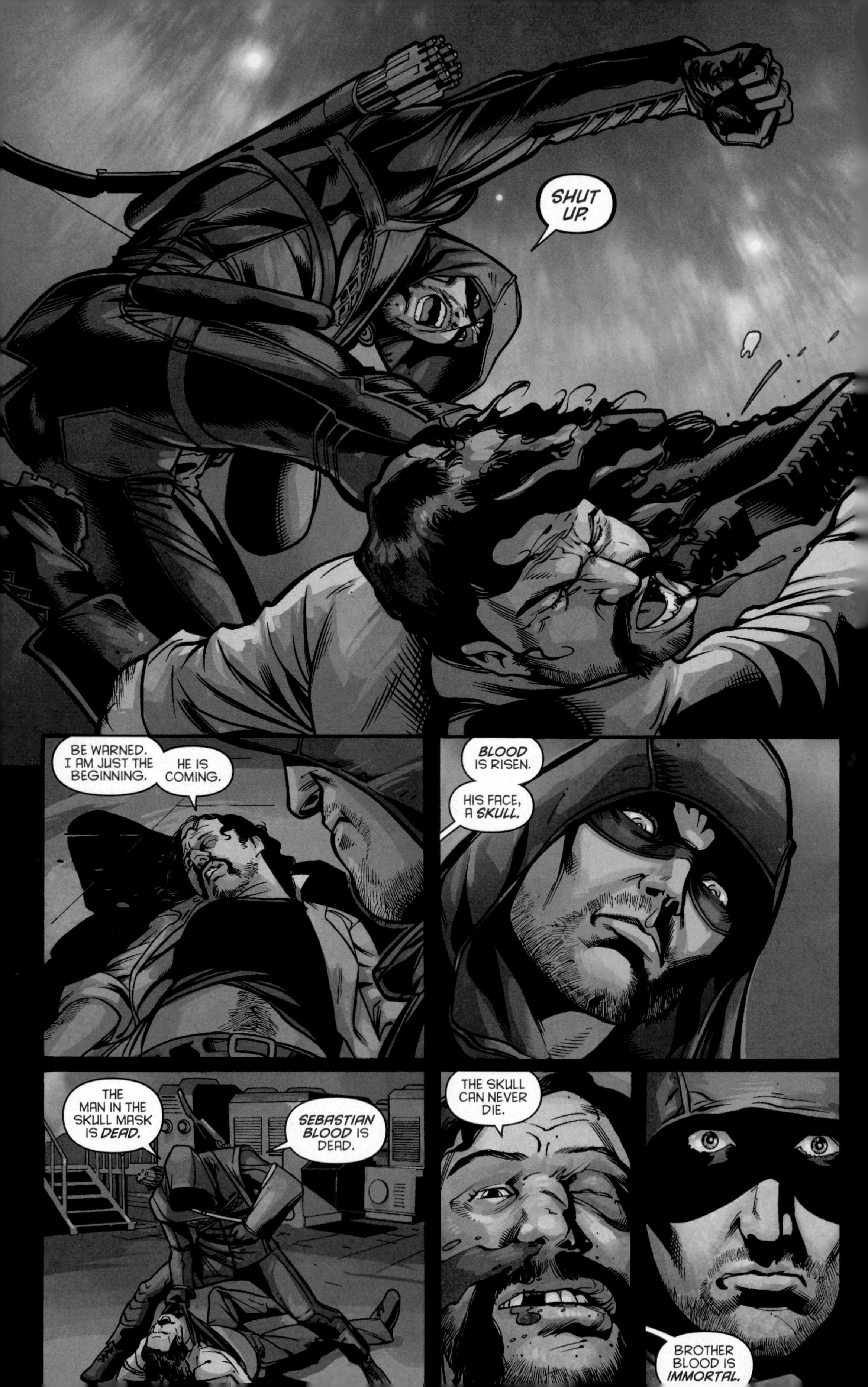
SHUT UP.
BE WARNED. I AM JUST THE BEGINNING.
HE IS COMING.
BLOOD IS RISEN.
HIS FACE, A SKULL.
THE MAN IN THE SKULL MASK IS DEAD.
SEBASTIAN BLOOD IS DEAD.
THE SKULL CAN NEVER DIE.
BROTHER BLOOD IS IMMORTAL.

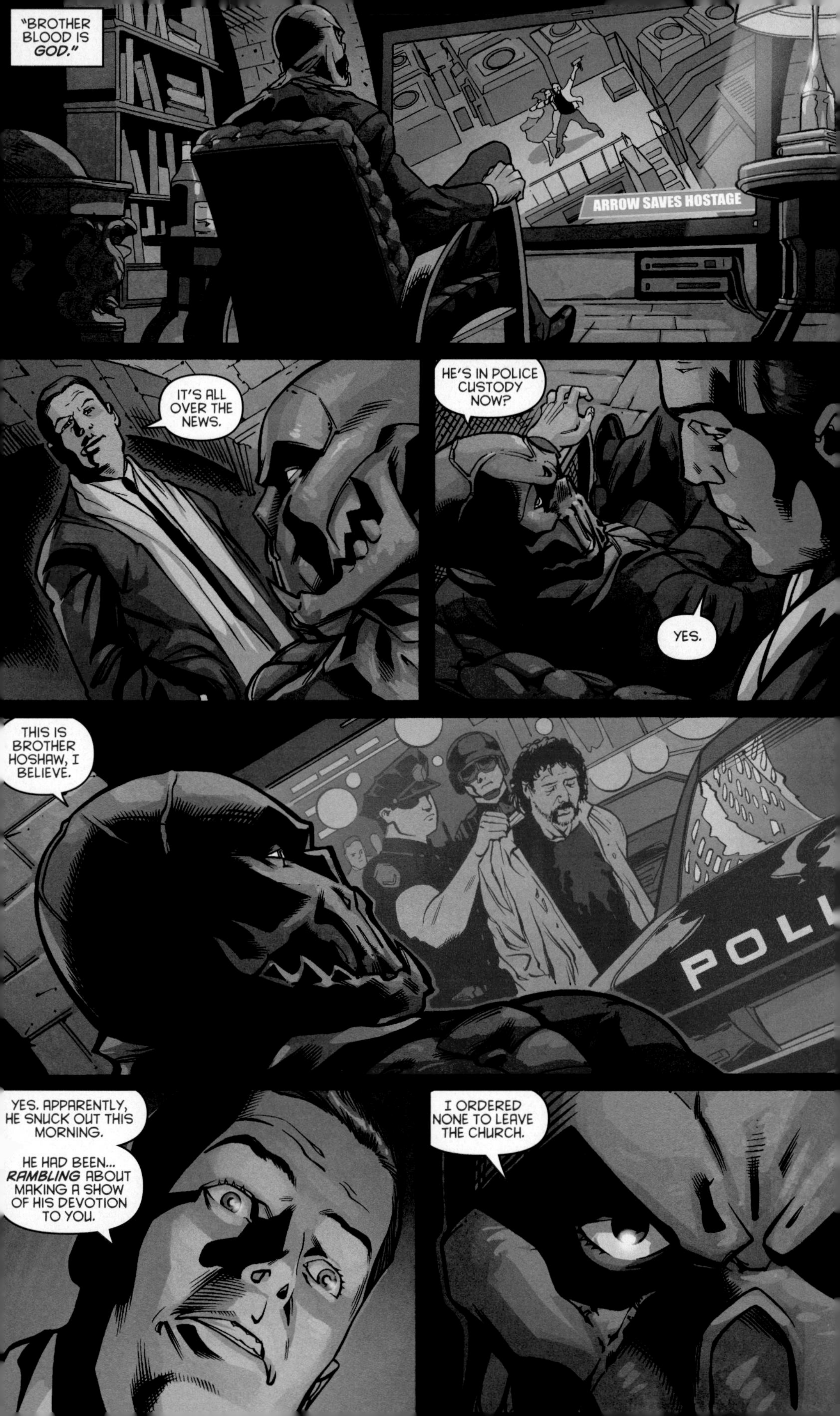
"BROTHER BLOOD IS *GOD.*"
ARROW SAVES HOSTAGE
IT'S ALL OVER THE NEWS.
HE'S IN POLICE CUSTODY NOW?
YES.
THIS IS BROTHER HOSHAW, I BELIEVE.
POLI
YES. APPARENTLY, HE SNUCK OUT THIS MORNING.
HE HAD BEEN... *RAMBLING* ABOUT MAKING A SHOW OF HIS DEVOTION TO YOU.
I ORDERED NONE TO LEAVE THE CHURCH.

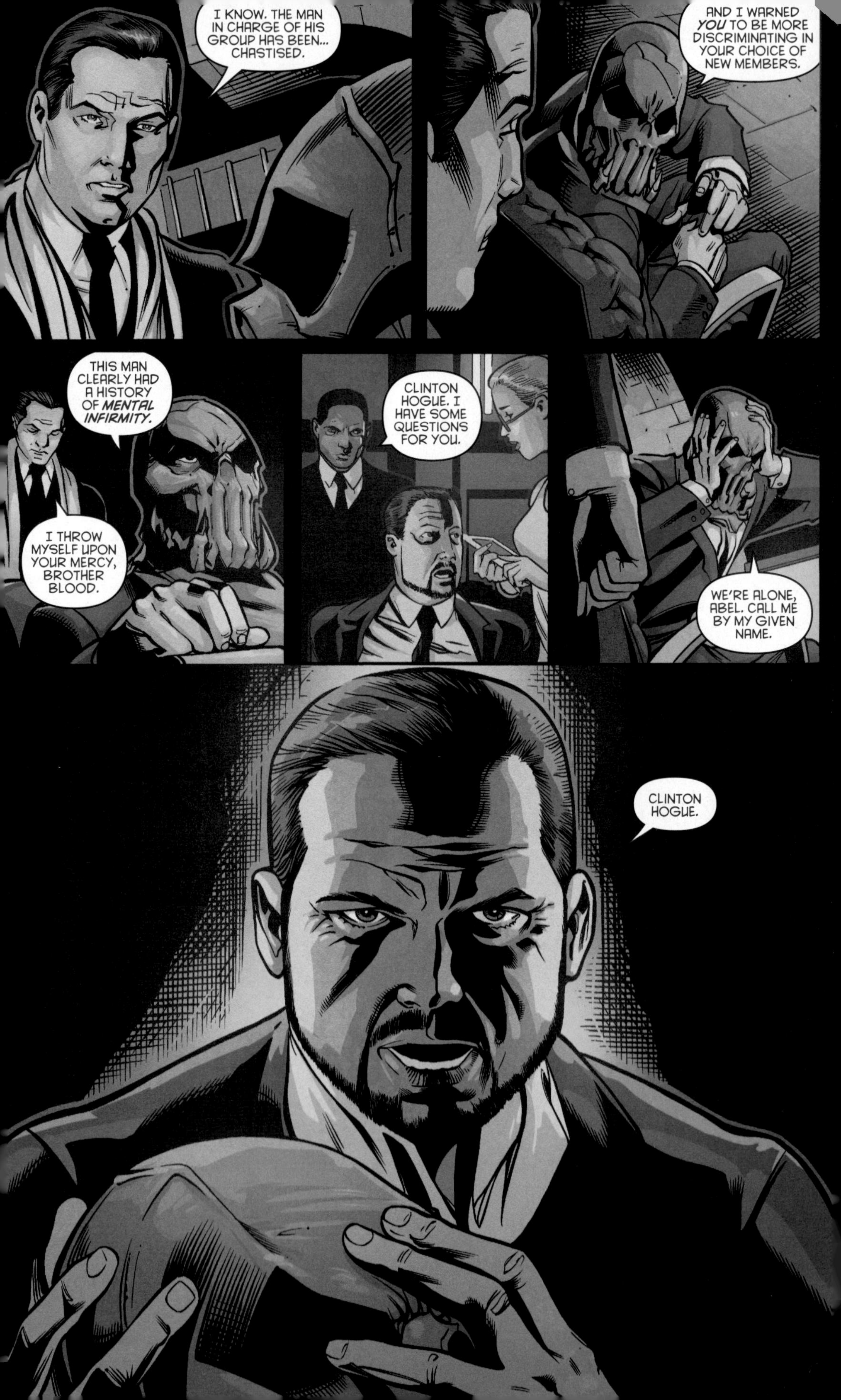

I KNOW. THE MAN IN CHARGE OF HIS GROUP HAS BEEN... CHASTISED.
AND I WARNED *YOU* TO BE MORE DISCRIMINATING IN YOUR CHOICE OF NEW MEMBERS.
THIS MAN CLEARLY HAD A HISTORY OF *MENTAL INFIRMITY.*
I THROW MYSELF UPON YOUR MERCY, BROTHER BLOOD.
CLINTON HOGUE. I HAVE SOME QUESTIONS FOR YOU.
WE'RE ALONE, ABEL. CALL ME BY MY GIVEN NAME.
CLINTON HOGUE.

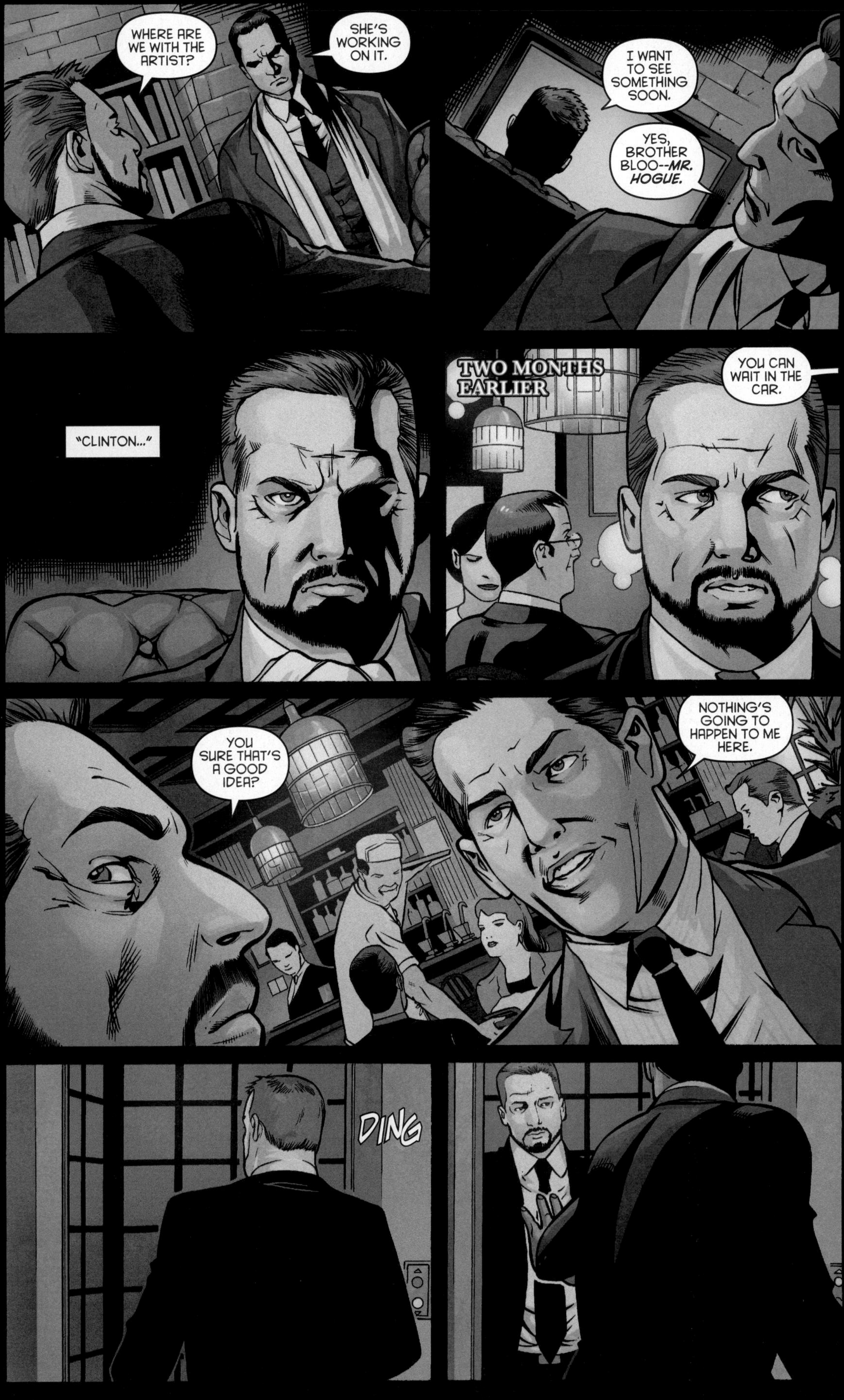
WHERE ARE WE WITH THE ARTIST?
SHE'S WORKING ON IT.
I WANT TO SEE SOMETHING SOON.
YES, BROTHER BLOO--MR. HOGUE.
"CLINTON..."
TWO MONTHS EARLIER
YOU CAN WAIT IN THE CAR.
YOU SURE THAT'S A GOOD IDEA?
NOTHING'S GOING TO HAPPEN TO ME HERE.
DING

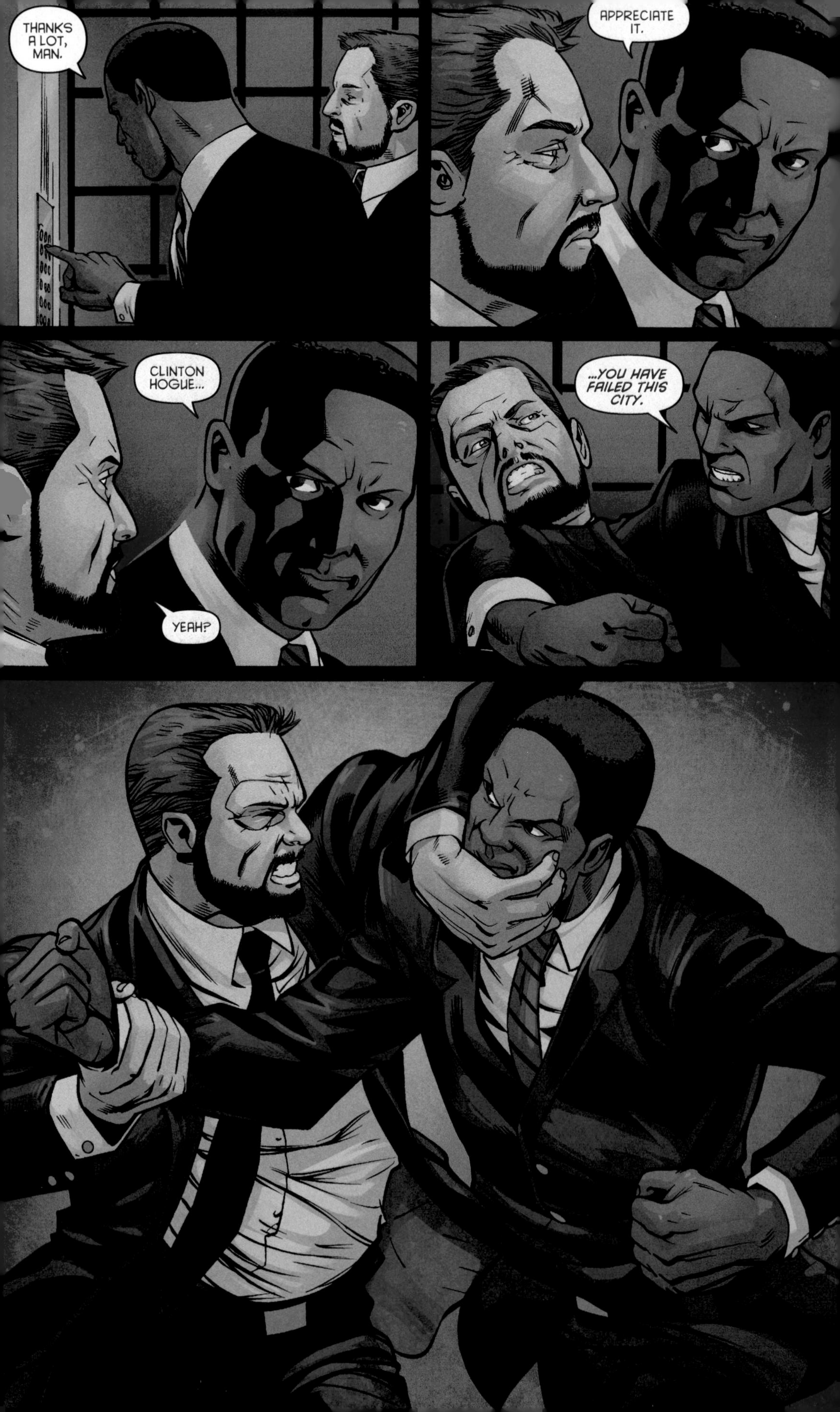
THANKS A LOT, MAN.
APPRECIATE IT.
CLINTON HOGUE...
YEAH?
...YOU HAVE FAILED THIS CITY.

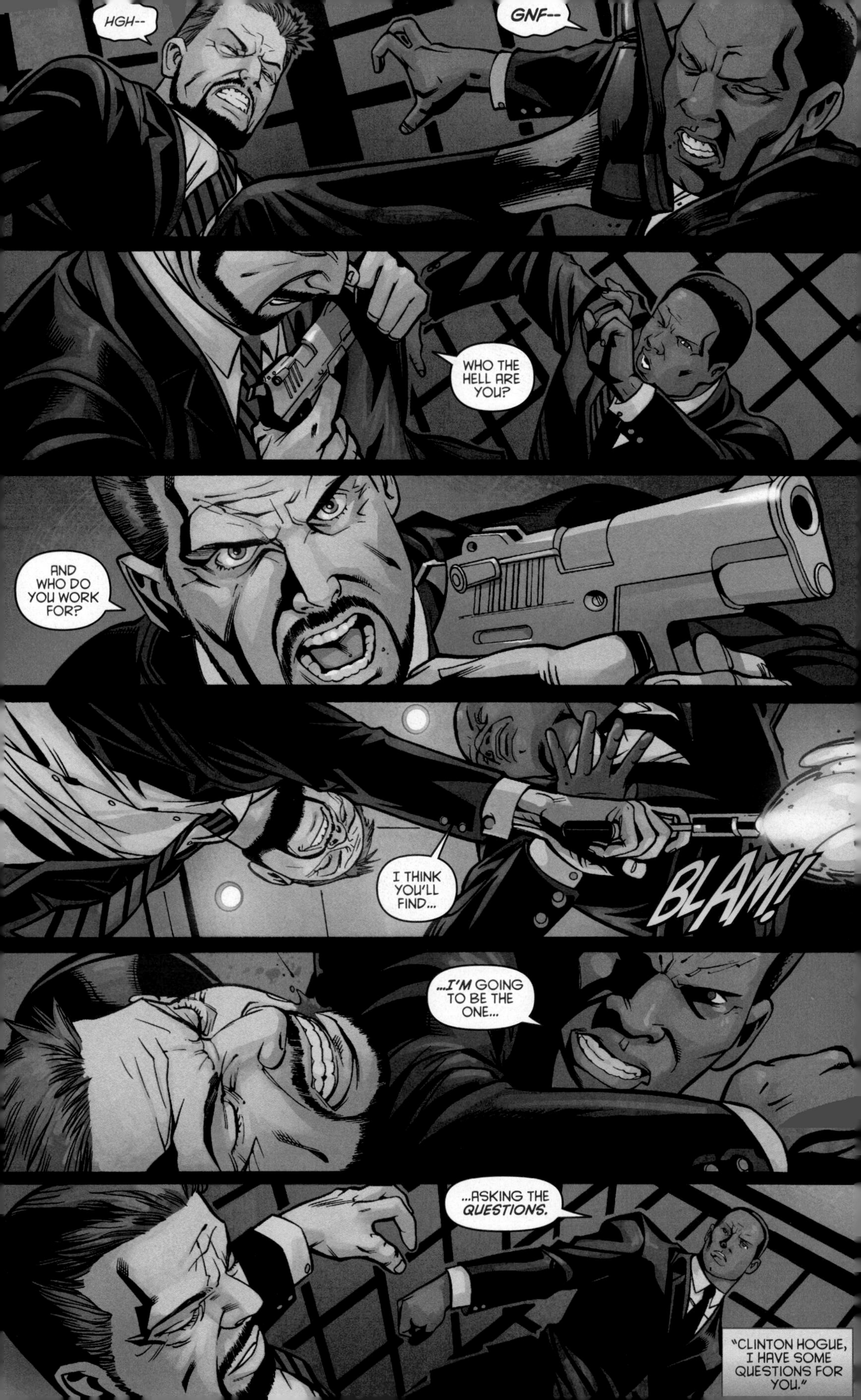
HGH--
GNF--
WHO THE HELL ARE YOU?
AND WHO DO YOU WORK FOR?
I THINK YOU'LL FIND...
BLAM!
...*I'M* GOING TO BE THE ONE...
...ASKING THE *QUESTIONS.*
"CLINTON HOGUE, I HAVE SOME QUESTIONS FOR YOU."

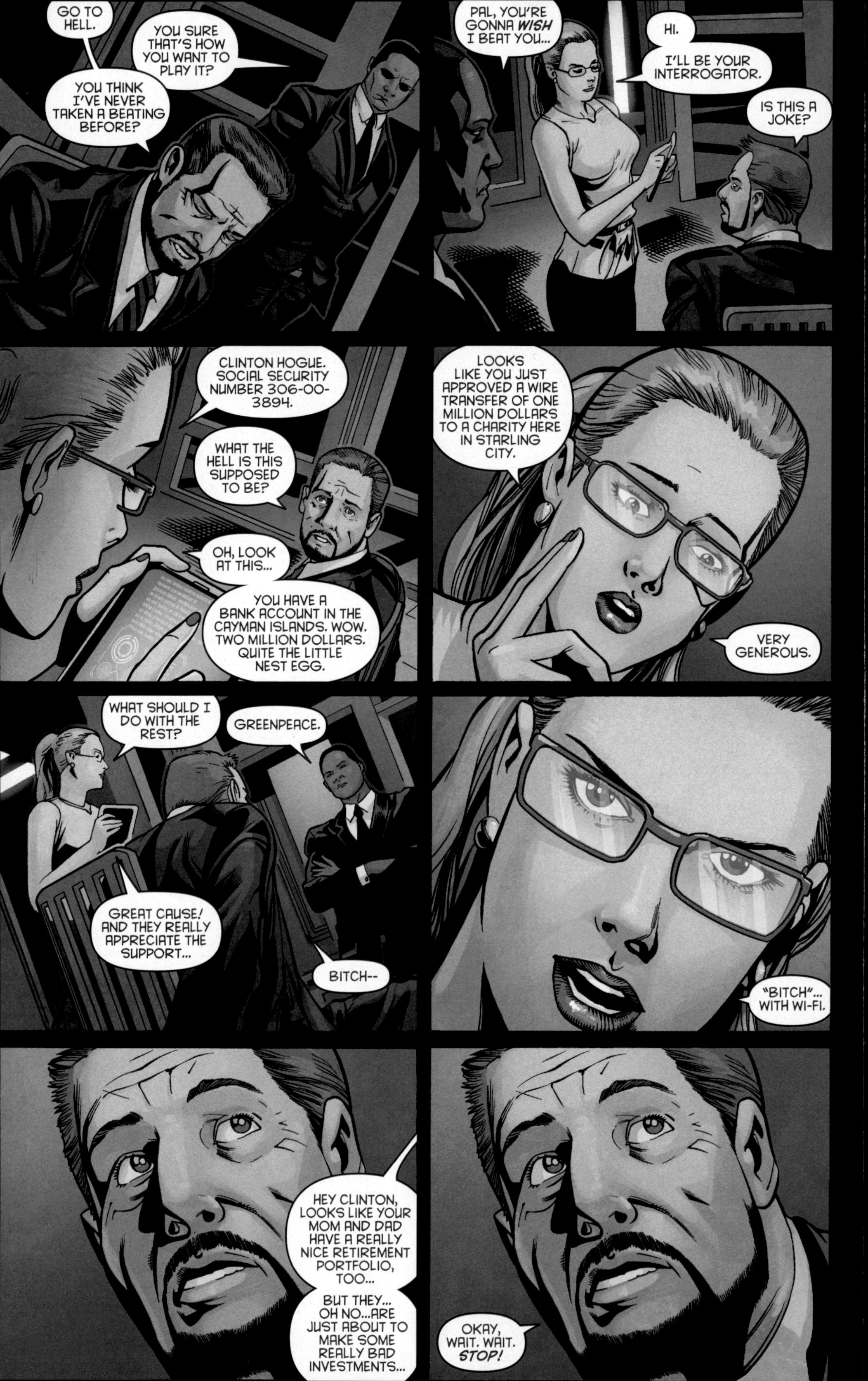
GO TO HELL.
YOU SURE THAT'S HOW YOU WANT TO PLAY IT?
YOU THINK I'VE NEVER TAKEN A BEATING BEFORE?
PAL, YOU'RE GONNA WISH I BEAT YOU...
HI.
I'LL BE YOUR INTERROGATOR.
IS THIS A JOKE?
CLINTON HOGUE. SOCIAL SECURITY NUMBER 306-00-3894.
WHAT THE HELL IS THIS SUPPOSED TO BE?
OH, LOOK AT THIS...
YOU HAVE A BANK ACCOUNT IN THE CAYMAN ISLANDS. WOW. TWO MILLION DOLLARS. QUITE THE LITTLE NEST EGG.
LOOKS LIKE YOU JUST APPROVED A WIRE TRANSFER OF ONE MILLION DOLLARS TO A CHARITY HERE IN STARLING CITY.
VERY GENEROUS.
WHAT SHOULD I DO WITH THE REST?
GREENPEACE.
GREAT CAUSE! AND THEY REALLY APPRECIATE THE SUPPORT...
BITCH--
"BITCH"... WITH WI-FI.
HEY CLINTON, LOOKS LIKE YOUR MOM AND DAD HAVE A REALLY NICE RETIREMENT PORTFOLIO, TOO...
BUT THEY... OH NO...ARE JUST ABOUT TO MAKE SOME REALLY BAD INVESTMENTS...
OKAY, WAIT. WAIT. STOP!

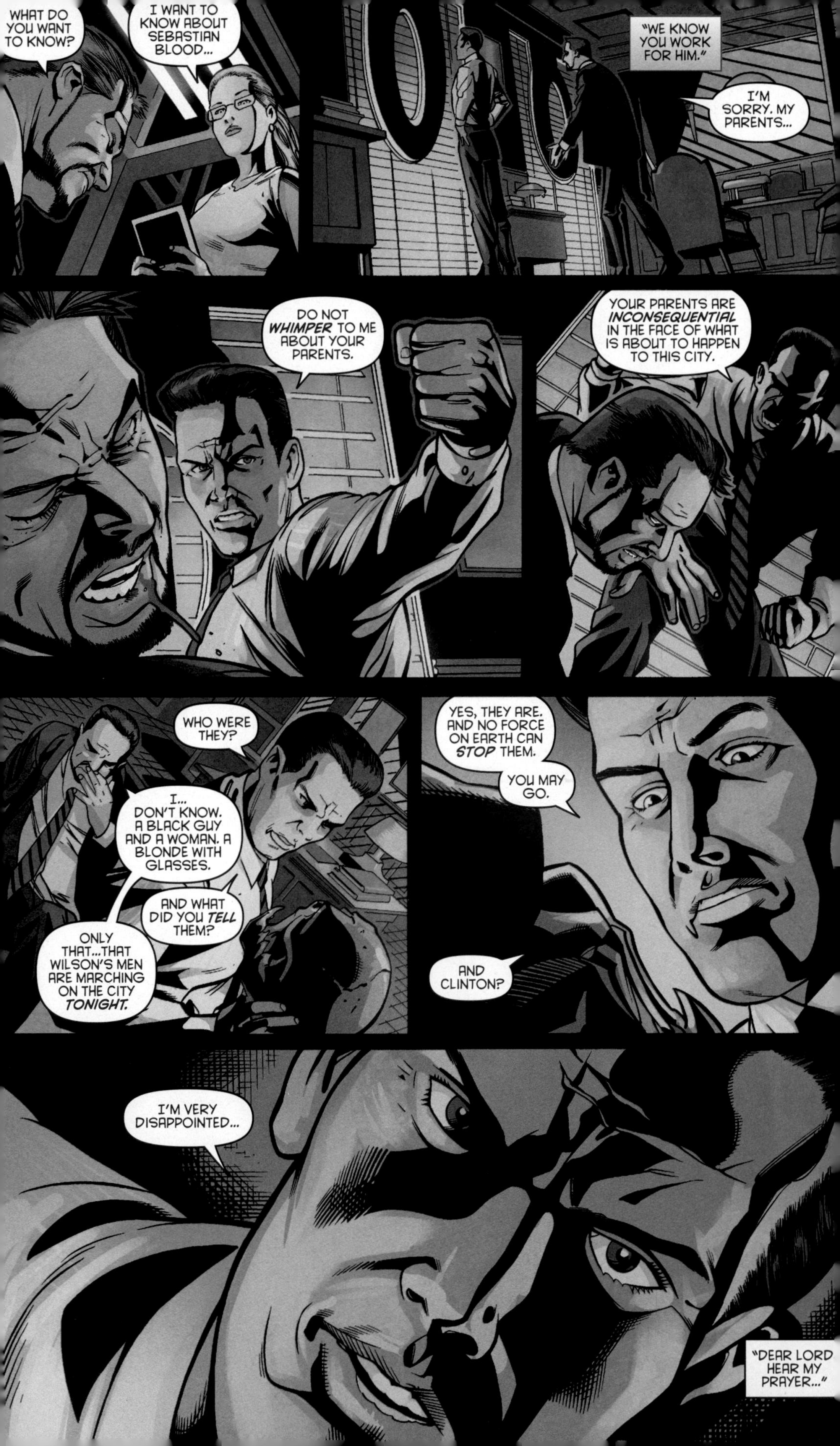
WHAT DO YOU WANT TO KNOW?
I WANT TO KNOW ABOUT SEBASTIAN BLOOD...
"WE KNOW YOU WORK FOR HIM."
I'M SORRY. MY PARENTS...
DO NOT WHIMPER TO ME ABOUT YOUR PARENTS.
YOUR PARENTS ARE INCONSEQUENTIAL IN THE FACE OF WHAT IS ABOUT TO HAPPEN TO THIS CITY.
WHO WERE THEY?
I... DON'T KNOW. A BLACK GUY AND A WOMAN. A BLONDE WITH GLASSES.
AND WHAT DID YOU TELL THEM?
ONLY THAT...THAT WILSON'S MEN ARE MARCHING ON THE CITY TONIGHT.
YES, THEY ARE. AND NO FORCE ON EARTH CAN STOP THEM.
YOU MAY GO.
AND CLINTON?
I'M VERY DISAPPOINTED...
"DEAR LORD HEAR MY PRAYER..."

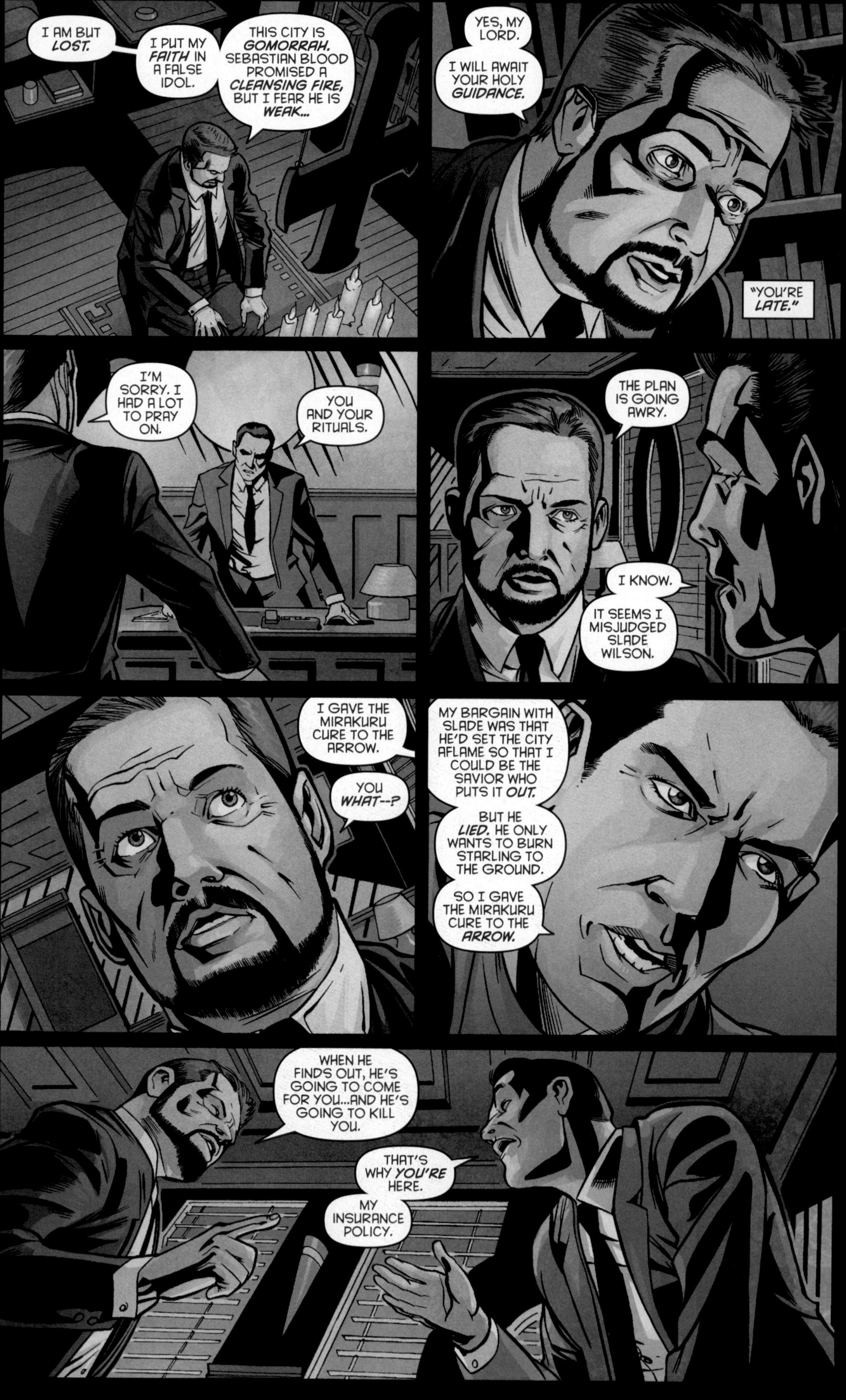

I AM BUT LOST.
I PUT MY FAITH IN A FALSE IDOL.
THIS CITY IS GOMORRAH. SEBASTIAN BLOOD PROMISED A CLEANSING FIRE, BUT I FEAR HE IS WEAK...
YES, MY LORD.
I WILL AWAIT YOUR HOLY GUIDANCE.
"YOU'RE LATE."
I'M SORRY. I HAD A LOT TO PRAY ON.
YOU AND YOUR RITUALS.
THE PLAN IS GOING AWRY.
I KNOW.
IT SEEMS I MISJUDGED SLADE WILSON.
I GAVE THE MIRAKURU CURE TO THE ARROW.
YOU WHAT--?
MY BARGAIN WITH SLADE WAS THAT HE'D SET THE CITY AFLAME SO THAT I COULD BE THE SAVIOR WHO PUTS IT OUT.
BUT HE LIED. HE ONLY WANTS TO BURN STARLING TO THE GROUND.
SO I GAVE THE MIRAKURU CURE TO THE ARROW.
WHEN HE FINDS OUT, HE'S GOING TO COME FOR YOU...AND HE'S GOING TO KILL YOU.
THAT'S WHY YOU'RE HERE.
MY INSURANCE POLICY.

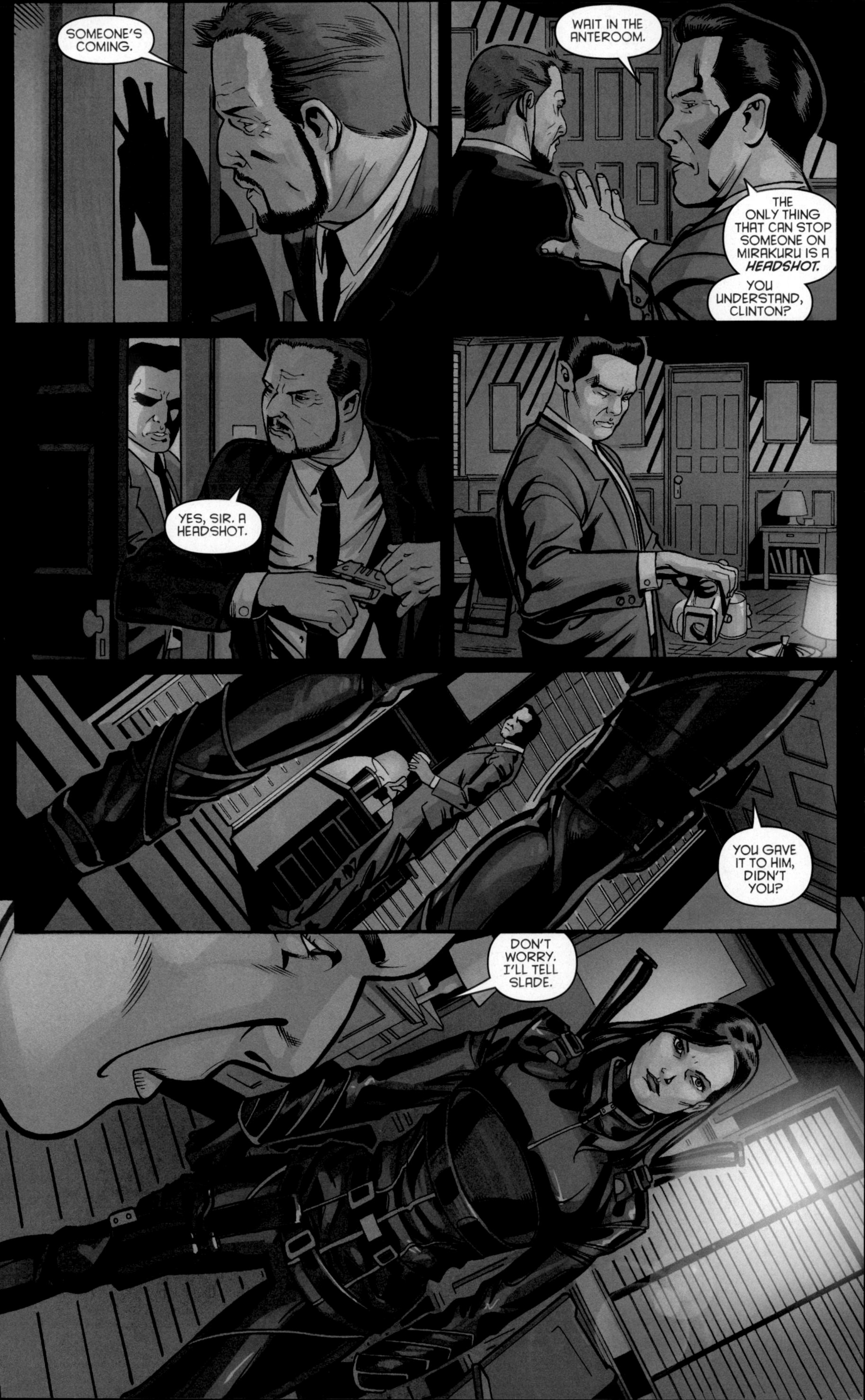
SOMEONE'S COMING.
WAIT IN THE ANTEROOM.
THE ONLY THING THAT CAN STOP SOMEONE ON MIRAKURU IS A *HEADSHOT.*
YOU UNDERSTAND, CLINTON?
YES, SIR. A HEADSHOT.
YOU GAVE IT TO HIM, DIDN'T YOU?
DON'T WORRY. I'LL TELL SLADE.

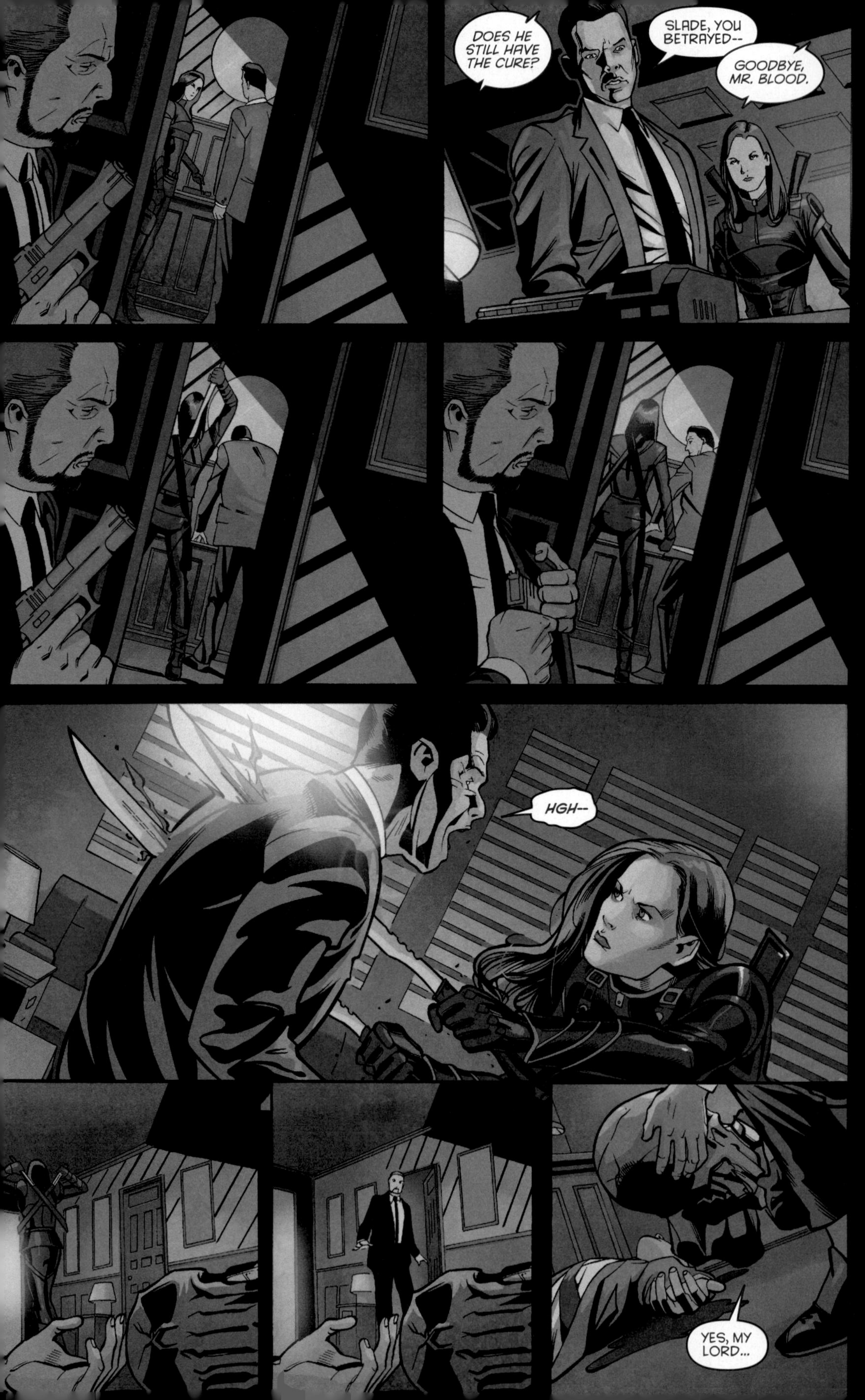
DOES HE STILL HAVE THE CURE?
SLADE, YOU BETRAYED--
GOODBYE, MR. BLOOD.
HGH--
YES, MY LORD...

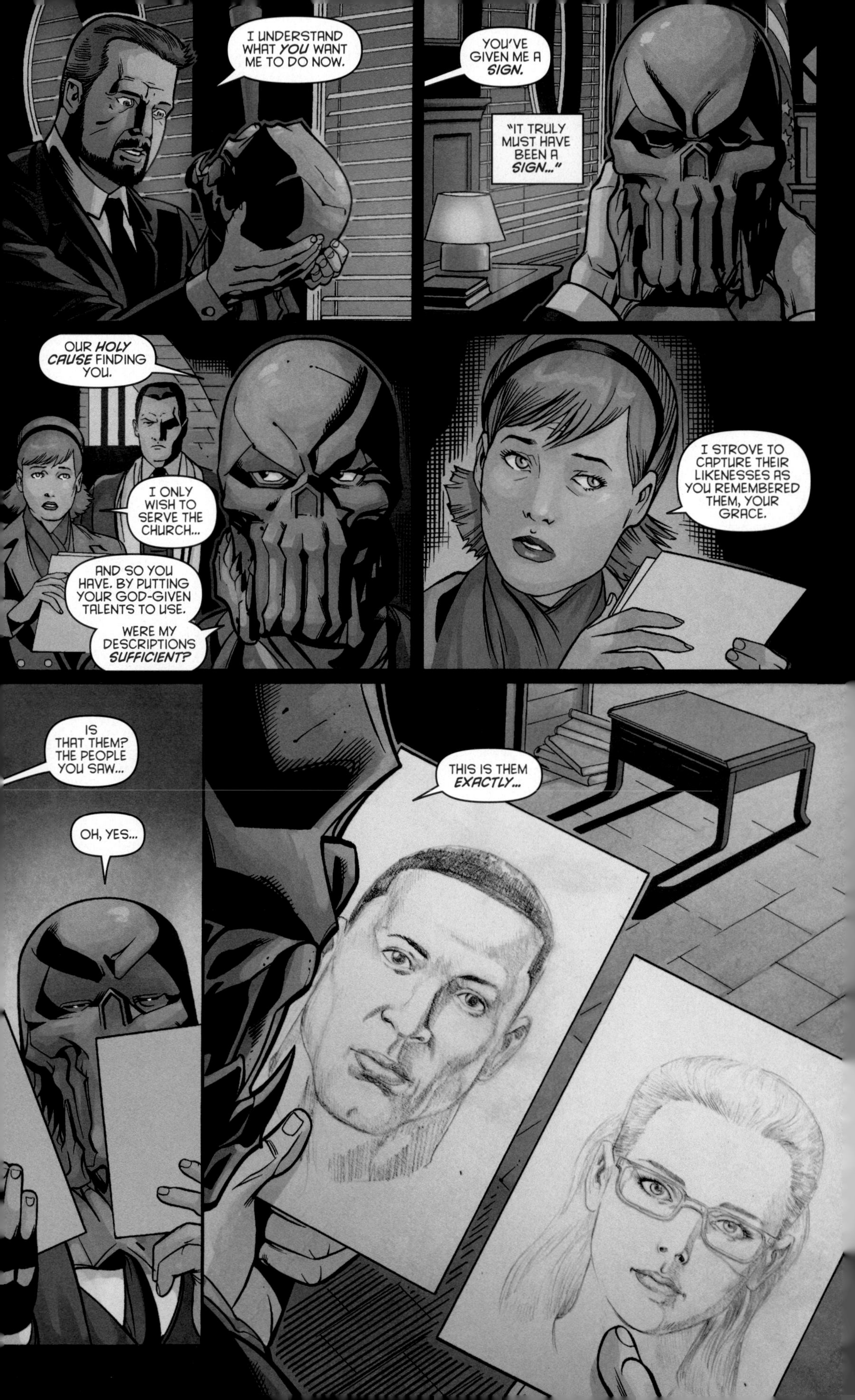

I UNDERSTAND WHAT YOU WANT ME TO DO NOW.
YOU'VE GIVEN ME A SIGN.
"IT TRULY MUST HAVE BEEN A SIGN..."
OUR HOLY CAUSE FINDING YOU.
I ONLY WISH TO SERVE THE CHURCH...
AND SO YOU HAVE. BY PUTTING YOUR GOD-GIVEN TALENTS TO USE.
WERE MY DESCRIPTIONS SUFFICIENT?
I STROVE TO CAPTURE THEIR LIKENESSES AS YOU REMEMBERED THEM, YOUR GRACE.
IS THAT THEM? THE PEOPLE YOU SAW...
OH, YES...
THIS IS THEM EXACTLY...

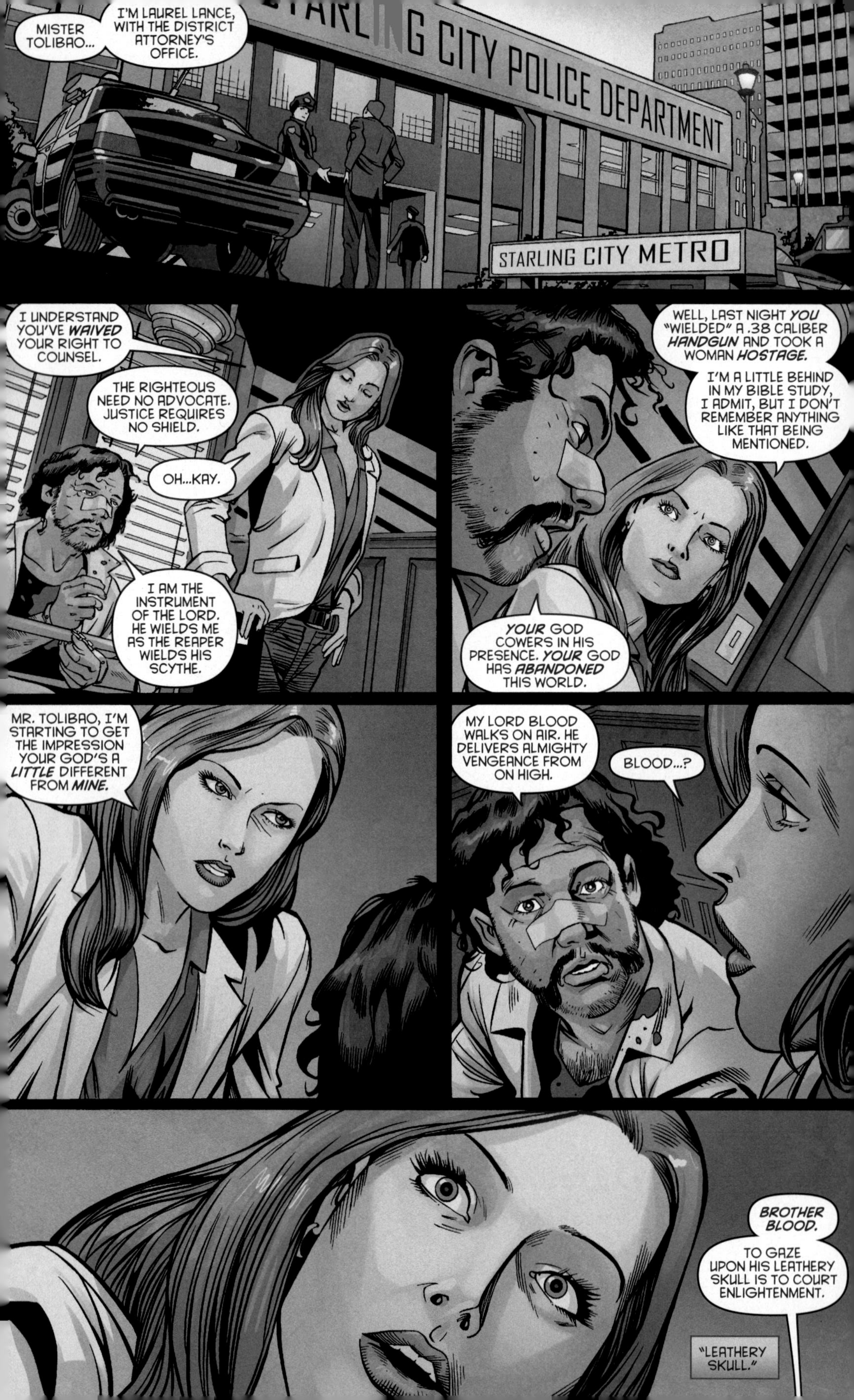
MISTER TOLIBAO...
I'M LAUREL LANCE, WITH THE DISTRICT ATTORNEY'S OFFICE.
STARLING CITY POLICE DEPARTMENT
STARLING CITY METRO
I UNDERSTAND YOU'VE *WAIVED* YOUR RIGHT TO COUNSEL.
THE RIGHTEOUS NEED NO ADVOCATE. JUSTICE REQUIRES NO SHIELD.
OH...KAY.
I AM THE INSTRUMENT OF THE LORD. HE WIELDS ME AS THE REAPER WIELDS HIS SCYTHE.
WELL, LAST NIGHT *YOU* "WIELDED" A .38 CALIBER *HANDGUN* AND TOOK A WOMAN *HOSTAGE.*
I'M A LITTLE BEHIND IN MY BIBLE STUDY, I ADMIT, BUT I DON'T REMEMBER ANYTHING LIKE THAT BEING MENTIONED.
YOUR GOD COWERS IN HIS PRESENCE. *YOUR* GOD HAS *ABANDONED* THIS WORLD.
MR. TOLIBAO, I'M STARTING TO GET THE IMPRESSION YOUR GOD'S A *LITTLE* DIFFERENT FROM *MINE.*
MY LORD BLOOD WALKS ON AIR. HE DELIVERS ALMIGHTY VENGEANCE FROM ON HIGH.
BLOOD...?
BROTHER BLOOD.
TO GAZE UPON HIS LEATHERY SKULL IS TO COURT ENLIGHTENMENT.
"LEATHERY SKULL."

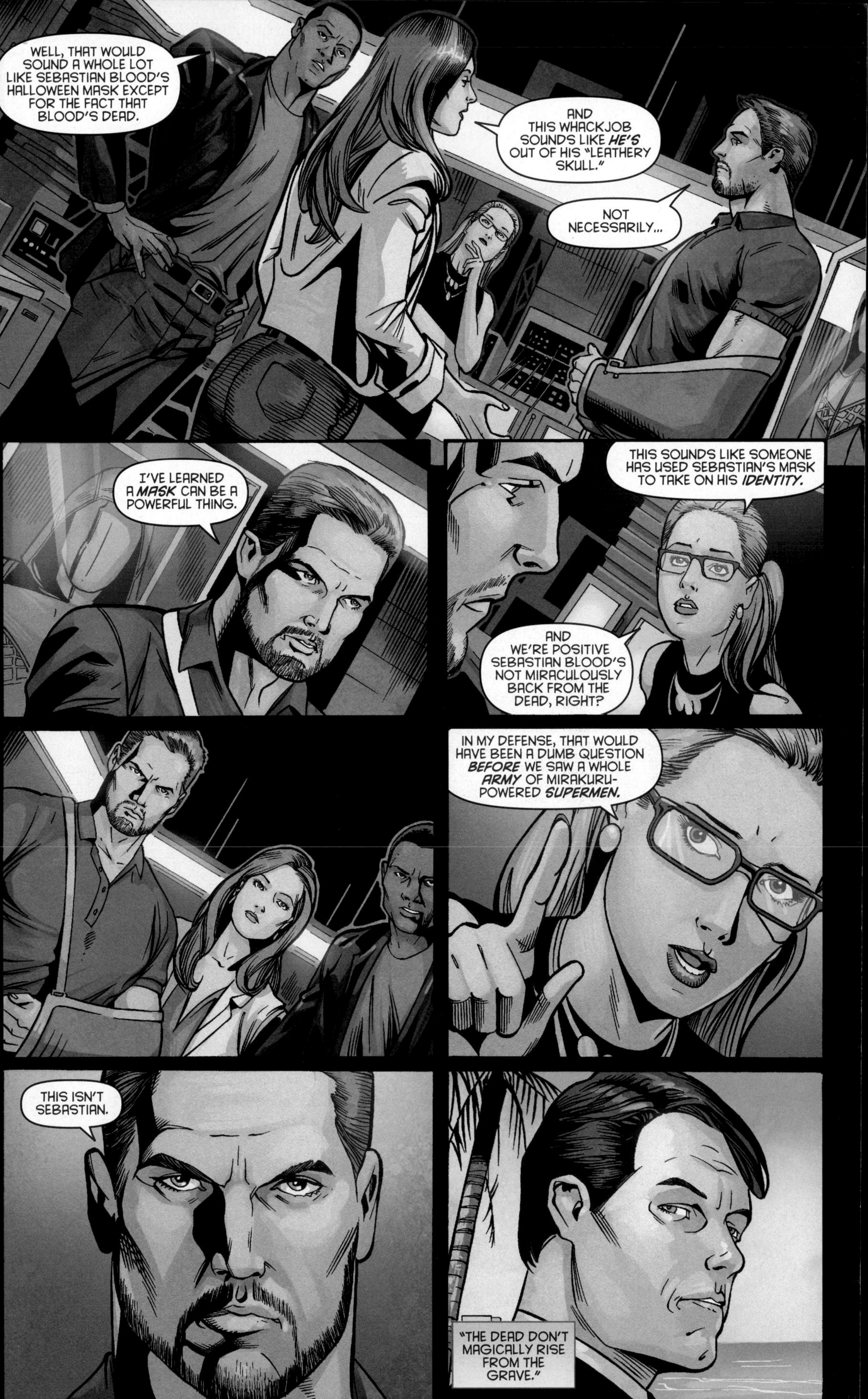

WELL, THAT WOULD SOUND A WHOLE LOT LIKE SEBASTIAN BLOOD'S HALLOWEEN MASK EXCEPT FOR THE FACT THAT BLOOD'S DEAD.
AND THIS WHACKJOB SOUNDS LIKE *HE'S* OUT OF HIS "LEATHERY SKULL."
NOT NECESSARILY...
I'VE LEARNED A *MASK* CAN BE A POWERFUL THING.
THIS SOUNDS LIKE SOMEONE HAS USED SEBASTIAN'S MASK TO TAKE ON HIS *IDENTITY.*
AND WE'RE POSITIVE SEBASTIAN BLOOD'S NOT MIRACULOUSLY BACK FROM THE DEAD, RIGHT?
IN MY DEFENSE, THAT WOULD HAVE BEEN A DUMB QUESTION *BEFORE* WE SAW A WHOLE *ARMY* OF MIRAKURU-POWERED *SUPERMEN.*
THIS ISN'T SEBASTIAN.
"THE DEAD DON'T MAGICALLY RISE FROM THE GRAVE."

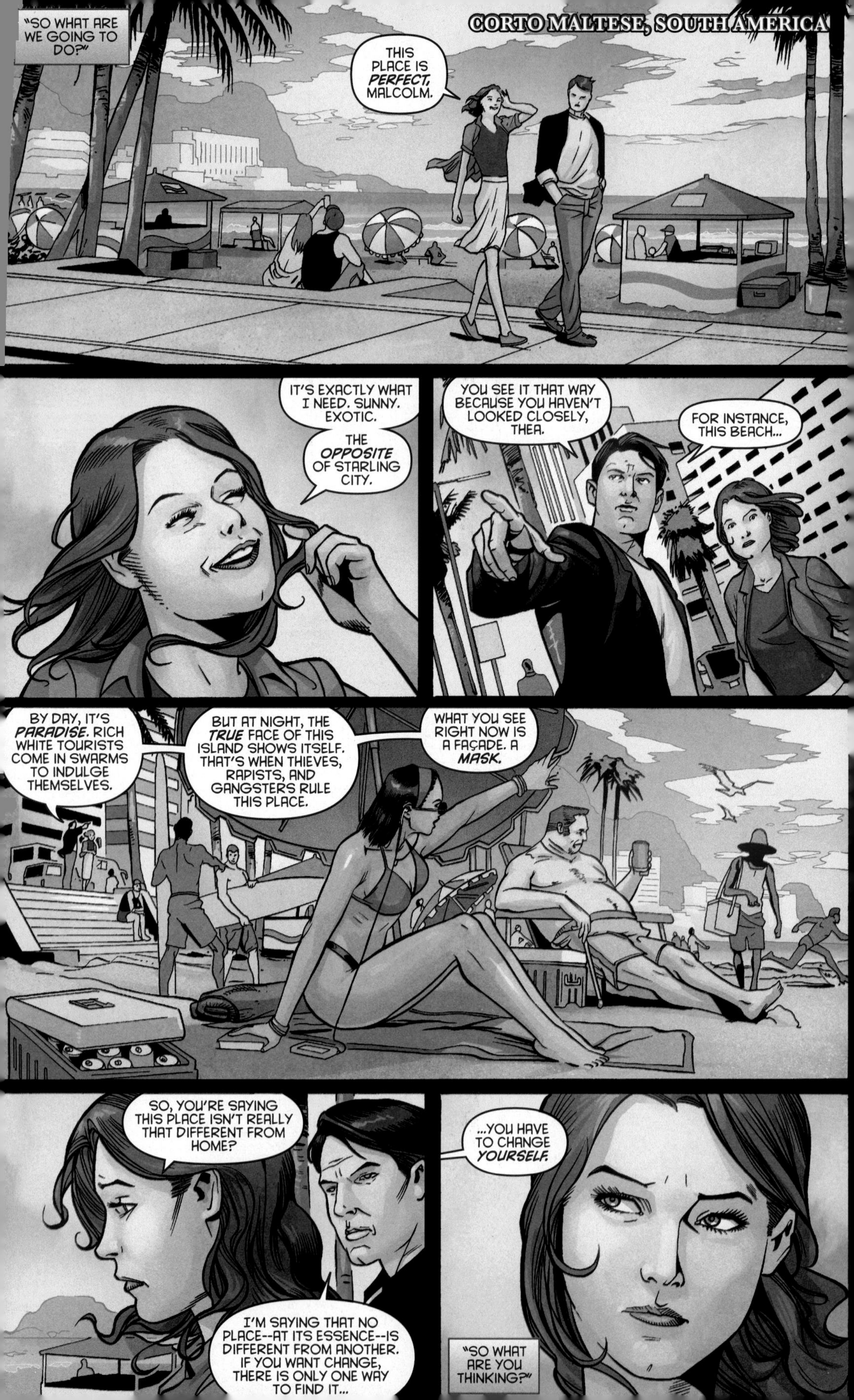
CORTO MALTESE, SOUTH AMERICA
"SO WHAT ARE WE GOING TO DO?"
THIS PLACE IS PERFECT, MALCOLM.
IT'S EXACTLY WHAT I NEED. SUNNY. EXOTIC.
THE OPPOSITE OF STARLING CITY.
YOU SEE IT THAT WAY BECAUSE YOU HAVEN'T LOOKED CLOSELY, THEA.
FOR INSTANCE, THIS BEACH...
BY DAY, IT'S PARADISE. RICH WHITE TOURISTS COME IN SWARMS TO INDULGE THEMSELVES.
BUT AT NIGHT, THE TRUE FACE OF THIS ISLAND SHOWS ITSELF. THAT'S WHEN THIEVES, RAPISTS, AND GANGSTERS RULE THIS PLACE.
WHAT YOU SEE RIGHT NOW IS A FAÇADE. A MASK.
SO, YOU'RE SAYING THIS PLACE ISN'T REALLY THAT DIFFERENT FROM HOME?
I'M SAYING THAT NO PLACE--AT ITS ESSENCE--IS DIFFERENT FROM ANOTHER. IF YOU WANT CHANGE, THERE IS ONLY ONE WAY TO FIND IT...
...YOU HAVE TO CHANGE YOURSELF.
"SO WHAT ARE YOU THINKING?"

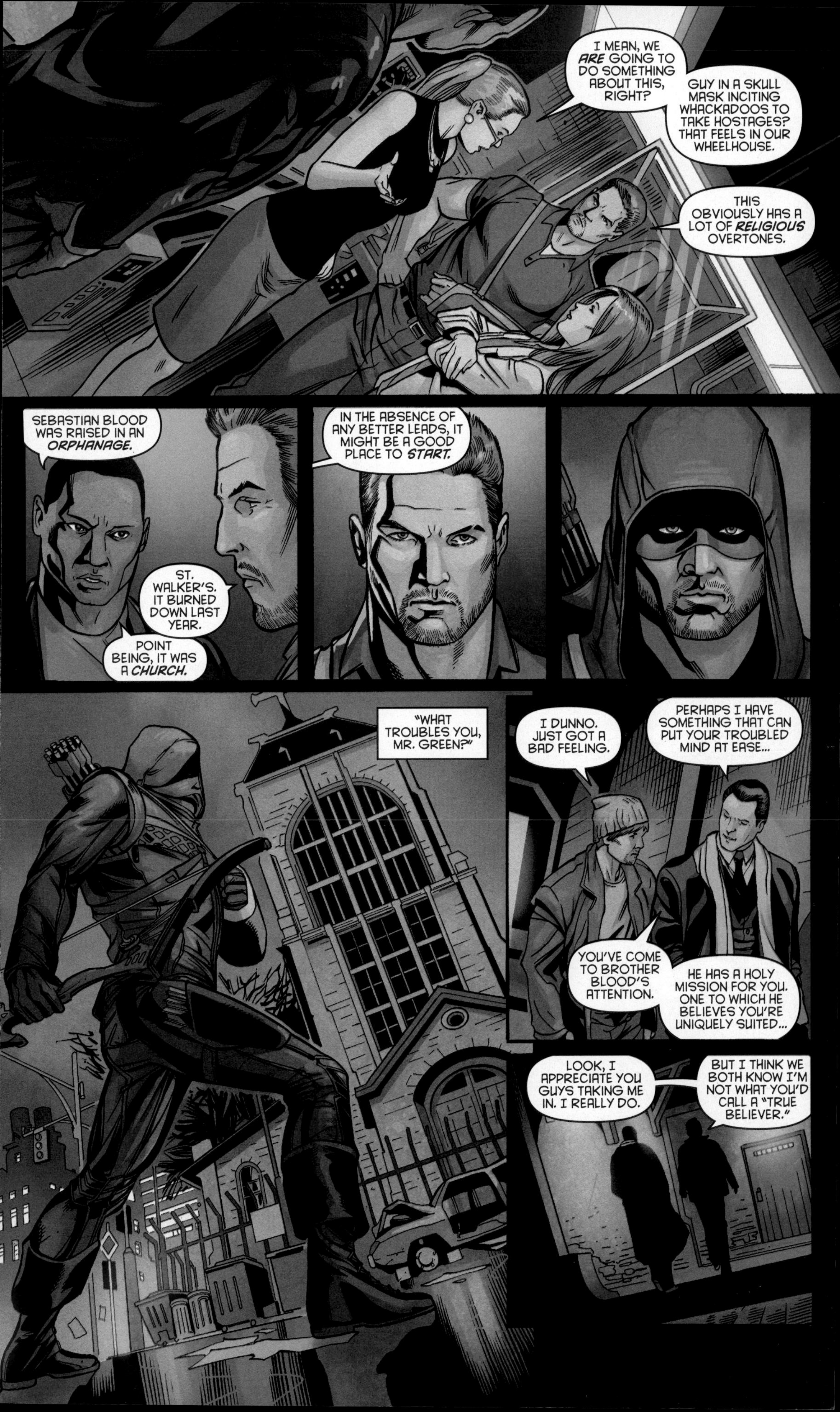
I MEAN, WE ARE GOING TO DO SOMETHING ABOUT THIS, RIGHT?
GUY IN A SKULL MASK INCITING WHACKADOOS TO TAKE HOSTAGES? THAT FEELS IN OUR WHEELHOUSE.
THIS OBVIOUSLY HAS A LOT OF RELIGIOUS OVERTONES.
SEBASTIAN BLOOD WAS RAISED IN AN ORPHANAGE.
ST. WALKER'S. IT BURNED DOWN LAST YEAR.
POINT BEING, IT WAS A CHURCH.
IN THE ABSENCE OF ANY BETTER LEADS, IT MIGHT BE A GOOD PLACE TO START.
"WHAT TROUBLES YOU, MR. GREEN?"
I DUNNO. JUST GOT A BAD FEELING.
PERHAPS I HAVE SOMETHING THAT CAN PUT YOUR TROUBLED MIND AT EASE...
YOU'VE COME TO BROTHER BLOOD'S ATTENTION.
HE HAS A HOLY MISSION FOR YOU. ONE TO WHICH HE BELIEVES YOU'RE UNIQUELY SUITED...
LOOK, I APPRECIATE YOU GUYS TAKING ME IN. I REALLY DO.
BUT I THINK WE BOTH KNOW I'M NOT WHAT YOU'D CALL A "TRUE BELIEVER."

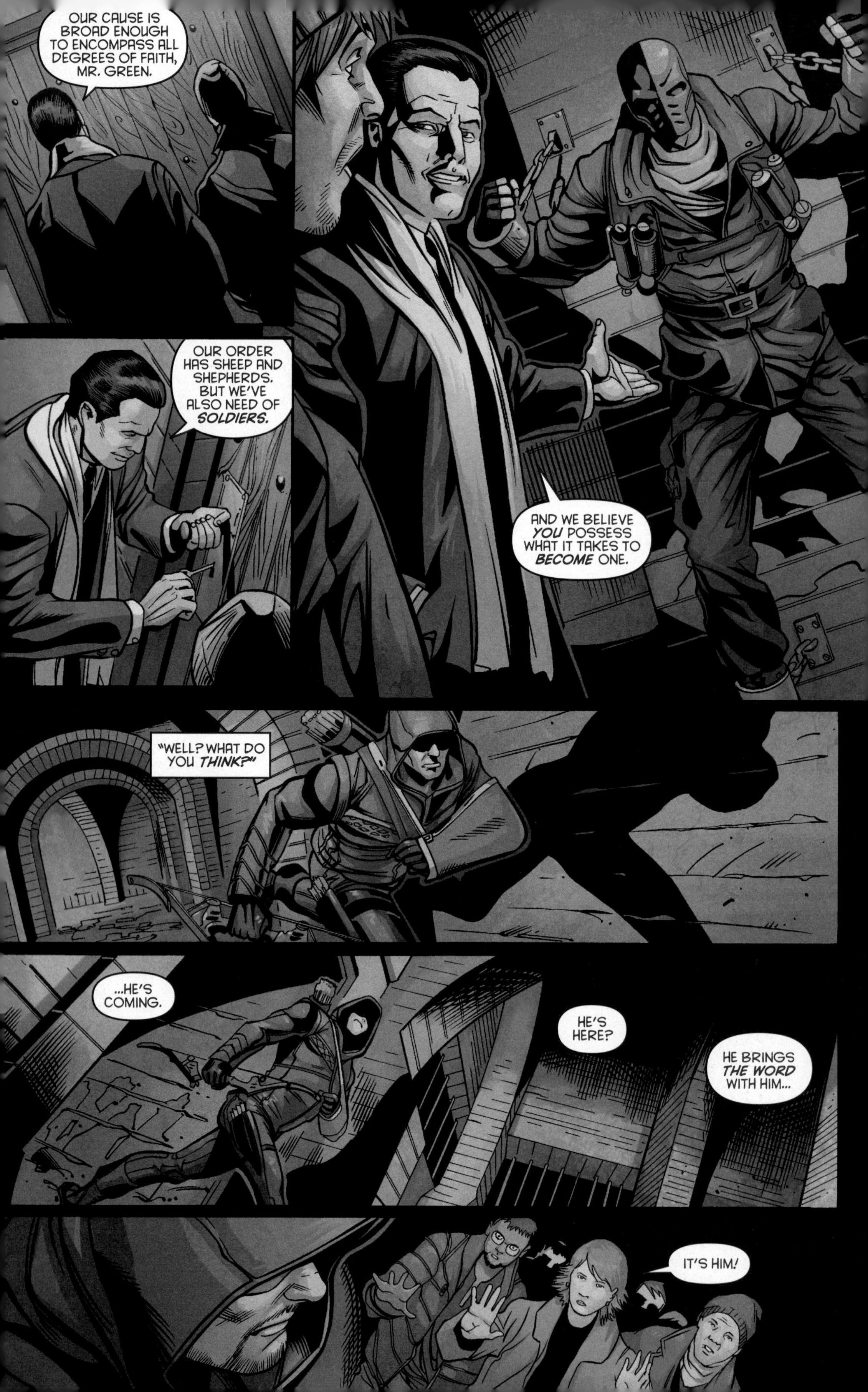
OUR CAUSE IS BROAD ENOUGH TO ENCOMPASS ALL DEGREES OF FAITH, MR. GREEN.
OUR ORDER HAS SHEEP AND SHEPHERDS. BUT WE'VE ALSO NEED OF **SOLDIERS.**
AND WE BELIEVE ***YOU*** POSSESS WHAT IT TAKES TO ***BECOME*** ONE.
"WELL? WHAT DO YOU ***THINK?***"
...HE'S COMING.
HE'S HERE?
HE BRINGS ***THE WORD*** WITH HIM...
IT'S HIM!

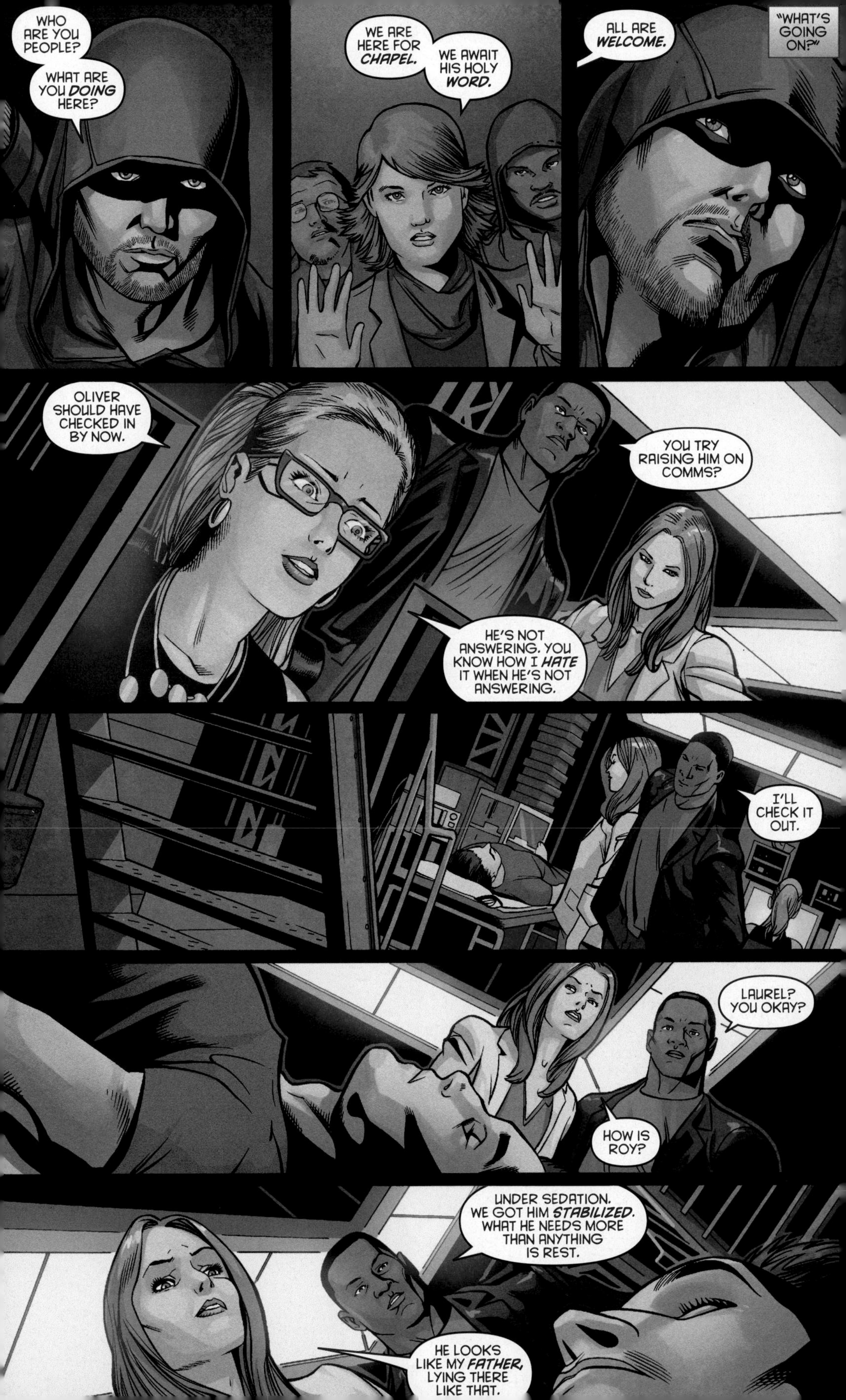
WHO ARE YOU PEOPLE?
WHAT ARE YOU DOING HERE?
WE ARE HERE FOR CHAPEL.
WE AWAIT HIS HOLY WORD.
ALL ARE WELCOME.
"WHAT'S GOING ON?"
OLIVER SHOULD HAVE CHECKED IN BY NOW.
YOU TRY RAISING HIM ON COMMS?
HE'S NOT ANSWERING. YOU KNOW HOW I HATE IT WHEN HE'S NOT ANSWERING.
I'LL CHECK IT OUT.
LAUREL? YOU OKAY?
HOW IS ROY?
UNDER SEDATION. WE GOT HIM STABILIZED. WHAT HE NEEDS MORE THAN ANYTHING IS REST.
HE LOOKS LIKE MY FATHER, LYING THERE LIKE THAT.

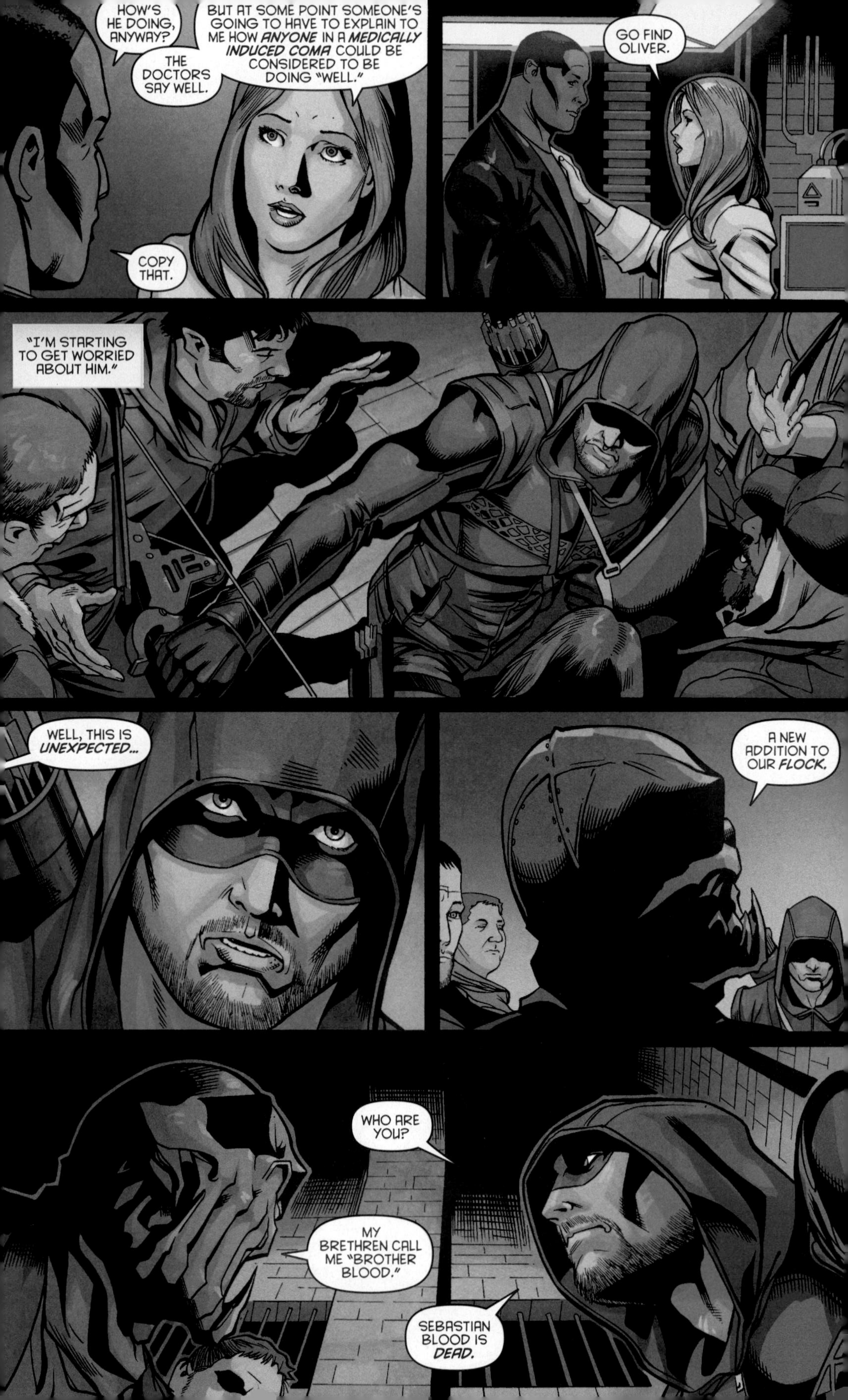
HOW'S HE DOING, ANYWAY?
THE DOCTORS SAY WELL.
BUT AT SOME POINT SOMEONE'S GOING TO HAVE TO EXPLAIN TO ME HOW ANYONE IN A MEDICALLY INDUCED COMA COULD BE CONSIDERED TO BE DOING "WELL."
COPY THAT.
GO FIND OLIVER.
"I'M STARTING TO GET WORRIED ABOUT HIM."
WELL, THIS IS UNEXPECTED...
A NEW ADDITION TO OUR FLOCK.
WHO ARE YOU?
MY BRETHREN CALL ME "BROTHER BLOOD."
SEBASTIAN BLOOD IS DEAD.

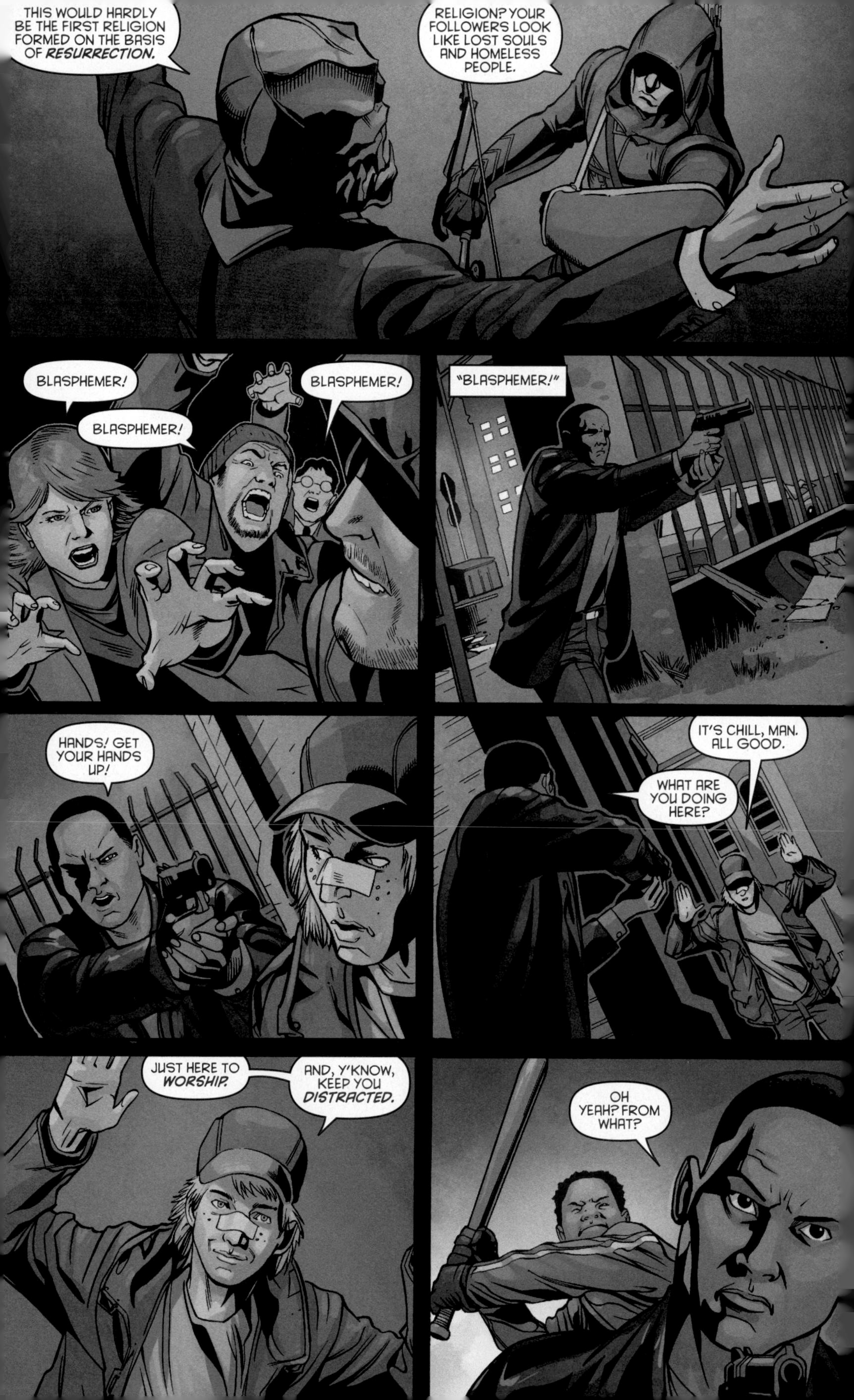
THIS WOULD HARDLY BE THE FIRST RELIGION FORMED ON THE BASIS OF *RESURRECTION.*
RELIGION? YOUR FOLLOWERS LOOK LIKE LOST SOULS AND HOMELESS PEOPLE.
BLASPHEMER!
BLASPHEMER!
BLASPHEMER!
"BLASPHEMER!"
HANDS! GET YOUR HANDS UP!
IT'S CHILL, MAN. ALL GOOD.
WHAT ARE YOU DOING HERE?
JUST HERE TO *WORSHIP.*
AND, Y'KNOW, KEEP YOU *DISTRACTED.*
OH YEAH? FROM WHAT?

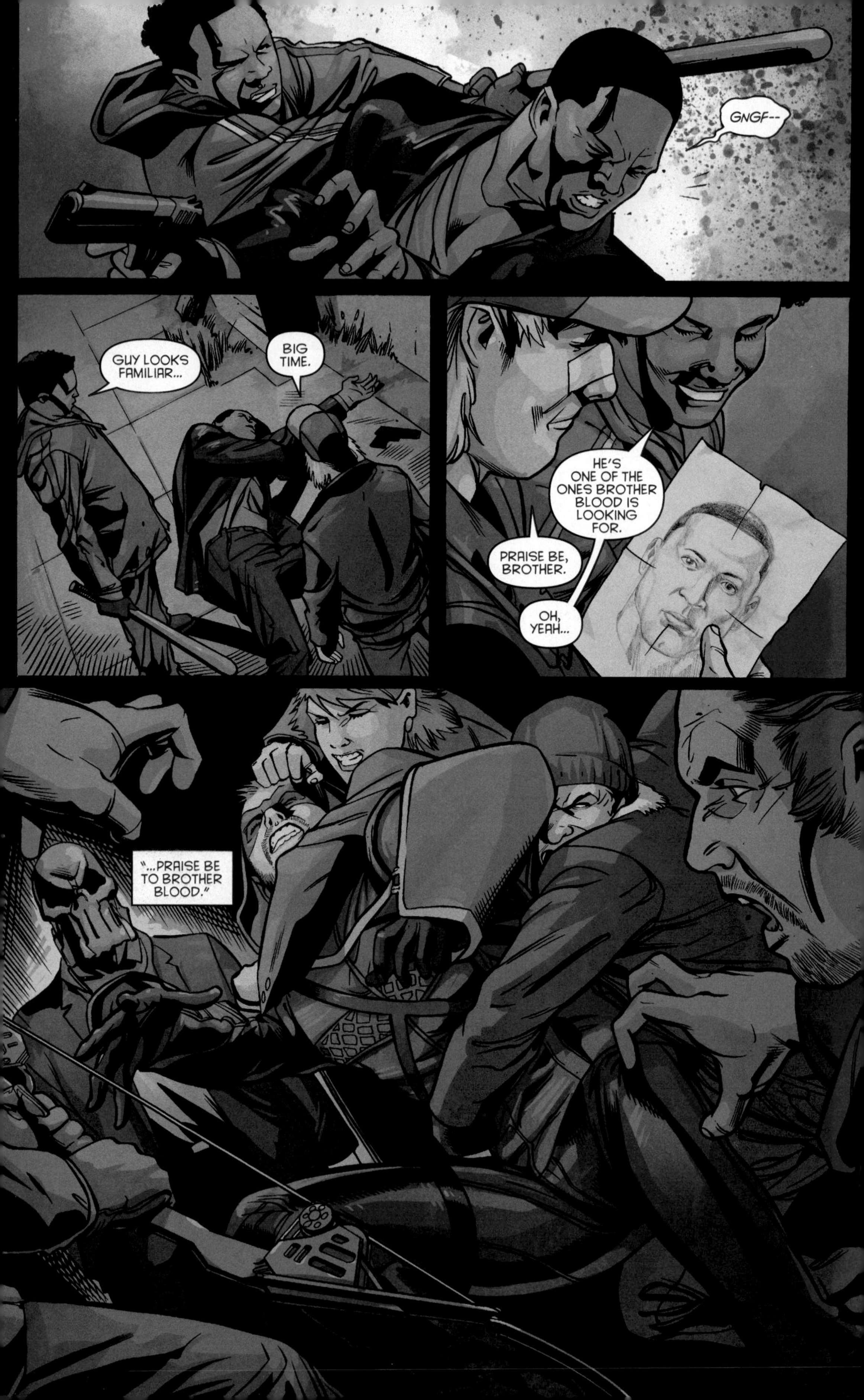
GNGF--
GUY LOOKS FAMILIAR...
BIG TIME.
HE'S ONE OF THE ONES BROTHER BLOOD IS LOOKING FOR.
PRAISE BE, BROTHER.
OH, YEAH...
"...PRAISE BE TO BROTHER BLOOD."

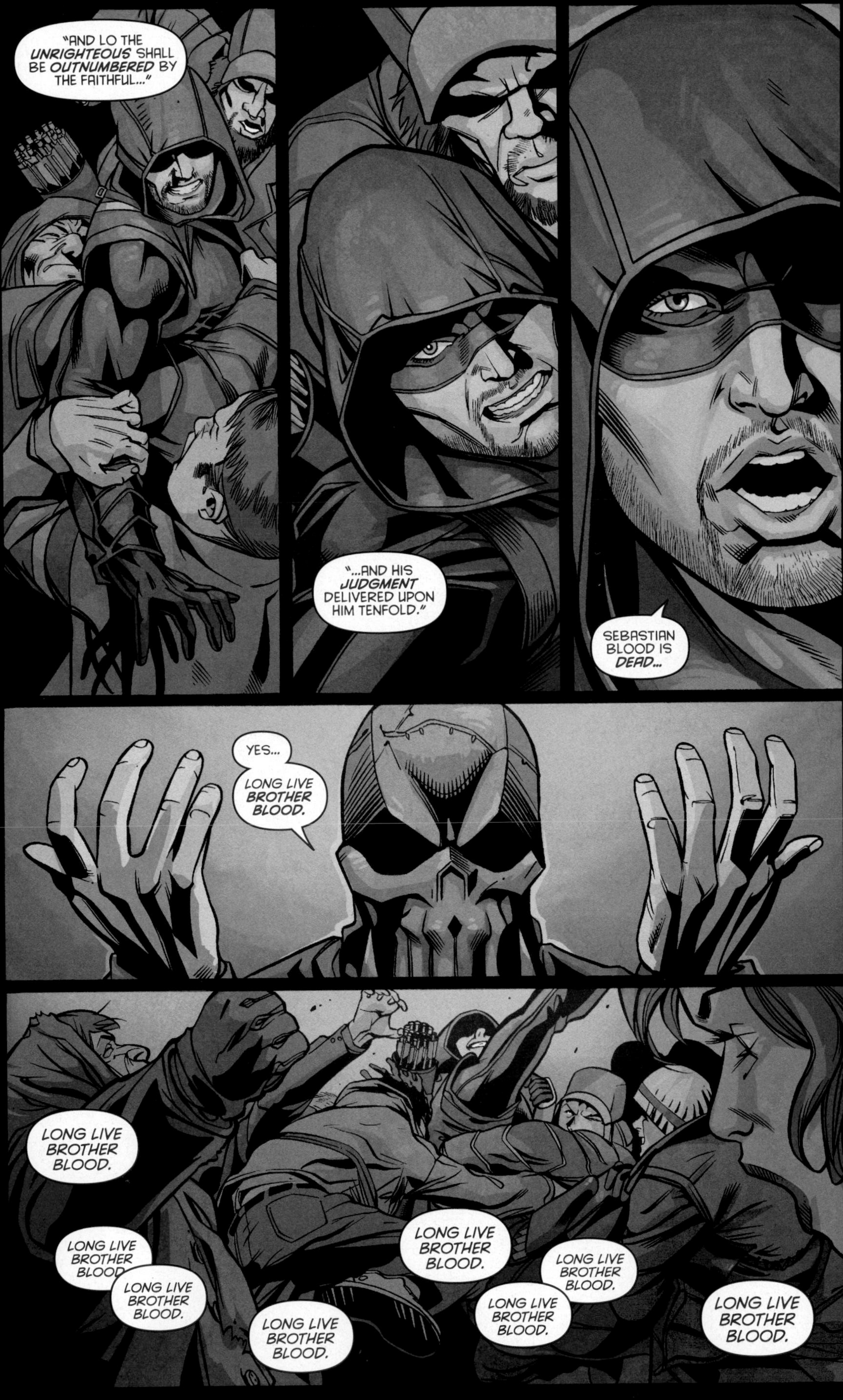
"AND LO THE UNRIGHTEOUS SHALL BE OUTNUMBERED BY THE FAITHFUL..."
"...AND HIS JUDGMENT DELIVERED UPON HIM TENFOLD."
SEBASTIAN BLOOD IS DEAD...
YES... LONG LIVE BROTHER BLOOD.
LONG LIVE BROTHER BLOOD.
LONG LIVE BROTHER BLOOD.
LONG LIVE BROTHER BLOOD.
LONG LIVE BROTHER BLOOD.
LONG LIVE BROTHER BLOOD.
LONG LIVE BROTHER BLOOD.
LONG LIVE BROTHER BLOOD.
LONG LIVE BROTHER BLOOD.

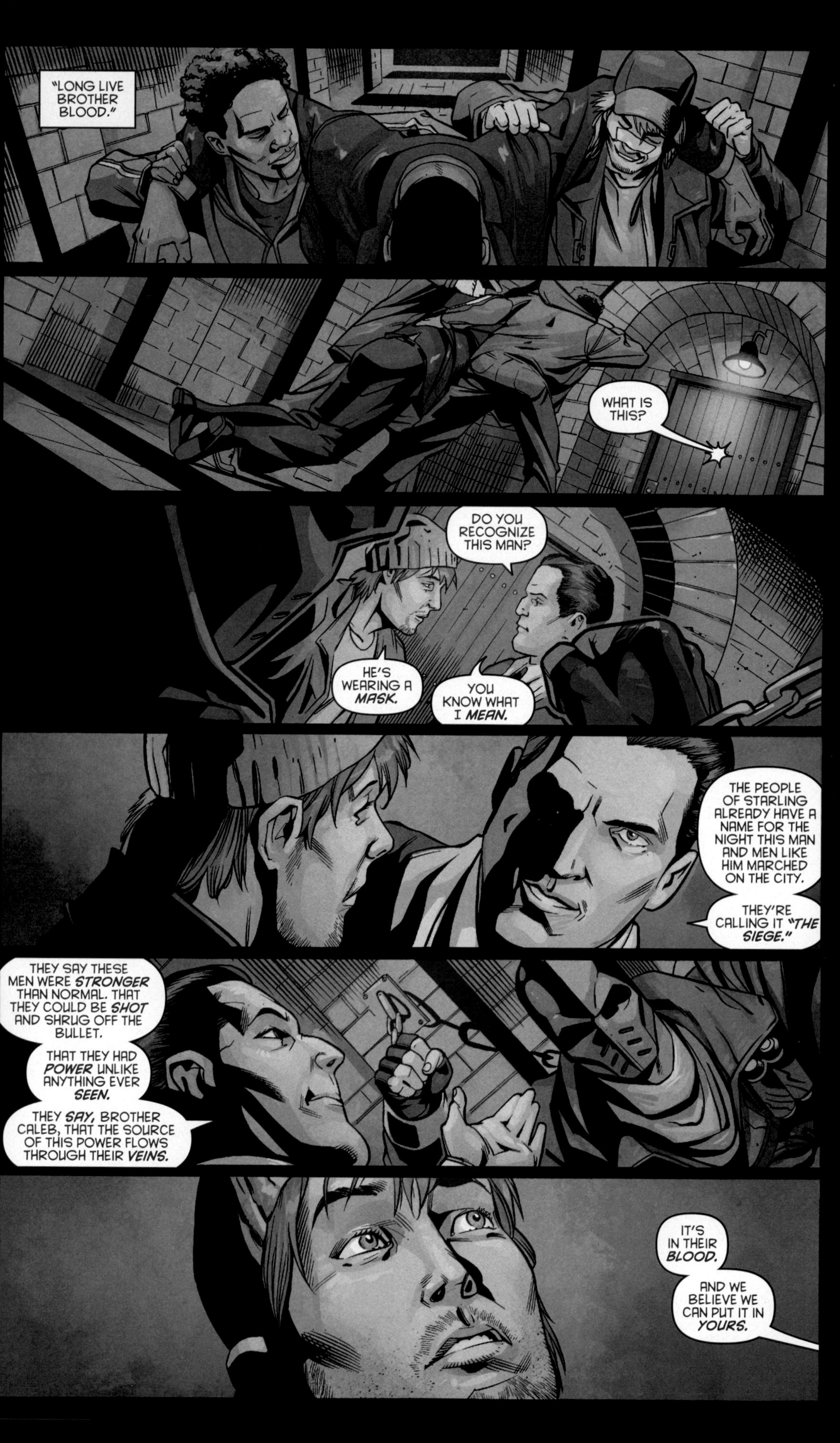
"LONG LIVE BROTHER BLOOD."
WHAT IS THIS?
DO YOU RECOGNIZE THIS MAN?
HE'S WEARING A MASK.
YOU KNOW WHAT I MEAN.
THE PEOPLE OF STARLING ALREADY HAVE A NAME FOR THE NIGHT THIS MAN AND MEN LIKE HIM MARCHED ON THE CITY.
THEY'RE CALLING IT "THE SIEGE."
THEY SAY THESE MEN WERE STRONGER THAN NORMAL. THAT THEY COULD BE SHOT AND SHRUG OFF THE BULLET.
THAT THEY HAD POWER UNLIKE ANYTHING EVER SEEN.
THEY SAY, BROTHER CALEB, THAT THE SOURCE OF THIS POWER FLOWS THROUGH THEIR VEINS.
IT'S IN THEIR BLOOD.
AND WE BELIEVE WE CAN PUT IT IN YOURS.

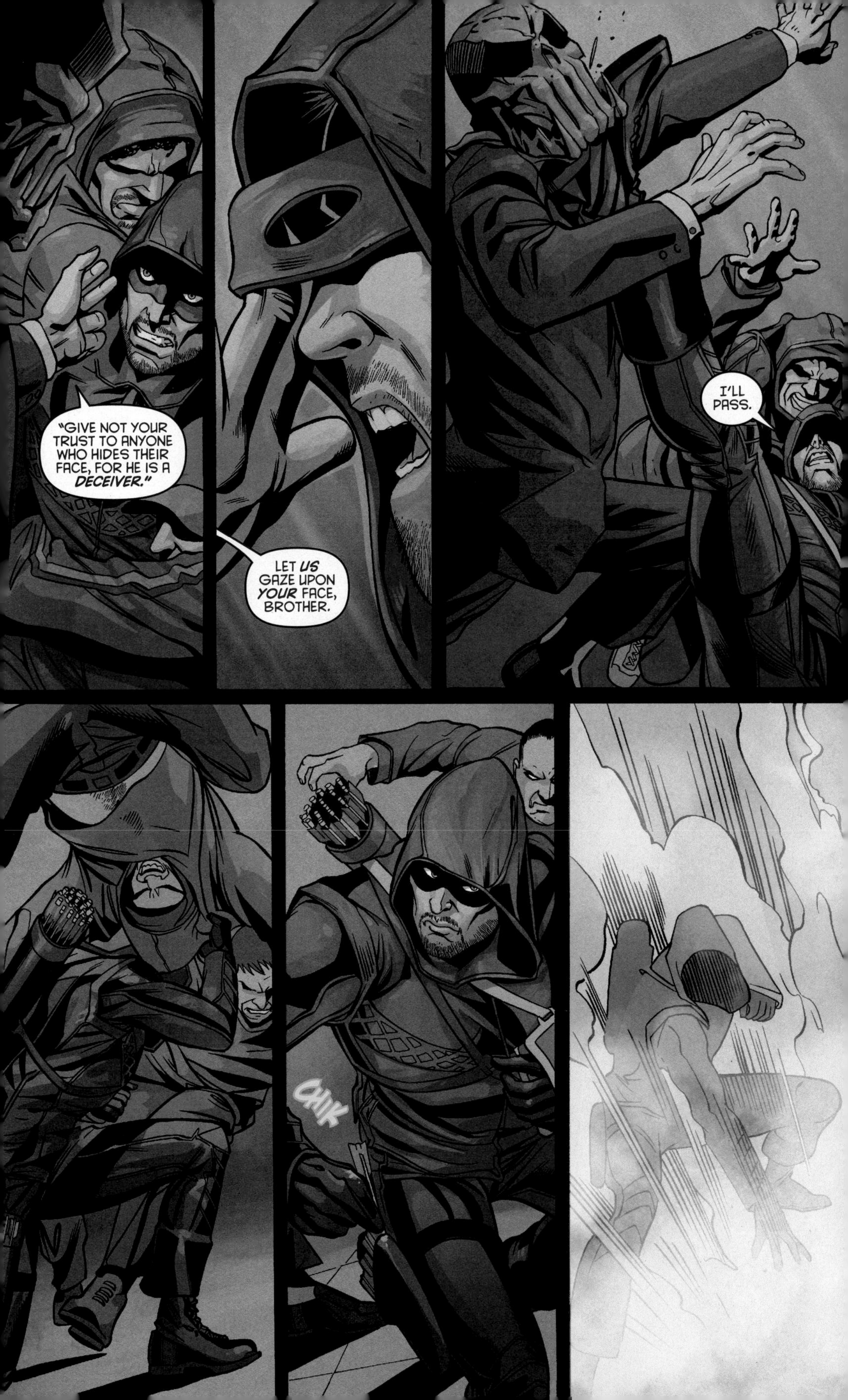
"GIVE NOT YOUR TRUST TO ANYONE WHO HIDES THEIR FACE, FOR HE IS A *DECEIVER*."
LET *US* GAZE UPON *YOUR* FACE, BROTHER.
I'LL PASS.
CHIK

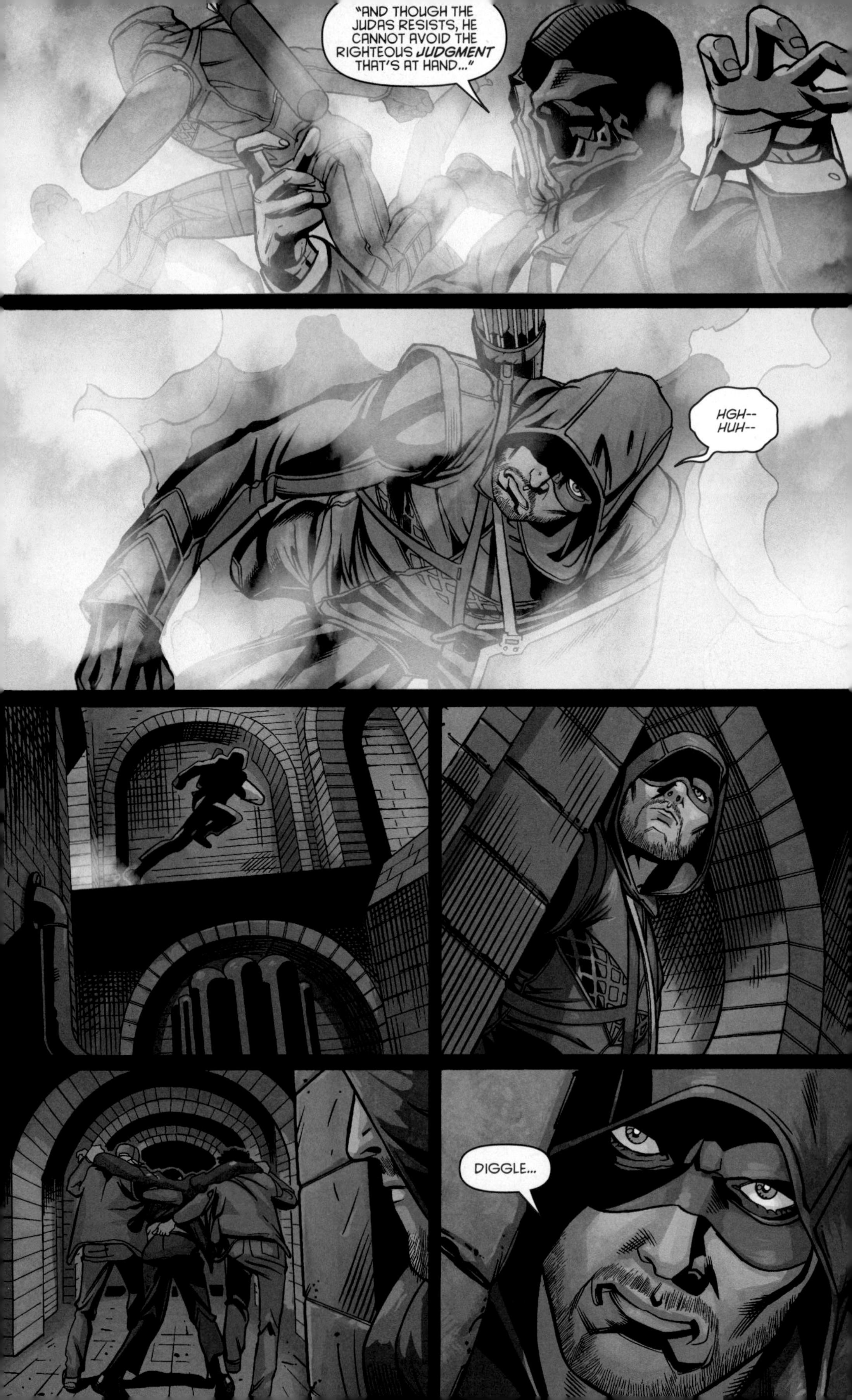
"AND THOUGH THE JUDAS RESISTS, HE CANNOT AVOID THE RIGHTEOUS JUDGMENT THAT'S AT HAND..."
HGH-- HUH--
DIGGLE...

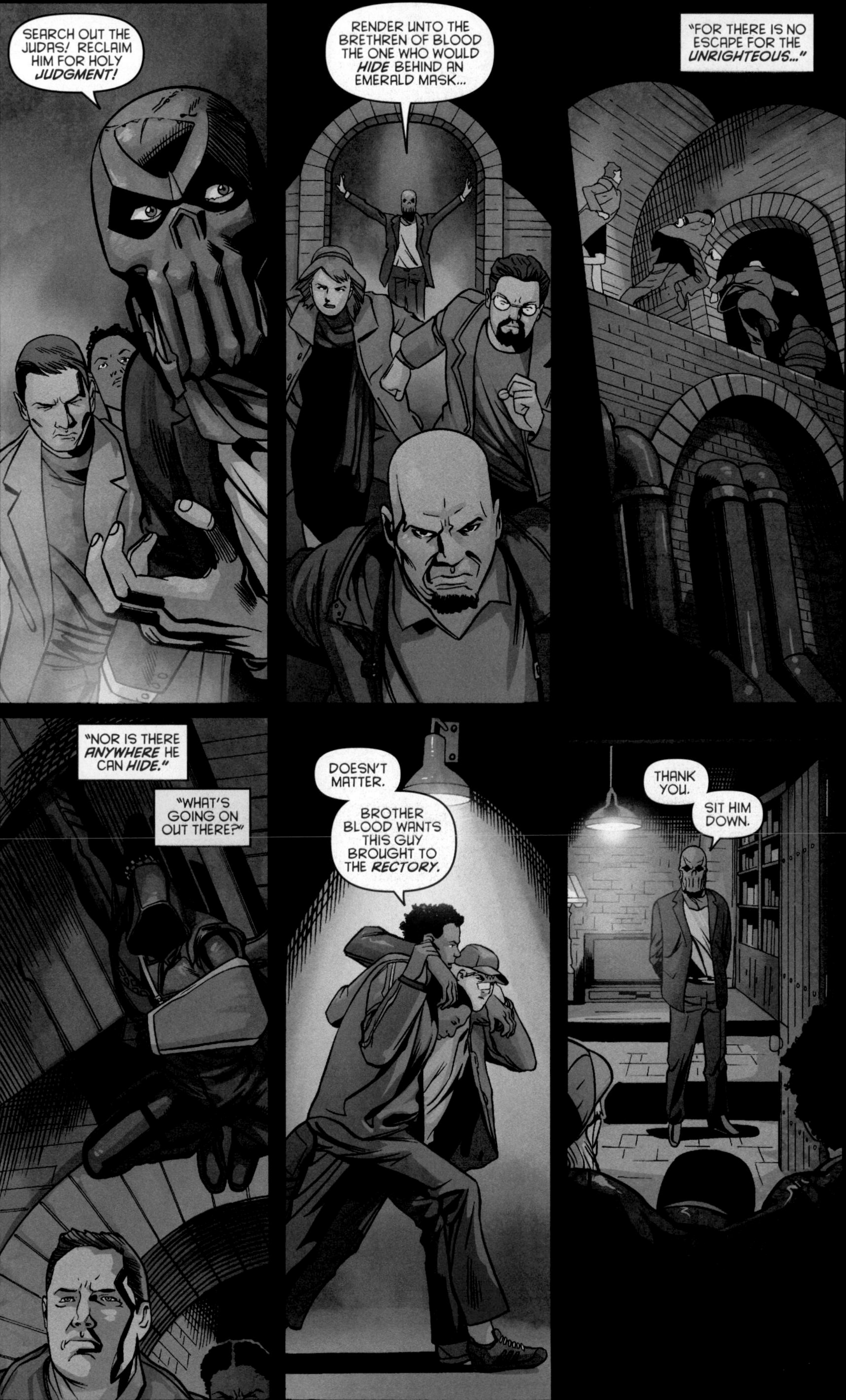
SEARCH OUT THE JUDAS! RECLAIM HIM FOR HOLY JUDGMENT!
RENDER UNTO THE BRETHREN OF BLOOD THE ONE WHO WOULD HIDE BEHIND AN EMERALD MASK...
"FOR THERE IS NO ESCAPE FOR THE UNRIGHTEOUS..."
"NOR IS THERE ANYWHERE HE CAN HIDE."
"WHAT'S GOING ON OUT THERE?"
DOESN'T MATTER.
BROTHER BLOOD WANTS THIS GUY BROUGHT TO THE RECTORY.
THANK YOU.
SIT HIM DOWN.

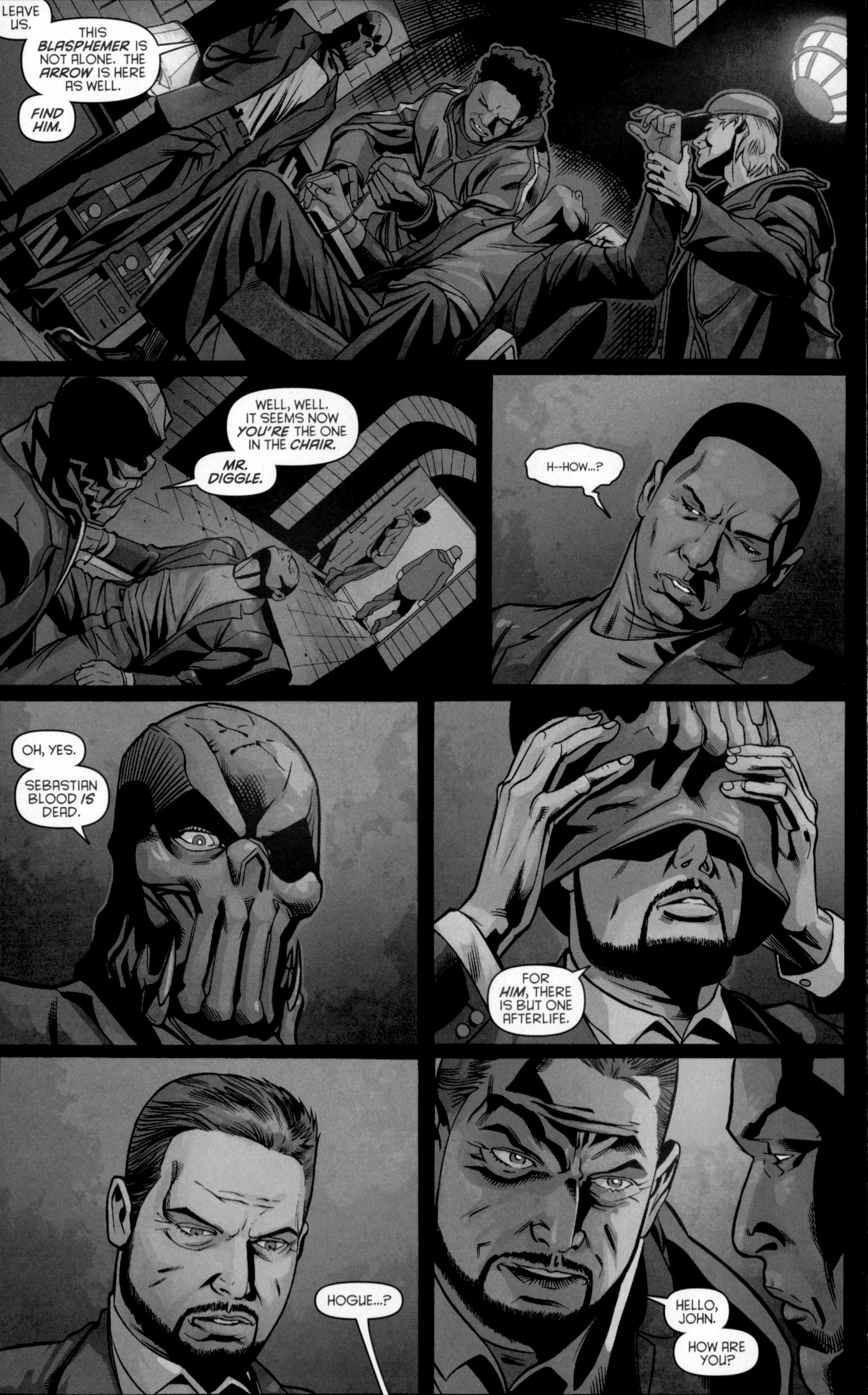

LEAVE US.
THIS BLASPHEMER IS NOT ALONE. THE ARROW IS HERE AS WELL.
FIND HIM.
WELL, WELL. IT SEEMS NOW YOU'RE THE ONE IN THE CHAIR.
MR. DIGGLE.
H--HOW...?
OH, YES.
SEBASTIAN BLOOD IS DEAD.
FOR HIM, THERE IS BUT ONE AFTERLIFE.
HOGUE...?
HELLO, JOHN.
HOW ARE YOU?

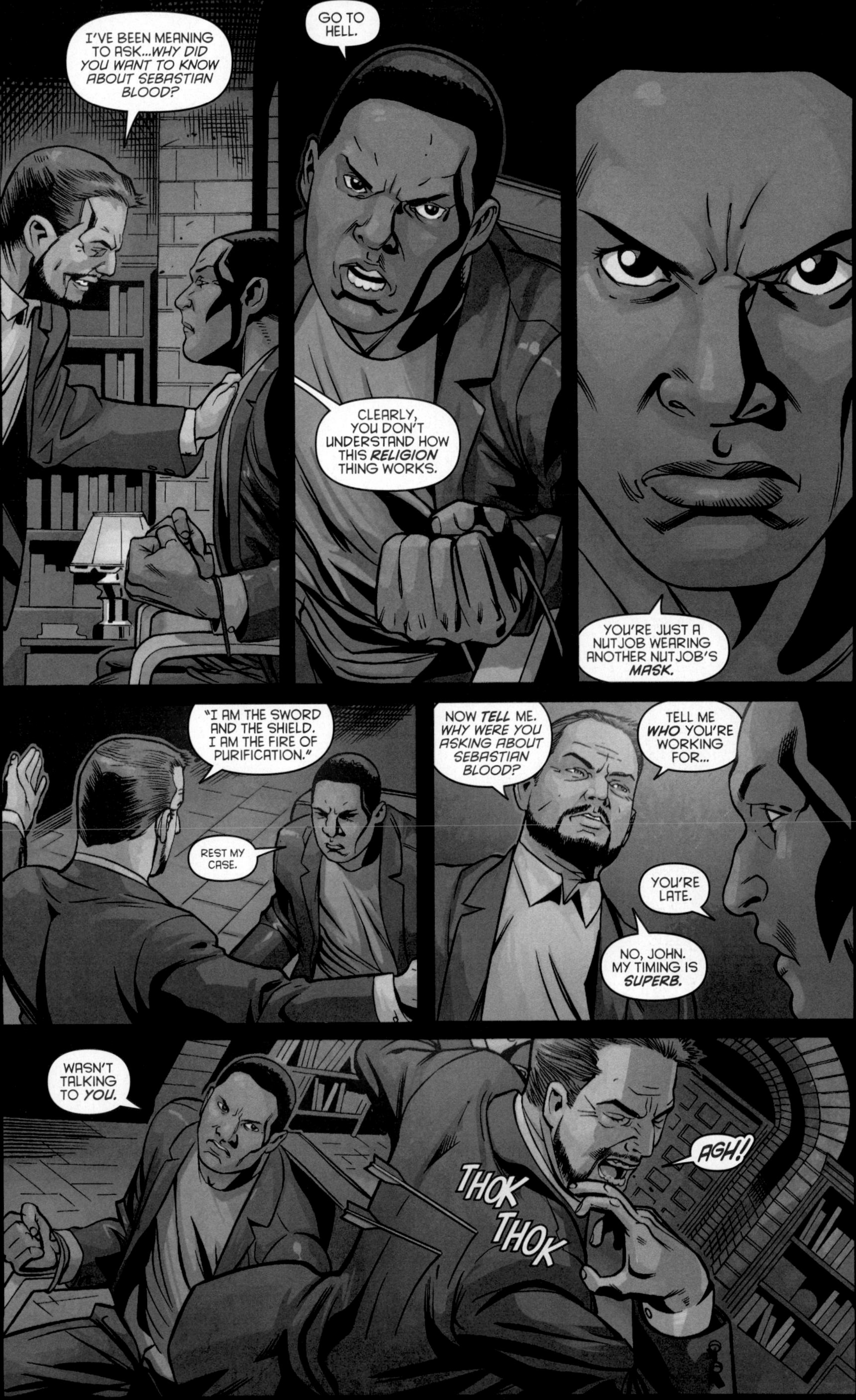
I'VE BEEN MEANING TO ASK...WHY DID YOU WANT TO KNOW ABOUT SEBASTIAN BLOOD?
GO TO HELL.
CLEARLY, YOU DON'T UNDERSTAND HOW THIS RELIGION THING WORKS.
YOU'RE JUST A NUTJOB WEARING ANOTHER NUTJOB'S MASK.
"I AM THE SWORD AND THE SHIELD. I AM THE FIRE OF PURIFICATION."
REST MY CASE.
NOW TELL ME. WHY WERE YOU ASKING ABOUT SEBASTIAN BLOOD?
TELL ME WHO YOU'RE WORKING FOR...
YOU'RE LATE.
NO, JOHN. MY TIMING IS SUPERB.
WASN'T TALKING TO YOU.
AGH!
THOK
THOK

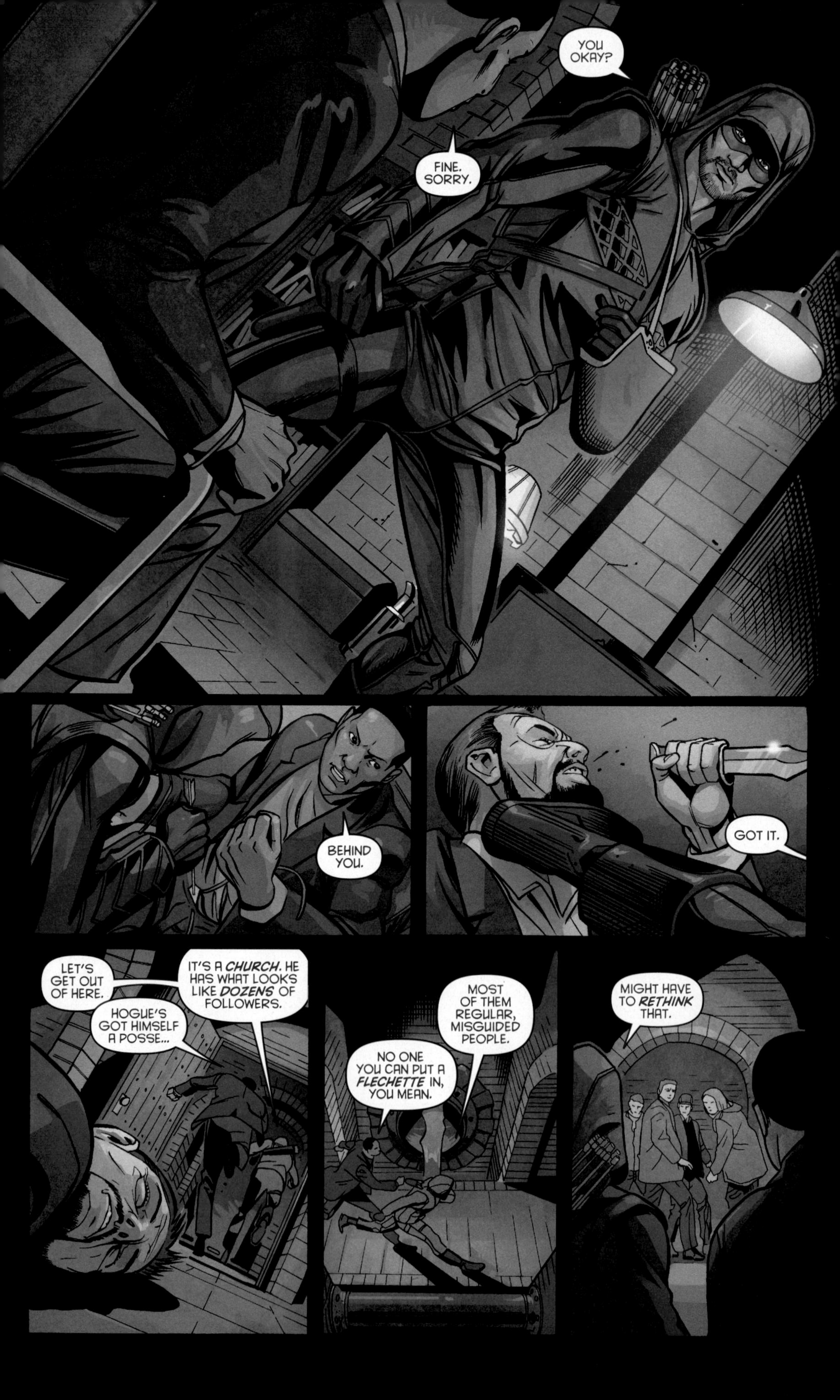
YOU OKAY?
FINE. SORRY.
BEHIND YOU.
GOT IT.
LET'S GET OUT OF HERE.
HOGUE'S GOT HIMSELF A POSSE...
IT'S A CHURCH. HE HAS WHAT LOOKS LIKE DOZENS OF FOLLOWERS.
MOST OF THEM REGULAR, MISGUIDED PEOPLE.
NO ONE YOU CAN PUT A FLECHETTE IN, YOU MEAN.
MIGHT HAVE TO RETHINK THAT.

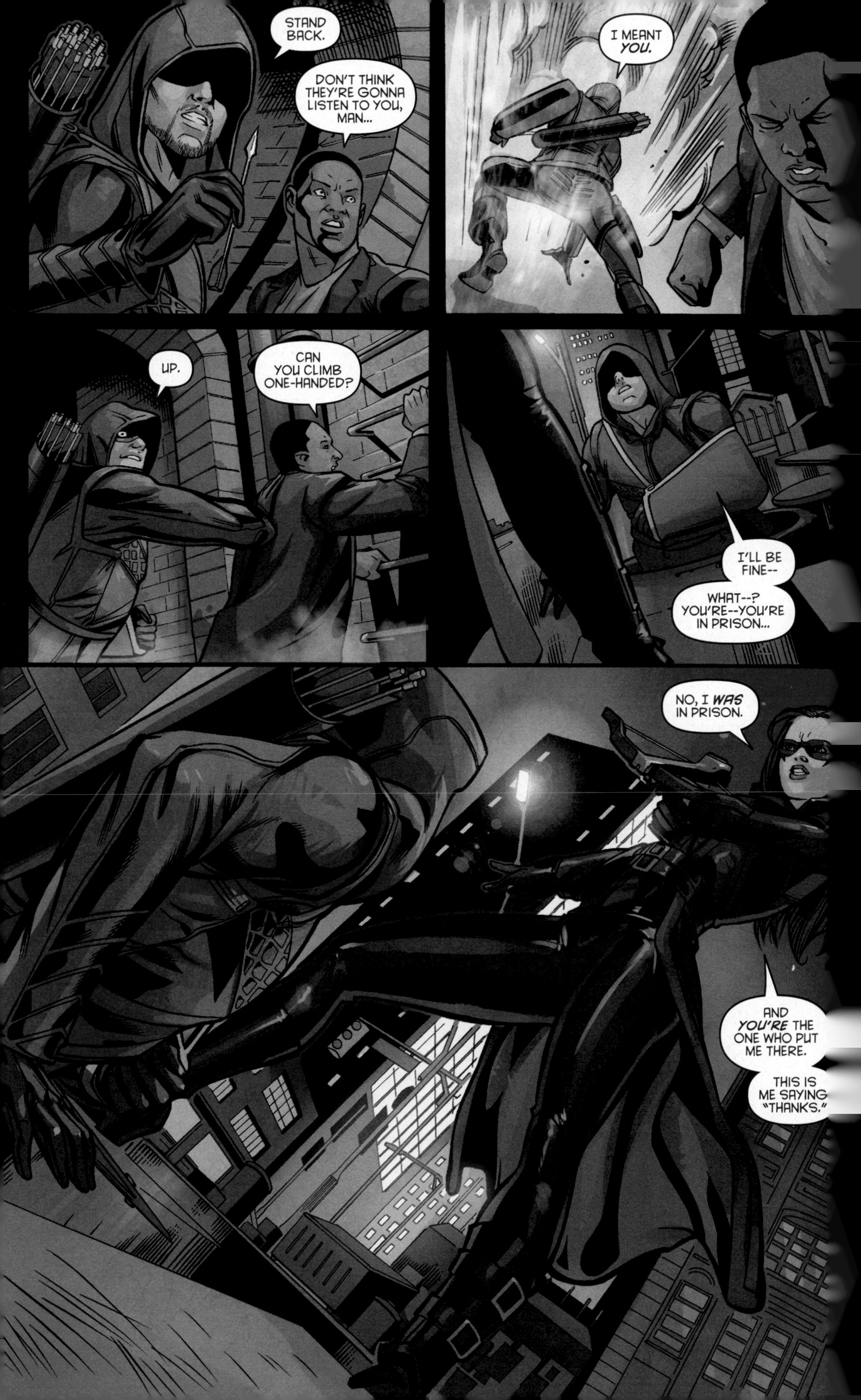
STAND BACK.
DON'T THINK THEY'RE GONNA LISTEN TO YOU, MAN...
I MEANT *YOU.*
UP.
CAN YOU CLIMB ONE-HANDED?
I'LL BE FINE--
WHAT--? YOU'RE--YOU'RE IN PRISON...
NO, I *WAS* IN PRISON.
AND *YOU'RE* THE ONE WHO PUT ME THERE.
THIS IS ME SAYING "THANKS."

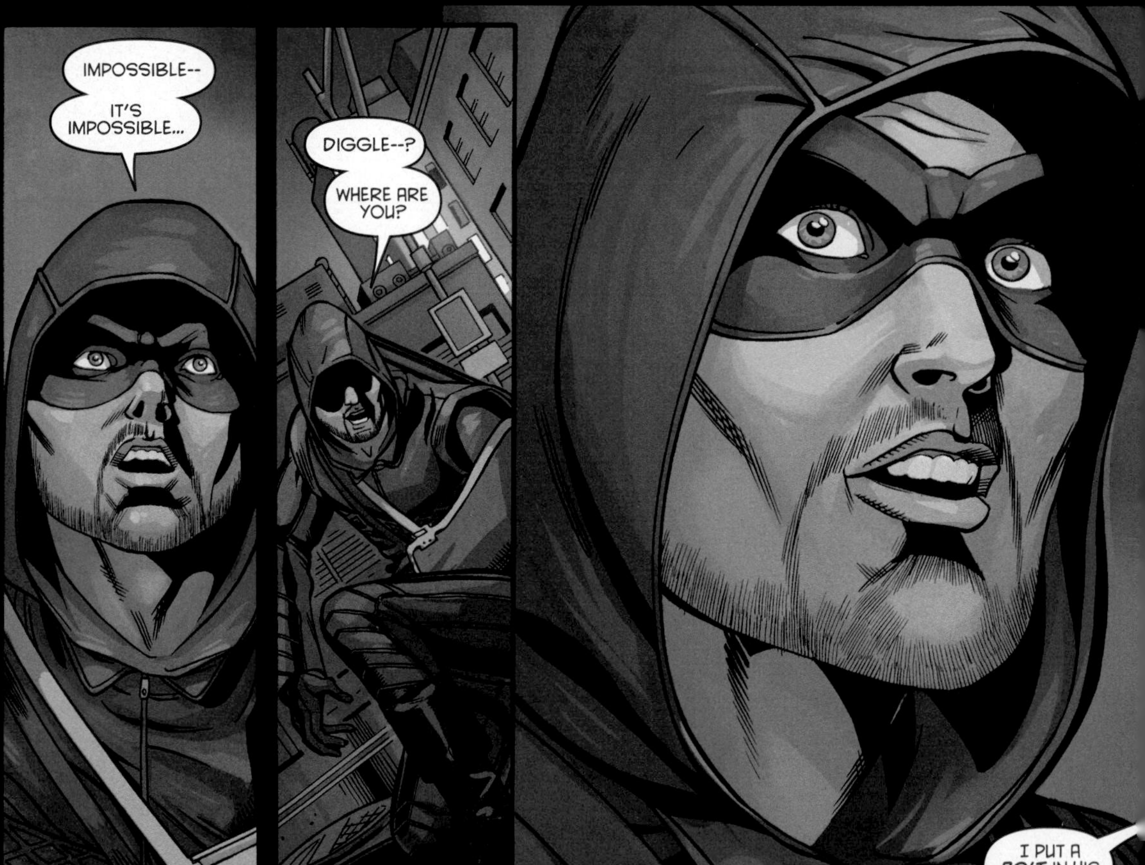
IMPOSSIBLE--
IT'S IMPOSSIBLE...
DIGGLE--?
WHERE ARE YOU?
I PUT A *BOLT* IN HIS HEART...

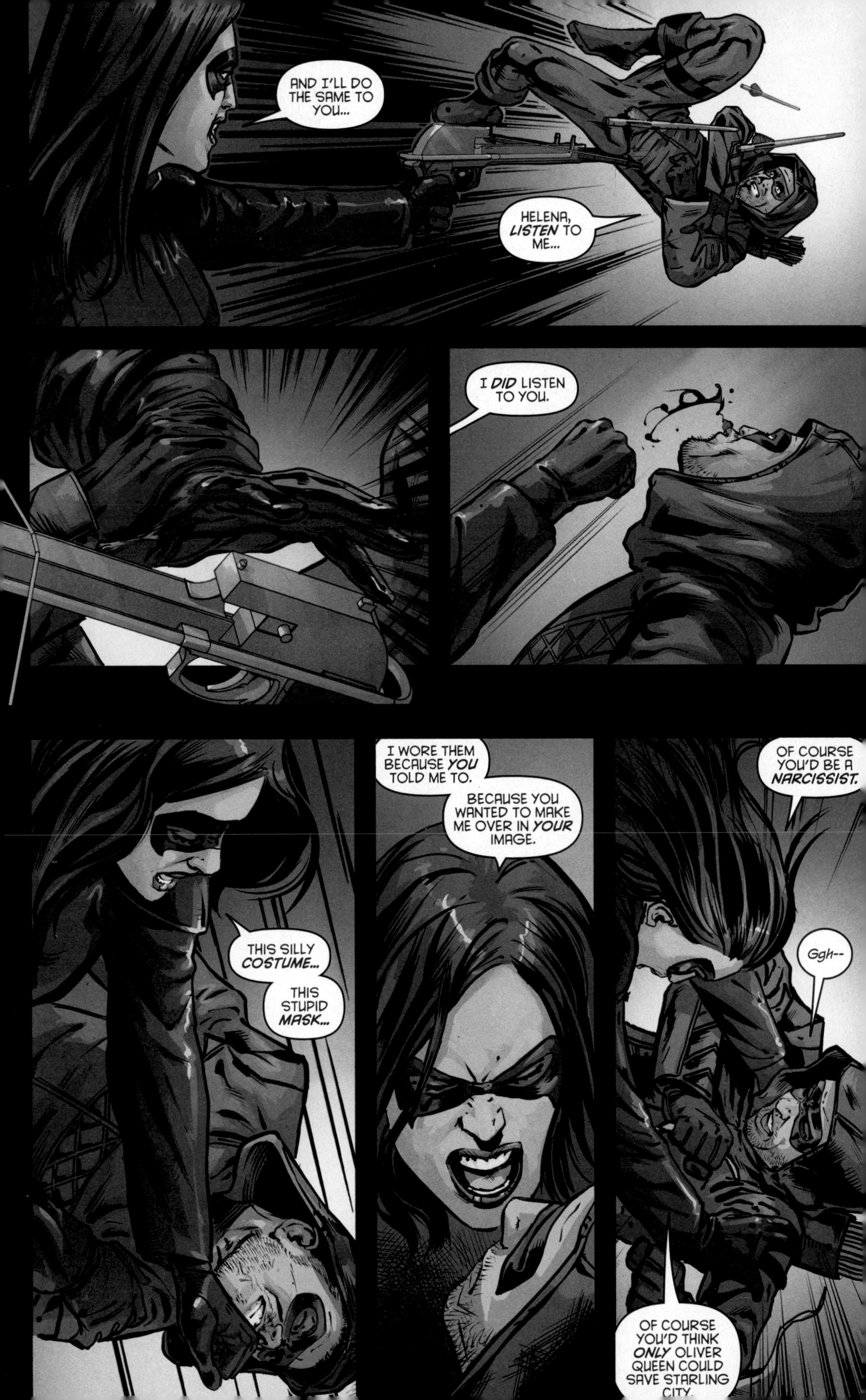
AND I'LL DO THE SAME TO YOU...
HELENA, LISTEN TO ME...
I DID LISTEN TO YOU.
THIS SILLY COSTUME...
THIS STUPID MASK...
I WORE THEM BECAUSE YOU TOLD ME TO.
BECAUSE YOU WANTED TO MAKE ME OVER IN YOUR IMAGE.
OF COURSE YOU'D BE A NARCISSIST.
Ggh--
OF COURSE YOU'D THINK ONLY OLIVER QUEEN COULD SAVE STARLING CITY.

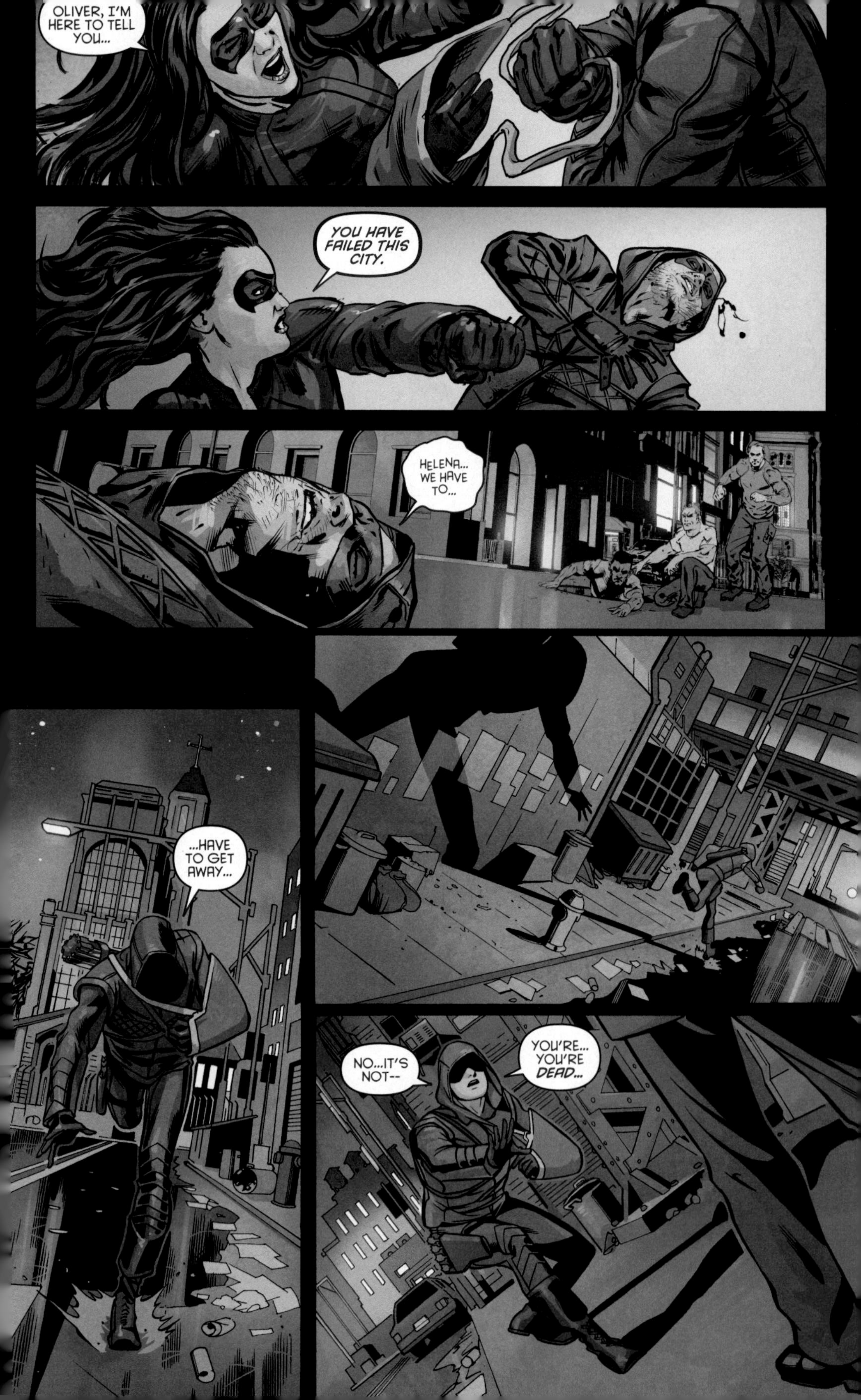
OLIVER, I'M HERE TO TELL YOU...
YOU HAVE FAILED THIS CITY.
HELENA... WE HAVE TO...
...HAVE TO GET AWAY...
NO...IT'S NOT--
YOU'RE... YOU'RE DEAD...

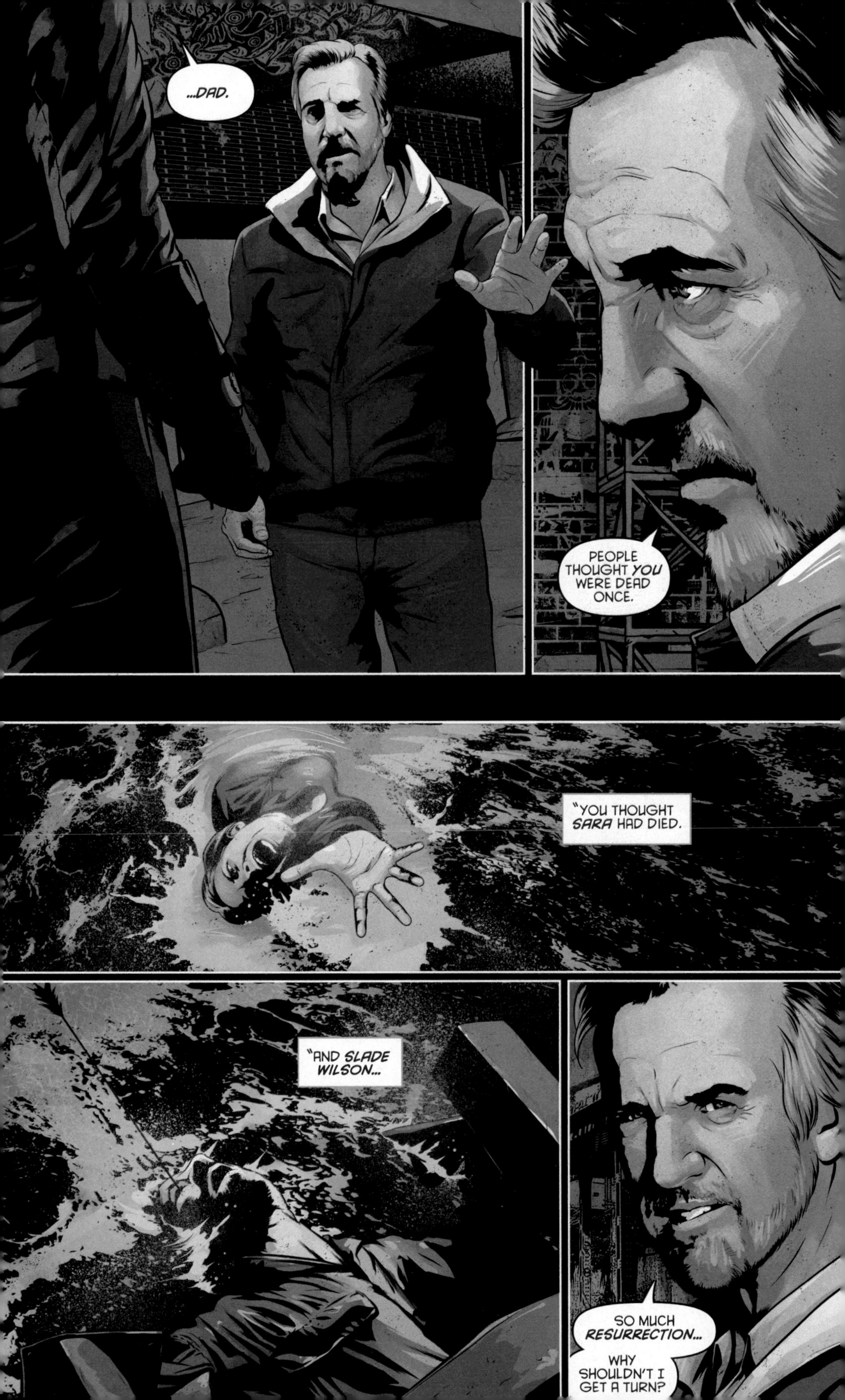
...DAD.
PEOPLE THOUGHT YOU WERE DEAD ONCE.
"YOU THOUGHT SARA HAD DIED.
"AND SLADE WILSON...
SO MUCH RESURRECTION...
WHY SHOULDN'T I GET A TURN?

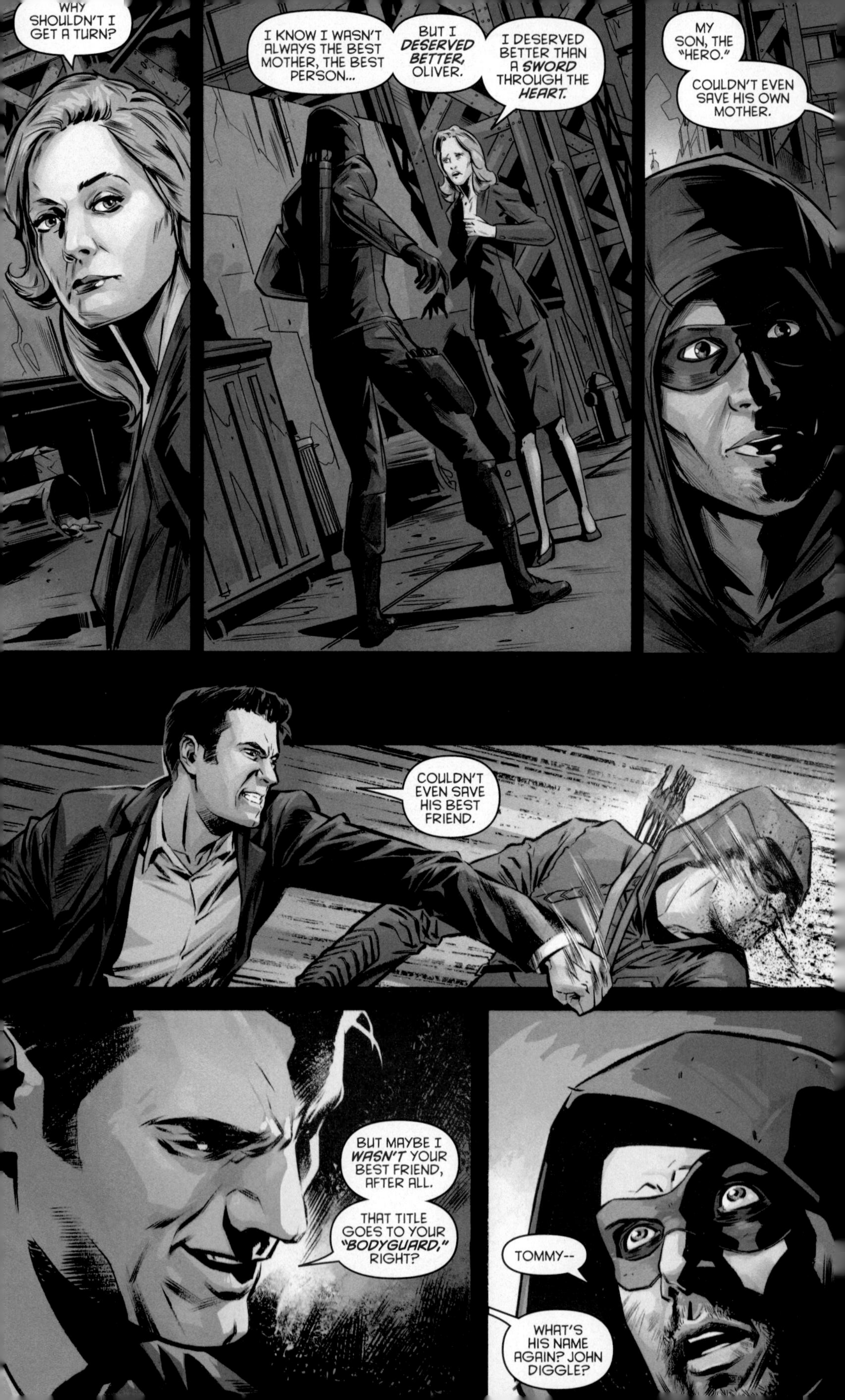
WHY SHOULDN'T I GET A TURN?
I KNOW I WASN'T ALWAYS THE BEST MOTHER, THE BEST PERSON...
BUT I DESERVED BETTER, OLIVER.
I DESERVED BETTER THAN A SWORD THROUGH THE HEART.
MY SON, THE "HERO."
COULDN'T EVEN SAVE HIS OWN MOTHER.
COULDN'T EVEN SAVE HIS BEST FRIEND.
BUT MAYBE I WASN'T YOUR BEST FRIEND, AFTER ALL.
THAT TITLE GOES TO YOUR "BODYGUARD," RIGHT?
TOMMY--
WHAT'S HIS NAME AGAIN? JOHN DIGGLE?

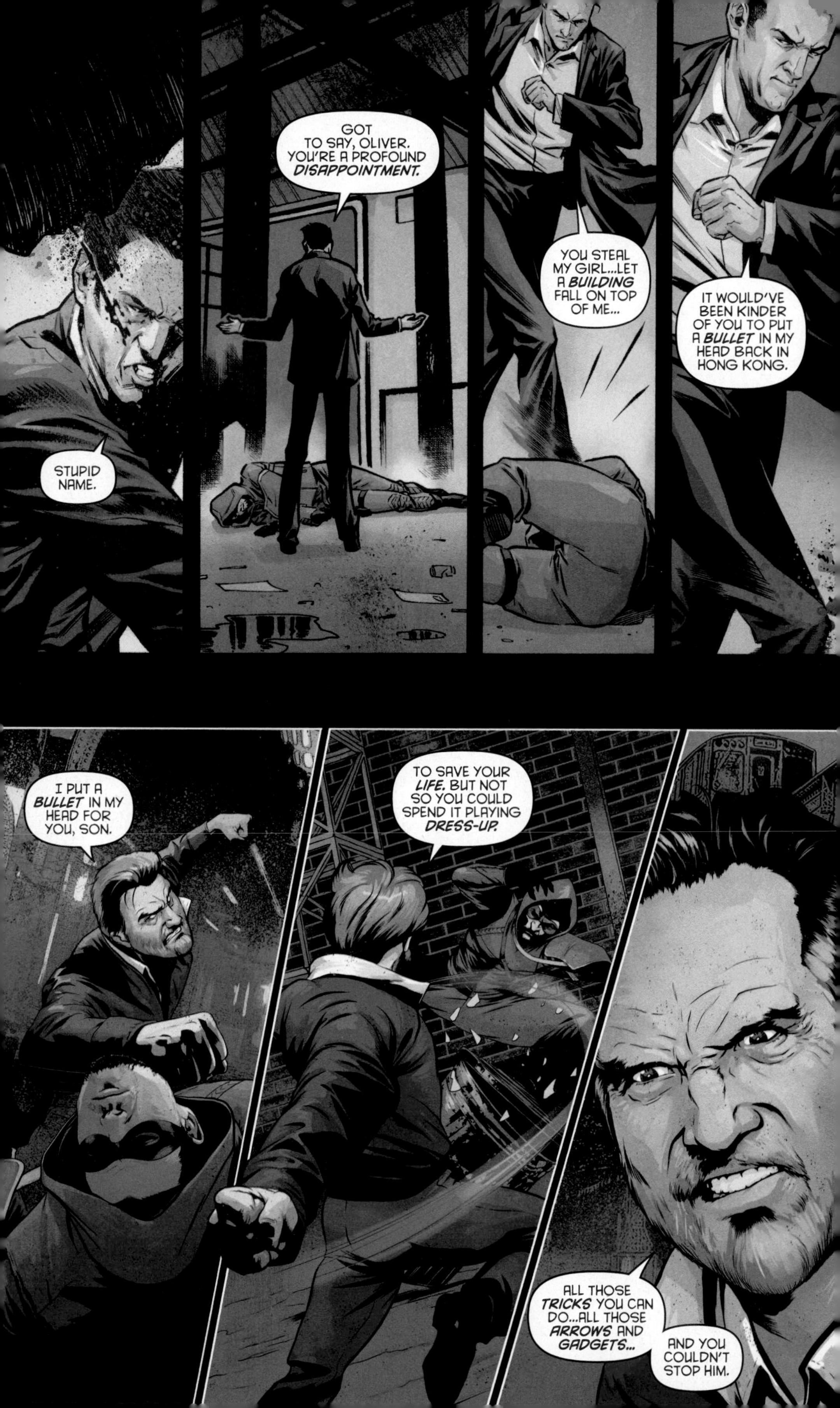
STUPID NAME.
GOT TO SAY, OLIVER. YOU'RE A PROFOUND DISAPPOINTMENT.
YOU STEAL MY GIRL...LET A BUILDING FALL ON TOP OF ME...
IT WOULD'VE BEEN KINDER OF YOU TO PUT A BULLET IN MY HEAD BACK IN HONG KONG.
I PUT A BULLET IN MY HEAD FOR YOU, SON.
TO SAVE YOUR LIFE. BUT NOT SO YOU COULD SPEND IT PLAYING DRESS-UP.
ALL THOSE TRICKS YOU CAN DO...ALL THOSE ARROWS AND GADGETS...
AND YOU COULDN'T STOP HIM.

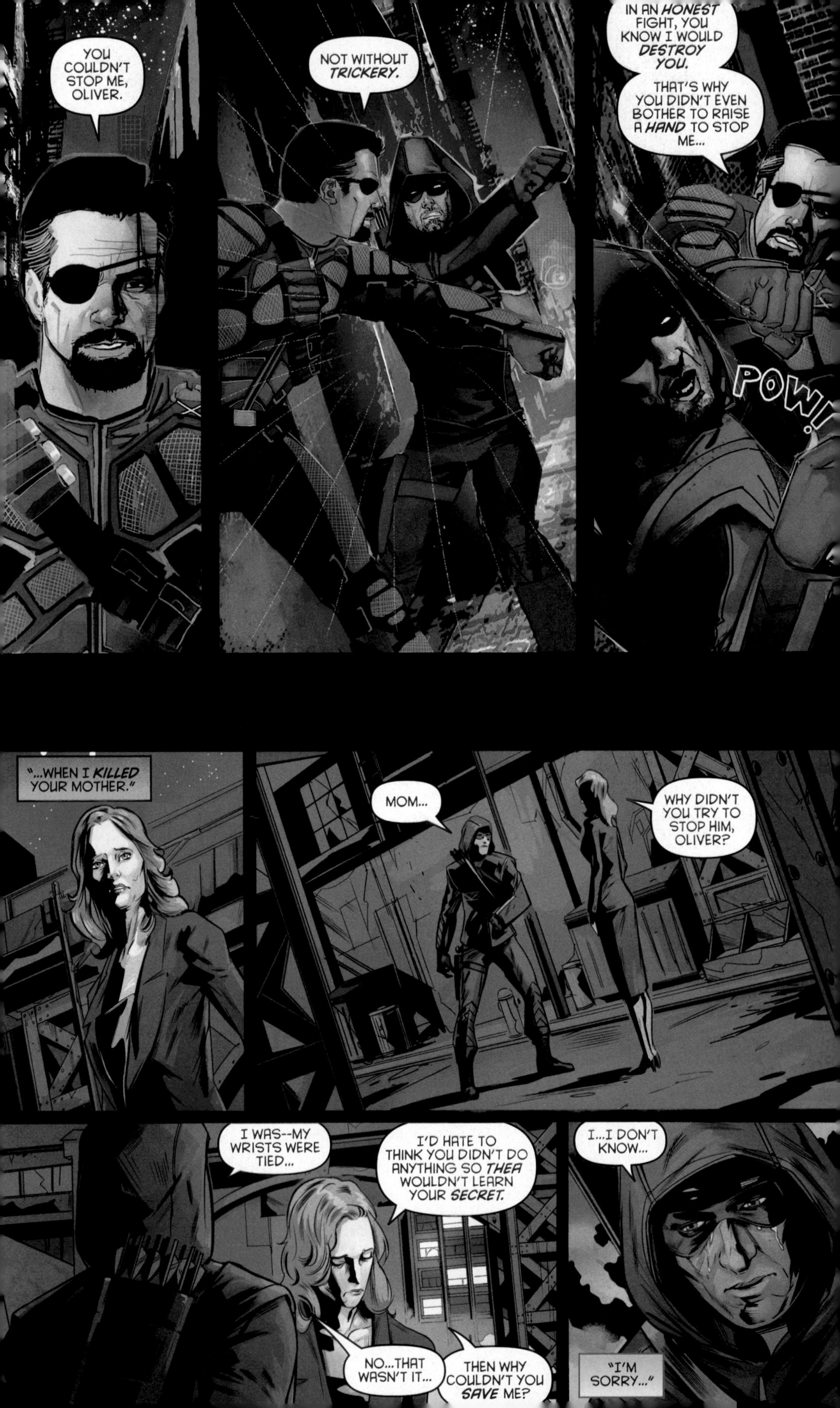

YOU COULDN'T STOP ME, OLIVER.
NOT WITHOUT *TRICKERY.*
IN AN *HONEST* FIGHT, YOU KNOW I WOULD *DESTROY YOU.*
THAT'S WHY YOU DIDN'T EVEN BOTHER TO RAISE A *HAND* TO STOP ME...
POW!
"...WHEN I *KILLED* YOUR MOTHER."
MOM...
WHY DIDN'T YOU TRY TO STOP HIM, OLIVER?
I WAS--MY WRISTS WERE TIED...
I'D HATE TO THINK YOU DIDN'T DO ANYTHING SO *THEA* WOULDN'T LEARN YOUR *SECRET.*
NO...THAT WASN'T IT...
THEN WHY COULDN'T YOU *SAVE* ME?
I...I DON'T KNOW...
"I'M SORRY..."

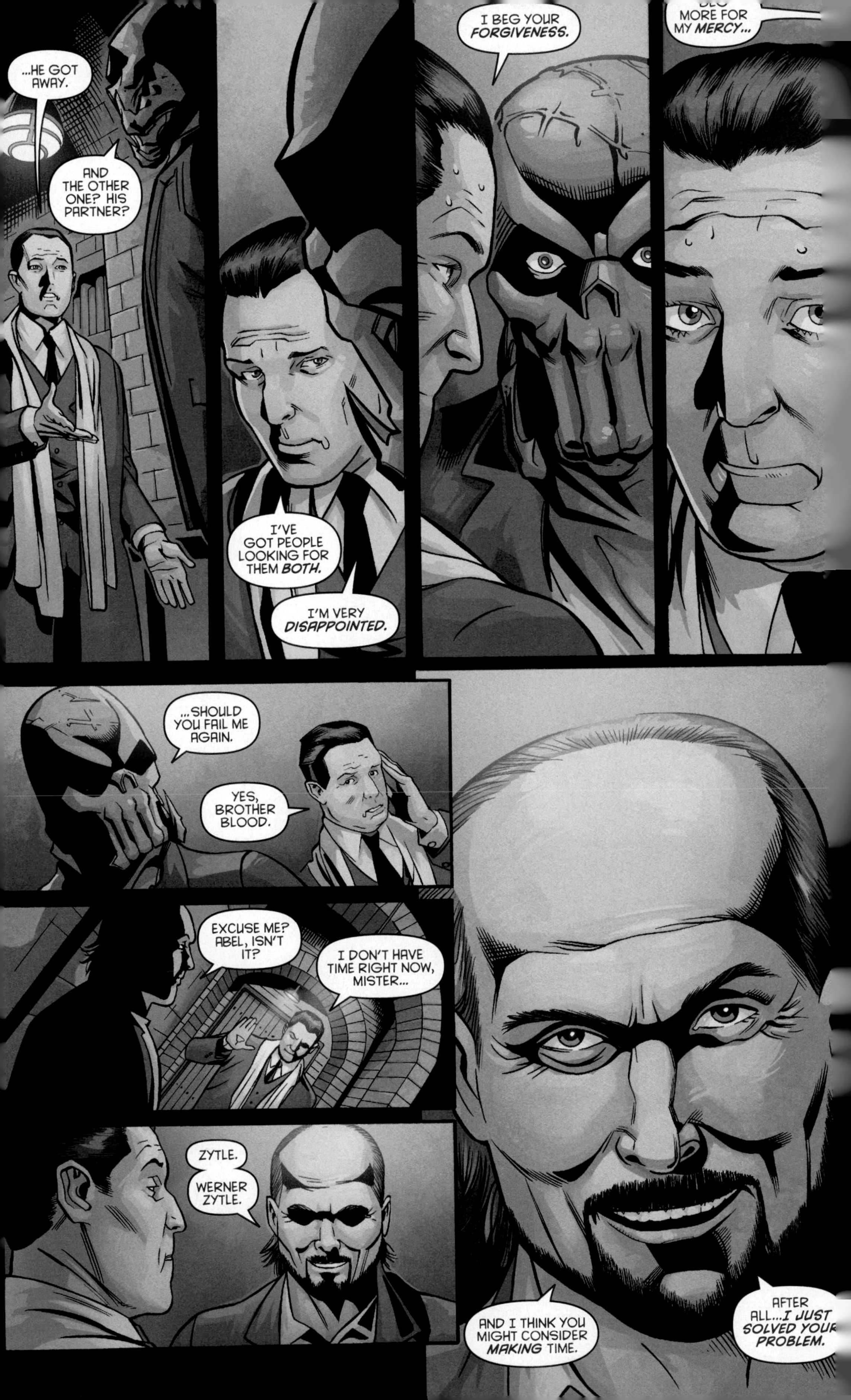
...HE GOT AWAY.
AND THE OTHER ONE? HIS PARTNER?
I'VE GOT PEOPLE LOOKING FOR THEM *BOTH.*
I'M VERY *DISAPPOINTED.*
I BEG YOUR *FORGIVENESS.*
MORE FOR MY *MERCY...*
...SHOULD YOU FAIL ME AGAIN.
YES, BROTHER BLOOD.
EXCUSE ME? ABEL, ISN'T IT?
I DON'T HAVE TIME RIGHT NOW, MISTER...
ZYTLE.
WERNER ZYTLE.
AND I THINK YOU MIGHT CONSIDER *MAKING* TIME.
AFTER ALL...*I JUST SOLVED YOUR PROBLEM.*

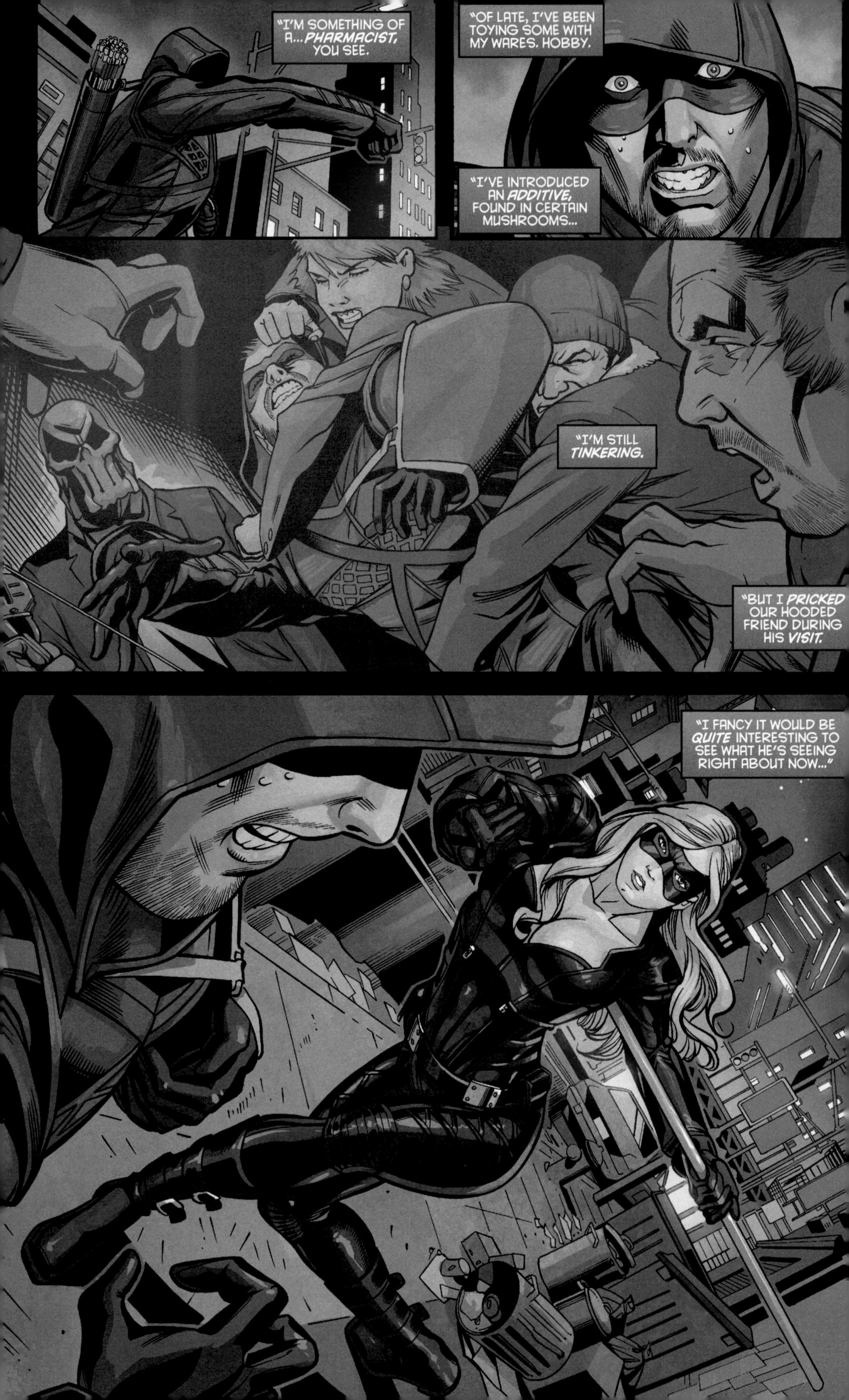
"I'M SOMETHING OF A...PHARMACIST, YOU SEE.
"OF LATE, I'VE BEEN TOYING SOME WITH MY WARES. HOBBY.
"I'VE INTRODUCED AN ADDITIVE, FOUND IN CERTAIN MUSHROOMS...
"I'M STILL TINKERING.
"BUT I PRICKED OUR HOODED FRIEND DURING HIS VISIT.
"I FANCY IT WOULD BE QUITE INTERESTING TO SEE WHAT HE'S SEEING RIGHT ABOUT NOW..."

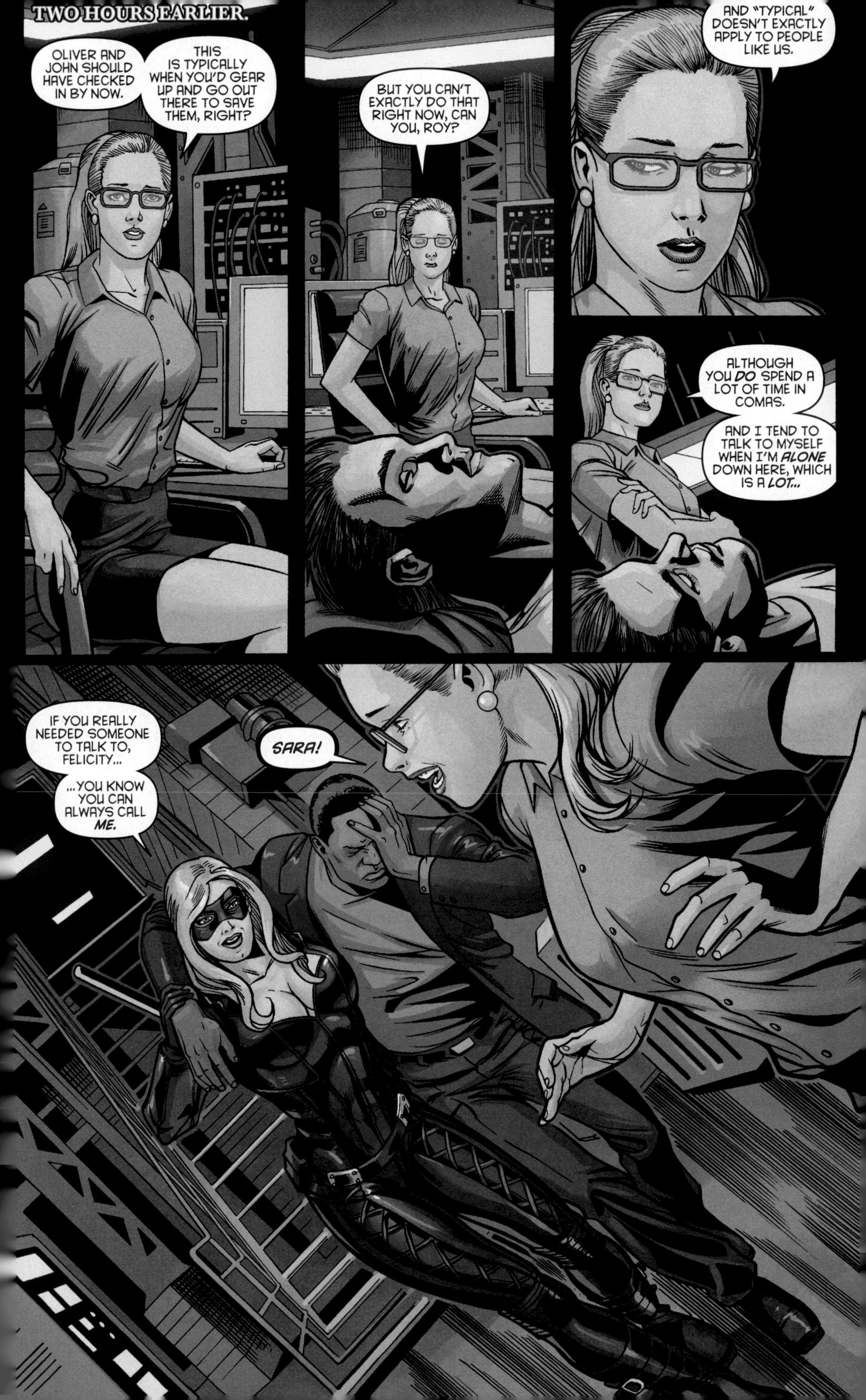
TWO HOURS EARLIER.
OLIVER AND JOHN SHOULD HAVE CHECKED IN BY NOW.
THIS IS TYPICALLY WHEN YOU'D GEAR UP AND GO OUT THERE TO SAVE THEM, RIGHT?
BUT YOU CAN'T EXACTLY DO THAT RIGHT NOW, CAN YOU, ROY?
AND "TYPICAL" DOESN'T EXACTLY APPLY TO PEOPLE LIKE US.
ALTHOUGH YOU DO SPEND A LOT OF TIME IN COMAS.
AND I TEND TO TALK TO MYSELF WHEN I'M ALONE DOWN HERE, WHICH IS A LOT...
IF YOU REALLY NEEDED SOMEONE TO TALK TO, FELICITY...
...YOU KNOW YOU CAN ALWAYS CALL ME.
SARA!

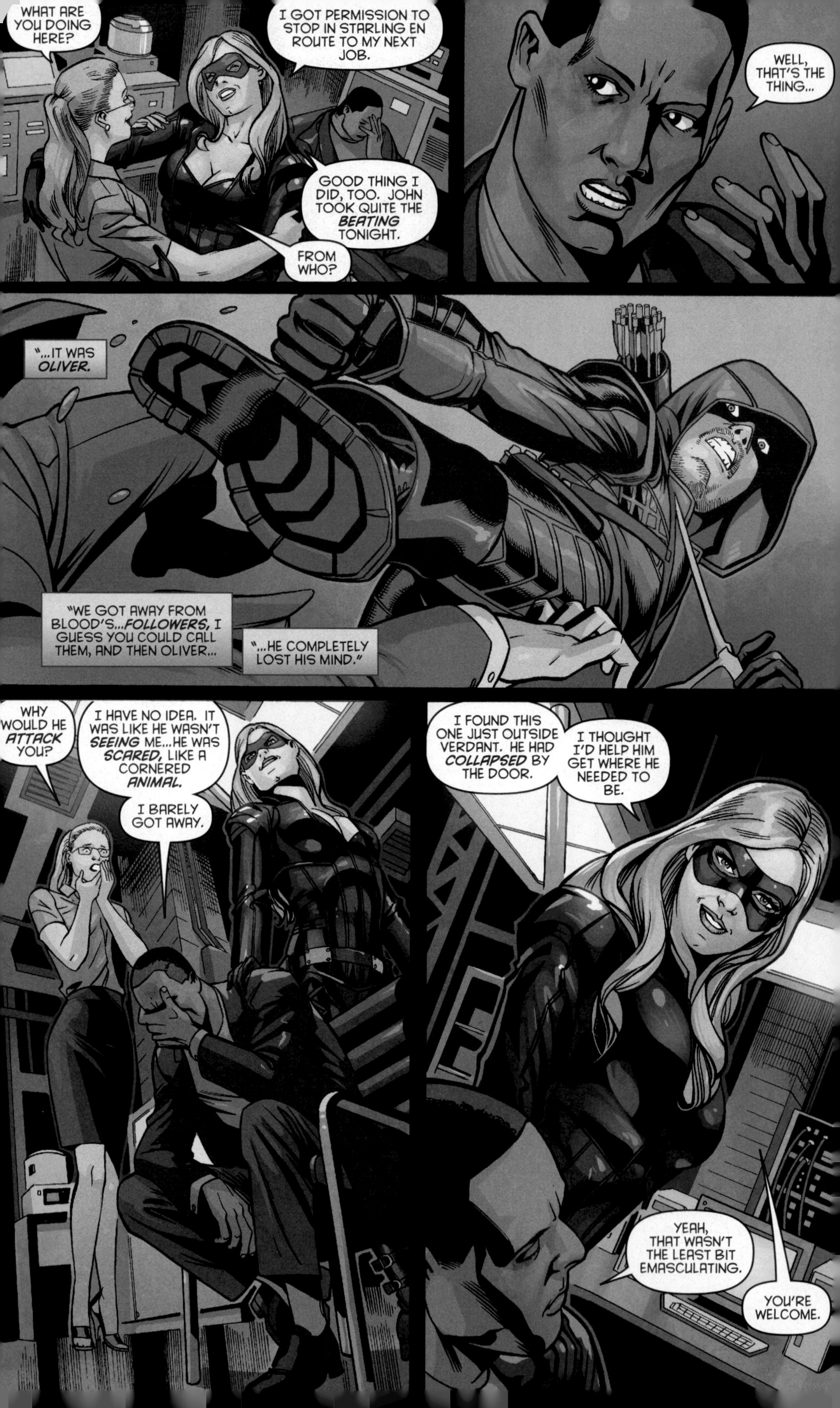
WHAT ARE YOU DOING HERE?
I GOT PERMISSION TO STOP IN STARLING EN ROUTE TO MY NEXT JOB.
GOOD THING I DID, TOO. JOHN TOOK QUITE THE BEATING TONIGHT.
FROM WHO?
WELL, THAT'S THE THING...
"...IT WAS OLIVER.
"WE GOT AWAY FROM BLOOD'S...FOLLOWERS, I GUESS YOU COULD CALL THEM, AND THEN OLIVER...
"...HE COMPLETELY LOST HIS MIND."
WHY WOULD HE ATTACK YOU?
I HAVE NO IDEA. IT WAS LIKE HE WASN'T SEEING ME...HE WAS SCARED, LIKE A CORNERED ANIMAL.
I BARELY GOT AWAY.
I FOUND THIS ONE JUST OUTSIDE VERDANT. HE HAD COLLAPSED BY THE DOOR.
I THOUGHT I'D HELP HIM GET WHERE HE NEEDED TO BE.
YEAH, THAT WASN'T THE LEAST BIT EMASCULATING.
YOU'RE WELCOME.

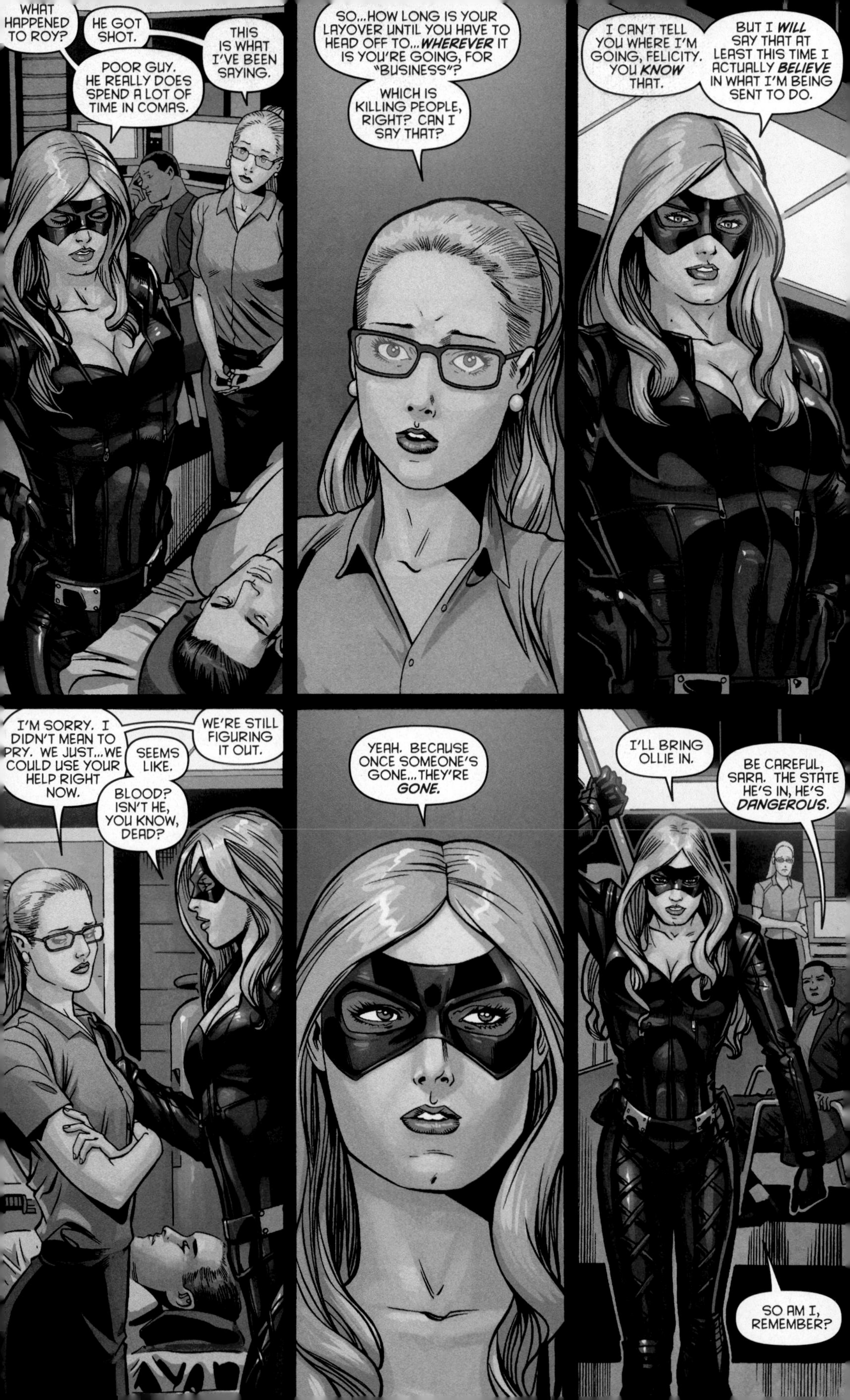
WHAT HAPPENED TO ROY?
HE GOT SHOT.
THIS IS WHAT I'VE BEEN SAYING.
POOR GUY. HE REALLY DOES SPEND A LOT OF TIME IN COMAS.
SO...HOW LONG IS YOUR LAYOVER UNTIL YOU HAVE TO HEAD OFF TO...*WHEREVER* IT IS YOU'RE GOING, FOR "BUSINESS"?
WHICH IS KILLING PEOPLE, RIGHT? CAN I SAY THAT?
I CAN'T TELL YOU WHERE I'M GOING, FELICITY. YOU *KNOW* THAT.
BUT I *WILL* SAY THAT AT LEAST THIS TIME I ACTUALLY *BELIEVE* IN WHAT I'M BEING SENT TO DO.
I'M SORRY. I DIDN'T MEAN TO PRY. WE JUST...WE COULD USE YOUR HELP RIGHT NOW.
WE'RE STILL FIGURING IT OUT.
SEEMS LIKE.
BLOOD? ISN'T HE, YOU KNOW, DEAD?
YEAH. BECAUSE ONCE SOMEONE'S GONE...THEY'RE *GONE.*
I'LL BRING OLLIE IN.
BE CAREFUL, SARA. THE STATE HE'S IN, HE'S *DANGEROUS*.
SO AM I, REMEMBER?

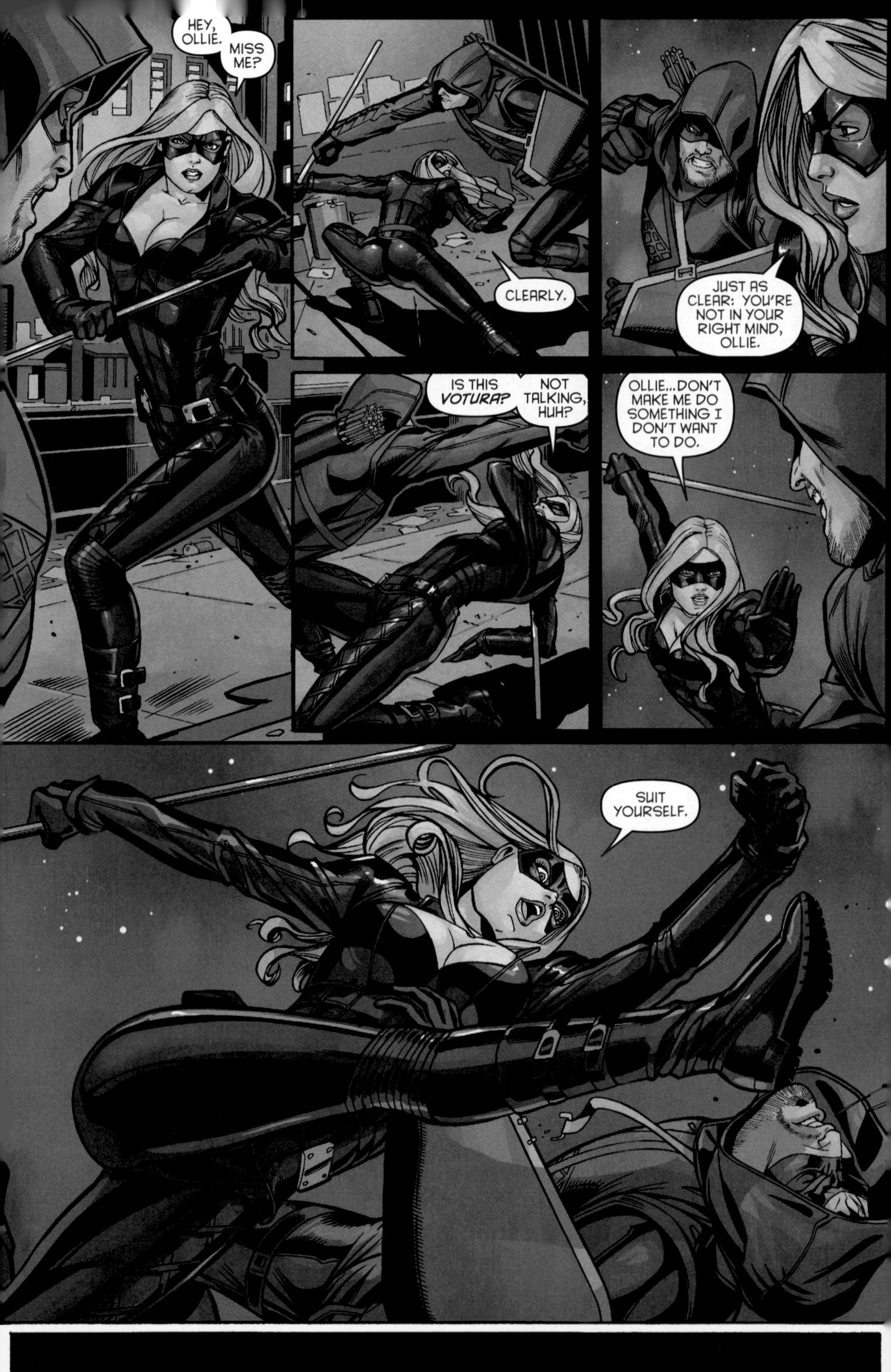
HEY, OLLIE.
MISS ME?
CLEARLY.
JUST AS CLEAR: YOU'RE NOT IN YOUR RIGHT MIND, OLLIE.
IS THIS *VOTURA?*
NOT TALKING, HUH?
OLLIE...DON'T MAKE ME DO SOMETHING I DON'T WANT TO DO.
SUIT YOURSELF.

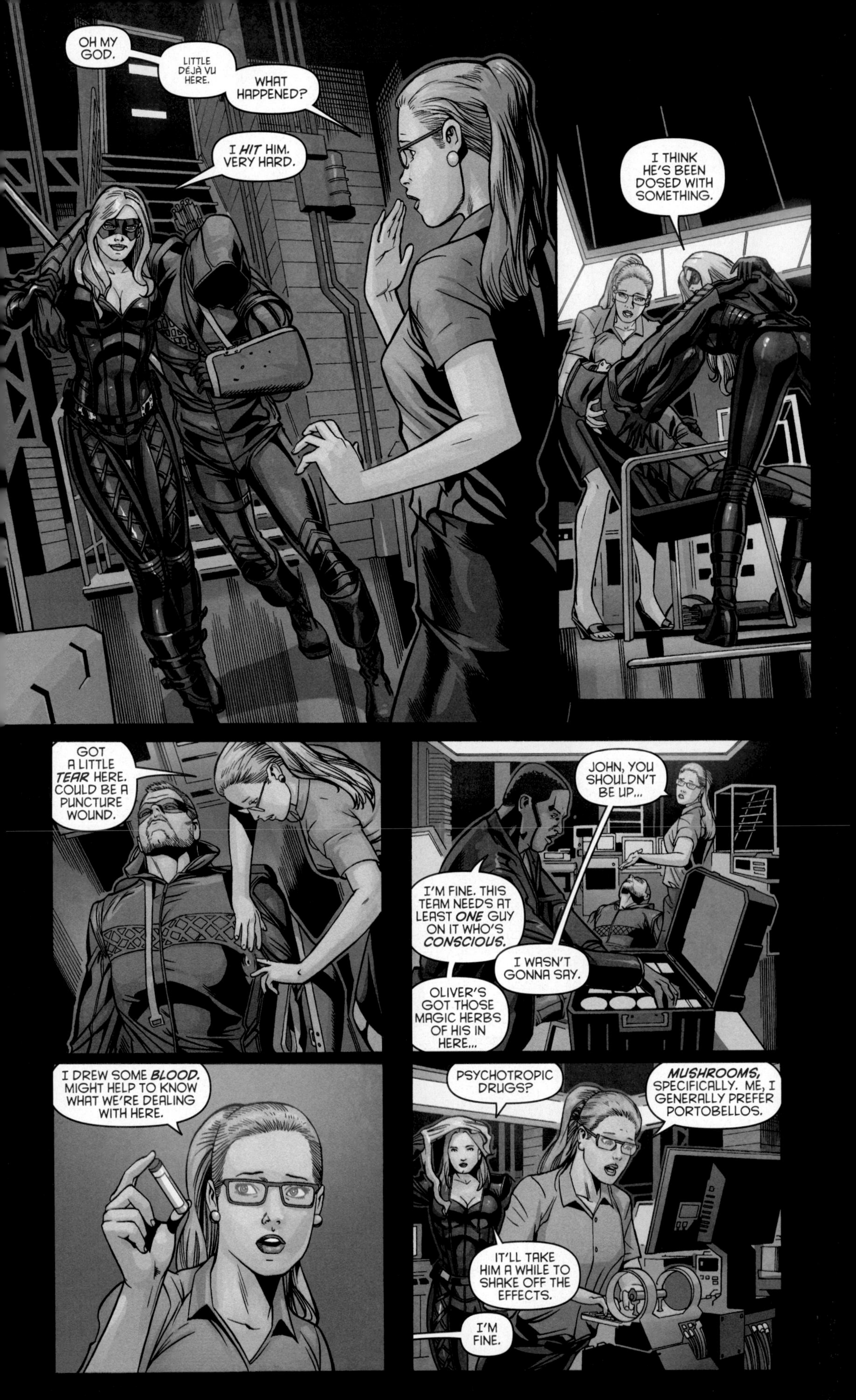

OH MY GOD.
LITTLE DÉJÀ VU HERE.
WHAT HAPPENED?
I *HIT* HIM. VERY HARD.
I THINK HE'S BEEN DOSED WITH SOMETHING.
GOT A LITTLE *TEAR* HERE. COULD BE A PUNCTURE WOUND.
JOHN, YOU SHOULDN'T BE UP...
I'M FINE. THIS TEAM NEEDS AT LEAST *ONE* GUY ON IT WHO'S *CONSCIOUS.*
I WASN'T GONNA SAY.
OLIVER'S GOT THOSE MAGIC HERBS OF HIS IN HERE...
I DREW SOME *BLOOD.* MIGHT HELP TO KNOW WHAT WE'RE DEALING WITH HERE.
PSYCHOTROPIC DRUGS?
MUSHROOMS, SPECIFICALLY. ME, I GENERALLY PREFER PORTOBELLOS.
IT'LL TAKE HIM A WHILE TO SHAKE OFF THE EFFECTS.
I'M FINE.

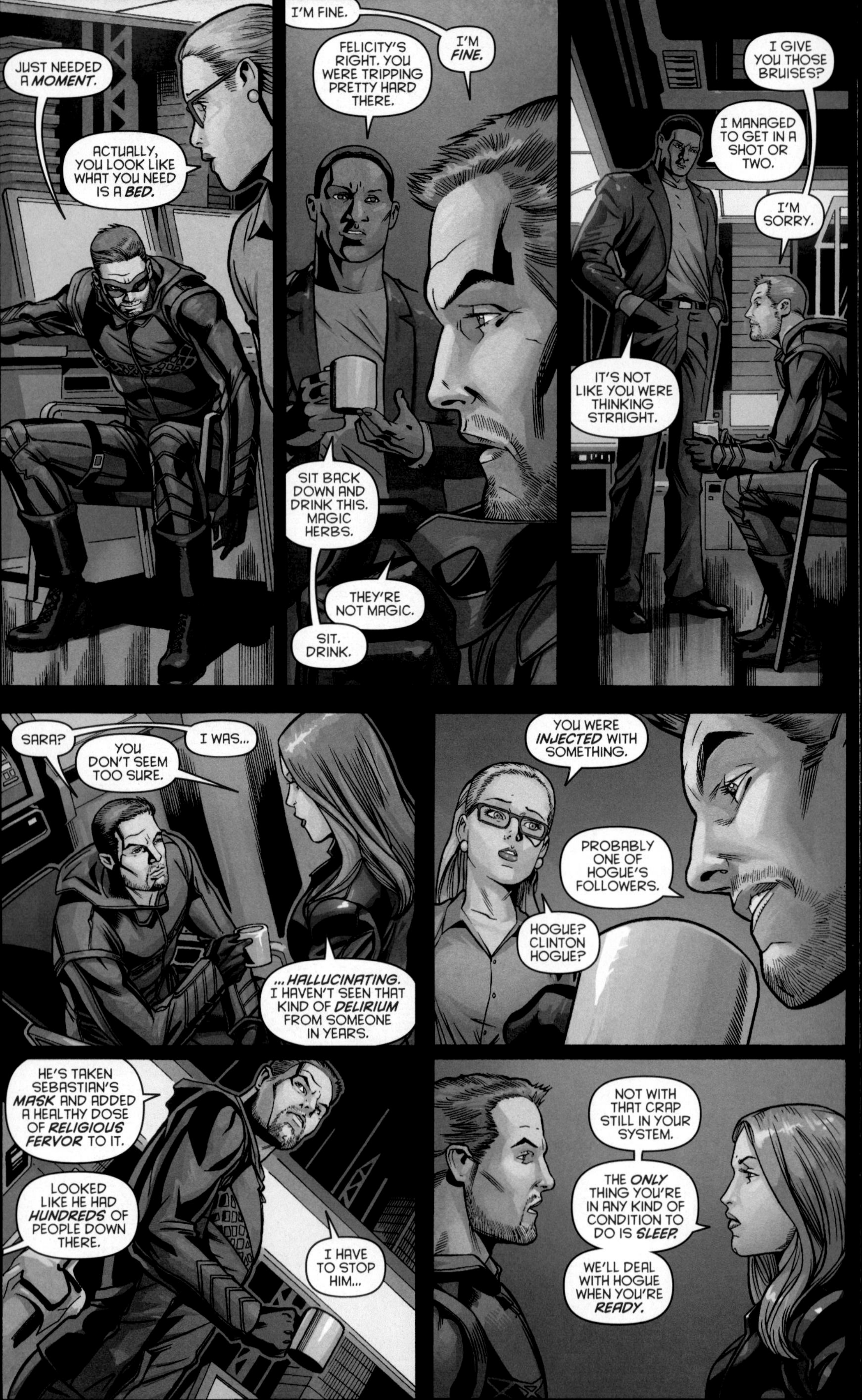

JUST NEEDED A *MOMENT*.
ACTUALLY, YOU LOOK LIKE WHAT YOU NEED IS A *BED*.
I'M FINE.
FELICITY'S RIGHT. YOU WERE TRIPPING PRETTY HARD THERE.
I'M *FINE.*
SIT BACK DOWN AND DRINK THIS. MAGIC HERBS.
THEY'RE NOT MAGIC.
SIT. DRINK.
I GIVE YOU THOSE BRUISES?
I MANAGED TO GET IN A SHOT OR TWO.
I'M SORRY.
IT'S NOT LIKE YOU WERE THINKING STRAIGHT.
SARA?
I WAS...
YOU DON'T SEEM TOO SURE.
...HALLUCINATING. I HAVEN'T SEEN THAT KIND OF *DELIRIUM* FROM SOMEONE IN YEARS.
YOU WERE *INJECTED* WITH SOMETHING.
PROBABLY ONE OF HOGUE'S FOLLOWERS.
HOGUE? CLINTON HOGUE?
HE'S TAKEN SEBASTIAN'S *MASK* AND ADDED A HEALTHY DOSE OF *RELIGIOUS FERVOR* TO IT.
LOOKED LIKE HE HAD *HUNDREDS* OF PEOPLE DOWN THERE.
I HAVE TO STOP HIM...
NOT WITH THAT CRAP STILL IN YOUR SYSTEM.
THE *ONLY* THING YOU'RE IN ANY KIND OF CONDITION TO DO IS *SLEEP.*
WE'LL DEAL WITH HOGUE WHEN YOU'RE *READY.*

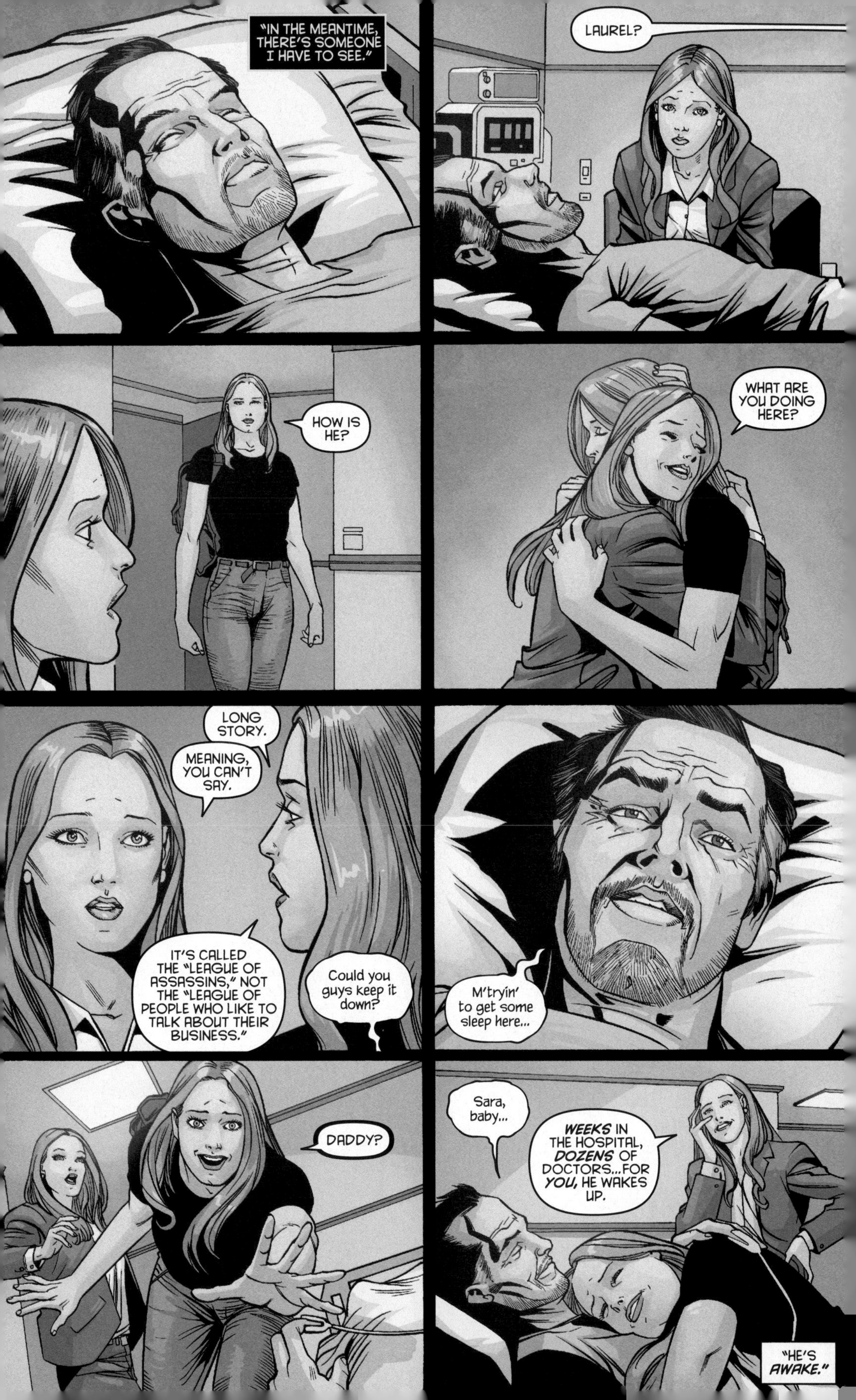
"IN THE MEANTIME, THERE'S SOMEONE I HAVE TO SEE."
LAUREL?
HOW IS HE?
WHAT ARE YOU DOING HERE?
LONG STORY.
MEANING, YOU CAN'T SAY.
IT'S CALLED THE "LEAGUE OF ASSASSINS," NOT THE "LEAGUE OF PEOPLE WHO LIKE TO TALK ABOUT THEIR BUSINESS."
Could you guys keep it down?
M'tryin' to get some sleep here...
DADDY?
Sara, baby...
WEEKS IN THE HOSPITAL, *DOZENS* OF DOCTORS...FOR *YOU,* HE WAKES UP.
"HE'S *AWAKE.*"

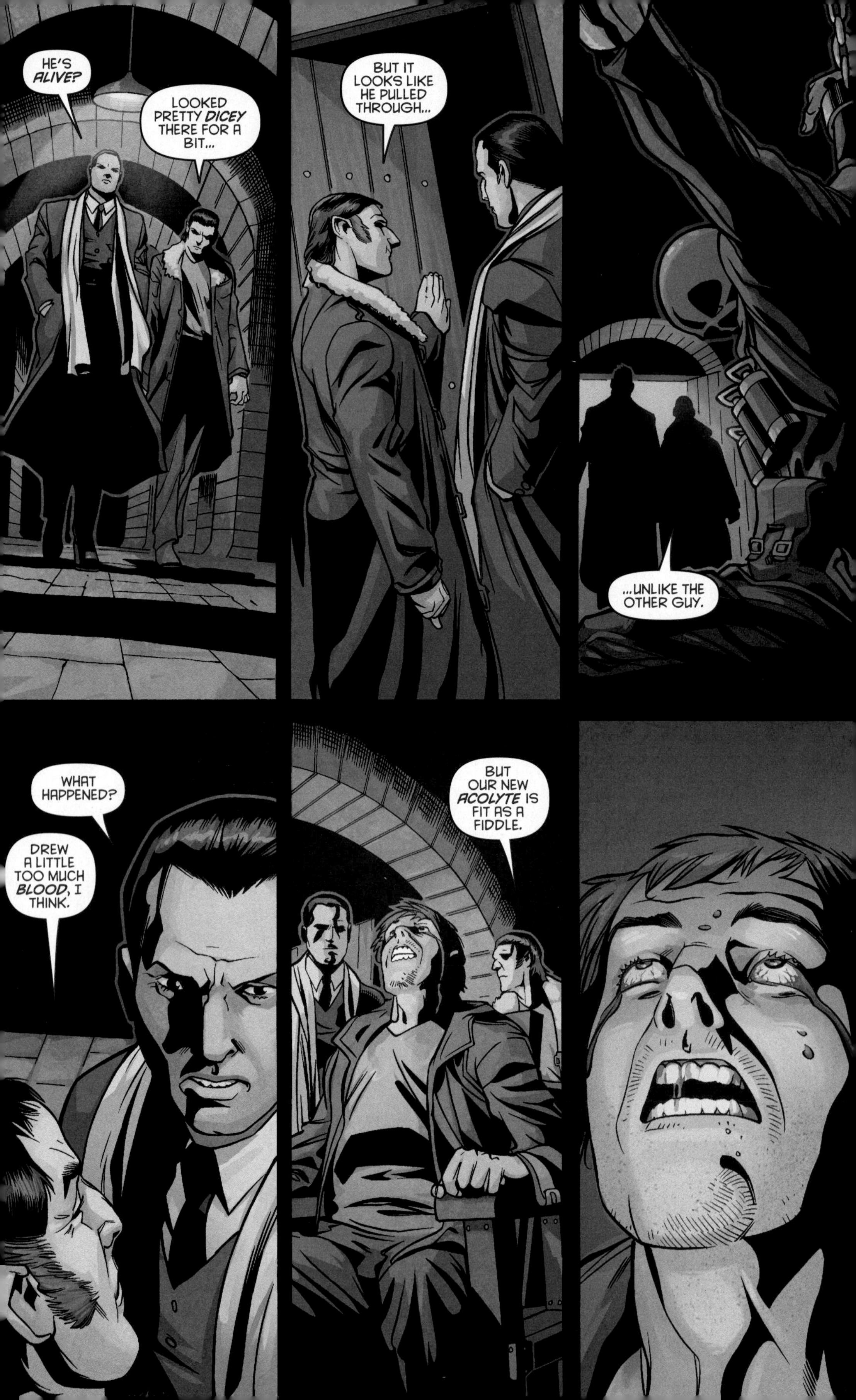
HE'S ALIVE?
LOOKED PRETTY DICEY THERE FOR A BIT...
BUT IT LOOKS LIKE HE PULLED THROUGH...
...UNLIKE THE OTHER GUY.
WHAT HAPPENED?
DREW A LITTLE TOO MUCH BLOOD, I THINK.
BUT OUR NEW ACOLYTE IS FIT AS A FIDDLE.

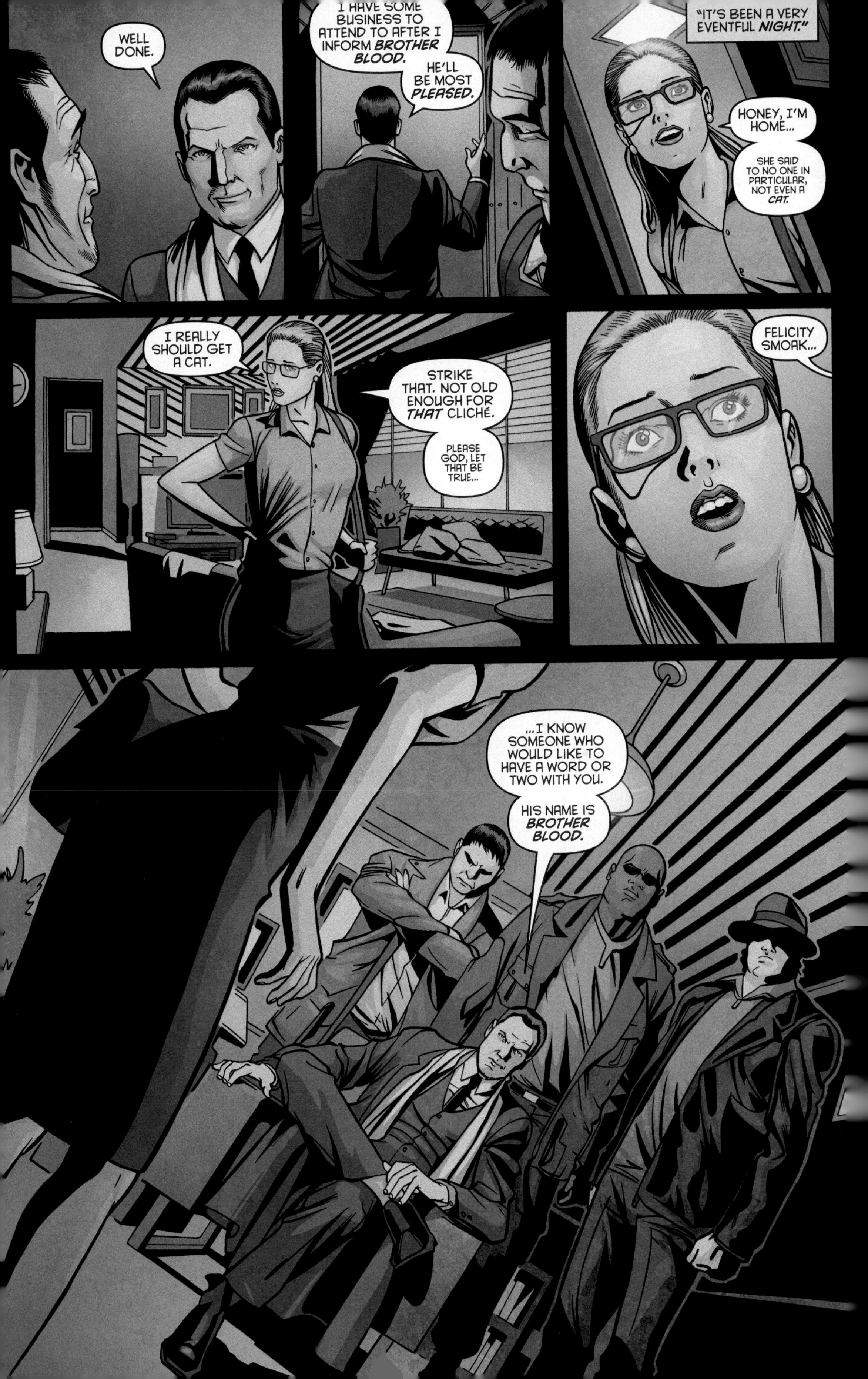
WELL DONE.
I HAVE SOME BUSINESS TO ATTEND TO AFTER I INFORM BROTHER BLOOD.
HE'LL BE MOST PLEASED.
"IT'S BEEN A VERY EVENTFUL NIGHT."
HONEY, I'M HOME...
SHE SAID TO NO ONE IN PARTICULAR, NOT EVEN A CAT.
I REALLY SHOULD GET A CAT.
STRIKE THAT. NOT OLD ENOUGH FOR THAT CLICHÉ.
PLEASE GOD, LET THAT BE TRUE...
FELICITY SMOAK...
...I KNOW SOMEONE WHO WOULD LIKE TO HAVE A WORD OR TWO WITH YOU.
HIS NAME IS BROTHER BLOOD.

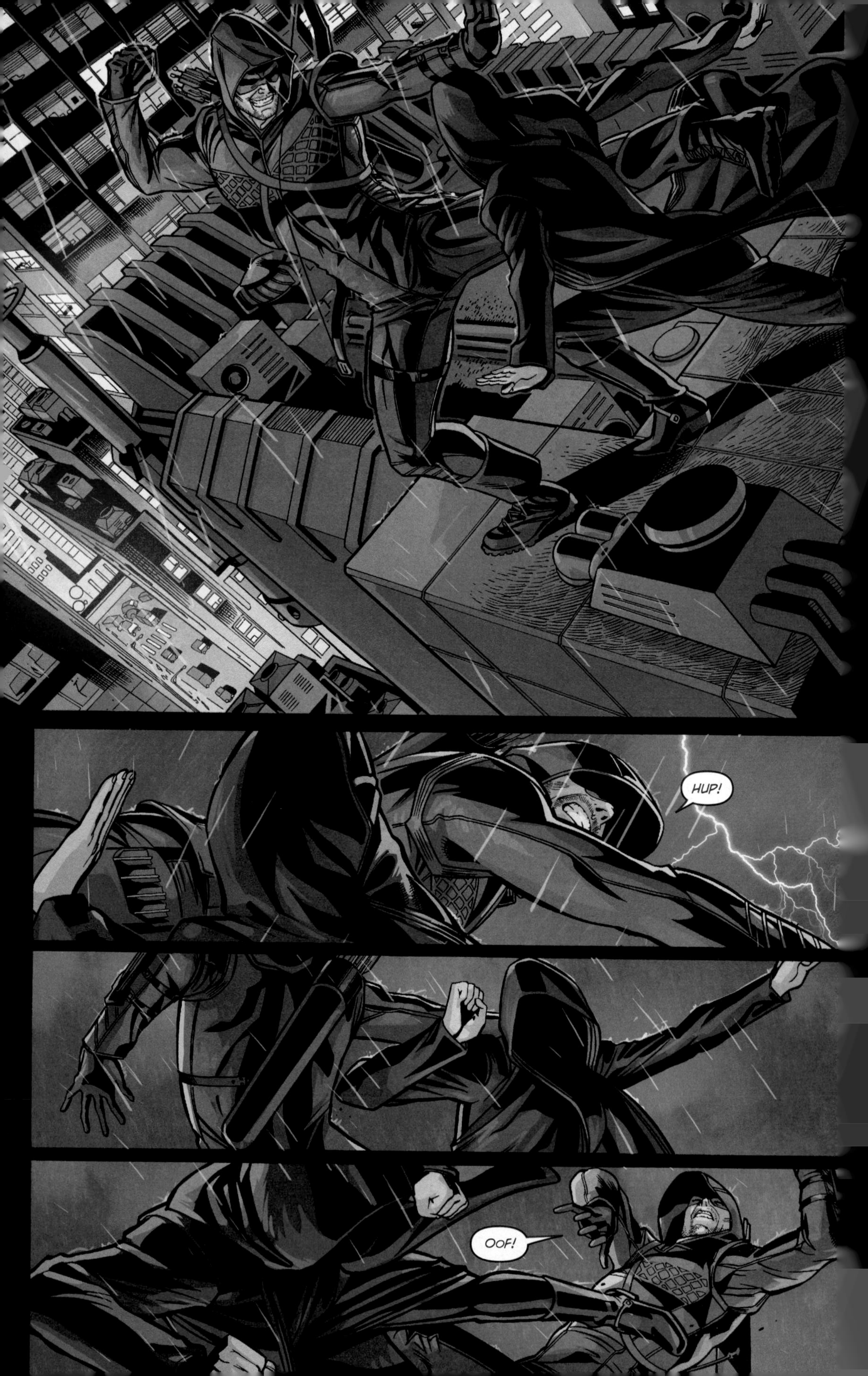
HUP!
OOF!

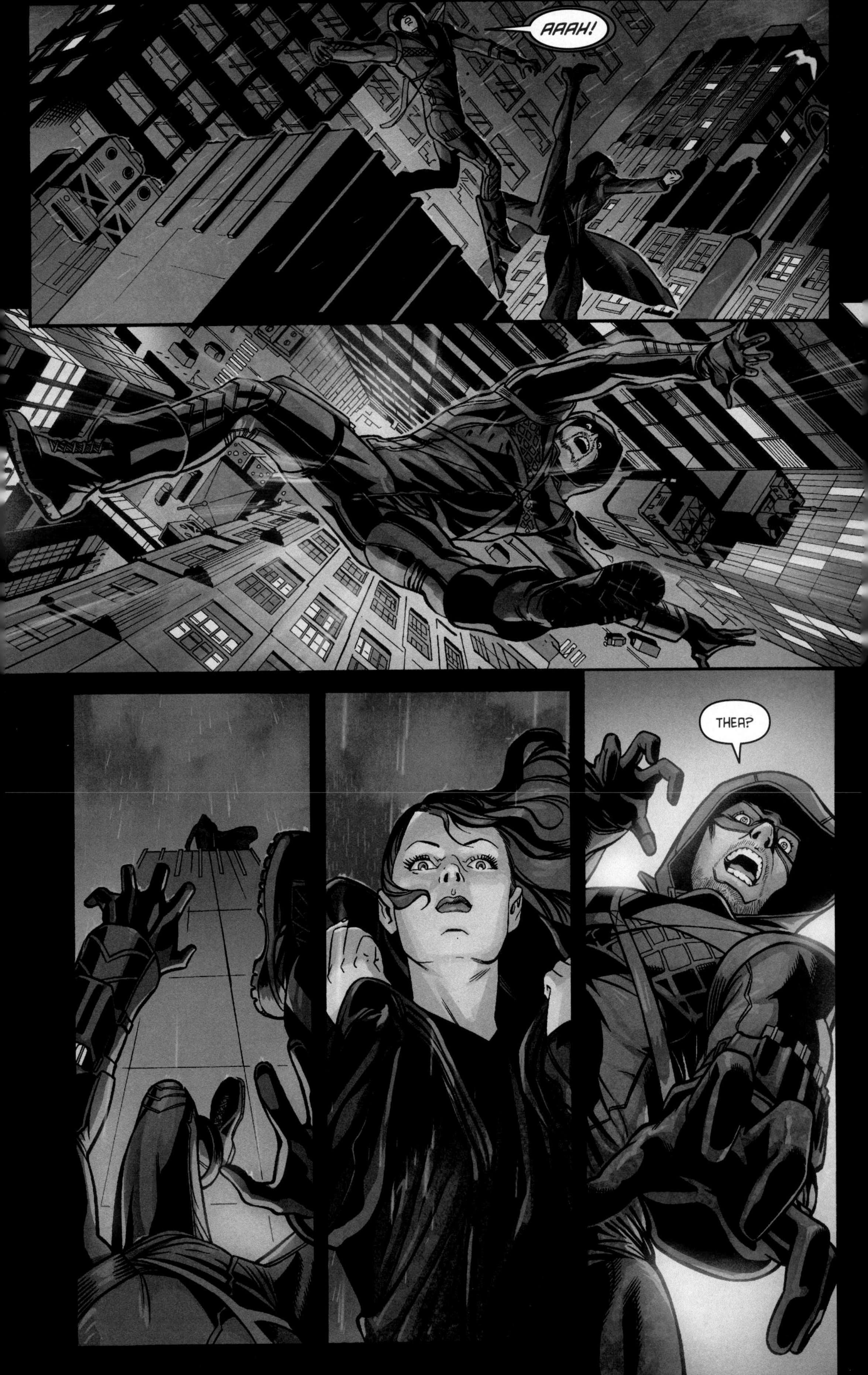
AAAH!
THEA?

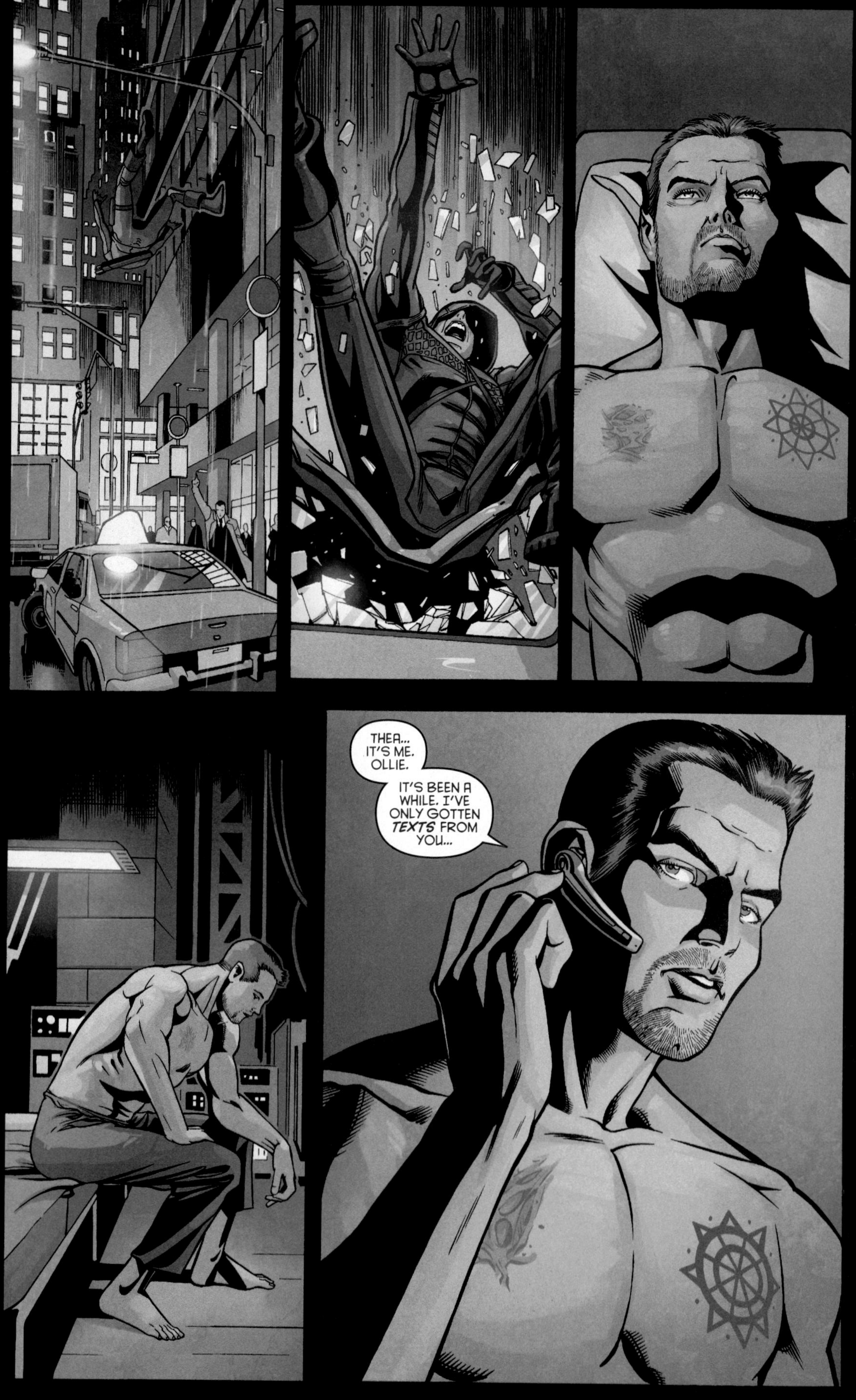
THEA... IT'S ME. OLLIE.
IT'S BEEN A WHILE. I'VE ONLY GOTTEN TEXTS FROM YOU...

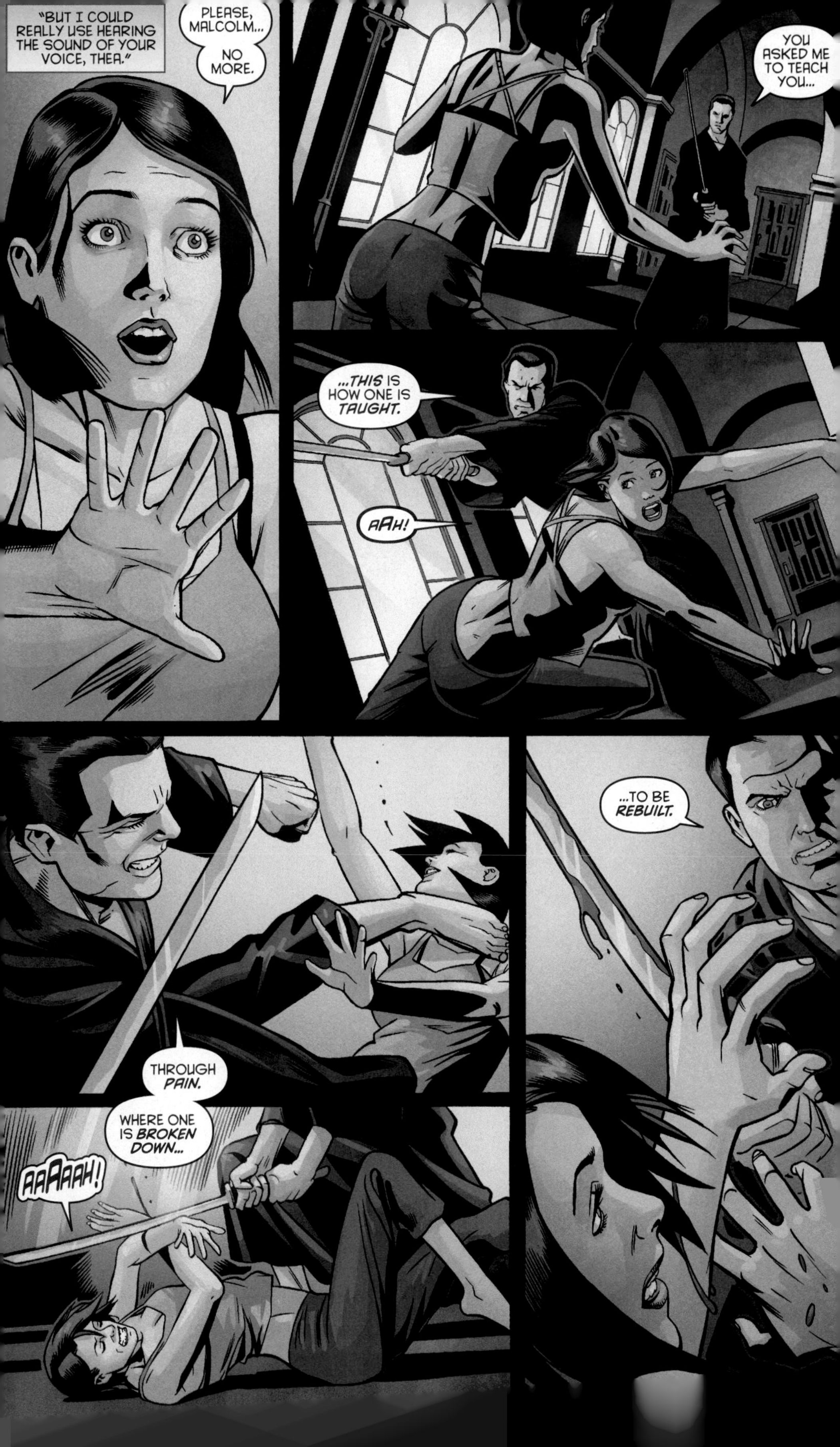
"BUT I COULD REALLY USE HEARING THE SOUND OF YOUR VOICE, THEA."
PLEASE, MALCOLM...
NO MORE.
YOU ASKED ME TO TEACH YOU...
...THIS IS HOW ONE IS TAUGHT.
AAH!
THROUGH PAIN.
WHERE ONE IS BROKEN DOWN...
AAAAAH!
...TO BE REBUILT.

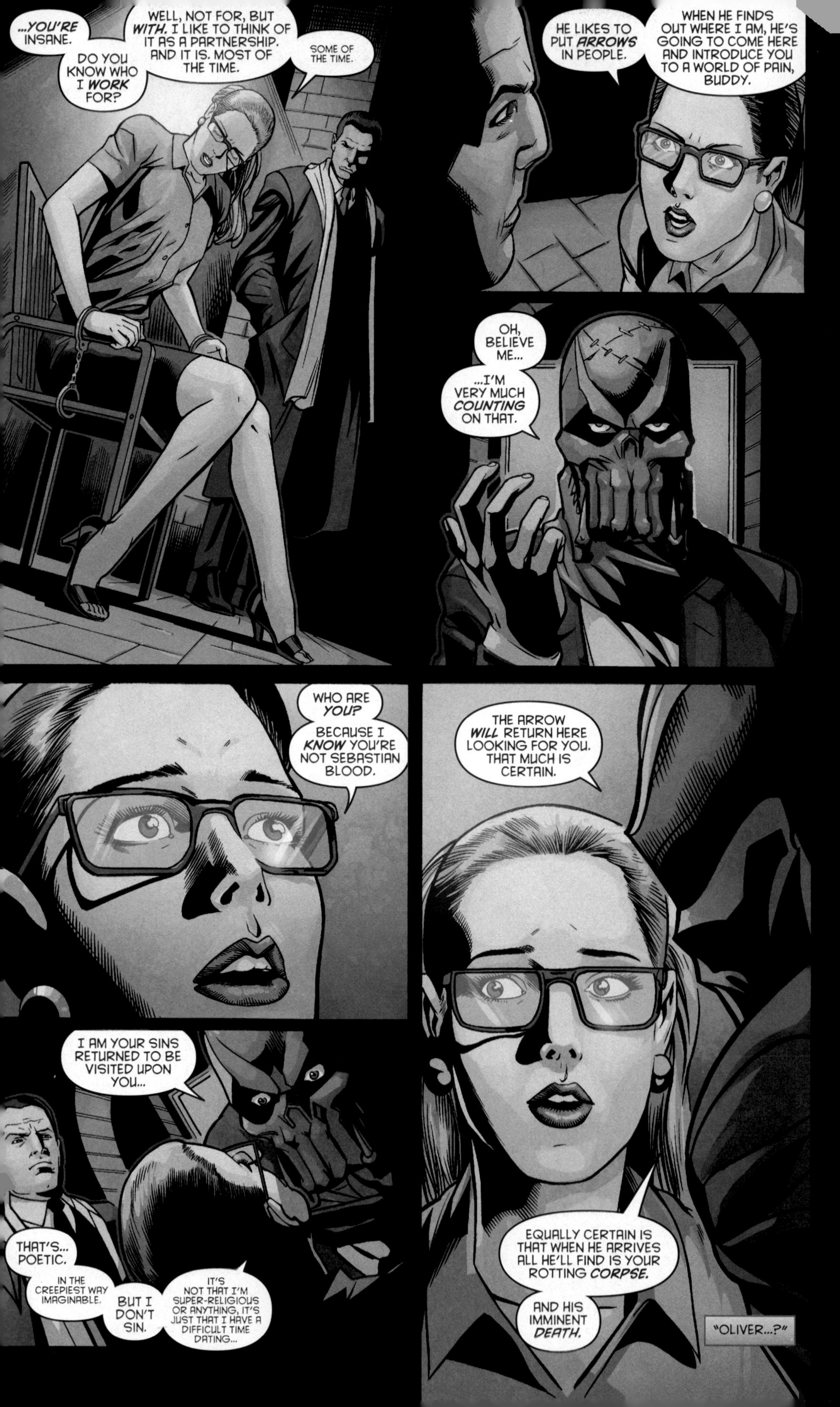
...YOU'RE INSANE.
DO YOU KNOW WHO I WORK FOR?
WELL, NOT FOR, BUT WITH. I LIKE TO THINK OF IT AS A PARTNERSHIP. AND IT IS. MOST OF THE TIME.
SOME OF THE TIME.
HE LIKES TO PUT ARROWS IN PEOPLE.
WHEN HE FINDS OUT WHERE I AM, HE'S GOING TO COME HERE AND INTRODUCE YOU TO A WORLD OF PAIN, BUDDY.
OH, BELIEVE ME...
...I'M VERY MUCH COUNTING ON THAT.
WHO ARE YOU?
BECAUSE I KNOW YOU'RE NOT SEBASTIAN BLOOD.
I AM YOUR SINS RETURNED TO BE VISITED UPON YOU...
THAT'S... POETIC.
IN THE CREEPIEST WAY IMAGINABLE.
BUT I DON'T SIN.
IT'S NOT THAT I'M SUPER-RELIGIOUS OR ANYTHING, IT'S JUST THAT I HAVE A DIFFICULT TIME DATING...
THE ARROW WILL RETURN HERE LOOKING FOR YOU. THAT MUCH IS CERTAIN.
EQUALLY CERTAIN IS THAT WHEN HE ARRIVES ALL HE'LL FIND IS YOUR ROTTING CORPSE.
AND HIS IMMINENT DEATH.
"OLIVER...?"

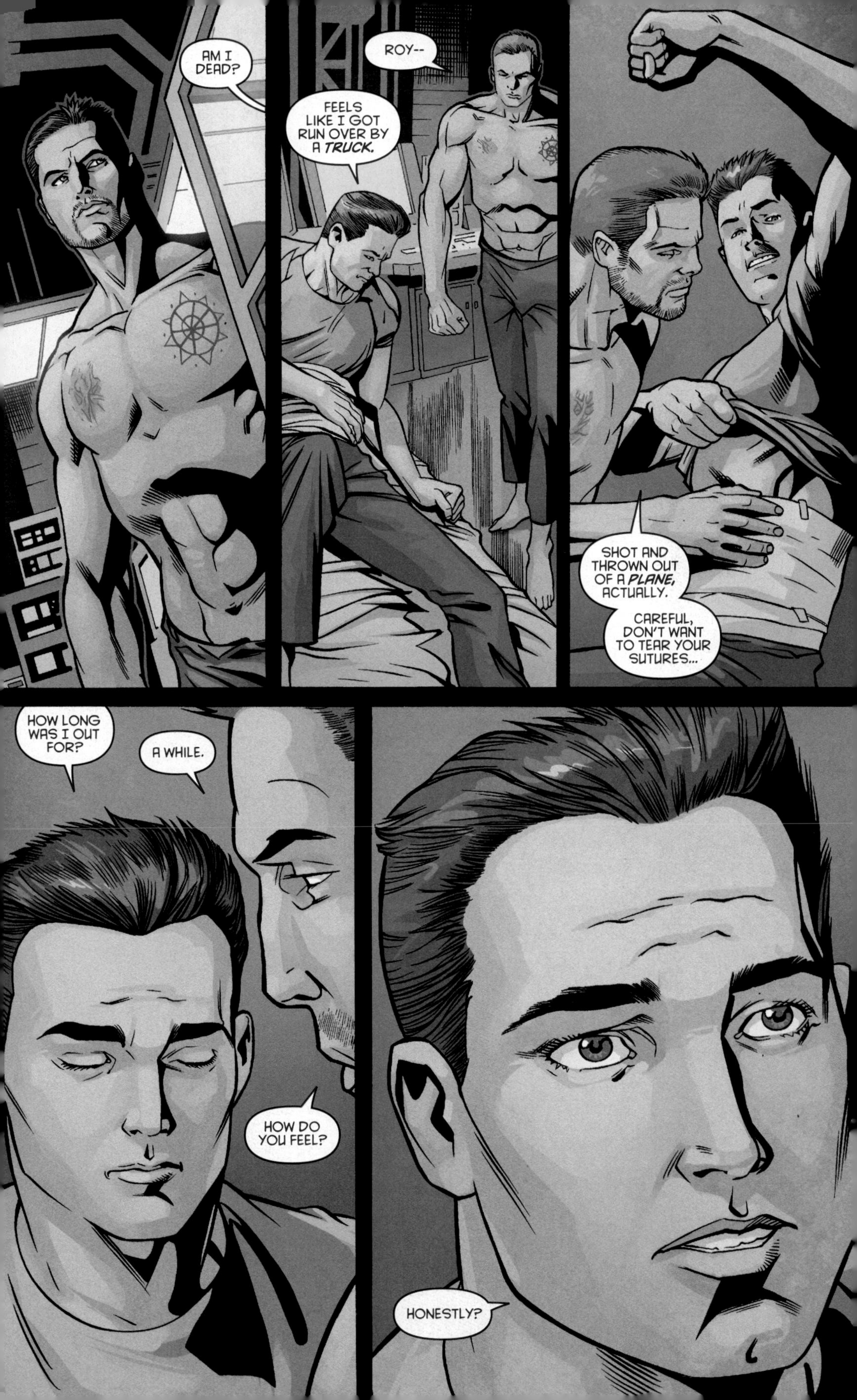
AM I DEAD?
ROY--
FEELS LIKE I GOT RUN OVER BY A *TRUCK.*
SHOT AND THROWN OUT OF A *PLANE,* ACTUALLY.
CAREFUL, DON'T WANT TO TEAR YOUR SUTURES...
HOW LONG WAS I OUT FOR?
A WHILE.
HOW DO YOU FEEL?
HONESTLY?

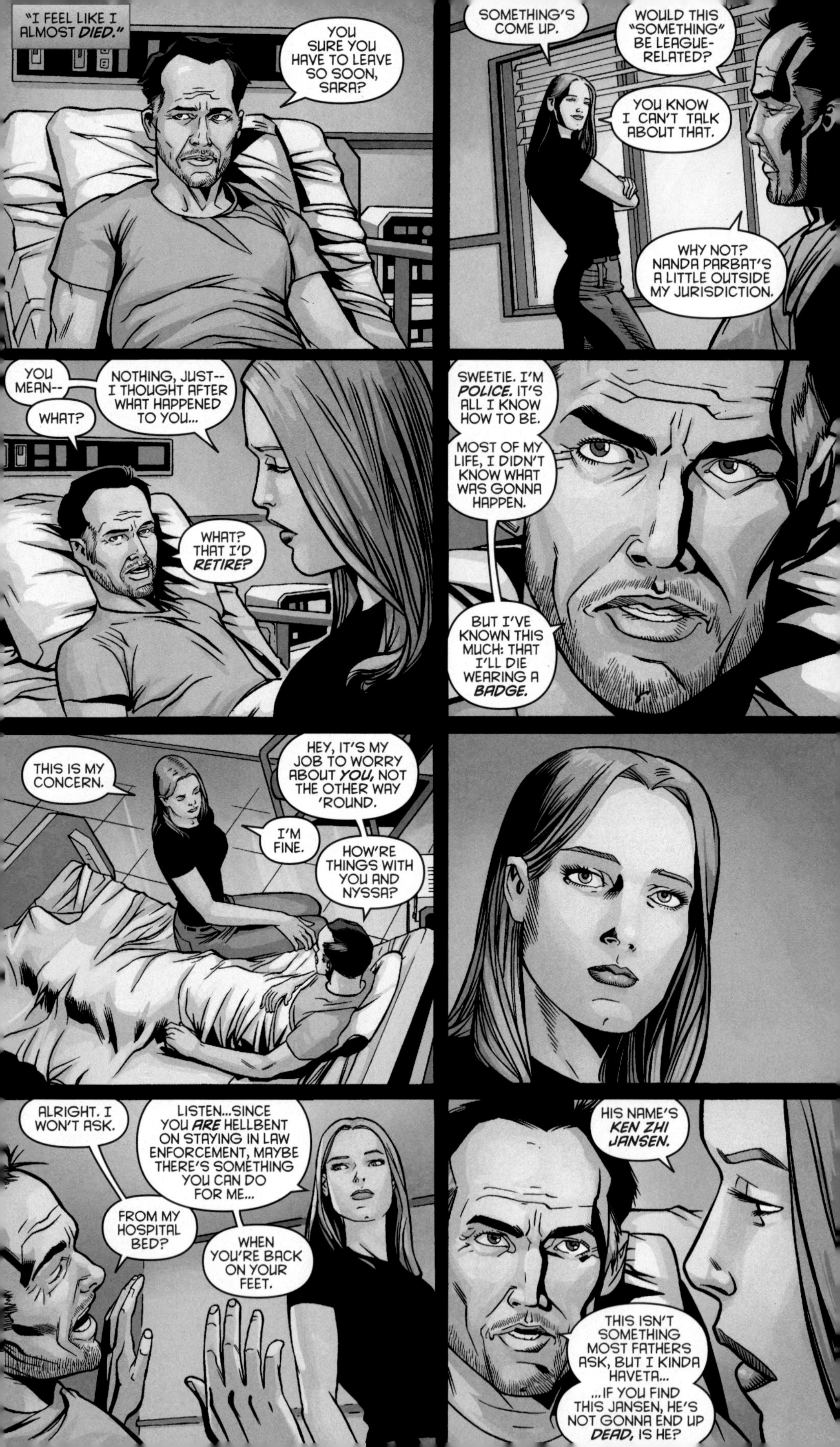

"I FEEL LIKE I ALMOST *DIED.*"
YOU SURE YOU HAVE TO LEAVE SO SOON, SARA?
SOMETHING'S COME UP.
WOULD THIS "SOMETHING" BE LEAGUE-RELATED?
YOU KNOW I CAN'T TALK ABOUT THAT.
WHY NOT? NANDA PARBAT'S A LITTLE OUTSIDE MY JURISDICTION.
YOU MEAN--
NOTHING, JUST-- I THOUGHT AFTER WHAT HAPPENED TO YOU...
WHAT?
WHAT? THAT I'D *RETIRE?*
SWEETIE. I'M *POLICE.* IT'S ALL I KNOW HOW TO BE.
MOST OF MY LIFE, I DIDN'T KNOW WHAT WAS GONNA HAPPEN.
BUT I'VE KNOWN THIS MUCH: THAT I'LL DIE WEARING A *BADGE.*
THIS IS MY CONCERN.
HEY, IT'S MY JOB TO WORRY ABOUT *YOU,* NOT THE OTHER WAY 'ROUND.
I'M FINE.
HOW'RE THINGS WITH YOU AND NYSSA?
ALRIGHT. I WON'T ASK.
LISTEN...SINCE YOU *ARE* HELLBENT ON STAYING IN LAW ENFORCEMENT, MAYBE THERE'S SOMETHING YOU CAN DO FOR ME...
FROM MY HOSPITAL BED?
WHEN YOU'RE BACK ON YOUR FEET.
HIS NAME'S *KEN ZHI JANSEN.*
THIS ISN'T SOMETHING MOST FATHERS ASK, BUT I KINDA HAVETA...
...IF YOU FIND THIS JANSEN, HE'S NOT GONNA END UP *DEAD,* IS HE?

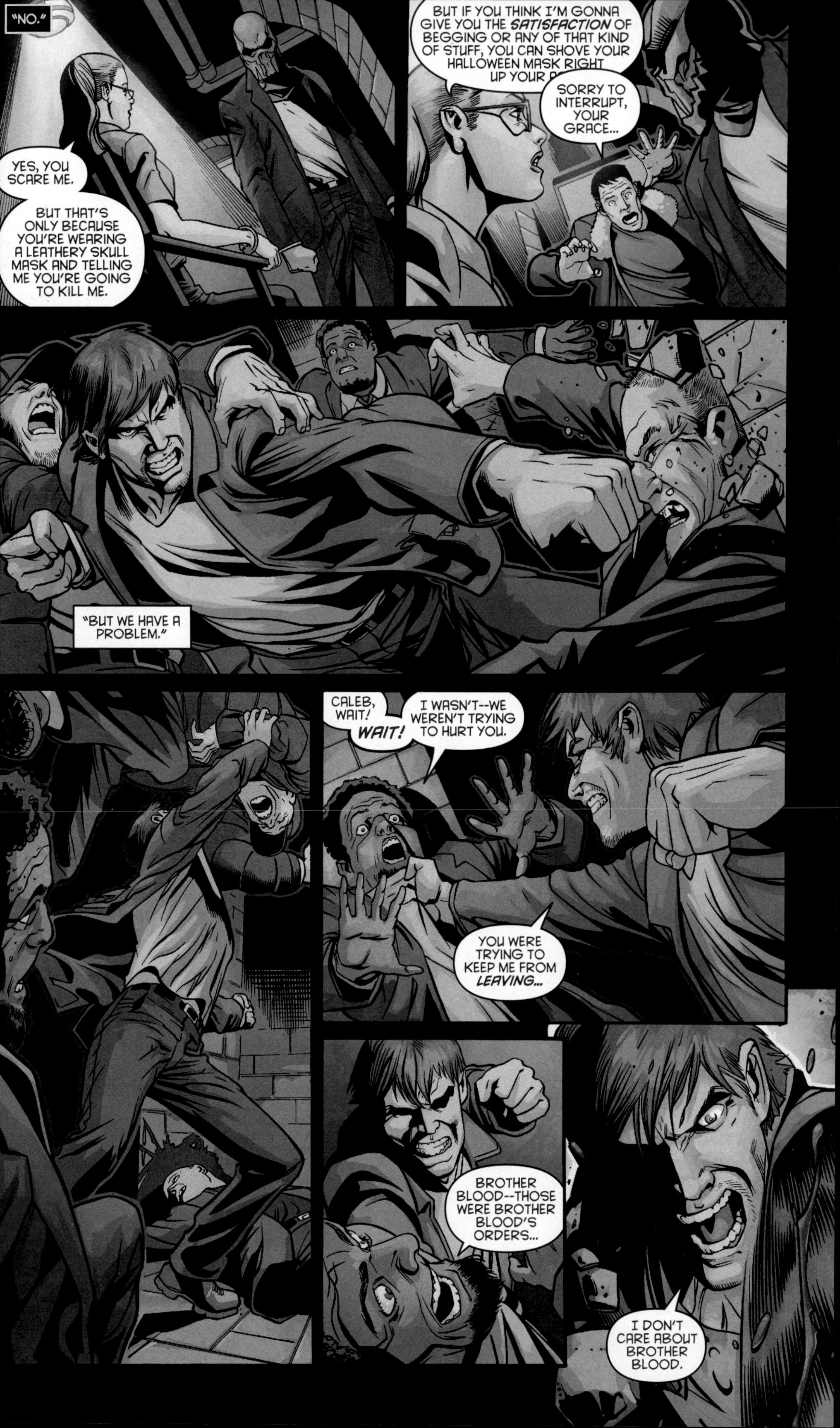
"NO."
YES, YOU SCARE ME.
BUT THAT'S ONLY BECAUSE YOU'RE WEARING A LEATHERY SKULL MASK AND TELLING ME YOU'RE GOING TO KILL ME.
BUT IF YOU THINK I'M GONNA GIVE YOU THE *SATISFACTION* OF BEGGING OR ANY OF THAT KIND OF STUFF, YOU CAN SHOVE YOUR HALLOWEEN MASK RIGHT UP YOUR A--
SORRY TO INTERRUPT, YOUR GRACE...
"BUT WE HAVE A PROBLEM."
CALEB, WAIT! *WAIT!*
I WASN'T--WE WEREN'T TRYING TO HURT YOU.
YOU WERE TRYING TO KEEP ME FROM *LEAVING*...
BROTHER BLOOD--THOSE WERE BROTHER BLOOD'S ORDERS...
I DON'T CARE ABOUT BROTHER BLOOD.

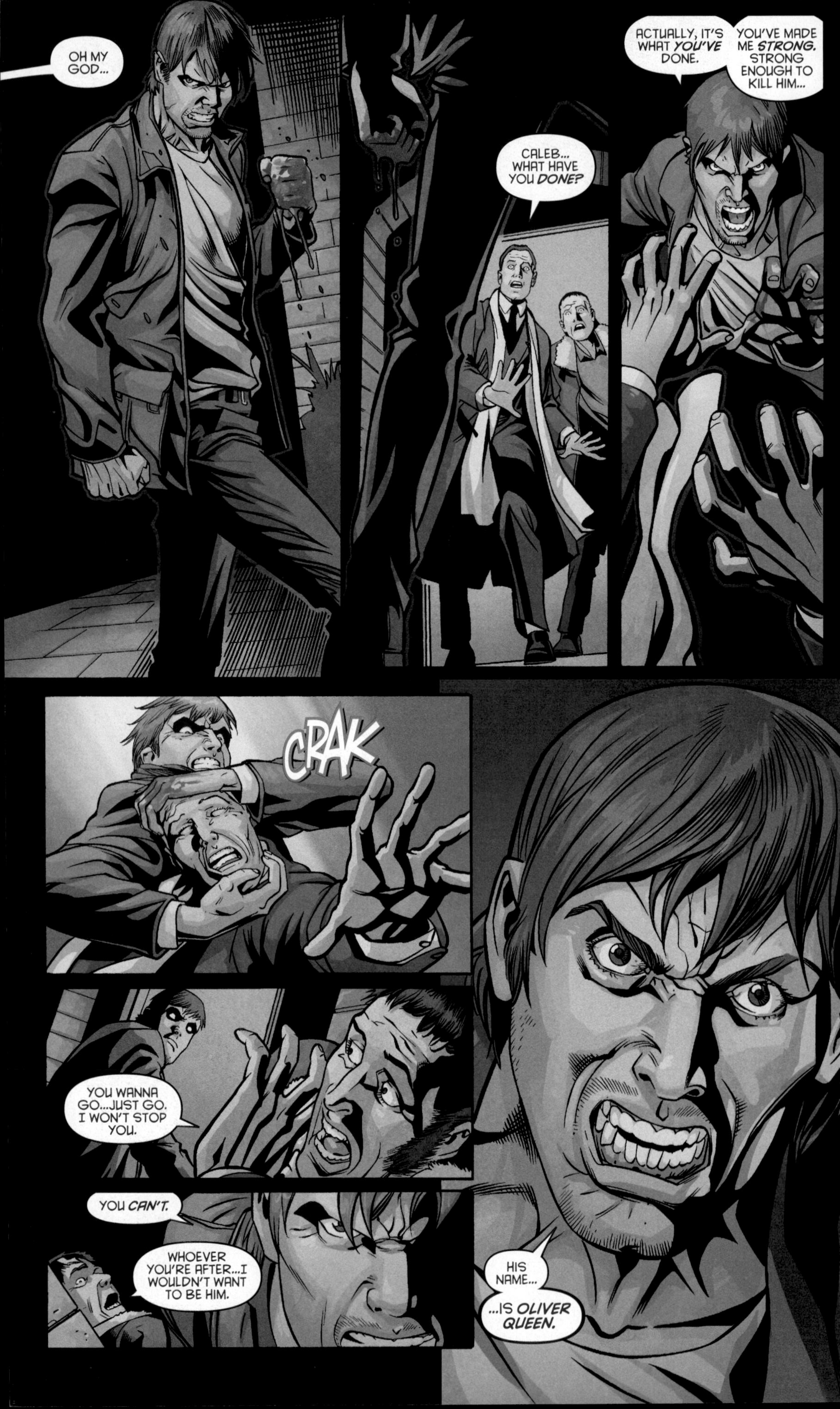
OH MY GOD...
CALEB... WHAT HAVE YOU DONE?
ACTUALLY, IT'S WHAT YOU'VE DONE.
YOU'VE MADE ME STRONG. STRONG ENOUGH TO KILL HIM...
CRAK
YOU WANNA GO...JUST GO. I WON'T STOP YOU.
YOU CAN'T.
WHOEVER YOU'RE AFTER...I WOULDN'T WANT TO BE HIM.
HIS NAME...
...IS OLIVER QUEEN.

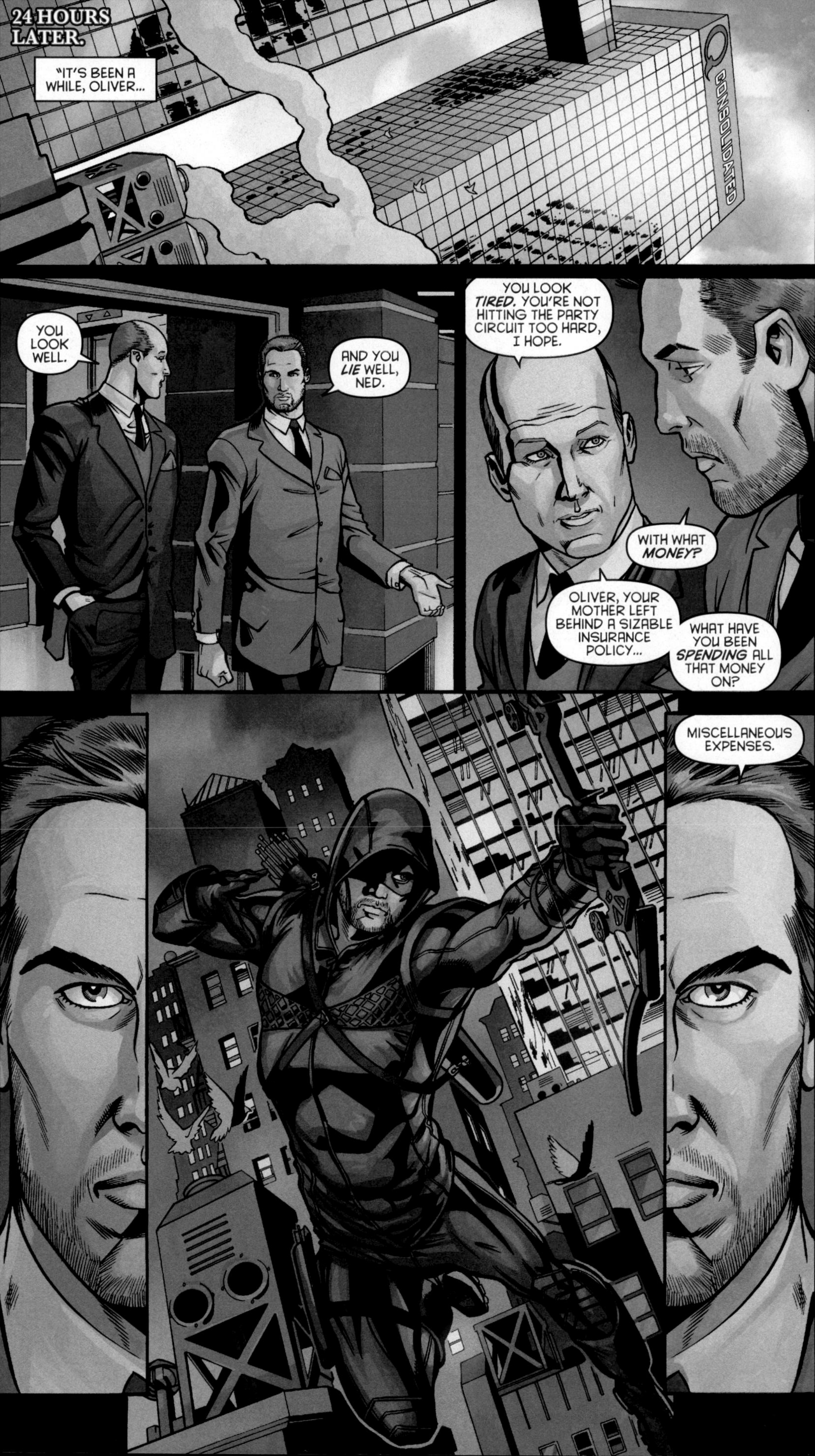
24 HOURS LATER.
"IT'S BEEN A WHILE, OLIVER...
CONSOLIDATED
YOU LOOK WELL.
AND YOU LIE WELL, NED.
YOU LOOK TIRED. YOU'RE NOT HITTING THE PARTY CIRCUIT TOO HARD, I HOPE.
WITH WHAT MONEY?
OLIVER, YOUR MOTHER LEFT BEHIND A SIZABLE INSURANCE POLICY...
WHAT HAVE YOU BEEN SPENDING ALL THAT MONEY ON?
MISCELLANEOUS EXPENSES.

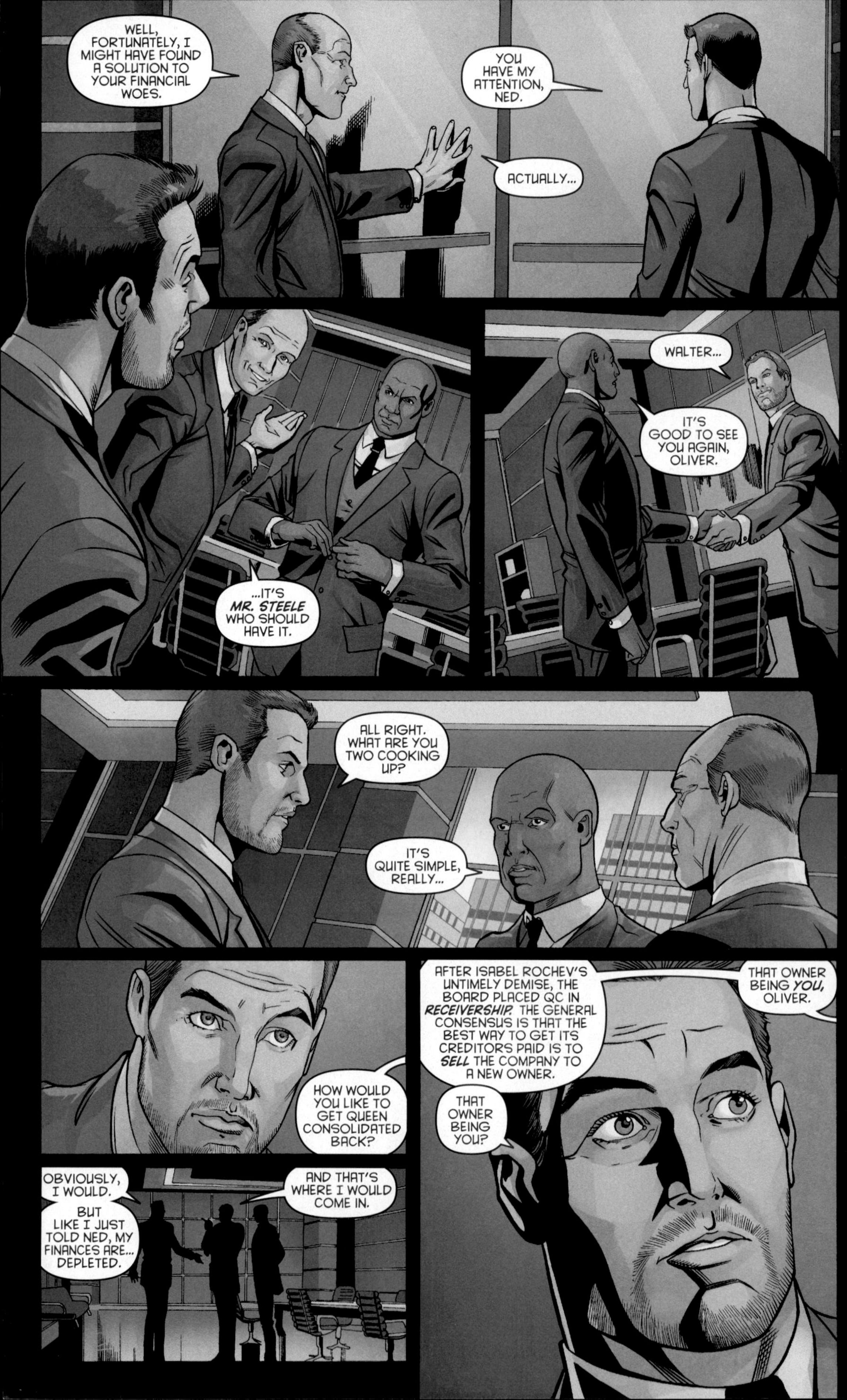
WELL, FORTUNATELY, I MIGHT HAVE FOUND A SOLUTION TO YOUR FINANCIAL WOES.
YOU HAVE MY ATTENTION, NED.
ACTUALLY...
...IT'S MR. STEELE WHO SHOULD HAVE IT.
WALTER...
IT'S GOOD TO SEE YOU AGAIN, OLIVER.
ALL RIGHT. WHAT ARE YOU TWO COOKING UP?
IT'S QUITE SIMPLE, REALLY...
HOW WOULD YOU LIKE TO GET QUEEN CONSOLIDATED BACK?
OBVIOUSLY, I WOULD.
BUT LIKE I JUST TOLD NED, MY FINANCES ARE... DEPLETED.
AND THAT'S WHERE I WOULD COME IN.
AFTER ISABEL ROCHEV'S UNTIMELY DEMISE, THE BOARD PLACED QC IN RECEIVERSHIP. THE GENERAL CONSENSUS IS THAT THE BEST WAY TO GET ITS CREDITORS PAID IS TO SELL THE COMPANY TO A NEW OWNER.
THAT OWNER BEING YOU?
THAT OWNER BEING YOU, OLIVER.

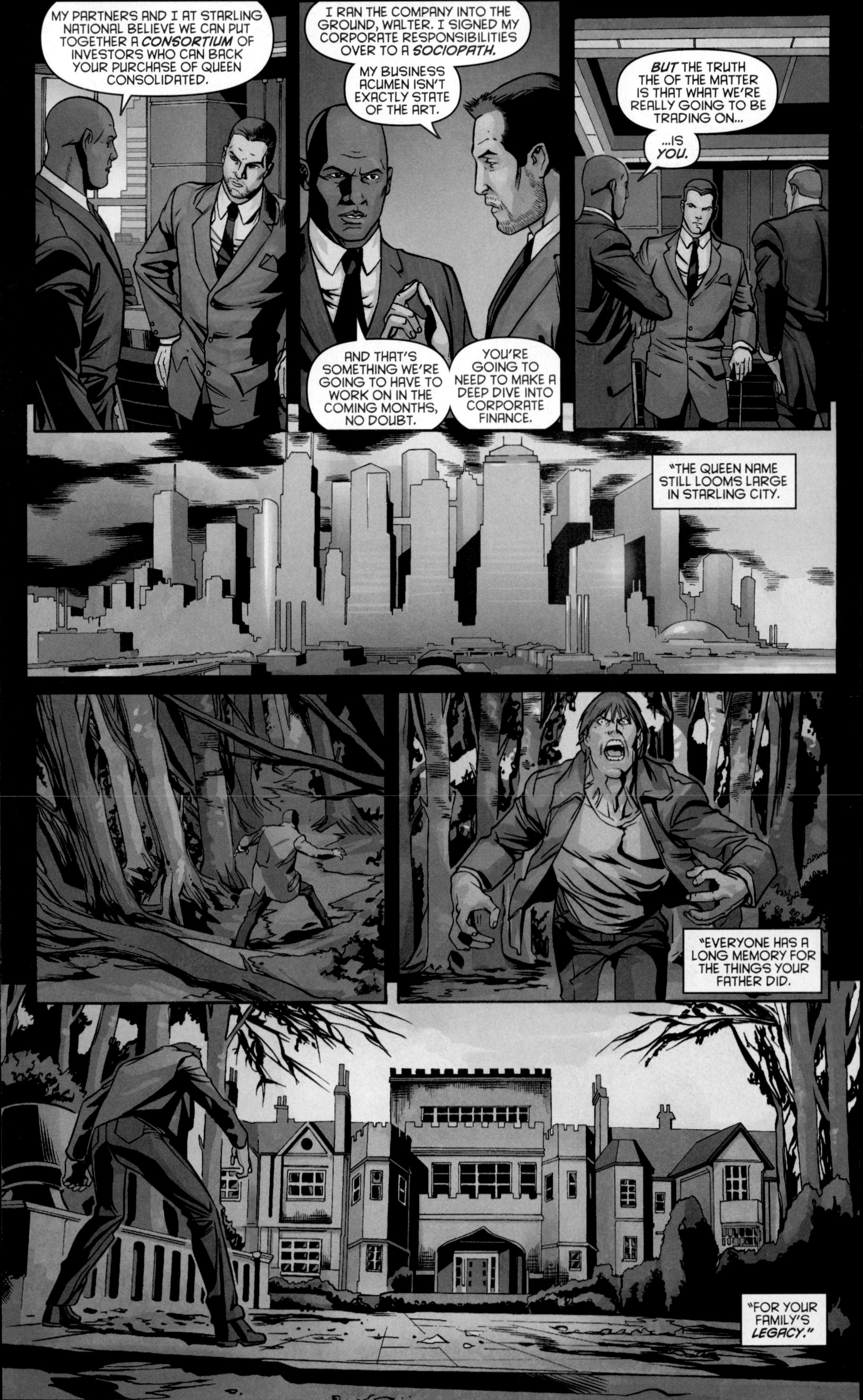
MY PARTNERS AND I AT STARLING NATIONAL BELIEVE WE CAN PUT TOGETHER A *CONSORTIUM* OF INVESTORS WHO CAN BACK YOUR PURCHASE OF QUEEN CONSOLIDATED.
I RAN THE COMPANY INTO THE GROUND, WALTER. I SIGNED MY CORPORATE RESPONSIBILITIES OVER TO A *SOCIOPATH.*
MY BUSINESS ACUMEN ISN'T EXACTLY STATE OF THE ART.
AND THAT'S SOMETHING WE'RE GOING TO HAVE TO WORK ON IN THE COMING MONTHS, NO DOUBT.
YOU'RE GOING TO NEED TO MAKE A DEEP DIVE INTO CORPORATE FINANCE.
BUT THE TRUTH THE OF THE MATTER IS THAT WHAT WE'RE REALLY GOING TO BE TRADING ON...
...IS *YOU.*
"THE QUEEN NAME STILL LOOMS LARGE IN STARLING CITY.
"EVERYONE HAS A LONG MEMORY FOR THE THINGS YOUR FATHER DID.
"FOR YOUR FAMILY'S *LEGACY.*"

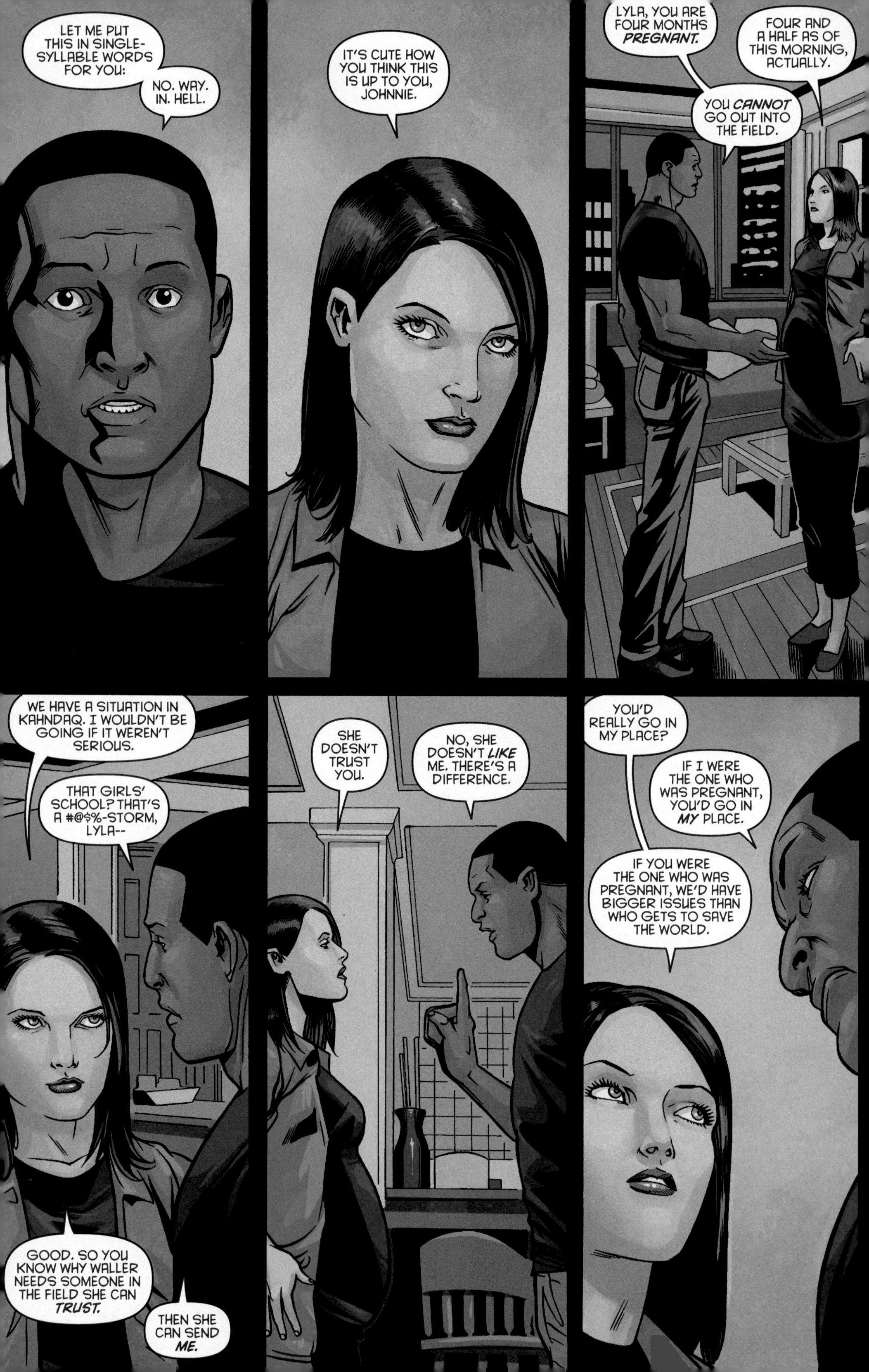
LET ME PUT THIS IN SINGLE-SYLLABLE WORDS FOR YOU:
NO. WAY. IN. HELL.
IT'S CUTE HOW YOU THINK THIS IS UP TO YOU, JOHNNIE.
LYLA, YOU ARE FOUR MONTHS *PREGNANT.*
YOU *CANNOT* GO OUT INTO THE FIELD.
FOUR AND A HALF AS OF THIS MORNING, ACTUALLY.
WE HAVE A SITUATION IN KAHNDAQ. I WOULDN'T BE GOING IF IT WEREN'T SERIOUS.
THAT GIRLS' SCHOOL? THAT'S A #@$%-STORM, LYLA--
GOOD. SO YOU KNOW WHY WALLER NEEDS SOMEONE IN THE FIELD SHE CAN *TRUST.*
THEN SHE CAN SEND *ME.*
SHE DOESN'T TRUST YOU.
NO, SHE DOESN'T *LIKE* ME. THERE'S A DIFFERENCE.
YOU'D REALLY GO IN MY PLACE?
IF I WERE THE ONE WHO WAS PREGNANT, YOU'D GO IN *MY* PLACE.
IF YOU WERE THE ONE WHO WAS PREGNANT, WE'D HAVE BIGGER ISSUES THAN WHO GETS TO SAVE THE WORLD.

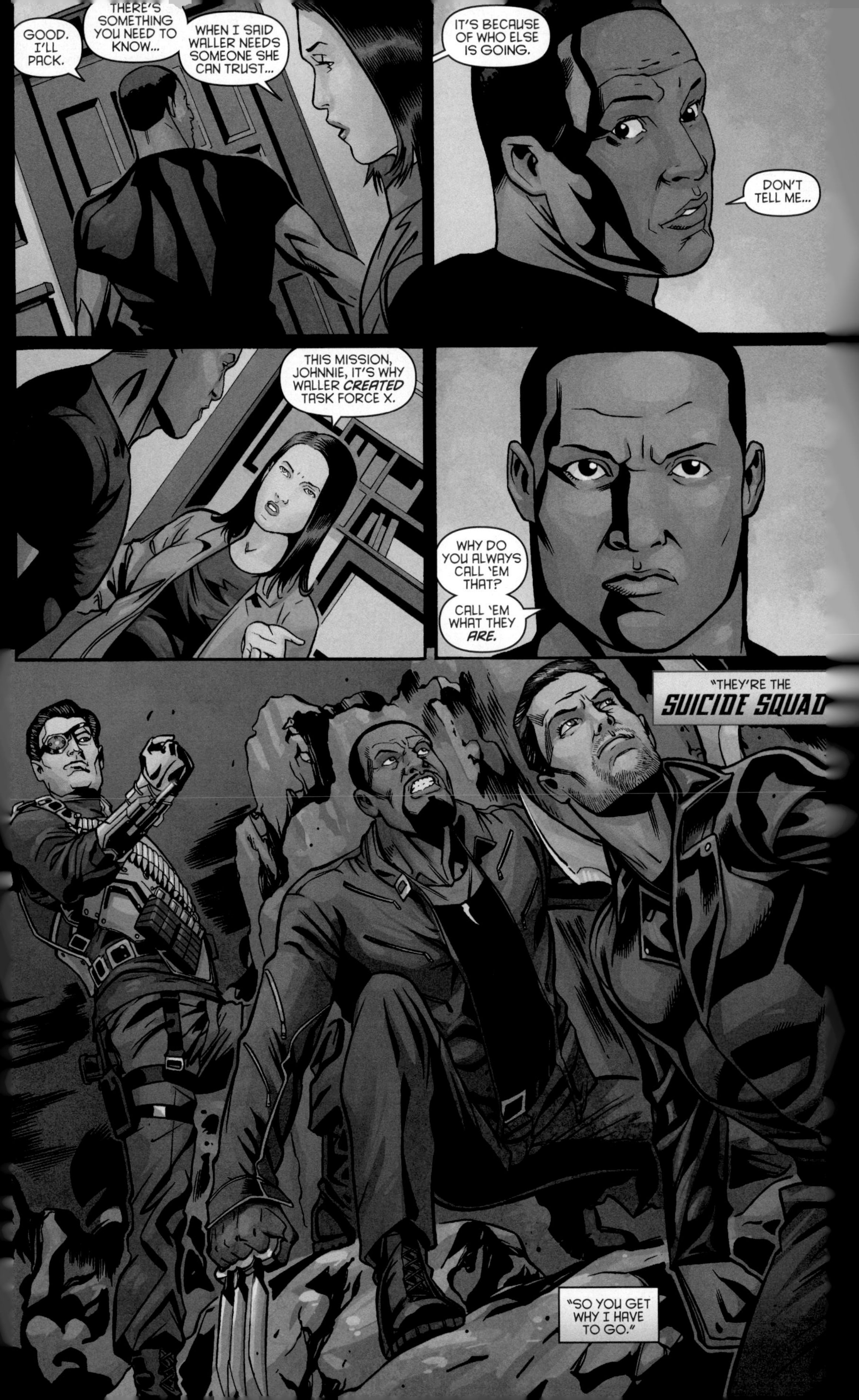
GOOD. I'LL PACK.
THERE'S SOMETHING YOU NEED TO KNOW...
WHEN I SAID WALLER NEEDS SOMEONE SHE CAN TRUST...
IT'S BECAUSE OF WHO ELSE IS GOING.
DON'T TELL ME...
THIS MISSION, JOHNNIE, IT'S WHY WALLER *CREATED* TASK FORCE X.
WHY DO YOU ALWAYS CALL 'EM THAT?
CALL 'EM WHAT THEY *ARE.*
"THEY'RE THE SUICIDE SQUAD
"SO YOU GET WHY I HAVE TO GO."

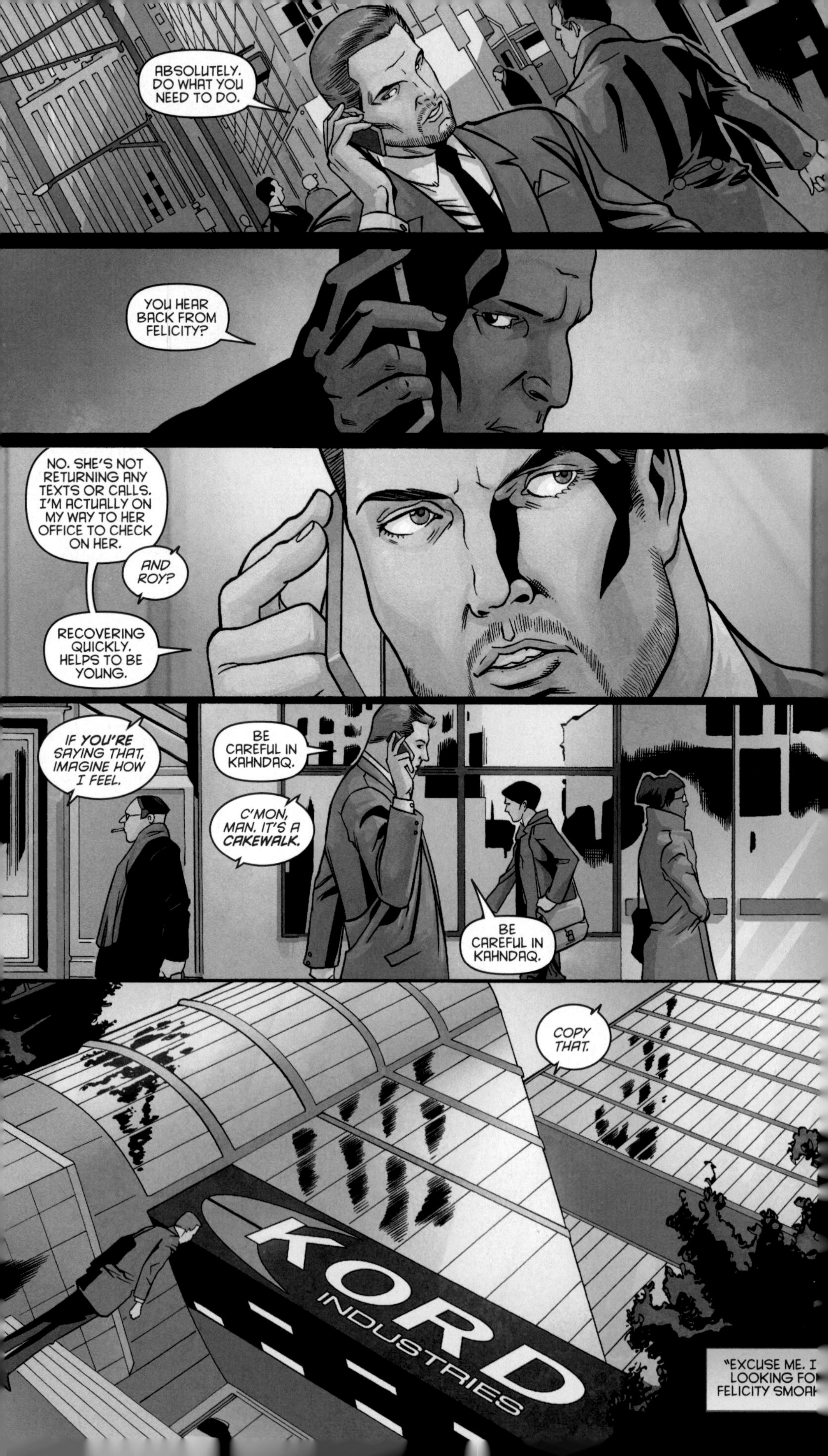
ABSOLUTELY. DO WHAT YOU NEED TO DO.
YOU HEAR BACK FROM FELICITY?
NO. SHE'S NOT RETURNING ANY TEXTS OR CALLS. I'M ACTUALLY ON MY WAY TO HER OFFICE TO CHECK ON HER.
AND ROY?
RECOVERING QUICKLY. HELPS TO BE YOUNG.
IF YOU'RE SAYING THAT, IMAGINE HOW I FEEL.
BE CAREFUL IN KAHNDAQ.
C'MON, MAN. IT'S A CAKEWALK.
BE CAREFUL IN KAHNDAQ.
COPY THAT.
KORD INDUSTRIES
"EXCUSE ME. I LOOKING FO FELICITY SMOA

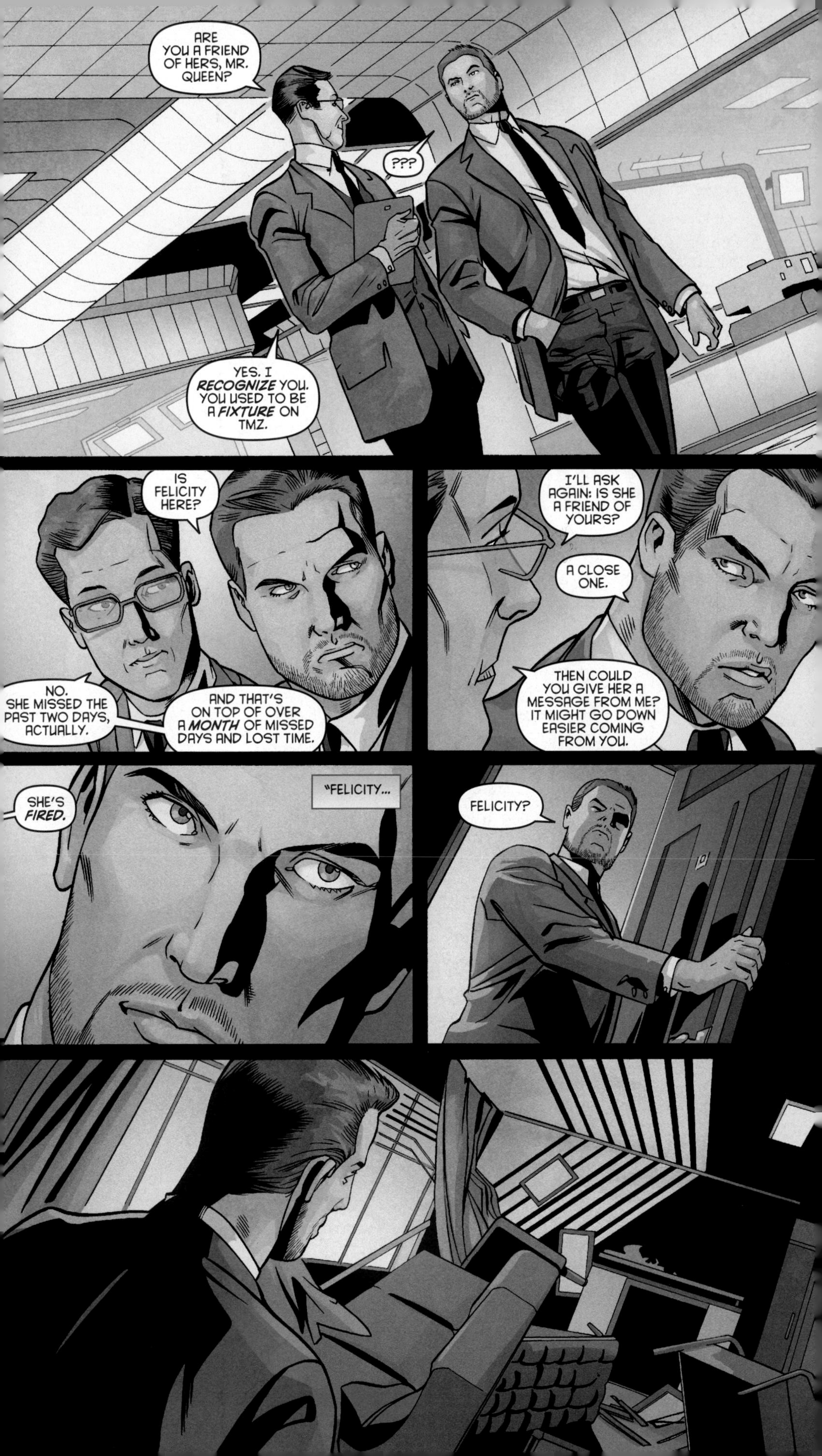
ARE YOU A FRIEND OF HERS, MR. QUEEN?
???
YES. I *RECOGNIZE* YOU. YOU USED TO BE A *FIXTURE* ON TMZ.
IS FELICITY HERE?
NO. SHE MISSED THE PAST TWO DAYS, ACTUALLY.
AND THAT'S ON TOP OF OVER A *MONTH* OF MISSED DAYS AND LOST TIME.
I'LL ASK AGAIN: IS SHE A FRIEND OF YOURS?
A CLOSE ONE.
THEN COULD YOU GIVE HER A MESSAGE FROM ME? IT MIGHT GO DOWN EASIER COMING FROM YOU.
SHE'S *FIRED.*
"FELICITY...
FELICITY?

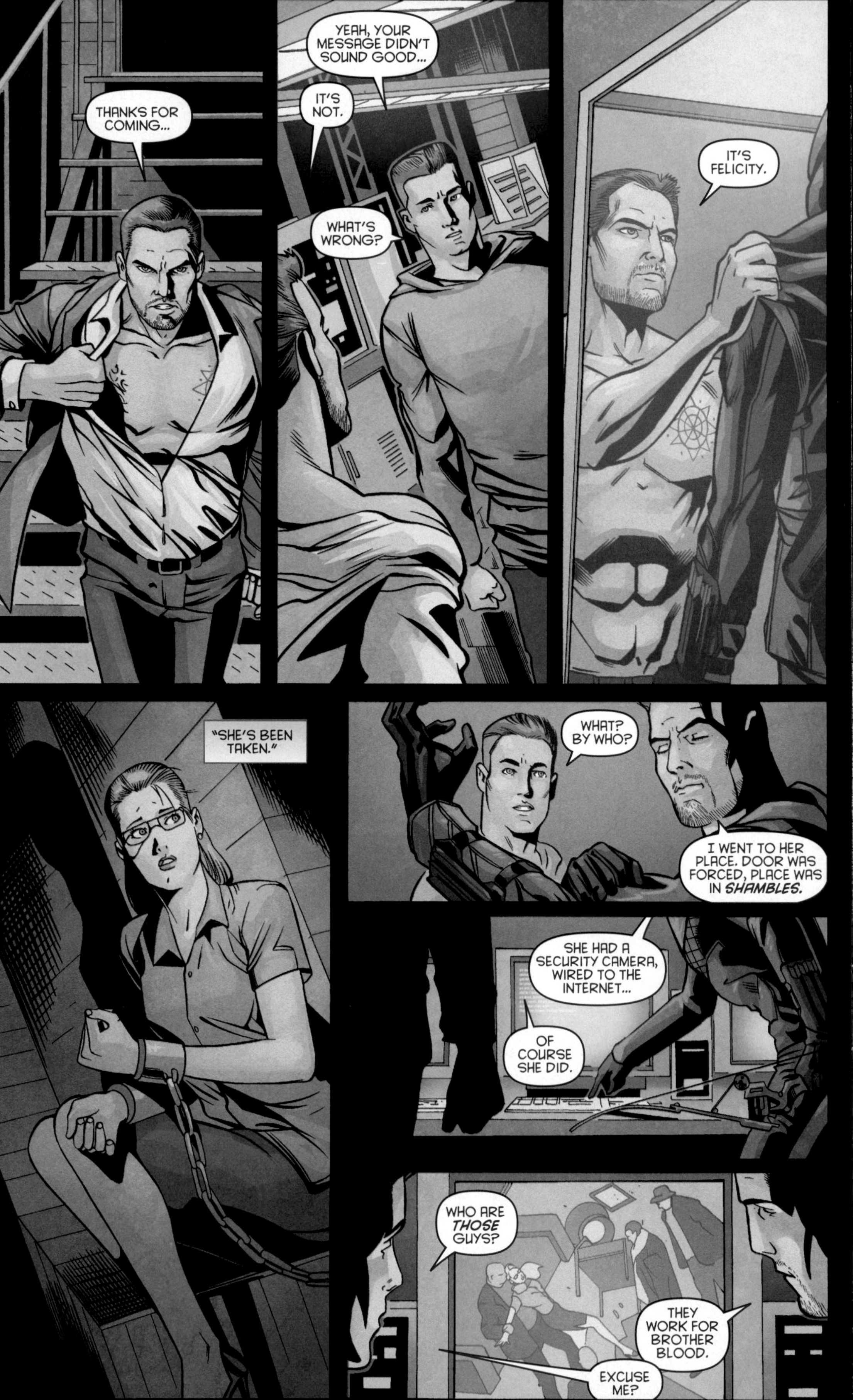
THANKS FOR COMING...
YEAH, YOUR MESSAGE DIDN'T SOUND GOOD...
IT'S NOT.
WHAT'S WRONG?
IT'S FELICITY.
"SHE'S BEEN TAKEN."
WHAT? BY WHO?
I WENT TO HER PLACE. DOOR WAS FORCED, PLACE WAS IN *SHAMBLES.*
SHE HAD A SECURITY CAMERA, WIRED TO THE INTERNET...
OF COURSE SHE DID.
WHO ARE *THOSE* GUYS?
THEY WORK FOR BROTHER BLOOD.
EXCUSE ME?

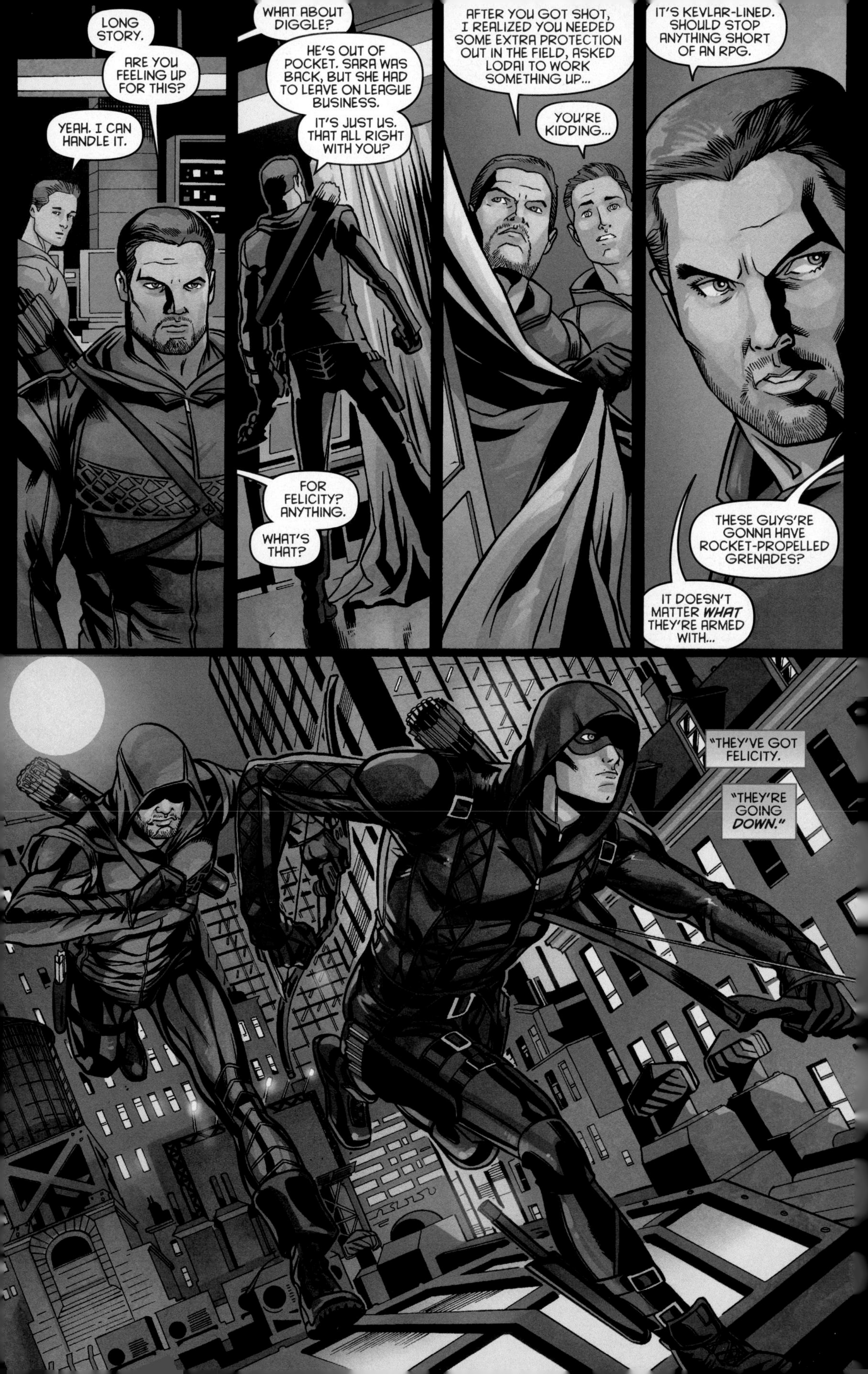
LONG STORY.
ARE YOU FEELING UP FOR THIS?
YEAH. I CAN HANDLE IT.
WHAT ABOUT DIGGLE?
HE'S OUT OF POCKET. SARA WAS BACK, BUT SHE HAD TO LEAVE ON LEAGUE BUSINESS.
IT'S JUST US. THAT ALL RIGHT WITH YOU?
FOR FELICITY? ANYTHING.
WHAT'S THAT?
AFTER YOU GOT SHOT, I REALIZED YOU NEEDED SOME EXTRA PROTECTION OUT IN THE FIELD, ASKED LODAI TO WORK SOMETHING UP...
YOU'RE KIDDING...
IT'S KEVLAR-LINED. SHOULD STOP ANYTHING SHORT OF AN RPG.
THESE GUYS'RE GONNA HAVE ROCKET-PROPELLED GRENADES?
IT DOESN'T MATTER *WHAT* THEY'RE ARMED WITH...
"THEY'VE GOT FELICITY.
"THEY'RE GOING *DOWN*."

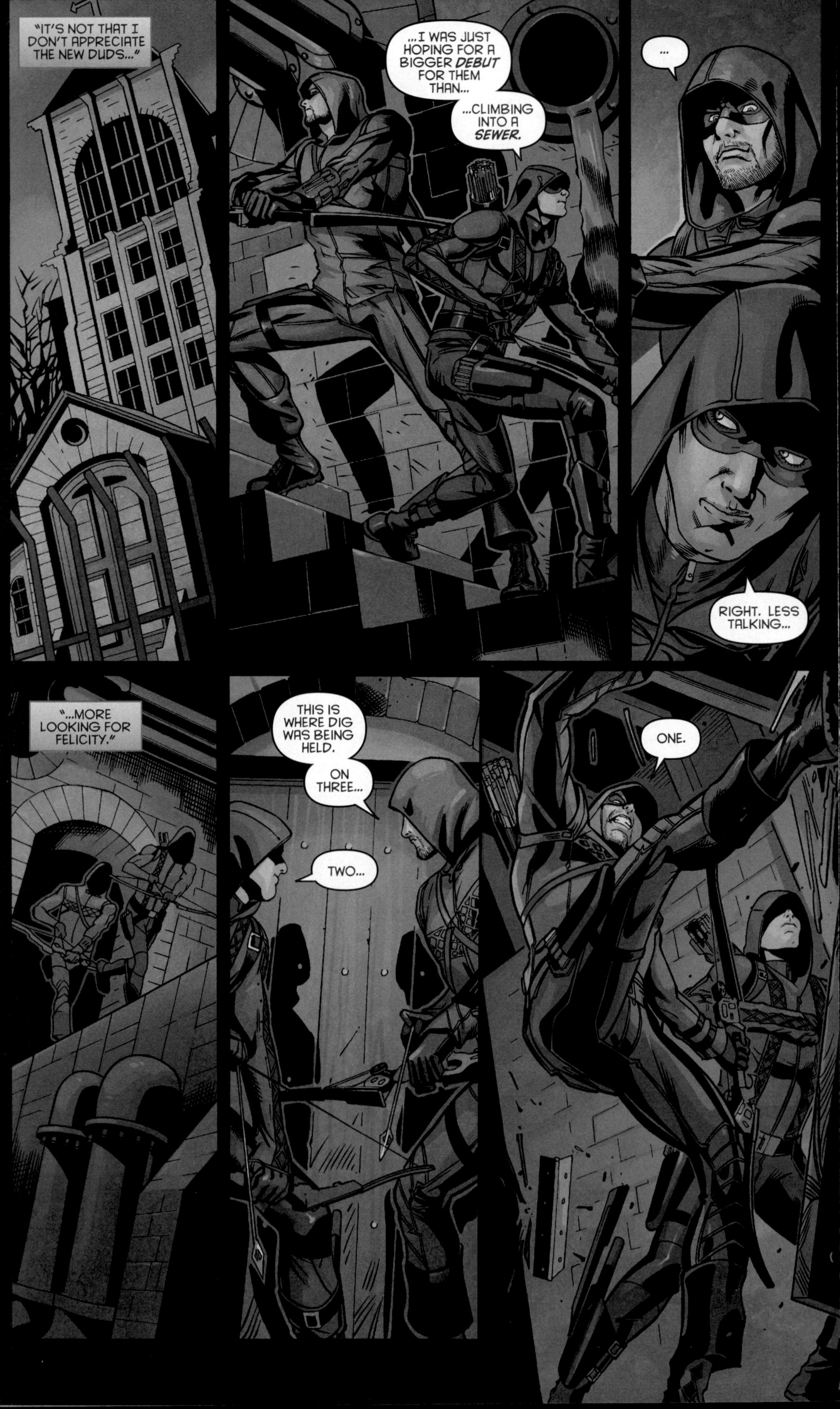
"IT'S NOT THAT I DON'T APPRECIATE THE NEW DUDS..."
...I WAS JUST HOPING FOR A BIGGER *DEBUT* FOR THEM THAN...
...CLIMBING INTO A *SEWER.*
...
RIGHT. LESS TALKING...
"...MORE LOOKING FOR FELICITY."
THIS IS WHERE DIG WAS BEING HELD.
ON THREE...
TWO...
ONE.

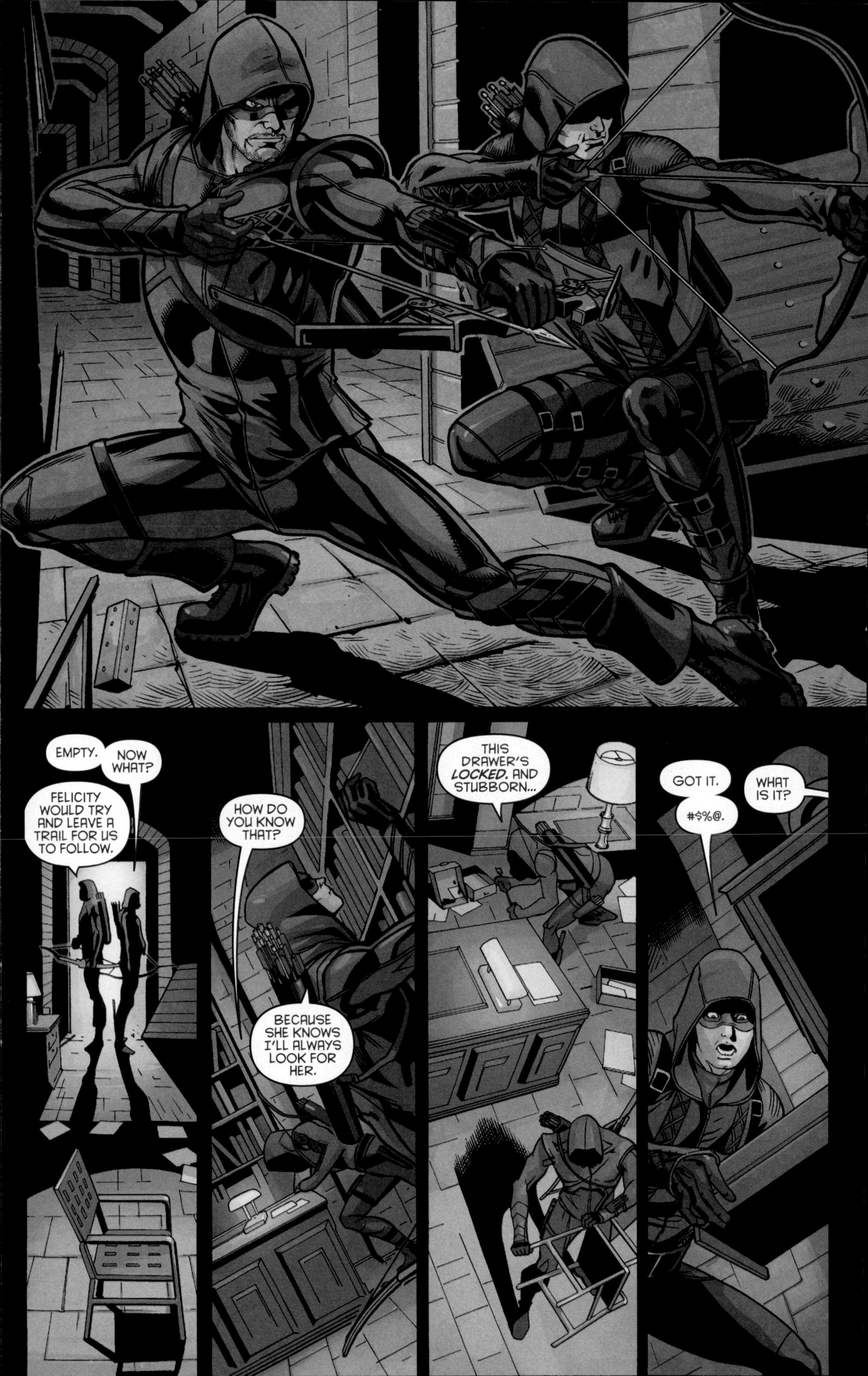

EMPTY.
NOW WHAT?
FELICITY WOULD TRY AND LEAVE A TRAIL FOR US TO FOLLOW.
HOW DO YOU KNOW THAT?
BECAUSE SHE KNOWS I'LL ALWAYS LOOK FOR HER.
THIS DRAWER'S LOCKED. AND STUBBORN...
GOT IT.
#$%@.
WHAT IS IT?

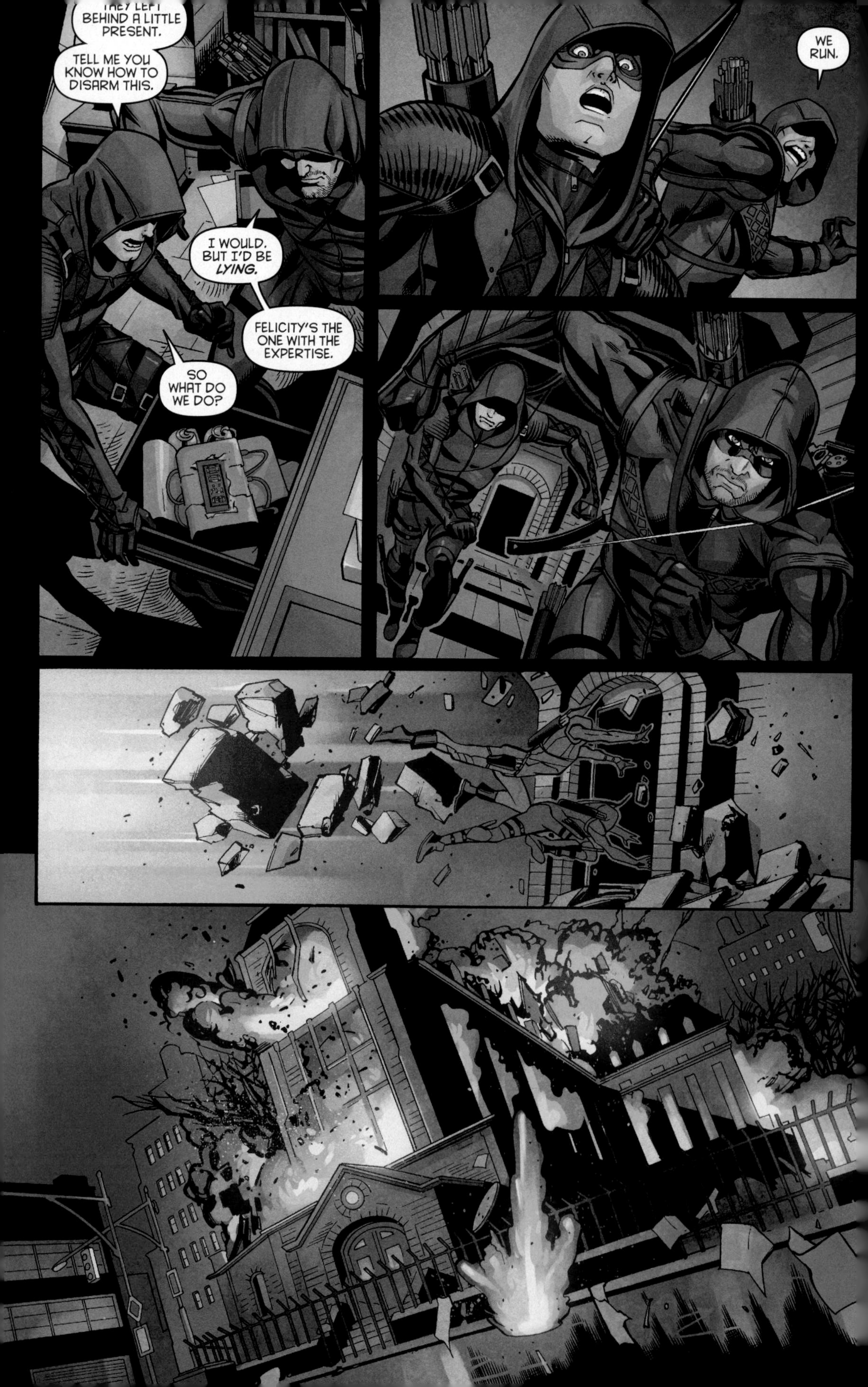
THEY LEFT BEHIND A LITTLE PRESENT.
TELL ME YOU KNOW HOW TO DISARM THIS.
I WOULD. BUT I'D BE *LYING.*
FELICITY'S THE ONE WITH THE EXPERTISE.
SO WHAT DO WE DO?
WE RUN.

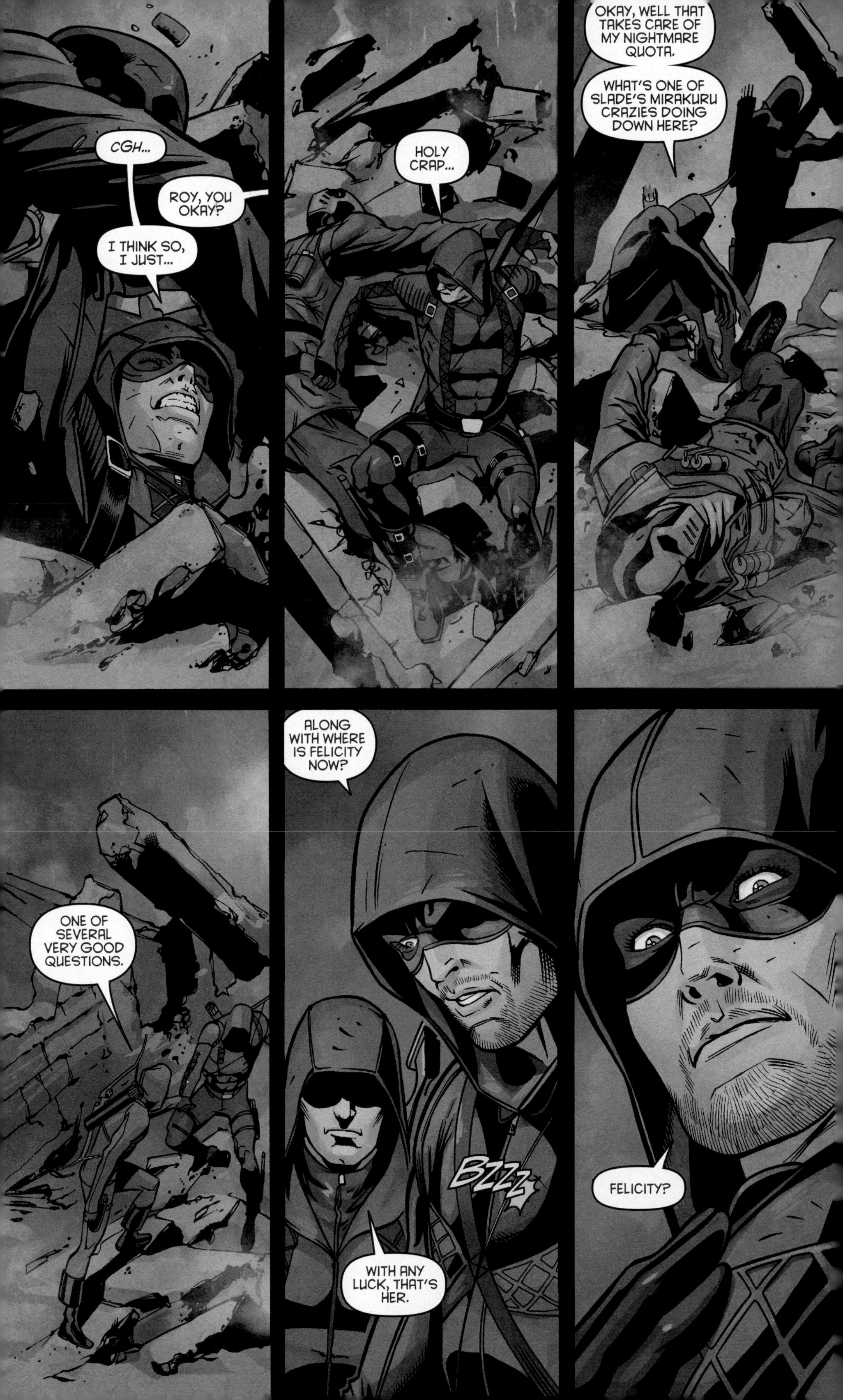
CGH...
ROY, YOU OKAY?
I THINK SO, I JUST...
HOLY CRAP...
OKAY, WELL THAT TAKES CARE OF MY NIGHTMARE QUOTA.
WHAT'S ONE OF SLADE'S MIRAKURU CRAZIES DOING DOWN HERE?
ONE OF SEVERAL VERY GOOD QUESTIONS.
ALONG WITH WHERE IS FELICITY NOW?
BZZZ
WITH ANY LUCK, THAT'S HER.
FELICITY?

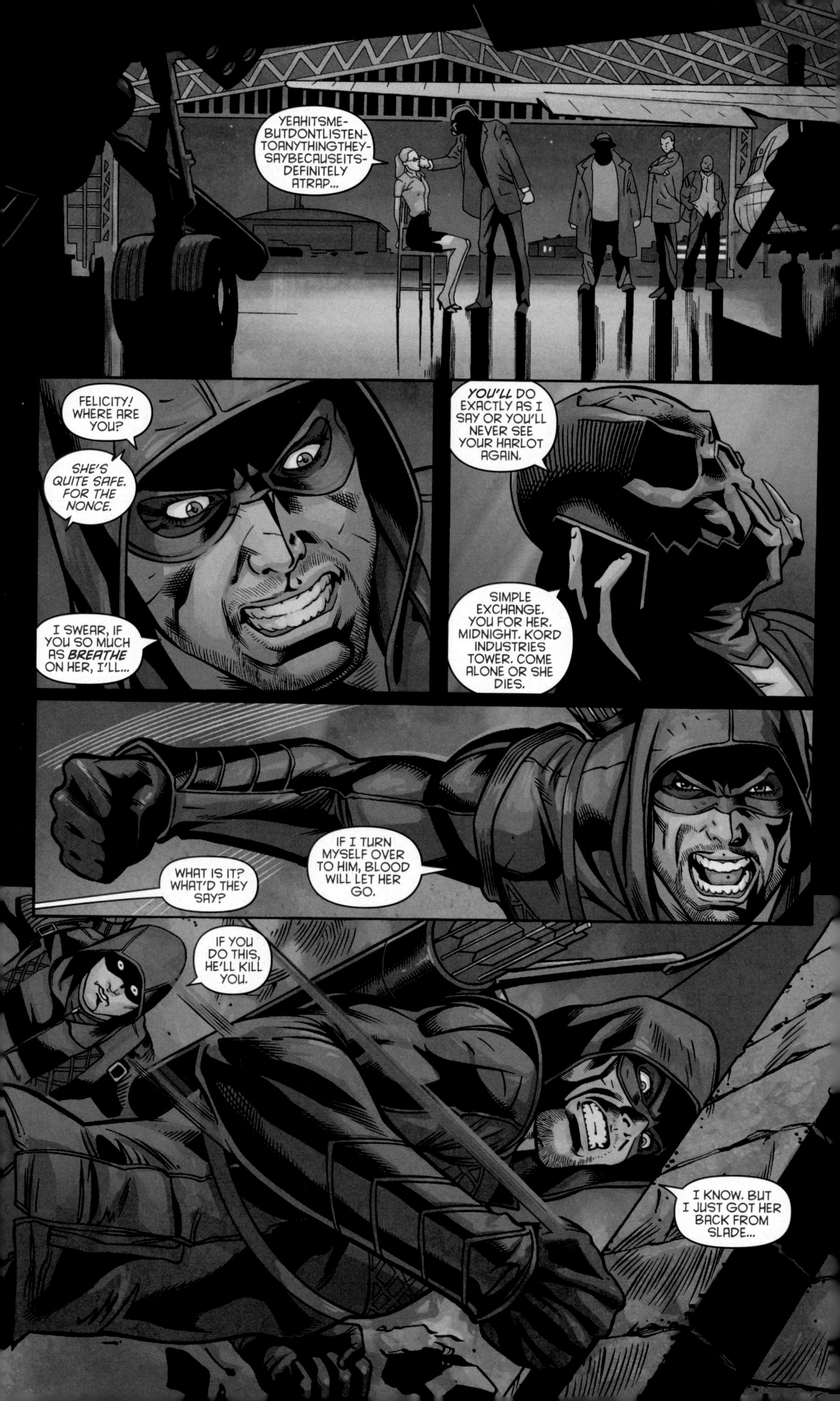
YEAHITSME-BUTDONTLISTEN-TOANYTHINGTHEY-SAYBECAUSEITS-DEFINITELY ATRAP...
FELICITY! WHERE ARE YOU?
SHE'S QUITE SAFE. FOR THE NONCE.
I SWEAR, IF YOU SO MUCH AS BREATHE ON HER, I'LL...
YOU'LL DO EXACTLY AS I SAY OR YOU'LL NEVER SEE YOUR HARLOT AGAIN.
SIMPLE EXCHANGE. YOU FOR HER. MIDNIGHT. KORD INDUSTRIES TOWER. COME ALONE OR SHE DIES.
WHAT IS IT? WHAT'D THEY SAY?
IF I TURN MYSELF OVER TO HIM, BLOOD WILL LET HER GO.
IF YOU DO THIS, HE'LL KILL YOU.
I KNOW. BUT I JUST GOT HER BACK FROM SLADE...

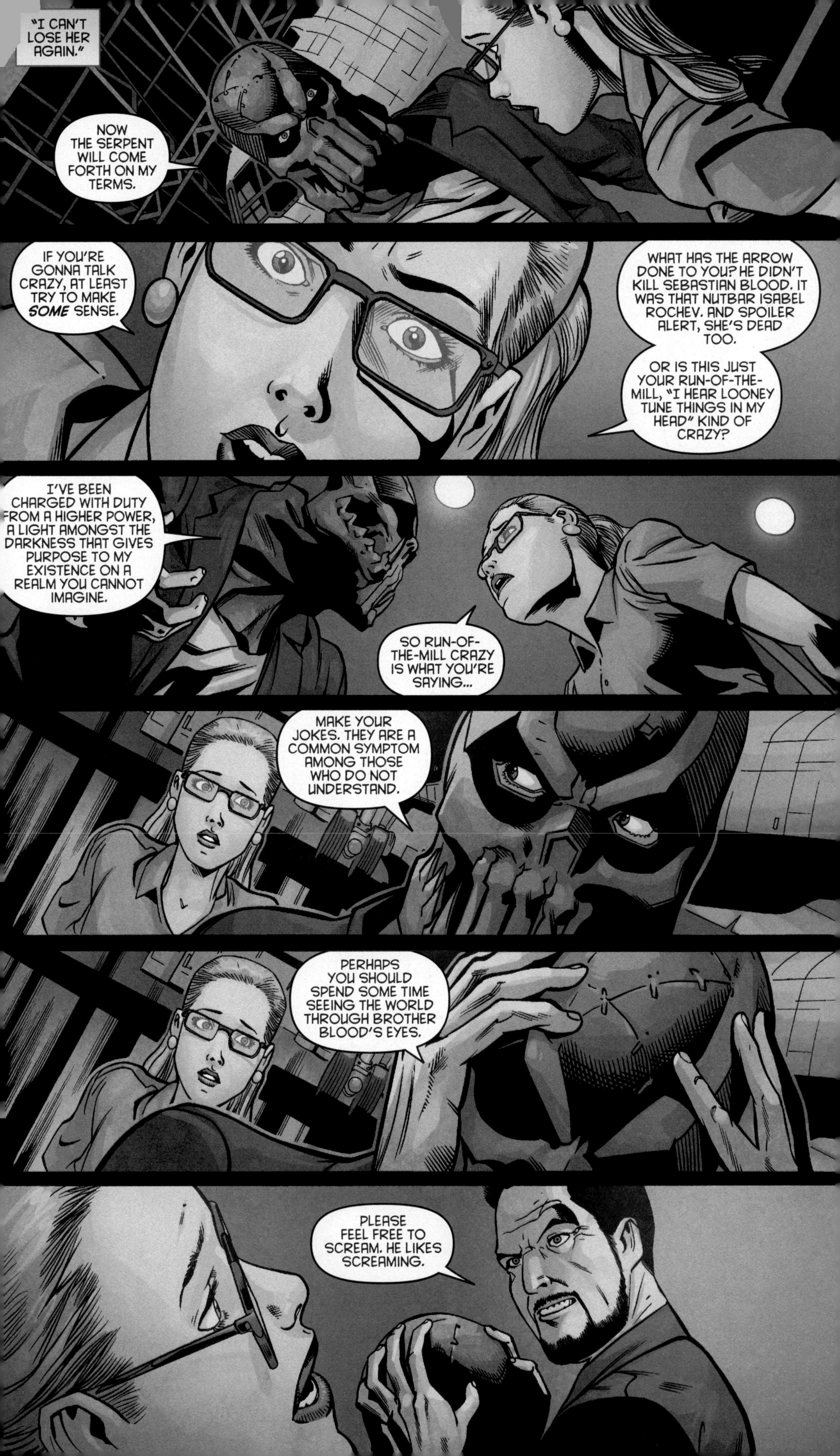
"I CAN'T LOSE HER AGAIN."
NOW THE SERPENT WILL COME FORTH ON MY TERMS.
IF YOU'RE GONNA TALK CRAZY, AT LEAST TRY TO MAKE SOME SENSE.
WHAT HAS THE ARROW DONE TO YOU? HE DIDN'T KILL SEBASTIAN BLOOD. IT WAS THAT NUTBAR ISABEL ROCHEV. AND SPOILER ALERT, SHE'S DEAD TOO.
OR IS THIS JUST YOUR RUN-OF-THE-MILL, "I HEAR LOONEY TUNE THINGS IN MY HEAD" KIND OF CRAZY?
I'VE BEEN CHARGED WITH DUTY FROM A HIGHER POWER, A LIGHT AMONGST THE DARKNESS THAT GIVES PURPOSE TO MY EXISTENCE ON A REALM YOU CANNOT IMAGINE.
SO RUN-OF-THE-MILL CRAZY IS WHAT YOU'RE SAYING...
MAKE YOUR JOKES. THEY ARE A COMMON SYMPTOM AMONG THOSE WHO DO NOT UNDERSTAND.
PERHAPS YOU SHOULD SPEND SOME TIME SEEING THE WORLD THROUGH BROTHER BLOOD'S EYES.
PLEASE FEEL FREE TO SCREAM. HE LIKES SCREAMING.

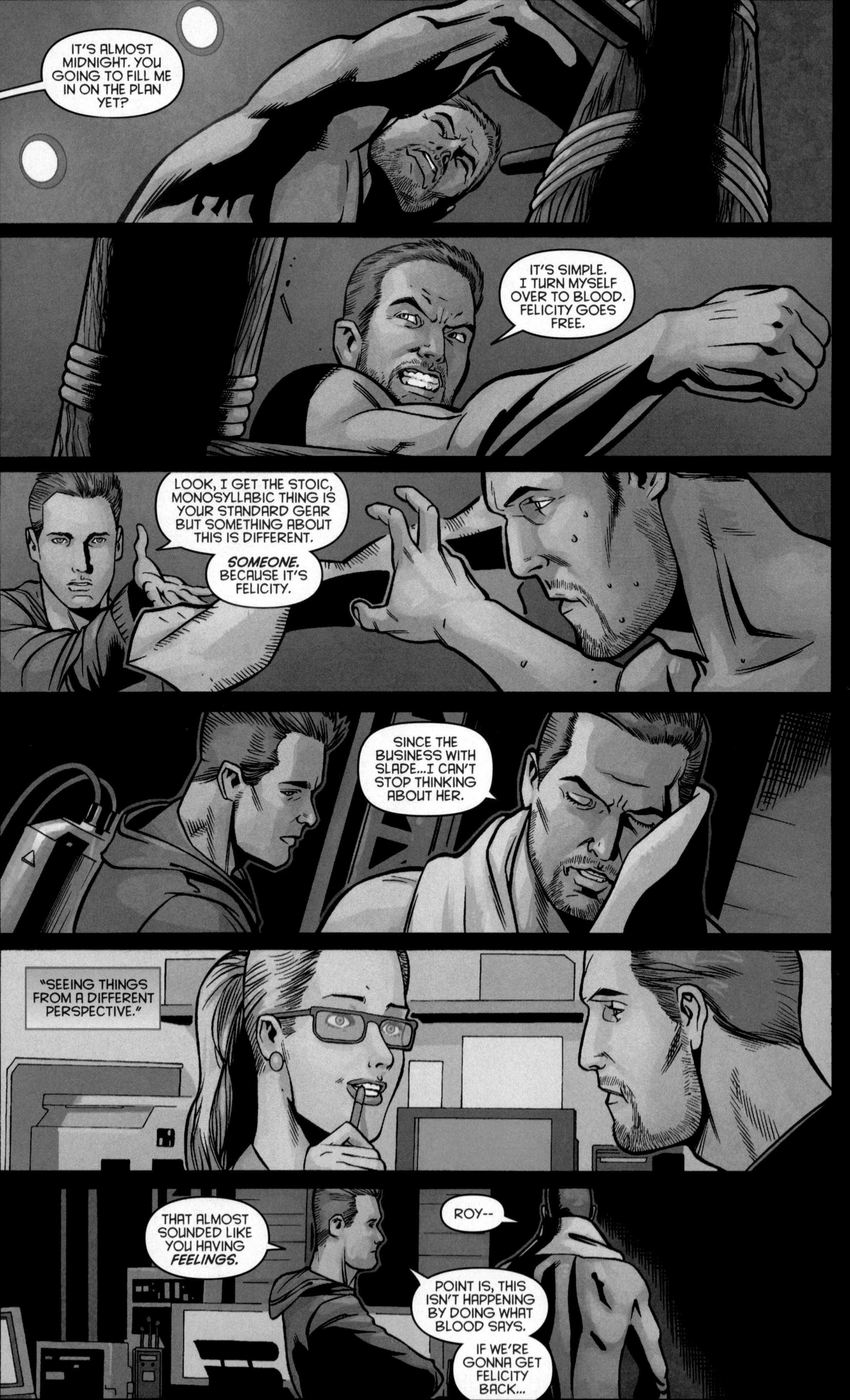
IT'S ALMOST MIDNIGHT. YOU GOING TO FILL ME IN ON THE PLAN YET?
IT'S SIMPLE. I TURN MYSELF OVER TO BLOOD. FELICITY GOES FREE.
LOOK, I GET THE STOIC, MONOSYLLABIC THING IS YOUR STANDARD GEAR BUT SOMETHING ABOUT THIS IS DIFFERENT.
SOMEONE. BECAUSE IT'S FELICITY.
SINCE THE BUSINESS WITH SLADE...I CAN'T STOP THINKING ABOUT HER.
"SEEING THINGS FROM A DIFFERENT PERSPECTIVE."
THAT ALMOST SOUNDED LIKE YOU HAVING *FEELINGS.*
ROY--
POINT IS, THIS ISN'T HAPPENING BY DOING WHAT BLOOD SAYS.
IF WE'RE GONNA GET FELICITY BACK...

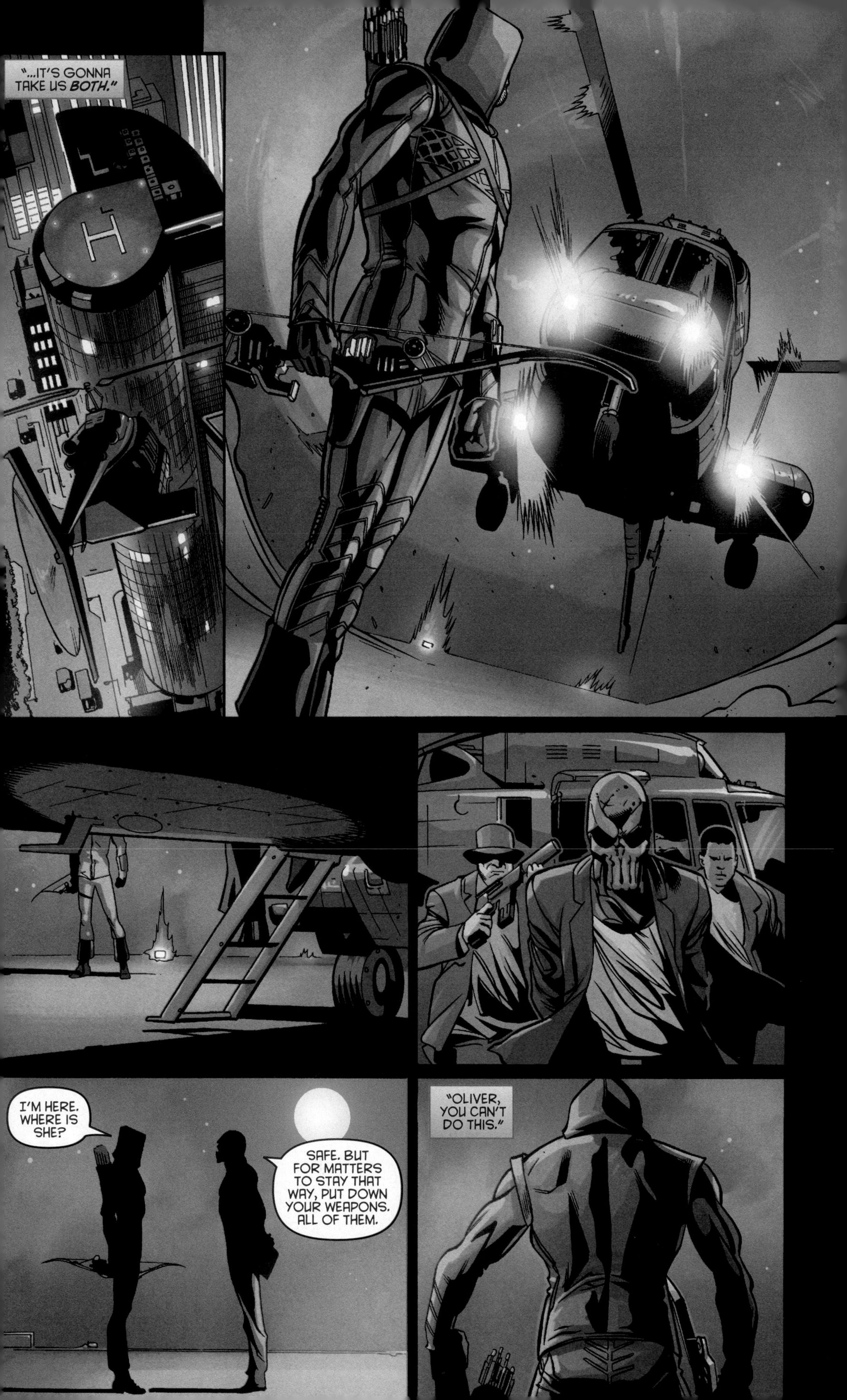
"...IT'S GONNA TAKE US *BOTH*."
I'M HERE. WHERE IS SHE?
SAFE. BUT FOR MATTERS TO STAY THAT WAY, PUT DOWN YOUR WEAPONS. ALL OF THEM.
"OLIVER, YOU CAN'T DO THIS."

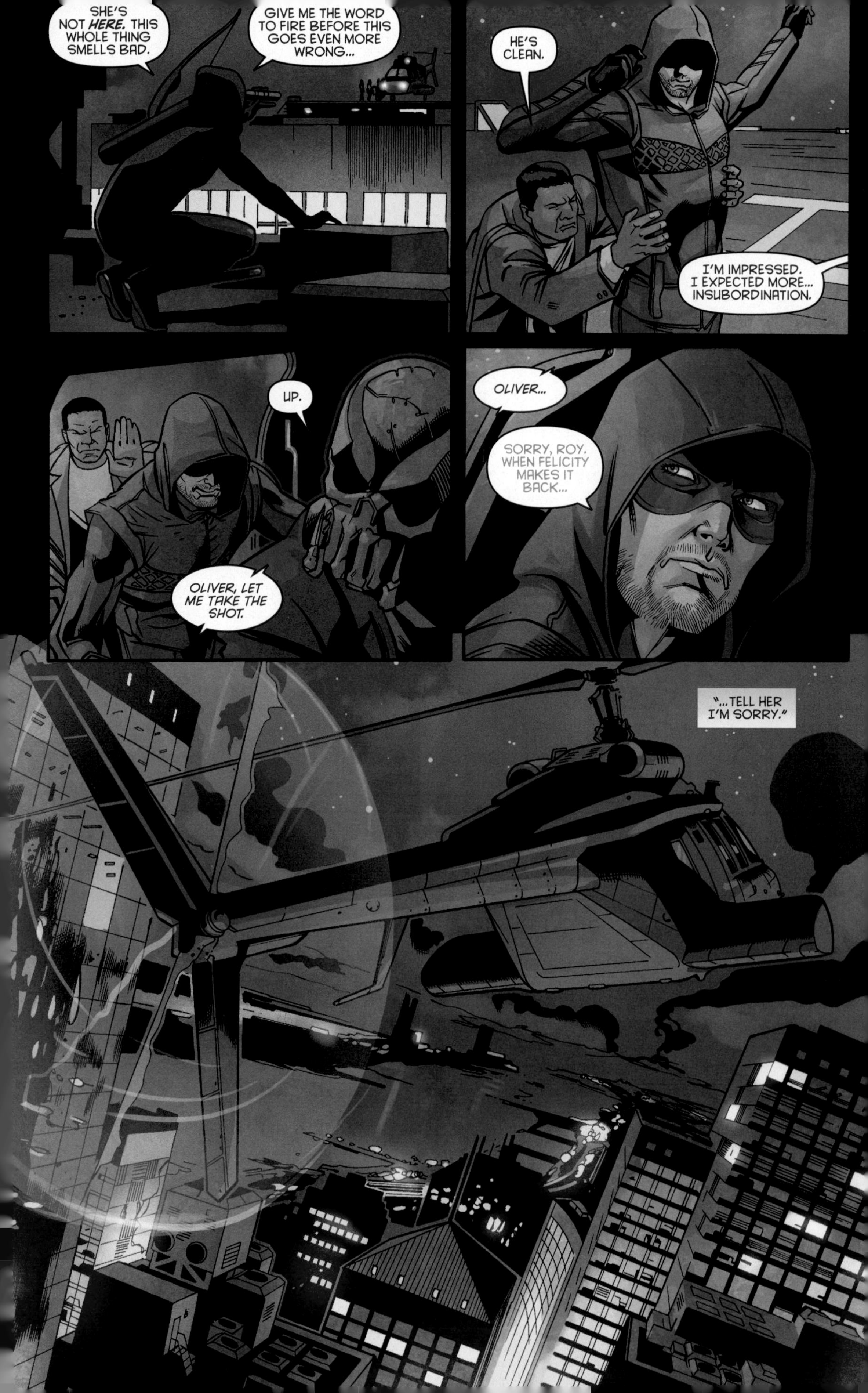
SHE'S NOT *HERE.* THIS WHOLE THING SMELLS BAD.
GIVE ME THE WORD TO FIRE BEFORE THIS GOES EVEN MORE WRONG...
HE'S CLEAN.
I'M IMPRESSED. I EXPECTED MORE... INSUBORDINATION.
UP.
OLIVER, LET ME TAKE THE SHOT.
OLIVER...
SORRY, ROY. WHEN FELICITY MAKES IT BACK...
"...TELL HER I'M SORRY."

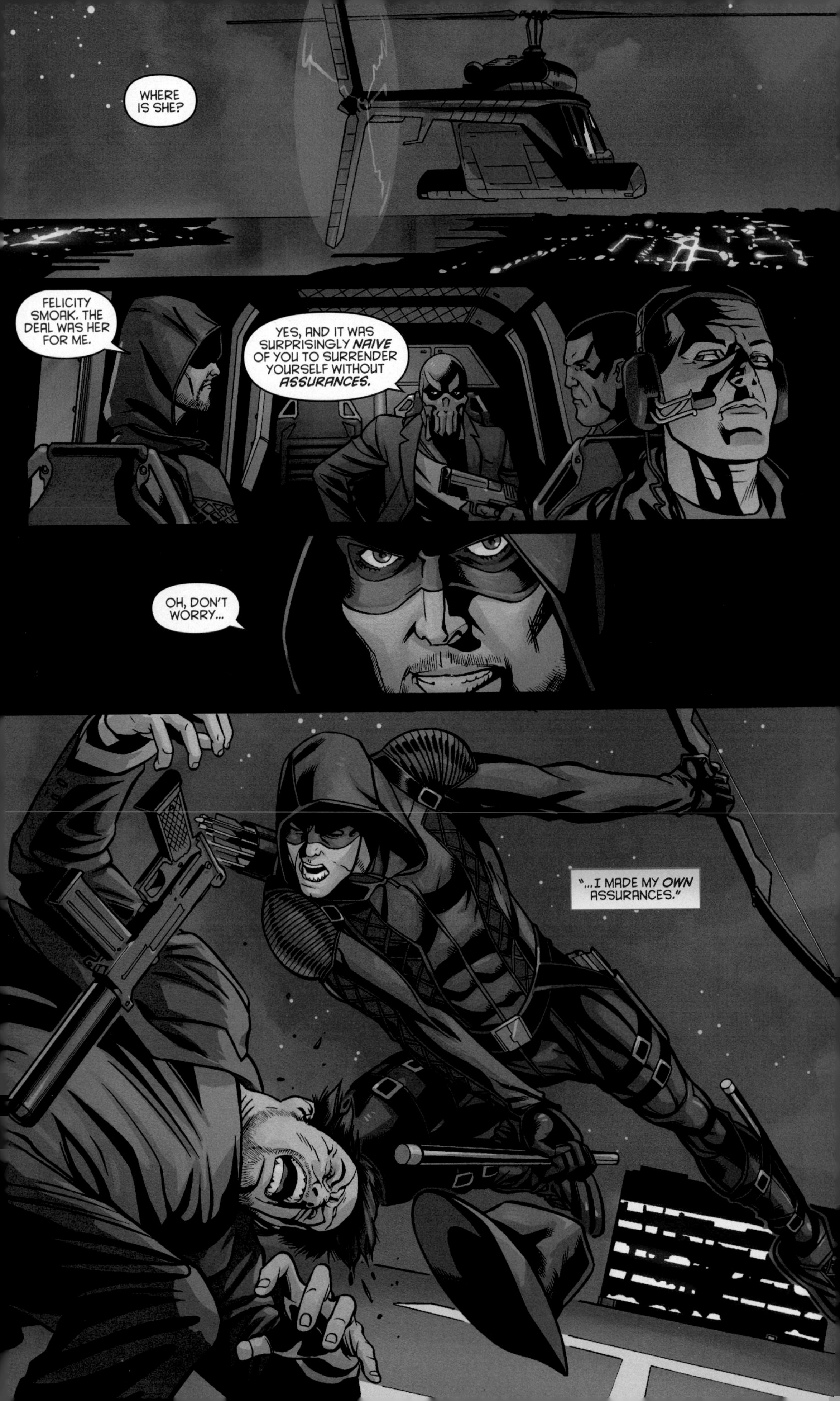
WHERE IS SHE?
FELICITY SMOAK. THE DEAL WAS HER FOR ME.
YES, AND IT WAS SURPRISINGLY NAIVE OF YOU TO SURRENDER YOURSELF WITHOUT ASSURANCES.
OH, DON'T WORRY...
"...I MADE MY OWN ASSURANCES."

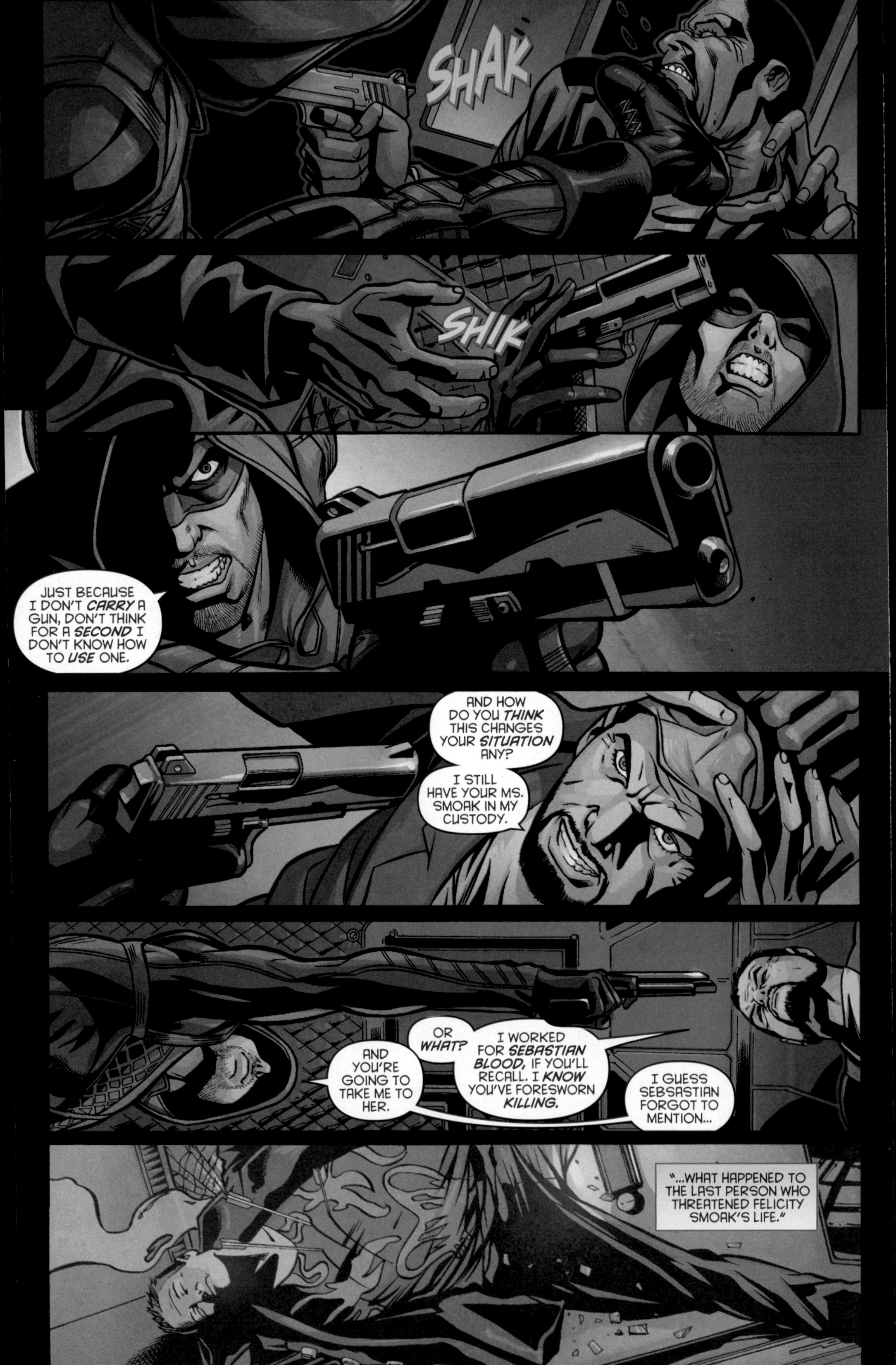
SHAK
SHIK
JUST BECAUSE I DON'T CARRY A GUN, DON'T THINK FOR A SECOND I DON'T KNOW HOW TO USE ONE.
AND HOW DO YOU THINK THIS CHANGES YOUR SITUATION ANY?
I STILL HAVE YOUR MS. SMOAK IN MY CUSTODY.
AND YOU'RE GOING TO TAKE ME TO HER.
OR WHAT?
I WORKED FOR SEBASTIAN BLOOD, IF YOU'LL RECALL. I KNOW YOU'VE FORESWORN KILLING.
I GUESS SEBSASTIAN FORGOT TO MENTION...
"...WHAT HAPPENED TO THE LAST PERSON WHO THREATENED FELICITY SMOAK'S LIFE."

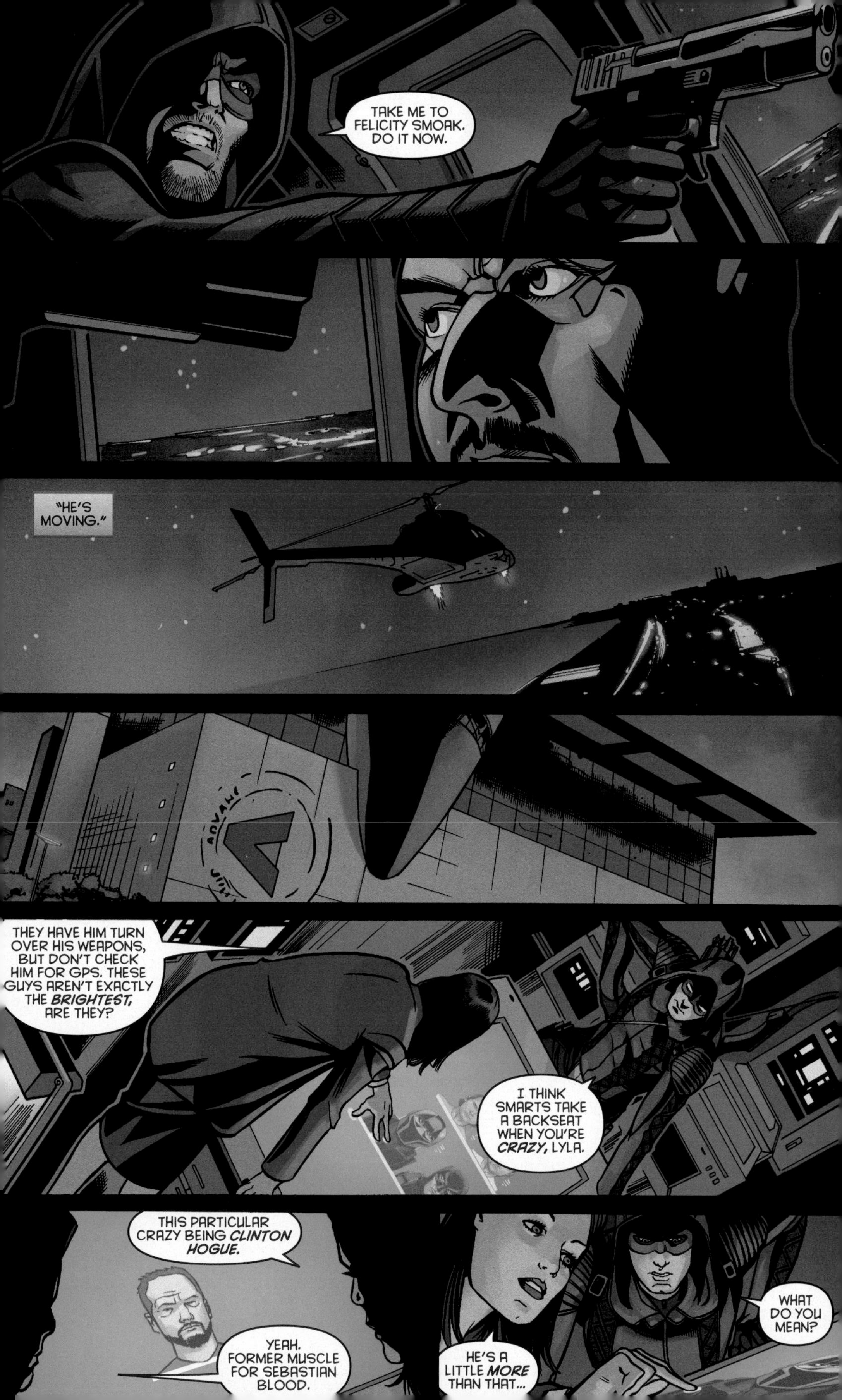
TAKE ME TO FELICITY SMOAK. DO IT NOW.
"HE'S MOVING."
THEY HAVE HIM TURN OVER HIS WEAPONS, BUT DON'T CHECK HIM FOR GPS. THESE GUYS AREN'T EXACTLY THE BRIGHTEST, ARE THEY?
I THINK SMARTS TAKE A BACKSEAT WHEN YOU'RE CRAZY, LYLA.
THIS PARTICULAR CRAZY BEING CLINTON HOGUE.
YEAH. FORMER MUSCLE FOR SEBASTIAN BLOOD.
HE'S A LITTLE MORE THAN THAT...
WHAT DO YOU MEAN?

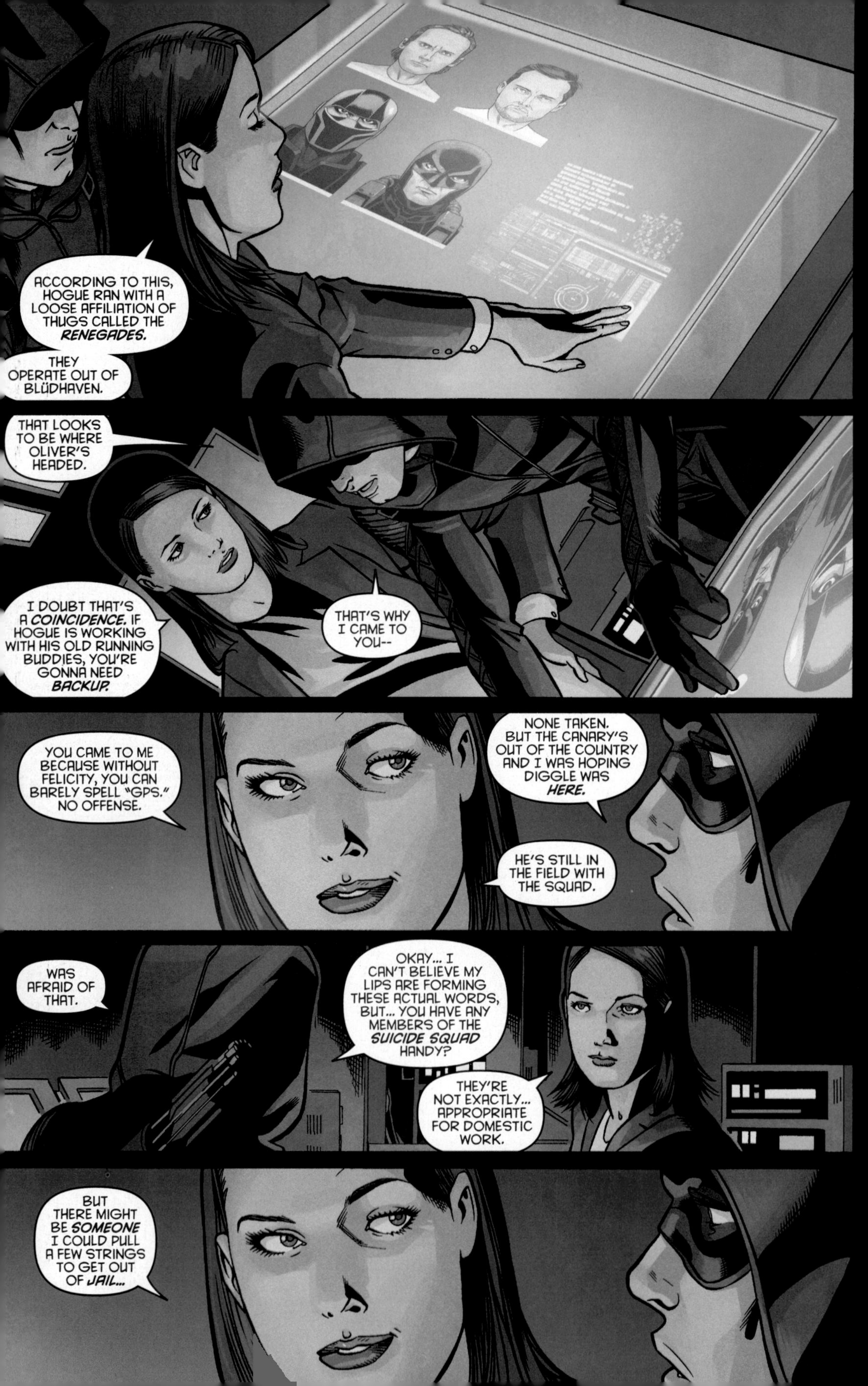
ACCORDING TO THIS, HOGUE RAN WITH A LOOSE AFFILIATION OF THUGS CALLED THE RENEGADES.
THEY OPERATE OUT OF BLÜDHAVEN.
THAT LOOKS TO BE WHERE OLIVER'S HEADED.
I DOUBT THAT'S A COINCIDENCE. IF HOGUE IS WORKING WITH HIS OLD RUNNING BUDDIES, YOU'RE GONNA NEED BACKUP.
THAT'S WHY I CAME TO YOU--
YOU CAME TO ME BECAUSE WITHOUT FELICITY, YOU CAN BARELY SPELL "GPS." NO OFFENSE.
NONE TAKEN. BUT THE CANARY'S OUT OF THE COUNTRY AND I WAS HOPING DIGGLE WAS HERE.
HE'S STILL IN THE FIELD WITH THE SQUAD.
WAS AFRAID OF THAT.
OKAY... I CAN'T BELIEVE MY LIPS ARE FORMING THESE ACTUAL WORDS, BUT... YOU HAVE ANY MEMBERS OF THE SUICIDE SQUAD HANDY?
THEY'RE NOT EXACTLY... APPROPRIATE FOR DOMESTIC WORK.
BUT THERE MIGHT BE SOMEONE I COULD PULL A FEW STRINGS TO GET OUT OF JAIL...

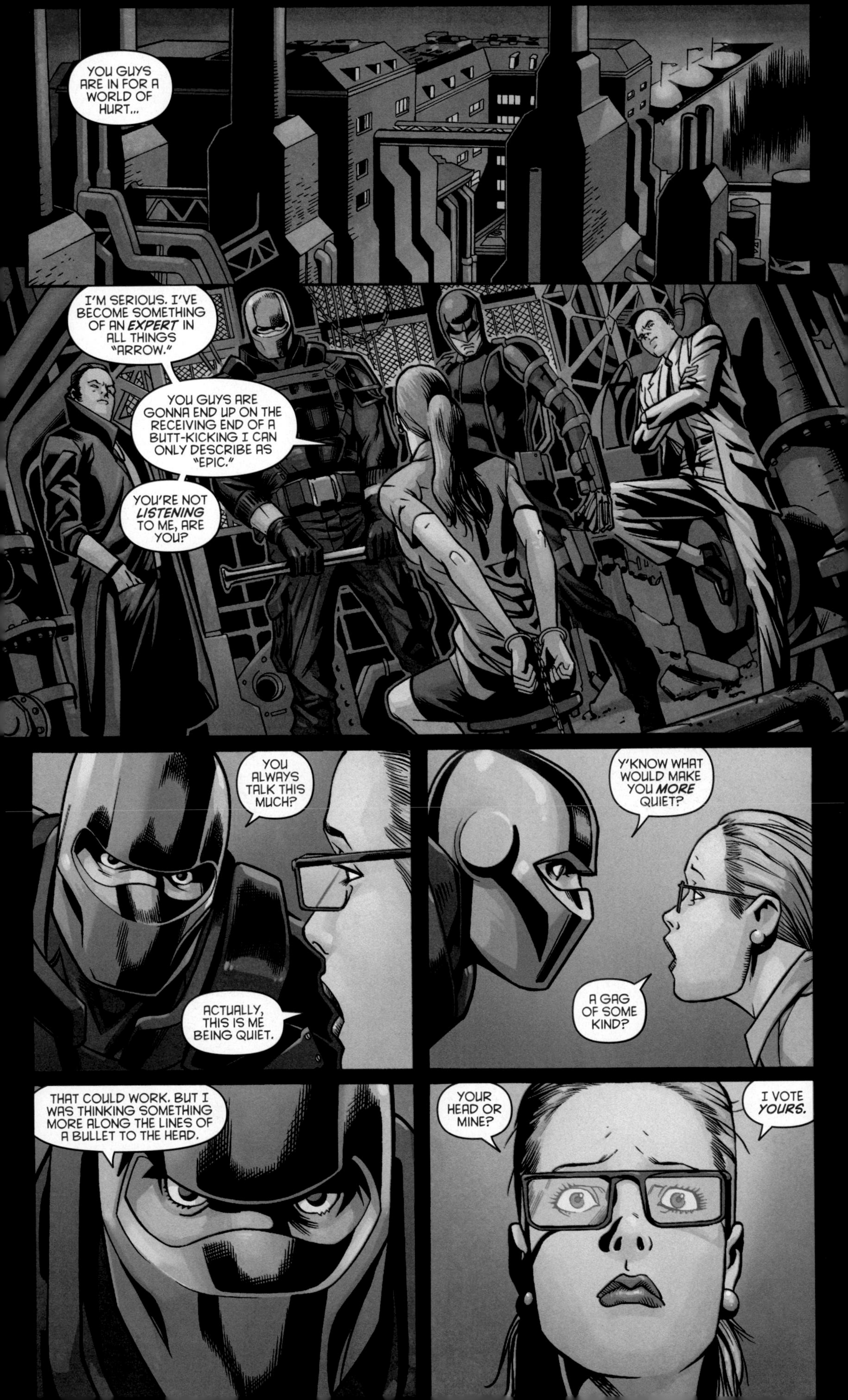
YOU GUYS ARE IN FOR A WORLD OF HURT...
I'M SERIOUS. I'VE BECOME SOMETHING OF AN EXPERT IN ALL THINGS "ARROW."
YOU GUYS ARE GONNA END UP ON THE RECEIVING END OF A BUTT-KICKING I CAN ONLY DESCRIBE AS "EPIC."
YOU'RE NOT LISTENING TO ME, ARE YOU?
YOU ALWAYS TALK THIS MUCH?
ACTUALLY, THIS IS ME BEING QUIET.
Y'KNOW WHAT WOULD MAKE YOU MORE QUIET?
A GAG OF SOME KIND?
THAT COULD WORK. BUT I WAS THINKING SOMETHING MORE ALONG THE LINES OF A BULLET TO THE HEAD.
YOUR HEAD OR MINE?
I VOTE YOURS.

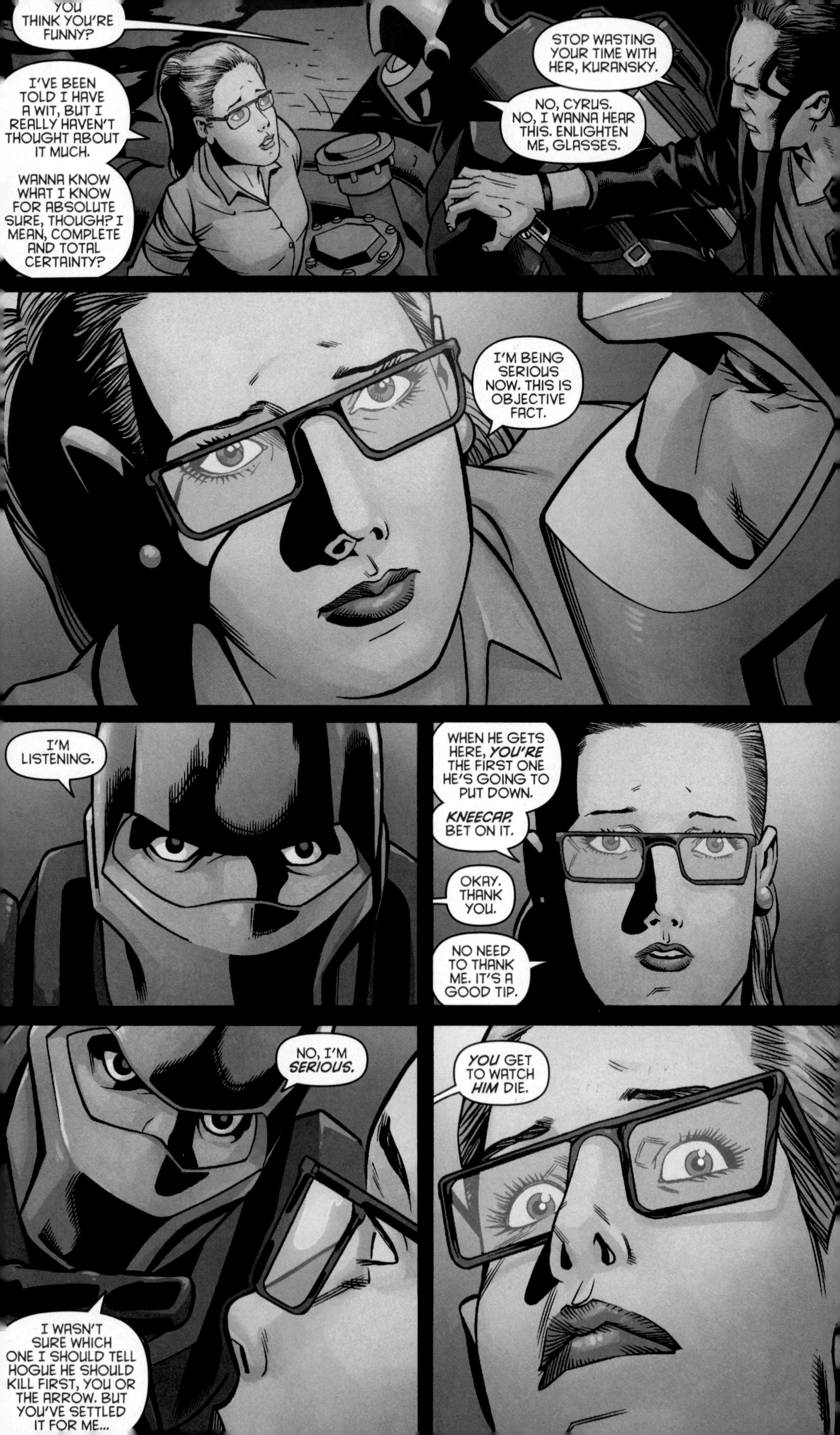
YOU THINK YOU'RE FUNNY?
I'VE BEEN TOLD I HAVE A WIT, BUT I REALLY HAVEN'T THOUGHT ABOUT IT MUCH.
WANNA KNOW WHAT I KNOW FOR ABSOLUTE SURE, THOUGH? I MEAN, COMPLETE AND TOTAL CERTAINTY?
STOP WASTING YOUR TIME WITH HER, KURANSKY.
NO, CYRUS. NO, I WANNA HEAR THIS. ENLIGHTEN ME, GLASSES.
I'M BEING SERIOUS NOW. THIS IS OBJECTIVE FACT.
I'M LISTENING.
WHEN HE GETS HERE, *YOU'RE* THE FIRST ONE HE'S GOING TO PUT DOWN.
KNEECAP. BET ON IT.
OKAY. THANK YOU.
NO NEED TO THANK ME. IT'S A GOOD TIP.
NO, I'M *SERIOUS.*
I WASN'T SURE WHICH ONE I SHOULD TELL HOGUE HE SHOULD KILL FIRST, YOU OR THE ARROW. BUT YOU'VE SETTLED IT FOR ME...
YOU GET TO WATCH *HIM* DIE.

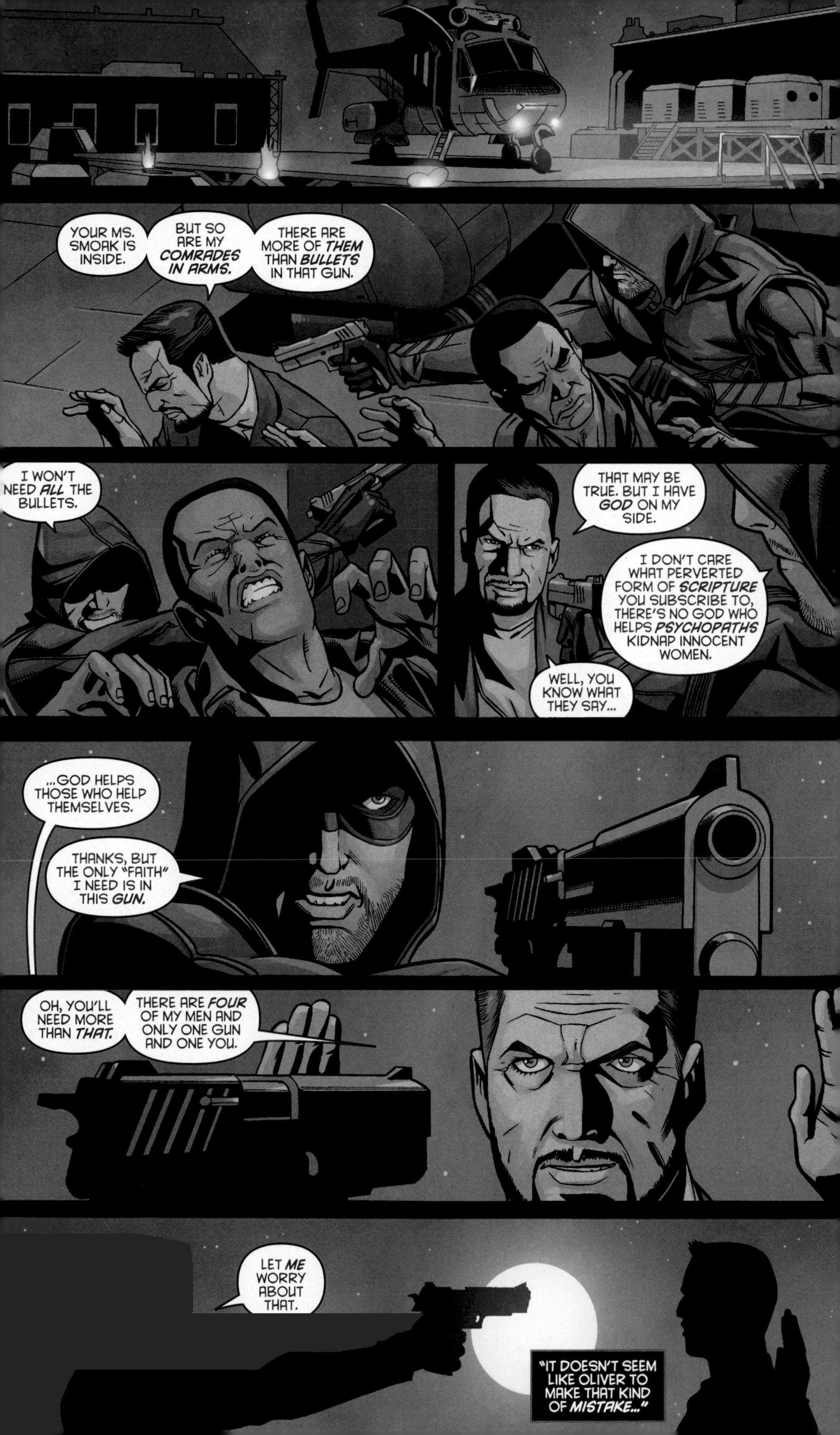
YOUR MS. SMOAK IS INSIDE.
BUT SO ARE MY COMRADES IN ARMS.
THERE ARE MORE OF THEM THAN BULLETS IN THAT GUN.
I WON'T NEED ALL THE BULLETS.
THAT MAY BE TRUE. BUT I HAVE GOD ON MY SIDE.
I DON'T CARE WHAT PERVERTED FORM OF SCRIPTURE YOU SUBSCRIBE TO, THERE'S NO GOD WHO HELPS PSYCHOPATHS KIDNAP INNOCENT WOMEN.
WELL, YOU KNOW WHAT THEY SAY...
...GOD HELPS THOSE WHO HELP THEMSELVES.
THANKS, BUT THE ONLY "FAITH" I NEED IS IN THIS GUN.
OH, YOU'LL NEED MORE THAN THAT.
THERE ARE FOUR OF MY MEN AND ONLY ONE GUN AND ONE YOU.
LET ME WORRY ABOUT THAT.
"IT DOESN'T SEEM LIKE OLIVER TO MAKE THAT KIND OF MISTAKE..."

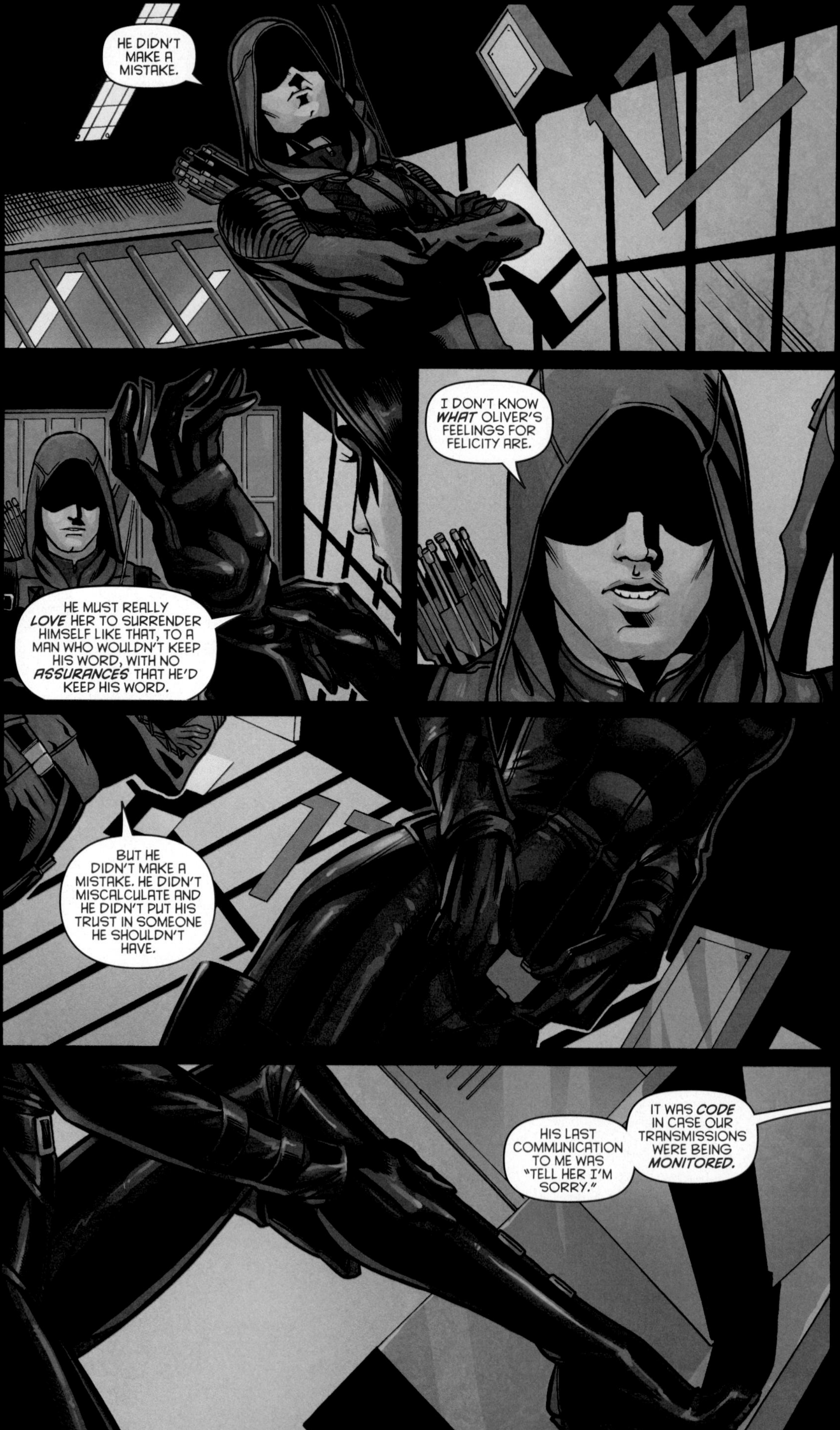

HE DIDN'T MAKE A MISTAKE.
I DON'T KNOW WHAT OLIVER'S FEELINGS FOR FELICITY ARE.
HE MUST REALLY LOVE HER TO SURRENDER HIMSELF LIKE THAT, TO A MAN WHO WOULDN'T KEEP HIS WORD, WITH NO ASSURANCES THAT HE'D KEEP HIS WORD.
BUT HE DIDN'T MAKE A MISTAKE. HE DIDN'T MISCALCULATE AND HE DIDN'T PUT HIS TRUST IN SOMEONE HE SHOULDN'T HAVE.
HIS LAST COMMUNICATION TO ME WAS "TELL HER I'M SORRY."
IT WAS CODE IN CASE OUR TRANSMISSIONS WERE BEING MONITORED.

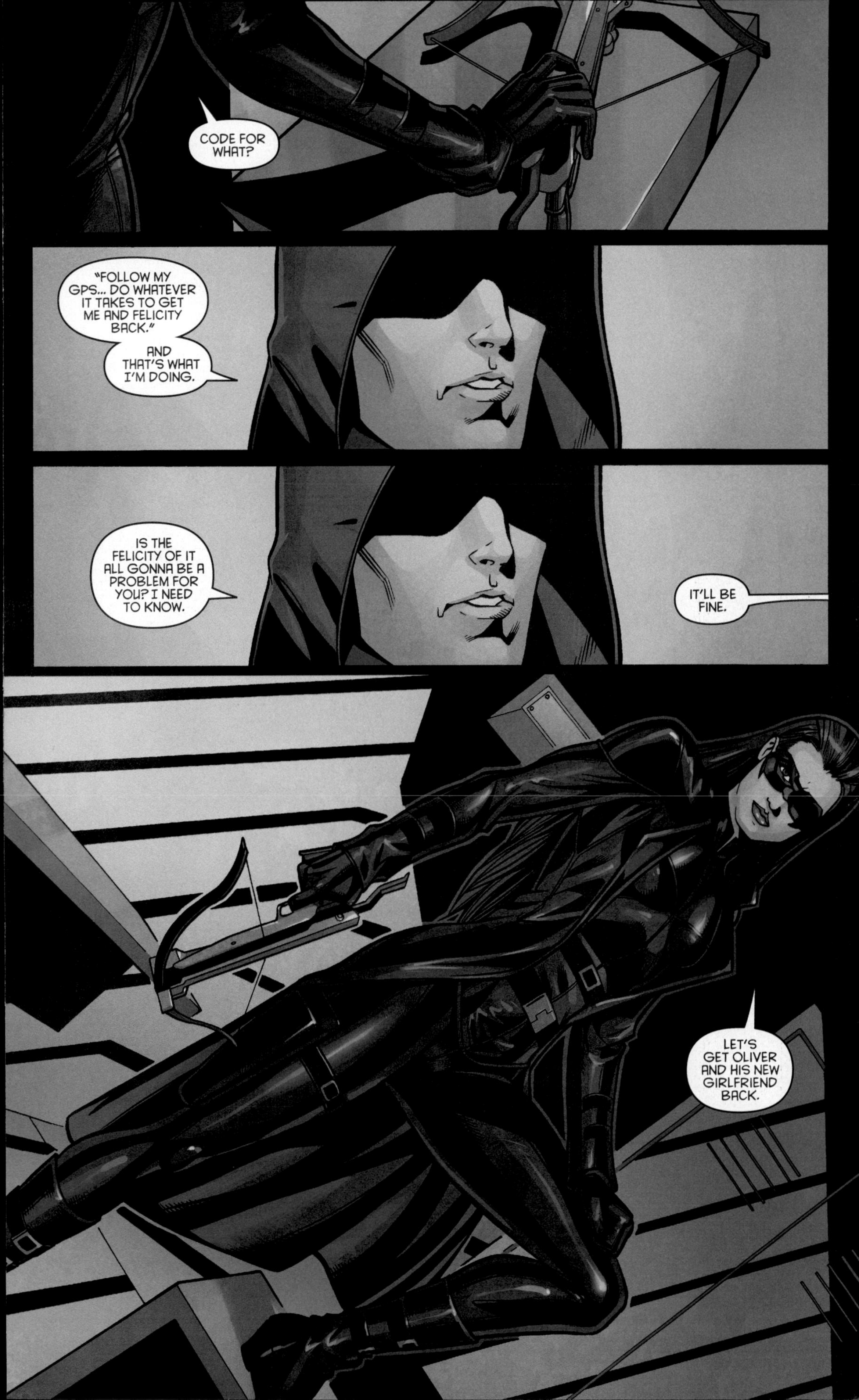
CODE FOR WHAT?
"FOLLOW MY GPS... DO WHATEVER IT TAKES TO GET ME AND FELICITY BACK."
AND THAT'S WHAT I'M DOING.
IS THE FELICITY OF IT ALL GONNA BE A PROBLEM FOR YOU? I NEED TO KNOW.
IT'LL BE FINE.
LET'S GET OLIVER AND HIS NEW GIRLFRIEND BACK.

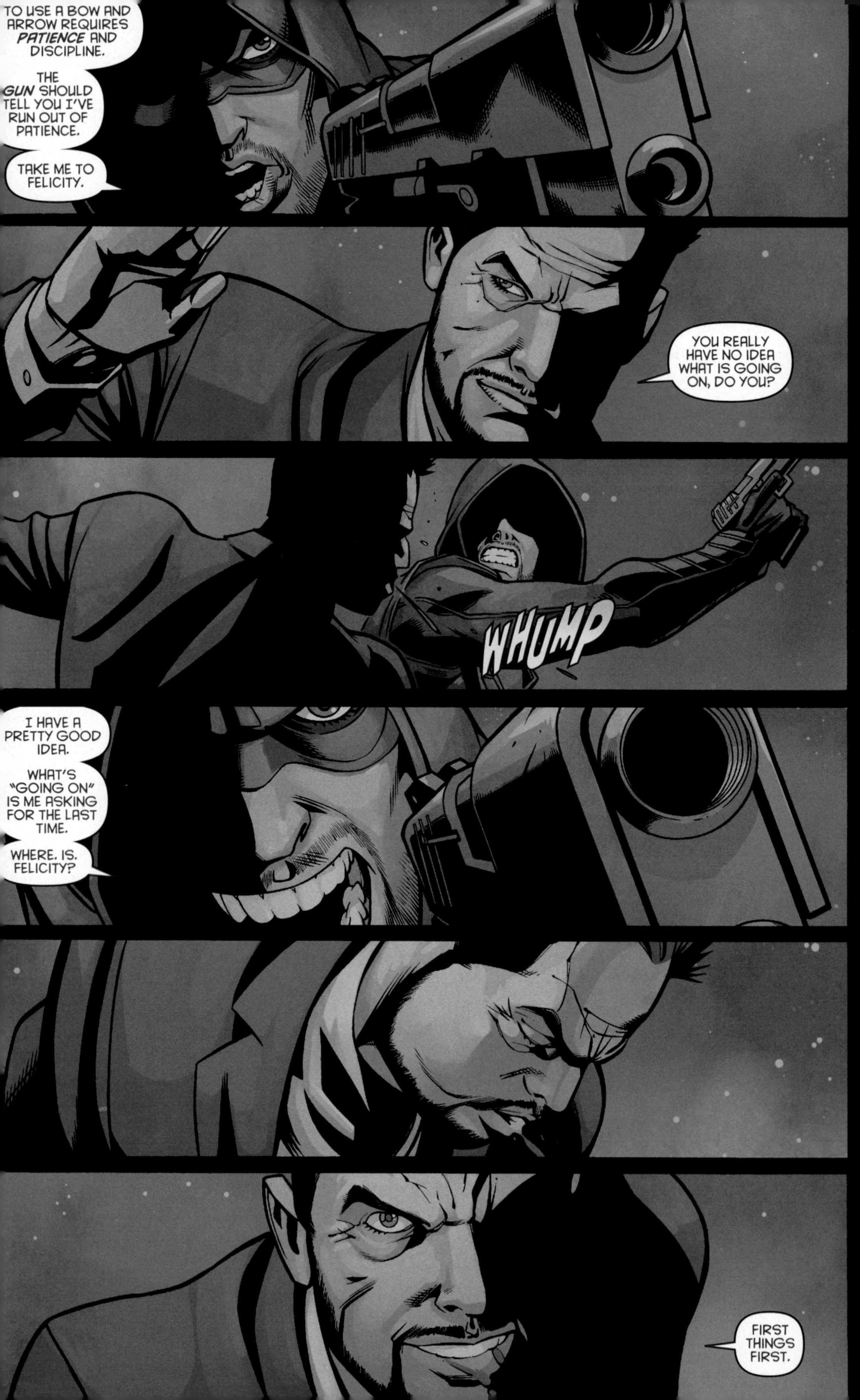
TO USE A BOW AND ARROW REQUIRES *PATIENCE* AND DISCIPLINE.
THE *GUN* SHOULD TELL YOU I'VE RUN OUT OF PATIENCE.
TAKE ME TO FELICITY.
YOU REALLY HAVE NO IDEA WHAT IS GOING ON, DO YOU?
WHUMP
I HAVE A PRETTY GOOD IDEA.
WHAT'S "GOING ON" IS ME ASKING FOR THE LAST TIME.
WHERE. IS. FELICITY?
FIRST THINGS FIRST.

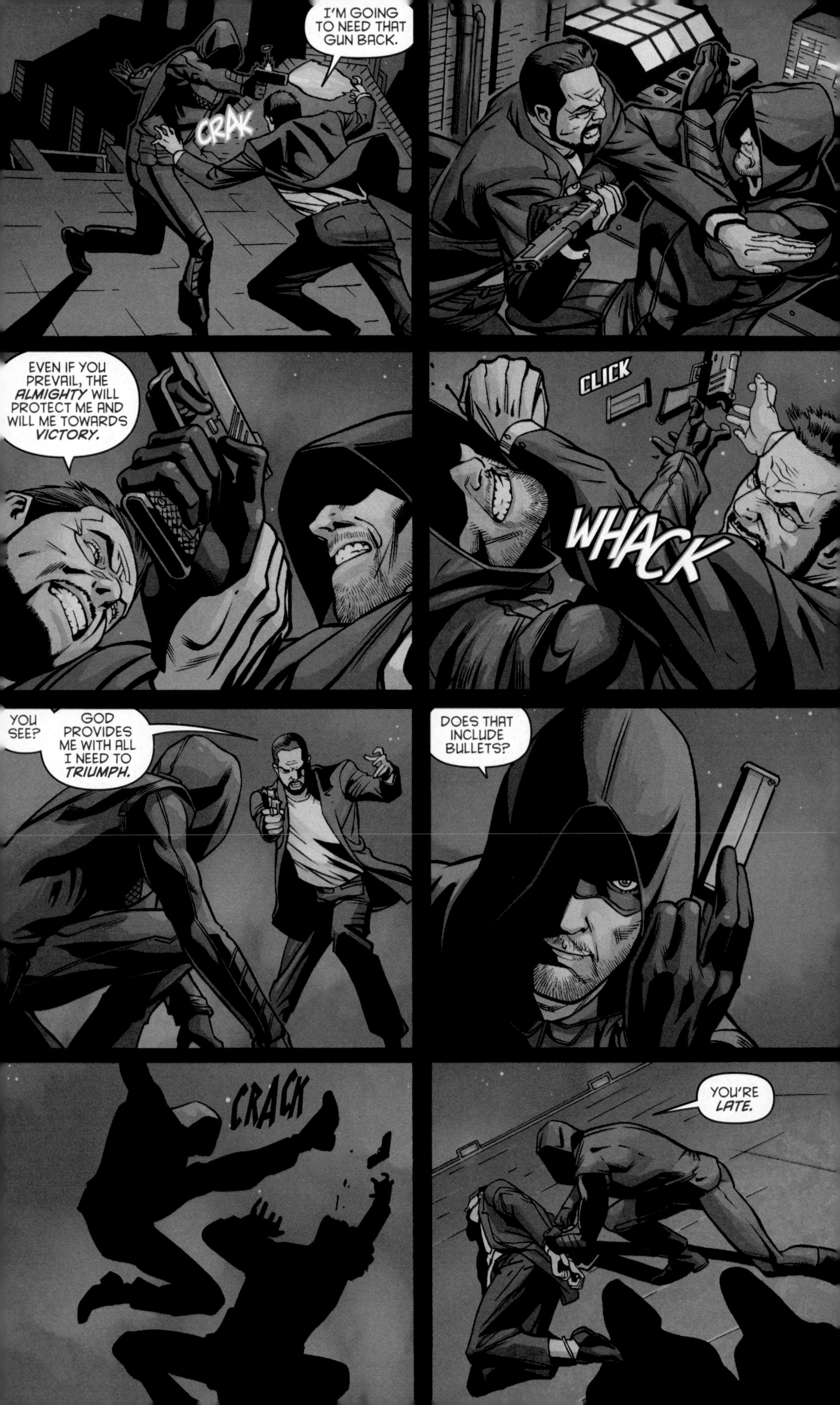
I'M GOING TO NEED THAT GUN BACK.
CRAK
EVEN IF YOU PREVAIL, THE *ALMIGHTY* WILL PROTECT ME AND WILL ME TOWARDS *VICTORY.*
CLICK
WHACK
YOU SEE?
GOD PROVIDES ME WITH ALL I NEED TO *TRIUMPH.*
DOES THAT INCLUDE BULLETS?
CRACK
YOU'RE *LATE.*

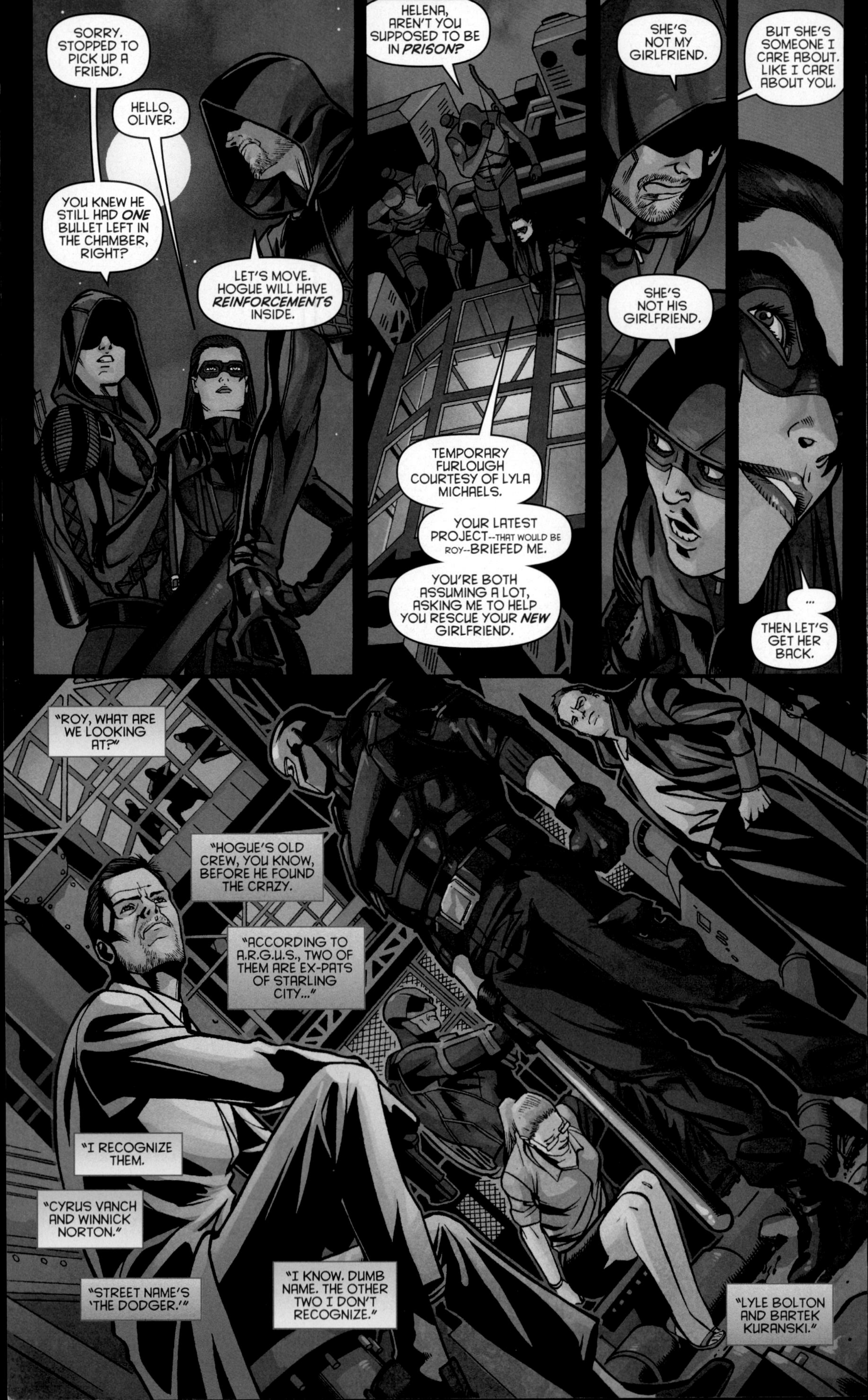
SORRY. STOPPED TO PICK UP A FRIEND.
HELLO, OLIVER.
YOU KNEW HE STILL HAD *ONE* BULLET LEFT IN THE CHAMBER, RIGHT?
LET'S MOVE. HOGUE WILL HAVE *REINFORCEMENTS* INSIDE.
HELENA, AREN'T YOU SUPPOSED TO BE IN *PRISON?*
TEMPORARY FURLOUGH COURTESY OF LYLA MICHAELS.
YOUR LATEST PROJECT--THAT WOULD BE ROY--BRIEFED ME.
YOU'RE BOTH ASSUMING A LOT, ASKING ME TO HELP YOU RESCUE YOUR *NEW* GIRLFRIEND.
SHE'S NOT MY GIRLFRIEND.
SHE'S NOT HIS GIRLFRIEND.
BUT SHE'S SOMEONE I CARE ABOUT. LIKE I CARE ABOUT YOU.
...
THEN LET'S GET HER BACK.
"ROY, WHAT ARE WE LOOKING AT?"
"HOGUE'S OLD CREW, YOU KNOW, BEFORE HE FOUND THE CRAZY.
"ACCORDING TO A.R.G.U.S., TWO OF THEM ARE EX-PATS OF STARLING CITY..."
"I RECOGNIZE THEM.
"CYRUS VANCH AND WINNICK NORTON."
"STREET NAME'S 'THE DODGER.'"
"I KNOW. DUMB NAME. THE OTHER TWO I DON'T RECOGNIZE."
"LYLE BOLTON AND BARTEK KURANSKI."

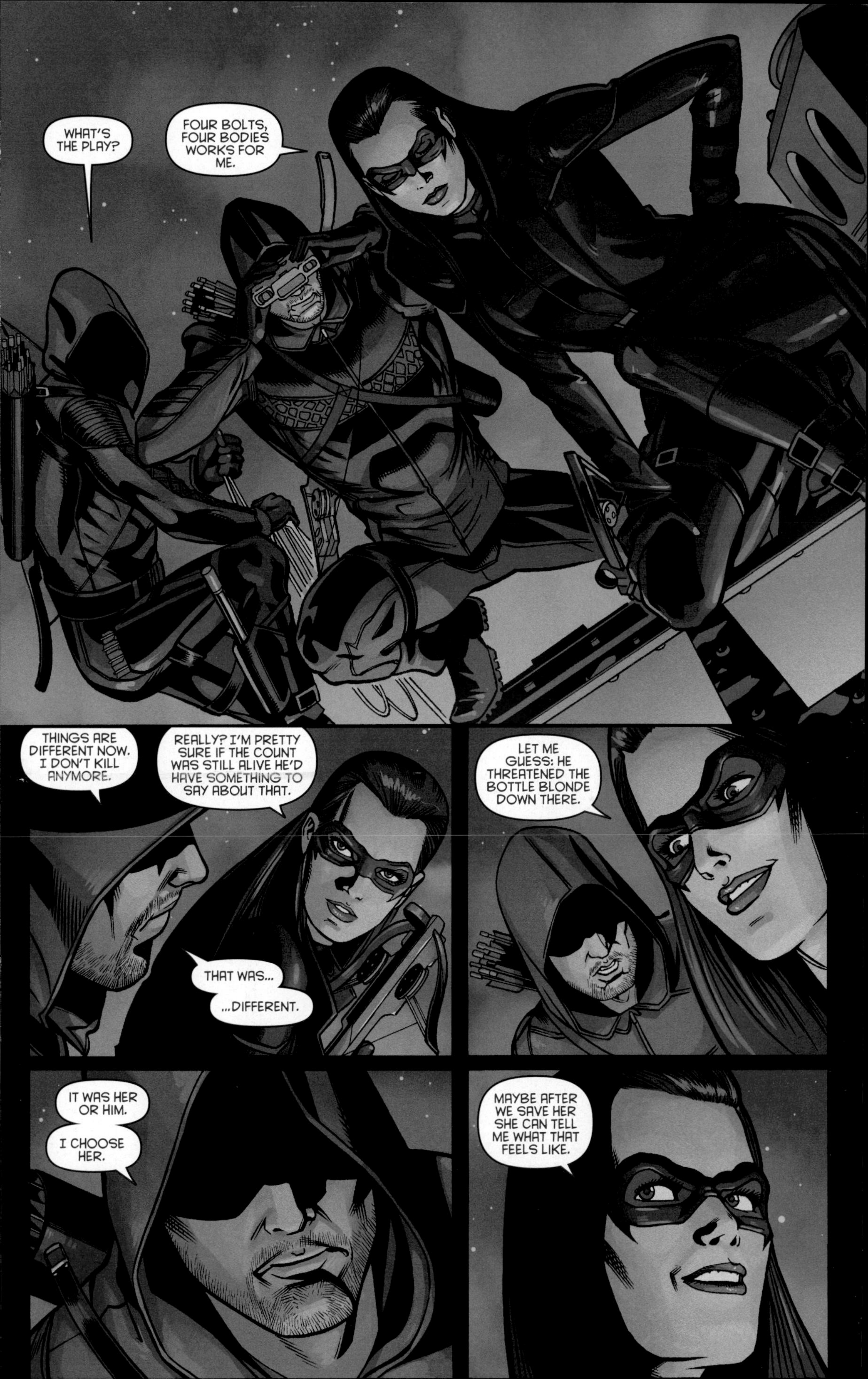
WHAT'S THE PLAY?
FOUR BOLTS, FOUR BODIES WORKS FOR ME.
THINGS ARE DIFFERENT NOW. I DON'T KILL ANYMORE.
REALLY? I'M PRETTY SURE IF THE COUNT WAS STILL ALIVE HE'D HAVE SOMETHING TO SAY ABOUT THAT.
THAT WAS...
...DIFFERENT.
LET ME GUESS: HE THREATENED THE BOTTLE BLONDE DOWN THERE.
IT WAS HER OR HIM.
I CHOOSE HER.
MAYBE AFTER WE SAVE HER SHE CAN TELL ME WHAT THAT FEELS LIKE.

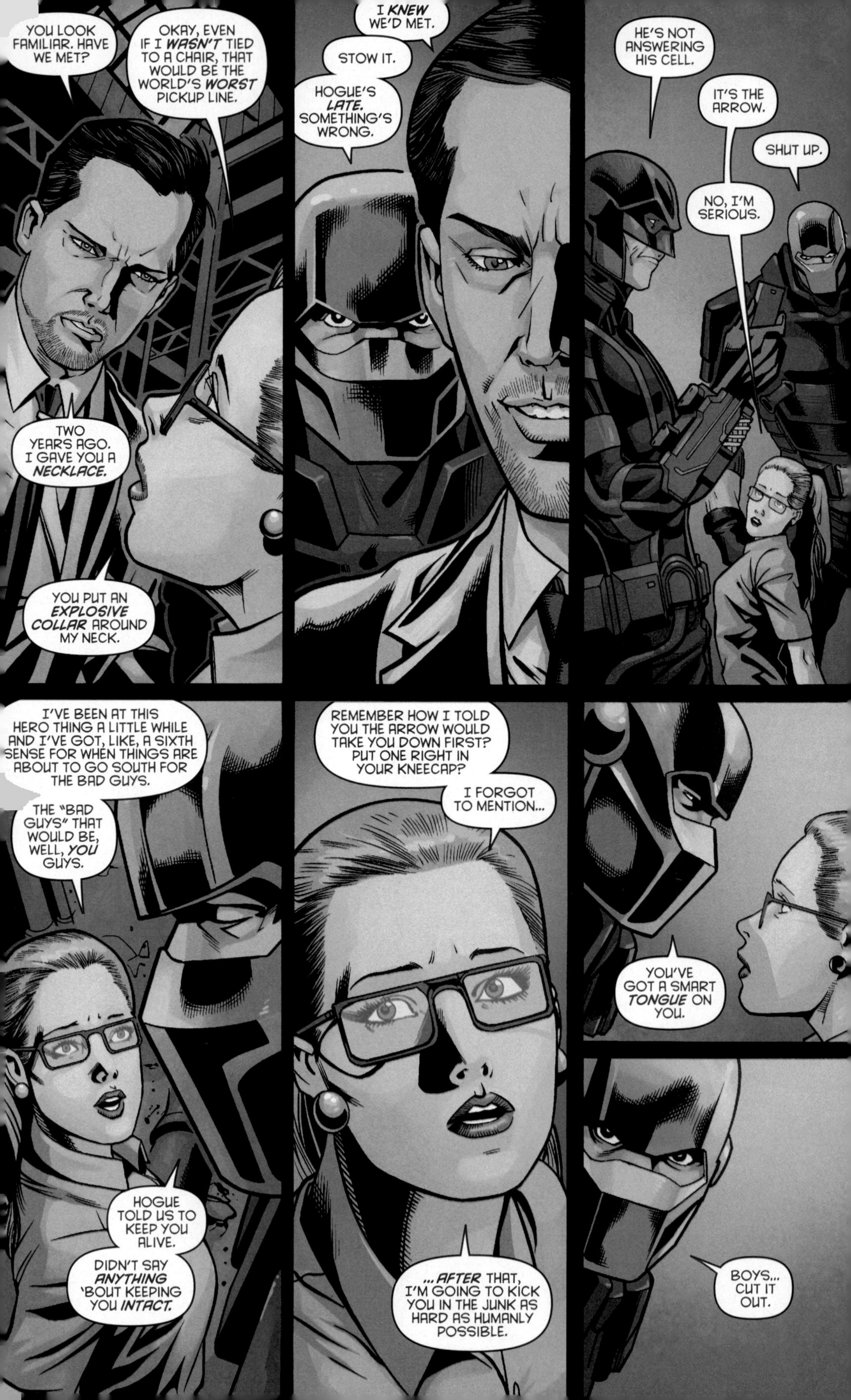
YOU LOOK FAMILIAR. HAVE WE MET?
OKAY, EVEN IF I WASN'T TIED TO A CHAIR, THAT WOULD BE THE WORLD'S WORST PICKUP LINE.
TWO YEARS AGO. I GAVE YOU A NECKLACE.
YOU PUT AN EXPLOSIVE COLLAR AROUND MY NECK.
I KNEW WE'D MET.
STOW IT.
HOGUE'S LATE. SOMETHING'S WRONG.
HE'S NOT ANSWERING HIS CELL.
IT'S THE ARROW.
SHUT UP.
NO, I'M SERIOUS.
I'VE BEEN AT THIS HERO THING A LITTLE WHILE AND I'VE GOT, LIKE, A SIXTH SENSE FOR WHEN THINGS ARE ABOUT TO GO SOUTH FOR THE BAD GUYS.
THE "BAD GUYS" THAT WOULD BE, WELL, YOU GUYS.
HOGUE TOLD US TO KEEP YOU ALIVE.
DIDN'T SAY ANYTHING 'BOUT KEEPING YOU INTACT.
REMEMBER HOW I TOLD YOU THE ARROW WOULD TAKE YOU DOWN FIRST? PUT ONE RIGHT IN YOUR KNEECAP?
I FORGOT TO MENTION...
...AFTER THAT, I'M GOING TO KICK YOU IN THE JUNK AS HARD AS HUMANLY POSSIBLE.
YOU'VE GOT A SMART TONGUE ON YOU.
BOYS... CUT IT OUT.

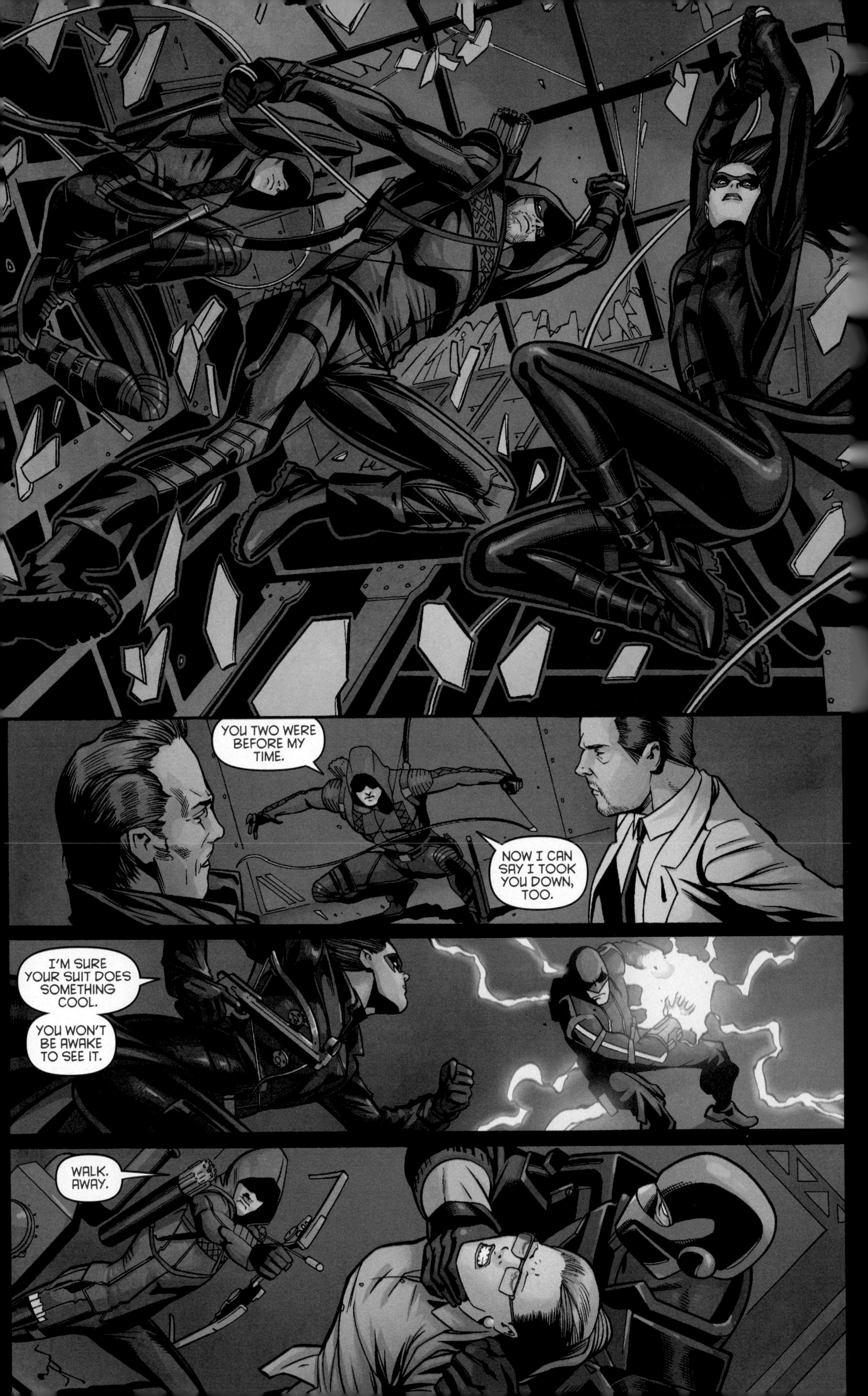
YOU TWO WERE BEFORE MY TIME.
NOW I CAN SAY I TOOK YOU DOWN, TOO.
I'M SURE YOUR SUIT DOES SOMETHING COOL.
YOU WON'T BE AWAKE TO SEE IT.
WALK. AWAY.

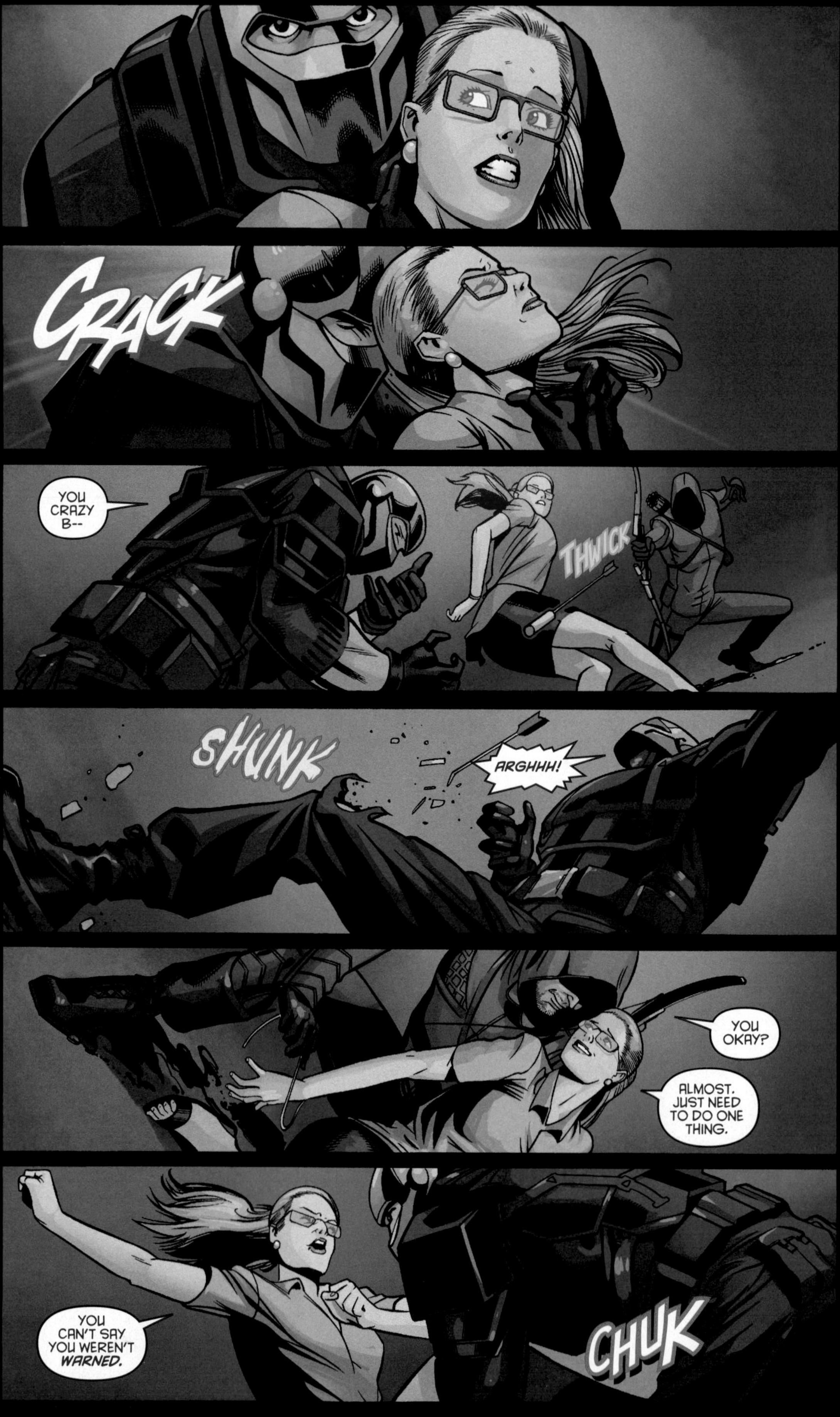

CRACK
YOU CRAZY B--
THWICK
SHUNK
ARGHHH!
YOU OKAY?
ALMOST. JUST NEED TO DO ONE THING.
YOU CAN'T SAY YOU WEREN'T *WARNED.*
CHUK

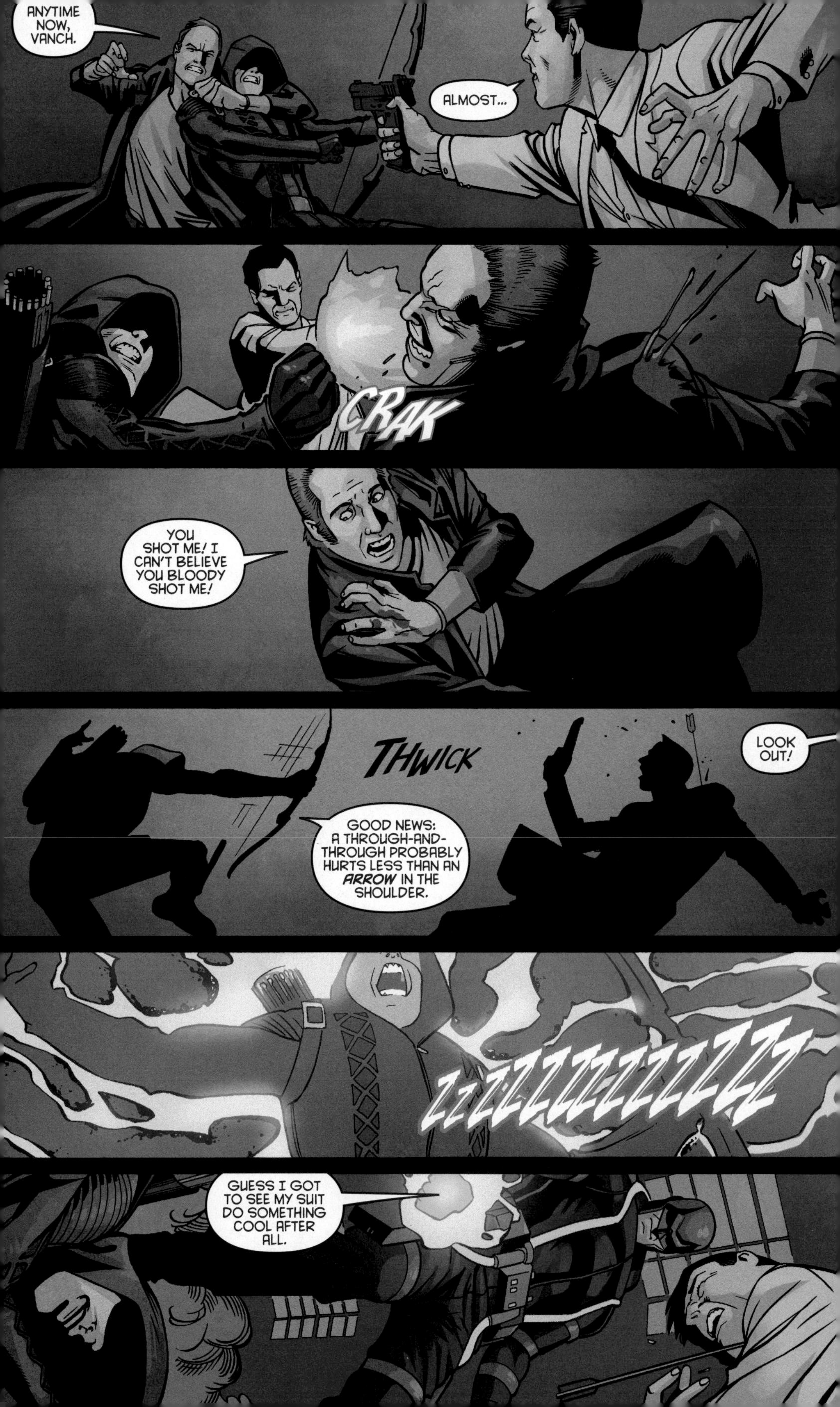
ANYTIME NOW, VANCH.
ALMOST...
CRAK
YOU SHOT ME! I CAN'T BELIEVE YOU BLOODY SHOT ME!
THWICK
LOOK OUT!
GOOD NEWS: A THROUGH-AND-THROUGH PROBABLY HURTS LESS THAN AN ARROW IN THE SHOULDER.
ZZZZZZZZZZZZZZZZZ
GUESS I GOT TO SEE MY SUIT DO SOMETHING COOL AFTER ALL.

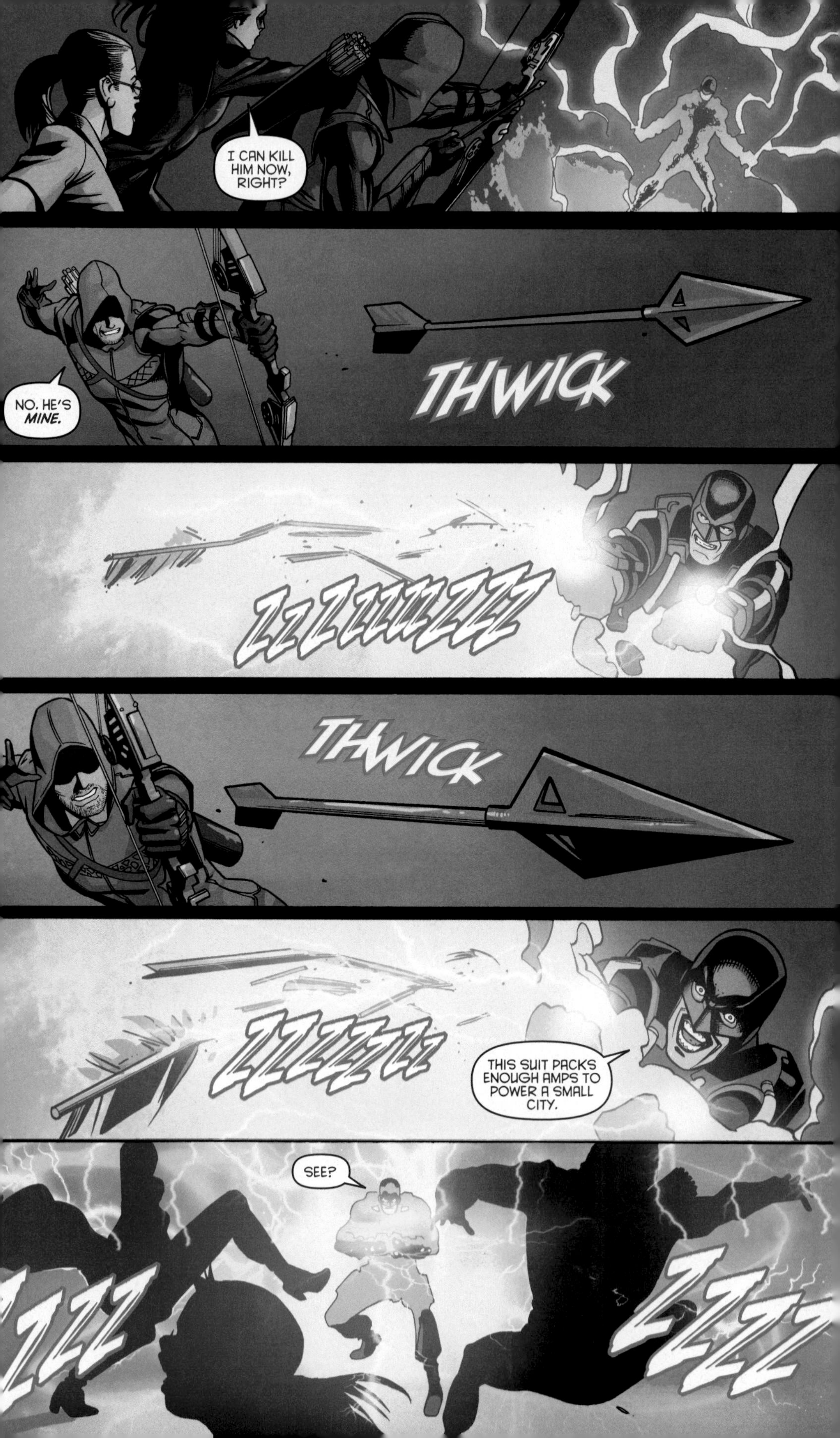
I CAN KILL HIM NOW, RIGHT?
NO. HE'S *MINE.*
THWICK
ZZZZZZZZZZZ
THWICK
ZZZZZZZ
THIS SUIT PACKS ENOUGH AMPS TO POWER A SMALL CITY.
SEE?
ZZZ
ZZZ

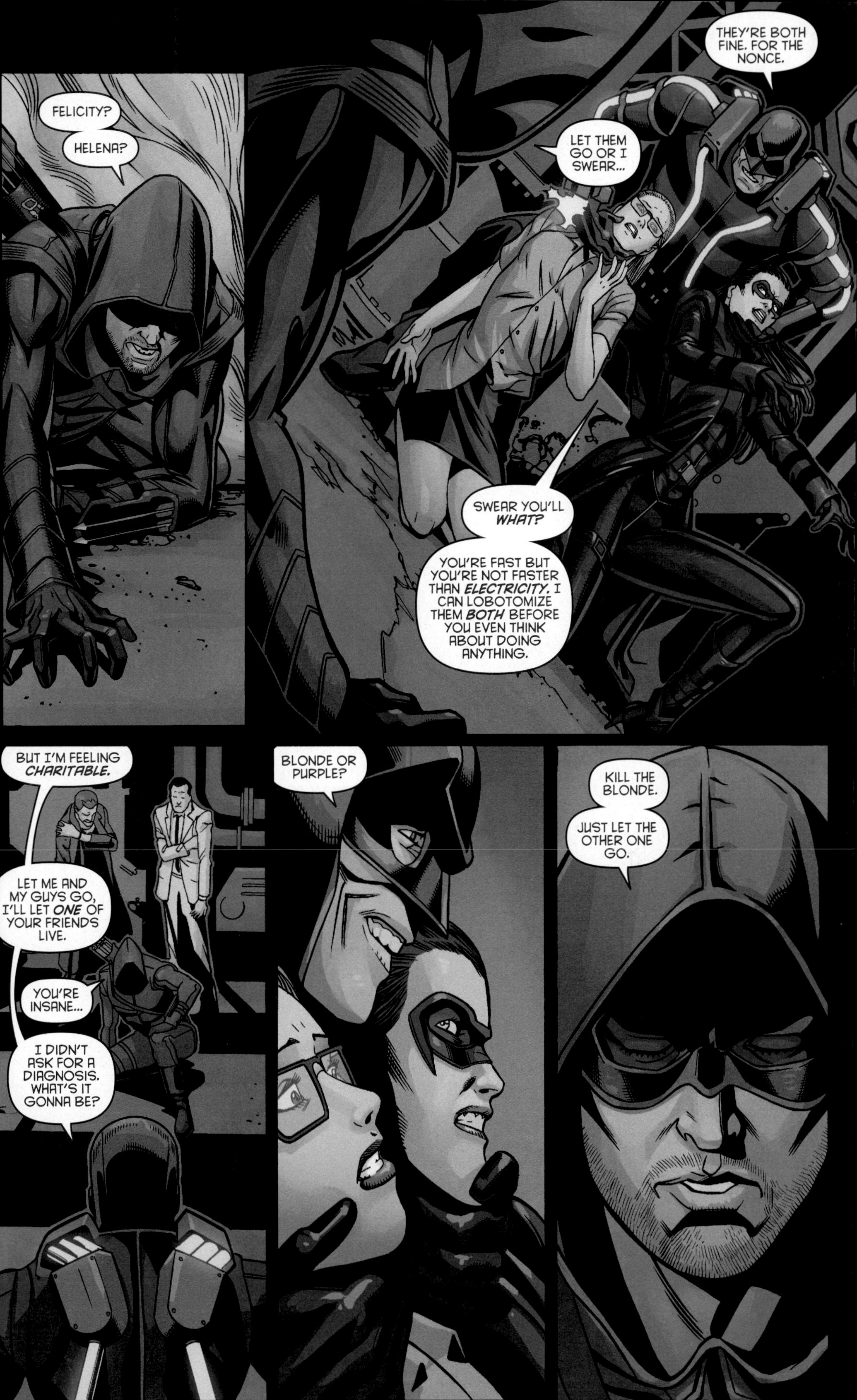
FELICITY?
HELENA?
THEY'RE BOTH FINE. FOR THE NONCE.
LET THEM GO OR I SWEAR...
SWEAR YOU'LL *WHAT?*
YOU'RE FAST BUT YOU'RE NOT FASTER THAN *ELECTRICITY.* I CAN LOBOTOMIZE THEM *BOTH* BEFORE YOU EVEN THINK ABOUT DOING ANYTHING.
BUT I'M FEELING *CHARITABLE.*
LET ME AND MY GUYS GO, I'LL LET *ONE* OF YOUR FRIENDS LIVE.
YOU'RE INSANE...
I DIDN'T ASK FOR A DIAGNOSIS. WHAT'S IT GONNA BE?
BLONDE OR PURPLE?
KILL THE BLONDE.
JUST LET THE OTHER ONE GO.

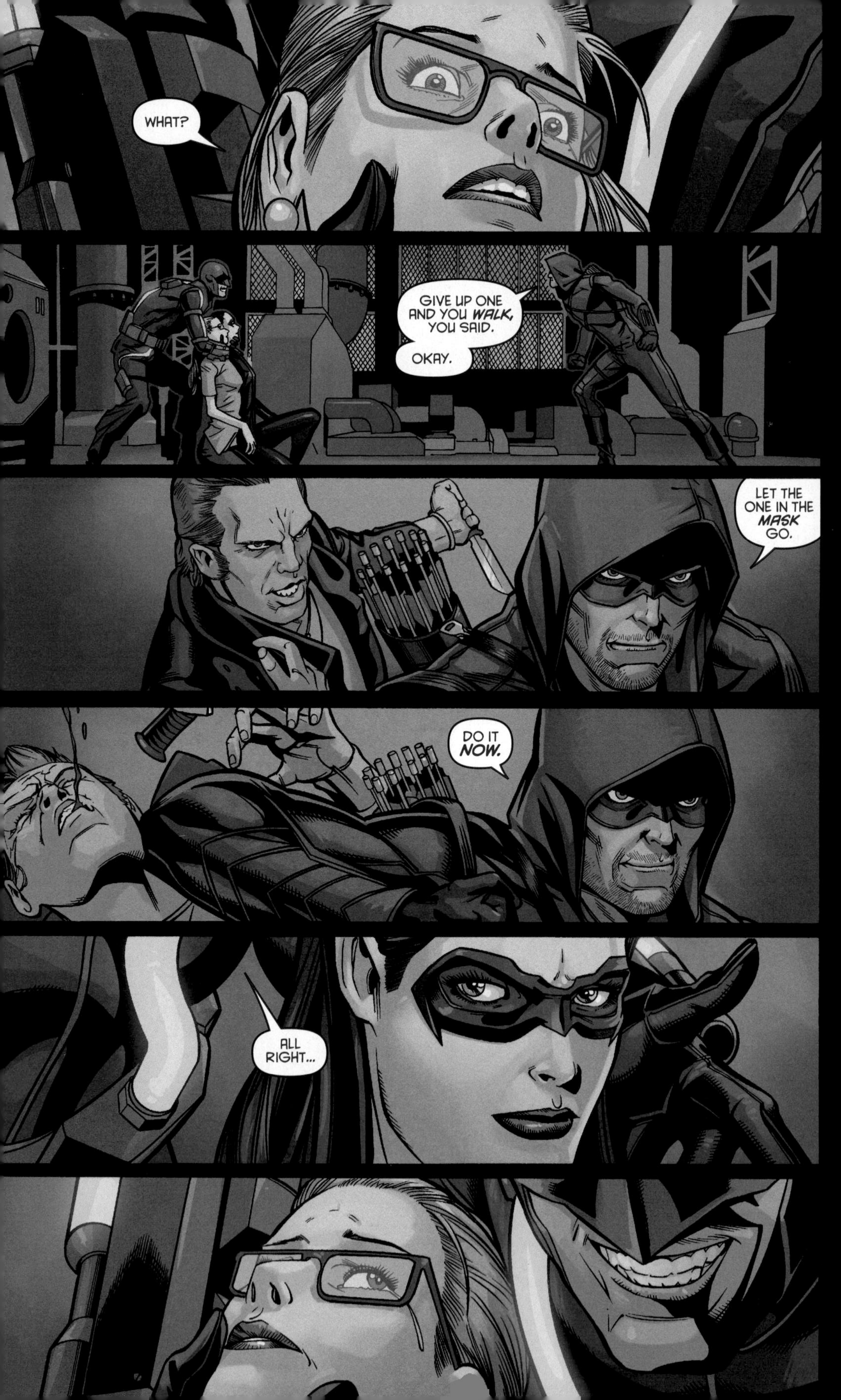
WHAT?
GIVE UP ONE AND YOU *WALK,* YOU SAID.
OKAY.
LET THE ONE IN THE *MASK* GO.
DO IT *NOW.*
ALL RIGHT...

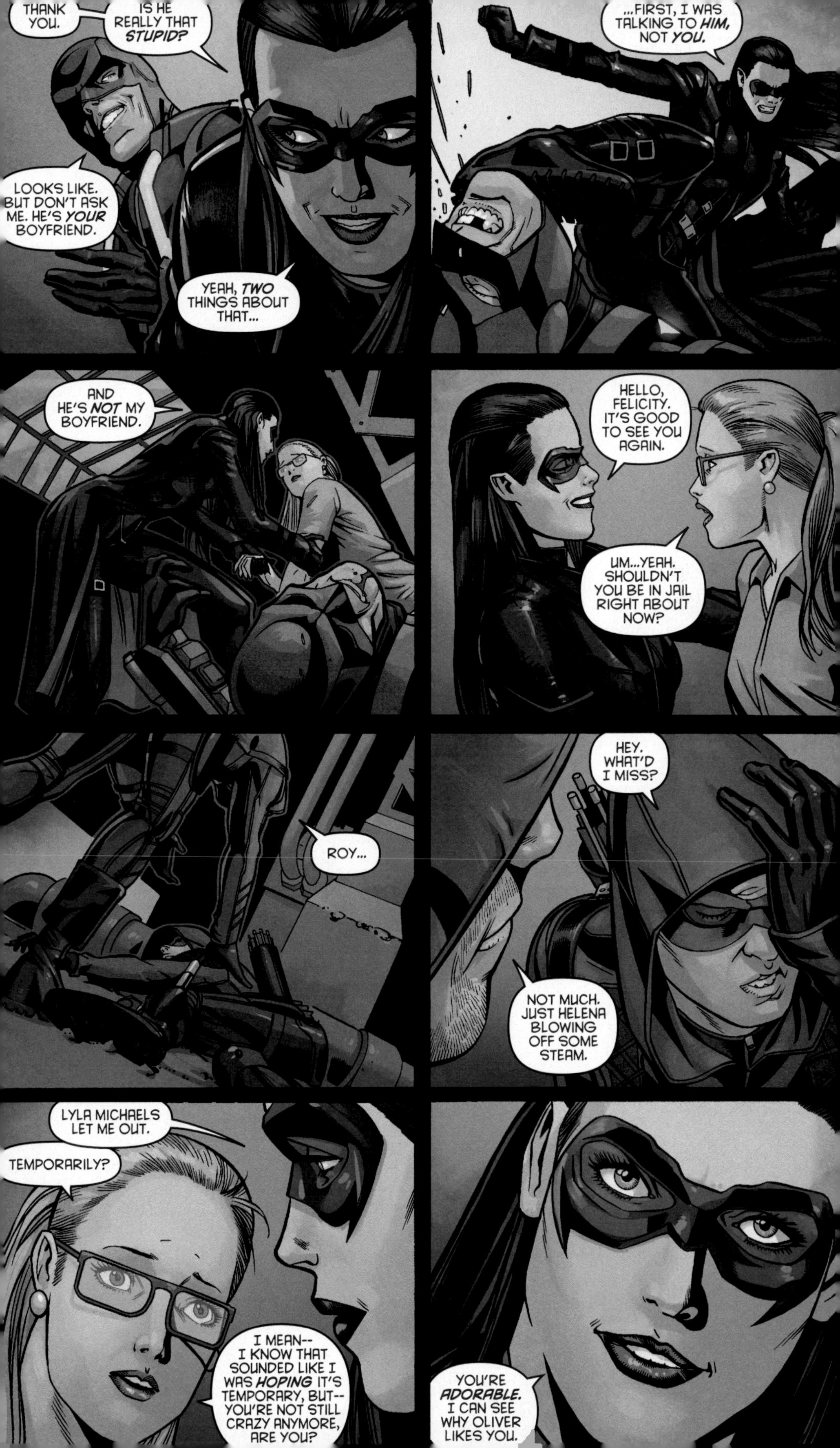
THANK YOU.
IS HE REALLY THAT STUPID?
LOOKS LIKE. BUT DON'T ASK ME. HE'S YOUR BOYFRIEND.
YEAH, TWO THINGS ABOUT THAT...
...FIRST, I WAS TALKING TO HIM, NOT YOU.
AND HE'S NOT MY BOYFRIEND.
HELLO, FELICITY. IT'S GOOD TO SEE YOU AGAIN.
UM...YEAH. SHOULDN'T YOU BE IN JAIL RIGHT ABOUT NOW?
ROY...
HEY. WHAT'D I MISS?
NOT MUCH. JUST HELENA BLOWING OFF SOME STEAM.
LYLA MICHAELS LET ME OUT.
TEMPORARILY?
I MEAN-- I KNOW THAT SOUNDED LIKE I WAS HOPING IT'S TEMPORARY, BUT-- YOU'RE NOT STILL CRAZY ANYMORE, ARE YOU?
YOU'RE ADORABLE. I CAN SEE WHY OLIVER LIKES YOU.

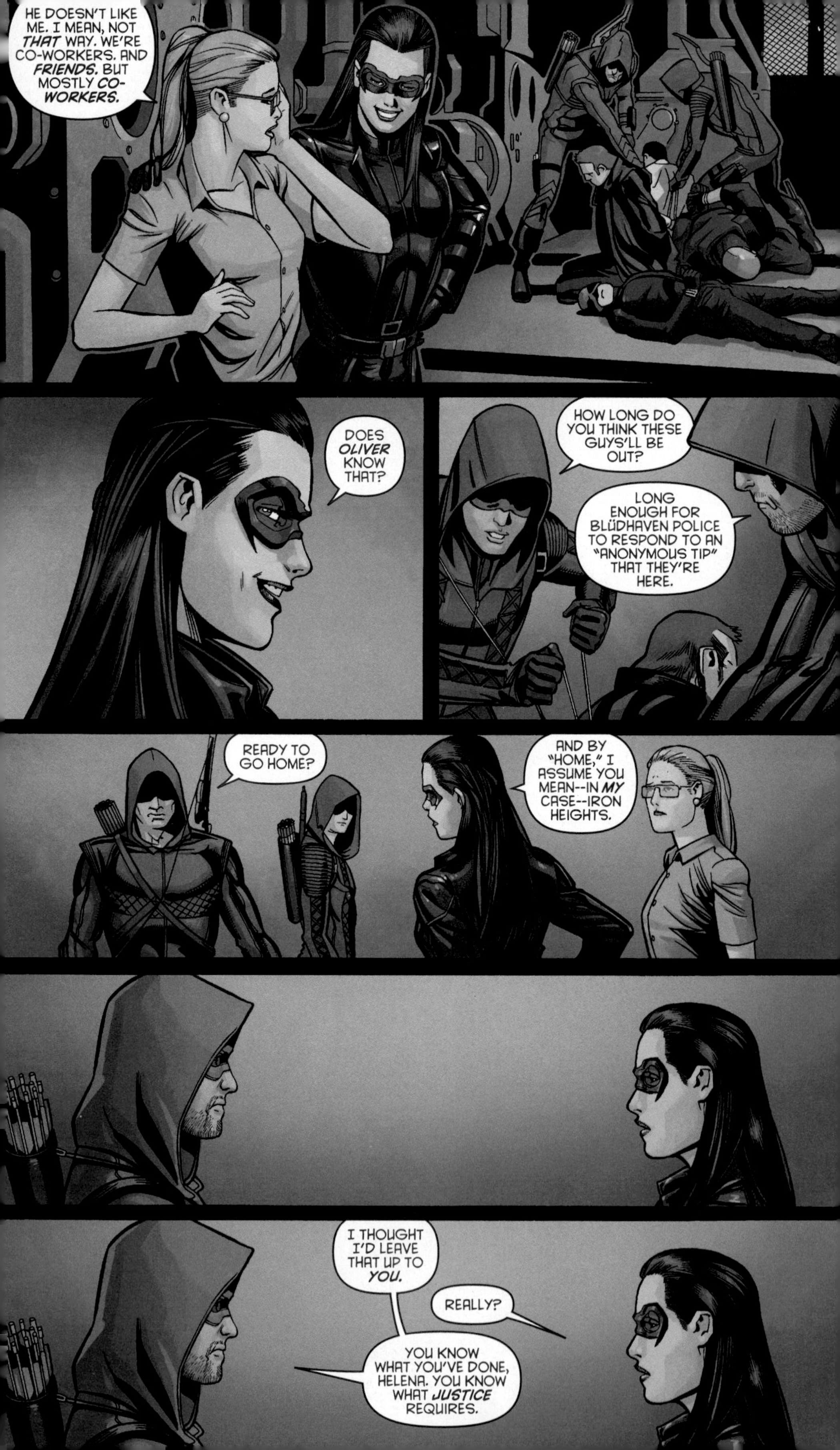

HE DOESN'T LIKE ME. I MEAN, NOT THAT WAY. WE'RE CO-WORKERS. AND FRIENDS. BUT MOSTLY CO-WORKERS.
DOES OLIVER KNOW THAT?
HOW LONG DO YOU THINK THESE GUYS'LL BE OUT?
LONG ENOUGH FOR BLÜDHAVEN POLICE TO RESPOND TO AN "ANONYMOUS TIP" THAT THEY'RE HERE.
READY TO GO HOME?
AND BY "HOME," I ASSUME YOU MEAN--IN MY CASE--IRON HEIGHTS.
I THOUGHT I'D LEAVE THAT UP TO YOU.
REALLY?
YOU KNOW WHAT YOU'VE DONE, HELENA. YOU KNOW WHAT JUSTICE REQUIRES.

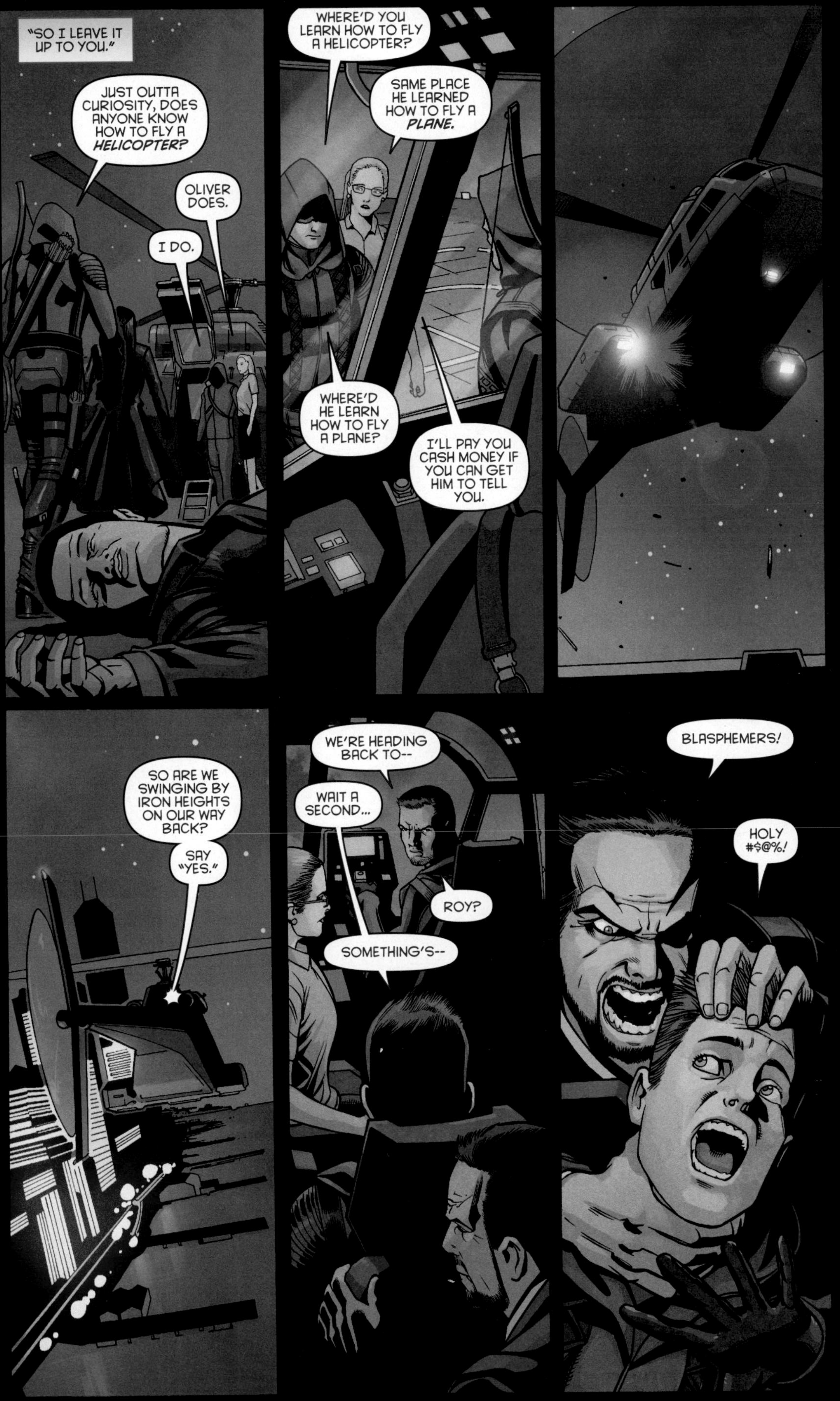
"SO I LEAVE IT UP TO YOU."
JUST OUTTA CURIOSITY, DOES ANYONE KNOW HOW TO FLY A HELICOPTER?
OLIVER DOES.
I DO.
WHERE'D YOU LEARN HOW TO FLY A HELICOPTER?
SAME PLACE HE LEARNED HOW TO FLY A PLANE.
WHERE'D HE LEARN HOW TO FLY A PLANE?
I'LL PAY YOU CASH MONEY IF YOU CAN GET HIM TO TELL YOU.
SO ARE WE SWINGING BY IRON HEIGHTS ON OUR WAY BACK?
SAY "YES."
WE'RE HEADING BACK TO--
WAIT A SECOND...
ROY?
SOMETHING'S--
BLASPHEMERS!
HOLY #$@%!

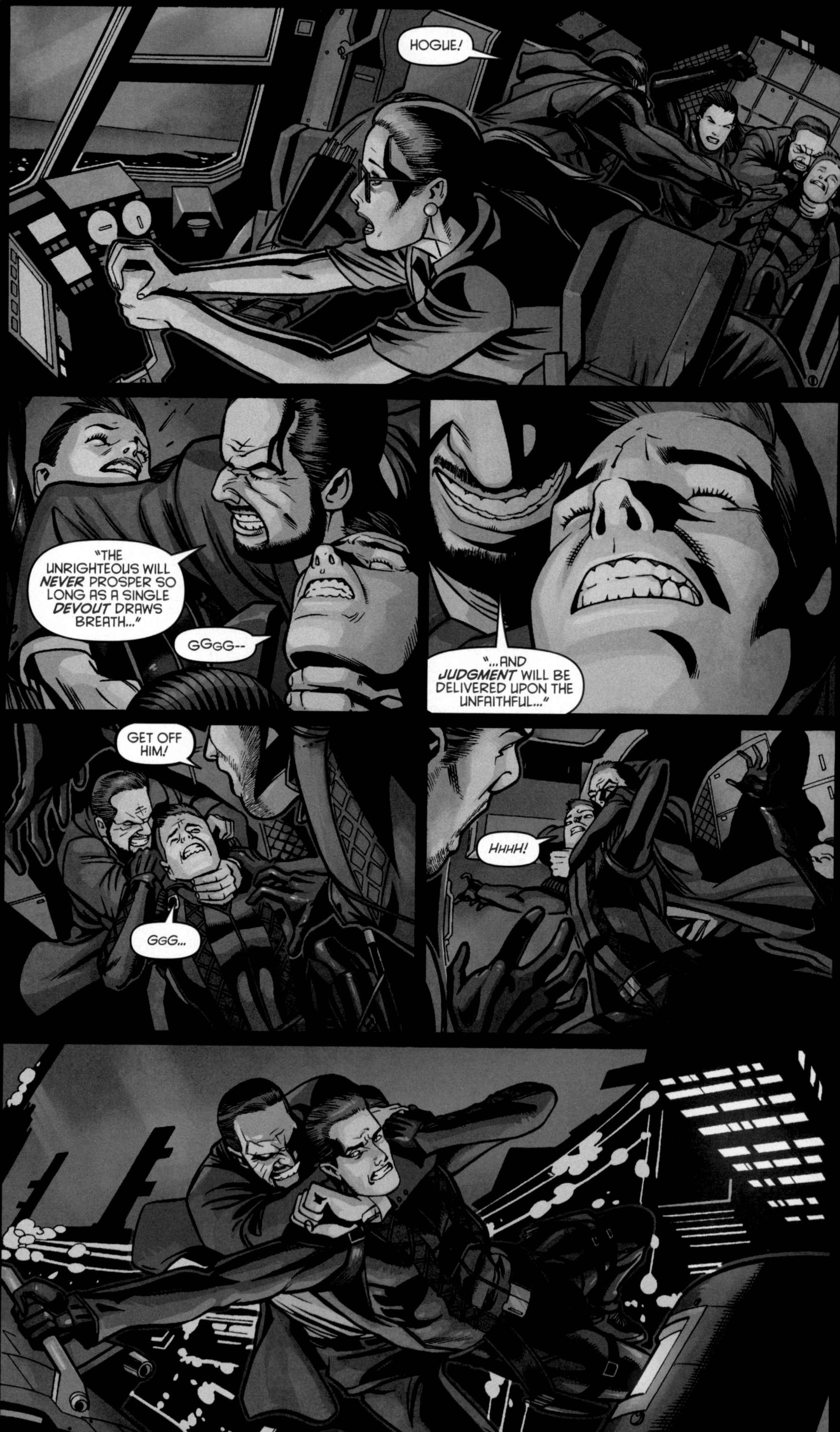
HOGUE!
"THE UNRIGHTEOUS WILL NEVER PROSPER SO LONG AS A SINGLE DEVOUT DRAWS BREATH..."
GGGG--
"...AND JUDGMENT WILL BE DELIVERED UPON THE UNFAITHFUL..."
GET OFF HIM!
GGG...
HHHH!

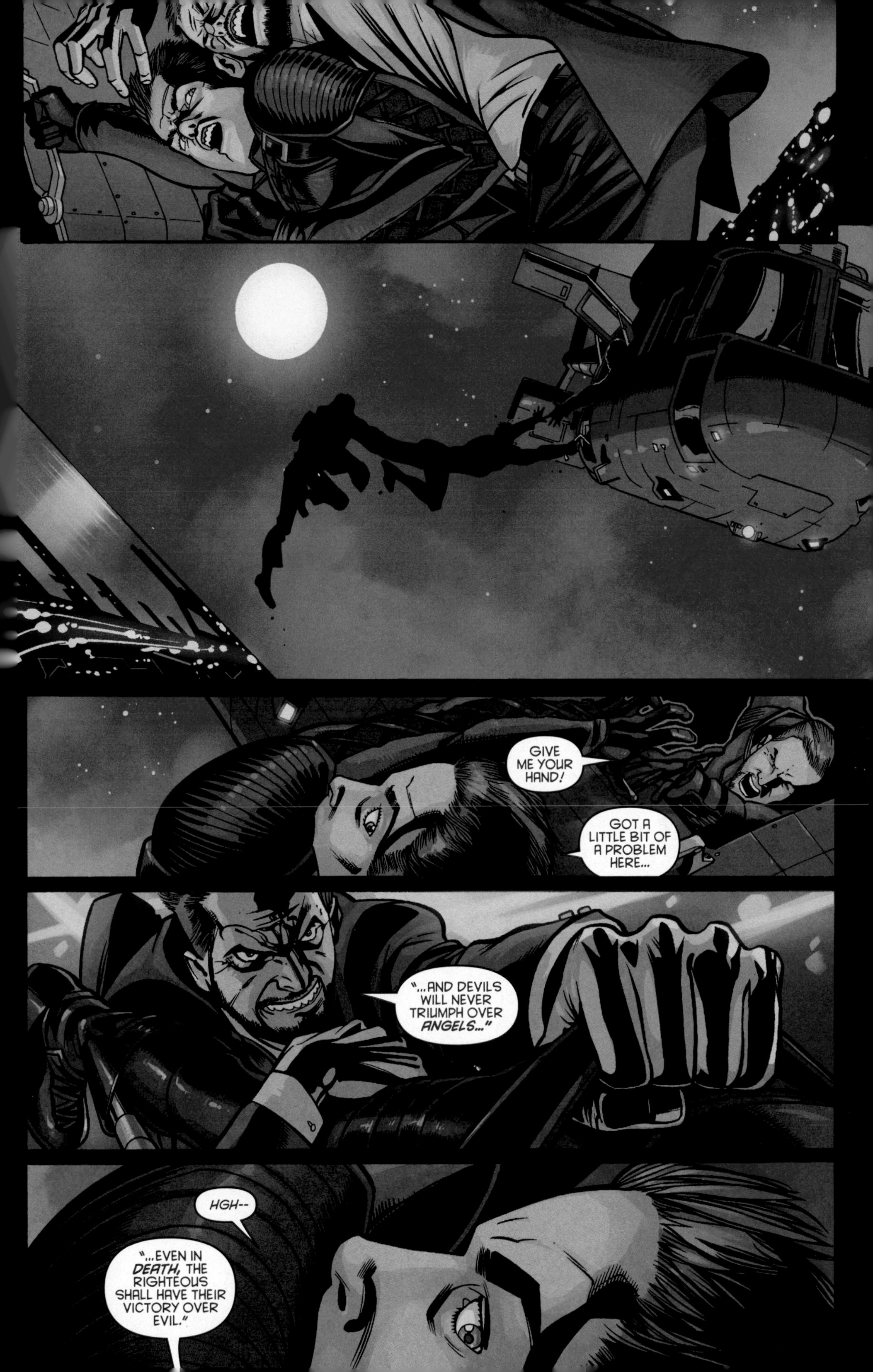
GIVE ME YOUR HAND!
GOT A LITTLE BIT OF A PROBLEM HERE...
"...AND DEVILS WILL NEVER TRIUMPH OVER *ANGELS...*"
HGH--
"...EVEN IN *DEATH,* THE RIGHTEOUS SHALL HAVE THEIR VICTORY OVER EVIL."

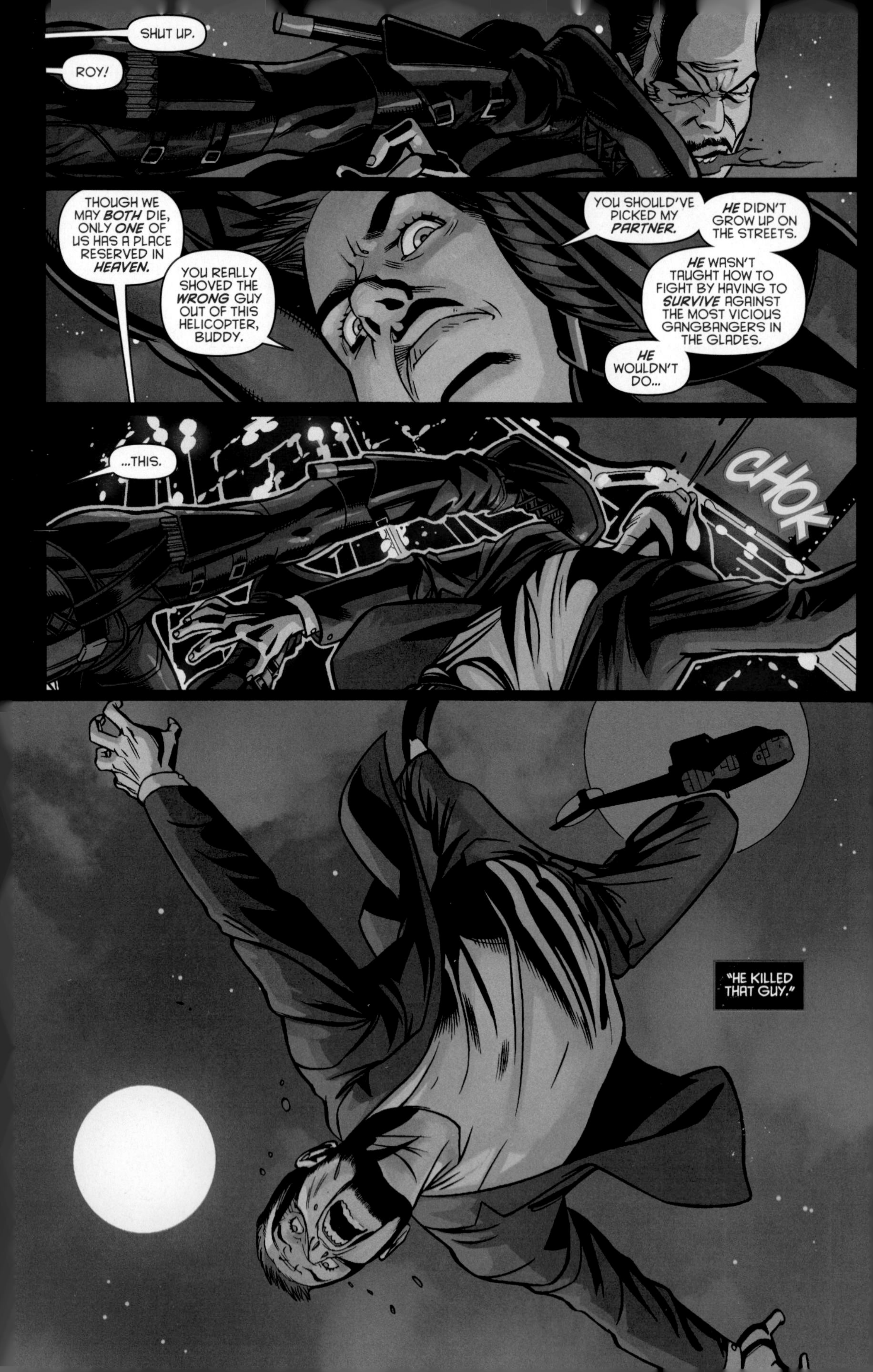
SHUT UP.
ROY!
THOUGH WE MAY BOTH DIE, ONLY ONE OF US HAS A PLACE RESERVED IN HEAVEN.
YOU REALLY SHOVED THE WRONG GUY OUT OF THIS HELICOPTER, BUDDY.
YOU SHOULD'VE PICKED MY PARTNER.
HE DIDN'T GROW UP ON THE STREETS.
HE WASN'T TAUGHT HOW TO FIGHT BY HAVING TO SURVIVE AGAINST THE MOST VICIOUS GANGBANGERS IN THE GLADES.
HE WOULDN'T DO...
...THIS.
CHOK
"HE KILLED THAT GUY."

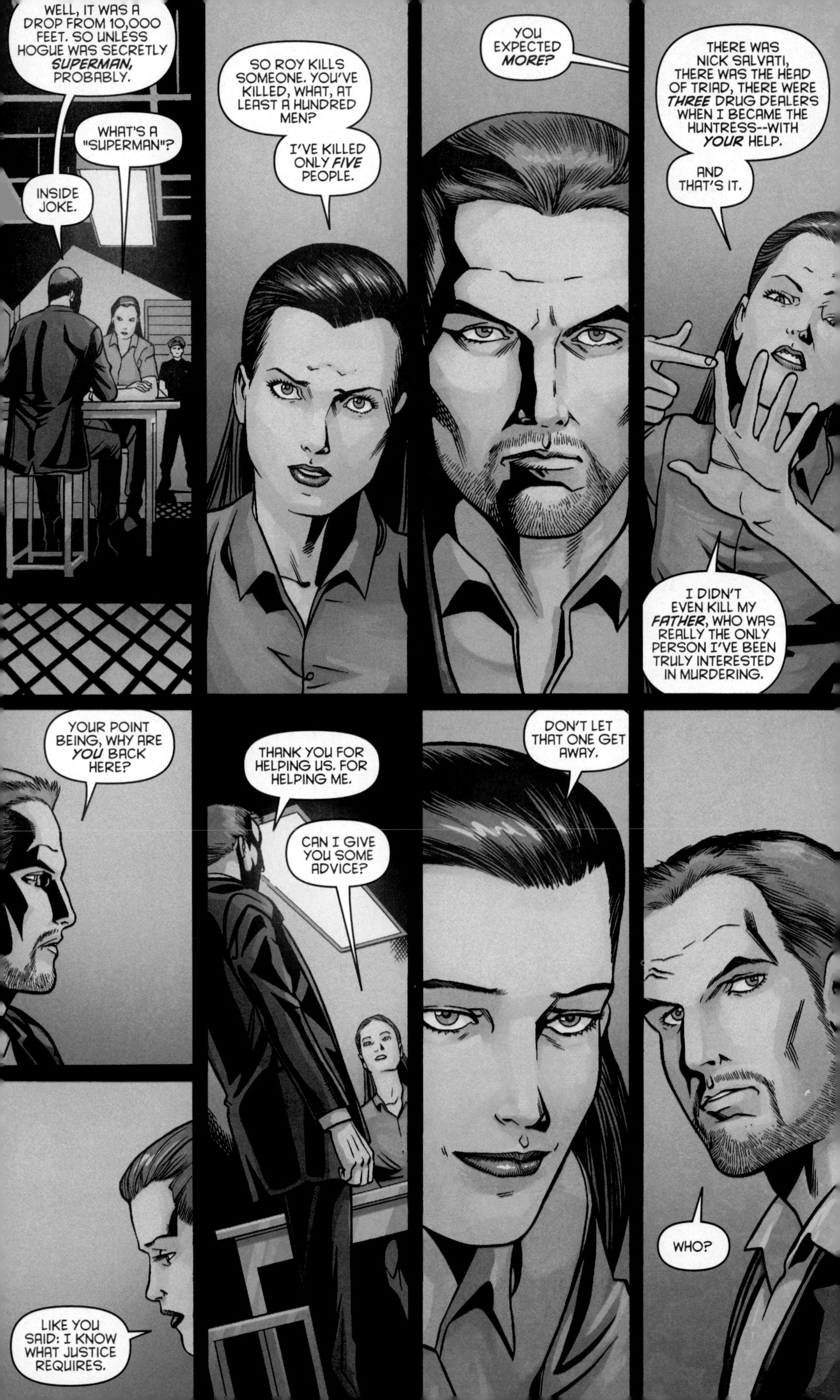
WELL, IT WAS A DROP FROM 10,000 FEET. SO UNLESS HOGUE WAS SECRETLY SUPERMAN, PROBABLY.
WHAT'S A "SUPERMAN"?
INSIDE JOKE.
SO ROY KILLS SOMEONE. YOU'VE KILLED, WHAT, AT LEAST A HUNDRED MEN?
I'VE KILLED ONLY FIVE PEOPLE.
YOU EXPECTED MORE?
THERE WAS NICK SALVATI, THERE WAS THE HEAD OF TRIAD, THERE WERE THREE DRUG DEALERS WHEN I BECAME THE HUNTRESS--WITH YOUR HELP.
AND THAT'S IT.
I DIDN'T EVEN KILL MY FATHER, WHO WAS REALLY THE ONLY PERSON I'VE BEEN TRULY INTERESTED IN MURDERING.
YOUR POINT BEING, WHY ARE YOU BACK HERE?
LIKE YOU SAID: I KNOW WHAT JUSTICE REQUIRES.
THANK YOU FOR HELPING US. FOR HELPING ME.
CAN I GIVE YOU SOME ADVICE?
DON'T LET THAT ONE GET AWAY.
WHO?

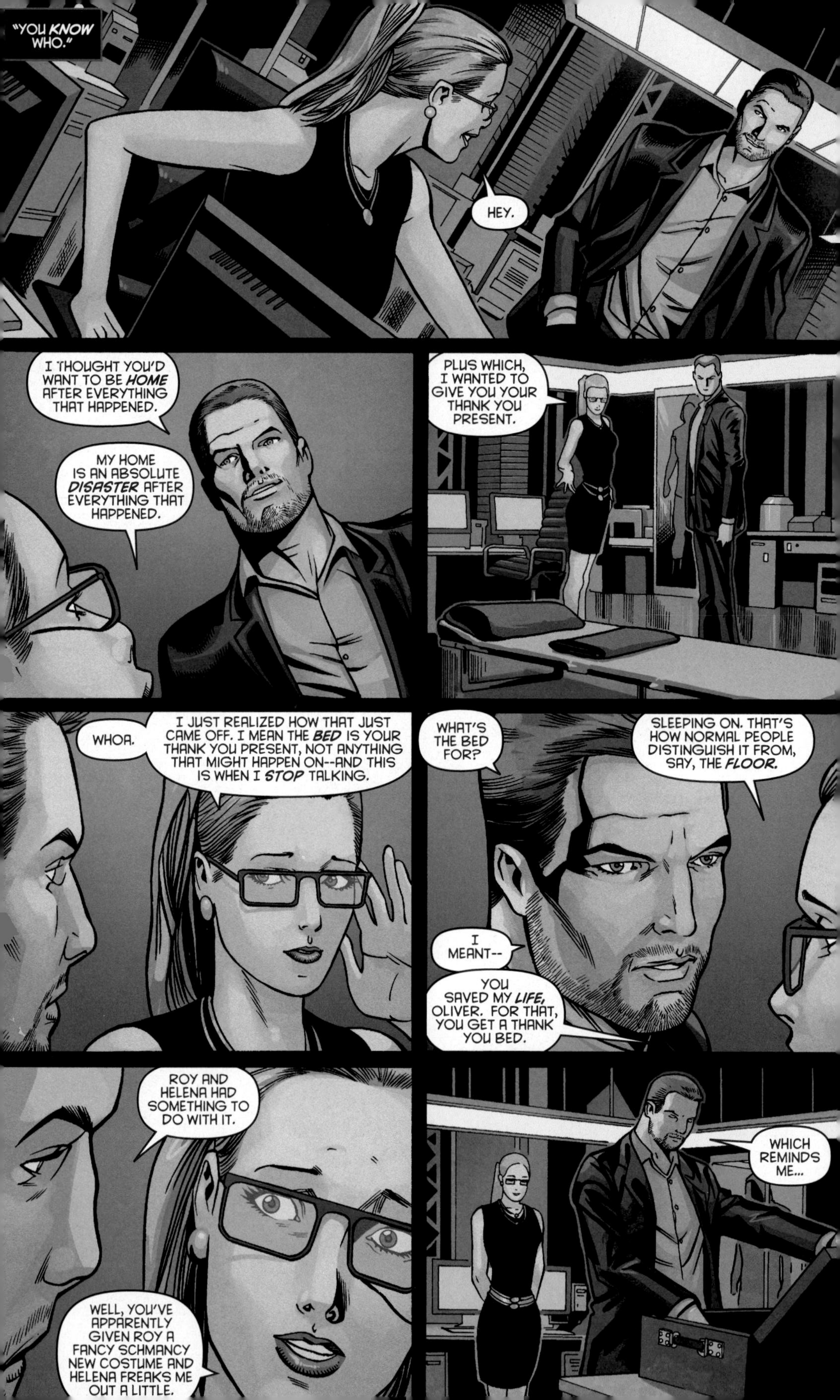
"YOU KNOW WHO."
HEY.
I THOUGHT YOU'D WANT TO BE HOME AFTER EVERYTHING THAT HAPPENED.
MY HOME IS AN ABSOLUTE DISASTER AFTER EVERYTHING THAT HAPPENED.
PLUS WHICH, I WANTED TO GIVE YOU YOUR THANK YOU PRESENT.
WHOA.
I JUST REALIZED HOW THAT JUST CAME OFF. I MEAN THE BED IS YOUR THANK YOU PRESENT, NOT ANYTHING THAT MIGHT HAPPEN ON--AND THIS IS WHEN I STOP TALKING.
WHAT'S THE BED FOR?
SLEEPING ON. THAT'S HOW NORMAL PEOPLE DISTINGUISH IT FROM, SAY, THE FLOOR.
I MEANT--
YOU SAVED MY LIFE, OLIVER. FOR THAT, YOU GET A THANK YOU BED.
ROY AND HELENA HAD SOMETHING TO DO WITH IT.
WELL, YOU'VE APPARENTLY GIVEN ROY A FANCY SCHMANCY NEW COSTUME AND HELENA FREAKS ME OUT A LITTLE.
WHICH REMINDS ME...

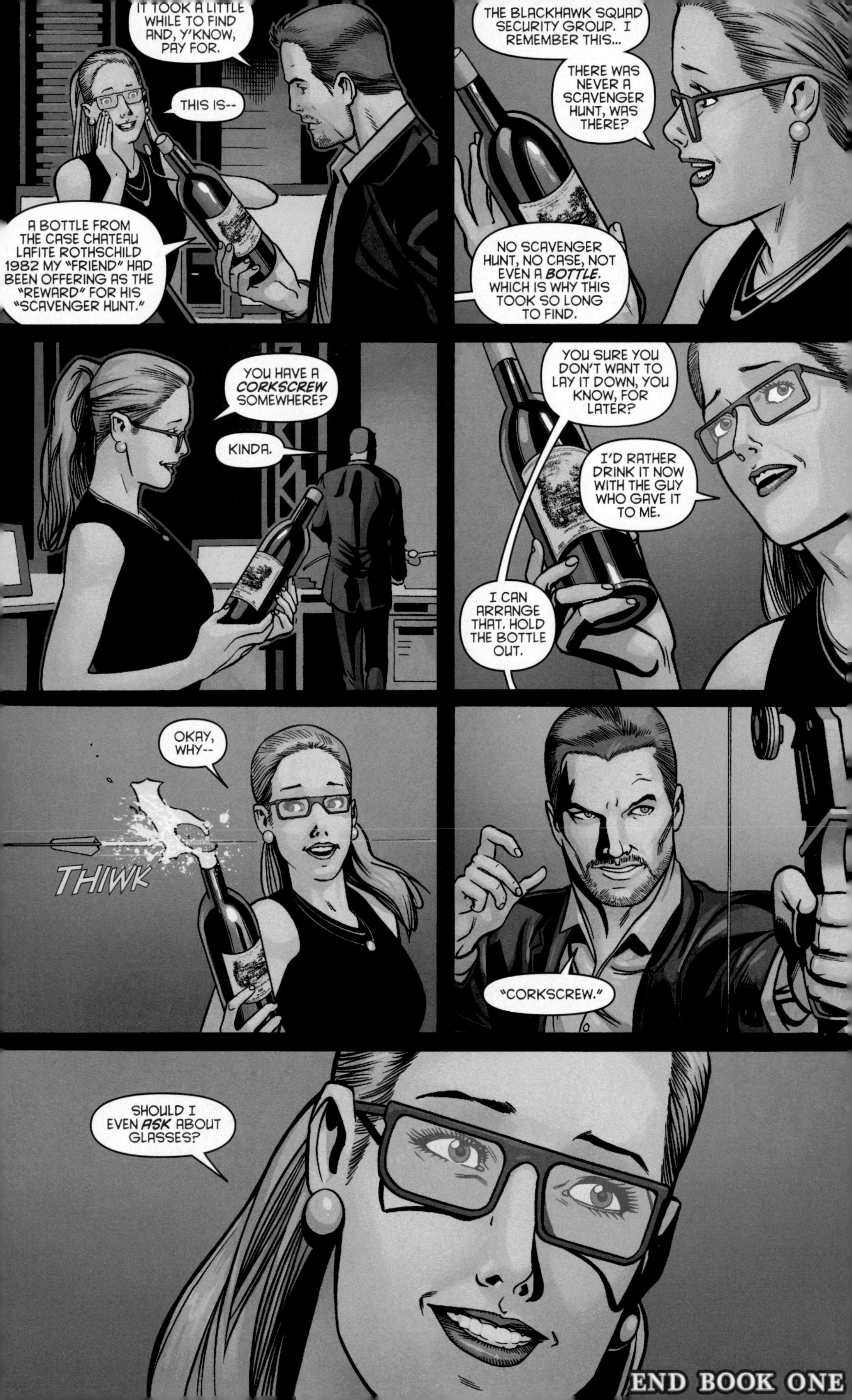
IT TOOK A LITTLE WHILE TO FIND AND, Y'KNOW, PAY FOR.
THIS IS--
A BOTTLE FROM THE CASE CHATEAU LAFITE ROTHSCHILD 1982 MY "FRIEND" HAD BEEN OFFERING AS THE "REWARD" FOR HIS "SCAVENGER HUNT."
THE BLACKHAWK SQUAD SECURITY GROUP. I REMEMBER THIS...
THERE WAS NEVER A SCAVENGER HUNT, WAS THERE?
NO SCAVENGER HUNT, NO CASE, NOT EVEN A BOTTLE. WHICH IS WHY THIS TOOK SO LONG TO FIND.
YOU HAVE A CORKSCREW SOMEWHERE?
KINDA.
YOU SURE YOU DON'T WANT TO LAY IT DOWN, YOU KNOW, FOR LATER?
I'D RATHER DRINK IT NOW WITH THE GUY WHO GAVE IT TO ME.
I CAN ARRANGE THAT. HOLD THE BOTTLE OUT.
OKAY, WHY--
THIWK
"CORKSCREW."
SHOULD I EVEN ASK ABOUT GLASSES?
END BOOK ONE

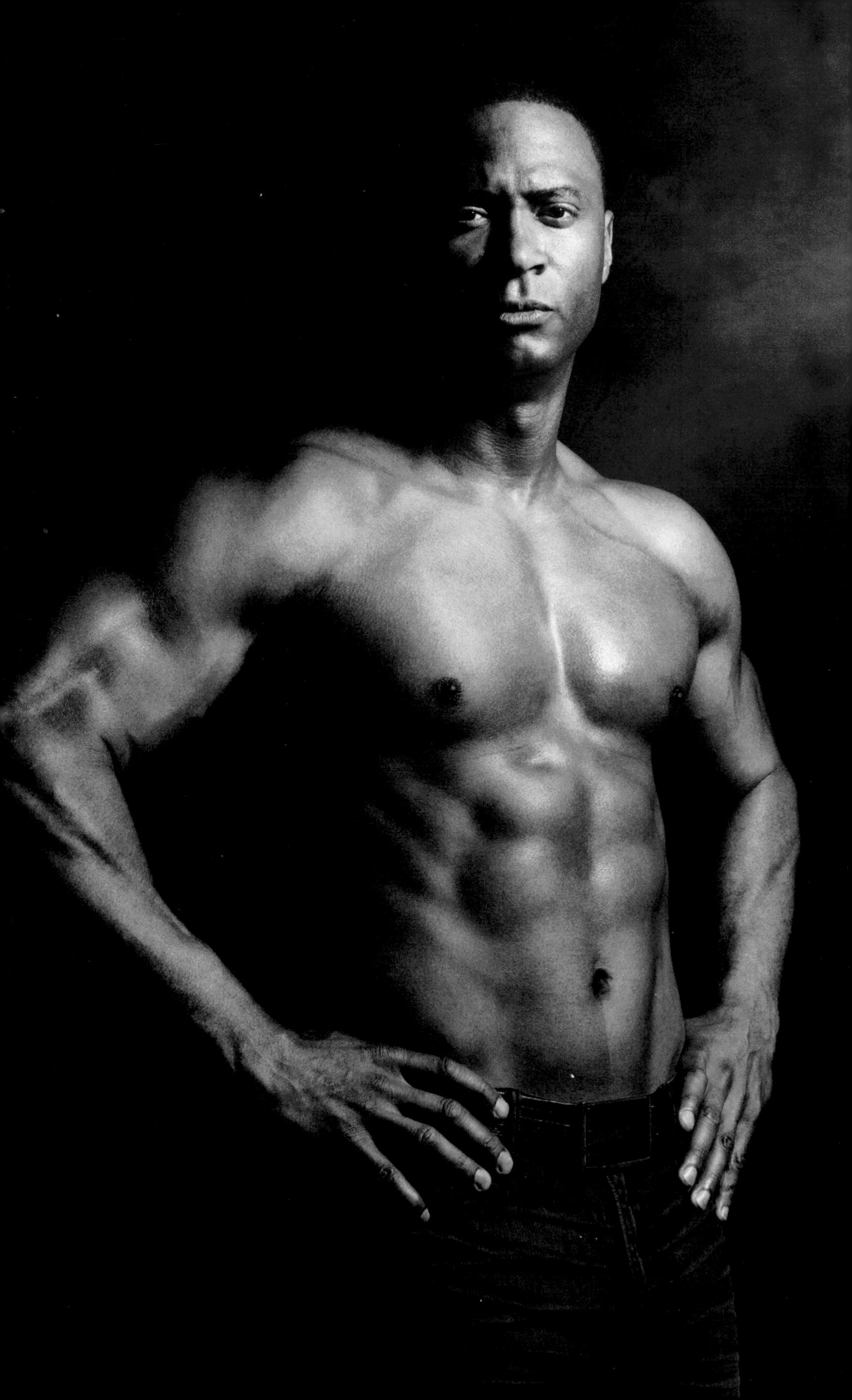

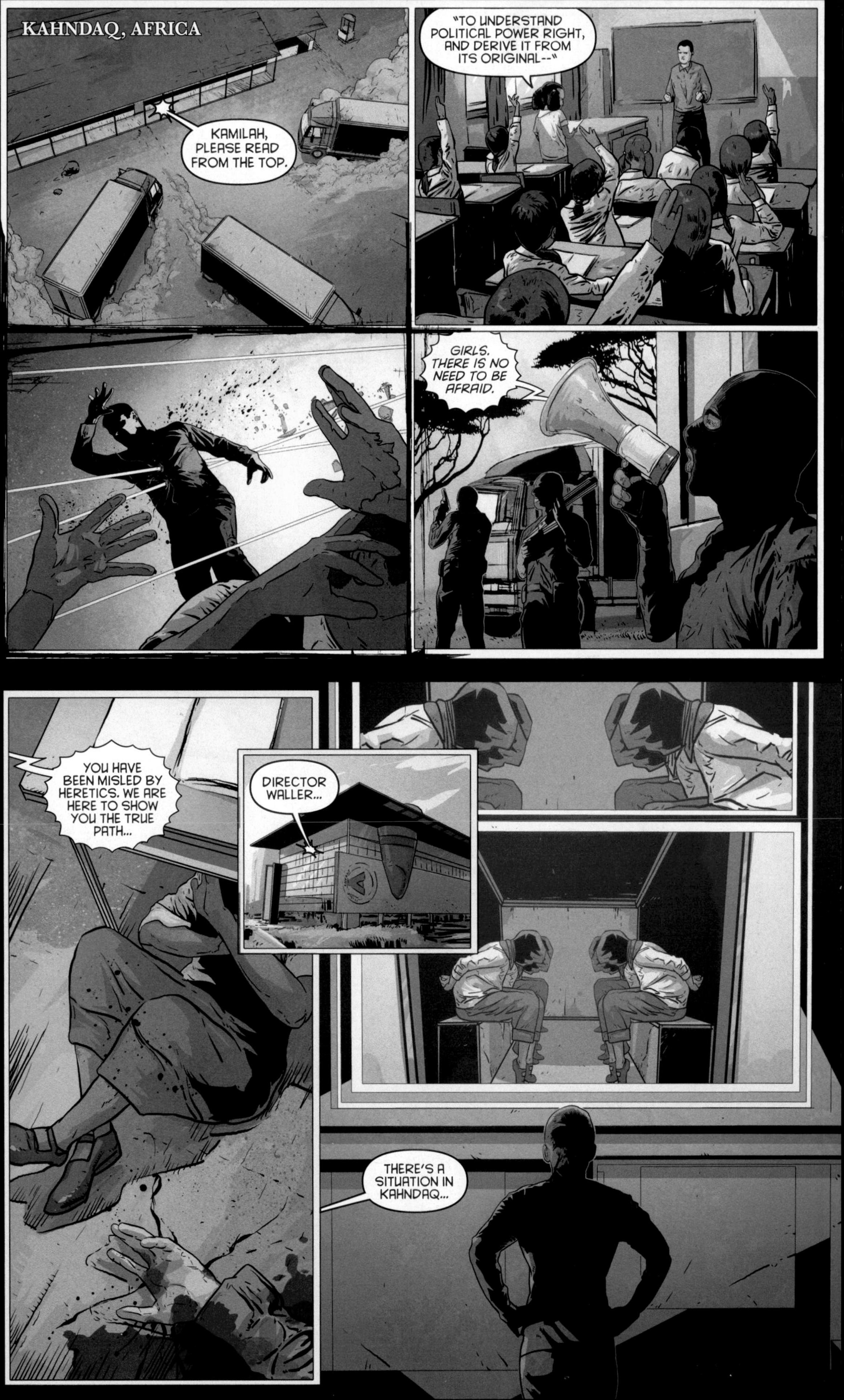
KAHNDAQ, AFRICA
KAMILAH, PLEASE READ FROM THE TOP.
"TO UNDERSTAND POLITICAL POWER RIGHT, AND DERIVE IT FROM ITS ORIGINAL--"
GIRLS. THERE IS NO NEED TO BE AFRAID.
YOU HAVE BEEN MISLED BY HERETICS. WE ARE HERE TO SHOW YOU THE TRUE PATH...
DIRECTOR WALLER...
THERE'S A SITUATION IN KAHNDAQ...

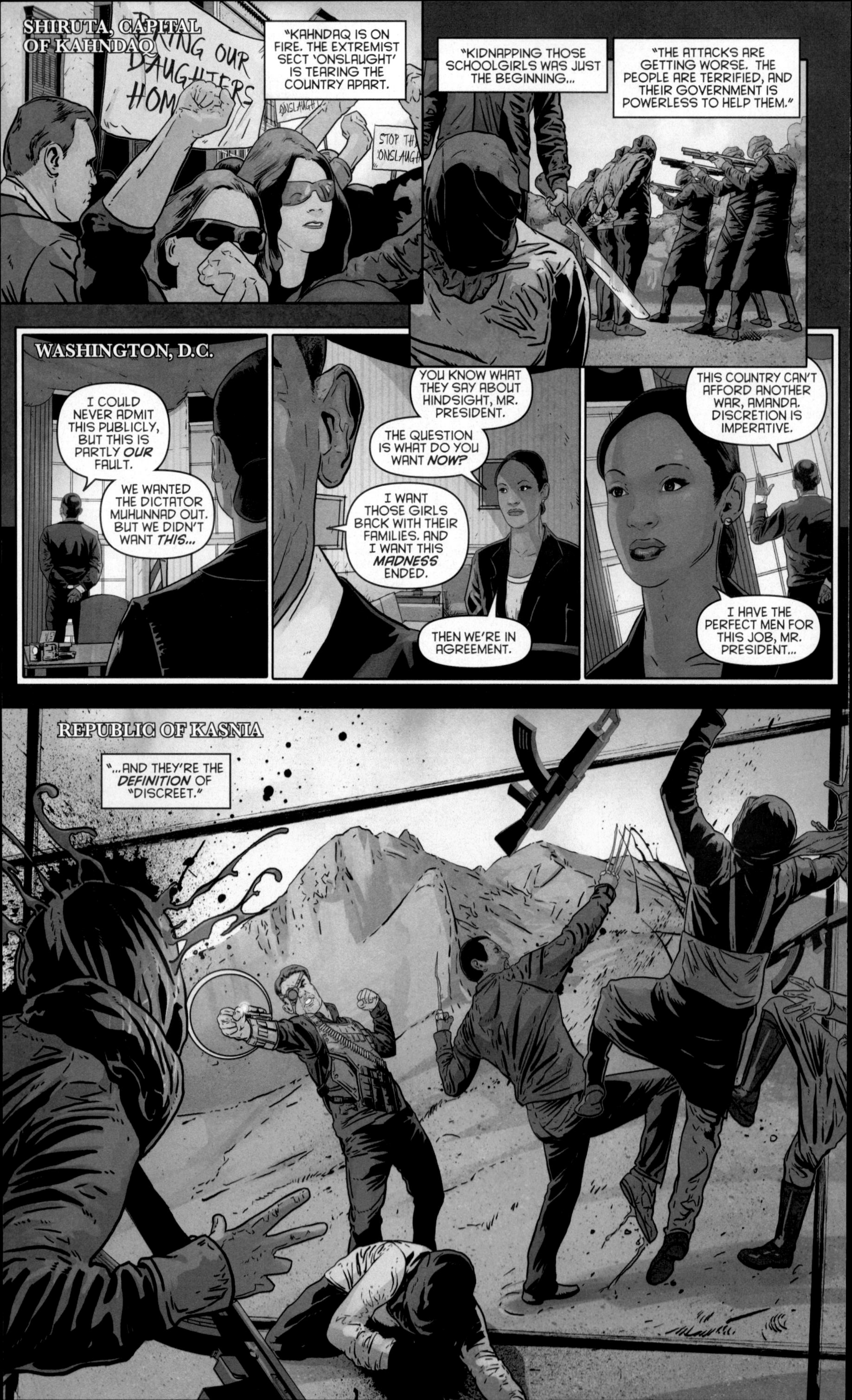
SHIRUTA, CAPITAL OF KAHNDAQ
"KAHNDAQ IS ON FIRE. THE EXTREMIST SECT 'ONSLAUGHT' IS TEARING THE COUNTRY APART.
"KIDNAPPING THOSE SCHOOLGIRLS WAS JUST THE BEGINNING...
"THE ATTACKS ARE GETTING WORSE. THE PEOPLE ARE TERRIFIED, AND THEIR GOVERNMENT IS POWERLESS TO HELP THEM."
WASHINGTON, D.C.
I COULD NEVER ADMIT THIS PUBLICLY, BUT THIS IS PARTLY *OUR* FAULT.
WE WANTED THE DICTATOR MUHUNNAD OUT. BUT WE DIDN'T WANT *THIS*...
YOU KNOW WHAT THEY SAY ABOUT HINDSIGHT, MR. PRESIDENT.
THE QUESTION IS WHAT DO YOU WANT *NOW?*
I WANT THOSE GIRLS BACK WITH THEIR FAMILIES. AND I WANT THIS *MADNESS* ENDED.
THEN WE'RE IN AGREEMENT.
THIS COUNTRY CAN'T AFFORD ANOTHER WAR, AMANDA. DISCRETION IS IMPERATIVE.
I HAVE THE PERFECT MEN FOR THIS JOB, MR. PRESIDENT...
REPUBLIC OF KASNIA
"...AND THEY'RE THE *DEFINITION* OF "DISCREET."

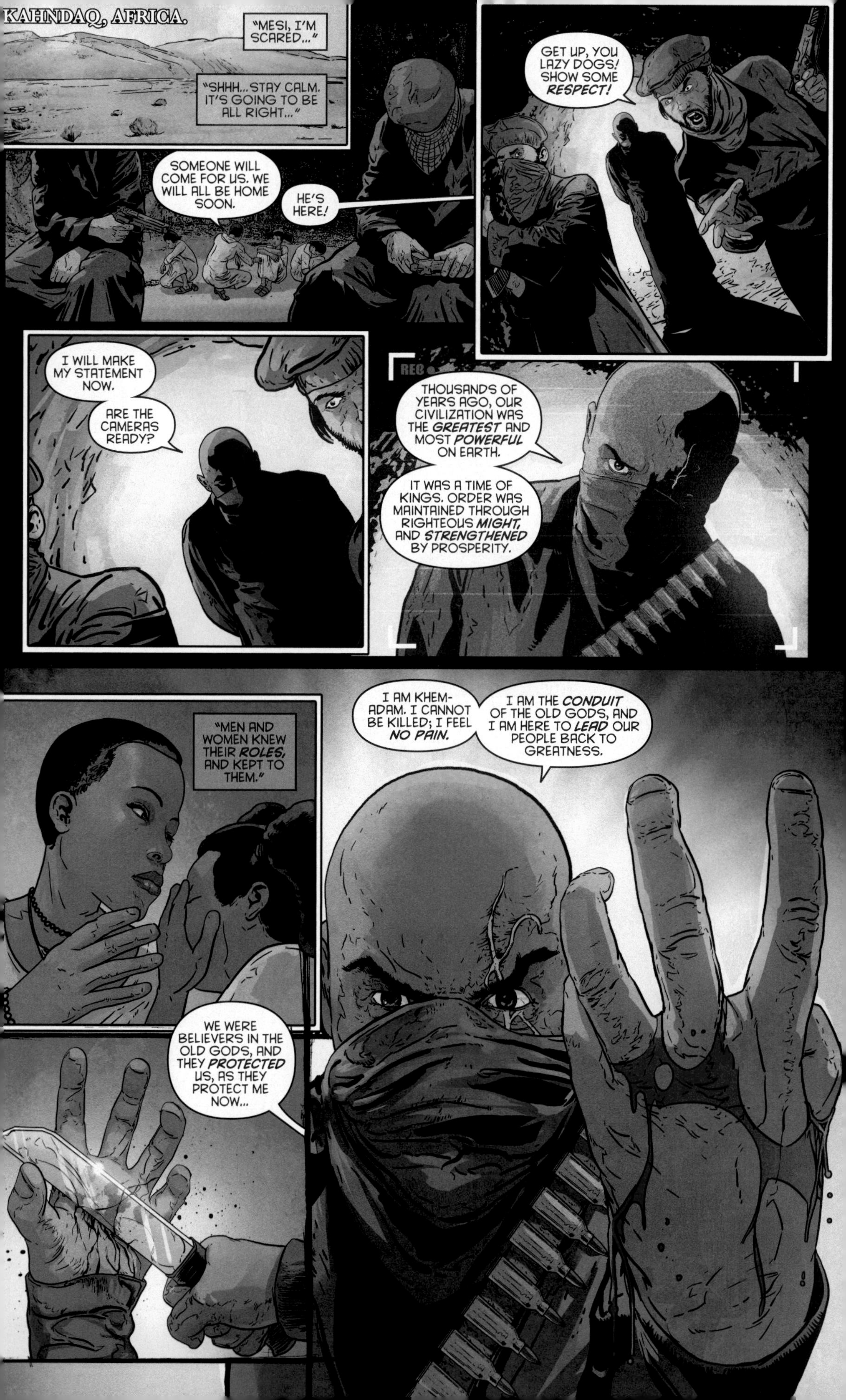
KAHNDAQ, AFRICA.
"MESI, I'M SCARED..."
"SHHH... STAY CALM. IT'S GOING TO BE ALL RIGHT..."
SOMEONE WILL COME FOR US. WE WILL ALL BE HOME SOON.
HE'S HERE!
GET UP, YOU LAZY DOGS! SHOW SOME RESPECT!
I WILL MAKE MY STATEMENT NOW.
ARE THE CAMERAS READY?
REC
THOUSANDS OF YEARS AGO, OUR CIVILIZATION WAS THE GREATEST AND MOST POWERFUL ON EARTH.
IT WAS A TIME OF KINGS. ORDER WAS MAINTAINED THROUGH RIGHTEOUS MIGHT, AND STRENGTHENED BY PROSPERITY.
"MEN AND WOMEN KNEW THEIR ROLES, AND KEPT TO THEM."
I AM KHEM-ADAM. I CANNOT BE KILLED; I FEEL NO PAIN.
I AM THE CONDUIT OF THE OLD GODS, AND I AM HERE TO LEAD OUR PEOPLE BACK TO GREATNESS.
WE WERE BELIEVERS IN THE OLD GODS, AND THEY PROTECTED US, AS THEY PROTECT ME NOW...

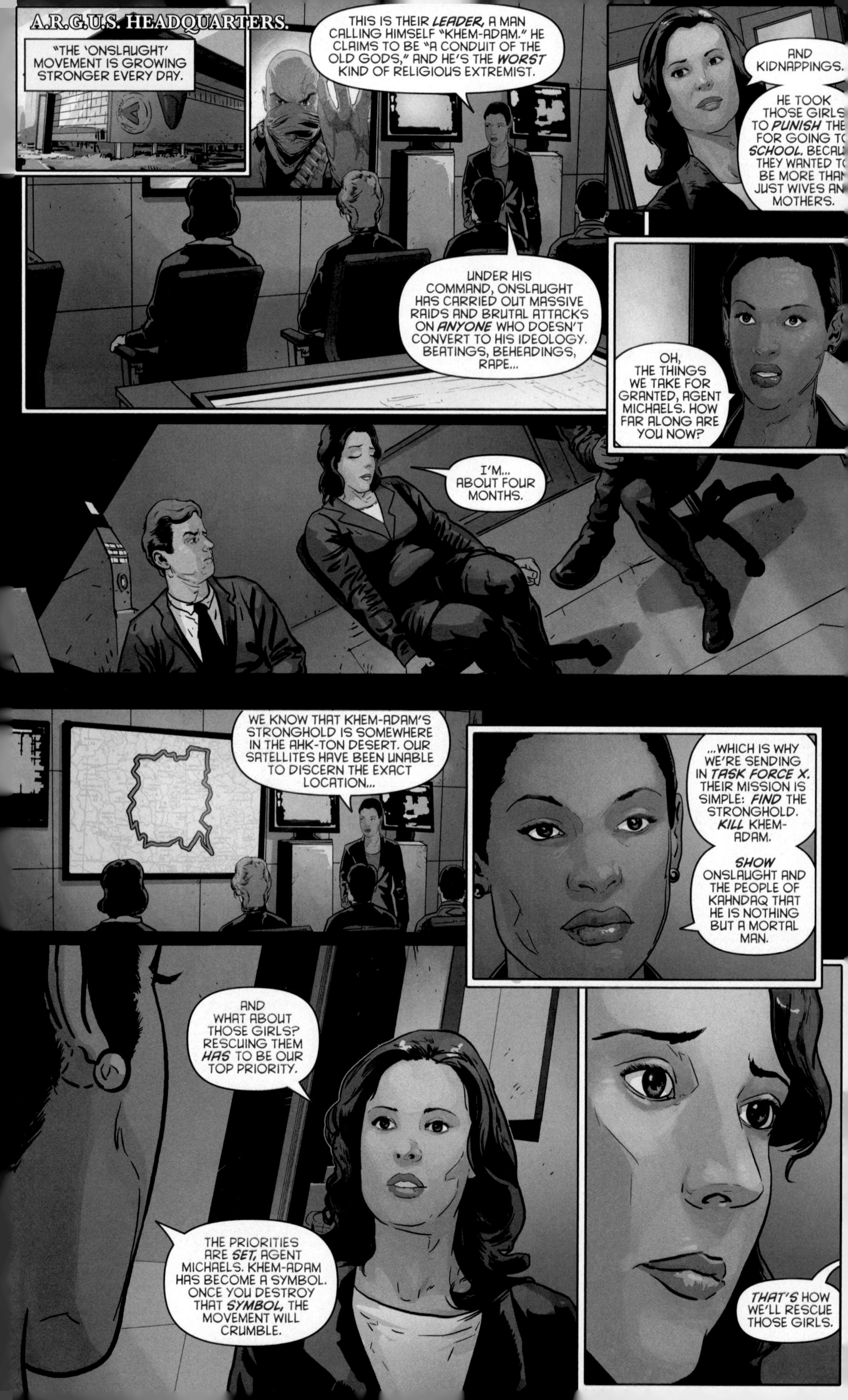
A.R.G.U.S. HEADQUARTERS.
"THE 'ONSLAUGHT' MOVEMENT IS GROWING STRONGER EVERY DAY.
THIS IS THEIR LEADER, A MAN CALLING HIMSELF "KHEM-ADAM." HE CLAIMS TO BE "A CONDUIT OF THE OLD GODS," AND HE'S THE WORST KIND OF RELIGIOUS EXTREMIST.
UNDER HIS COMMAND, ONSLAUGHT HAS CARRIED OUT MASSIVE RAIDS AND BRUTAL ATTACKS ON ANYONE WHO DOESN'T CONVERT TO HIS IDEOLOGY. BEATINGS, BEHEADINGS, RAPE...
AND KIDNAPPINGS.
OH, THE THINGS WE TAKE FOR GRANTED, AGENT MICHAELS. HOW FAR ALONG ARE YOU NOW?
I'M... ABOUT FOUR MONTHS.
WE KNOW THAT KHEM-ADAM'S STRONGHOLD IS SOMEWHERE IN THE AHK-TON DESERT. OUR SATELLITES HAVE BEEN UNABLE TO DISCERN THE EXACT LOCATION...
...WHICH IS WHY WE'RE SENDING IN TASK FORCE X. THEIR MISSION IS SIMPLE: FIND THE STRONGHOLD. KILL KHEM-ADAM.
SHOW ONSLAUGHT AND THE PEOPLE OF KAHNDAQ THAT HE IS NOTHING BUT A MORTAL MAN.
AND WHAT ABOUT THOSE GIRLS? RESCUING THEM HAS TO BE OUR TOP PRIORITY.
THE PRIORITIES ARE SET, AGENT MICHAELS. KHEM-ADAM HAS BECOME A SYMBOL. ONCE YOU DESTROY THAT SYMBOL, THE MOVEMENT WILL CRUMBLE.
THAT'S HOW WE'LL RESCUE THOSE GIRLS.

HE HASN'T SAID A WORD SINCE HE ARRIVED.

THAT WAS OVER TWO YEARS AGO.

RAVAN NASSAR...

IT'S BEEN FAR TOO LONG.

LYLA MICHAELS.

I THOUGHT YOU WEREN'T SPEAKING THESE DAYS.

IT WOULD BE *RUDE* NOT TO ACKNOWLEDGE AN *OLD FRIEND.* WHAT CAN I DO FOR YOU?

IT'S MORE WHAT WE CAN DO FOR *EACH OTHER.* THERE'S TROUBLE IN YOUR HOME COUNTRY.

AS I *WARNED* YOU THERE WOULD BE. BEFORE YOU AND YOUR ARMED FORCES *OUSTED* MY PRESIDENT AND PUT ME IN THIS CELL.

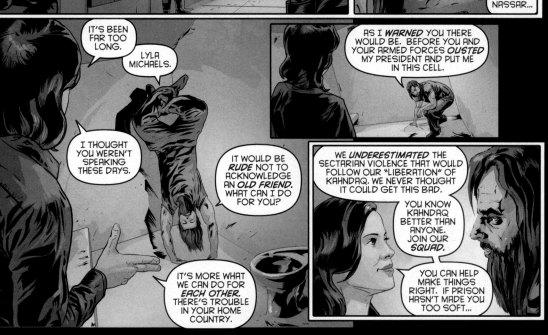

WE *UNDERESTIMATED* THE SECTARIAN VIOLENCE THAT WOULD FOLLOW OUR "LIBERATION" OF KAHNDAQ. WE NEVER THOUGHT IT COULD GET THIS BAD.

YOU KNOW KAHNDAQ BETTER THAN ANYONE. JOIN OUR *SQUAD.*

YOU CAN HELP MAKE THINGS RIGHT. IF PRISON HASN'T MADE YOU TOO SOFT...

THAT "SOFT" ENOUGH FOR YOU?

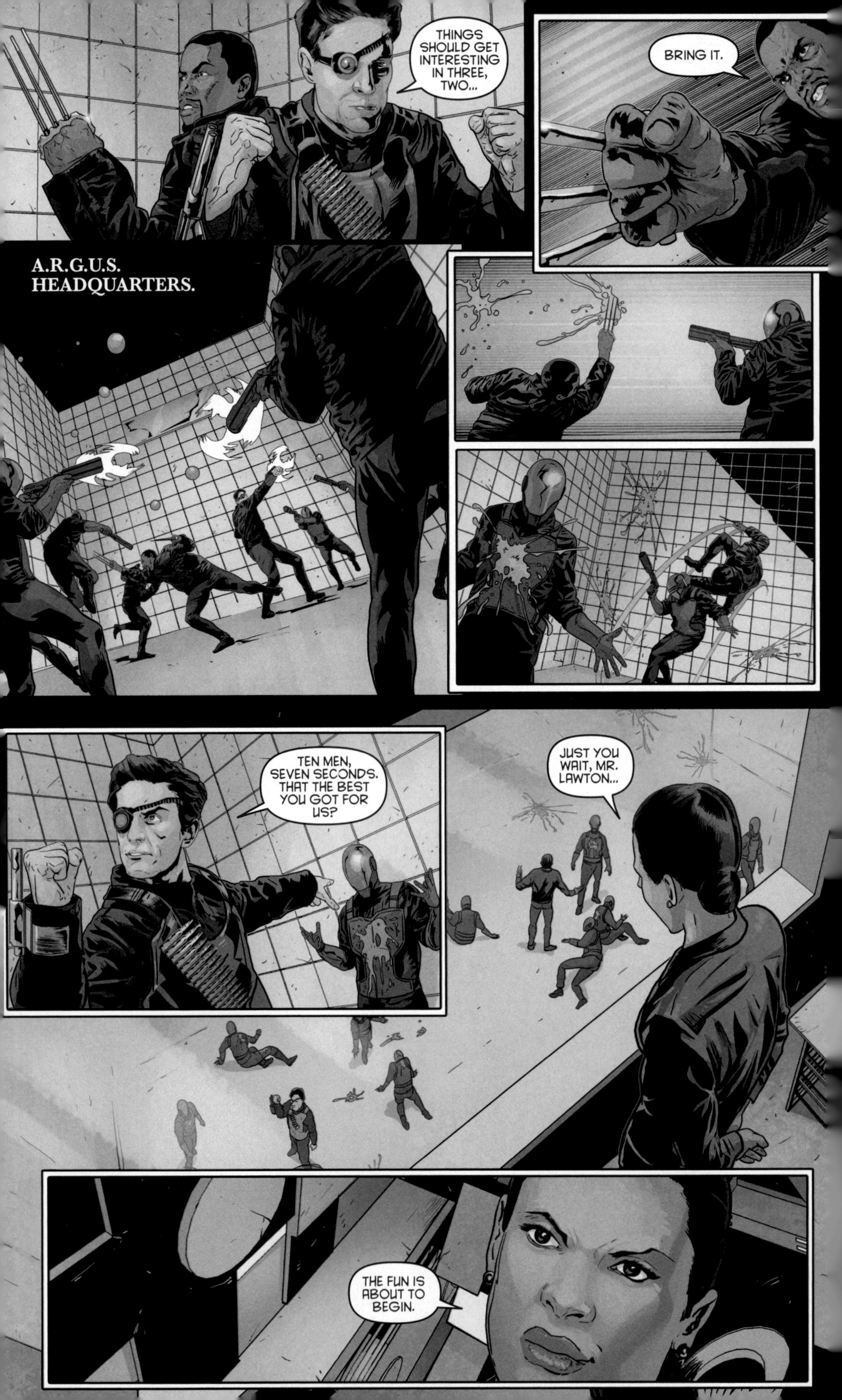
THINGS SHOULD GET INTERESTING IN THREE, TWO...
BRING IT.
A.R.G.U.S. HEADQUARTERS.
TEN MEN, SEVEN SECONDS. THAT THE BEST YOU GOT FOR US?
JUST YOU WAIT, MR. LAWTON...
THE FUN IS ABOUT TO BEGIN.

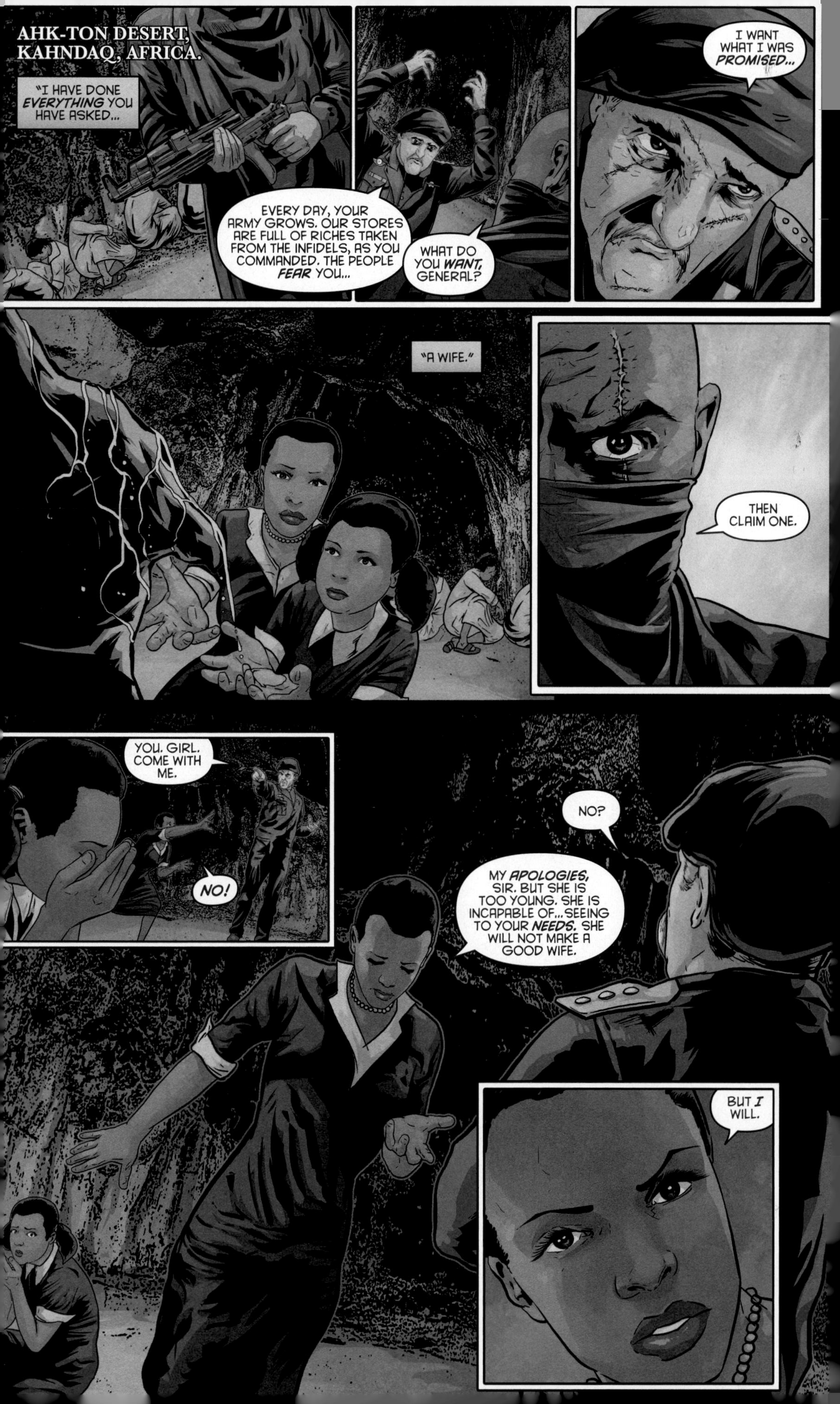
AHK-TON DESERT, KAHNDAQ, AFRICA.
"I HAVE DONE EVERYTHING YOU HAVE ASKED...
EVERY DAY, YOUR ARMY GROWS. OUR STORES ARE FULL OF RICHES TAKEN FROM THE INFIDELS, AS YOU COMMANDED. THE PEOPLE FEAR YOU...
WHAT DO YOU WANT, GENERAL?
I WANT WHAT I WAS PROMISED...
"A WIFE."
THEN CLAIM ONE.
YOU. GIRL. COME WITH ME.
NO!
NO?
MY APOLOGIES, SIR. BUT SHE IS TOO YOUNG. SHE IS INCAPABLE OF... SEEING TO YOUR NEEDS. SHE WILL NOT MAKE A GOOD WIFE.
BUT I WILL.

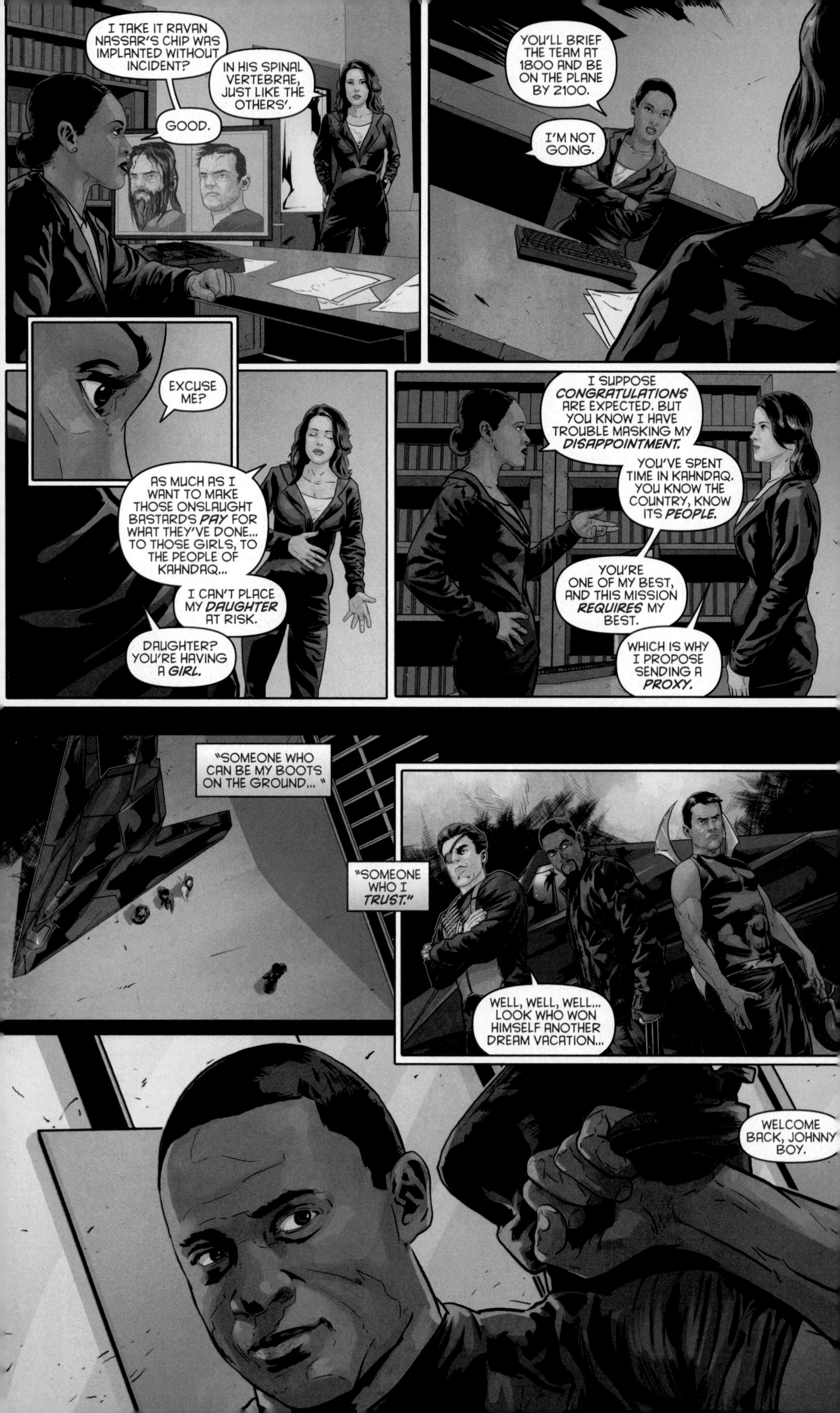

I TAKE IT RAVAN NASSAR'S CHIP WAS IMPLANTED WITHOUT INCIDENT?
IN HIS SPINAL VERTEBRAE, JUST LIKE THE OTHERS'.
GOOD.
YOU'LL BRIEF THE TEAM AT 1800 AND BE ON THE PLANE BY 2100.
I'M NOT GOING.
EXCUSE ME?
AS MUCH AS I WANT TO MAKE THOSE ONSLAUGHT BASTARDS *PAY* FOR WHAT THEY'VE DONE... TO THOSE GIRLS, TO THE PEOPLE OF KAHNDAQ...
I CAN'T PLACE MY *DAUGHTER* AT RISK.
DAUGHTER? YOU'RE HAVING A *GIRL.*
I SUPPOSE *CONGRATULATIONS* ARE EXPECTED. BUT YOU KNOW I HAVE TROUBLE MASKING MY *DISAPPOINTMENT.*
YOU'VE SPENT TIME IN KAHNDAQ. YOU KNOW THE COUNTRY, KNOW ITS *PEOPLE.*
YOU'RE ONE OF MY BEST, AND THIS MISSION *REQUIRES* MY BEST.
WHICH IS WHY I PROPOSE SENDING A *PROXY.*
"SOMEONE WHO CAN BE MY BOOTS ON THE GROUND... "
"SOMEONE WHO I *TRUST.*"
WELL, WELL, WELL... LOOK WHO WON HIMSELF ANOTHER DREAM VACATION...
WELCOME BACK, JOHNNY BOY.

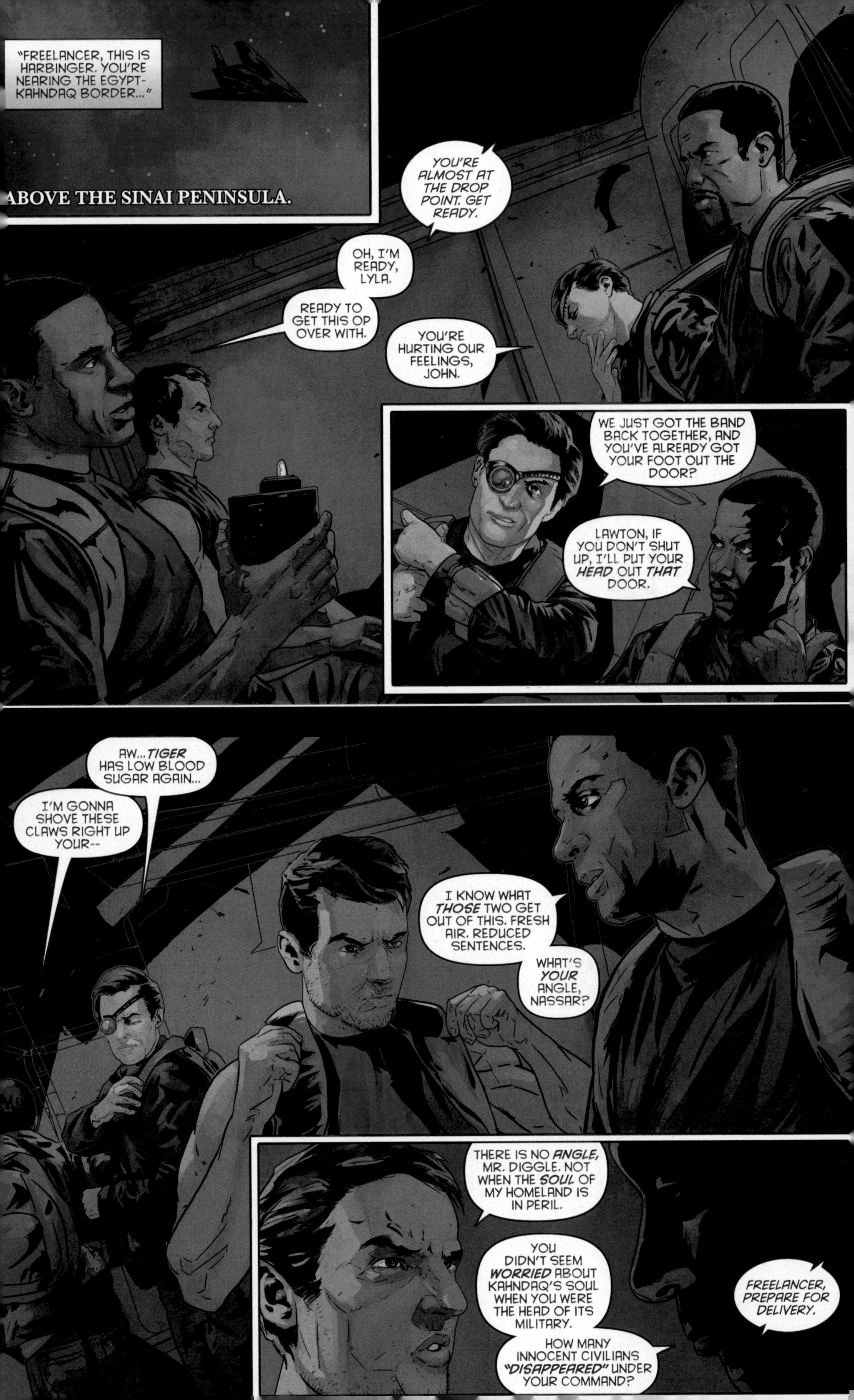
"FREELANCER, THIS IS HARBINGER. YOU'RE NEARING THE EGYPT-KAHNDAQ BORDER..."
ABOVE THE SINAI PENINSULA.
YOU'RE ALMOST AT THE DROP POINT. GET READY.
OH, I'M READY, LYLA.
READY TO GET THIS OP OVER WITH.
YOU'RE HURTING OUR FEELINGS, JOHN.
WE JUST GOT THE BAND BACK TOGETHER, AND YOU'VE ALREADY GOT YOUR FOOT OUT THE DOOR?
LAWTON, IF YOU DON'T SHUT UP, I'LL PUT YOUR HEAD OUT THAT DOOR.
AW... TIGER HAS LOW BLOOD SUGAR AGAIN...
I'M GONNA SHOVE THESE CLAWS RIGHT UP YOUR--
I KNOW WHAT THOSE TWO GET OUT OF THIS. FRESH AIR. REDUCED SENTENCES.
WHAT'S YOUR ANGLE, NASSAR?
THERE IS NO ANGLE, MR. DIGGLE. NOT WHEN THE SOUL OF MY HOMELAND IS IN PERIL.
YOU DIDN'T SEEM WORRIED ABOUT KAHNDAQ'S SOUL WHEN YOU WERE THE HEAD OF ITS MILITARY.
HOW MANY INNOCENT CIVILIANS "DISAPPEARED" UNDER YOUR COMMAND?
FREELANCER, PREPARE FOR DELIVERY.

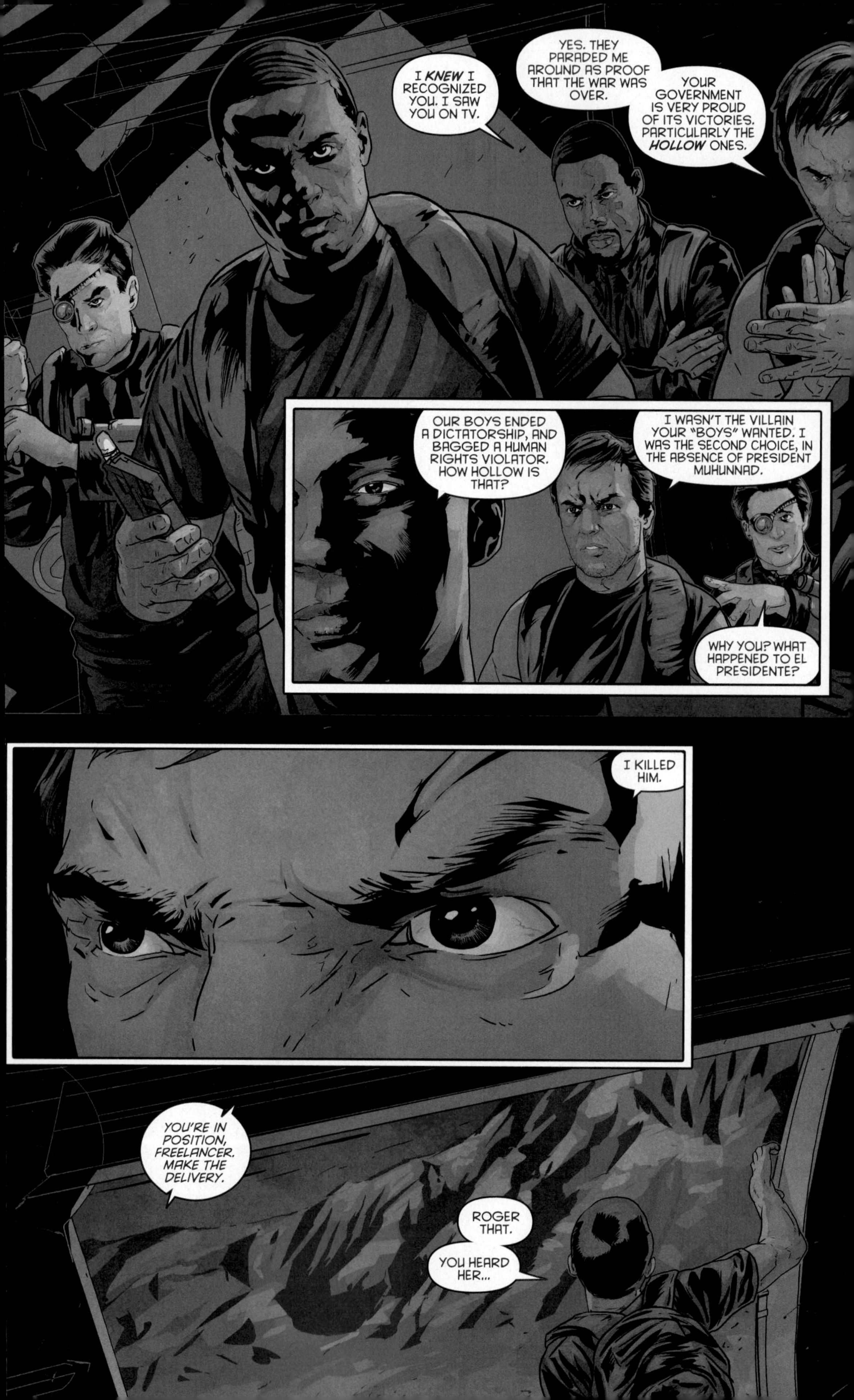
I KNEW I RECOGNIZED YOU. I SAW YOU ON TV.
YES. THEY PARADED ME AROUND AS PROOF THAT THE WAR WAS OVER.
YOUR GOVERNMENT IS VERY PROUD OF ITS VICTORIES. PARTICULARLY THE HOLLOW ONES.
OUR BOYS ENDED A DICTATORSHIP, AND BAGGED A HUMAN RIGHTS VIOLATOR. HOW HOLLOW IS THAT?
I WASN'T THE VILLAIN YOUR "BOYS" WANTED. I WAS THE SECOND CHOICE, IN THE ABSENCE OF PRESIDENT MUHUNNAD.
WHY YOU? WHAT HAPPENED TO EL PRESIDENTE?
I KILLED HIM.
YOU'RE IN POSITION, FREELANCER. MAKE THE DELIVERY.
ROGER THAT.
YOU HEARD HER...

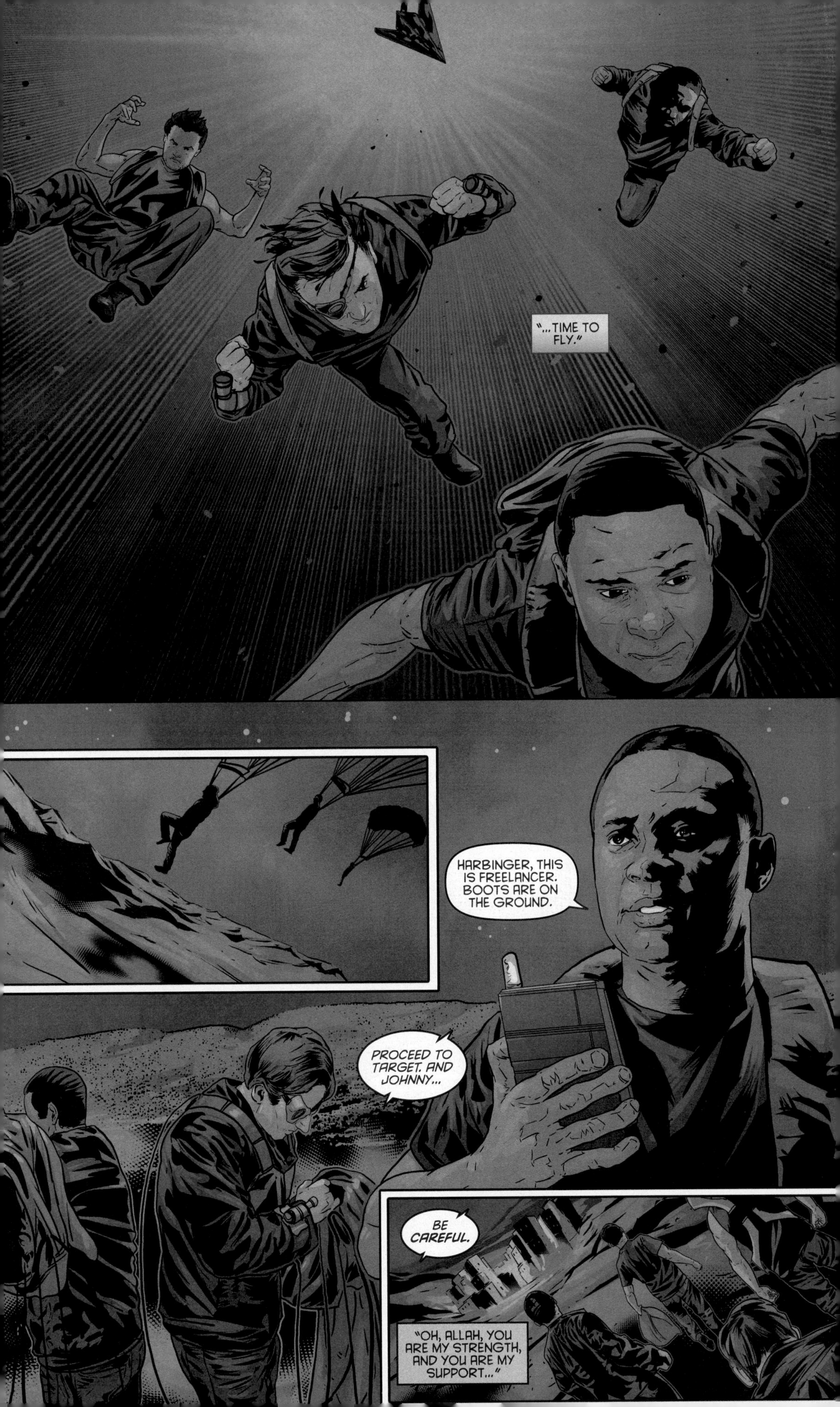
"...TIME TO FLY."
HARBINGER, THIS IS FREELANCER. BOOTS ARE ON THE GROUND.
PROCEED TO TARGET. AND JOHNNY...
BE CAREFUL.
"OH, ALLAH, YOU ARE MY STRENGTH, AND YOU ARE MY SUPPORT..."

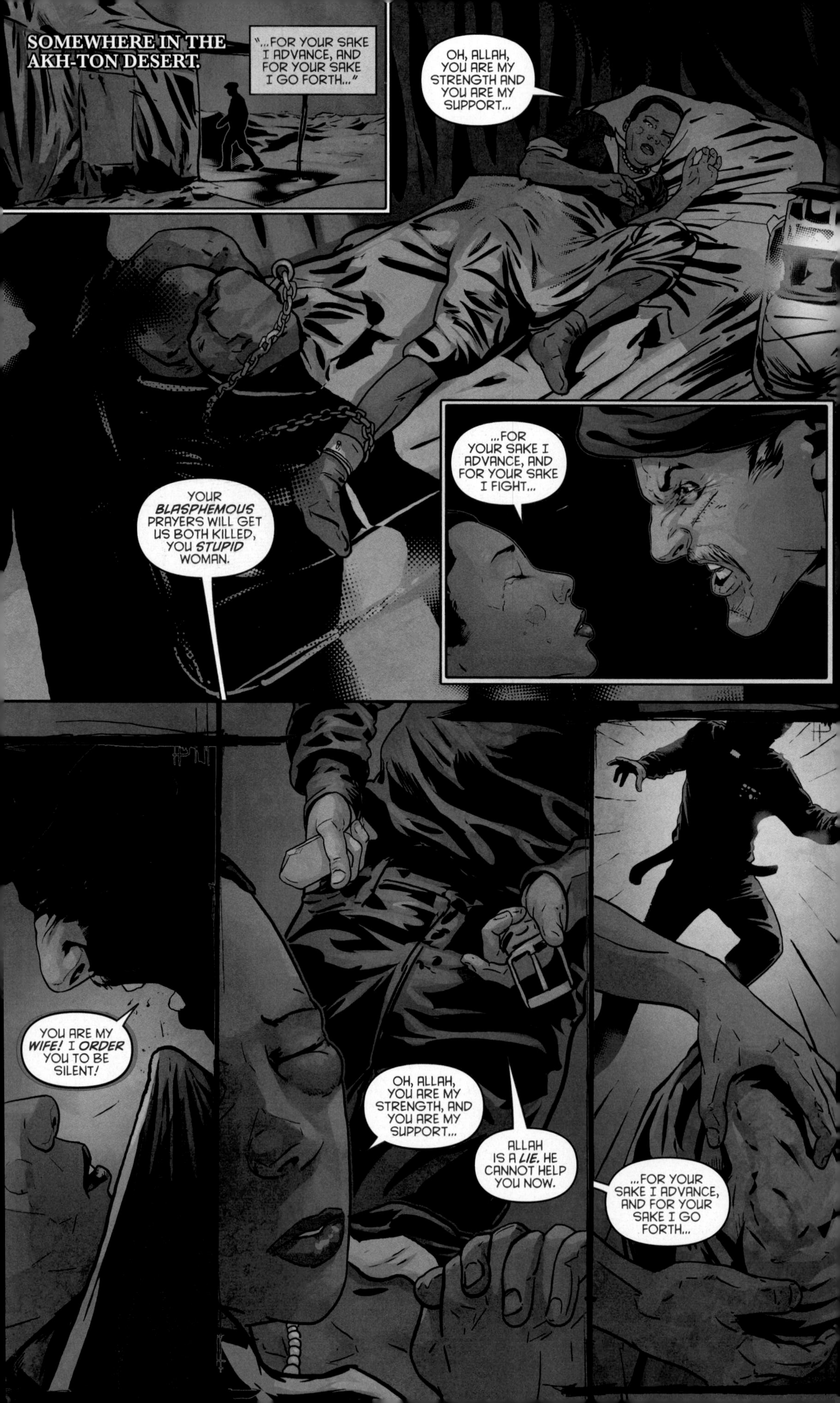

SOMEWHERE IN THE AKH-TON DESERT.
"...FOR YOUR SAKE I ADVANCE, AND FOR YOUR SAKE I GO FORTH..."
OH, ALLAH, YOU ARE MY STRENGTH AND YOU ARE MY SUPPORT...
YOUR *BLASPHEMOUS* PRAYERS WILL GET US BOTH KILLED, YOU *STUPID* WOMAN.
...FOR YOUR SAKE I ADVANCE, AND FOR YOUR SAKE I FIGHT...
YOU ARE MY *WIFE!* I *ORDER* YOU TO BE SILENT!
OH, ALLAH, YOU ARE MY STRENGTH, AND YOU ARE MY SUPPORT...
ALLAH IS A *LIE.* HE CANNOT HELP YOU NOW.
...FOR YOUR SAKE I ADVANCE, AND FOR YOUR SAKE I GO FORTH...

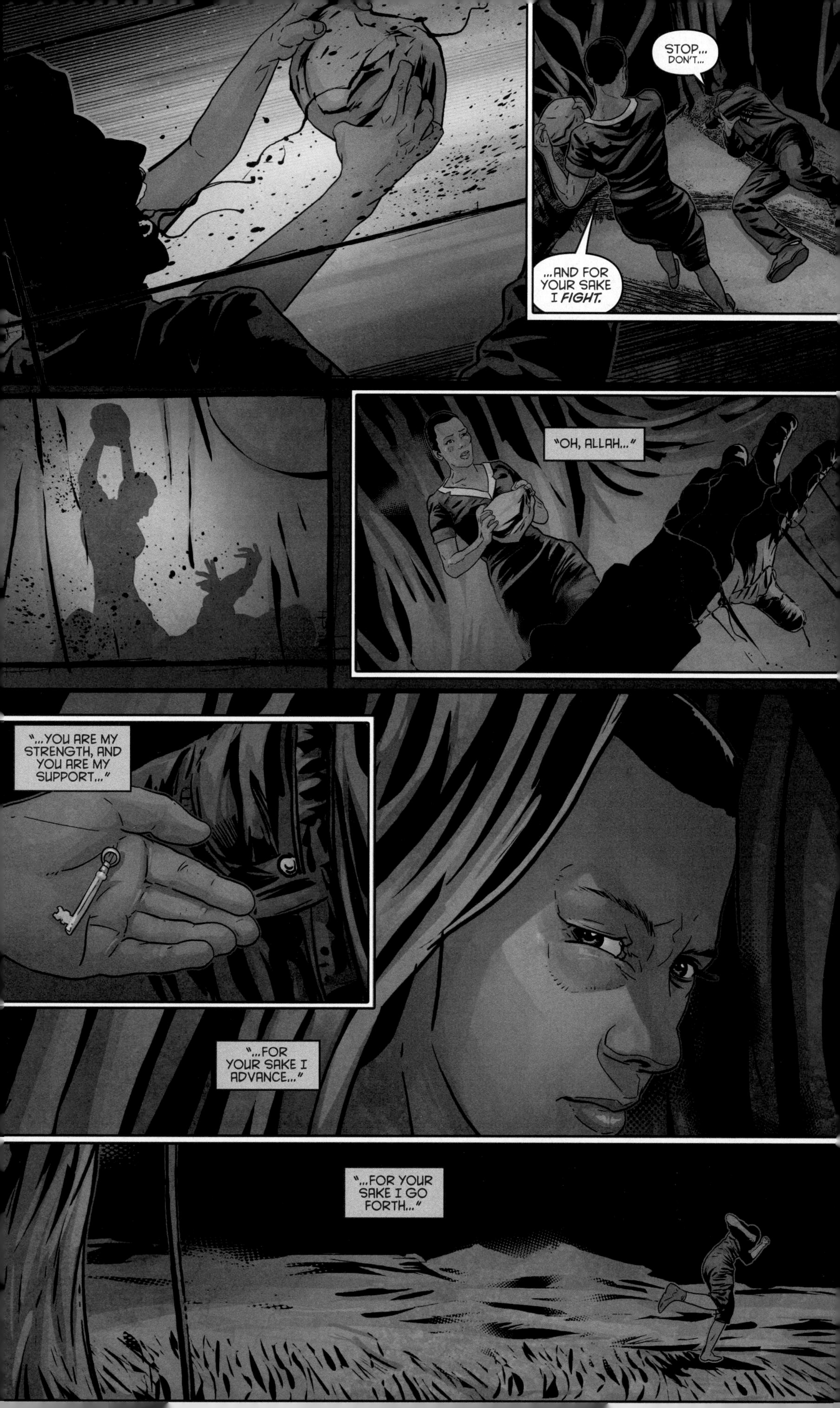
STOP... DON'T...
...AND FOR YOUR SAKE I FIGHT.
"OH, ALLAH..."
"...YOU ARE MY STRENGTH, AND YOU ARE MY SUPPORT..."
"...FOR YOUR SAKE I ADVANCE..."
"...FOR YOUR SAKE I GO FORTH..."

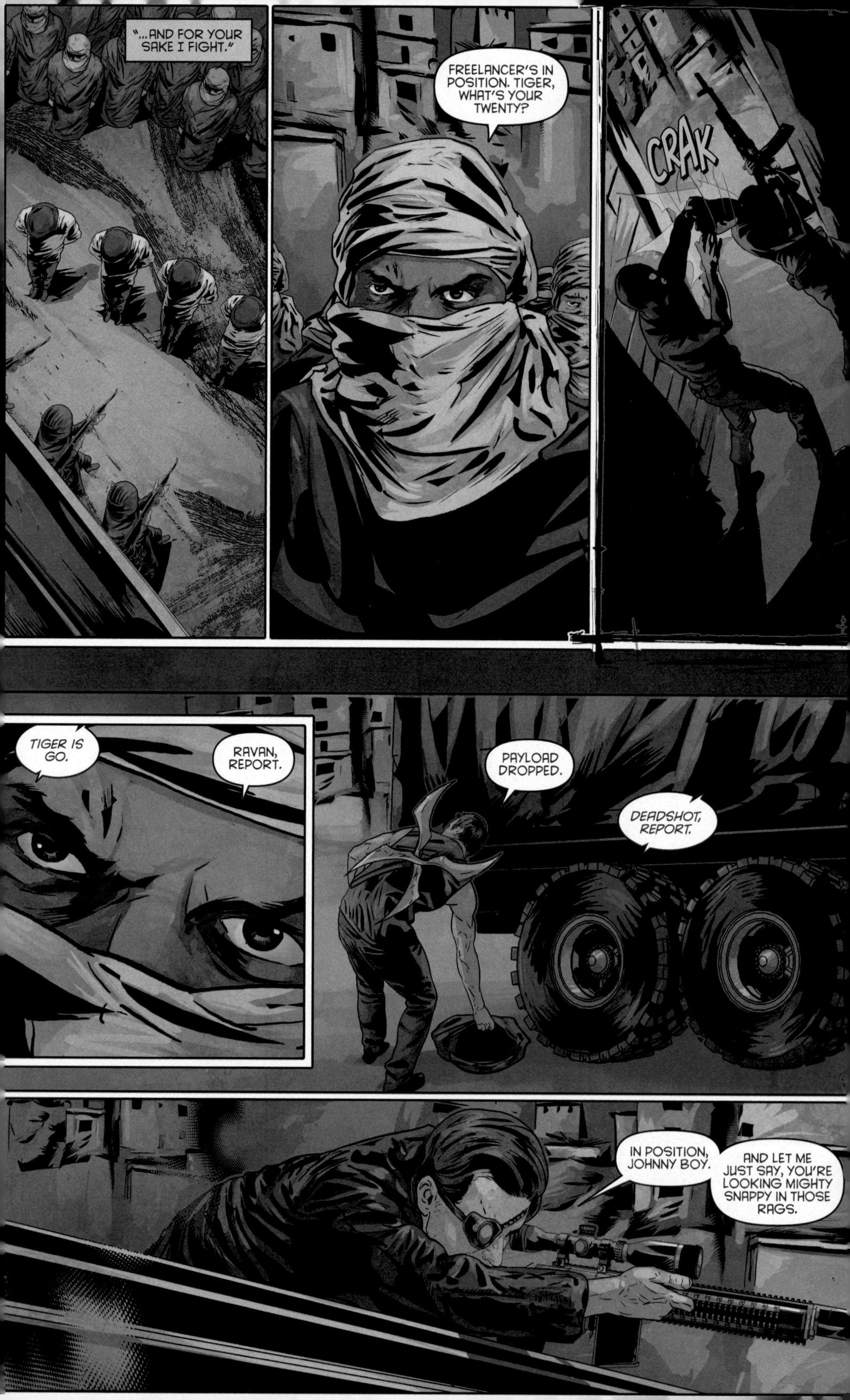
"...AND FOR YOUR SAKE I FIGHT."
FREELANCER'S IN POSITION. TIGER, WHAT'S YOUR TWENTY?
CRAK
TIGER IS GO.
RAVAN, REPORT.
PAYLOAD DROPPED.
DEADSHOT, REPORT.
IN POSITION, JOHNNY BOY.
AND LET ME JUST SAY, YOU'RE LOOKING MIGHTY SNAPPY IN THOSE RAGS.

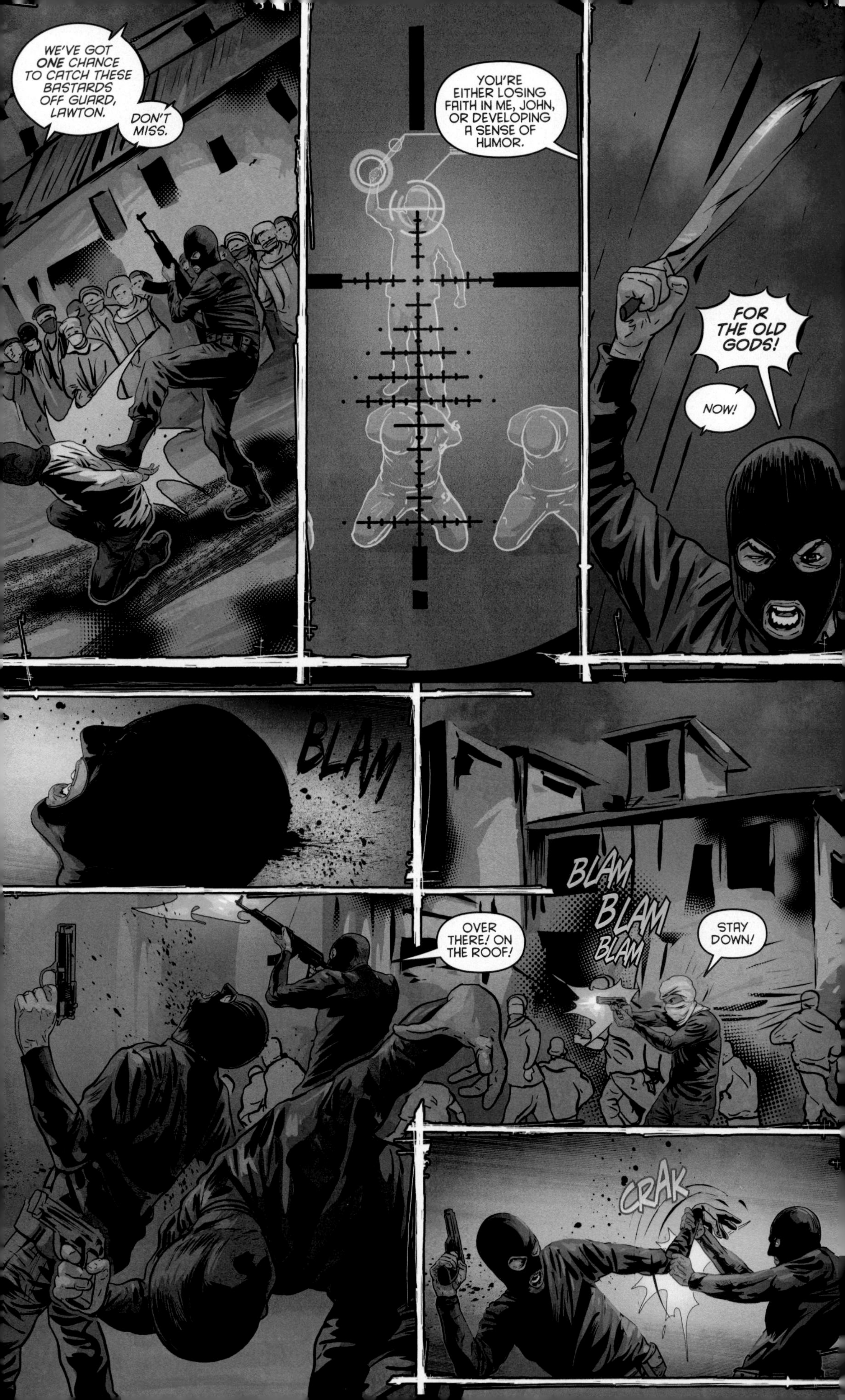
WE'VE GOT ONE CHANCE TO CATCH THESE BASTARDS OFF GUARD, LAWTON.
DON'T MISS.
YOU'RE EITHER LOSING FAITH IN ME, JOHN, OR DEVELOPING A SENSE OF HUMOR.
FOR THE OLD GODS!
NOW!
BLAM
BLAM
BLAM
BLAM
OVER THERE! ON THE ROOF!
STAY DOWN!
CRAK

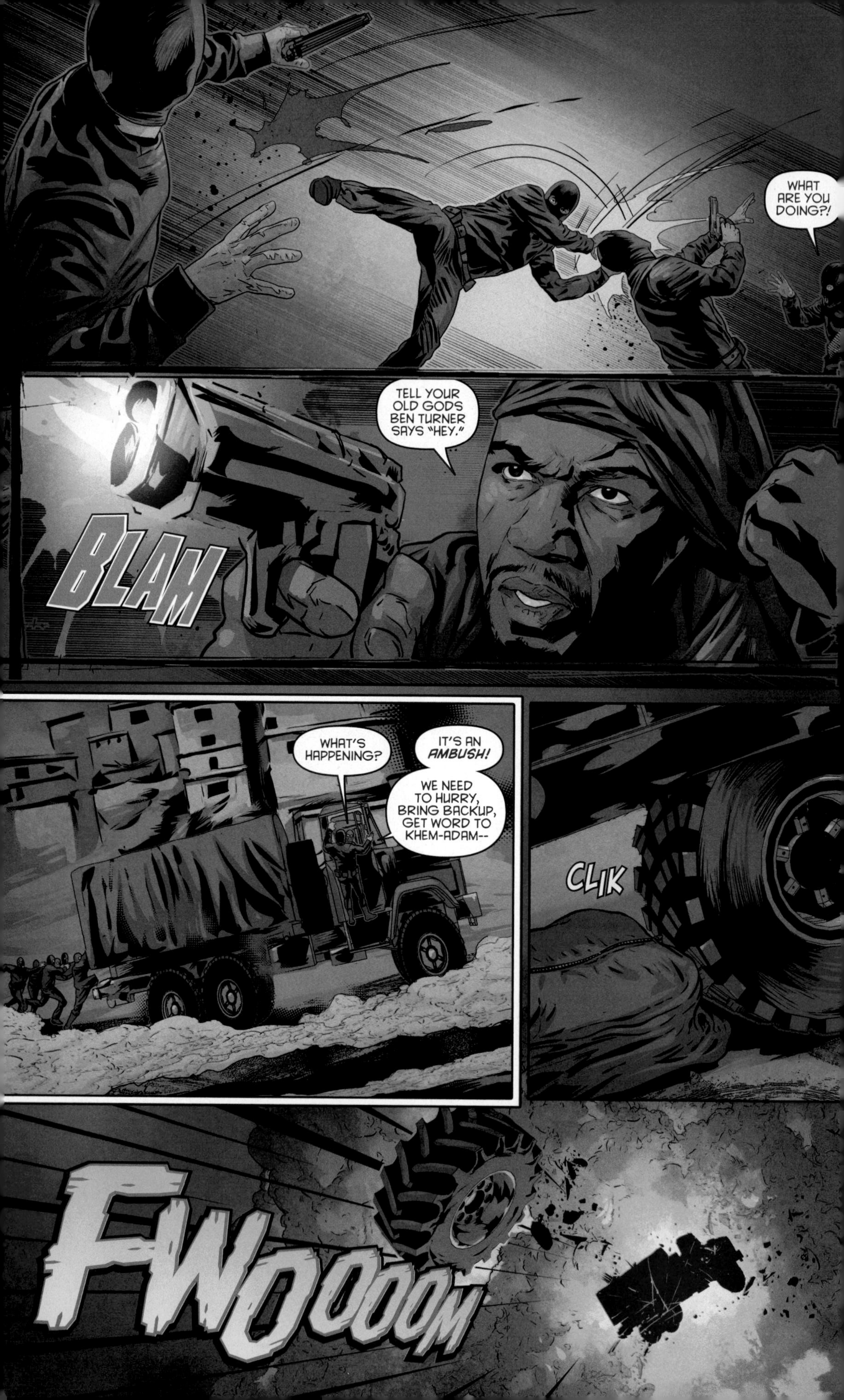
WHAT ARE YOU DOING?!
TELL YOUR OLD GODS BEN TURNER SAYS "HEY."
BLAM
WHAT'S HAPPENING?
IT'S AN *AMBUSH!*
WE NEED TO HURRY, BRING BACKUP, GET WORD TO KHEM-ADAM--
CLIK
FWOOOOM

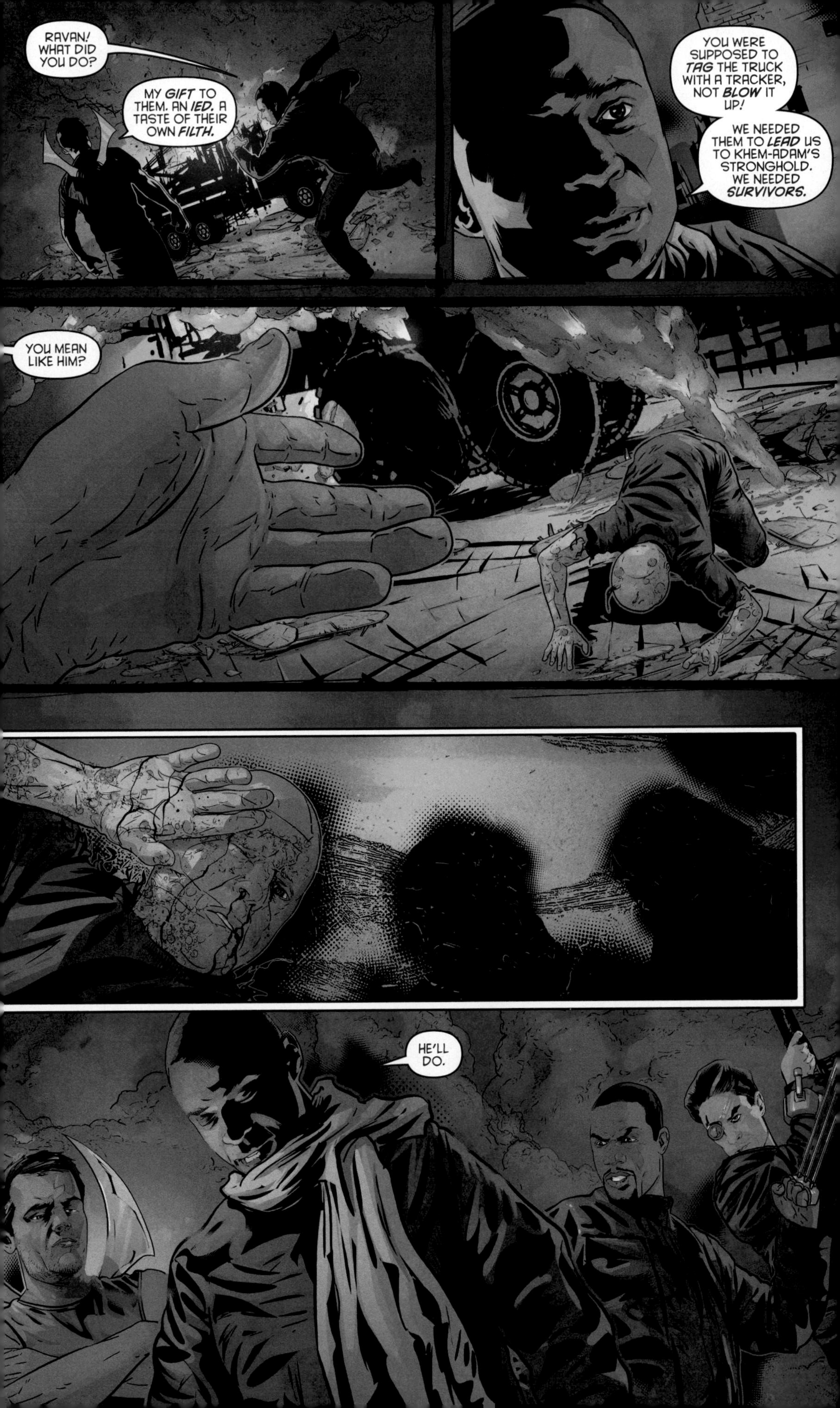
RAVAN! WHAT DID YOU DO?
MY GIFT TO THEM. AN IED. A TASTE OF THEIR OWN FILTH.
YOU WERE SUPPOSED TO TAG THE TRUCK WITH A TRACKER, NOT BLOW IT UP!
WE NEEDED THEM TO LEAD US TO KHEM-ADAM'S STRONGHOLD. WE NEEDED SURVIVORS.
YOU MEAN LIKE HIM?
HE'LL DO.

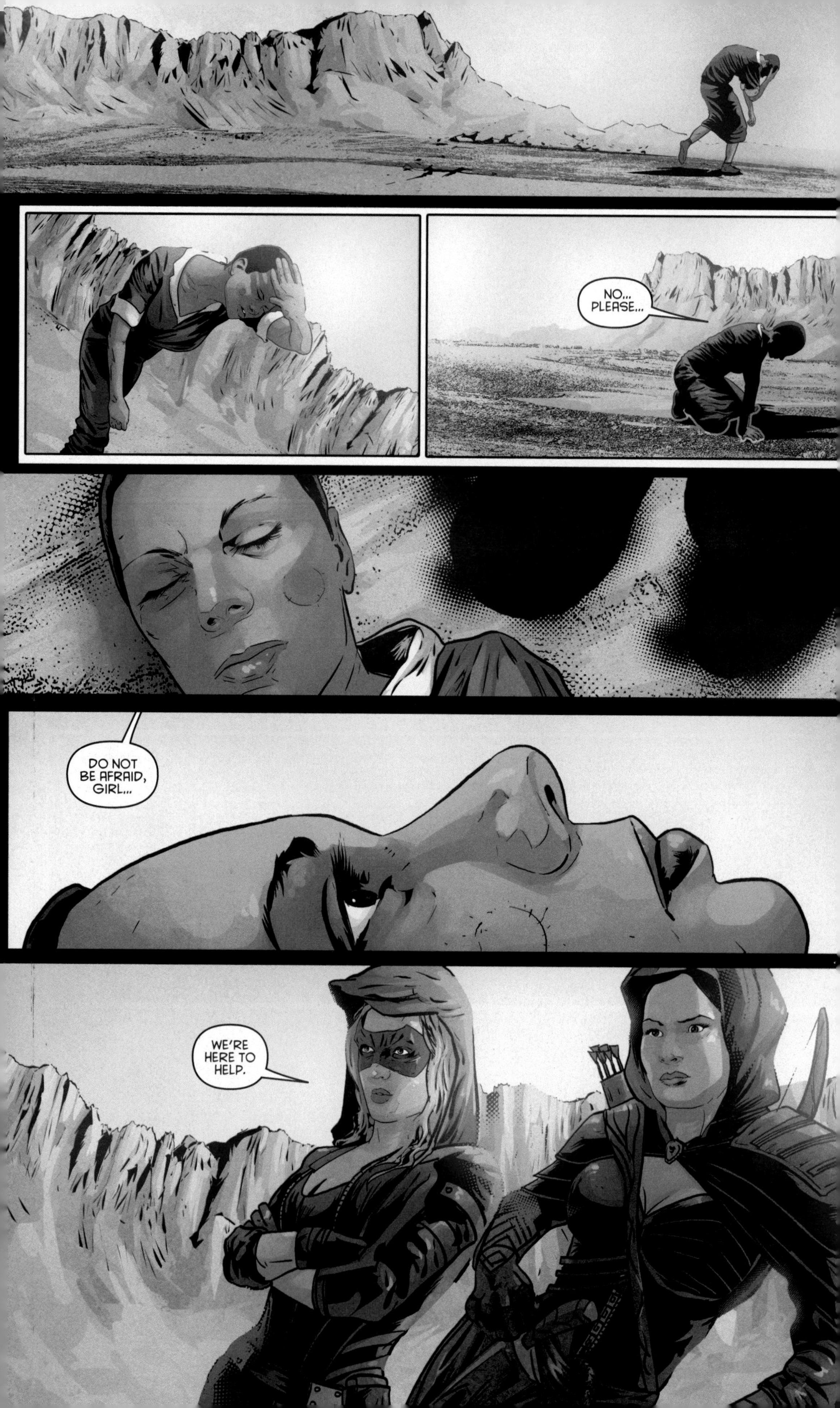
NO... PLEASE...
DO NOT BE AFRAID, GIRL...
WE'RE HERE TO HELP.

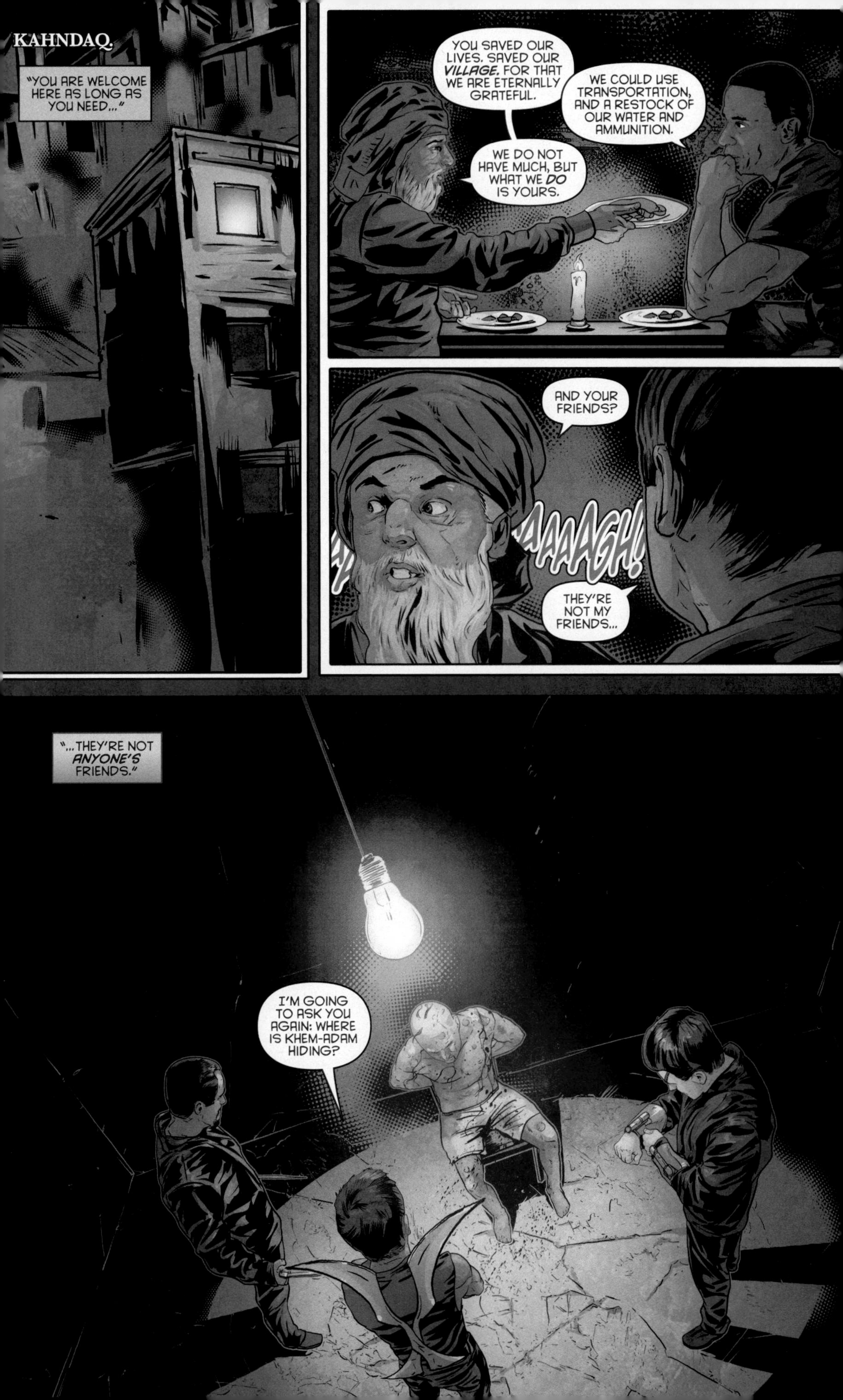
KAHNDAQ.
"YOU ARE WELCOME HERE AS LONG AS YOU NEED..."
YOU SAVED OUR LIVES. SAVED OUR VILLAGE. FOR THAT WE ARE ETERNALLY GRATEFUL.
WE DO NOT HAVE MUCH, BUT WHAT WE DO IS YOURS.
WE COULD USE TRANSPORTATION, AND A RESTOCK OF OUR WATER AND AMMUNITION.
AND YOUR FRIENDS?
AAAAGH!
THEY'RE NOT MY FRIENDS...
"...THEY'RE NOT ANYONE'S FRIENDS."
I'M GOING TO ASK YOU AGAIN: WHERE IS KHEM-ADAM HIDING?

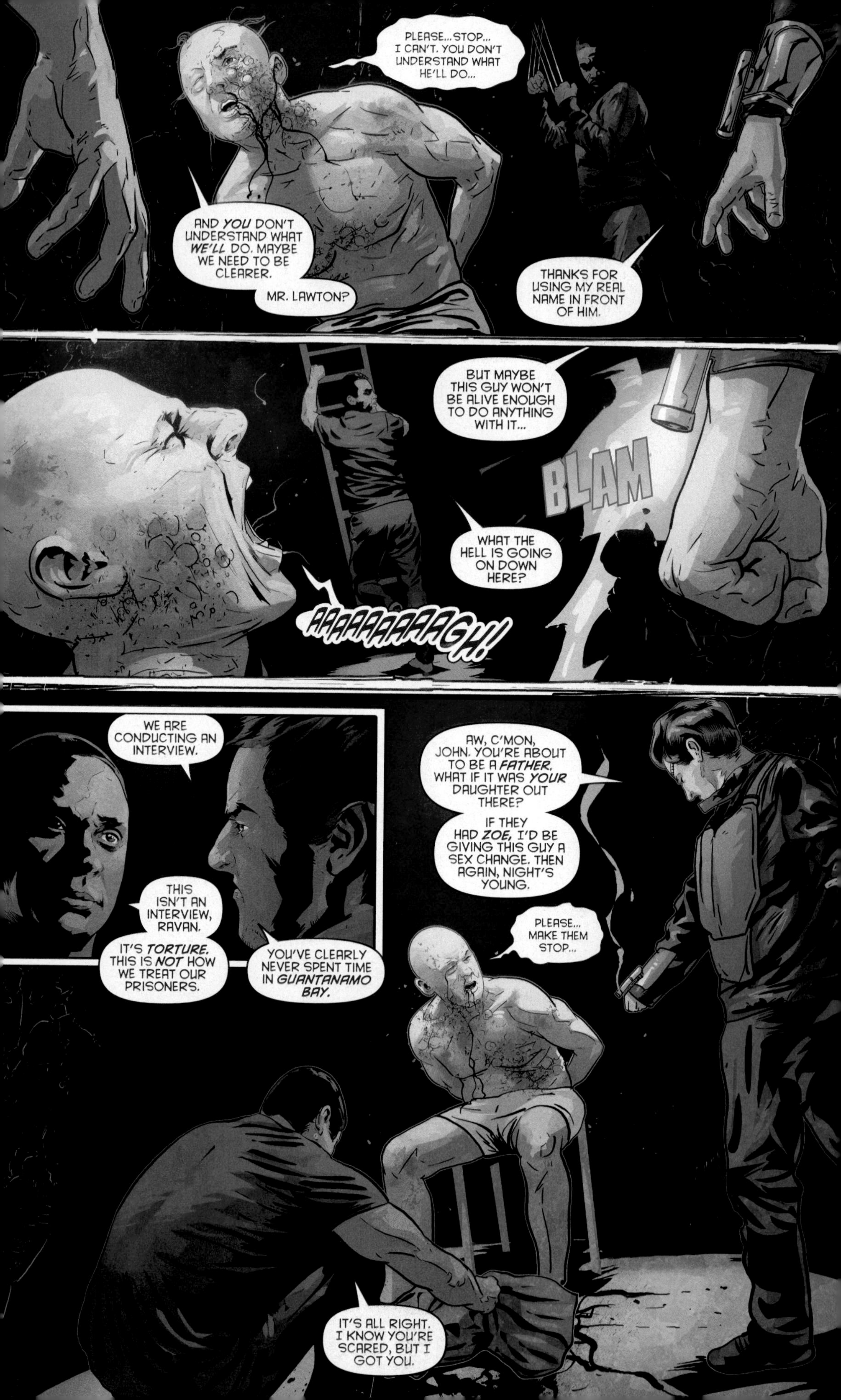
PLEASE... STOP... I CAN'T. YOU DON'T UNDERSTAND WHAT HE'LL DO...
AND YOU DON'T UNDERSTAND WHAT WE'LL DO. MAYBE WE NEED TO BE CLEARER.
MR. LAWTON?
THANKS FOR USING MY REAL NAME IN FRONT OF HIM.
BUT MAYBE THIS GUY WON'T BE ALIVE ENOUGH TO DO ANYTHING WITH IT...
BLAM
WHAT THE HELL IS GOING ON DOWN HERE?
AAAAAAAAAAGH!
WE ARE CONDUCTING AN INTERVIEW.
THIS ISN'T AN INTERVIEW, RAVAN.
IT'S TORTURE. THIS IS NOT HOW WE TREAT OUR PRISONERS.
YOU'VE CLEARLY NEVER SPENT TIME IN GUANTANAMO BAY.
AW, C'MON, JOHN. YOU'RE ABOUT TO BE A FATHER. WHAT IF IT WAS YOUR DAUGHTER OUT THERE?
IF THEY HAD ZOE, I'D BE GIVING THIS GUY A SEX CHANGE. THEN AGAIN, NIGHT'S YOUNG.
PLEASE... MAKE THEM STOP...
IT'S ALL RIGHT. I KNOW YOU'RE SCARED, BUT I GOT YOU.

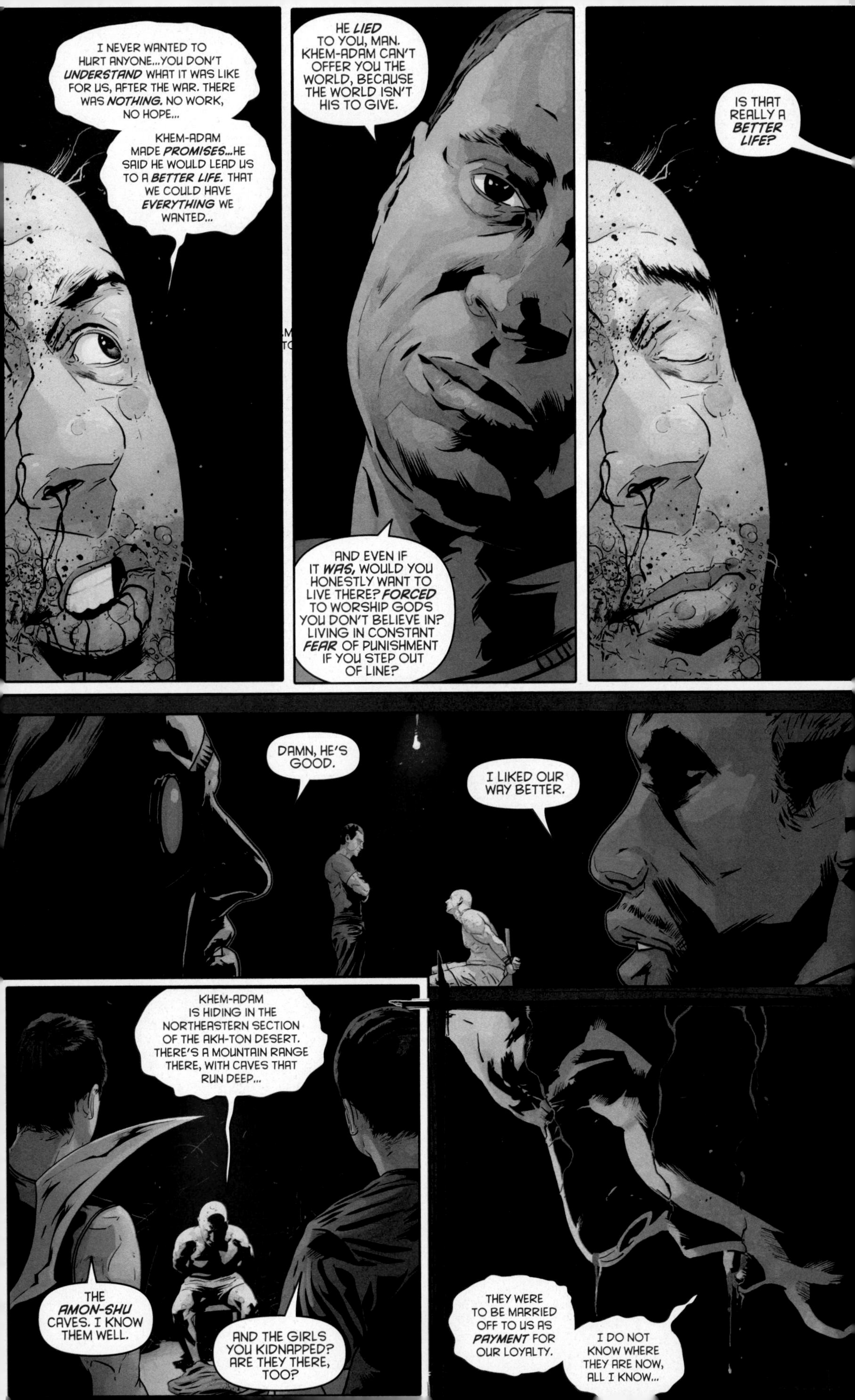
I NEVER WANTED TO HURT ANYONE...YOU DON'T UNDERSTAND WHAT IT WAS LIKE FOR US, AFTER THE WAR. THERE WAS NOTHING. NO WORK, NO HOPE...
KHEM-ADAM MADE PROMISES...HE SAID HE WOULD LEAD US TO A BETTER LIFE. THAT WE COULD HAVE EVERYTHING WE WANTED...
HE LIED TO YOU, MAN. KHEM-ADAM CAN'T OFFER YOU THE WORLD, BECAUSE THE WORLD ISN'T HIS TO GIVE.
AND EVEN IF IT WAS, WOULD YOU HONESTLY WANT TO LIVE THERE? FORCED TO WORSHIP GODS YOU DON'T BELIEVE IN? LIVING IN CONSTANT FEAR OF PUNISHMENT IF YOU STEP OUT OF LINE?
IS THAT REALLY A BETTER LIFE?
DAMN, HE'S GOOD.
I LIKED OUR WAY BETTER.
KHEM-ADAM IS HIDING IN THE NORTHEASTERN SECTION OF THE AKH-TON DESERT. THERE'S A MOUNTAIN RANGE THERE, WITH CAVES THAT RUN DEEP...
THE AMON-SHU CAVES. I KNOW THEM WELL.
AND THE GIRLS YOU KIDNAPPED? ARE THEY THERE, TOO?
THEY WERE TO BE MARRIED OFF TO US AS PAYMENT FOR OUR LOYALTY.
I DO NOT KNOW WHERE THEY ARE NOW, ALL I KNOW...

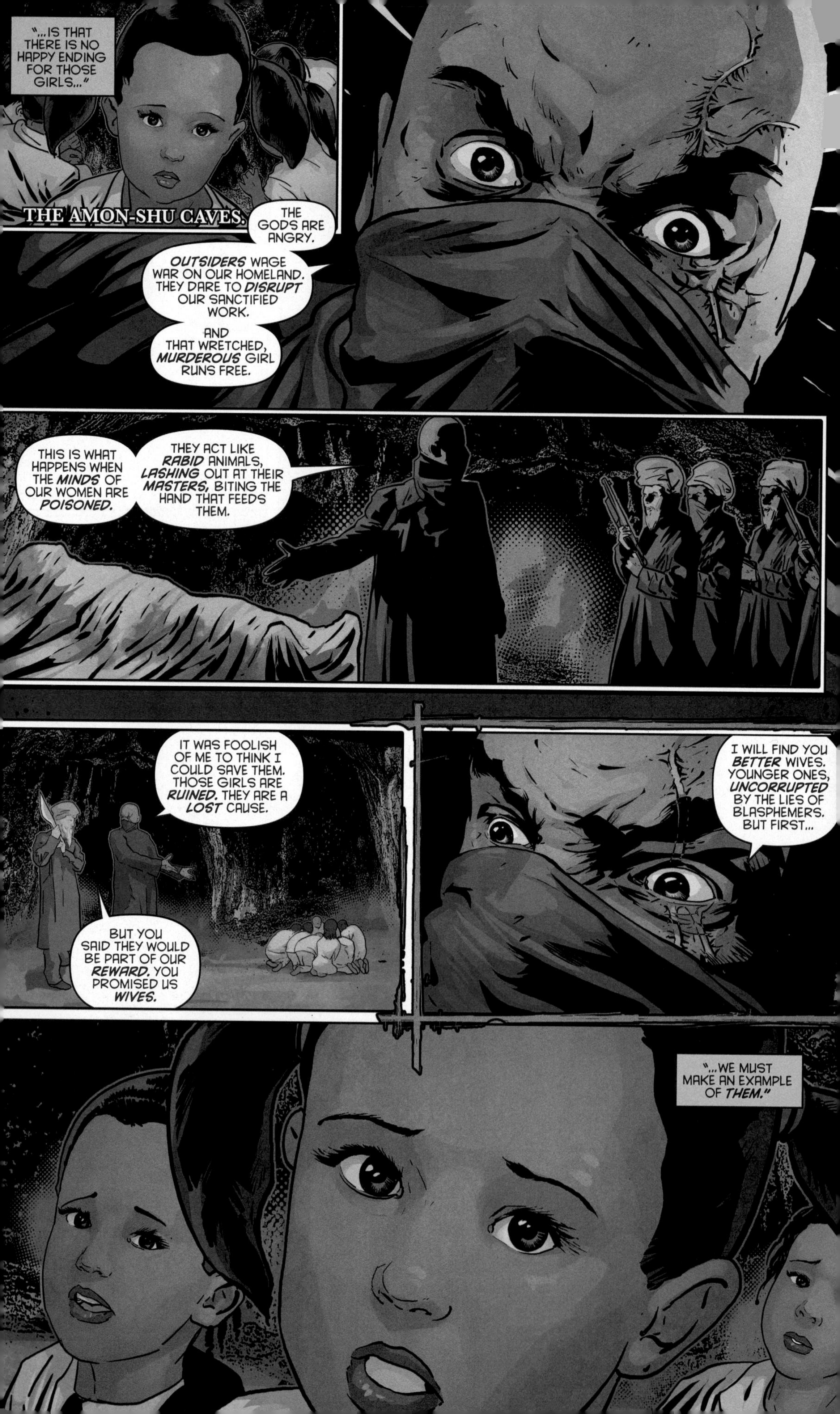
"...IS THAT THERE IS NO HAPPY ENDING FOR THOSE GIRLS..."
THE AMON-SHU CAVES.
THE GOD'S ARE ANGRY.
OUTSIDERS WAGE WAR ON OUR HOMELAND. THEY DARE TO DISRUPT OUR SANCTIFIED WORK.
AND THAT WRETCHED, MURDEROUS GIRL RUNS FREE.
THIS IS WHAT HAPPENS WHEN THE MINDS OF OUR WOMEN ARE POISONED.
THEY ACT LIKE RABID ANIMALS, LASHING OUT AT THEIR MASTERS, BITING THE HAND THAT FEEDS THEM.
IT WAS FOOLISH OF ME TO THINK I COULD SAVE THEM. THOSE GIRLS ARE RUINED. THEY ARE A LOST CAUSE.
BUT YOU SAID THEY WOULD BE PART OF OUR REWARD. YOU PROMISED US WIVES.
I WILL FIND YOU BETTER WIVES. YOUNGER ONES, UNCORRUPTED BY THE LIES OF BLASPHEMERS. BUT FIRST...
"...WE MUST MAKE AN EXAMPLE OF THEM."

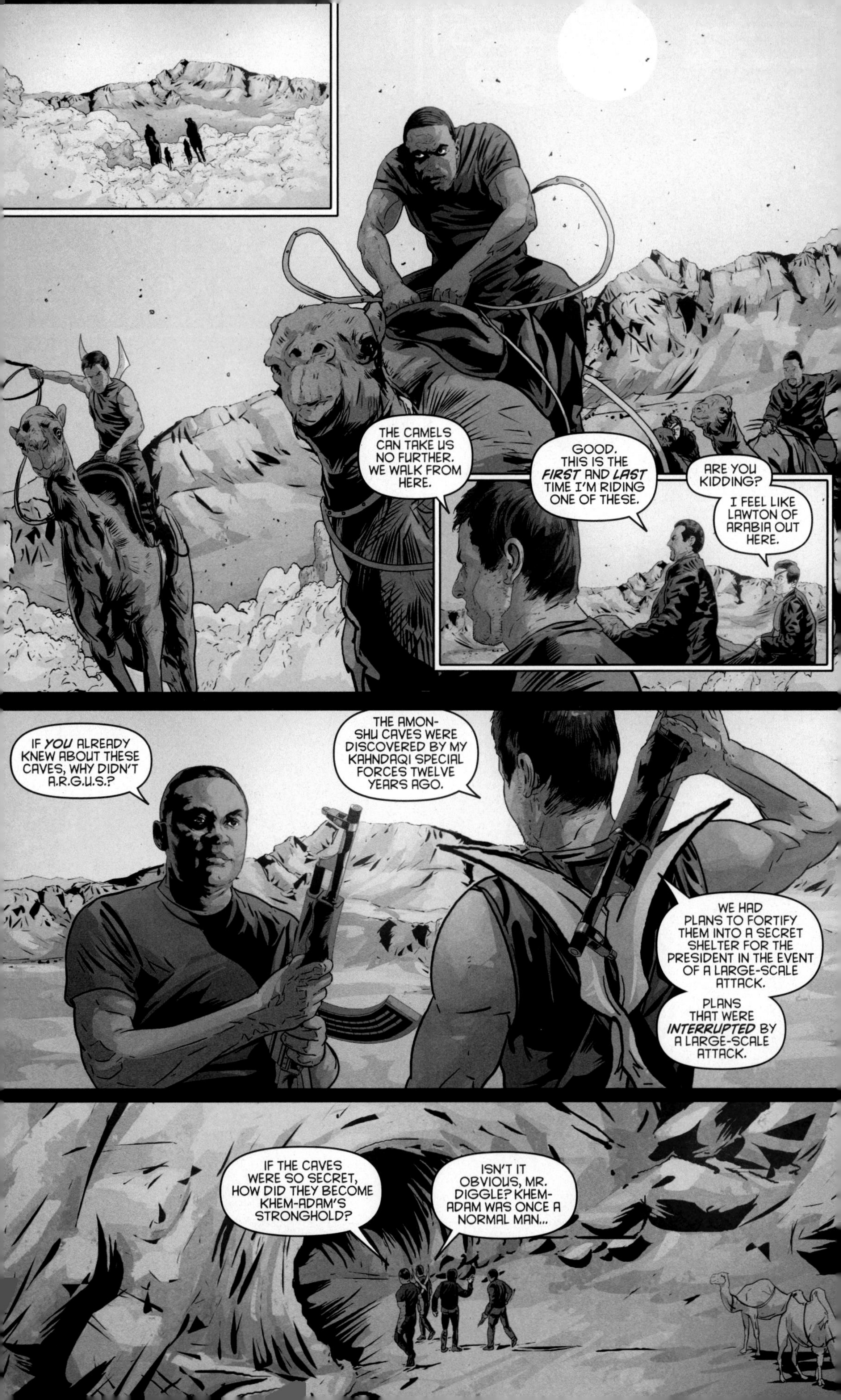
THE CAMELS CAN TAKE US NO FURTHER. WE WALK FROM HERE.
GOOD. THIS IS THE *FIRST* AND *LAST* TIME I'M RIDING ONE OF THESE.
ARE YOU KIDDING?
I FEEL LIKE LAWTON OF ARABIA OUT HERE.
IF *YOU* ALREADY KNEW ABOUT THESE CAVES, WHY DIDN'T A.R.G.U.S.?
THE AMON-SHU CAVES WERE DISCOVERED BY MY KAHNDAQI SPECIAL FORCES TWELVE YEARS AGO.
WE HAD PLANS TO FORTIFY THEM INTO A SECRET SHELTER FOR THE PRESIDENT IN THE EVENT OF A LARGE-SCALE ATTACK.
PLANS THAT WERE *INTERRUPTED* BY A LARGE-SCALE ATTACK.
IF THE CAVES WERE SO SECRET, HOW DID THEY BECOME KHEM-ADAM'S STRONGHOLD?
ISN'T IT OBVIOUS, MR. DIGGLE? KHEM-ADAM WAS ONCE A NORMAL MAN...

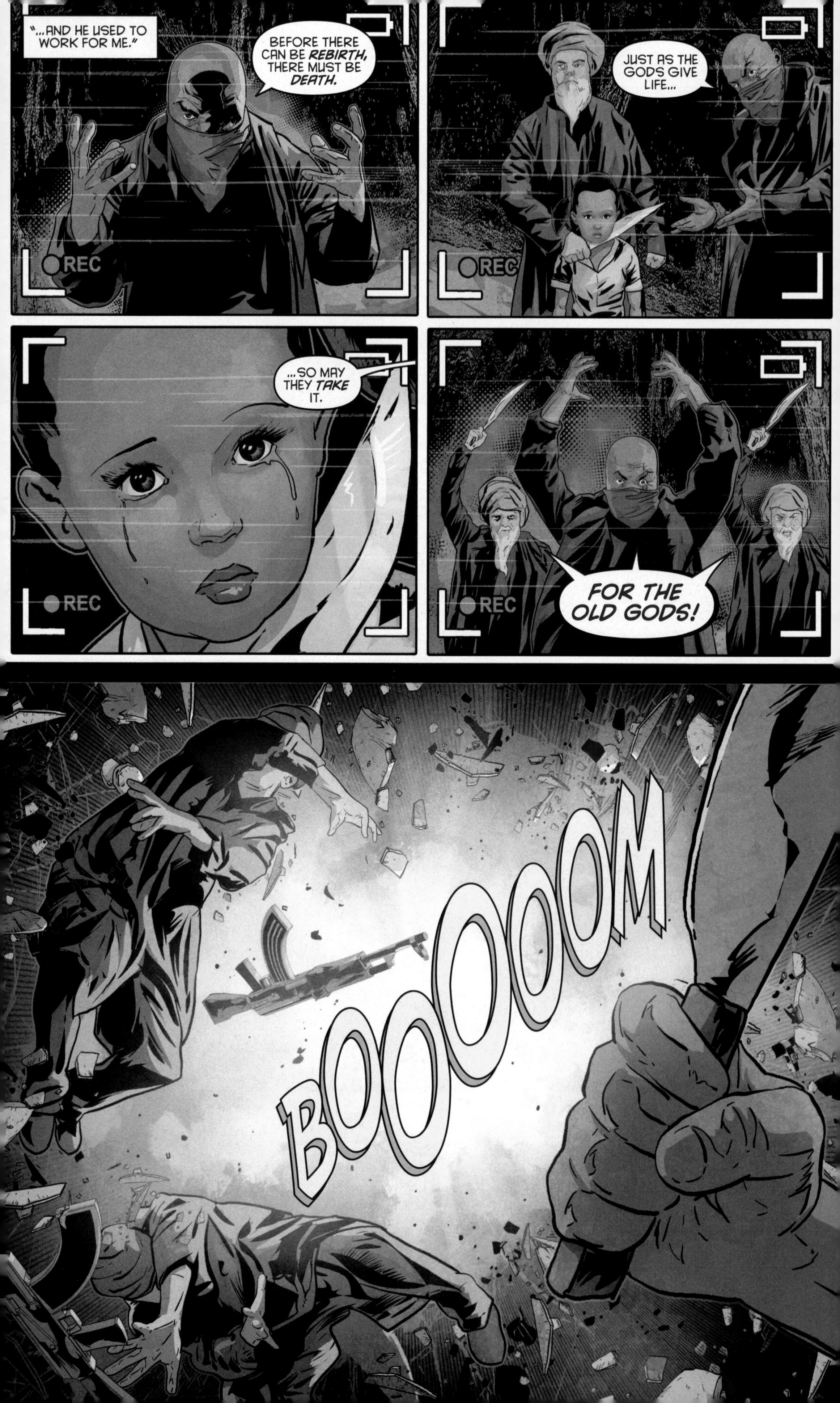
"...AND HE USED TO WORK FOR ME."
BEFORE THERE CAN BE *REBIRTH,* THERE MUST BE *DEATH.*
REC
JUST AS THE GODS GIVE LIFE...
REC
...SO MAY THEY *TAKE* IT.
REC
FOR THE OLD GODS!
REC
BOOOOOOM

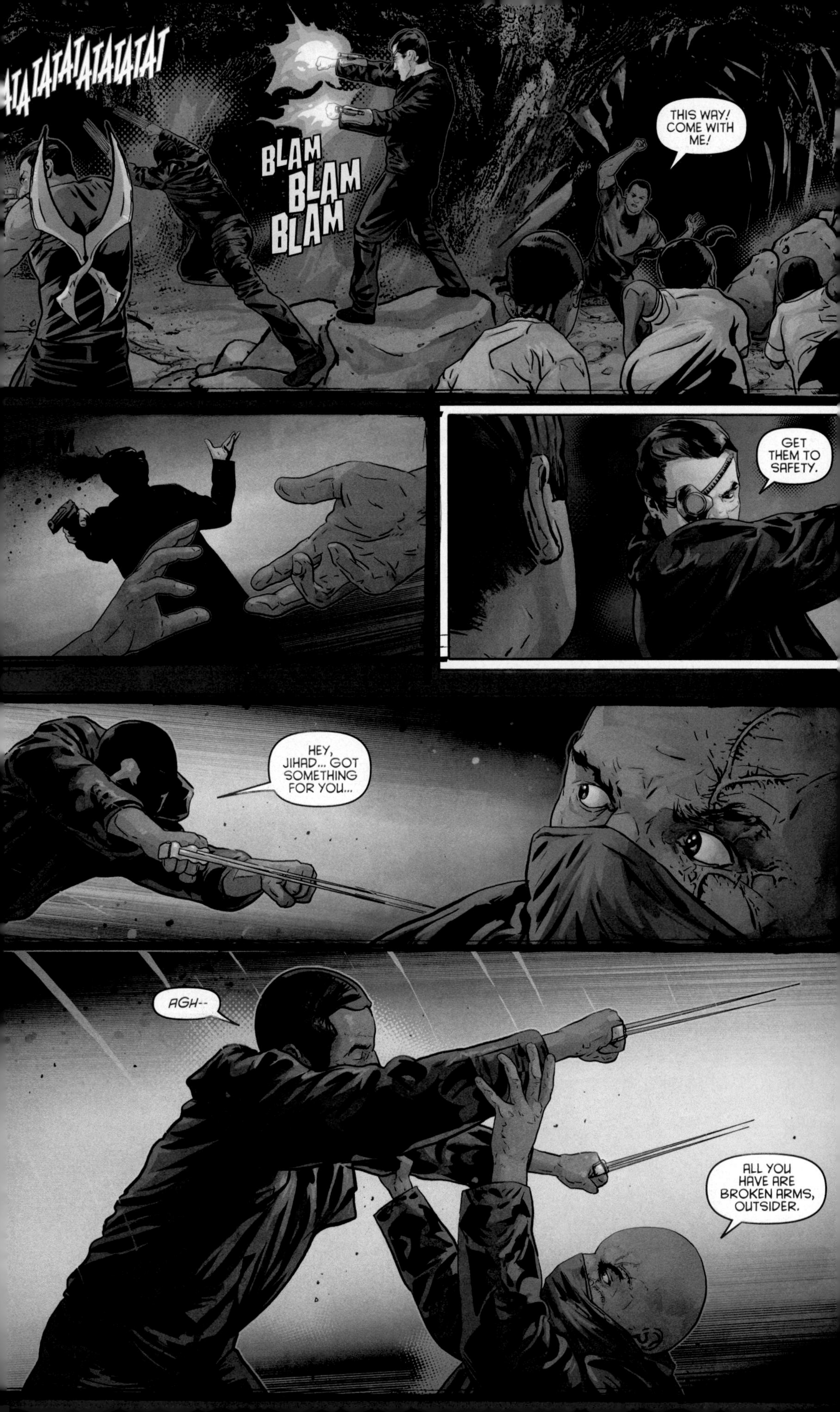
TATATATATATATAT
BLAM BLAM BLAM
THIS WAY! COME WITH ME!
GET THEM TO SAFETY.
HEY, JIHAD... GOT SOMETHING FOR YOU...
AGH--
ALL YOU HAVE ARE BROKEN ARMS, OUTSIDER.

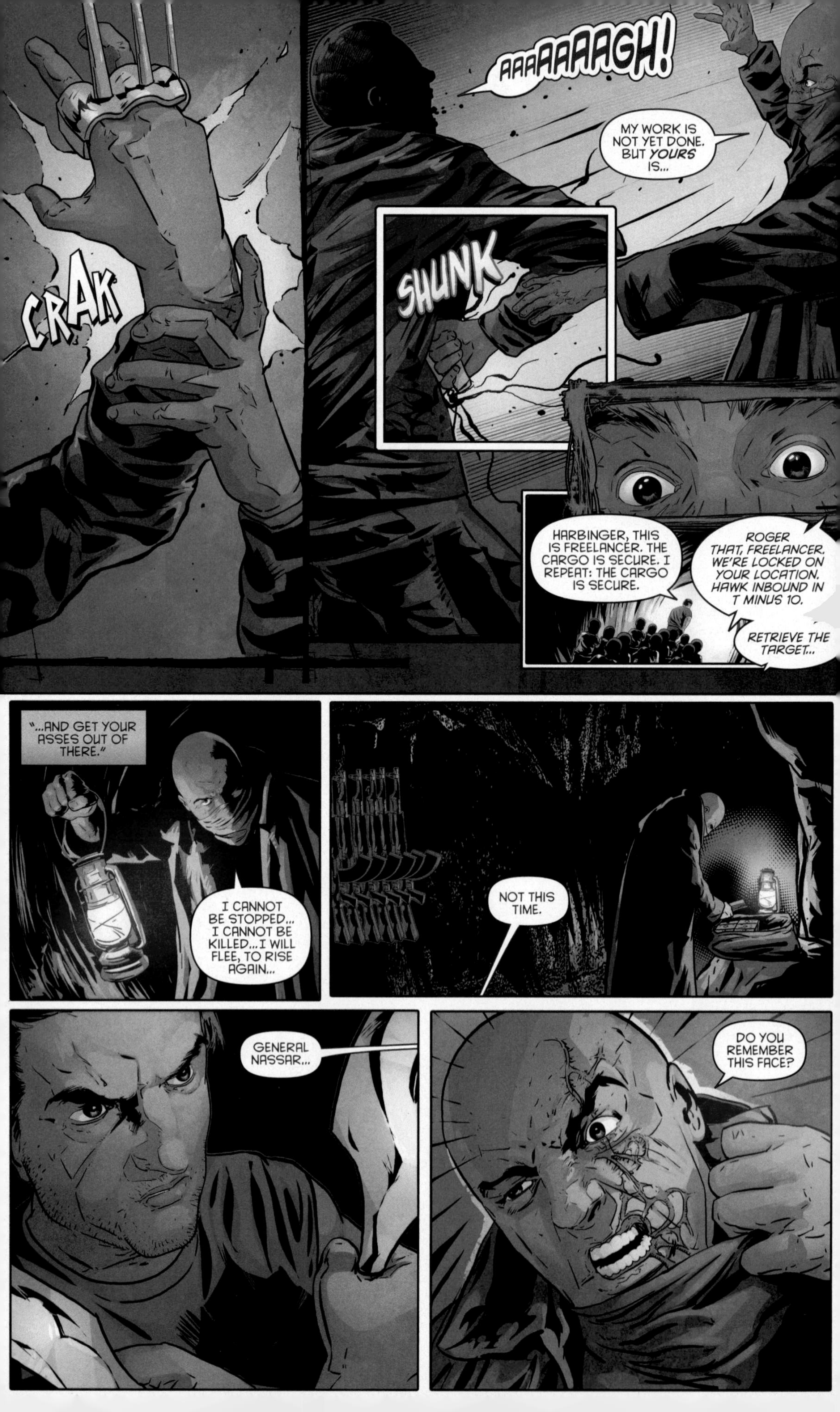
CRAK
AAAAAAAAGH!
MY WORK IS NOT YET DONE. BUT YOURS IS...
SHUNK
HARBINGER, THIS IS FREELANCER. THE CARGO IS SECURE. I REPEAT: THE CARGO IS SECURE.
ROGER THAT, FREELANCER. WE'RE LOCKED ON YOUR LOCATION. HAWK INBOUND IN T MINUS 10.
RETRIEVE THE TARGET...
"...AND GET YOUR ASSES OUT OF THERE."
I CANNOT BE STOPPED... I CANNOT BE KILLED... I WILL FLEE, TO RISE AGAIN...
NOT THIS TIME.
GENERAL NASSAR...
DO YOU REMEMBER THIS FACE?

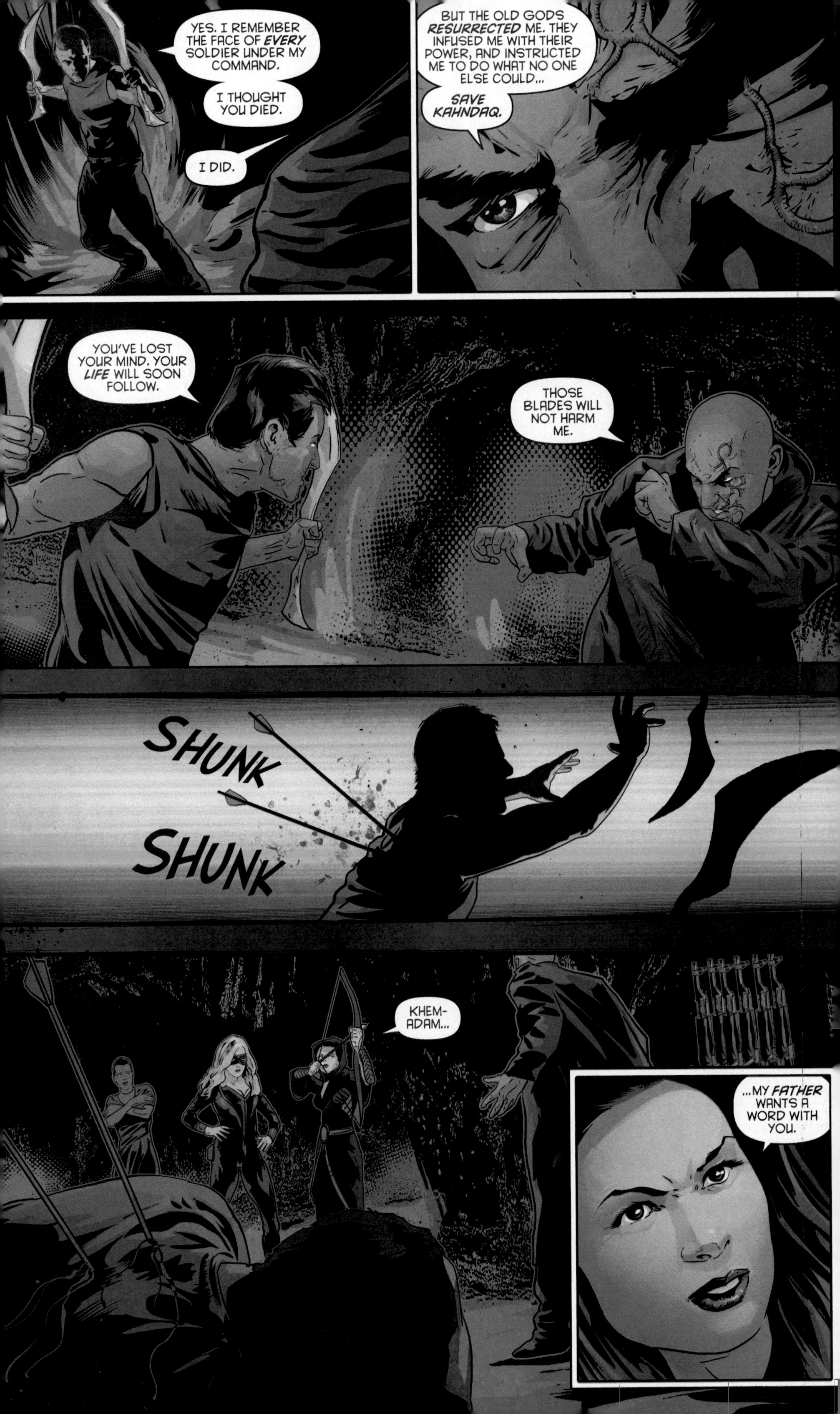
YES. I REMEMBER THE FACE OF *EVERY* SOLDIER UNDER MY COMMAND.
I THOUGHT YOU DIED.
I DID.
BUT THE OLD GODS *RESURRECTED* ME. THEY INFUSED ME WITH THEIR POWER, AND INSTRUCTED ME TO DO WHAT NO ONE ELSE COULD...
SAVE KAHNDAQ.
YOU'VE LOST YOUR MIND. YOUR *LIFE* WILL SOON FOLLOW.
THOSE BLADES WILL NOT HARM ME.
SHUNK
SHUNK
KHEM-ADAM...
...MY *FATHER* WANTS A WORD WITH YOU.

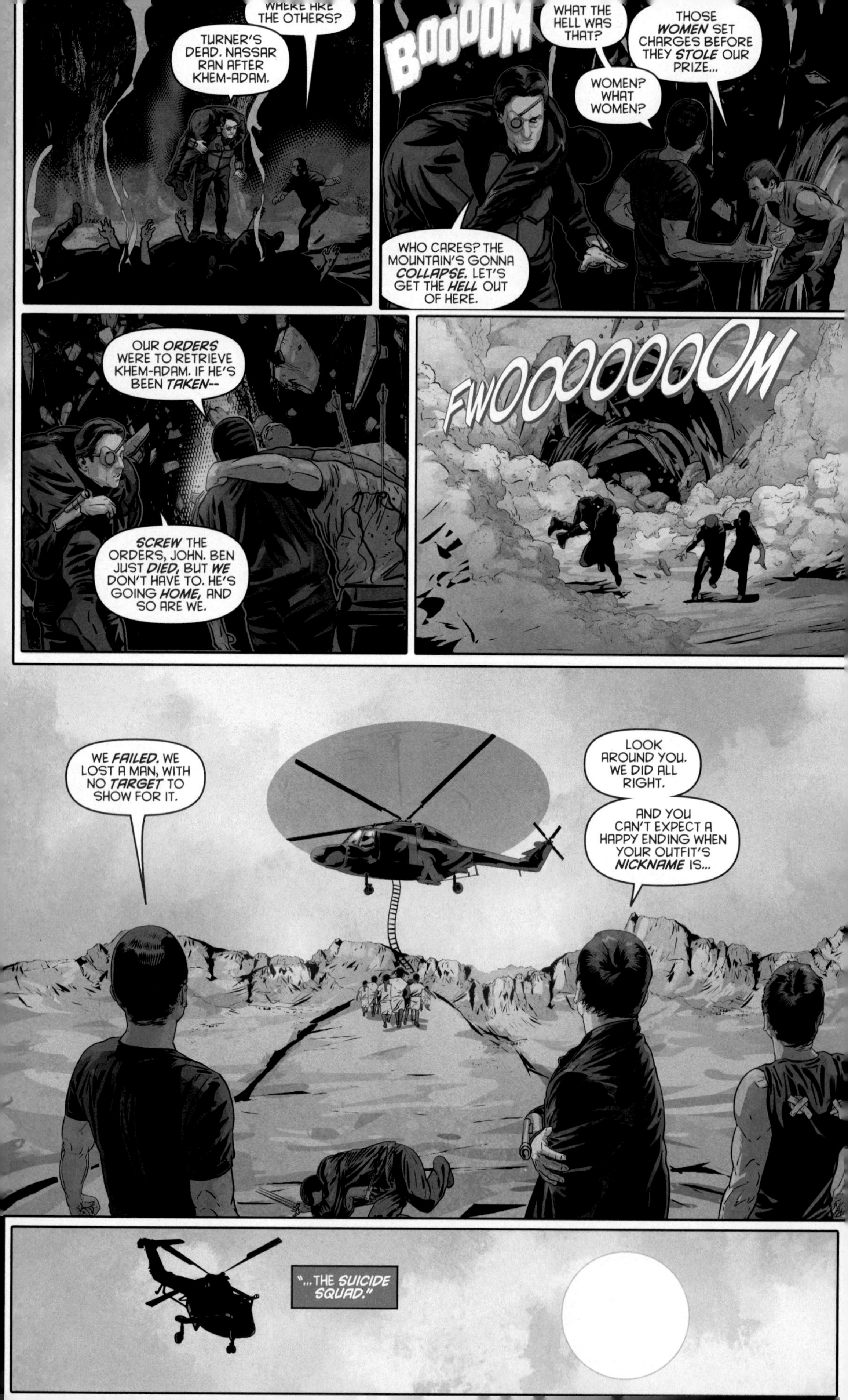
WHERE ARE THE OTHERS?
TURNER'S DEAD. NASSAR RAN AFTER KHEM-ADAM.
BOOOOM
WHAT THE HELL WAS THAT?
THOSE WOMEN SET CHARGES BEFORE THEY STOLE OUR PRIZE...
WOMEN? WHAT WOMEN?
WHO CARES? THE MOUNTAIN'S GONNA COLLAPSE. LET'S GET THE HELL OUT OF HERE.
OUR ORDERS WERE TO RETRIEVE KHEM-ADAM. IF HE'S BEEN TAKEN--
SCREW THE ORDERS, JOHN. BEN JUST DIED, BUT WE DON'T HAVE TO. HE'S GOING HOME, AND SO ARE WE.
FWOOOOOOOOM
WE FAILED. WE LOST A MAN, WITH NO TARGET TO SHOW FOR IT.
LOOK AROUND YOU. WE DID ALL RIGHT.
AND YOU CAN'T EXPECT A HAPPY ENDING WHEN YOUR OUTFIT'S NICKNAME IS...
"...THE SUICIDE SQUAD."

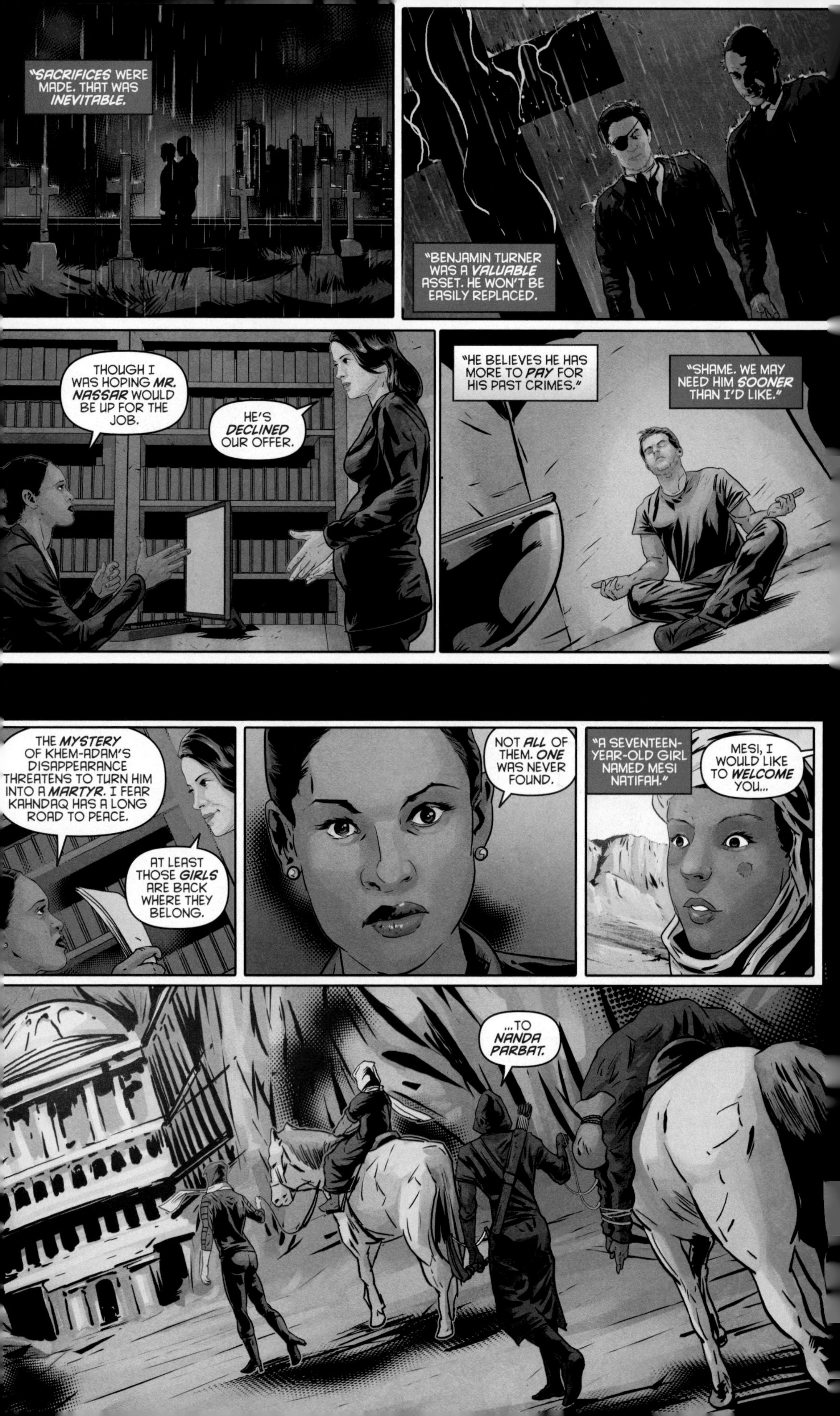
"SACRIFICES WERE MADE. THAT WAS INEVITABLE.
"BENJAMIN TURNER WAS A VALUABLE ASSET. HE WON'T BE EASILY REPLACED.
THOUGH I WAS HOPING MR. NASSAR WOULD BE UP FOR THE JOB.
HE'S DECLINED OUR OFFER.
"HE BELIEVES HE HAS MORE TO PAY FOR HIS PAST CRIMES."
"SHAME. WE MAY NEED HIM SOONER THAN I'D LIKE."
THE MYSTERY OF KHEM-ADAM'S DISAPPEARANCE THREATENS TO TURN HIM INTO A MARTYR. I FEAR KAHNDAQ HAS A LONG ROAD TO PEACE.
AT LEAST THOSE GIRLS ARE BACK WHERE THEY BELONG.
NOT ALL OF THEM. ONE WAS NEVER FOUND.
"A SEVENTEEN-YEAR-OLD GIRL NAMED MESI NATIFAH."
MESI, I WOULD LIKE TO WELCOME YOU...
...TO NANDA PARBAT.

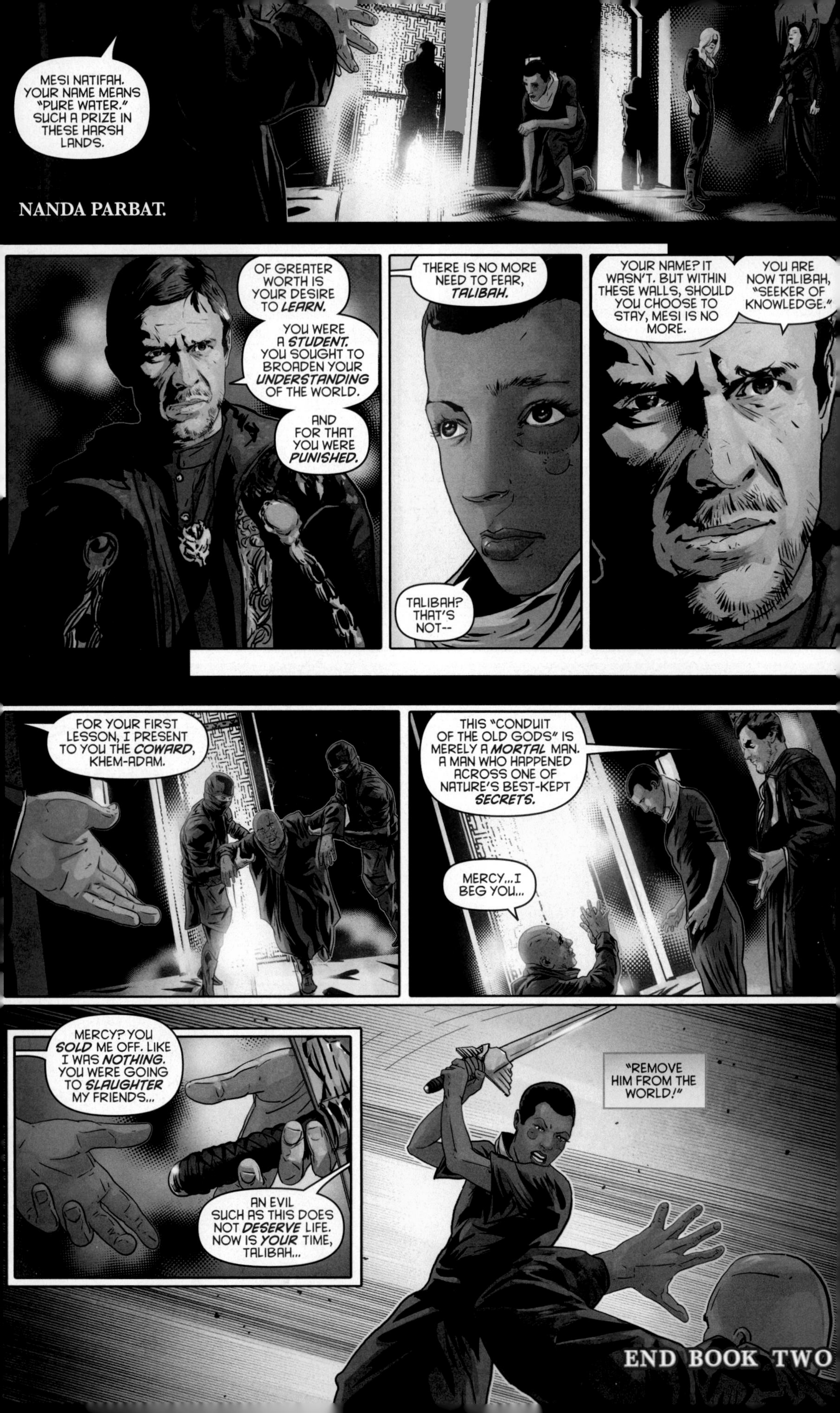
MESI NATIFAH. YOUR NAME MEANS "PURE WATER." SUCH A PRIZE IN THESE HARSH LANDS.
NANDA PARBAT.
OF GREATER WORTH IS YOUR DESIRE TO LEARN.
YOU WERE A STUDENT. YOU SOUGHT TO BROADEN YOUR UNDERSTANDING OF THE WORLD.
AND FOR THAT YOU WERE PUNISHED.
THERE IS NO MORE NEED TO FEAR, TALIBAH.
TALIBAH? THAT'S NOT--
YOUR NAME? IT WASN'T. BUT WITHIN THESE WALLS, SHOULD YOU CHOOSE TO STAY, MESI IS NO MORE.
YOU ARE NOW TALIBAH, "SEEKER OF KNOWLEDGE."
FOR YOUR FIRST LESSON, I PRESENT TO YOU THE COWARD, KHEM-ADAM.
THIS "CONDUIT OF THE OLD GODS" IS MERELY A MORTAL MAN. A MAN WHO HAPPENED ACROSS ONE OF NATURE'S BEST-KEPT SECRETS.
MERCY... I BEG YOU...
MERCY? YOU SOLD ME OFF. LIKE I WAS NOTHING. YOU WERE GOING TO SLAUGHTER MY FRIENDS...
AN EVIL SUCH AS THIS DOES NOT DESERVE LIFE. NOW IS YOUR TIME, TALIBAH...
"REMOVE HIM FROM THE WORLD!"
END BOOK TWO

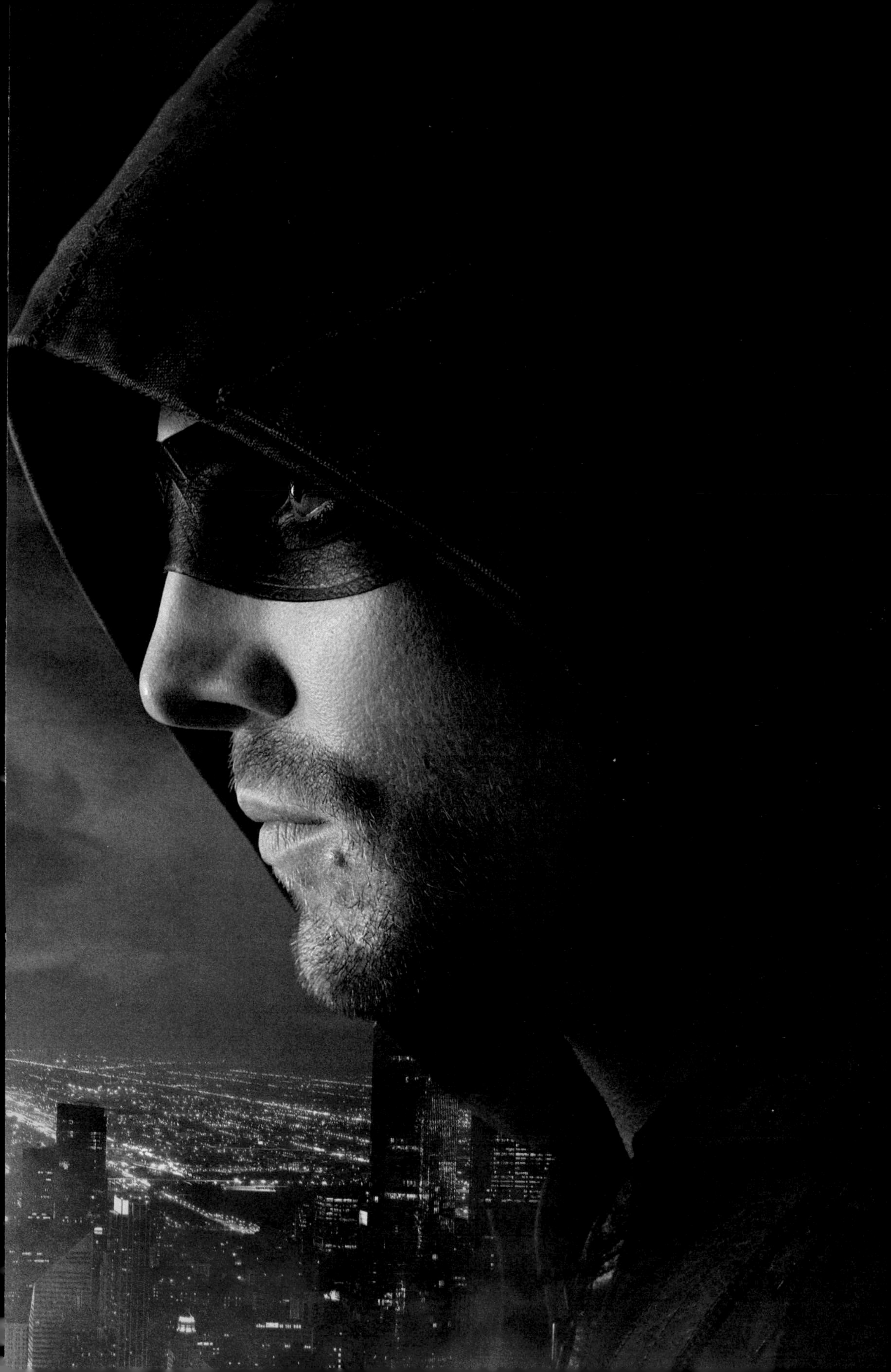

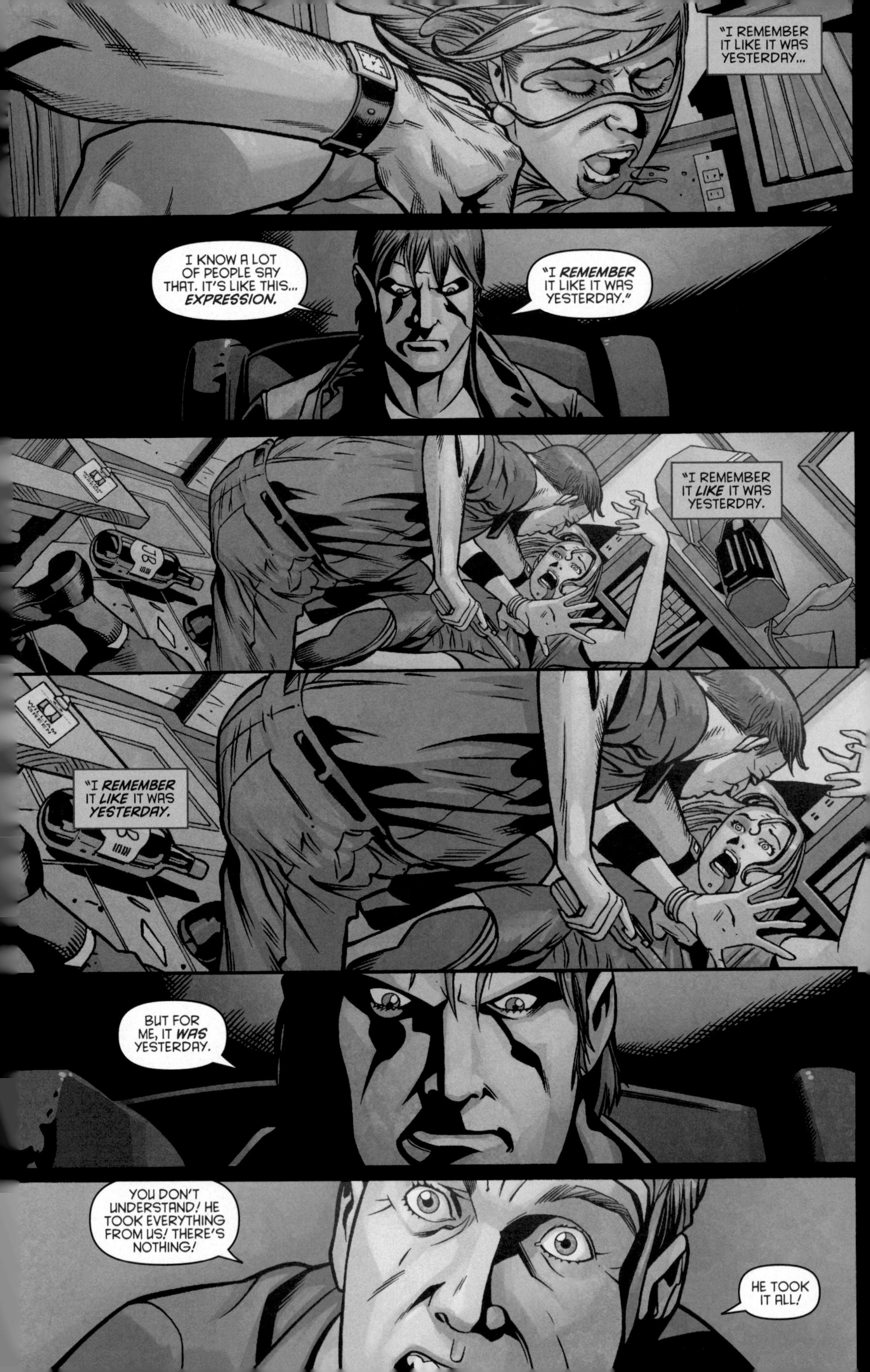
"I REMEMBER IT LIKE IT WAS YESTERDAY...
I KNOW A LOT OF PEOPLE SAY THAT. IT'S LIKE THIS... EXPRESSION.
"I REMEMBER IT LIKE IT WAS YESTERDAY."
"I REMEMBER IT LIKE IT WAS YESTERDAY.
"I REMEMBER IT LIKE IT WAS YESTERDAY.
BUT FOR ME, IT WAS YESTERDAY.
YOU DON'T UNDERSTAND! HE TOOK EVERYTHING FROM US! THERE'S NOTHING!
HE TOOK IT ALL!

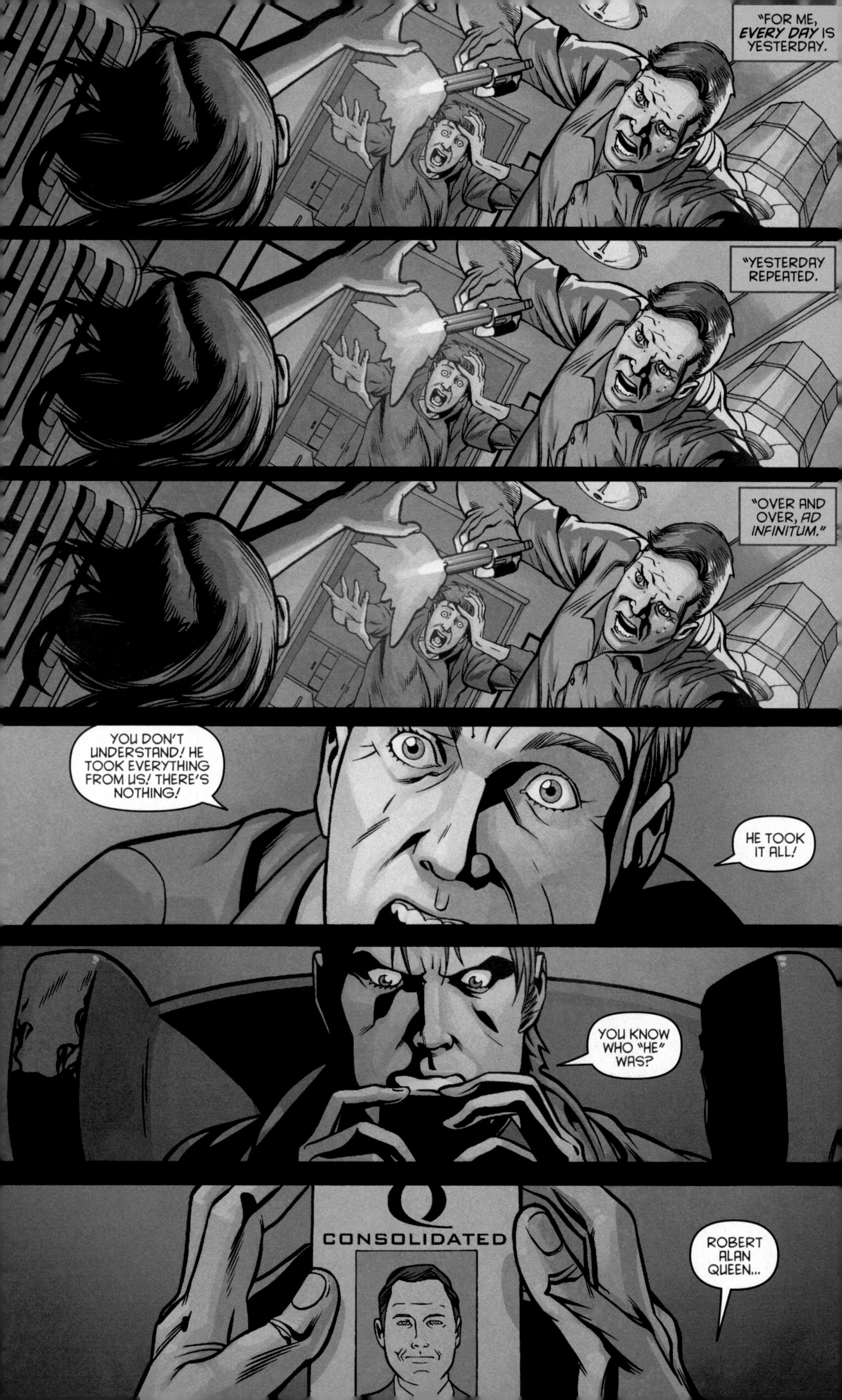
"FOR ME, EVERY DAY IS YESTERDAY.
"YESTERDAY REPEATED.
"OVER AND OVER, AD INFINITUM."
YOU DON'T UNDERSTAND! HE TOOK EVERYTHING FROM US! THERE'S NOTHING!
HE TOOK IT ALL!
YOU KNOW WHO "HE" WAS?
CONSOLIDATED
ROBERT ALAN QUEEN...

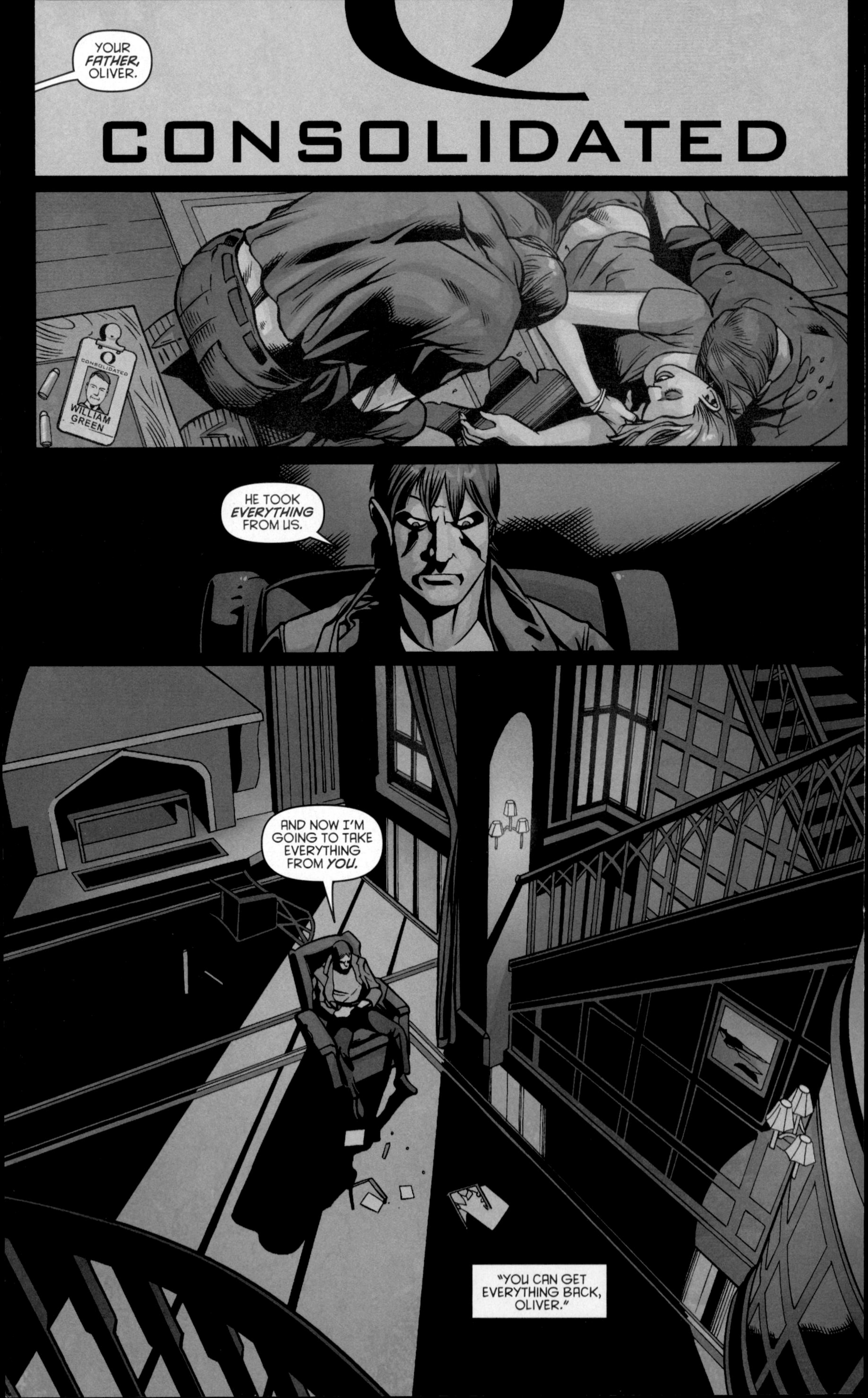

YOUR FATHER, OLIVER.
CONSOLIDATED
Q CONSOLIDATED WILLIAM GREEN
HE TOOK EVERYTHING FROM US.
AND NOW I'M GOING TO TAKE EVERYTHING FROM YOU.
"YOU CAN GET EVERYTHING BACK, OLIVER."

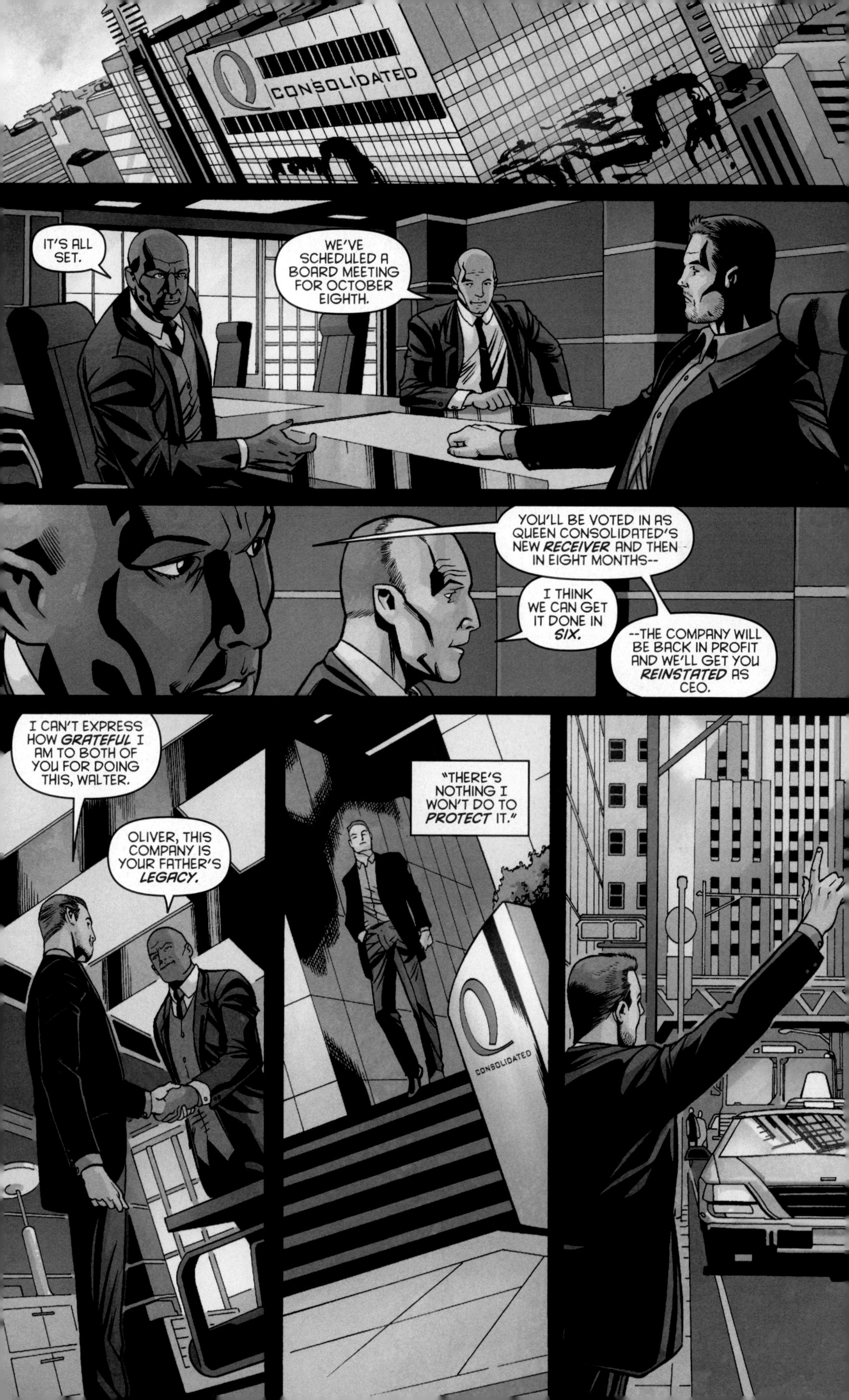
CONSOLIDATED
IT'S ALL SET.
WE'VE SCHEDULED A BOARD MEETING FOR OCTOBER EIGHTH.
YOU'LL BE VOTED IN AS QUEEN CONSOLIDATED'S NEW RECEIVER AND THEN IN EIGHT MONTHS--
I THINK WE CAN GET IT DONE IN SIX.
--THE COMPANY WILL BE BACK IN PROFIT AND WE'LL GET YOU REINSTATED AS CEO.
I CAN'T EXPRESS HOW GRATEFUL I AM TO BOTH OF YOU FOR DOING THIS, WALTER.
OLIVER, THIS COMPANY IS YOUR FATHER'S LEGACY.
"THERE'S NOTHING I WON'T DO TO PROTECT IT."
CONSOLIDATED

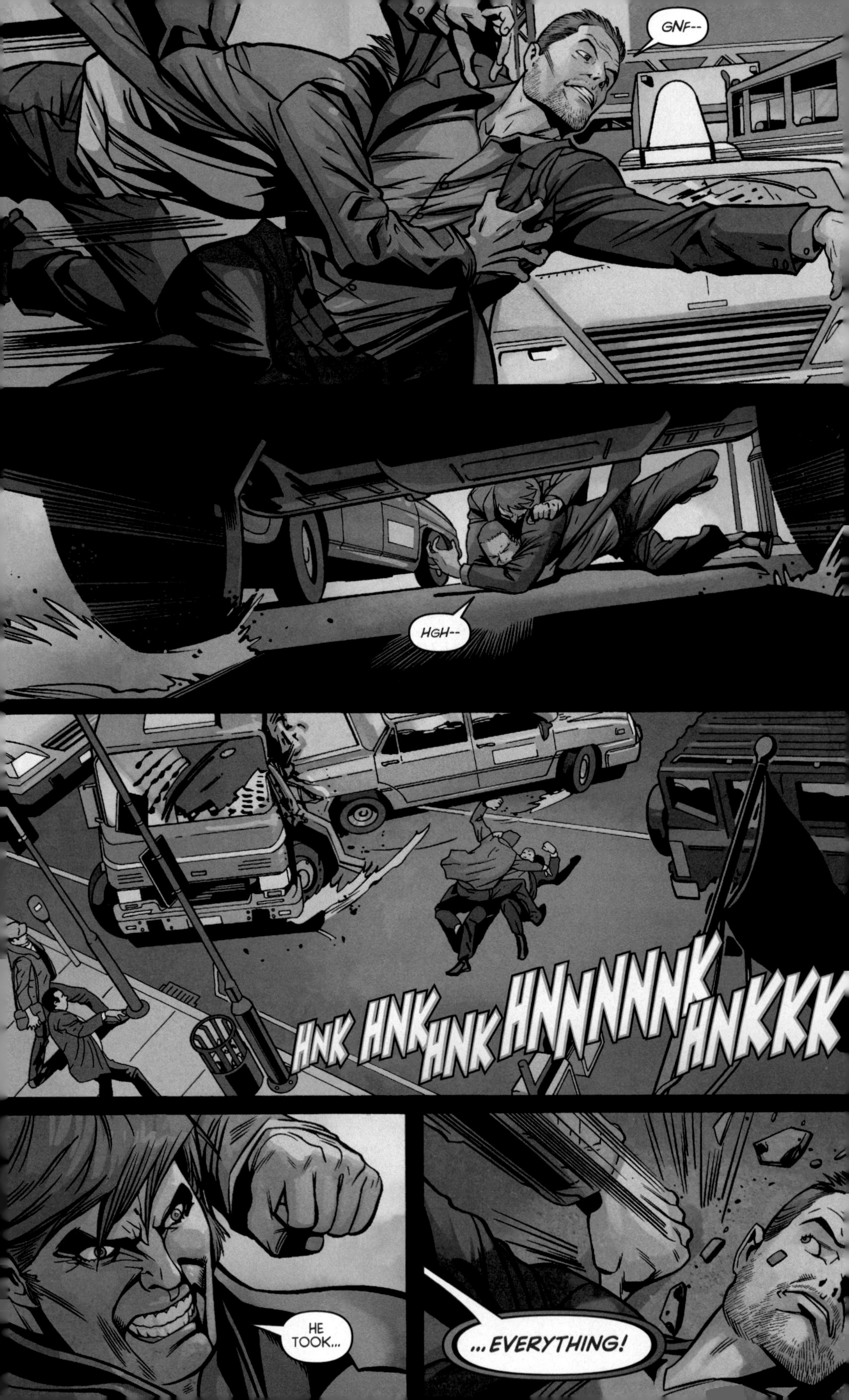
GNF--
HGH--
HNK HNK HNK HNNNNNK HNKKK
HE TOOK...
...EVERYTHING!

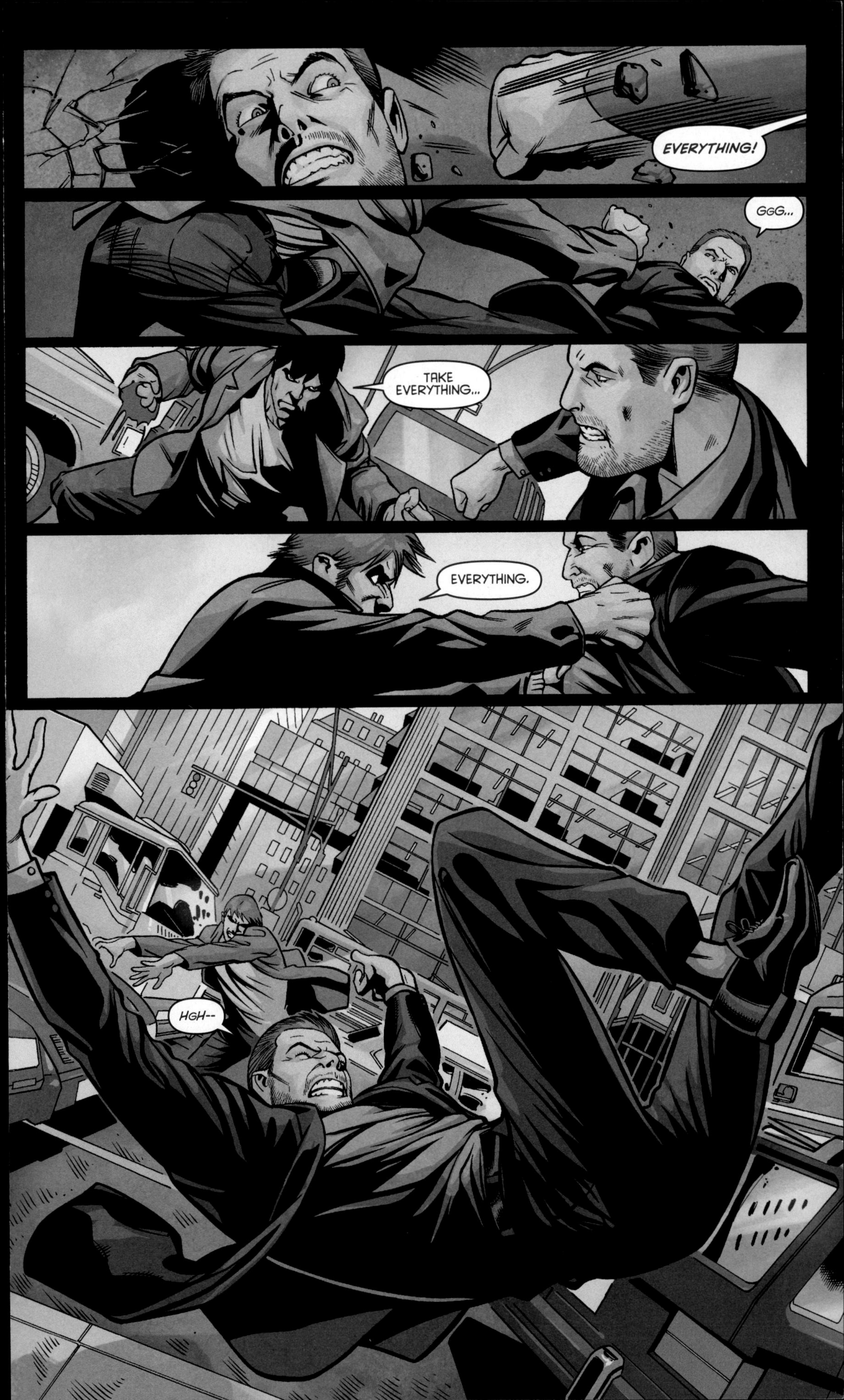
EVERYTHING!
GGG...
TAKE EVERYTHING...
EVERYTHING.
HGH--

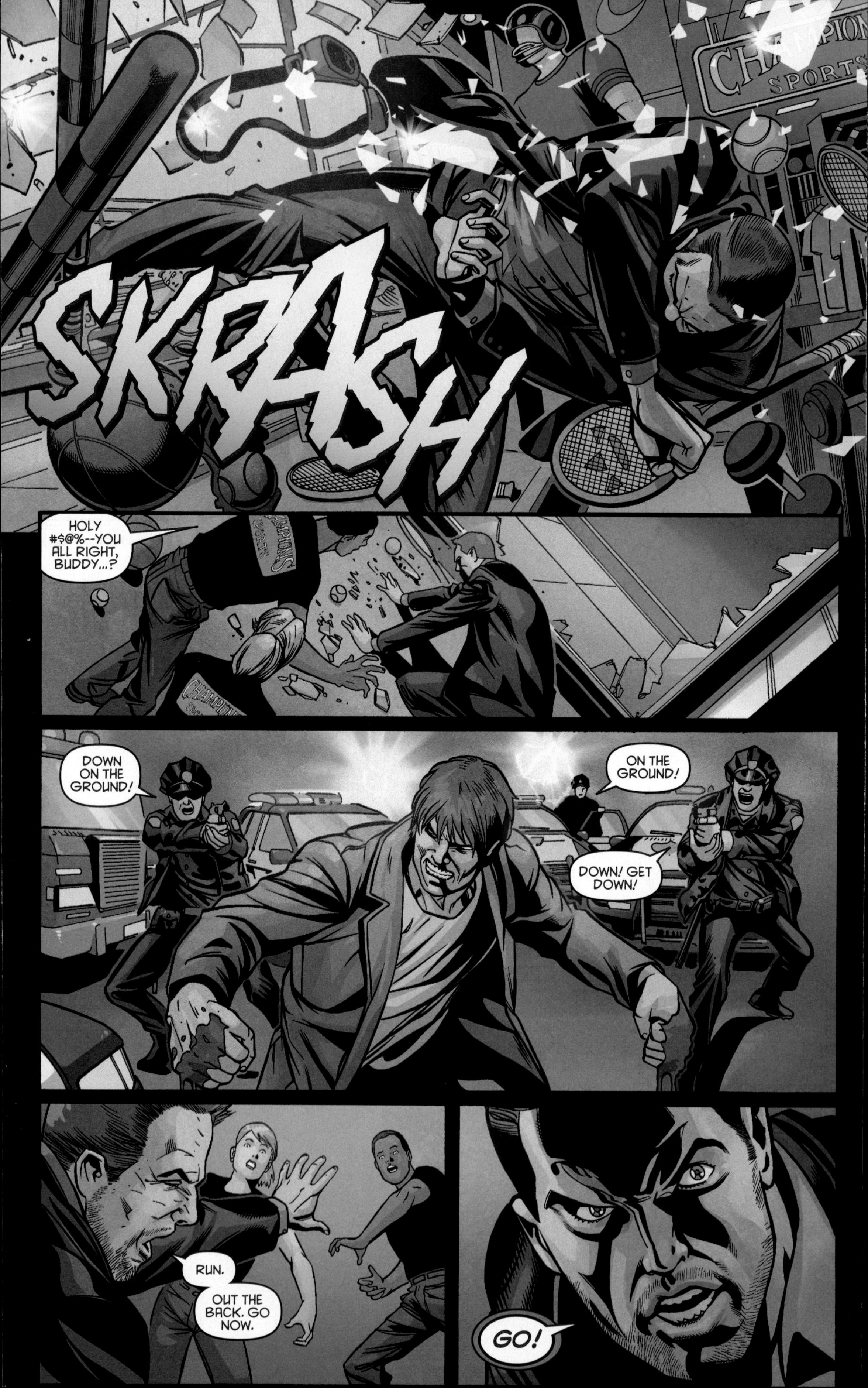
SKRASH
CHAMPIONS SPORTS
HOLY #$@%--YOU ALL RIGHT, BUDDY...?
DOWN ON THE GROUND!
ON THE GROUND!
DOWN! GET DOWN!
RUN.
OUT THE BACK. GO NOW.
GO!

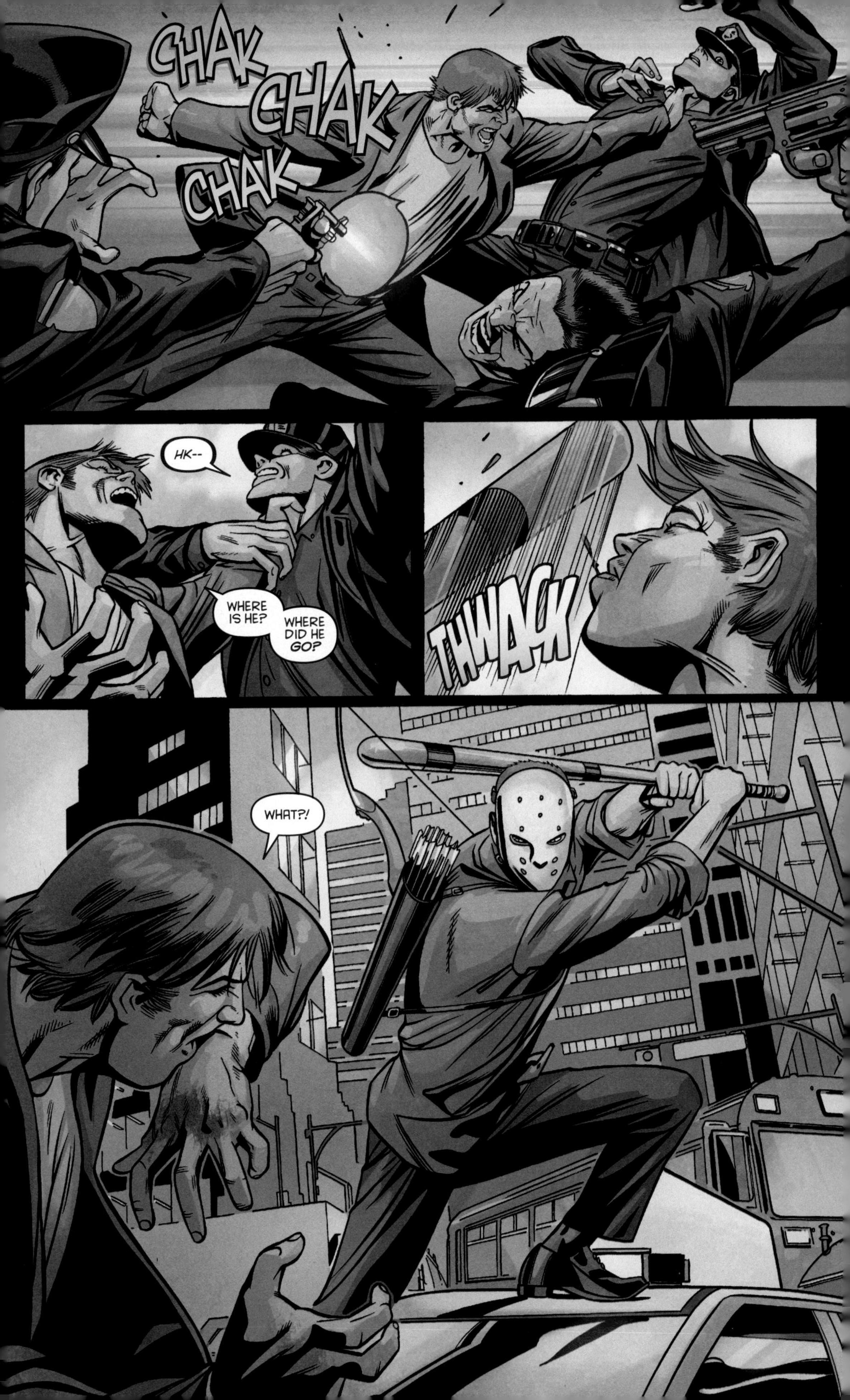
CHAK
CHAK
CHAK
HK--
WHERE IS HE?
WHERE DID HE GO?
THWACK
WHAT?!

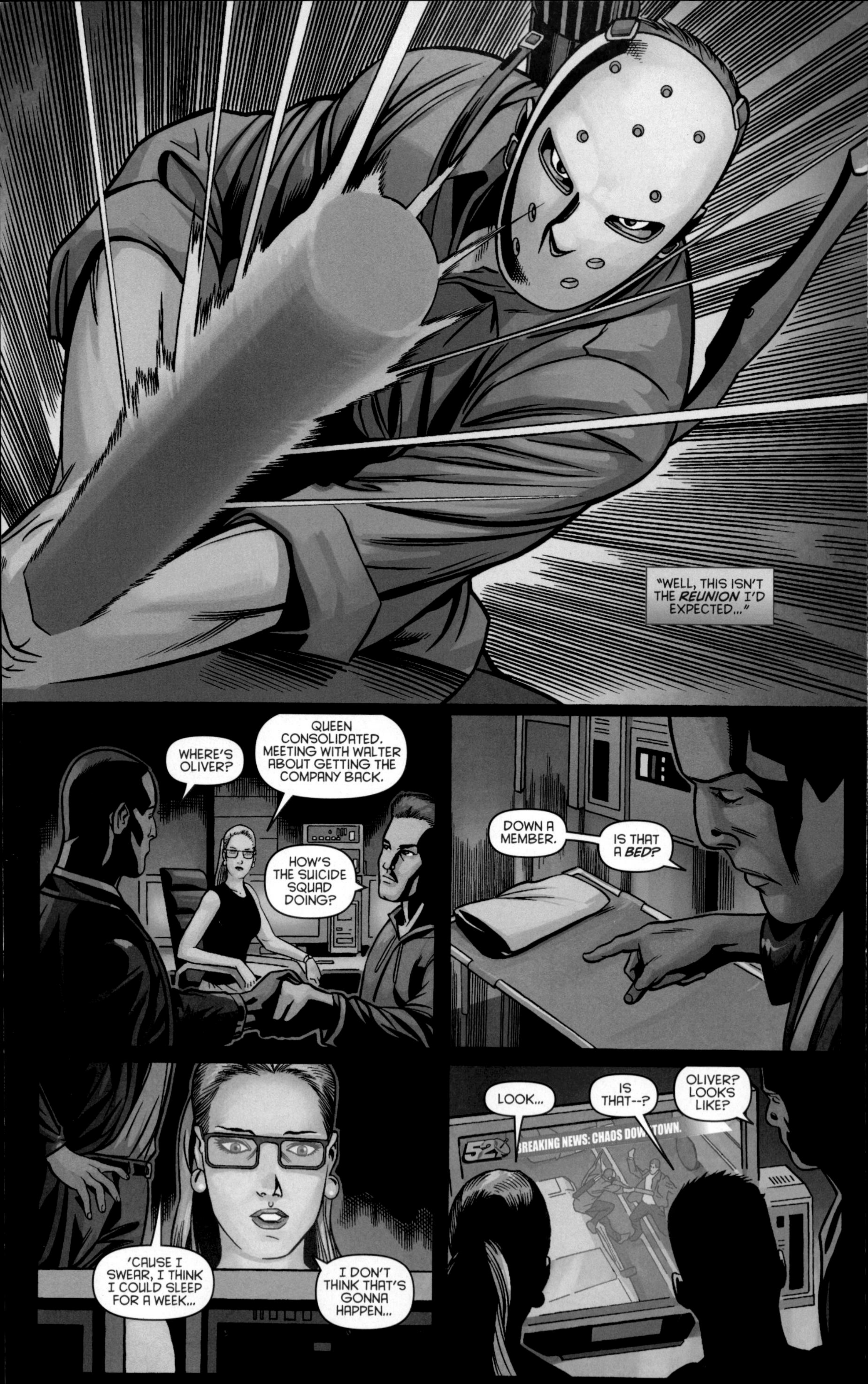
"WELL, THIS ISN'T THE *REUNION* I'D EXPECTED..."
WHERE'S OLIVER?
QUEEN CONSOLIDATED. MEETING WITH WALTER ABOUT GETTING THE COMPANY BACK.
HOW'S THE SUICIDE SQUAD DOING?
DOWN A MEMBER.
IS THAT A *BED?*
'CAUSE I SWEAR, I THINK I COULD SLEEP FOR A WEEK...
I DON'T THINK THAT'S GONNA HAPPEN...
LOOK...
IS THAT--?
OLIVER? LOOKS LIKE?
52
BREAKING NEWS: CHAOS DOWNTOWN.

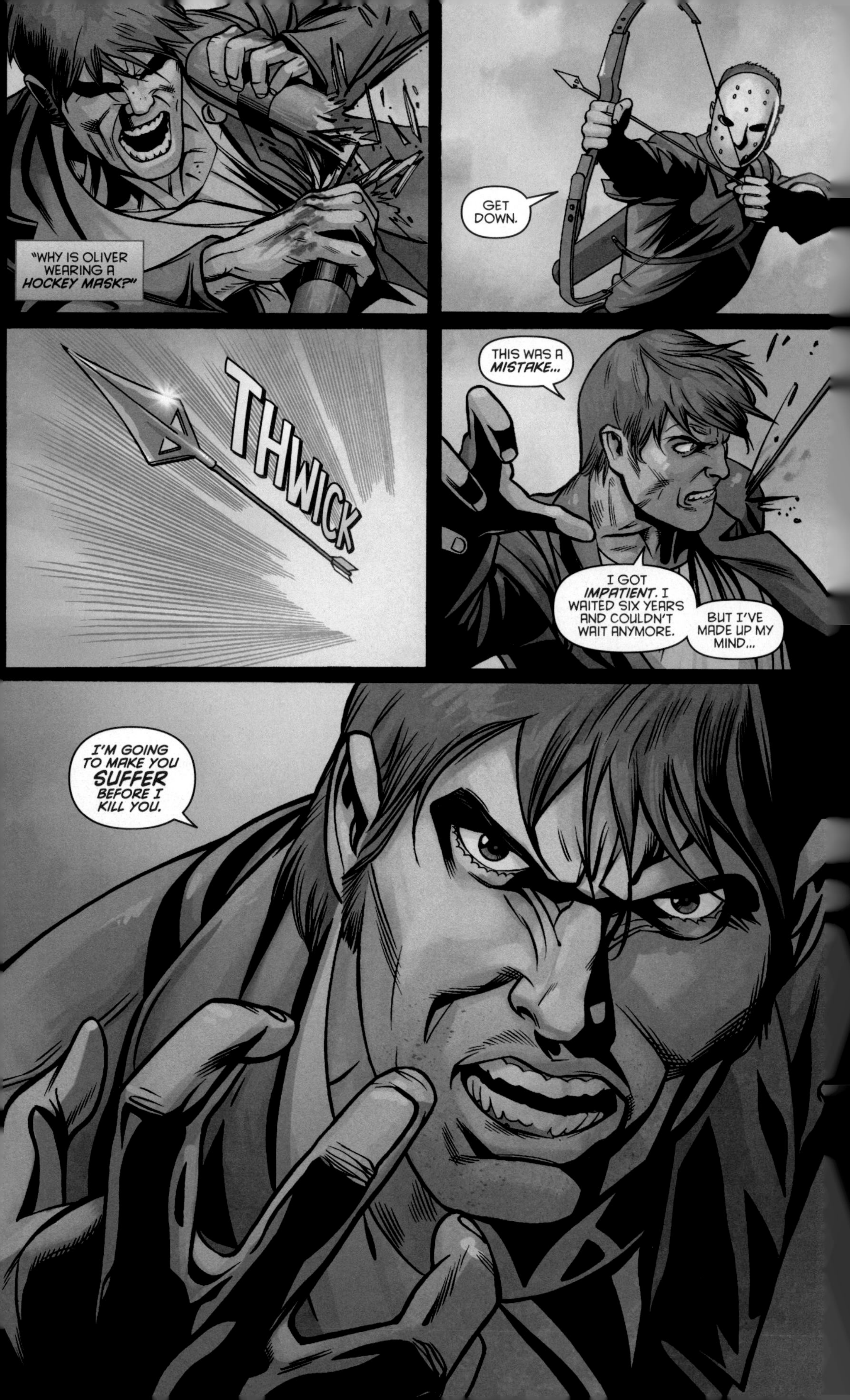
"WHY IS OLIVER WEARING A HOCKEY MASK?"
GET DOWN.
THWICK
THIS WAS A MISTAKE...
I GOT IMPATIENT. I WAITED SIX YEARS AND COULDN'T WAIT ANYMORE.
BUT I'VE MADE UP MY MIND...
I'M GOING TO MAKE YOU SUFFER BEFORE I KILL YOU.

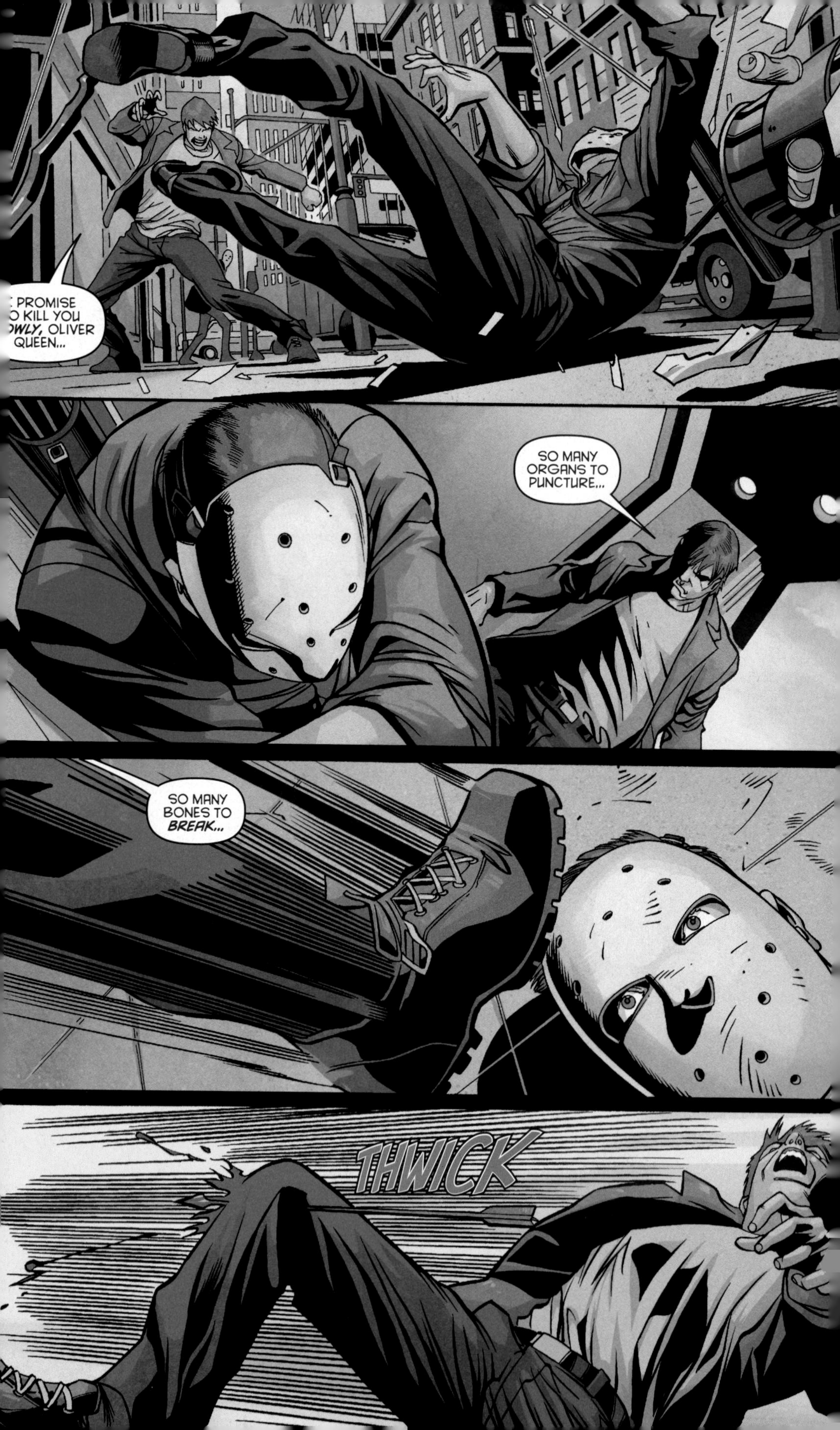
PROMISE O KILL YOU OWLY, OLIVER QUEEN...
SO MANY ORGANS TO PUNCTURE...
SO MANY BONES TO *BREAK...*
THWICK

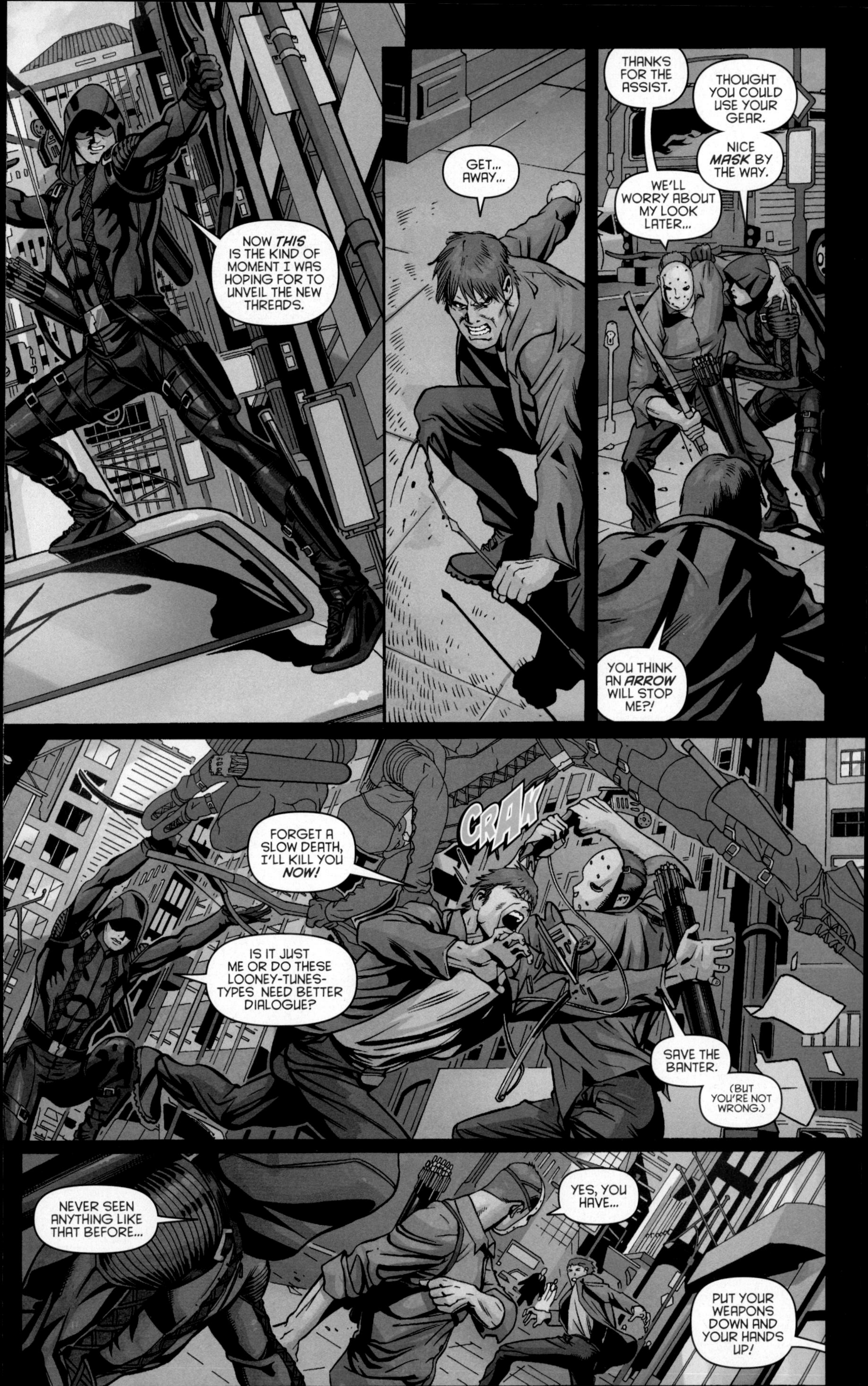
NOW THIS IS THE KIND OF MOMENT I WAS HOPING FOR TO UNVEIL THE NEW THREADS.
GET... AWAY...
THANKS FOR THE ASSIST.
THOUGHT YOU COULD USE YOUR GEAR.
NICE MASK BY THE WAY.
WE'LL WORRY ABOUT MY LOOK LATER...
YOU THINK AN ARROW WILL STOP ME?!
CRAK
FORGET A SLOW DEATH, I'LL KILL YOU NOW!
IS IT JUST ME OR DO THESE LOONEY-TUNES-TYPES NEED BETTER DIALOGUE?
SAVE THE BANTER.
(BUT YOU'RE NOT WRONG.)
NEVER SEEN ANYTHING LIKE THAT BEFORE...
YES, YOU HAVE...
PUT YOUR WEAPONS DOWN AND YOUR HANDS UP!

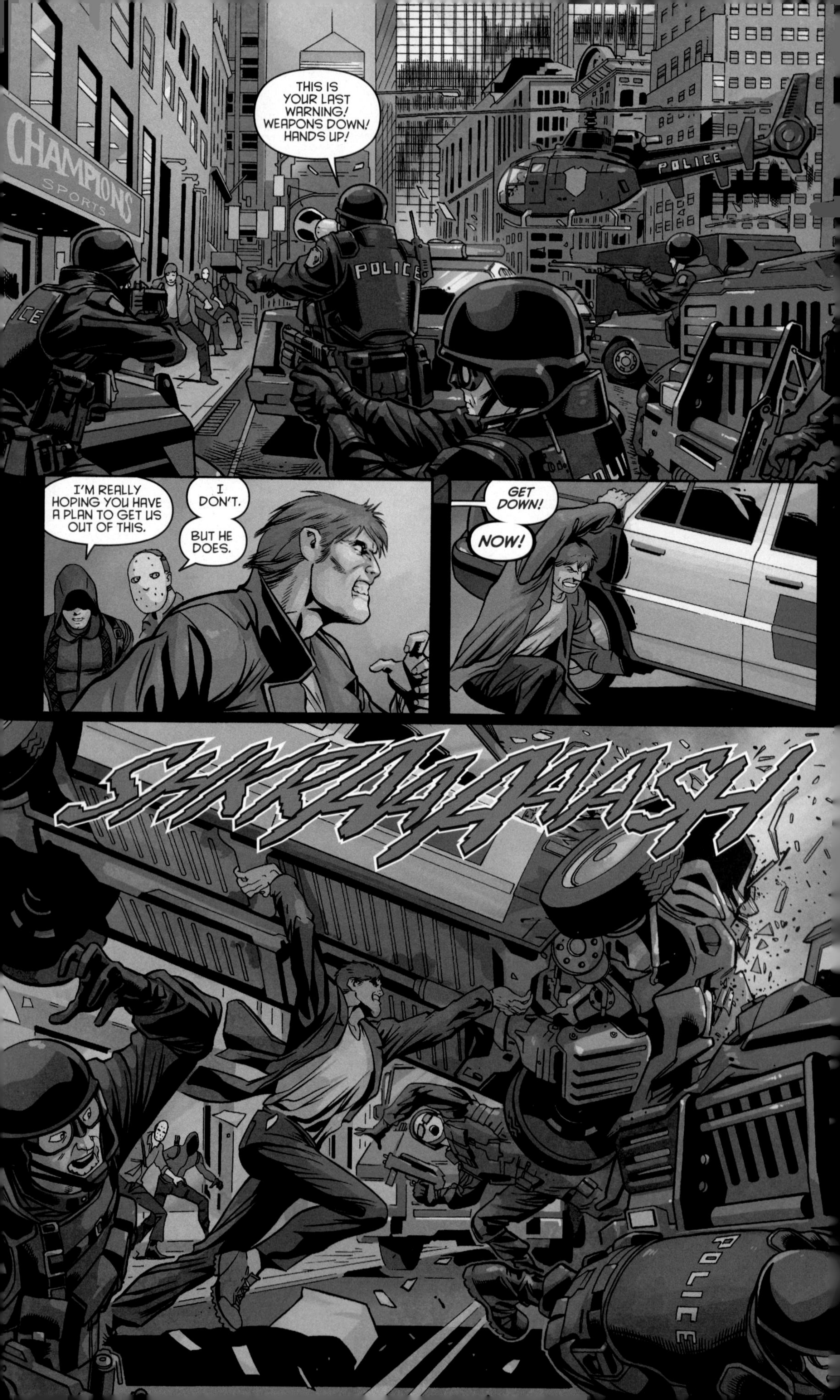
CHAMPIONS
SPORTS
THIS IS YOUR LAST WARNING! WEAPONS DOWN! HANDS UP!
POLICE
POLICE
I'M REALLY HOPING YOU HAVE A PLAN TO GET US OUT OF THIS.
I DON'T.
BUT HE DOES.
GET DOWN!
NOW!
SHKRAAAAAASH
POLICE

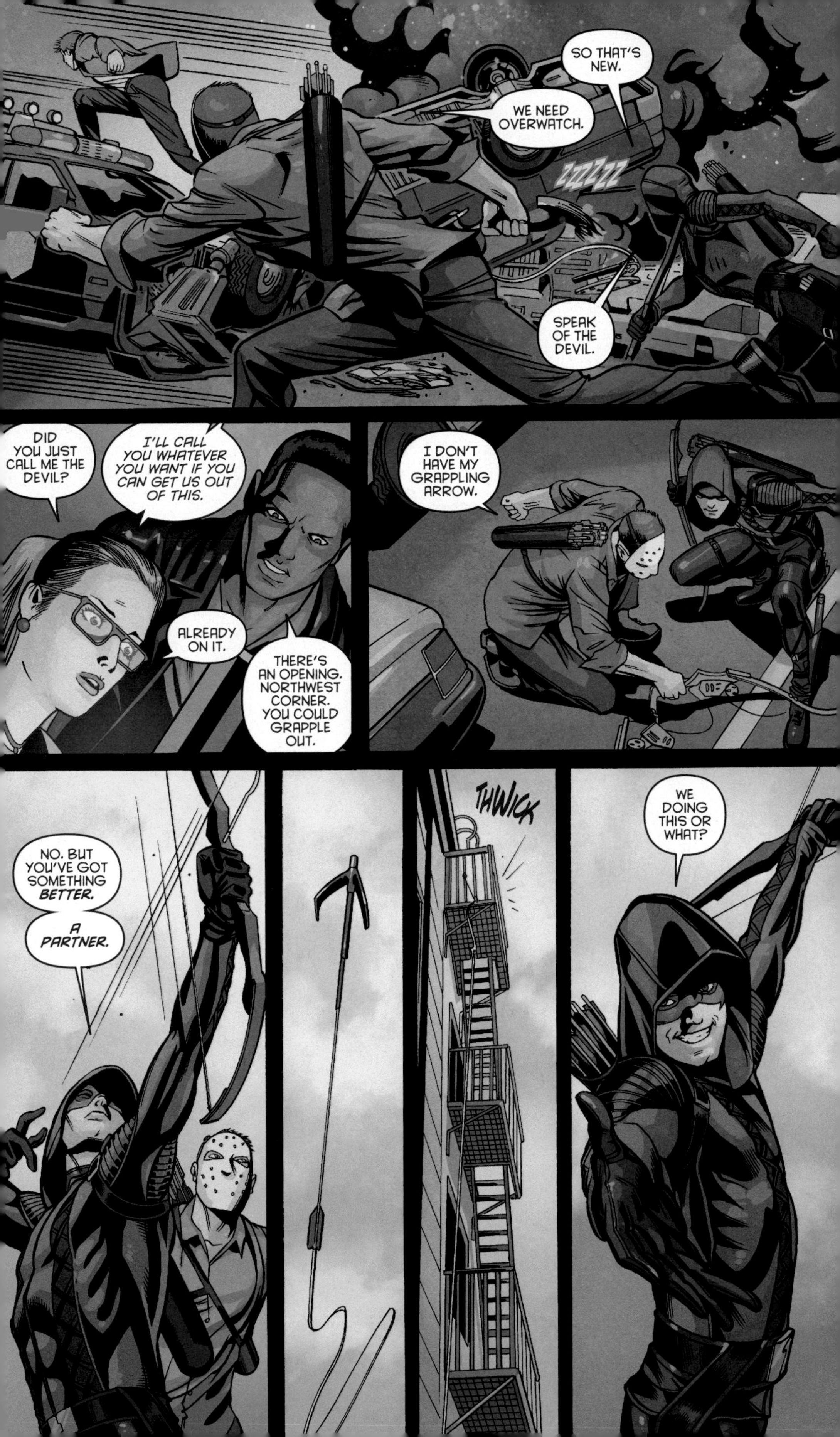
SO THAT'S NEW.
WE NEED OVERWATCH.
ZZZZZZ
SPEAK OF THE DEVIL.
DID YOU JUST CALL ME THE DEVIL?
I'LL CALL YOU WHATEVER YOU WANT IF YOU CAN GET US OUT OF THIS.
ALREADY ON IT.
THERE'S AN OPENING. NORTHWEST CORNER. YOU COULD GRAPPLE OUT.
I DON'T HAVE MY GRAPPLING ARROW.
NO. BUT YOU'VE GOT SOMETHING *BETTER.*
A *PARTNER.*
THWICK
WE DOING THIS OR WHAT?

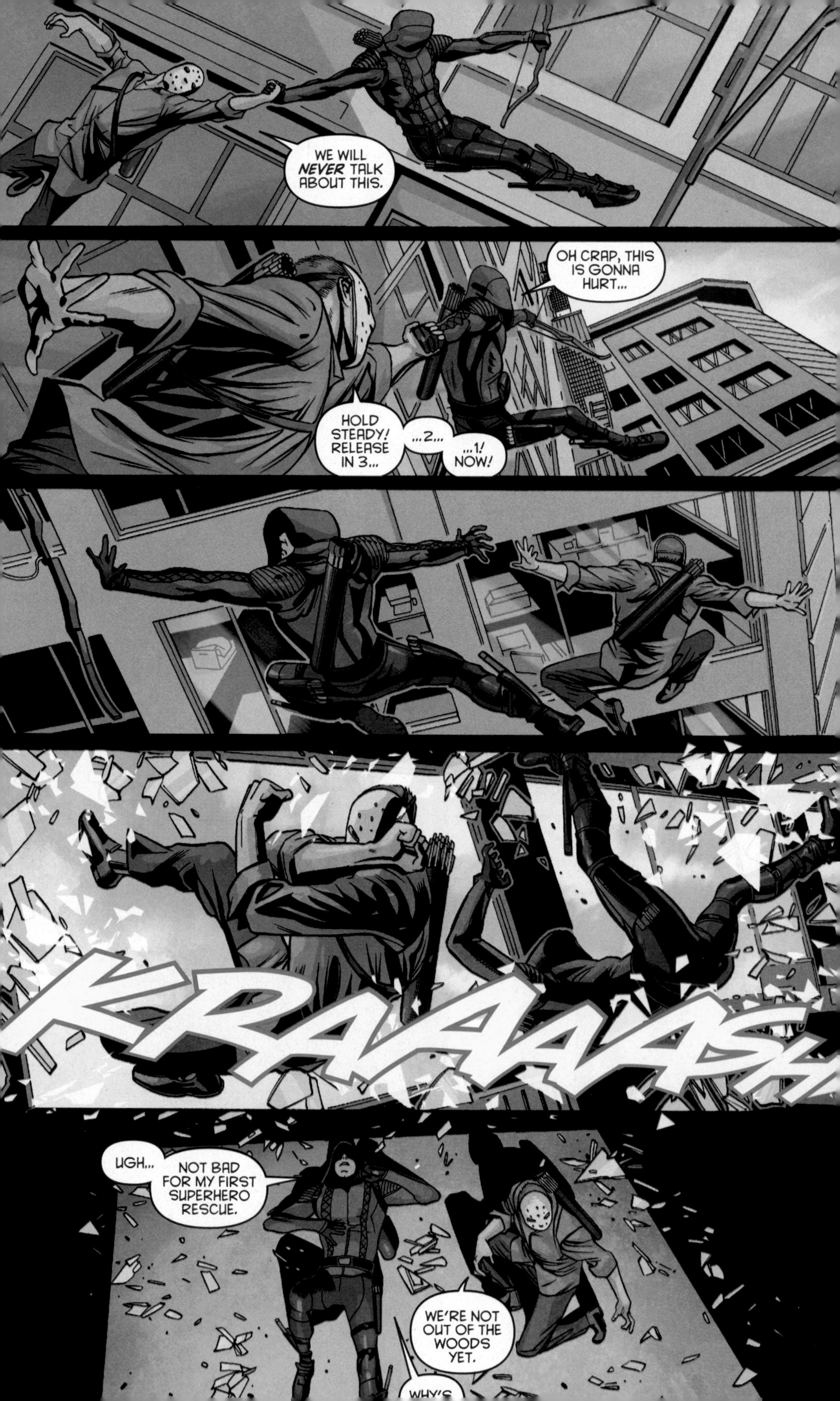
WE WILL NEVER TALK ABOUT THIS.
OH CRAP, THIS IS GONNA HURT...
HOLD STEADY! RELEASE IN 3...
...2...
...1! NOW!
KRAAAASH
UGH...
NOT BAD FOR MY FIRST SUPERHERO RESCUE.
WE'RE NOT OUT OF THE WOODS YET.
WHY'S

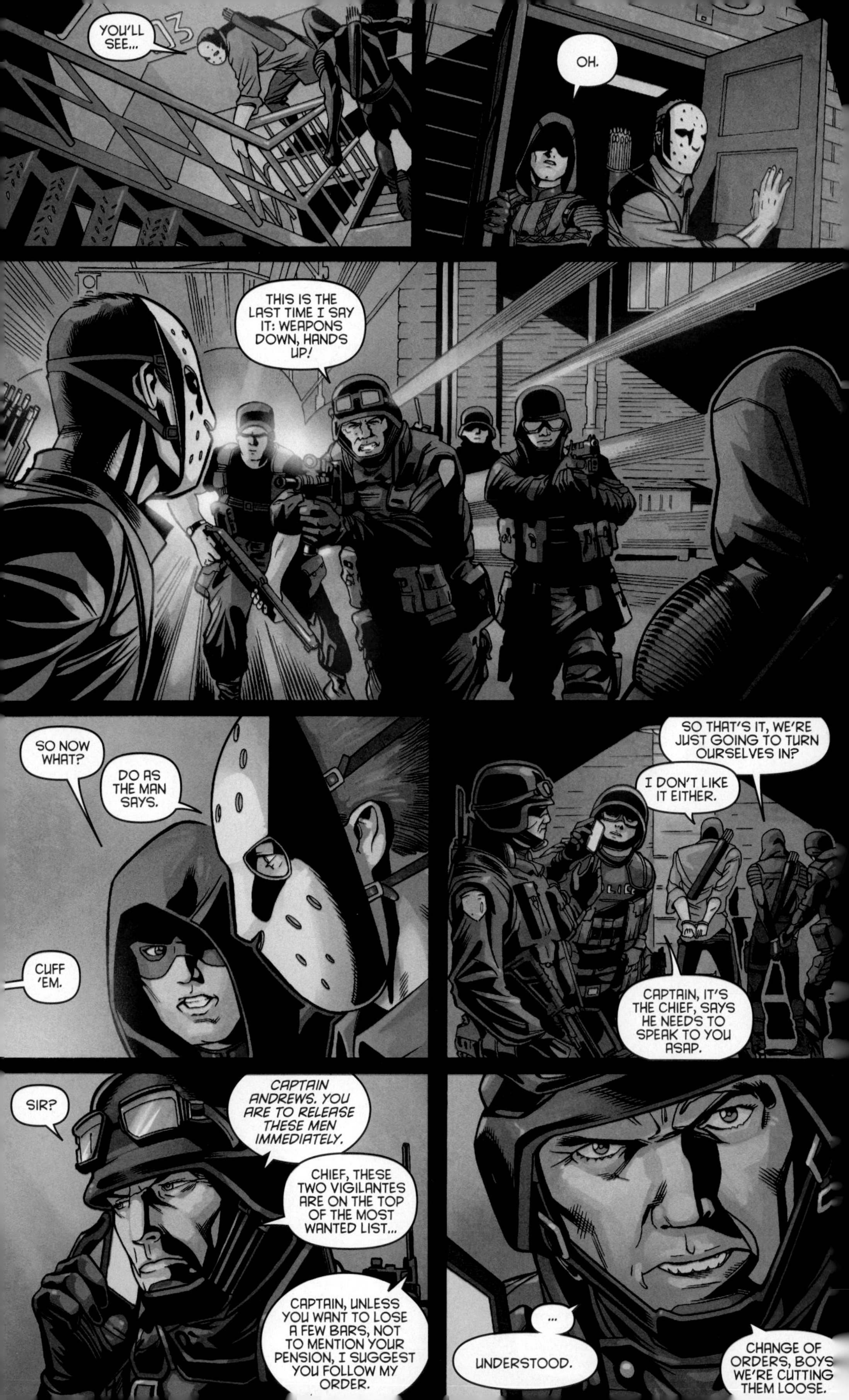
YOU'LL SEE...
OH.
THIS IS THE LAST TIME I SAY IT: WEAPONS DOWN, HANDS UP!
SO NOW WHAT?
DO AS THE MAN SAYS.
CUFF 'EM.
SO THAT'S IT, WE'RE JUST GOING TO TURN OURSELVES IN?
I DON'T LIKE IT EITHER.
CAPTAIN, IT'S THE CHIEF, SAYS HE NEEDS TO SPEAK TO YOU ASAP.
SIR?
CAPTAIN ANDREWS. YOU ARE TO RELEASE THESE MEN IMMEDIATELY.
CHIEF, THESE TWO VIGILANTES ARE ON THE TOP OF THE MOST WANTED LIST...
CAPTAIN, UNLESS YOU WANT TO LOSE A FEW BARS, NOT TO MENTION YOUR PENSION, I SUGGEST YOU FOLLOW MY ORDER.
...
UNDERSTOOD.
CHANGE OF ORDERS, BOYS. WE'RE CUTTING THEM LOOSE.

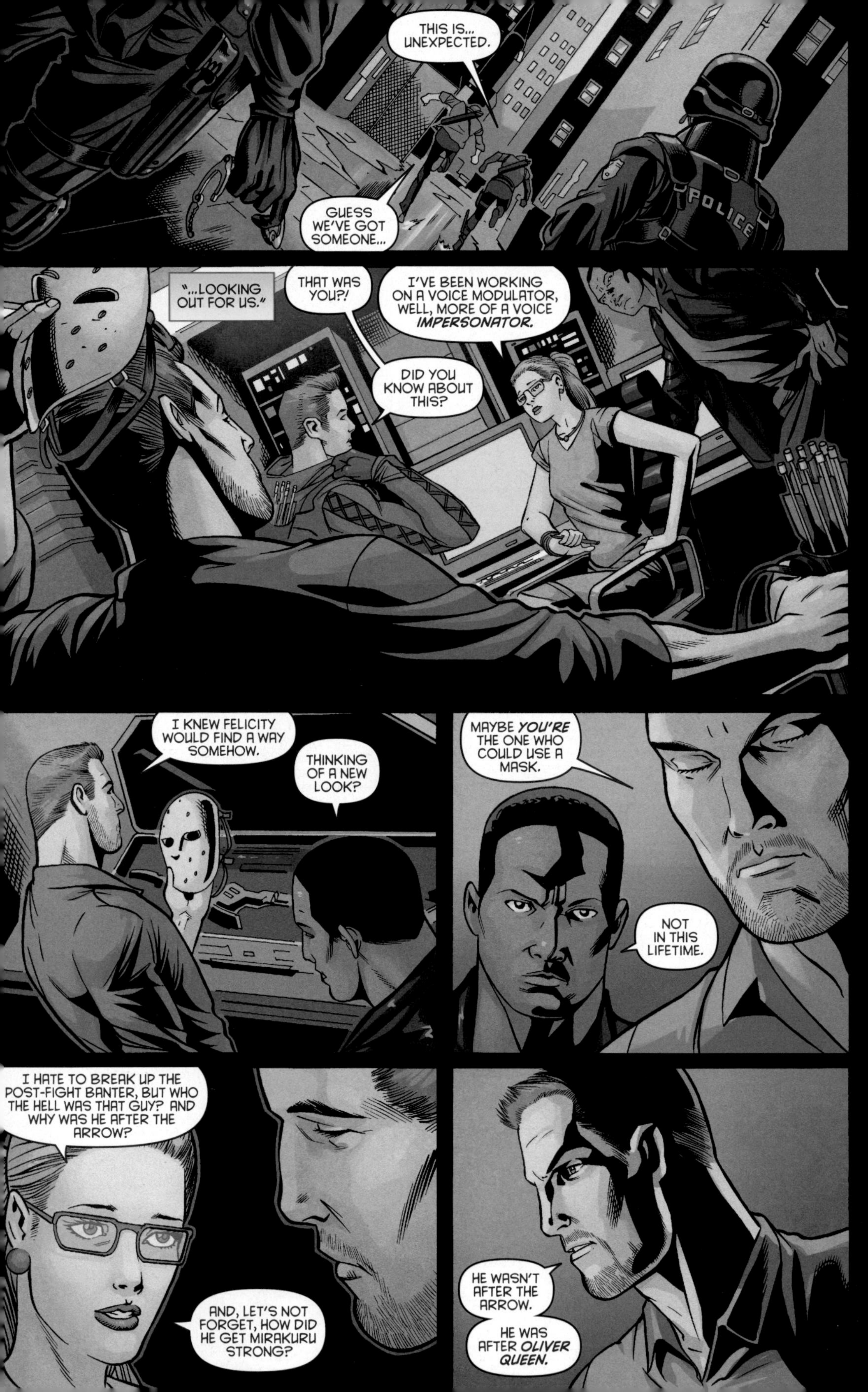
THIS IS... UNEXPECTED.
GUESS WE'VE GOT SOMEONE...
"...LOOKING OUT FOR US."
THAT WAS YOU?!
I'VE BEEN WORKING ON A VOICE MODULATOR, WELL, MORE OF A VOICE *IMPERSONATOR.*
DID YOU KNOW ABOUT THIS?
I KNEW FELICITY WOULD FIND A WAY SOMEHOW.
THINKING OF A NEW LOOK?
MAYBE *YOU'RE* THE ONE WHO COULD USE A MASK.
NOT IN THIS LIFETIME.
I HATE TO BREAK UP THE POST-FIGHT BANTER, BUT WHO THE HELL WAS THAT GUY? AND WHY WAS HE AFTER THE ARROW?
AND, LET'S NOT FORGET, HOW DID HE GET MIRAKURU STRONG?
HE WASN'T AFTER THE ARROW.
HE WAS AFTER *OLIVER QUEEN.*

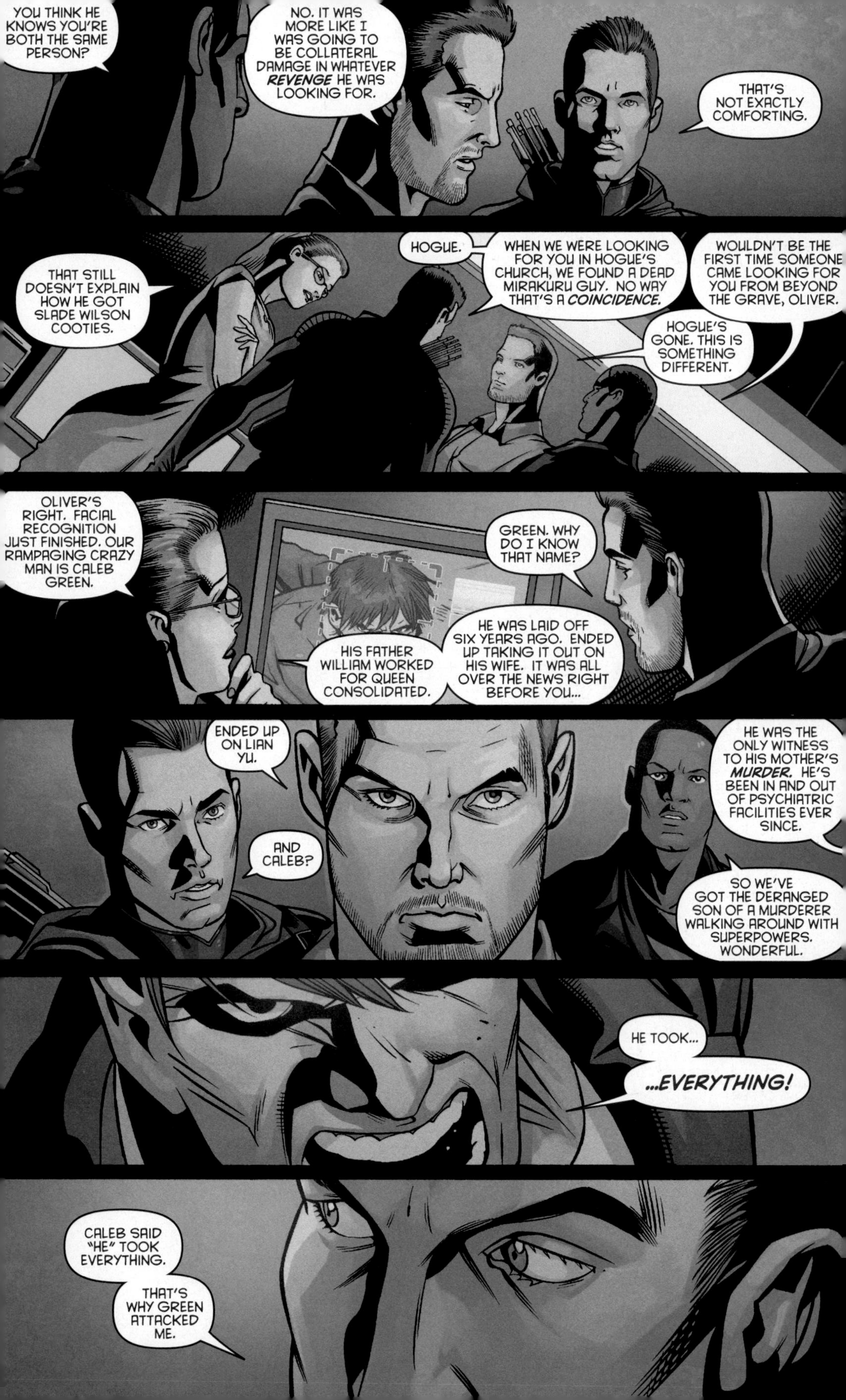

YOU THINK HE KNOWS YOU'RE BOTH THE SAME PERSON?
NO. IT WAS MORE LIKE I WAS GOING TO BE COLLATERAL DAMAGE IN WHATEVER REVENGE HE WAS LOOKING FOR.
THAT'S NOT EXACTLY COMFORTING.
THAT STILL DOESN'T EXPLAIN HOW HE GOT SLADE WILSON COOTIES.
HOGUE.
WHEN WE WERE LOOKING FOR YOU IN HOGUE'S CHURCH, WE FOUND A DEAD MIRAKURU GUY. NO WAY THAT'S A COINCIDENCE.
WOULDN'T BE THE FIRST TIME SOMEONE CAME LOOKING FOR YOU FROM BEYOND THE GRAVE, OLIVER.
HOGUE'S GONE. THIS IS SOMETHING DIFFERENT.
OLIVER'S RIGHT. FACIAL RECOGNITION JUST FINISHED. OUR RAMPAGING CRAZY MAN IS CALEB GREEN.
GREEN. WHY DO I KNOW THAT NAME?
HIS FATHER WILLIAM WORKED FOR QUEEN CONSOLIDATED.
HE WAS LAID OFF SIX YEARS AGO. ENDED UP TAKING IT OUT ON HIS WIFE. IT WAS ALL OVER THE NEWS RIGHT BEFORE YOU...
ENDED UP ON LIAN YU.
AND CALEB?
HE WAS THE ONLY WITNESS TO HIS MOTHER'S MURDER. HE'S BEEN IN AND OUT OF PSYCHIATRIC FACILITIES EVER SINCE.
SO WE'VE GOT THE DERANGED SON OF A MURDERER WALKING AROUND WITH SUPERPOWERS. WONDERFUL.
HE TOOK...
...EVERYTHING!
CALEB SAID "HE" TOOK EVERYTHING.
THAT'S WHY GREEN ATTACKED ME.

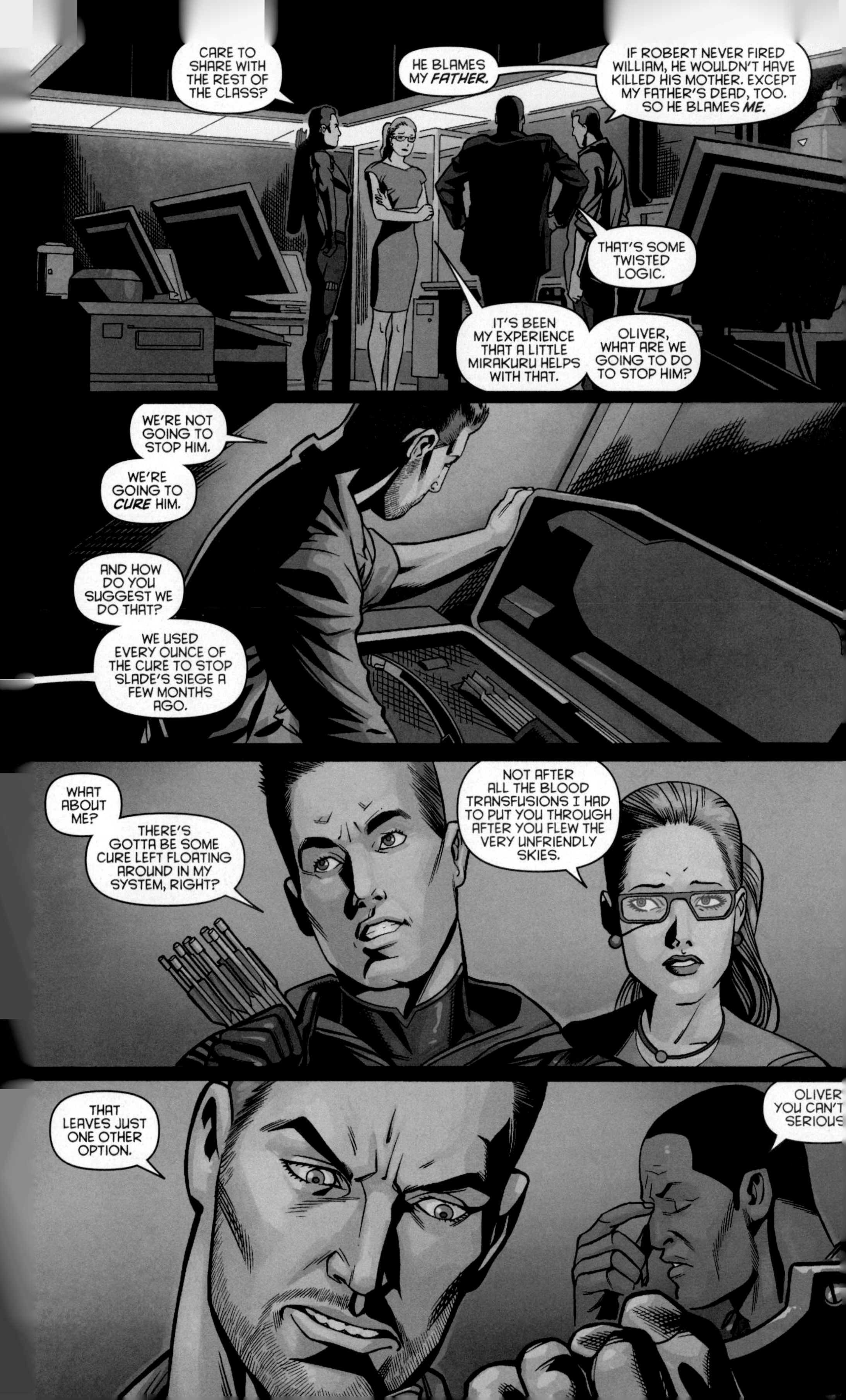
CARE TO SHARE WITH THE REST OF THE CLASS?
HE BLAMES MY *FATHER.*
IF ROBERT NEVER FIRED WILLIAM, HE WOULDN'T HAVE KILLED HIS MOTHER. EXCEPT MY FATHER'S DEAD, TOO. SO HE BLAMES *ME.*
THAT'S SOME TWISTED LOGIC.
IT'S BEEN MY EXPERIENCE THAT A LITTLE MIRAKURU HELPS WITH THAT.
OLIVER, WHAT ARE WE GOING TO DO TO STOP HIM?
WE'RE NOT GOING TO STOP HIM.
WE'RE GOING TO *CURE* HIM.
AND HOW DO YOU SUGGEST WE DO THAT?
WE USED EVERY OUNCE OF THE CURE TO STOP SLADE'S SIEGE A FEW MONTHS AGO.
WHAT ABOUT ME?
THERE'S GOTTA BE SOME CURE LEFT FLOATING AROUND IN MY SYSTEM, RIGHT?
NOT AFTER ALL THE BLOOD TRANSFUSIONS I HAD TO PUT YOU THROUGH AFTER YOU FLEW THE VERY UNFRIENDLY SKIES.
THAT LEAVES JUST ONE OTHER OPTION.

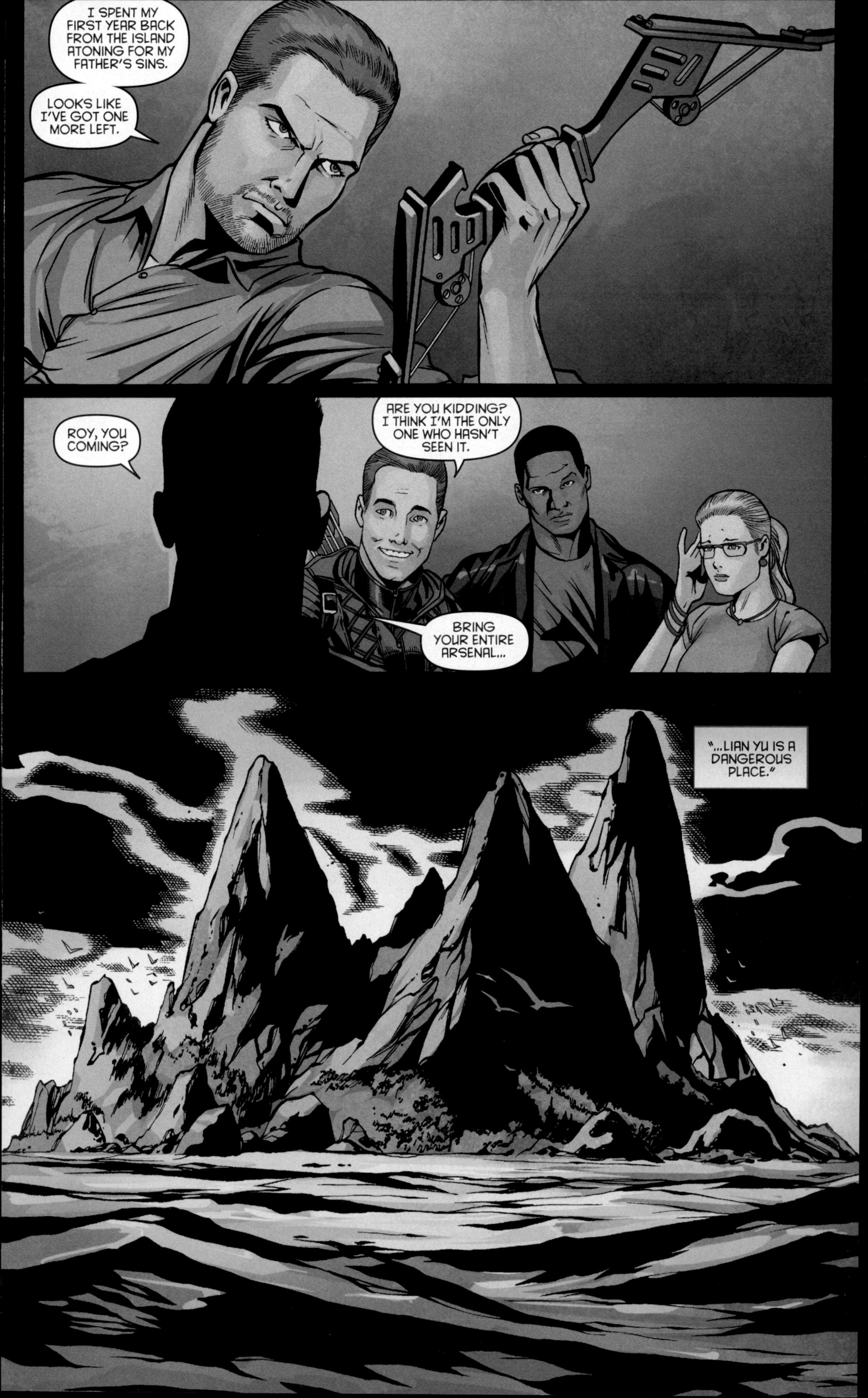
I SPENT MY FIRST YEAR BACK FROM THE ISLAND ATONING FOR MY FATHER'S SINS.
LOOKS LIKE I'VE GOT ONE MORE LEFT.
ROY, YOU COMING?
ARE YOU KIDDING? I THINK I'M THE ONLY ONE WHO HASN'T SEEN IT.
BRING YOUR ENTIRE ARSENAL...
"...LIAN YU IS A DANGEROUS PLACE."

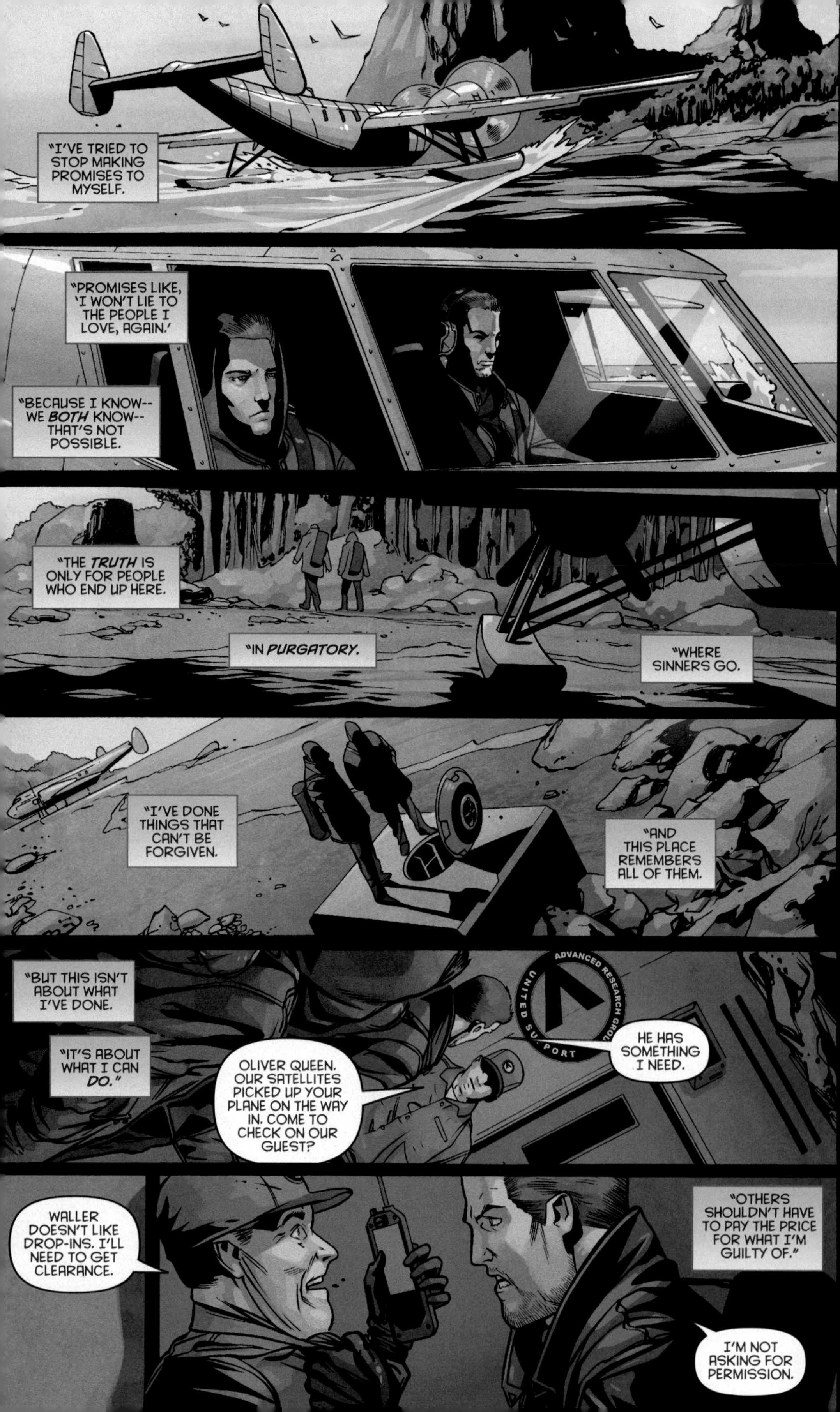
"I'VE TRIED TO STOP MAKING PROMISES TO MYSELF.
"PROMISES LIKE, 'I WON'T LIE TO THE PEOPLE I LOVE, AGAIN.'
"BECAUSE I KNOW-- WE BOTH KNOW-- THAT'S NOT POSSIBLE.
"THE TRUTH IS ONLY FOR PEOPLE WHO END UP HERE.
"IN PURGATORY.
"WHERE SINNERS GO.
"I'VE DONE THINGS THAT CAN'T BE FORGIVEN.
"AND THIS PLACE REMEMBERS ALL OF THEM.
"BUT THIS ISN'T ABOUT WHAT I'VE DONE.
"IT'S ABOUT WHAT I CAN DO."
ADVANCED RESEARCH GROU
UNITED SU PORT
OLIVER QUEEN. OUR SATELLITES PICKED UP YOUR PLANE ON THE WAY IN. COME TO CHECK ON OUR GUEST?
HE HAS SOMETHING I NEED.
WALLER DOESN'T LIKE DROP-INS. I'LL NEED TO GET CLEARANCE.
"OTHERS SHOULDN'T HAVE TO PAY THE PRICE FOR WHAT I'M GUILTY OF."
I'M NOT ASKING FOR PERMISSION.

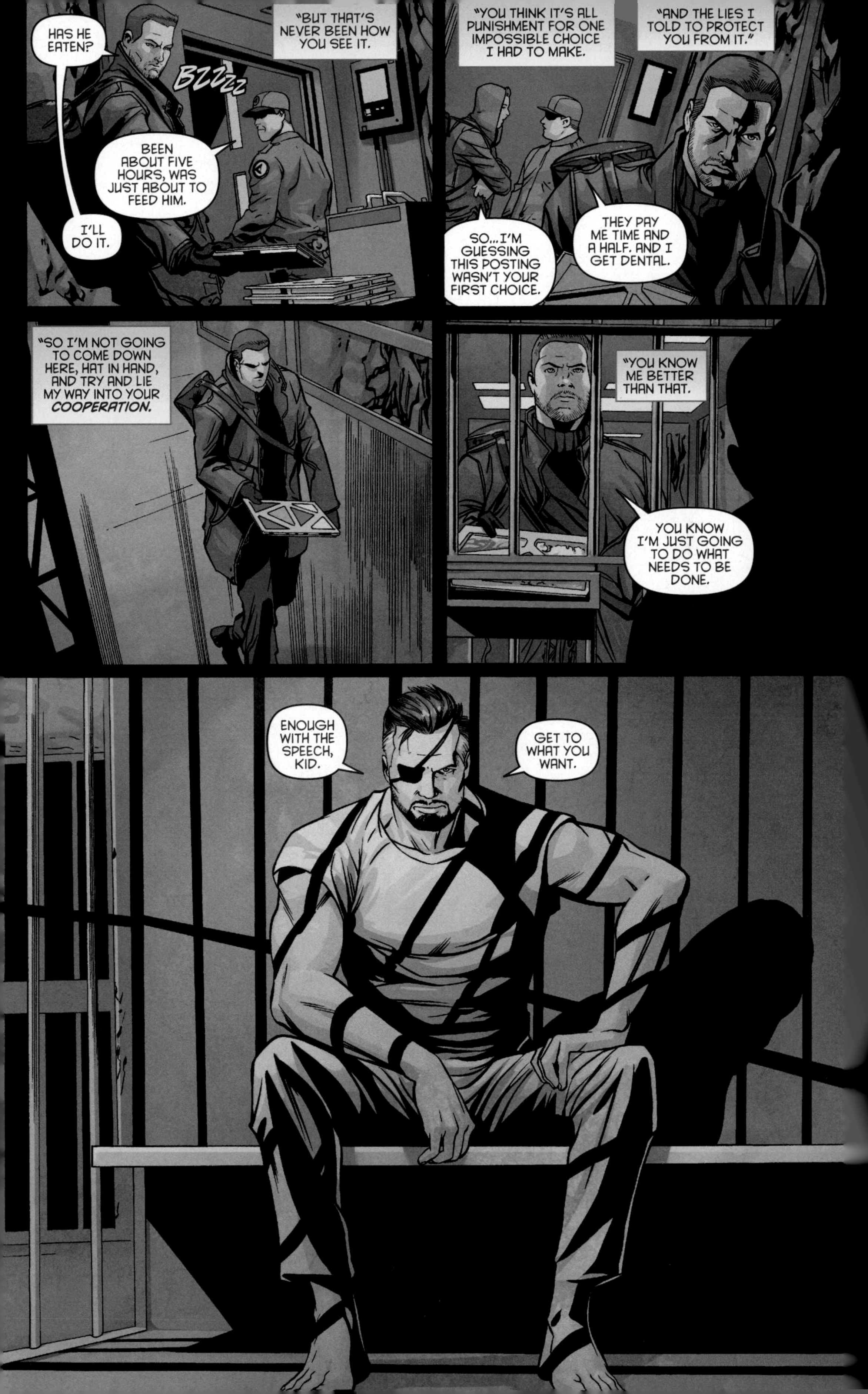
HAS HE EATEN?
"BUT THAT'S NEVER BEEN HOW YOU SEE IT.
BZZZZ
BEEN ABOUT FIVE HOURS, WAS JUST ABOUT TO FEED HIM.
I'LL DO IT.
"YOU THINK IT'S ALL PUNISHMENT FOR ONE IMPOSSIBLE CHOICE I HAD TO MAKE.
"AND THE LIES I TOLD TO PROTECT YOU FROM IT."
SO...I'M GUESSING THIS POSTING WASN'T YOUR FIRST CHOICE.
THEY PAY ME TIME AND A HALF. AND I GET DENTAL.
"SO I'M NOT GOING TO COME DOWN HERE, HAT IN HAND, AND TRY AND LIE MY WAY INTO YOUR *COOPERATION.*
"YOU KNOW ME BETTER THAN THAT.
YOU KNOW I'M JUST GOING TO DO WHAT NEEDS TO BE DONE.
ENOUGH WITH THE SPEECH, KID.
GET TO WHAT YOU WANT.

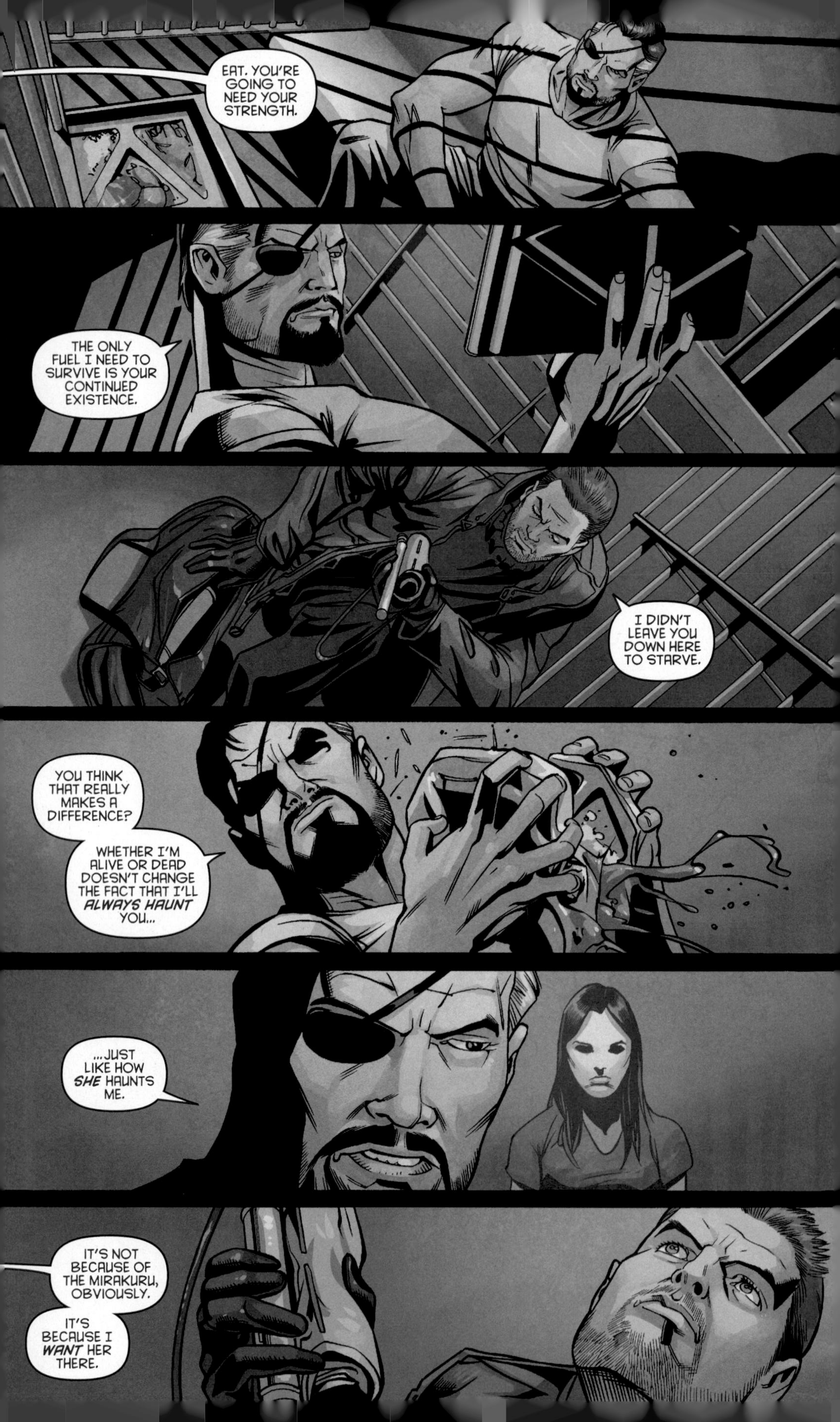
EAT. YOU'RE GOING TO NEED YOUR STRENGTH.
THE ONLY FUEL I NEED TO SURVIVE IS YOUR CONTINUED EXISTENCE.
I DIDN'T LEAVE YOU DOWN HERE TO STARVE.
YOU THINK THAT REALLY MAKES A DIFFERENCE?
WHETHER I'M ALIVE OR DEAD DOESN'T CHANGE THE FACT THAT I'LL *ALWAYS HAUNT* YOU...
...JUST LIKE HOW *SHE* HAUNTS ME.
IT'S NOT BECAUSE OF THE MIRAKURU, OBVIOUSLY.
IT'S BECAUSE I *WANT* HER THERE.

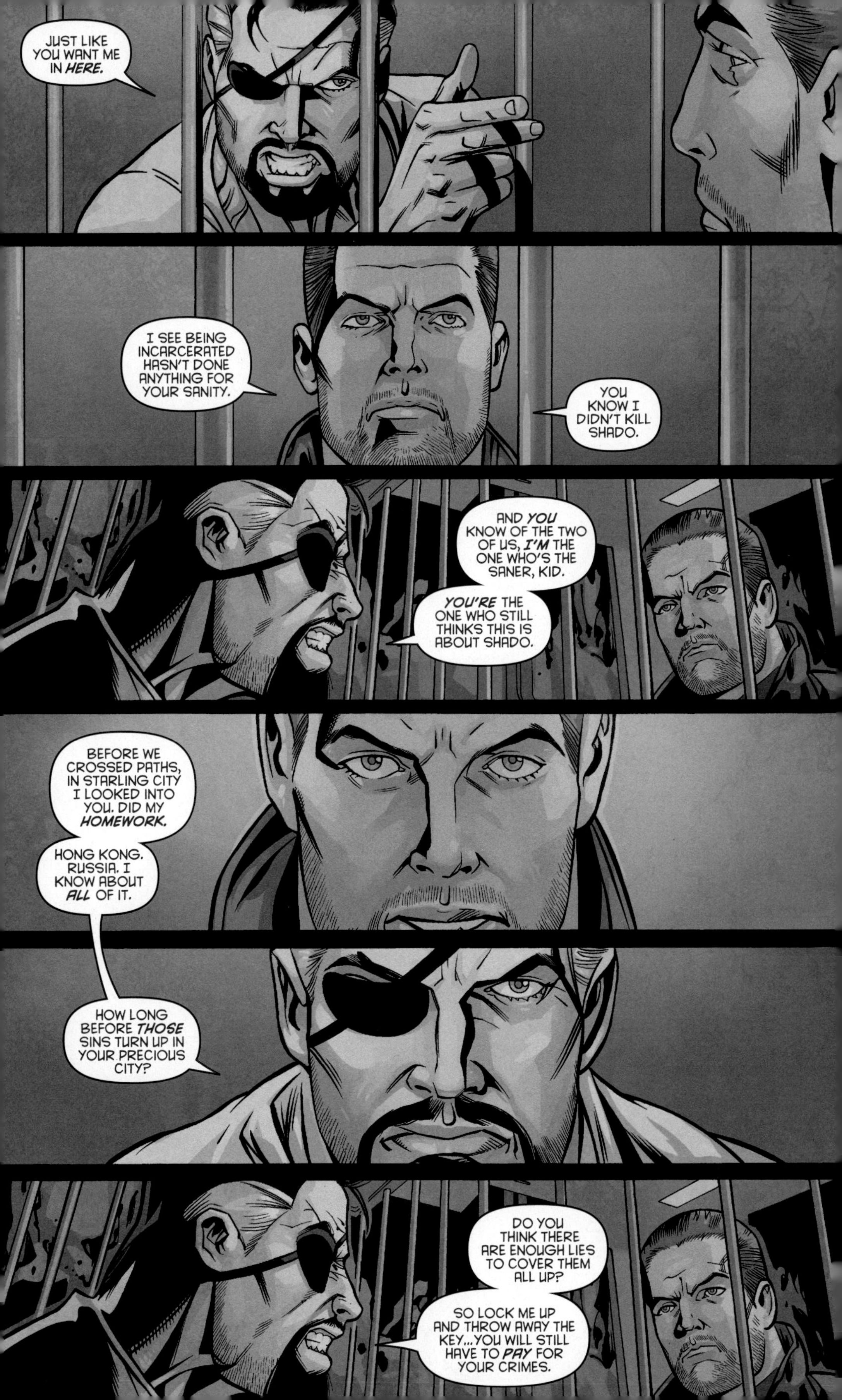
JUST LIKE YOU WANT ME IN HERE.
I SEE BEING INCARCERATED HASN'T DONE ANYTHING FOR YOUR SANITY.
YOU KNOW I DIDN'T KILL SHADO.
AND YOU KNOW OF THE TWO OF US, I'M THE ONE WHO'S THE SANER, KID.
YOU'RE THE ONE WHO STILL THINKS THIS IS ABOUT SHADO.
BEFORE WE CROSSED PATHS, IN STARLING CITY I LOOKED INTO YOU. DID MY HOMEWORK.
HONG KONG. RUSSIA. I KNOW ABOUT ALL OF IT.
HOW LONG BEFORE THOSE SINS TURN UP IN YOUR PRECIOUS CITY?
DO YOU THINK THERE ARE ENOUGH LIES TO COVER THEM ALL UP?
SO LOCK ME UP AND THROW AWAY THE KEY... YOU WILL STILL HAVE TO PAY FOR YOUR CRIMES.

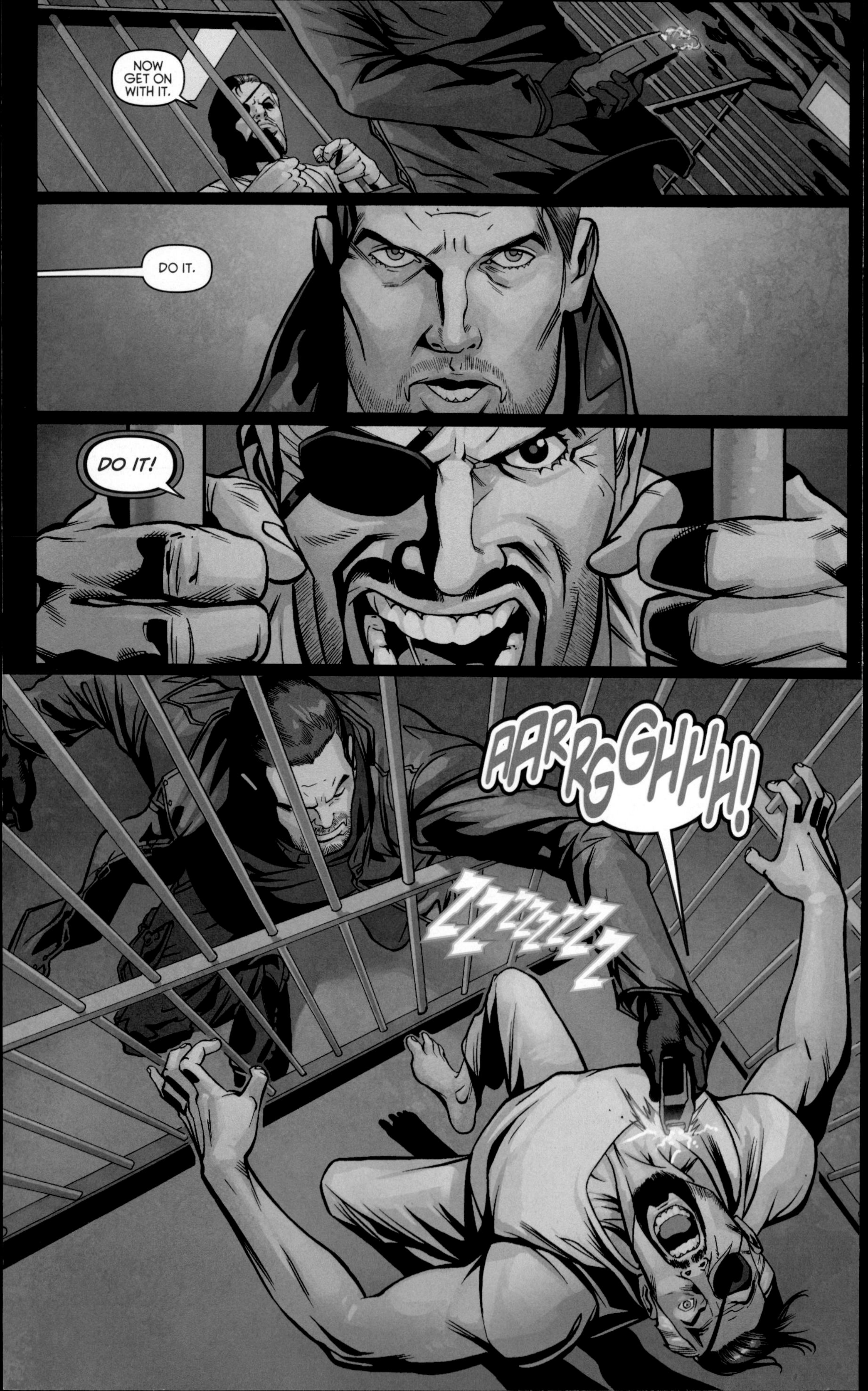
NOW GET ON WITH IT.
DO IT.
DO IT!
AARRGGHHH!
ZZZZZZZZZ

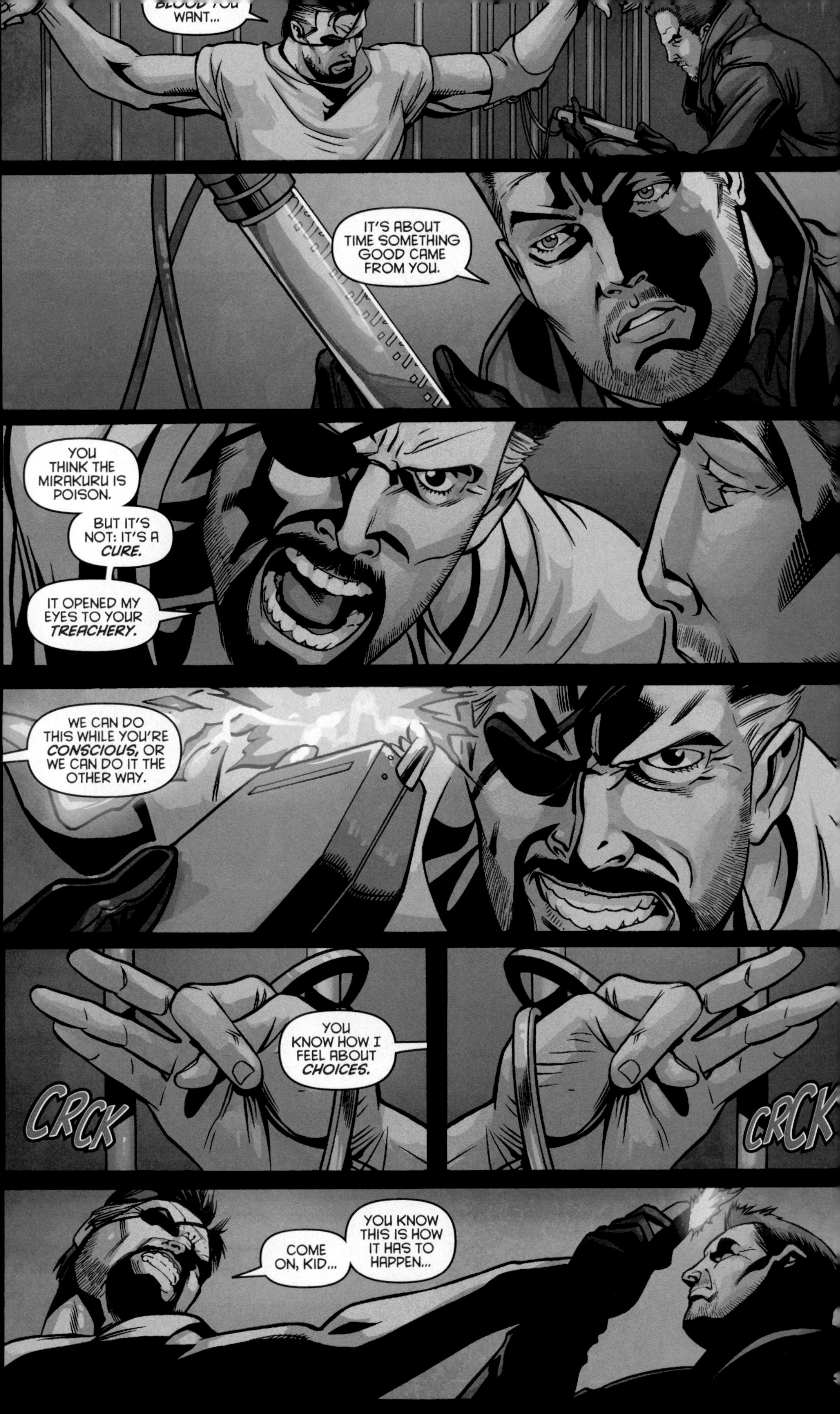
WANT...
IT'S ABOUT TIME SOMETHING GOOD CAME FROM YOU.
YOU THINK THE MIRAKURU IS POISON.
BUT IT'S NOT: IT'S A CURE.
IT OPENED MY EYES TO YOUR TREACHERY.
WE CAN DO THIS WHILE YOU'RE CONSCIOUS, OR WE CAN DO IT THE OTHER WAY.
YOU KNOW HOW I FEEL ABOUT CHOICES.
CRCK
CRCK
COME ON, KID...
YOU KNOW THIS IS HOW IT HAS TO HAPPEN...

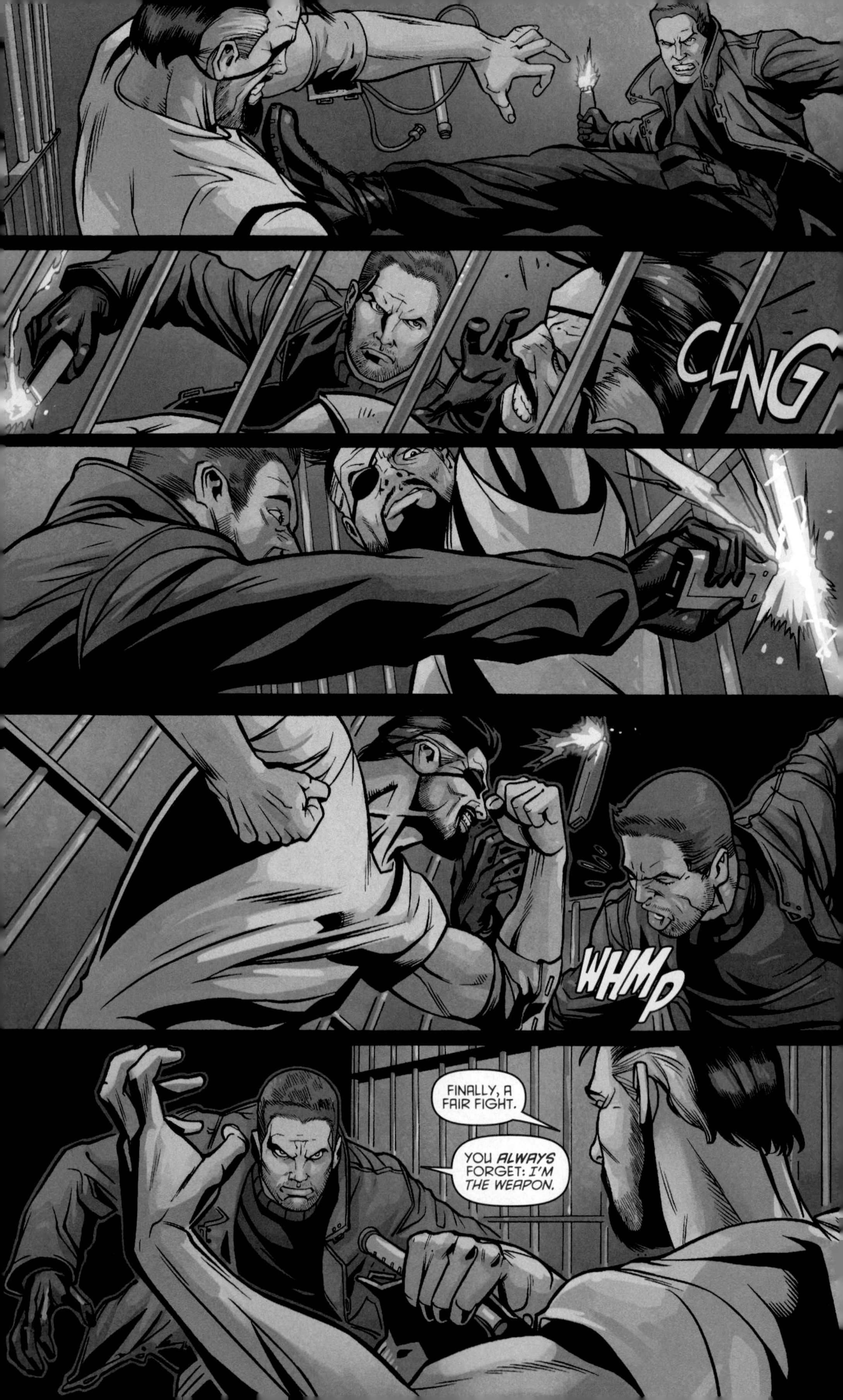
CLNG
WHMP
FINALLY, A FAIR FIGHT.
YOU *ALWAYS* FORGET: I'M *THE WEAPON.*

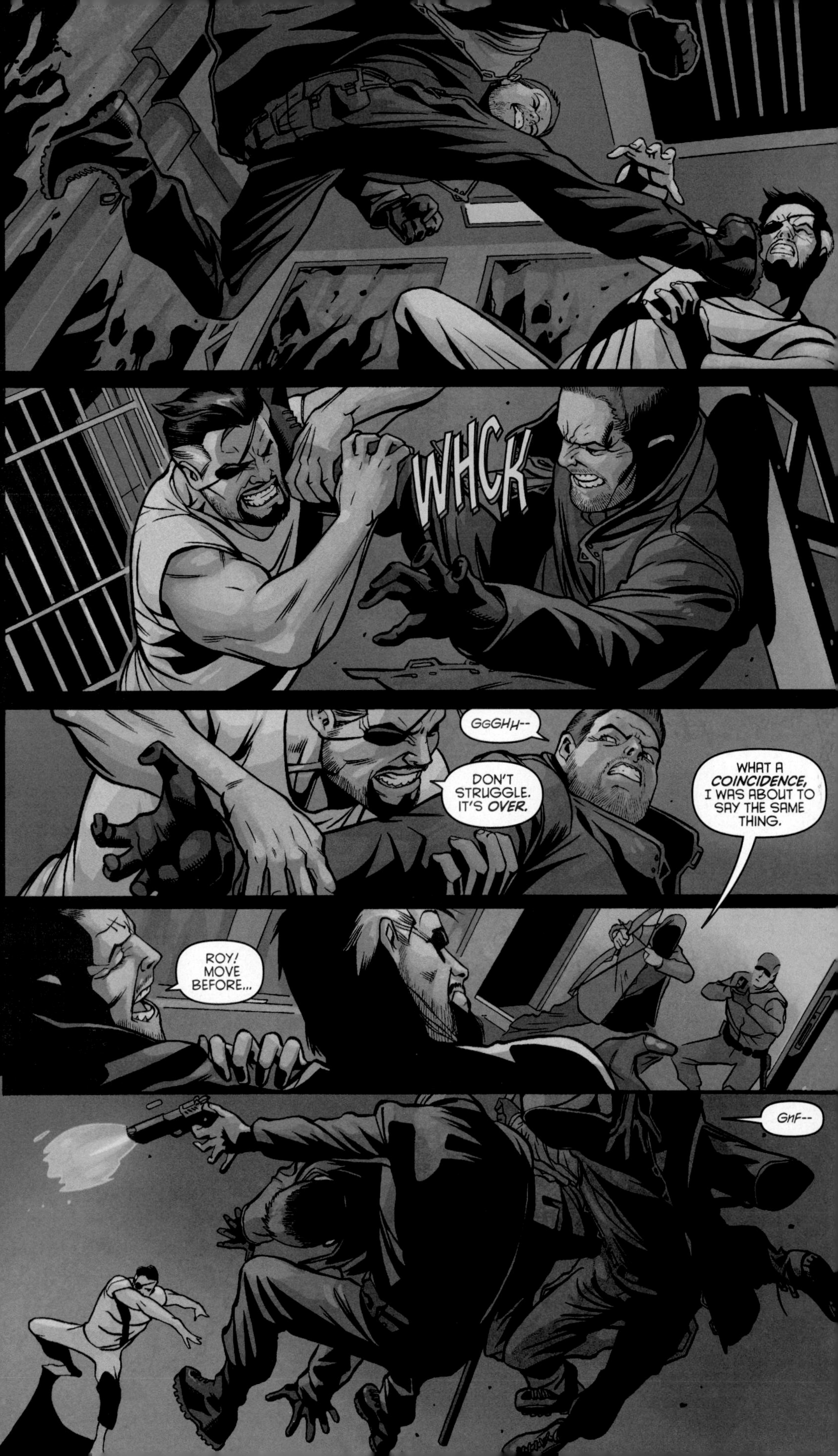
WHCK
GGGHH--
DON'T STRUGGLE. IT'S OVER.
WHAT A COINCIDENCE, I WAS ABOUT TO SAY THE SAME THING.
ROY! MOVE BEFORE...
GNF--

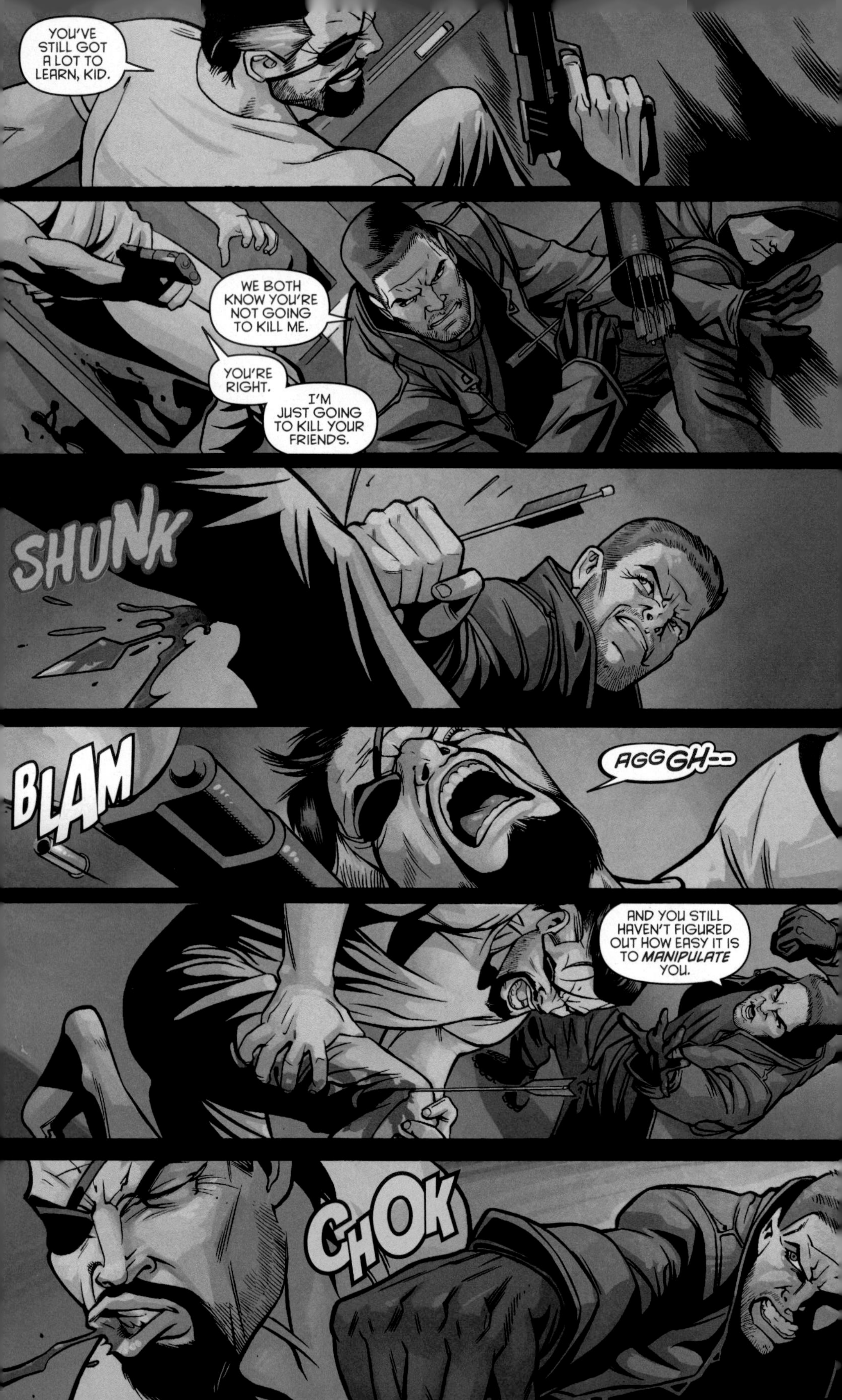

YOU'VE STILL GOT A LOT TO LEARN, KID.
WE BOTH KNOW YOU'RE NOT GOING TO KILL ME.
YOU'RE RIGHT.
I'M JUST GOING TO KILL YOUR FRIENDS.
SHUNK
BLAM
AGGGH--
AND YOU STILL HAVEN'T FIGURED OUT HOW EASY IT IS TO *MANIPULATE* YOU.
CHOK

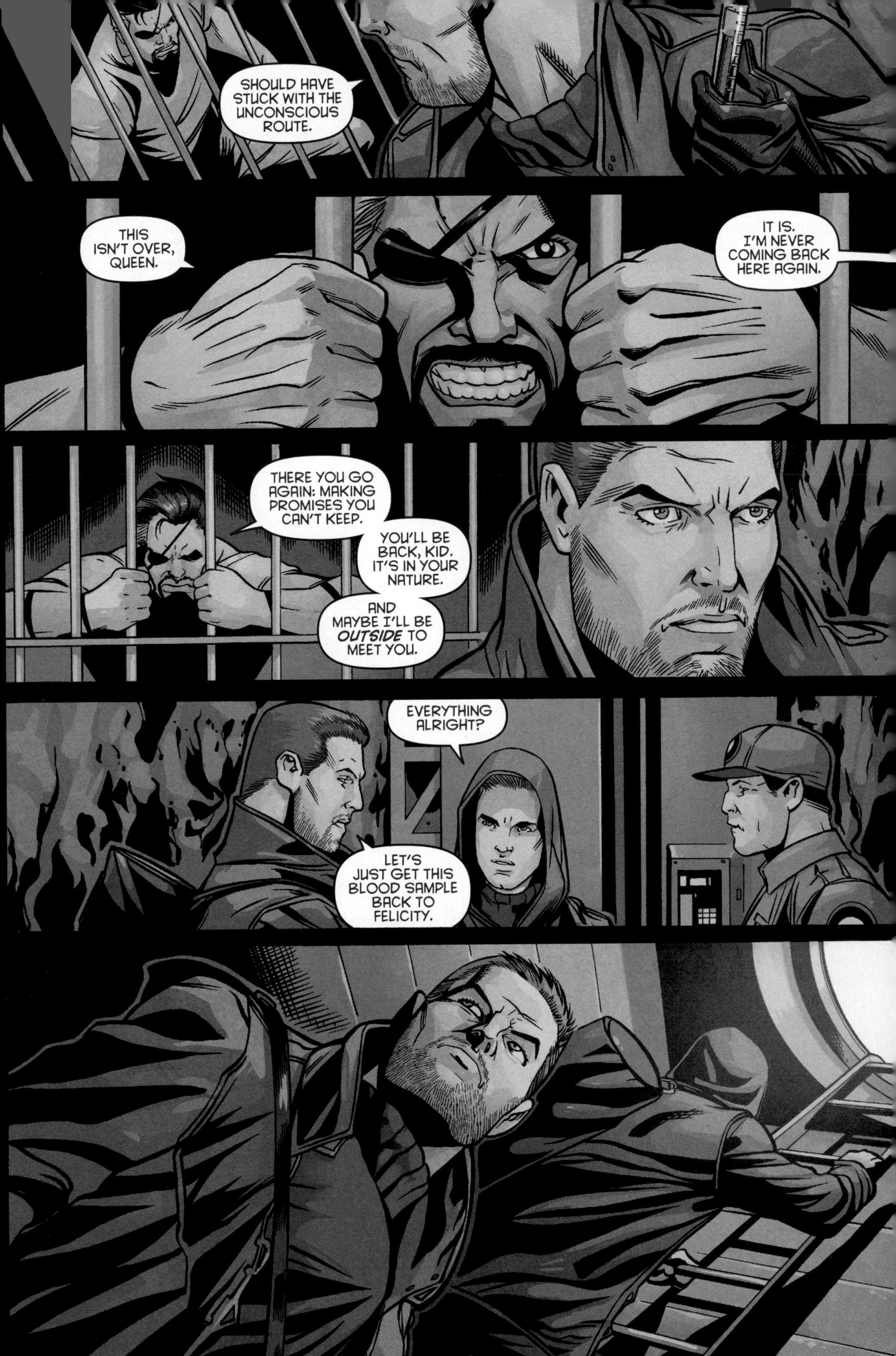
SHOULD HAVE STUCK WITH THE UNCONSCIOUS ROUTE.
THIS ISN'T OVER, QUEEN.
IT IS. I'M NEVER COMING BACK HERE AGAIN.
THERE YOU GO AGAIN: MAKING PROMISES YOU CAN'T KEEP.
YOU'LL BE BACK, KID. IT'S IN YOUR NATURE.
AND MAYBE I'LL BE *OUTSIDE* TO MEET YOU.
EVERYTHING ALRIGHT?
LET'S JUST GET THIS BLOOD SAMPLE BACK TO FELICITY.

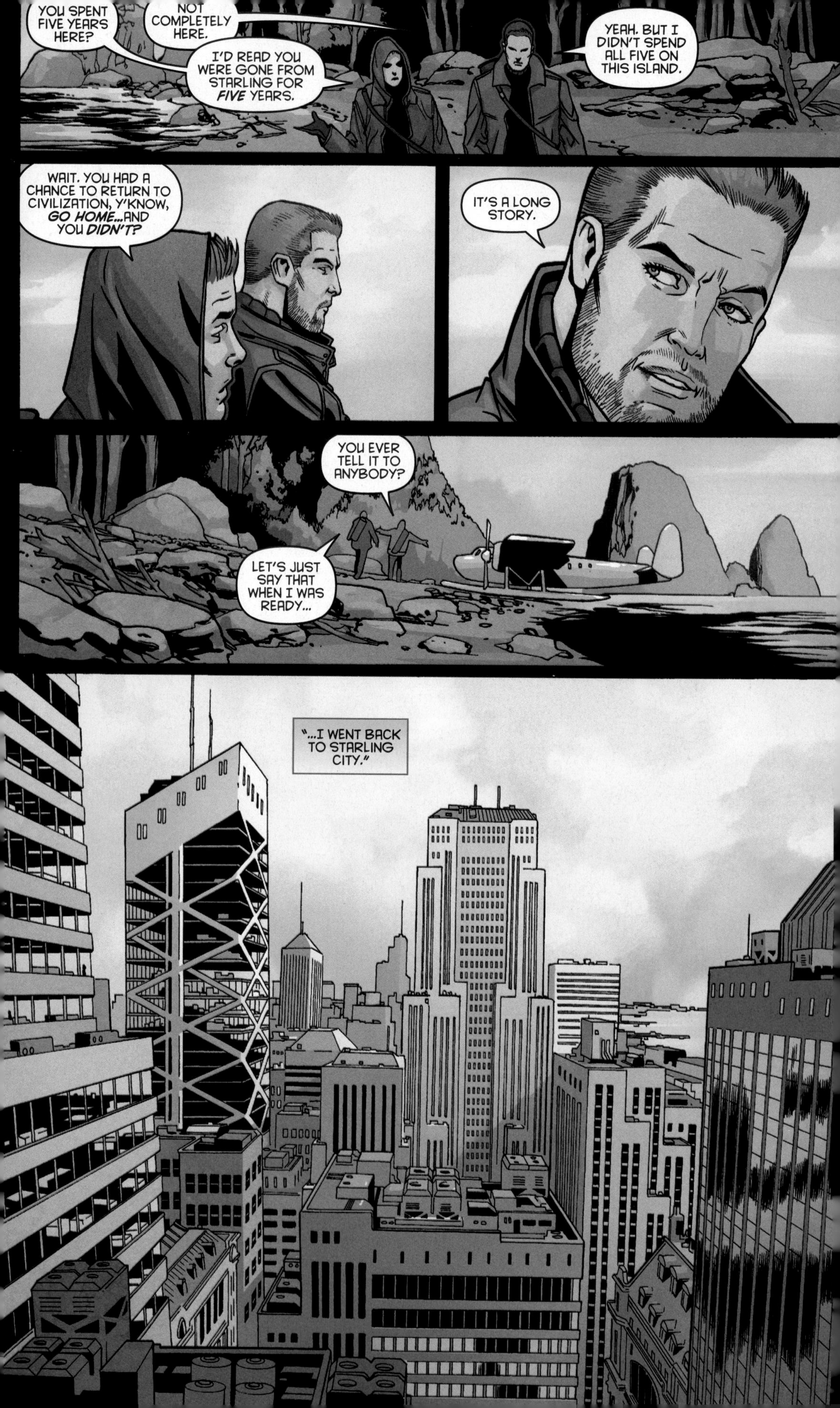
YOU SPENT FIVE YEARS HERE?
NOT COMPLETELY HERE.
I'D READ YOU WERE GONE FROM STARLING FOR FIVE YEARS.
YEAH. BUT I DIDN'T SPEND ALL FIVE ON THIS ISLAND.
WAIT. YOU HAD A CHANCE TO RETURN TO CIVILIZATION, Y'KNOW, GO HOME...AND YOU DIDN'T?
IT'S A LONG STORY.
YOU EVER TELL IT TO ANYBODY?
LET'S JUST SAY THAT WHEN I WAS READY...
"...I WENT BACK TO STARLING CITY."

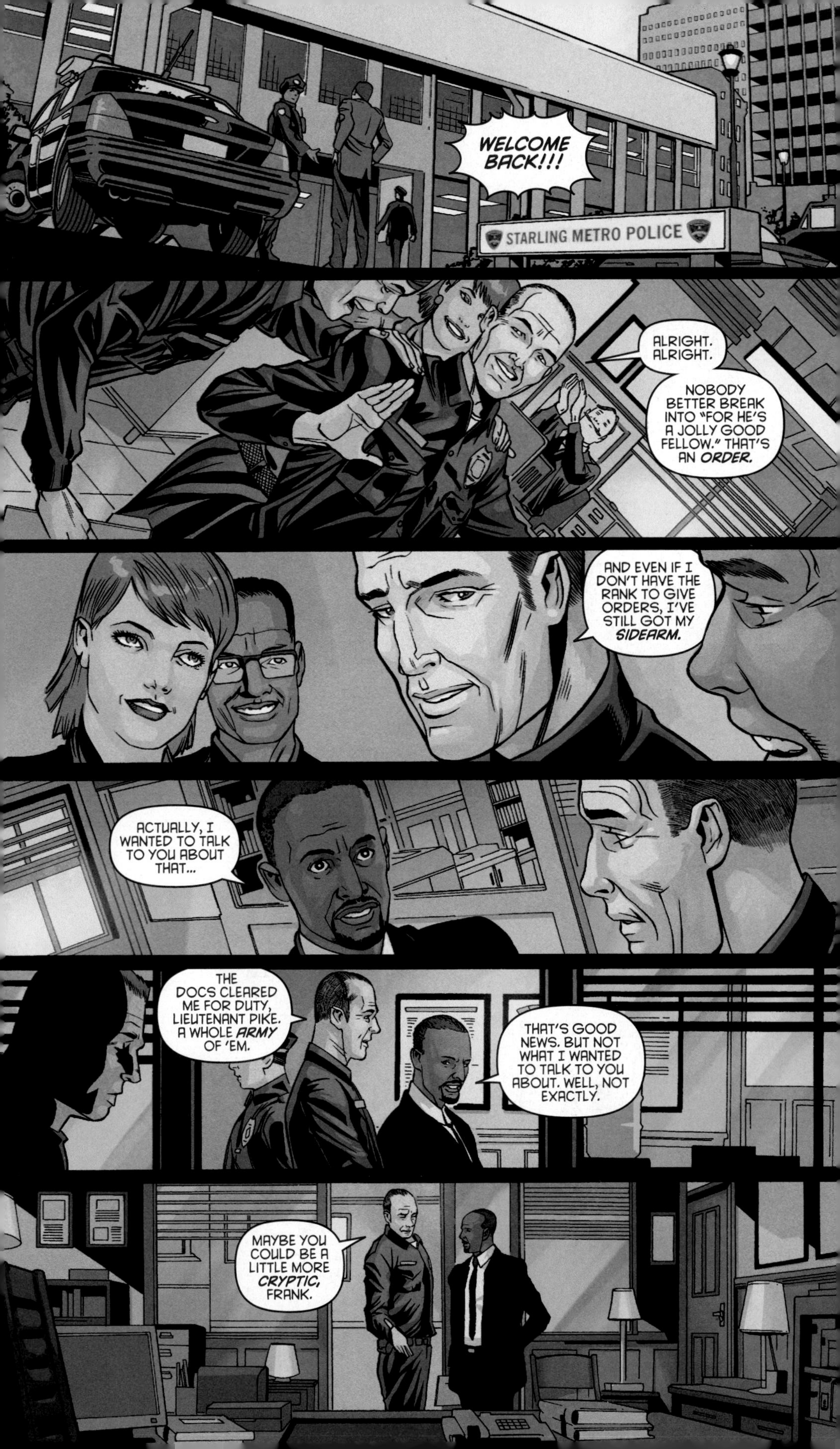

WELCOME BACK!!!
STARLING METRO POLICE
ALRIGHT. ALRIGHT.
NOBODY BETTER BREAK INTO "FOR HE'S A JOLLY GOOD FELLOW." THAT'S AN *ORDER.*
AND EVEN IF I DON'T HAVE THE RANK TO GIVE ORDERS, I'VE STILL GOT MY *SIDEARM.*
ACTUALLY, I WANTED TO TALK TO YOU ABOUT THAT...
THE DOCS CLEARED ME FOR DUTY, LIEUTENANT PIKE. A WHOLE *ARMY* OF 'EM.
THAT'S GOOD NEWS. BUT NOT WHAT I WANTED TO TALK TO YOU ABOUT. WELL, NOT EXACTLY.
MAYBE YOU COULD BE A LITTLE MORE *CRYPTIC,* FRANK.

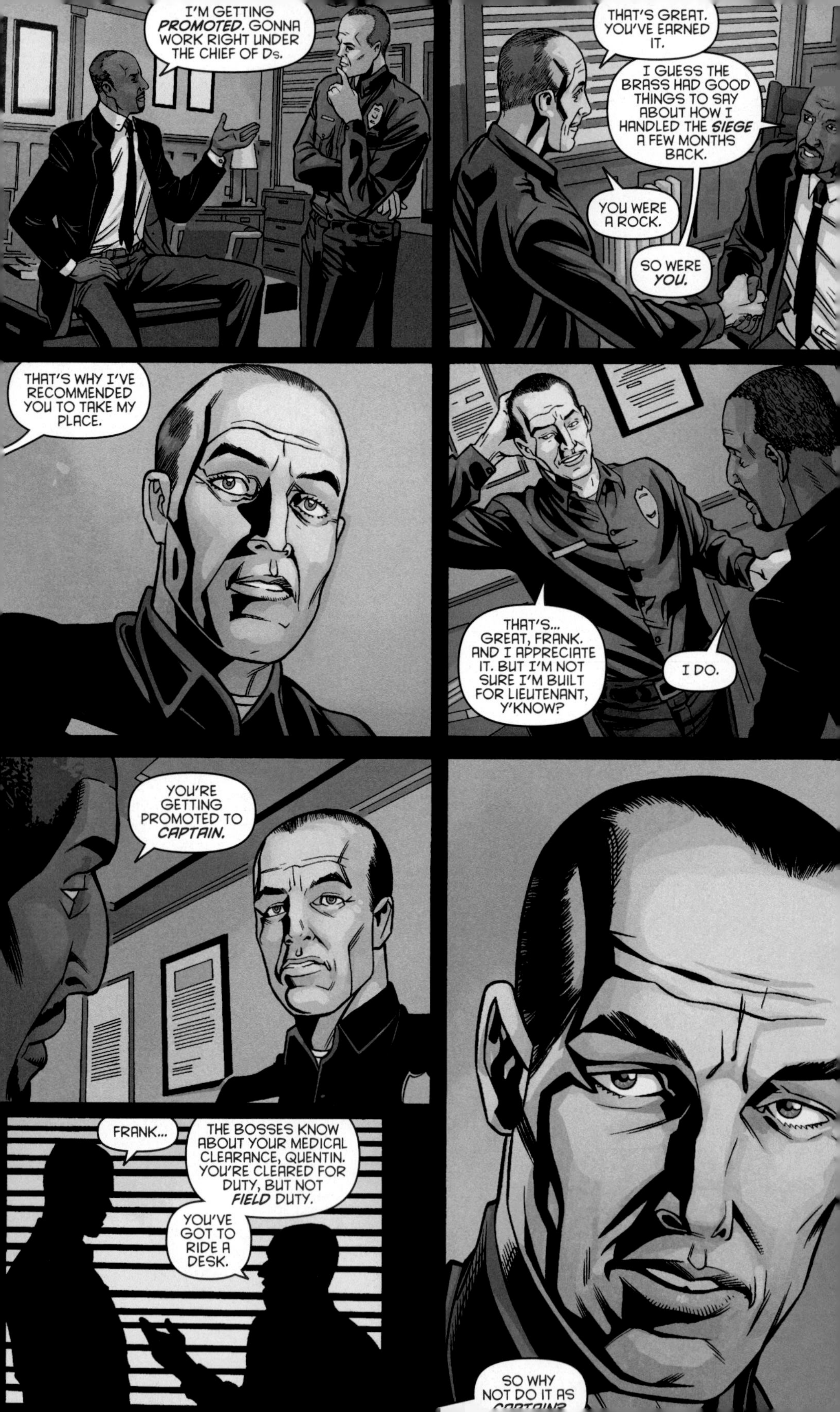
I'M GETTING *PROMOTED.* GONNA WORK RIGHT UNDER THE CHIEF OF Ds.
THAT'S GREAT. YOU'VE EARNED IT.
I GUESS THE BRASS HAD GOOD THINGS TO SAY ABOUT HOW I HANDLED THE *SIEGE* A FEW MONTHS BACK.
YOU WERE A ROCK.
SO WERE *YOU.*
THAT'S WHY I'VE RECOMMENDED YOU TO TAKE MY PLACE.
THAT'S... GREAT, FRANK. AND I APPRECIATE IT. BUT I'M NOT SURE I'M BUILT FOR LIEUTENANT, Y'KNOW?
I DO.
YOU'RE GETTING PROMOTED TO *CAPTAIN.*
FRANK...
THE BOSSES KNOW ABOUT YOUR MEDICAL CLEARANCE, QUENTIN. YOU'RE CLEARED FOR DUTY, BUT NOT *FIELD* DUTY.
YOU'VE GOT TO RIDE A DESK.
SO WHY NOT DO IT AS

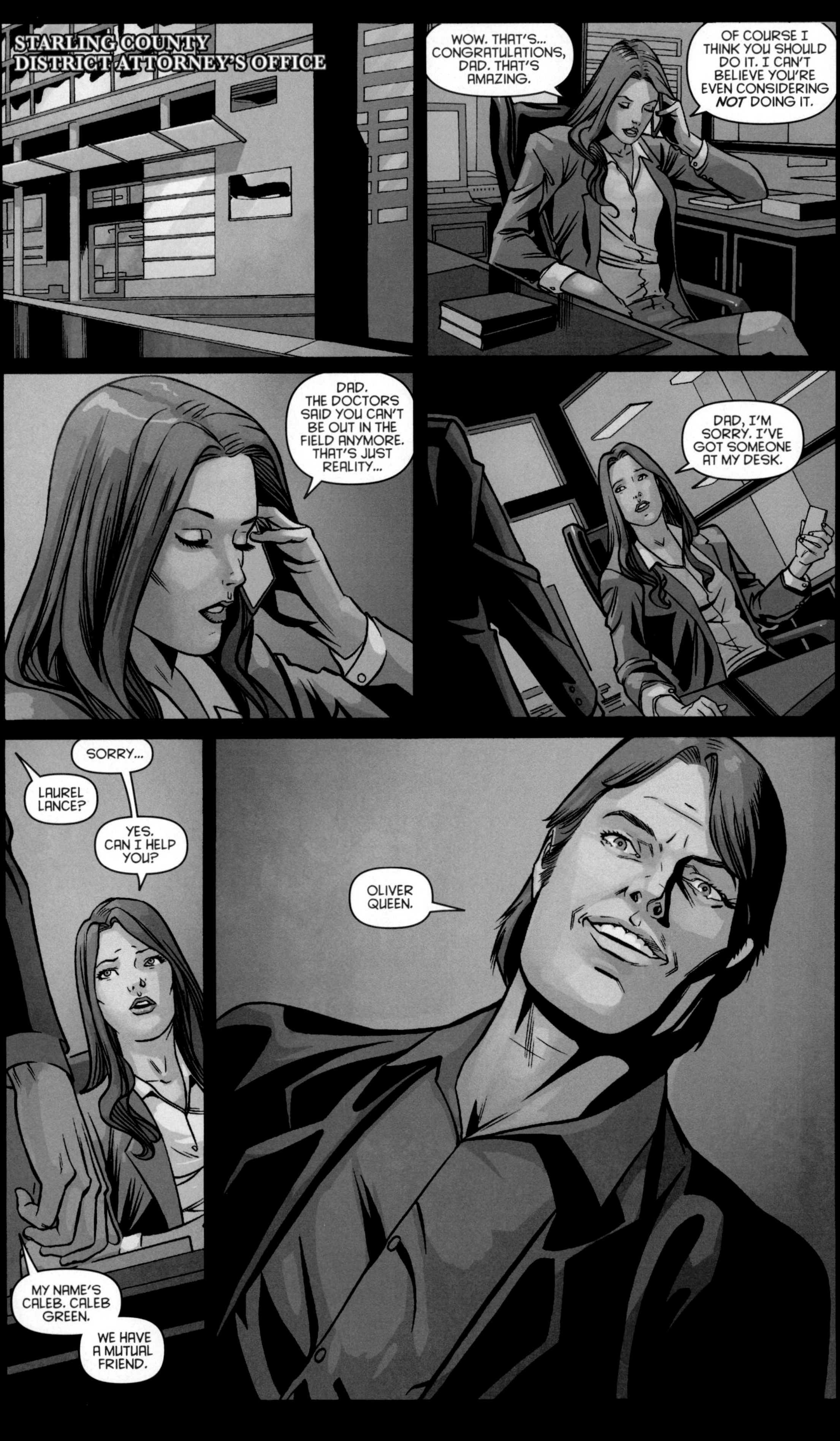
STARLING COUNTY
DISTRICT ATTORNEY'S OFFICE
WOW. THAT'S... CONGRATULATIONS, DAD. THAT'S AMAZING.
OF COURSE I THINK YOU SHOULD DO IT. I CAN'T BELIEVE YOU'RE EVEN CONSIDERING *NOT* DOING IT.
DAD. THE DOCTORS SAID YOU CAN'T BE OUT IN THE FIELD ANYMORE. THAT'S JUST REALITY...
DAD, I'M SORRY. I'VE GOT SOMEONE AT MY DESK.
SORRY...
LAUREL LANCE?
YES. CAN I HELP YOU?
MY NAME'S CALEB. CALEB GREEN.
WE HAVE A MUTUAL FRIEND.
OLIVER QUEEN.

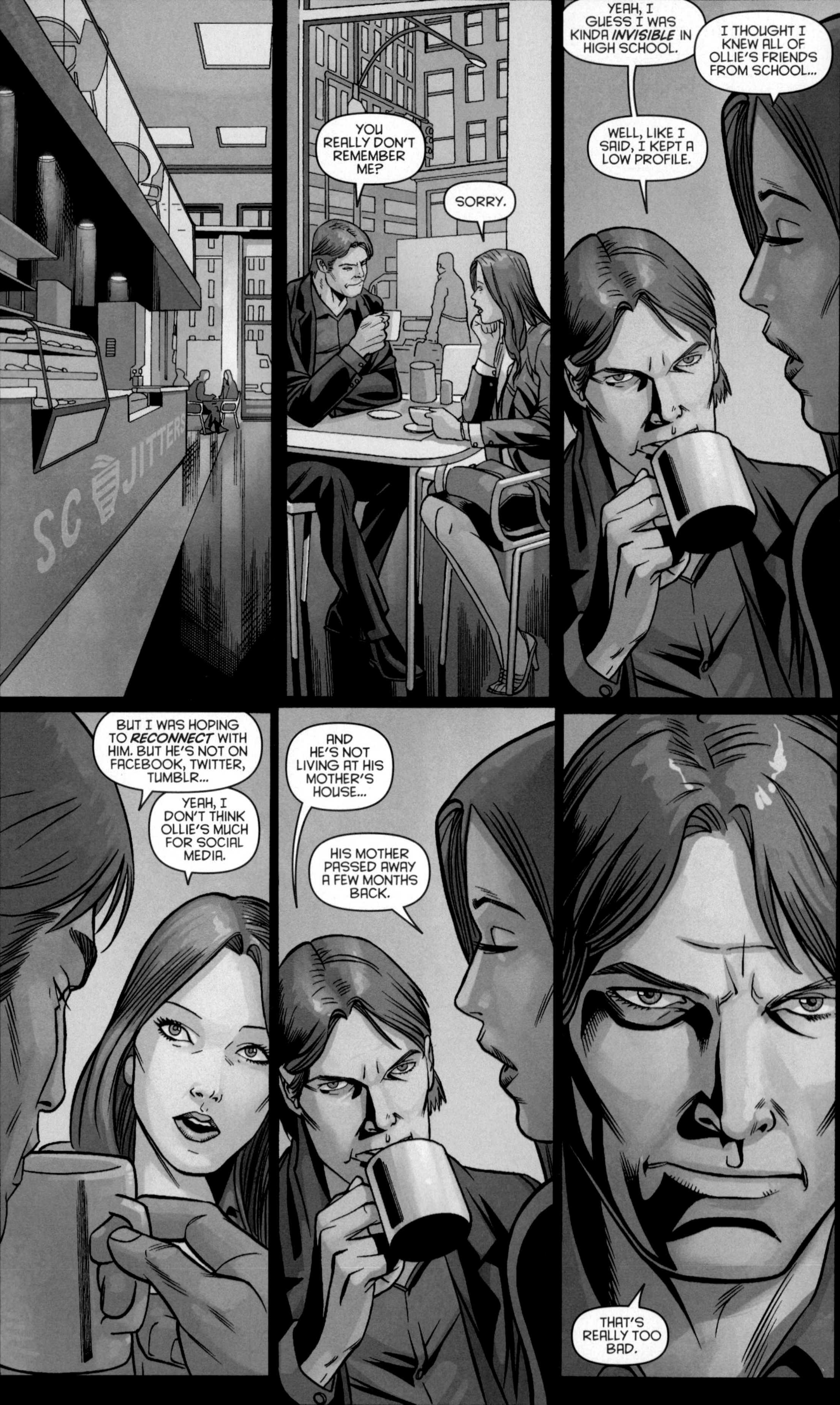
S.C JITTERS
YOU REALLY DON'T REMEMBER ME?
SORRY.
YEAH, I GUESS I WAS KINDA *INVISIBLE* IN HIGH SCHOOL.
I THOUGHT I KNEW ALL OF OLLIE'S FRIENDS FROM SCHOOL...
WELL, LIKE I SAID, I KEPT A LOW PROFILE.
BUT I WAS HOPING TO *RECONNECT* WITH HIM. BUT HE'S NOT ON FACEBOOK, TWITTER, TUMBLR...
YEAH, I DON'T THINK OLLIE'S MUCH FOR SOCIAL MEDIA.
AND HE'S NOT LIVING AT HIS MOTHER'S HOUSE...
HIS MOTHER PASSED AWAY A FEW MONTHS BACK.
THAT'S REALLY TOO BAD.

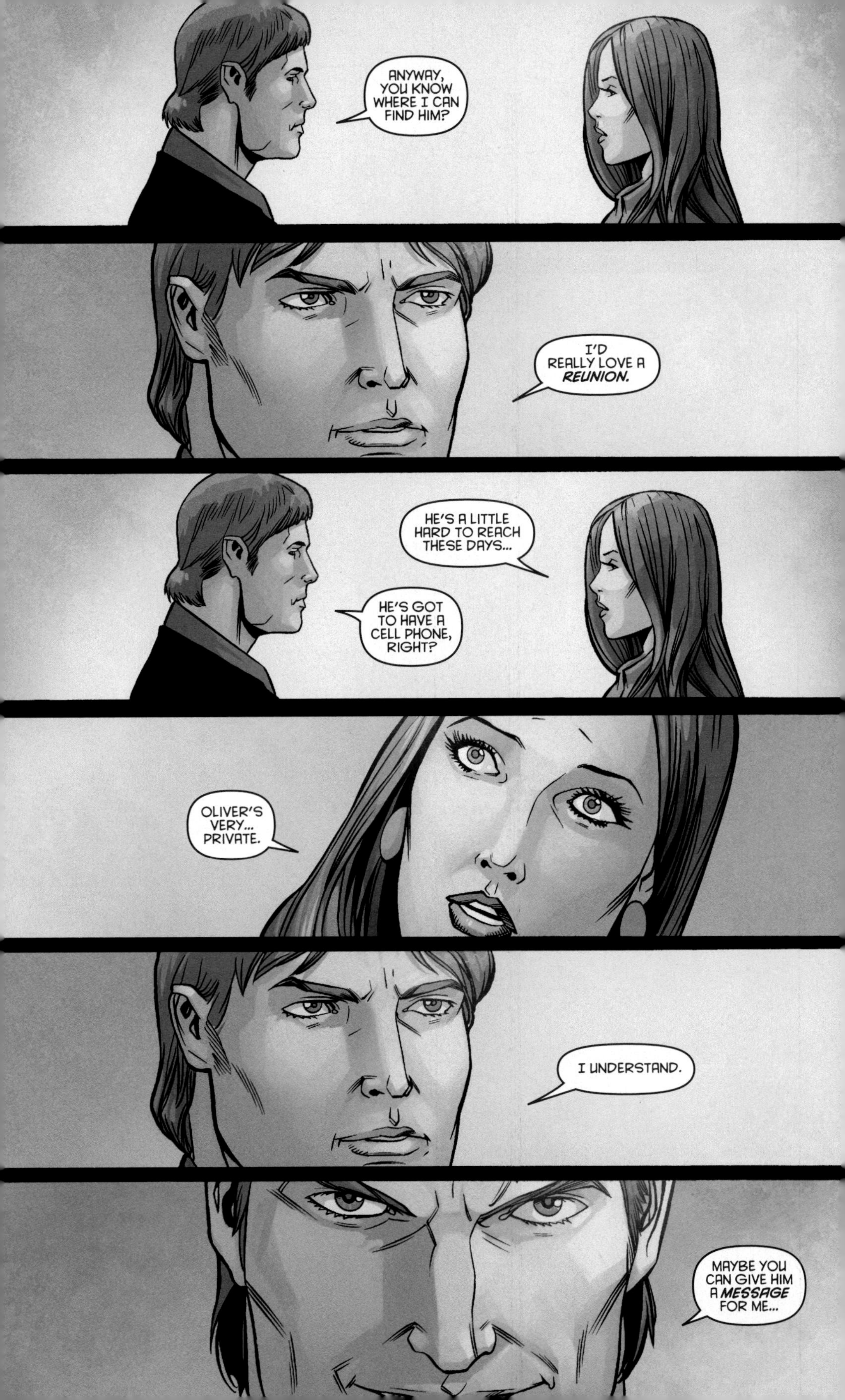
ANYWAY, YOU KNOW WHERE I CAN FIND HIM?
I'D REALLY LOVE A *REUNION.*
HE'S A LITTLE HARD TO REACH THESE DAYS...
HE'S GOT TO HAVE A CELL PHONE, RIGHT?
OLIVER'S VERY... PRIVATE.
I UNDERSTAND.
MAYBE YOU CAN GIVE HIM A *MESSAGE* FOR ME...

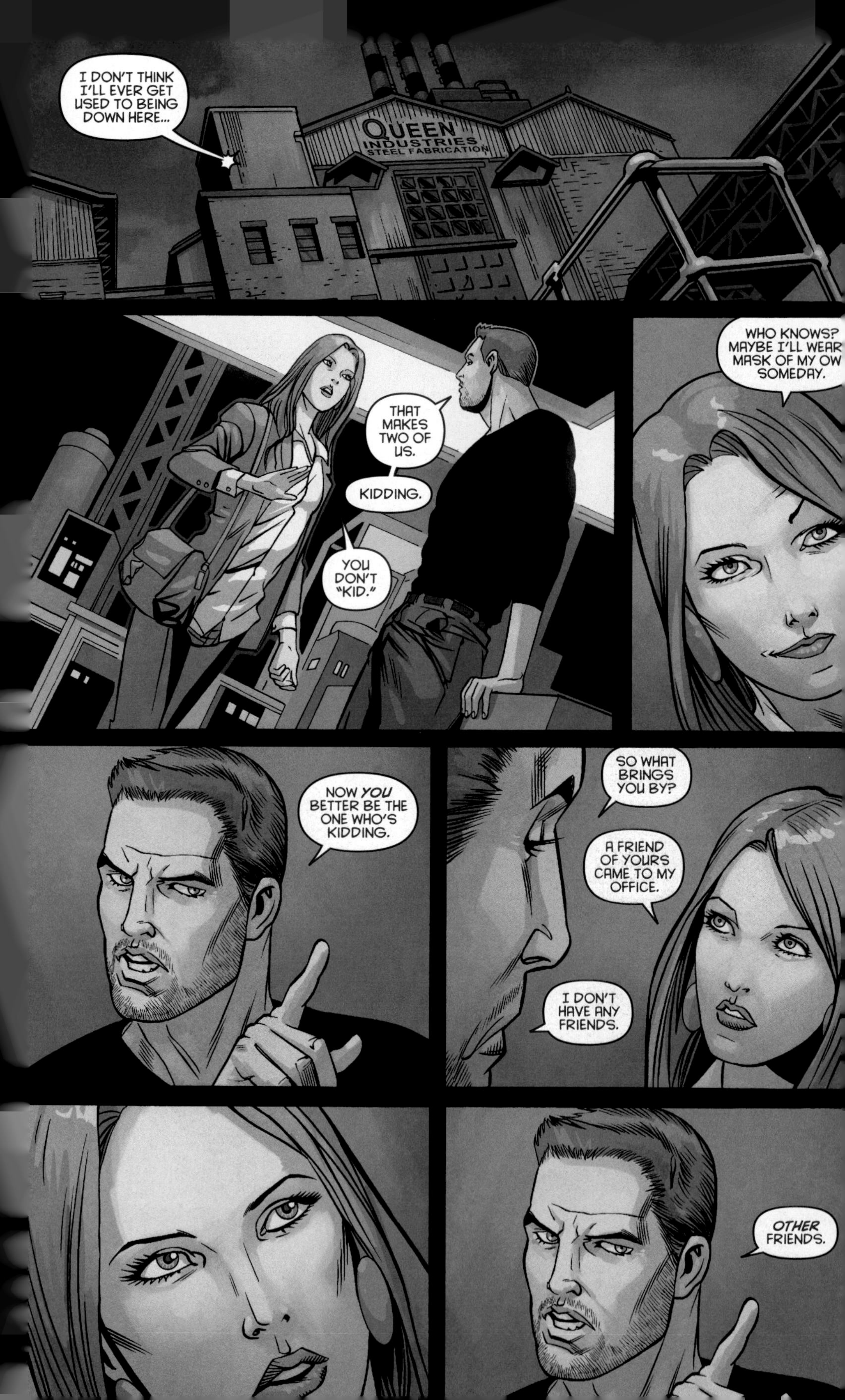

QUEEN INDUSTRIES STEEL FABRICATION
I DON'T THINK I'LL EVER GET USED TO BEING DOWN HERE...
THAT MAKES TWO OF US.
KIDDING.
YOU DON'T "KID."
WHO KNOWS? MAYBE I'LL WEAR MASK OF MY OW SOMEDAY.
NOW *YOU* BETTER BE THE ONE WHO'S KIDDING.
SO WHAT BRINGS YOU BY?
A FRIEND OF YOURS CAME TO MY OFFICE.
I DON'T HAVE ANY FRIENDS.
OTHER FRIENDS.

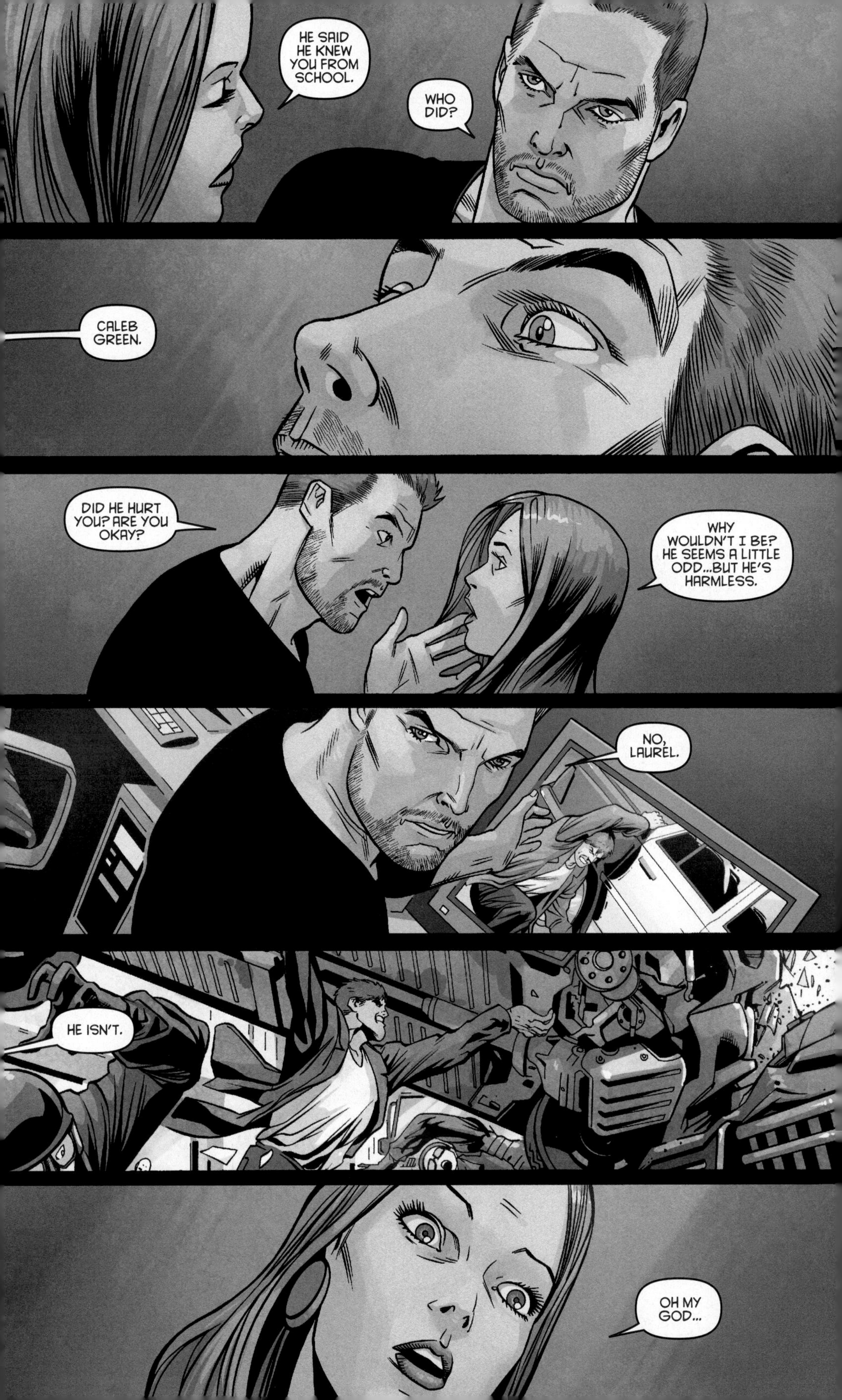
HE SAID HE KNEW YOU FROM SCHOOL.
WHO DID?
CALEB GREEN.
DID HE HURT YOU? ARE YOU OKAY?
WHY WOULDN'T I BE? HE SEEMS A LITTLE ODD...BUT HE'S HARMLESS.
NO, LAUREL.
HE ISN'T.
OH MY GOD...

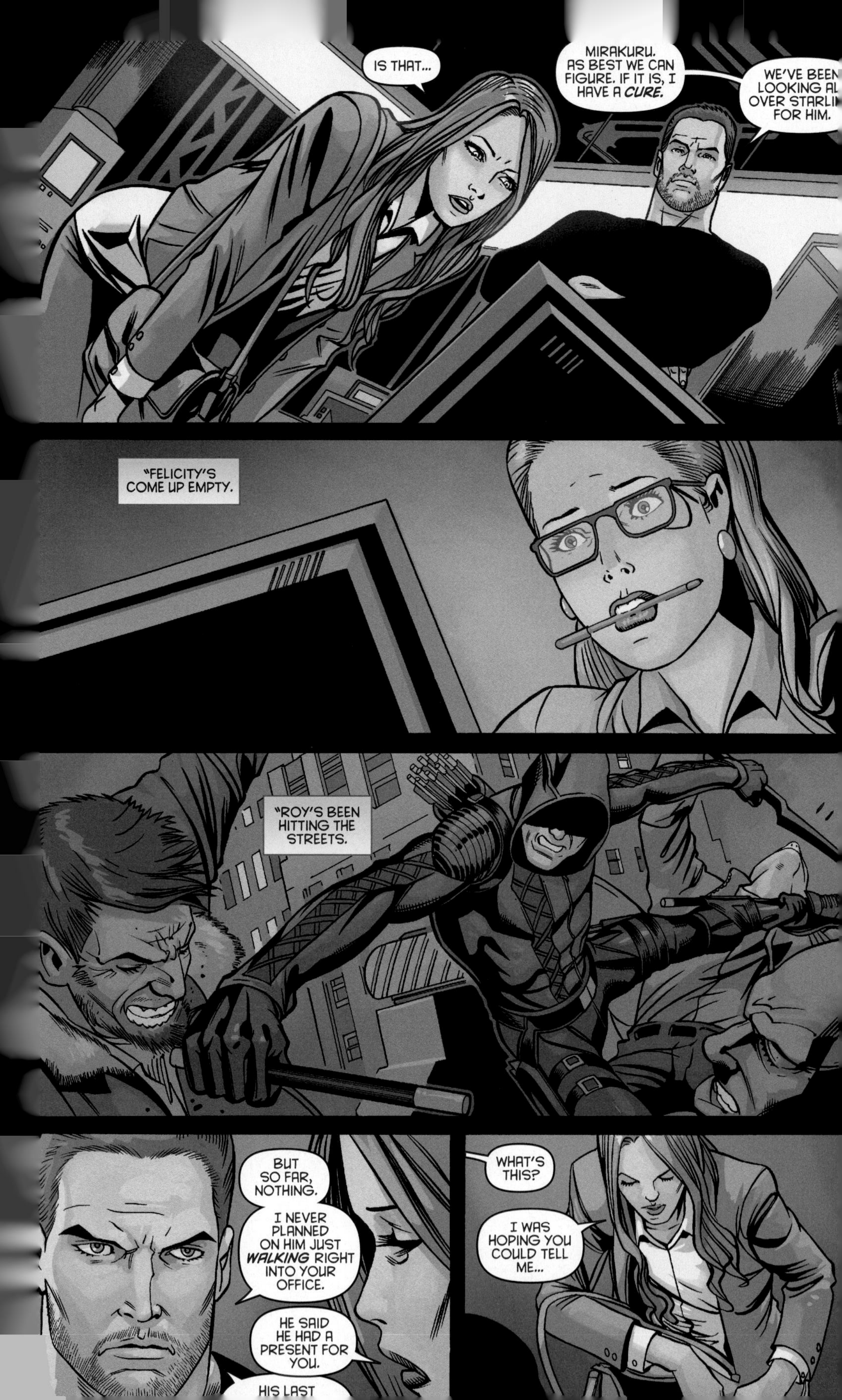
IS THAT...
MIRAKURU. AS BEST WE CAN FIGURE. IF IT IS, I HAVE A CURE.
WE'VE BEEN LOOKING AL OVER STARLI FOR HIM.
"FELICITY'S COME UP EMPTY.
"ROY'S BEEN HITTING THE STREETS.
BUT SO FAR, NOTHING.
I NEVER PLANNED ON HIM JUST WALKING RIGHT INTO YOUR OFFICE.
HE SAID HE HAD A PRESENT FOR YOU.
HIS LAST
WHAT'S THIS?
I WAS HOPING YOU COULD TELL ME...

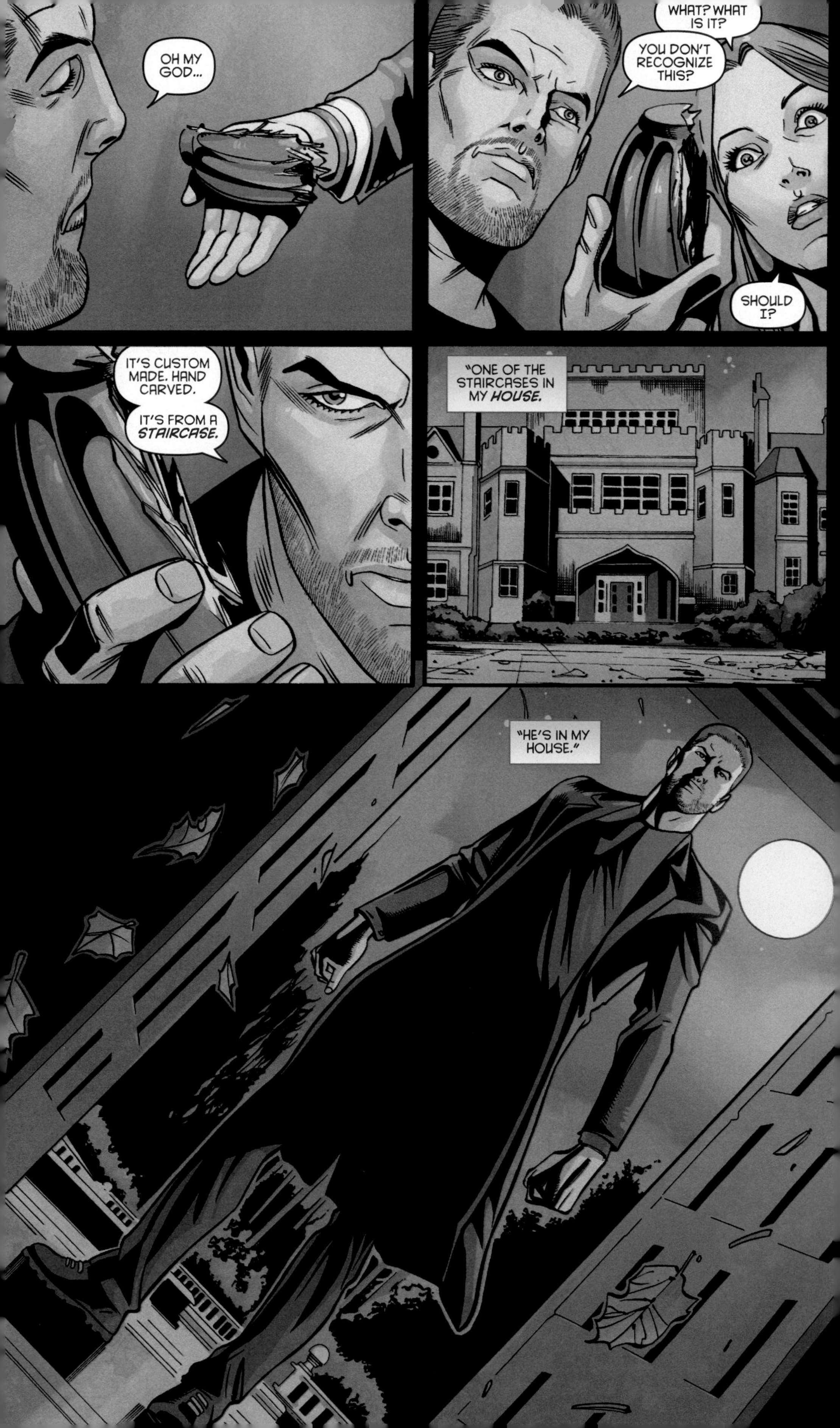
OH MY GOD...
WHAT? WHAT IS IT?
YOU DON'T RECOGNIZE THIS?
SHOULD I?
IT'S CUSTOM MADE. HAND CARVED.
IT'S FROM A *STAIRCASE.*
"ONE OF THE STAIRCASES IN MY *HOUSE.*
"HE'S IN MY HOUSE."

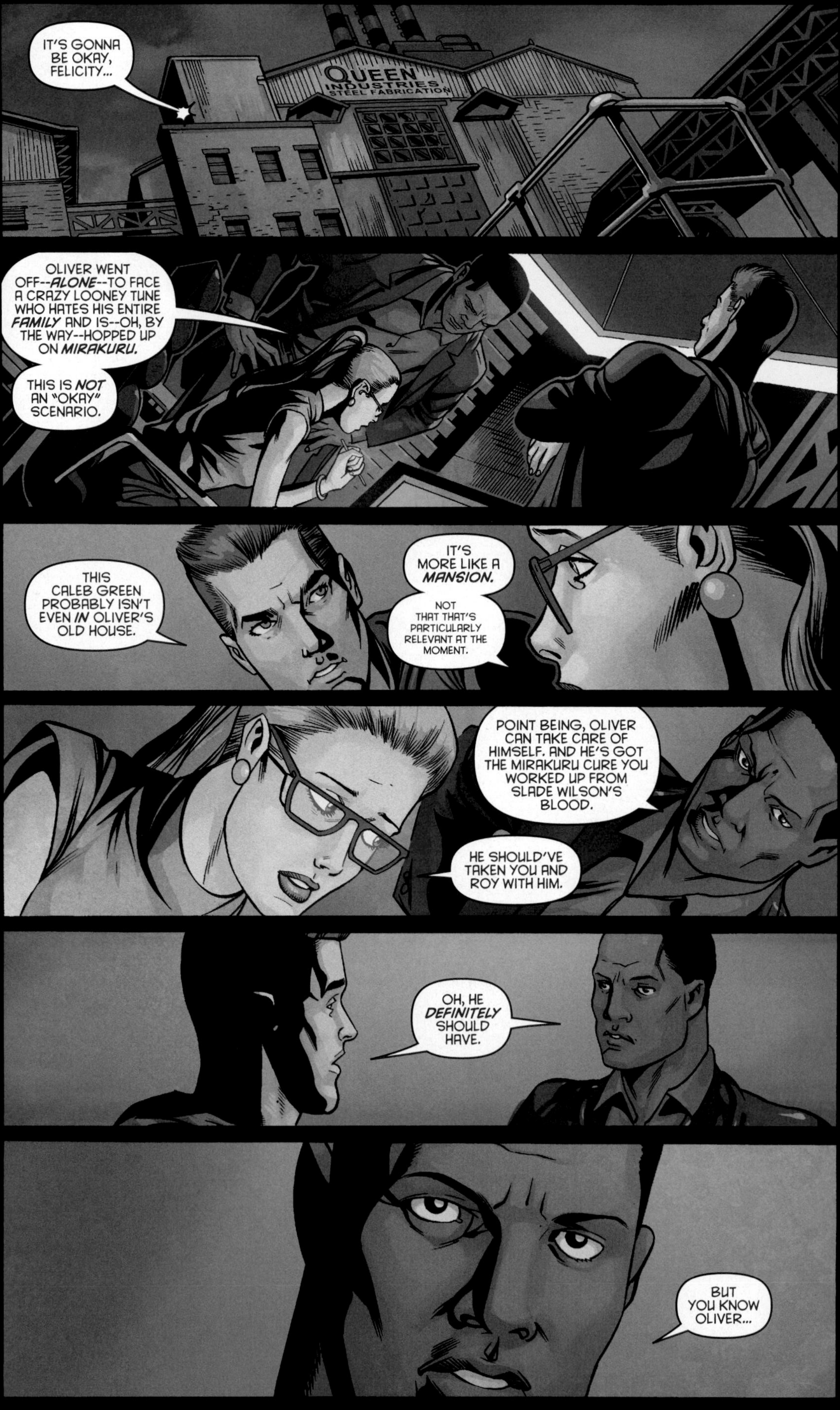
IT'S GONNA BE OKAY, FELICITY...
QUEEN INDUSTRIES STEEL FABRICATION
OLIVER WENT OFF--*ALONE*--TO FACE A CRAZY LOONEY TUNE WHO HATES HIS ENTIRE *FAMILY* AND IS--OH, BY THE WAY--HOPPED UP ON *MIRAKURU.*
THIS IS *NOT* AN "OKAY" SCENARIO.
THIS CALEB GREEN PROBABLY ISN'T EVEN *IN* OLIVER'S OLD HOUSE.
IT'S MORE LIKE A *MANSION.*
NOT THAT THAT'S PARTICULARLY RELEVANT AT THE MOMENT.
POINT BEING, OLIVER CAN TAKE CARE OF HIMSELF. AND HE'S GOT THE MIRAKURU CURE YOU WORKED UP FROM SLADE WILSON'S BLOOD.
HE SHOULD'VE TAKEN YOU AND ROY WITH HIM.
OH, HE *DEFINITELY* SHOULD HAVE.
BUT YOU KNOW OLIVER...

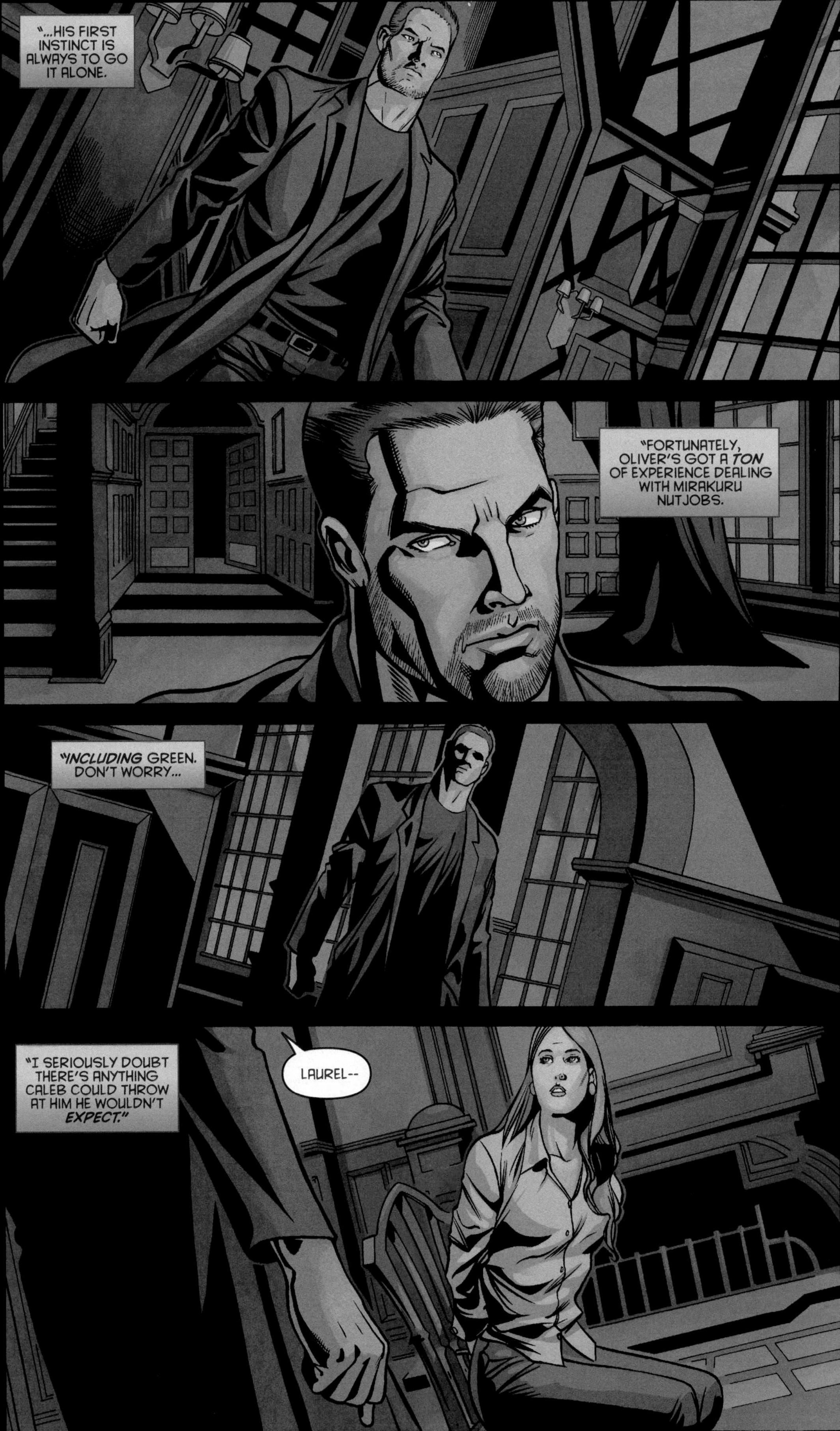
"...HIS FIRST INSTINCT IS ALWAYS TO GO IT ALONE.
"FORTUNATELY, OLIVER'S GOT A *TON* OF EXPERIENCE DEALING WITH MIRAKURU NUTJOBS.
"*INCLUDING* GREEN. DON'T WORRY...
"I SERIOUSLY DOUBT THERE'S ANYTHING CALEB COULD THROW AT HIM HE WOULDN'T *EXPECT.*"
LAUREL--

OLIVER—

WHAT HAPPENED?

I LEFT YOUR PLACE AND WENT HOME. HE WAS THERE...

"...HE WAS WAITING FOR ME.

IT'S LIKE THE HUNDREDTH TIME MY APARTMENT'S BEEN BROKEN INTO. I REALLY NEED TO MOVE...

LET'S WORRY ABOUT THAT LATER. I'M GETTING YOU OUT OF HERE...

WHERE'S GREEN?

I DON'T KNOW. HE KNOCKED ME OUT. I WOKE UP HERE.

HELLO, OLIVER.

I'M GLAD YOU COULD JOIN THE PARTY.

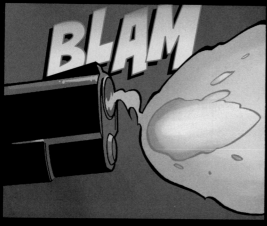

BLAM

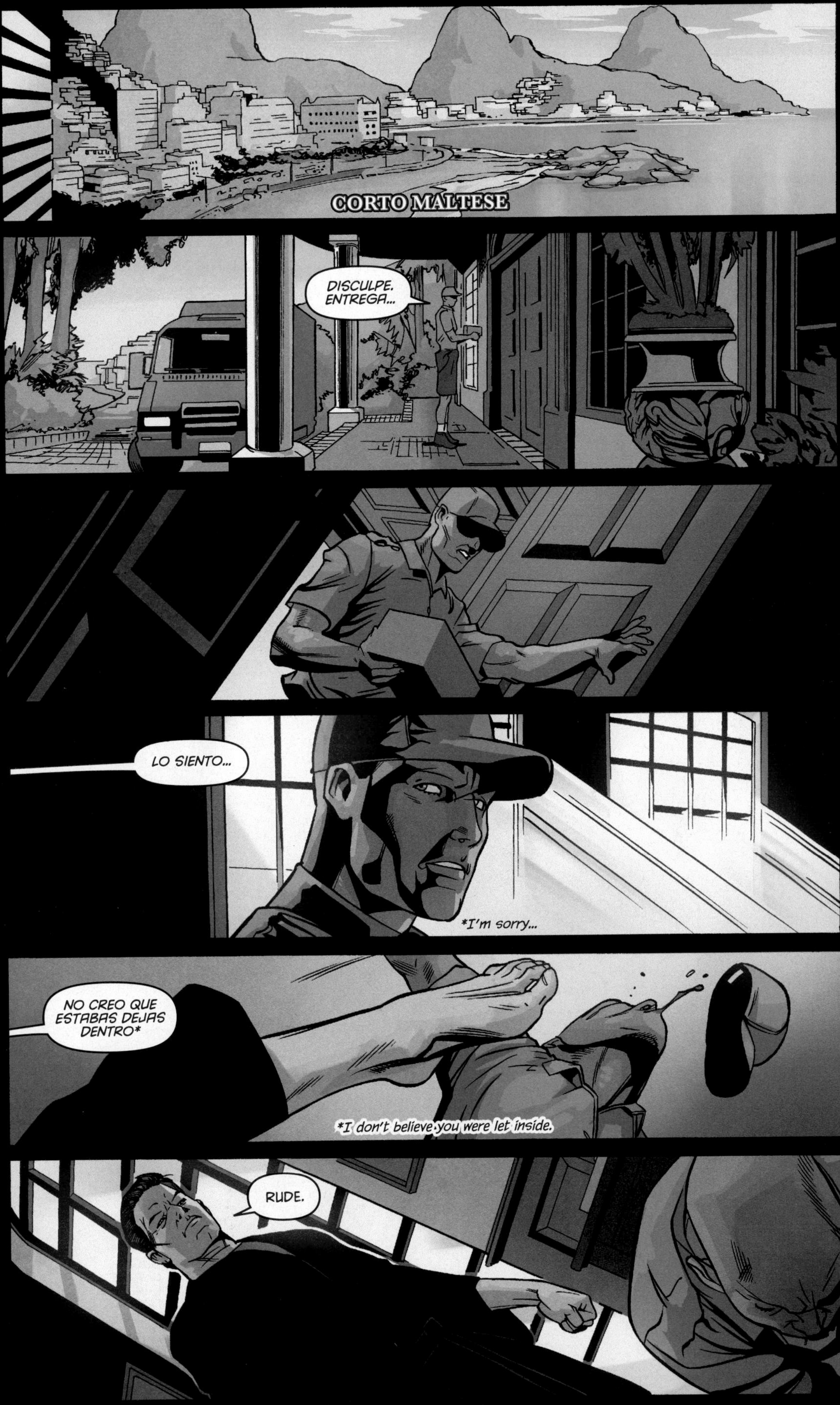
CORTO MALTESE
DISCULPE. ENTREGA...
LO SIENTO...
*I'm sorry...
NO CREO QUE ESTABAS DEJAS DENTRO*
*I don't believe you were let inside.
RUDE.

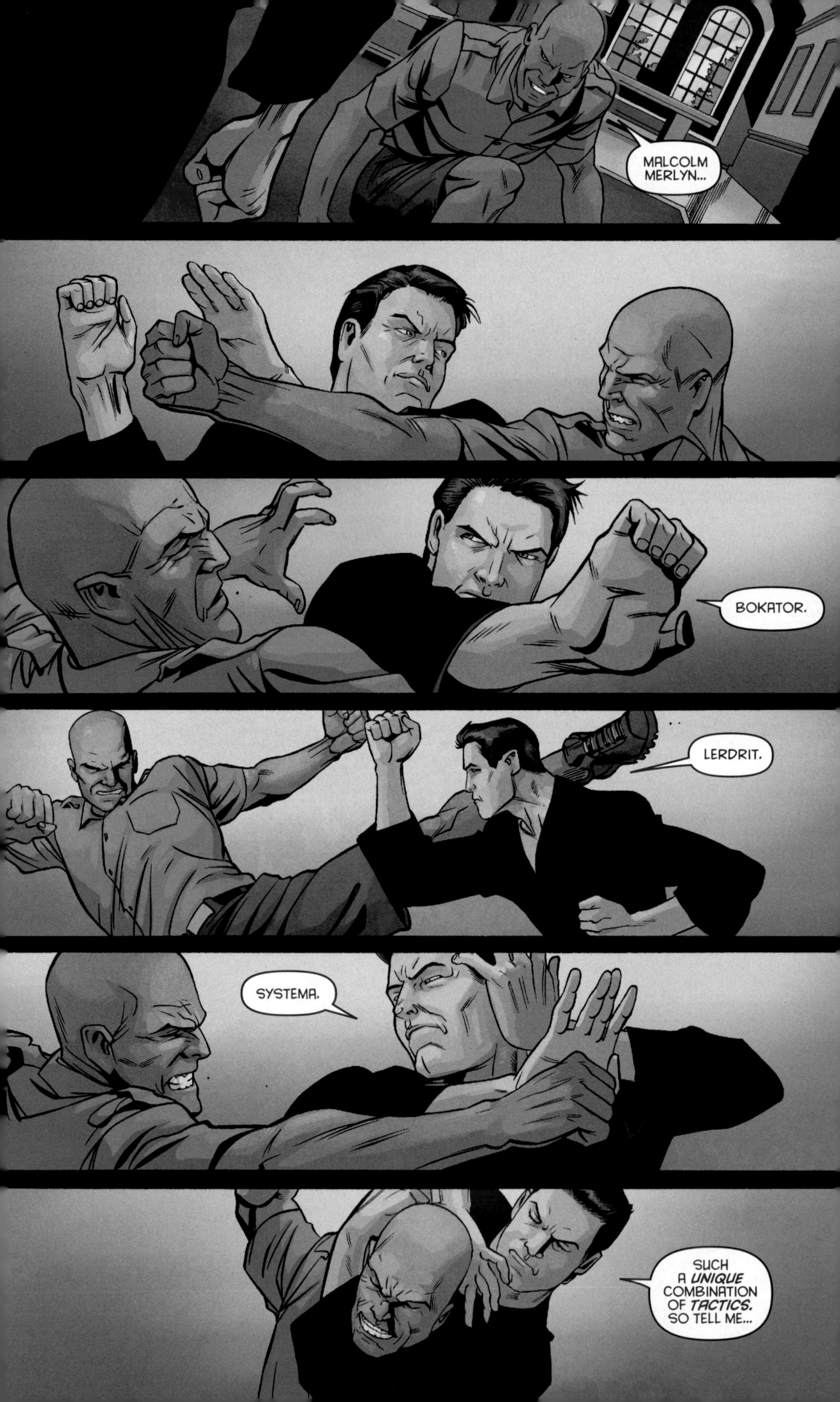
MALCOLM MERLYN...
BOKATOR.
LERDRIT.
SYSTEMA.
SUCH A *UNIQUE* COMBINATION OF *TACTICS.* SO TELL ME...

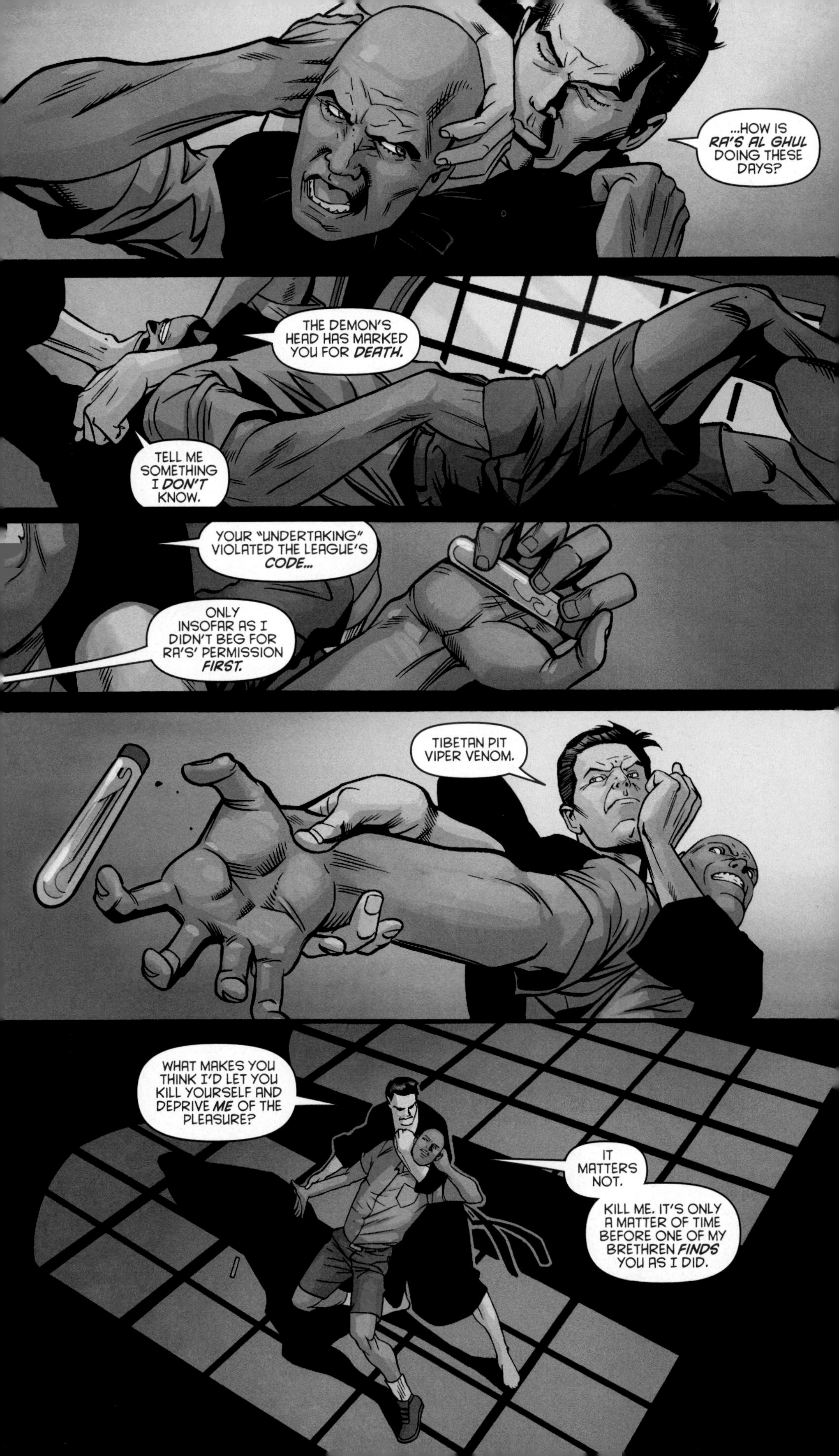
...HOW IS RA'S AL GHUL DOING THESE DAYS?
THE DEMON'S HEAD HAS MARKED YOU FOR DEATH.
TELL ME SOMETHING I DON'T KNOW.
YOUR "UNDERTAKING" VIOLATED THE LEAGUE'S CODE...
ONLY INSOFAR AS I DIDN'T BEG FOR RA'S' PERMISSION FIRST.
TIBETAN PIT VIPER VENOM.
WHAT MAKES YOU THINK I'D LET YOU KILL YOURSELF AND DEPRIVE ME OF THE PLEASURE?
IT MATTERS NOT.
KILL ME. IT'S ONLY A MATTER OF TIME BEFORE ONE OF MY BRETHREN FINDS YOU AS I DID.

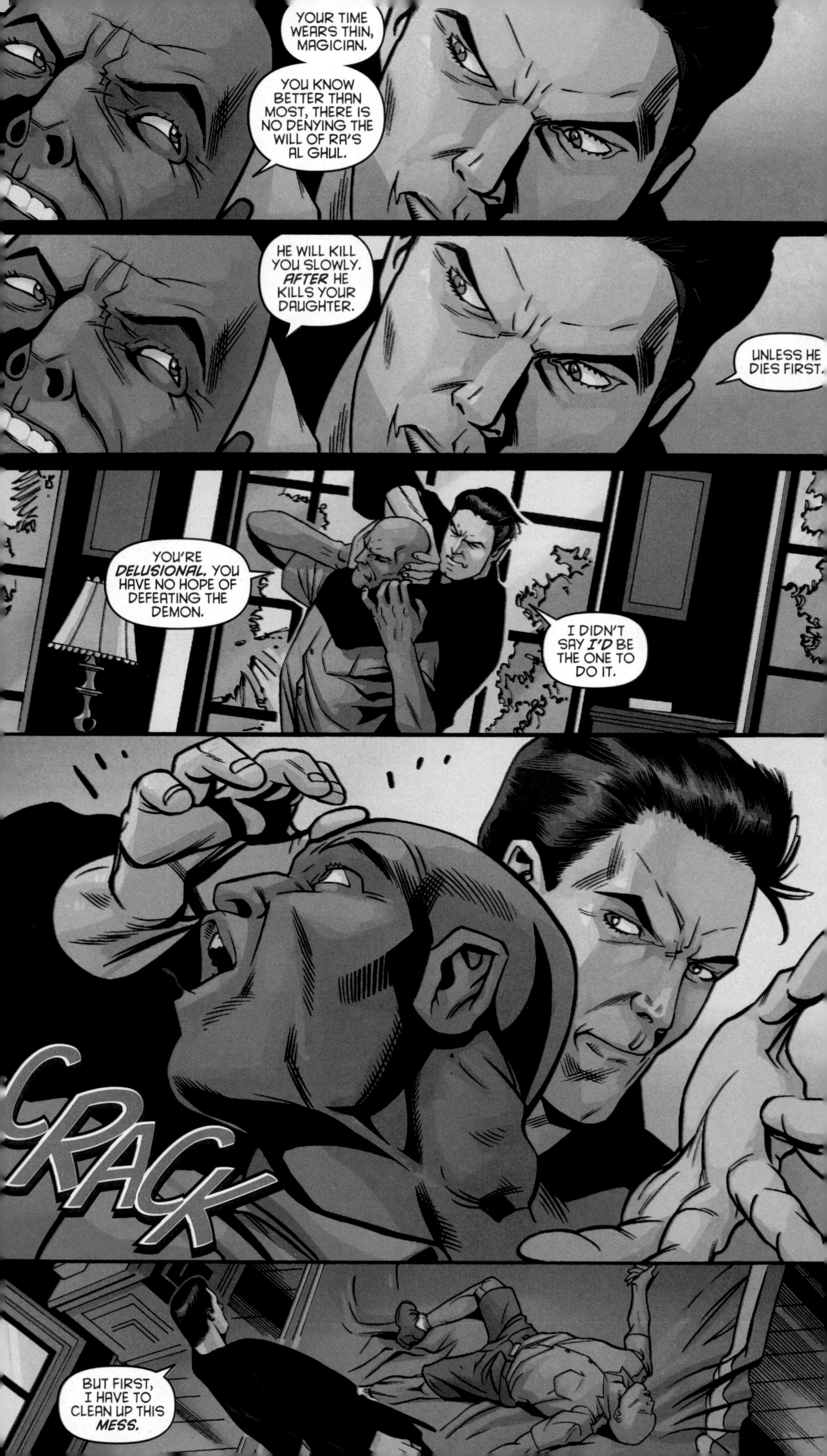

YOUR TIME WEARS THIN, MAGICIAN.
YOU KNOW BETTER THAN MOST, THERE IS NO DENYING THE WILL OF RA'S AL GHUL.
HE WILL KILL YOU SLOWLY. *AFTER* HE KILLS YOUR DAUGHTER.
UNLESS HE DIES FIRST.
YOU'RE *DELUSIONAL.* YOU HAVE NO HOPE OF DEFEATING THE DEMON.
I DIDN'T SAY *I'D* BE THE ONE TO DO IT.
CRACK
BUT FIRST, I HAVE TO CLEAN UP THIS *MESS.*

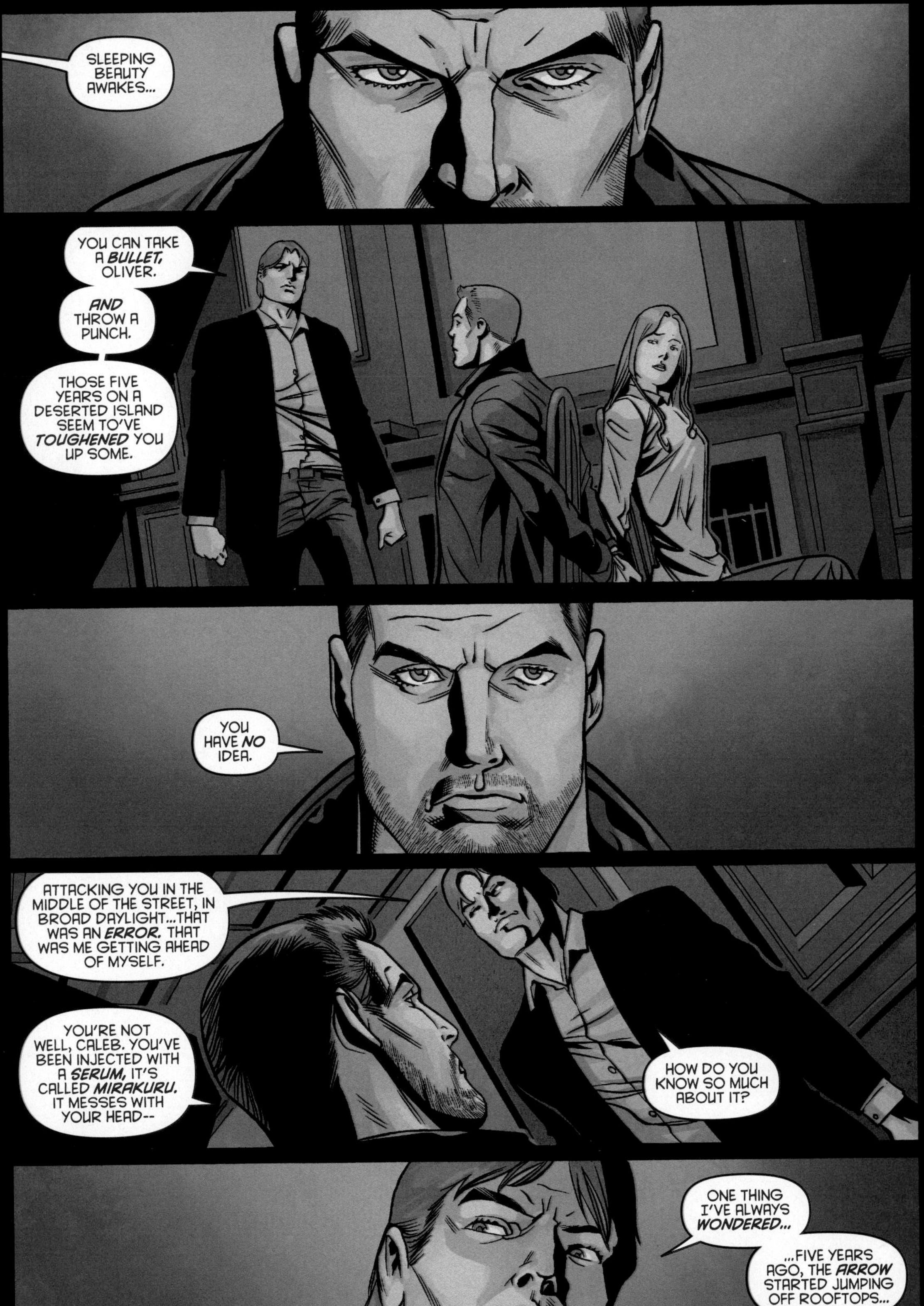
SLEEPING BEAUTY AWAKES...
YOU CAN TAKE A BULLET, OLIVER.
AND THROW A PUNCH.
THOSE FIVE YEARS ON A DESERTED ISLAND SEEM TO'VE TOUGHENED YOU UP SOME.
YOU HAVE NO IDEA.
ATTACKING YOU IN THE MIDDLE OF THE STREET, IN BROAD DAYLIGHT...THAT WAS AN ERROR. THAT WAS ME GETTING AHEAD OF MYSELF.
YOU'RE NOT WELL, CALEB. YOU'VE BEEN INJECTED WITH A SERUM, IT'S CALLED MIRAKURU. IT MESSES WITH YOUR HEAD--
HOW DO YOU KNOW SO MUCH ABOUT IT?
ONE THING I'VE ALWAYS WONDERED...
...FIVE YEARS AGO, THE ARROW STARTED JUMPING OFF ROOFTOPS...

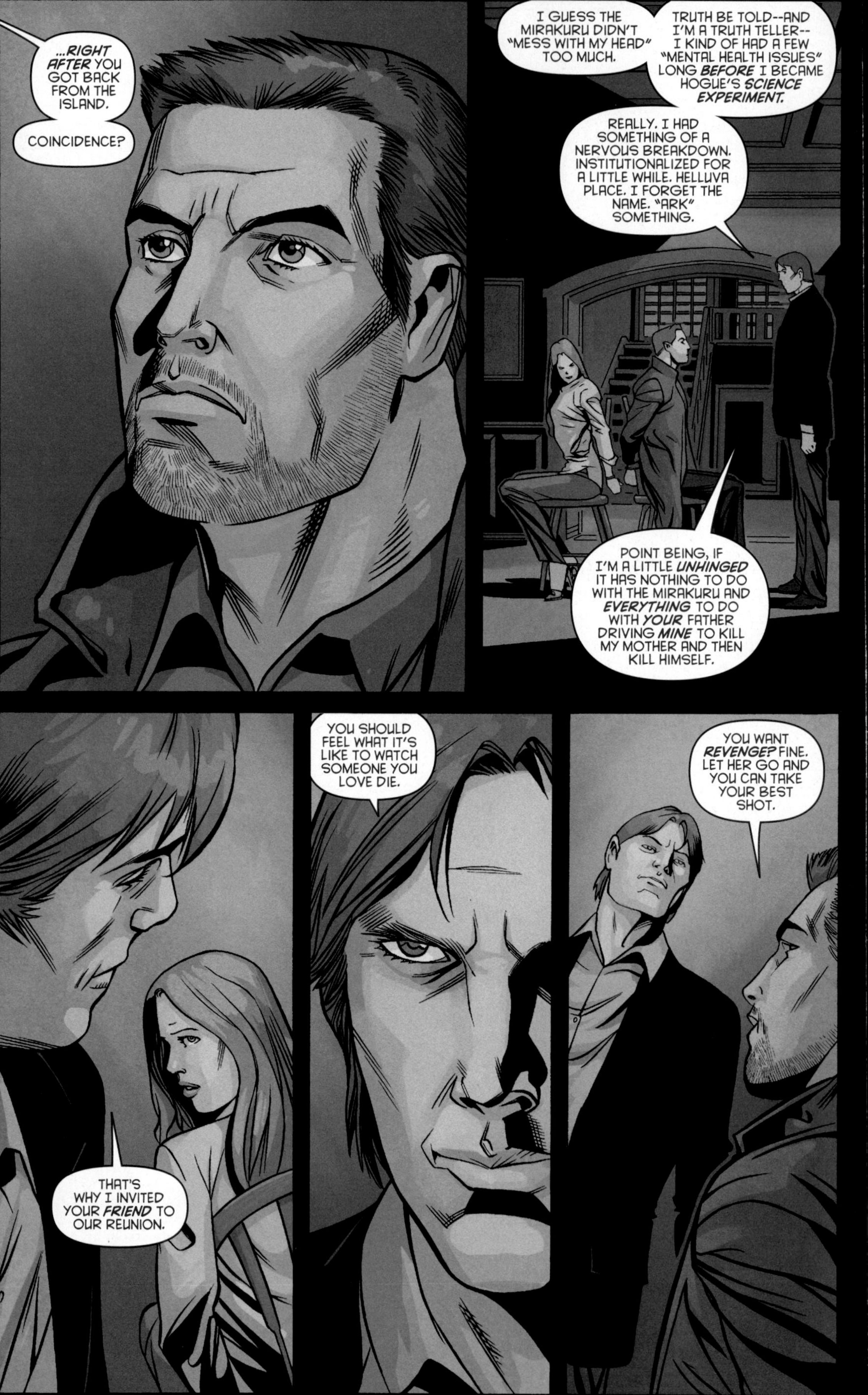
...RIGHT AFTER YOU GOT BACK FROM THE ISLAND.
COINCIDENCE?
I GUESS THE MIRAKURU DIDN'T "MESS WITH MY HEAD" TOO MUCH.
TRUTH BE TOLD--AND I'M A TRUTH TELLER--I KIND OF HAD A FEW "MENTAL HEALTH ISSUES" LONG BEFORE I BECAME HOGUE'S SCIENCE EXPERIMENT.
REALLY. I HAD SOMETHING OF A NERVOUS BREAKDOWN. INSTITUTIONALIZED FOR A LITTLE WHILE. HELLUVA PLACE. I FORGET THE NAME. "ARK" SOMETHING.
POINT BEING, IF I'M A LITTLE UNHINGED IT HAS NOTHING TO DO WITH THE MIRAKURU AND EVERYTHING TO DO WITH YOUR FATHER DRIVING MINE TO KILL MY MOTHER AND THEN KILL HIMSELF.
THAT'S WHY I INVITED YOUR FRIEND TO OUR REUNION.
YOU SHOULD FEEL WHAT IT'S LIKE TO WATCH SOMEONE YOU LOVE DIE.
YOU WANT REVENGE? FINE. LET HER GO AND YOU CAN TAKE YOUR BEST SHOT.

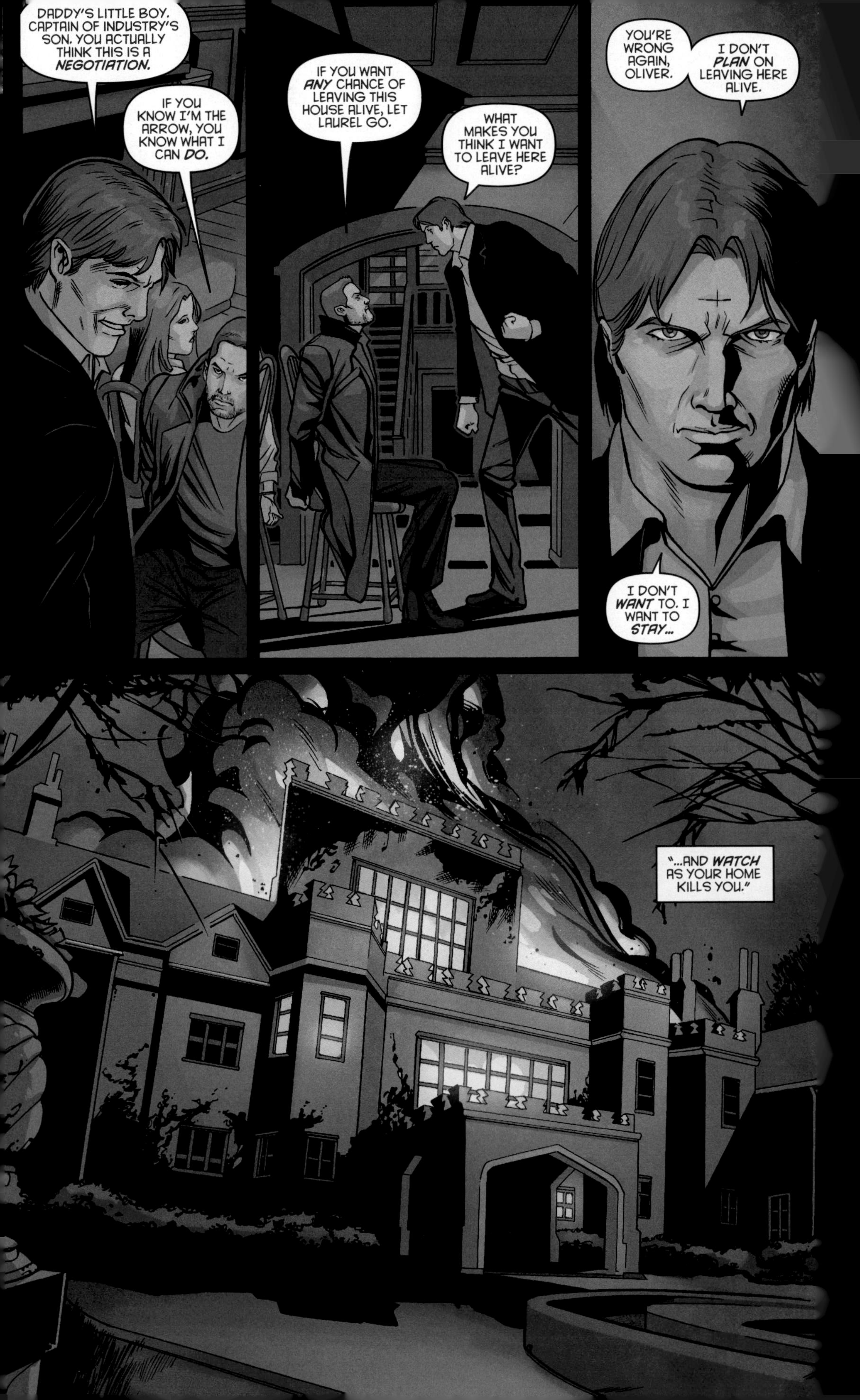
DADDY'S LITTLE BOY. CAPTAIN OF INDUSTRY'S SON. YOU ACTUALLY THINK THIS IS A NEGOTIATION.
IF YOU KNOW I'M THE ARROW, YOU KNOW WHAT I CAN DO.
IF YOU WANT ANY CHANCE OF LEAVING THIS HOUSE ALIVE, LET LAUREL GO.
WHAT MAKES YOU THINK I WANT TO LEAVE HERE ALIVE?
YOU'RE WRONG AGAIN, OLIVER.
I DON'T PLAN ON LEAVING HERE ALIVE.
I DON'T WANT TO. I WANT TO STAY...
"...AND WATCH AS YOUR HOME KILLS YOU."

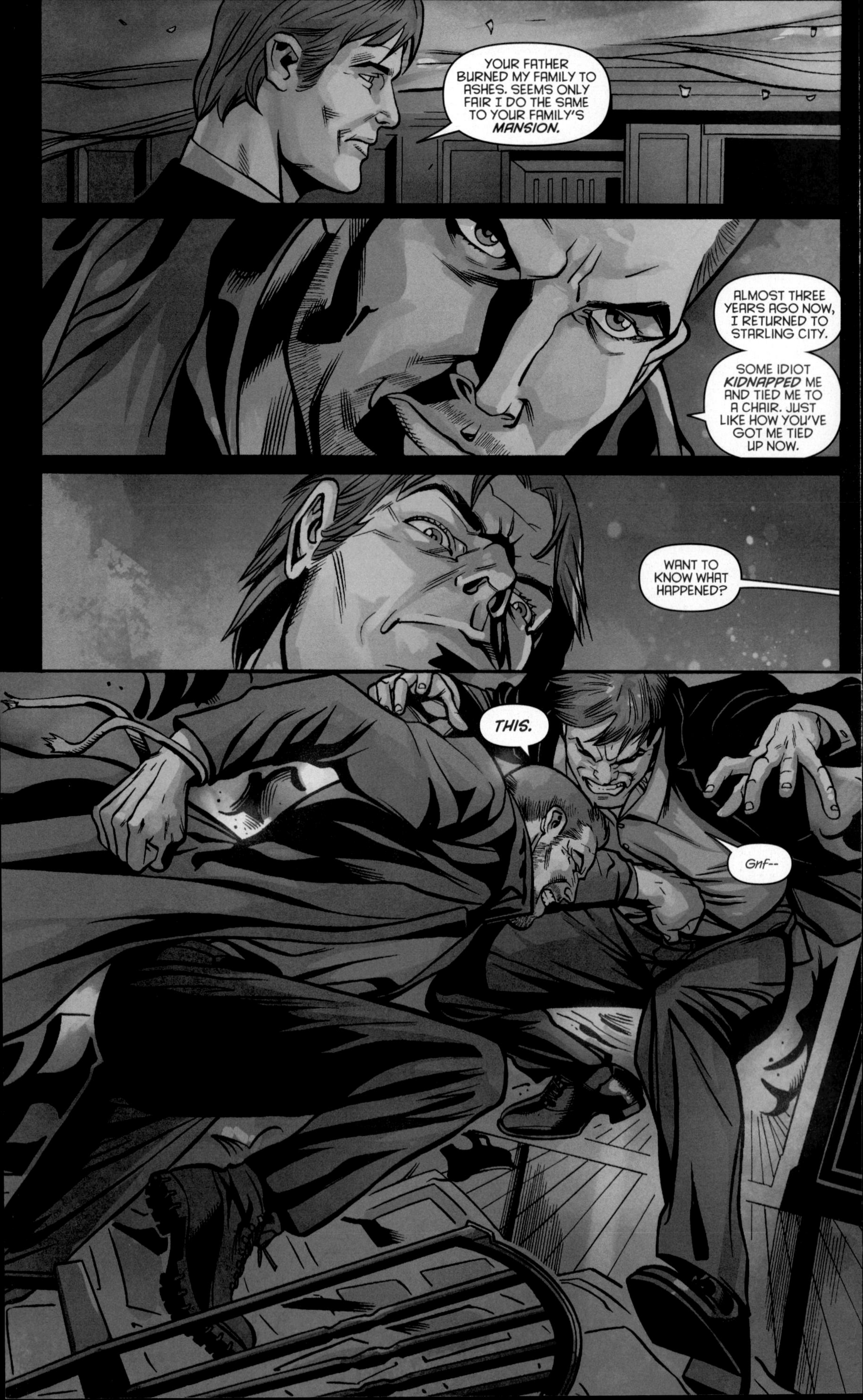
YOUR FATHER BURNED MY FAMILY TO ASHES. SEEMS ONLY FAIR I DO THE SAME TO YOUR FAMILY'S MANSION.
ALMOST THREE YEARS AGO NOW, I RETURNED TO STARLING CITY.
SOME IDIOT KIDNAPPED ME AND TIED ME TO A CHAIR. JUST LIKE HOW YOU'VE GOT ME TIED UP NOW.
WANT TO KNOW WHAT HAPPENED?
THIS.
Gnf--

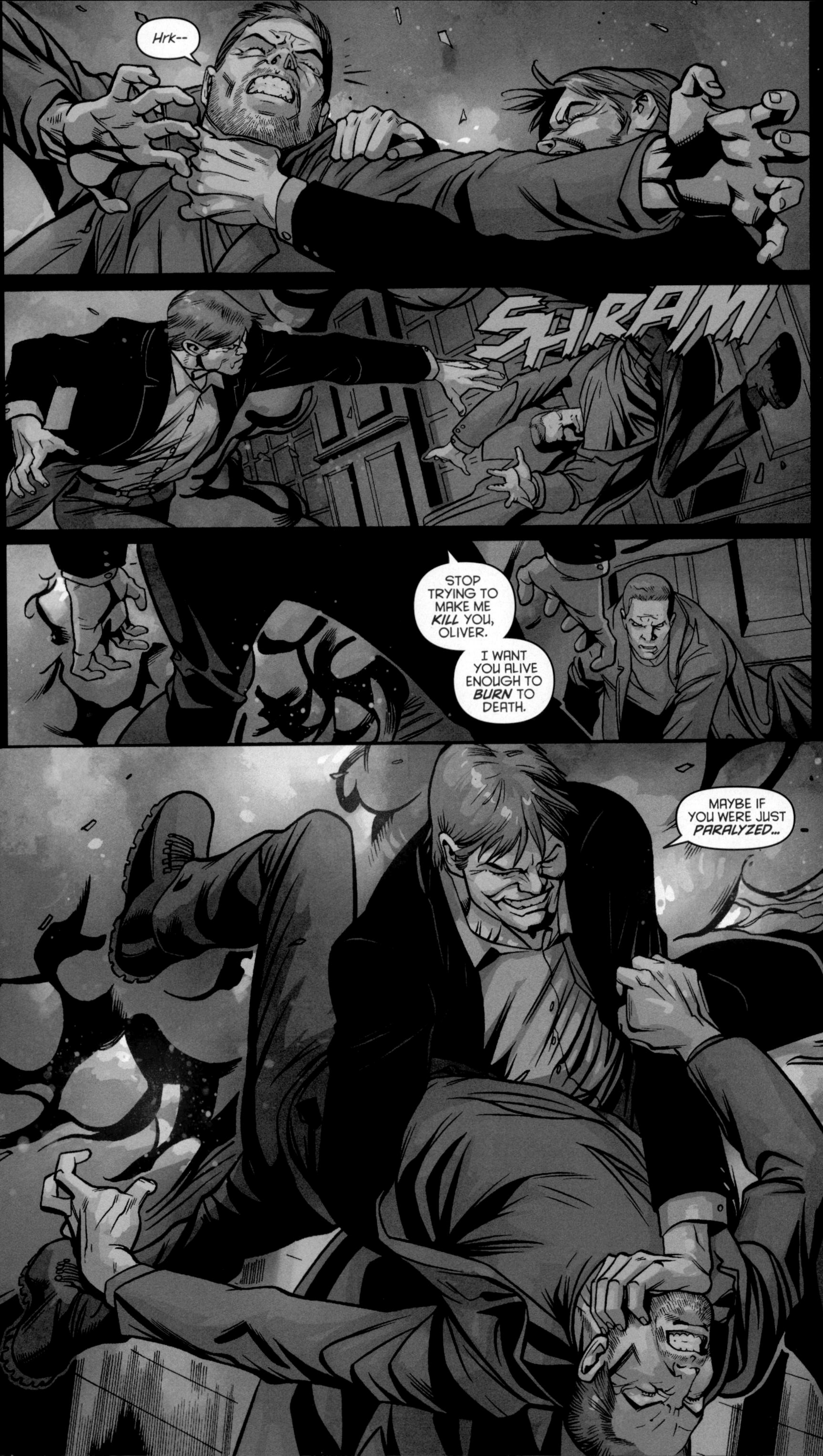
Hrk--
SHRAM
STOP TRYING TO MAKE ME KILL YOU, OLIVER.
I WANT YOU ALIVE ENOUGH TO BURN TO DEATH.
MAYBE IF YOU WERE JUST PARALYZED...

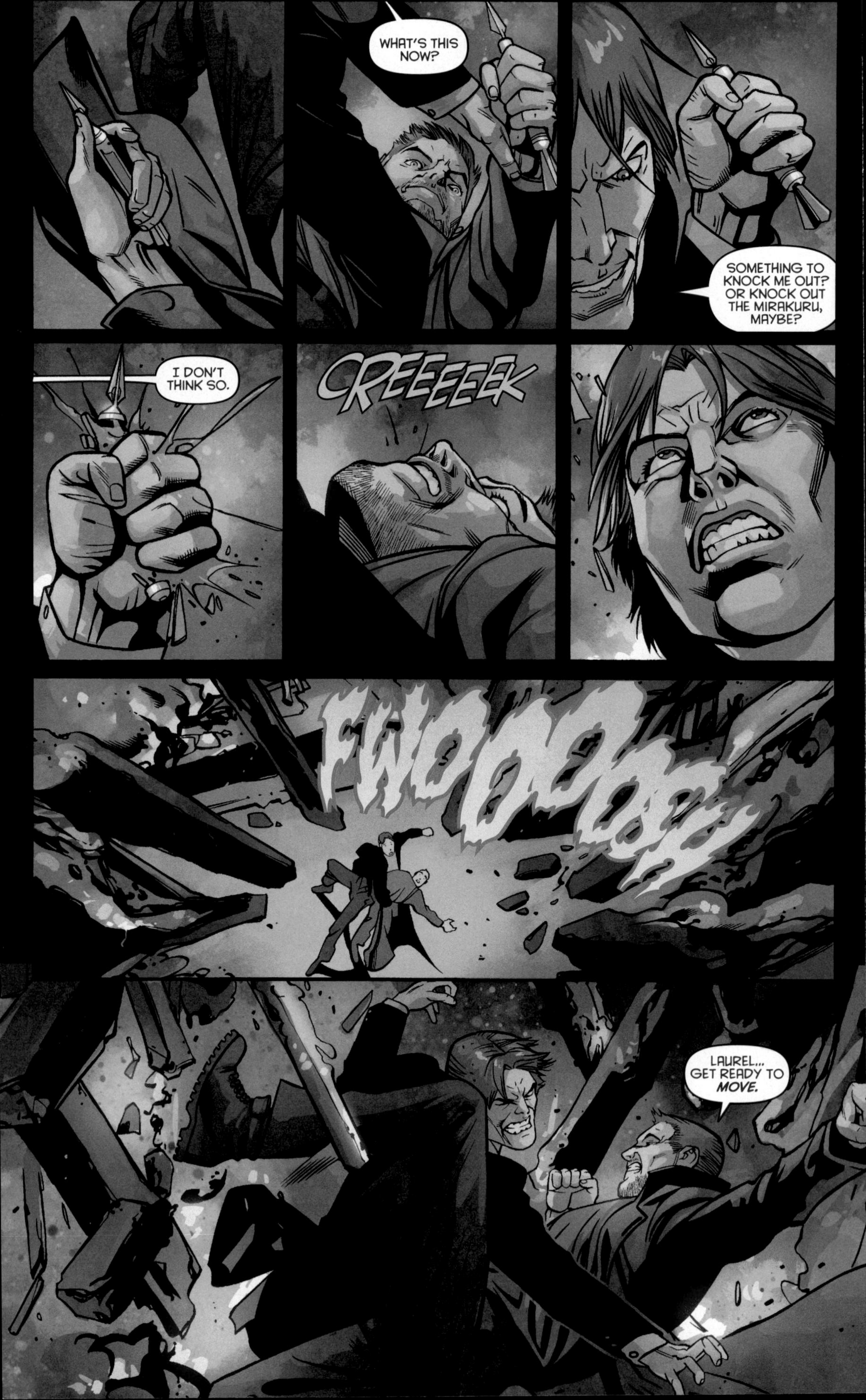
WHAT'S THIS NOW?
SOMETHING TO KNOCK ME OUT? OR KNOCK OUT THE MIRAKURU, MAYBE?
I DON'T THINK SO.
CREEEEEEK
FWOOOOM
LAUREL... GET READY TO *MOVE.*

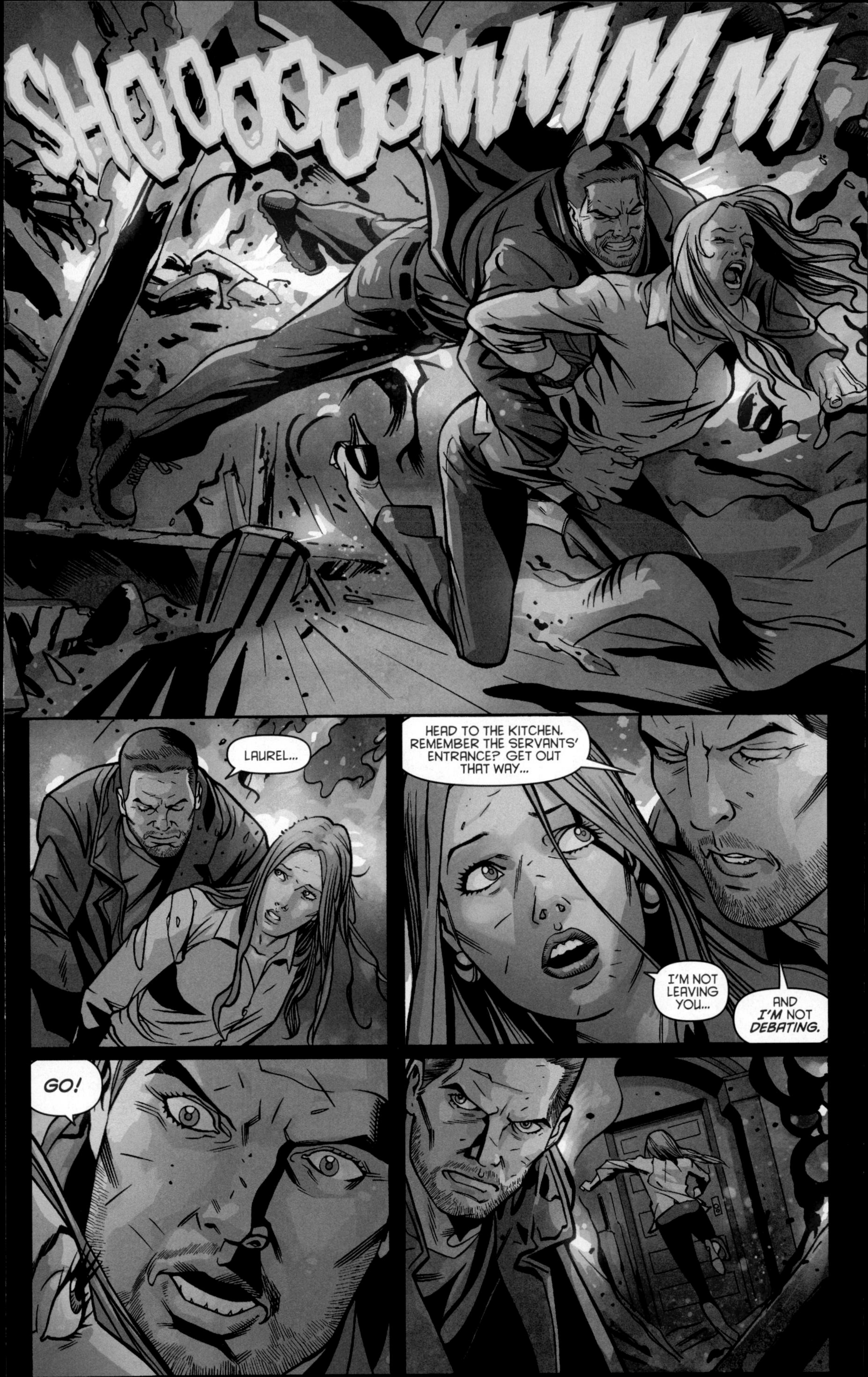
SHOOOOOOMMMMM
LAUREL...
HEAD TO THE KITCHEN. REMEMBER THE SERVANTS' ENTRANCE? GET OUT THAT WAY...
I'M NOT LEAVING YOU...
AND *I'M* NOT *DEBATING.*
GO!

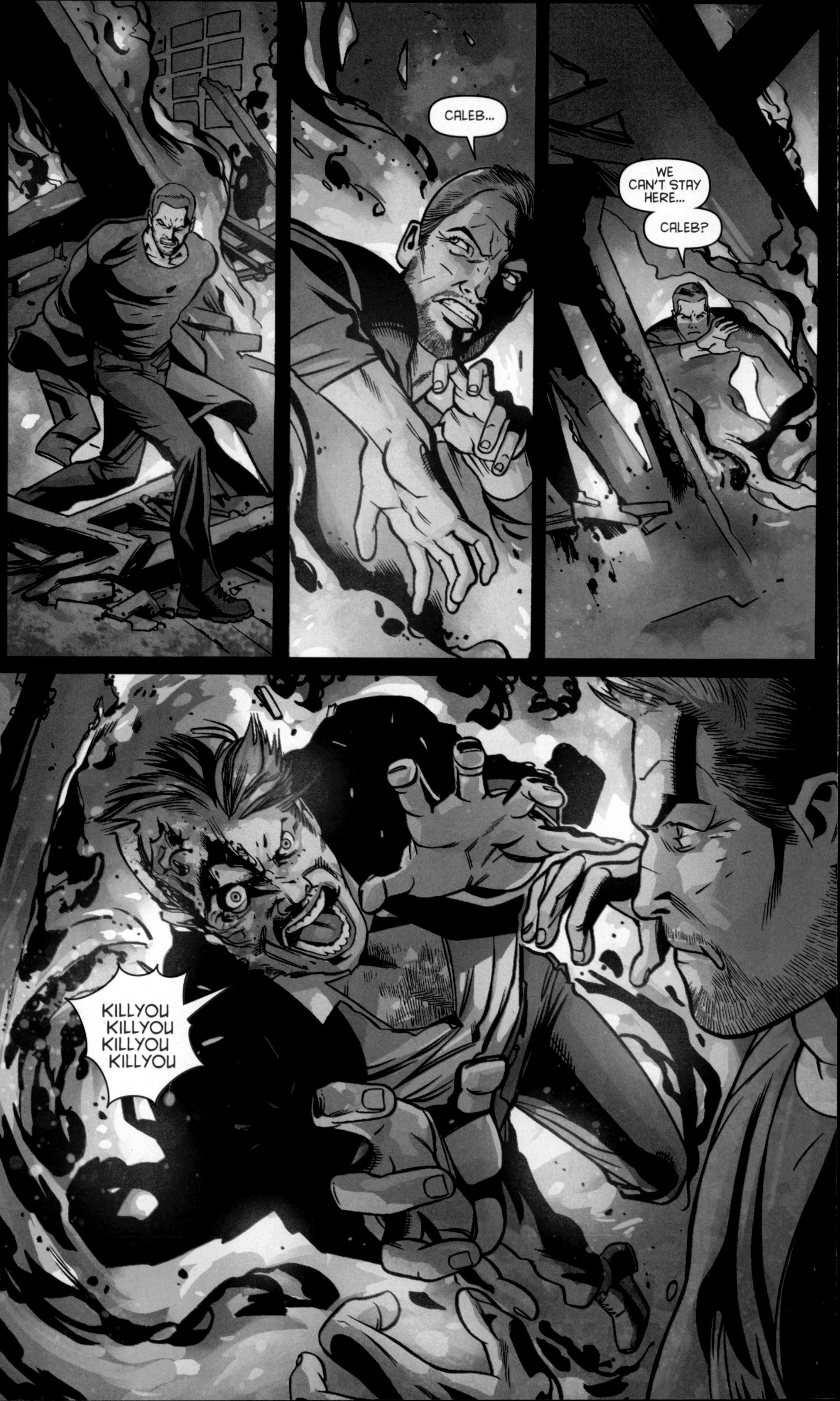
CALEB...
WE CAN'T STAY HERE...
CALEB?
KILLYOU KILLYOU KILLYOU KILLYOU

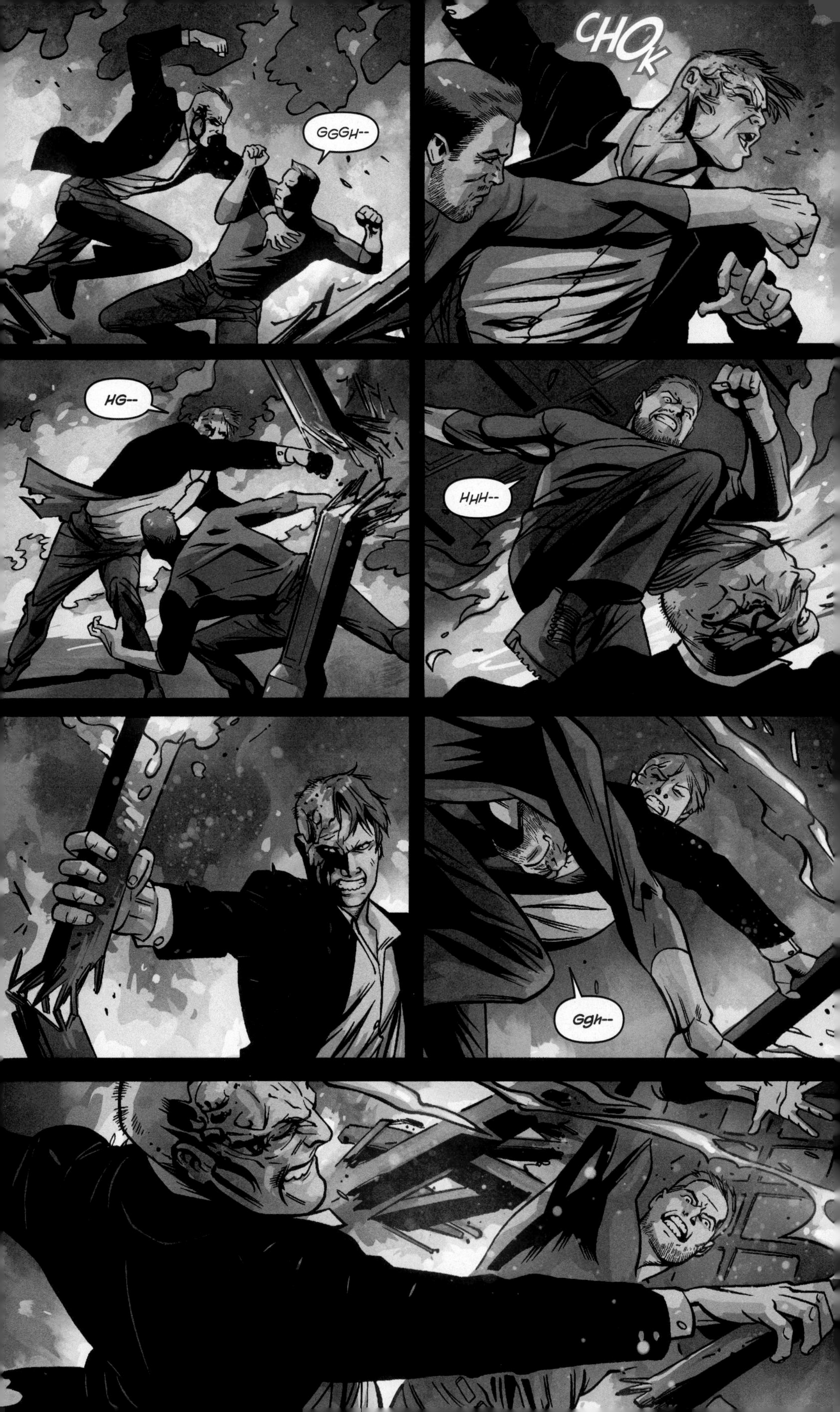
GGGH--
CHOK
HG--
HHH--
Ggh--

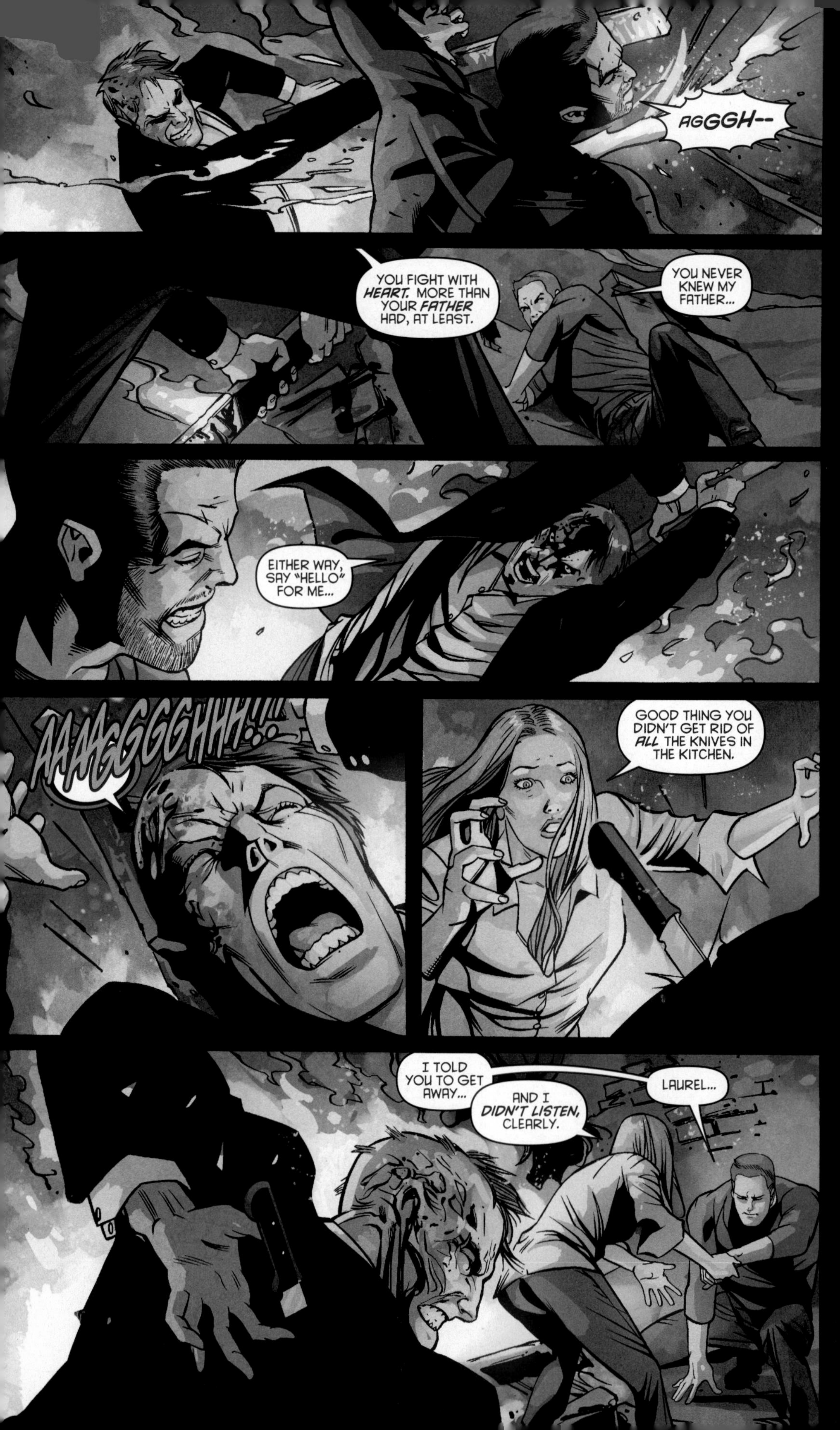
AGGGH--
YOU FIGHT WITH HEART. MORE THAN YOUR FATHER HAD, AT LEAST.
YOU NEVER KNEW MY FATHER...
EITHER WAY, SAY "HELLO" FOR ME...
AAAAGGGHHH!!!
GOOD THING YOU DIDN'T GET RID OF ALL THE KNIVES IN THE KITCHEN.
I TOLD YOU TO GET AWAY...
LAUREL...
AND I DIDN'T LISTEN, CLEARLY.

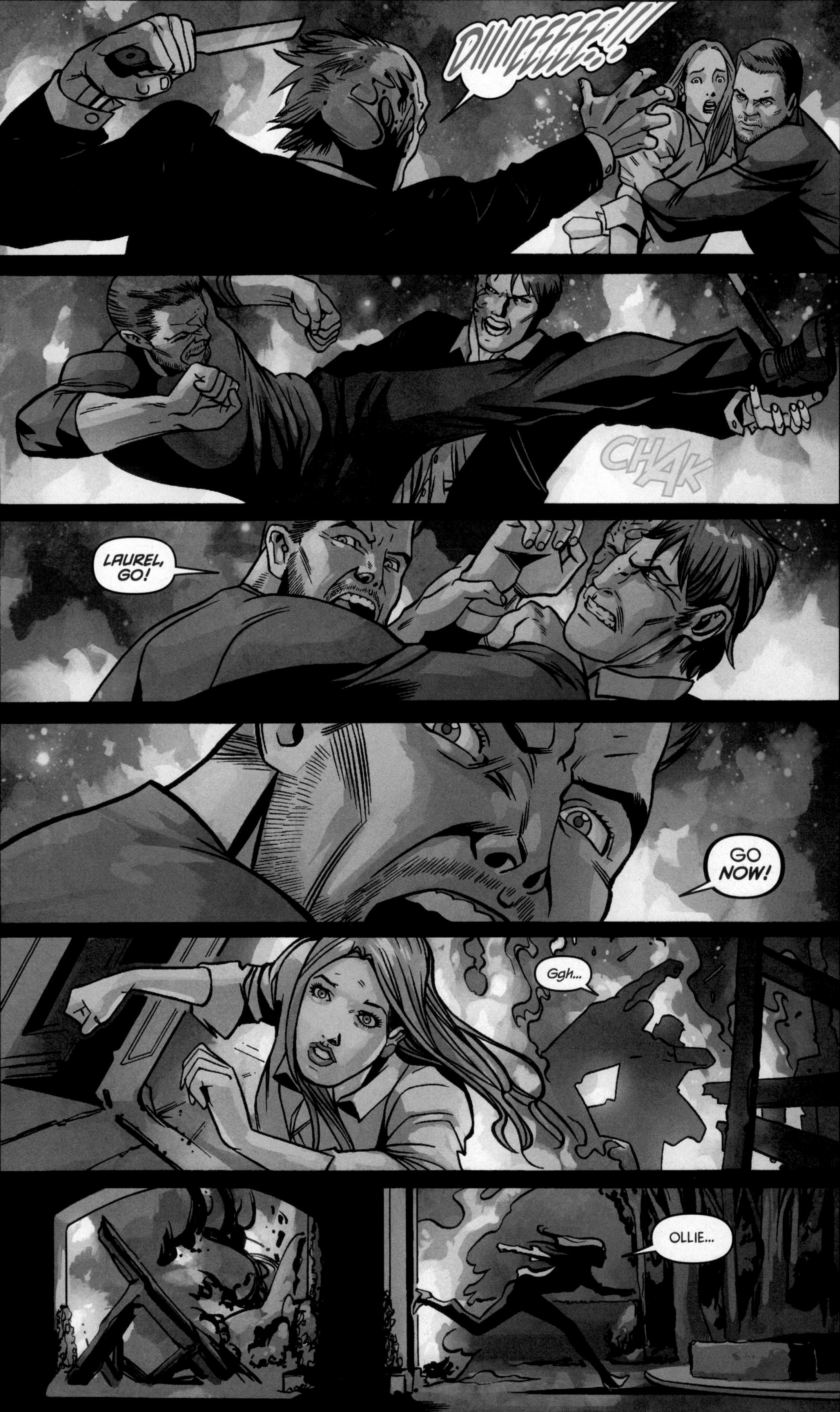
DIIIEEEEE!!!
CHAK
LAUREL, GO!
GO NOW!
Ggh...
OLLIE...

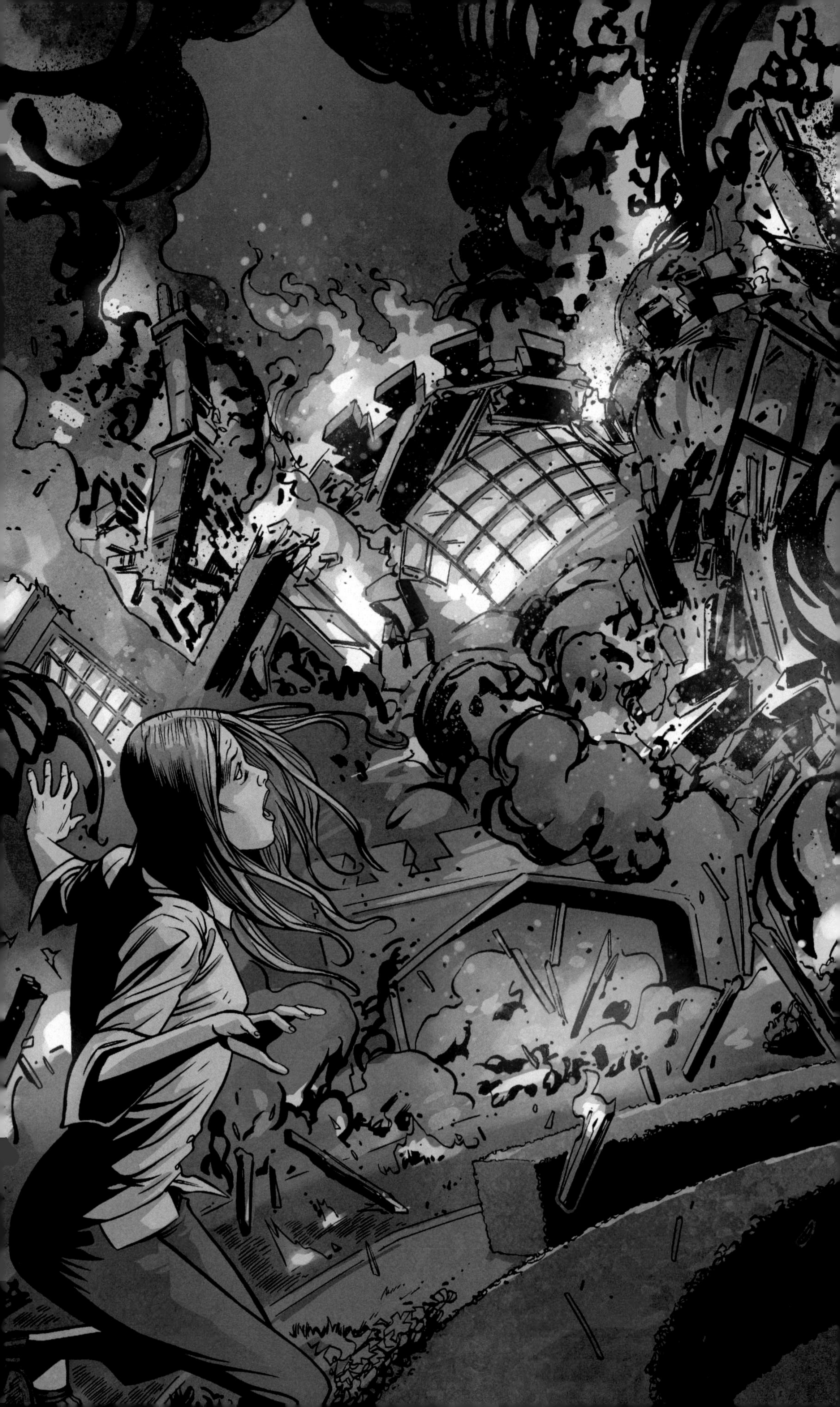

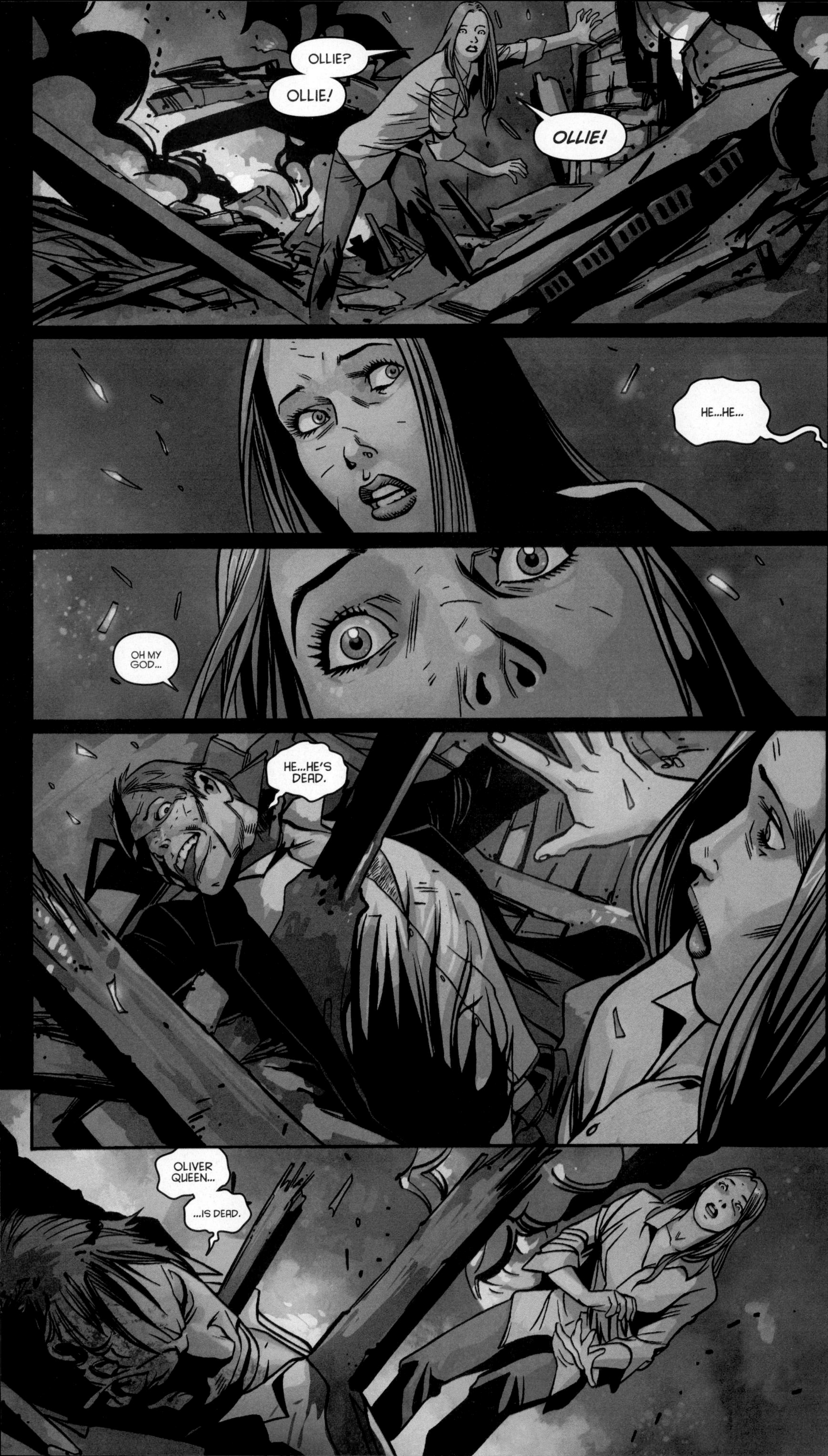
OLLIE?
OLLIE!
OLLIE!
HE...HE...
OH MY GOD...
HE...HE'S DEAD.
OLIVER QUEEN...
...IS DEAD.

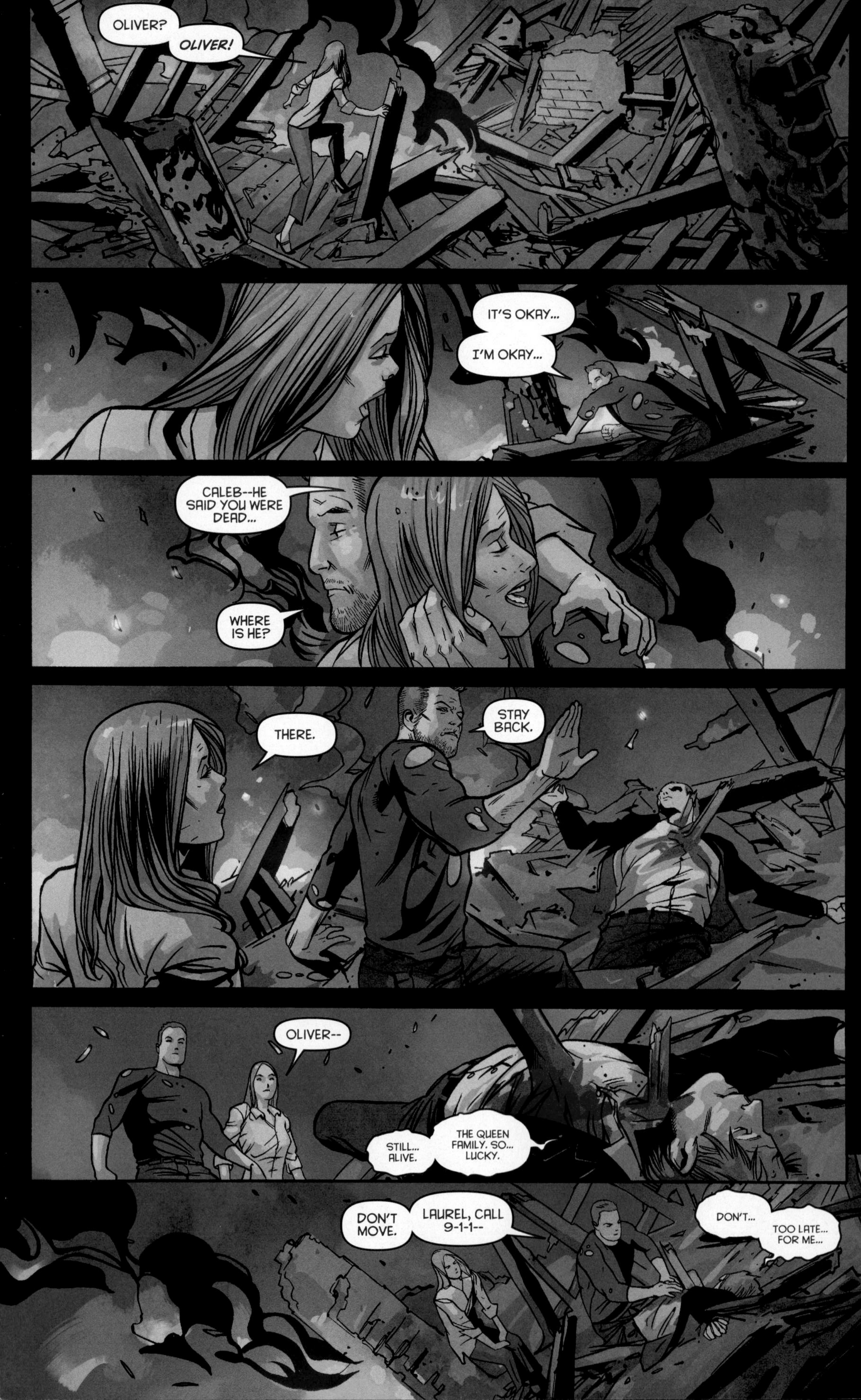
OLIVER?
OLIVER!
IT'S OKAY...
I'M OKAY...
CALEB--HE SAID YOU WERE DEAD...
WHERE IS HE?
THERE.
STAY BACK.
OLIVER--
THE QUEEN FAMILY. SO... LUCKY.
STILL... ALIVE.
LAUREL, CALL 9-1-1--
DON'T MOVE.
DON'T...
TOO LATE... FOR ME...

LIVE WITH IT. THE GUILT. OF WHAT YOUR FAMILY DID...TO *MY* FAMILY...

YOU THINK-- YOU THINK YOU'RE SOME... SOME *HERO* NOW.

YOU THINK... WHATEVER YOU DO...IN THAT HOOD...

IT CAN'T MAKE UP FOR WHAT...FOR WHAT YOU'VE DONE.

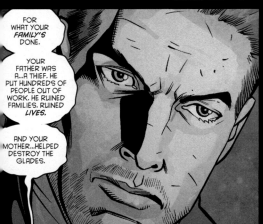

FOR WHAT YOUR *FAMILY'S* DONE.

YOUR FATHER WAS A...A THIEF. HE PUT HUNDREDS OF PEOPLE OUT OF WORK. HE RUINED FAMILIES. RUINED *LIVES.*

AND YOUR MOTHER...HELPED DESTROY THE GLADES.

BUT I BET...I BET THEY KNEW WHO THEY WERE.

NOT LIKE *YOU.*

I KNOW WHO YOU WERE BEFORE THAT BOAT WENT DOWN.

SELFISH. ONLY OUT FOR...FOR *YOURSELF.*

NO HOOD... NO MASK CAN CHANGE THAT.

I TRIED TO KILL YOU, BUT...BUT I COULDN'T. SO YOU LIVE.

YOU LIVE WITH WHO YOU ARE. YOU LIVE...LIVE WITH *WHAT* YOU...

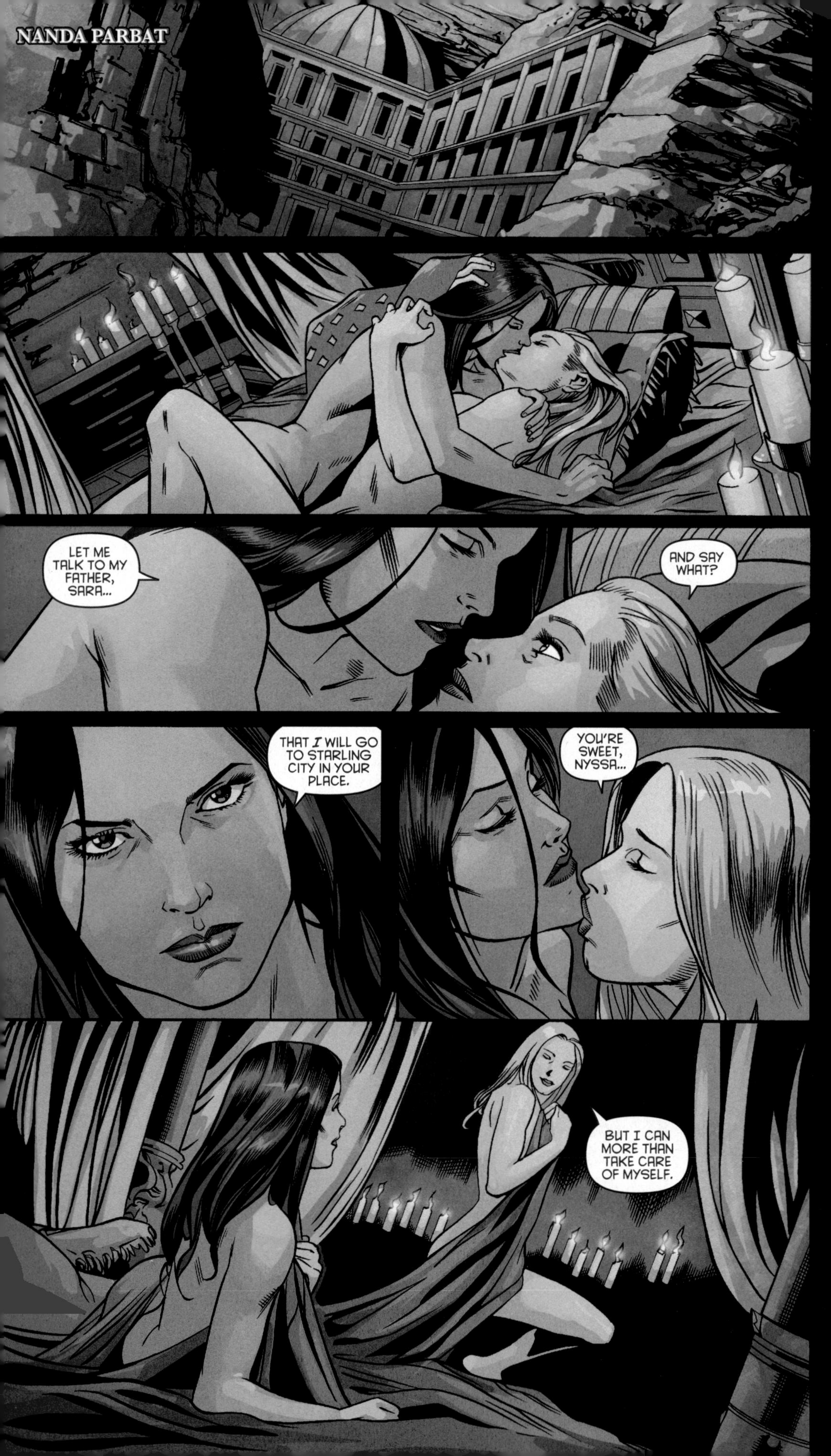
NANDA PARBAT
LET ME TALK TO MY FATHER, SARA...
AND SAY WHAT?
THAT I WILL GO TO STARLING CITY IN YOUR PLACE.
YOU'RE SWEET, NYSSA...
BUT I CAN MORE THAN TAKE CARE OF MYSELF.

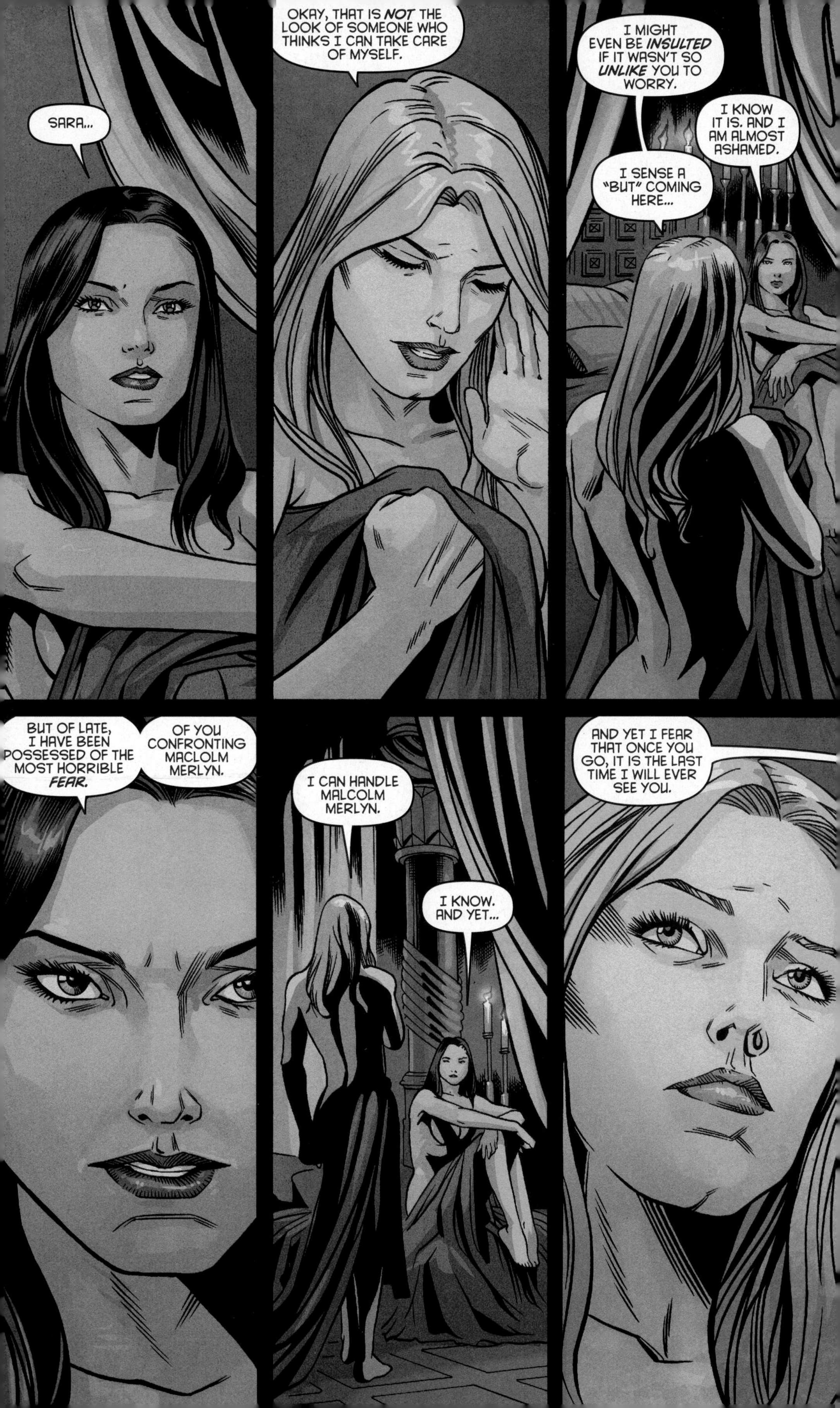
SARA...
OKAY, THAT IS NOT THE LOOK OF SOMEONE WHO THINKS I CAN TAKE CARE OF MYSELF.
I MIGHT EVEN BE INSULTED IF IT WASN'T SO UNLIKE YOU TO WORRY.
I KNOW IT IS. AND I AM ALMOST ASHAMED.
I SENSE A "BUT" COMING HERE...
BUT OF LATE, I HAVE BEEN POSSESSED OF THE MOST HORRIBLE FEAR.
OF YOU CONFRONTING MACLOLM MERLYN.
I CAN HANDLE MALCOLM MERLYN.
I KNOW. AND YET...
AND YET I FEAR THAT ONCE YOU GO, IT IS THE LAST TIME I WILL EVER SEE YOU.

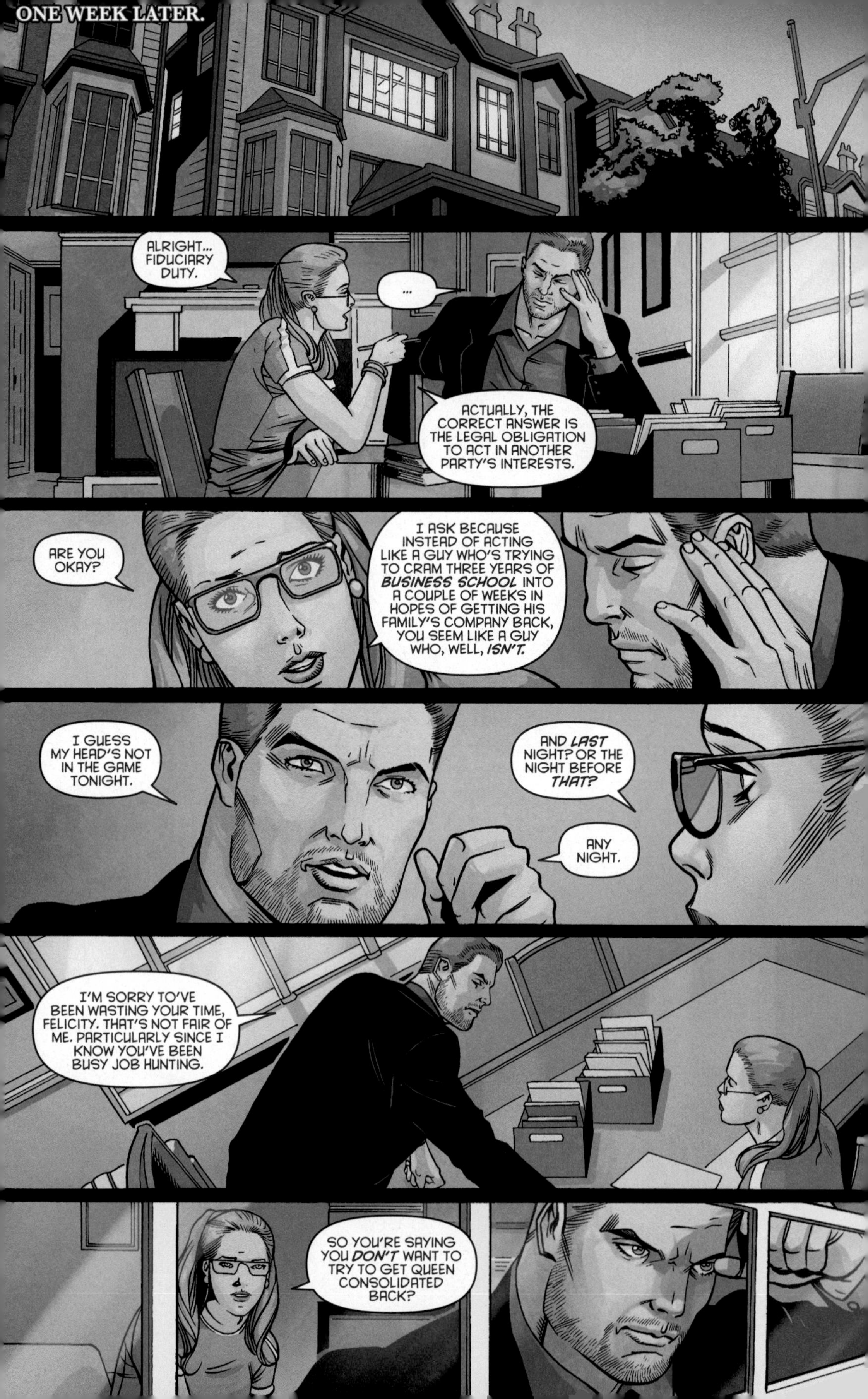
ONE WEEK LATER.
ALRIGHT... FIDUCIARY DUTY.
...
ACTUALLY, THE CORRECT ANSWER IS THE LEGAL OBLIGATION TO ACT IN ANOTHER PARTY'S INTERESTS.
ARE YOU OKAY?
I ASK BECAUSE INSTEAD OF ACTING LIKE A GUY WHO'S TRYING TO CRAM THREE YEARS OF *BUSINESS SCHOOL* INTO A COUPLE OF WEEKS IN HOPES OF GETTING HIS FAMILY'S COMPANY BACK, YOU SEEM LIKE A GUY WHO, WELL, *ISN'T.*
I GUESS MY HEAD'S NOT IN THE GAME TONIGHT.
AND *LAST* NIGHT? OR THE NIGHT BEFORE *THAT?*
ANY NIGHT.
I'M SORRY TO'VE BEEN WASTING YOUR TIME, FELICITY. THAT'S NOT FAIR OF ME. PARTICULARLY SINCE I KNOW YOU'VE BEEN BUSY JOB HUNTING.
SO YOU'RE SAYING YOU *DON'T* WANT TO TRY TO GET QUEEN CONSOLIDATED BACK?

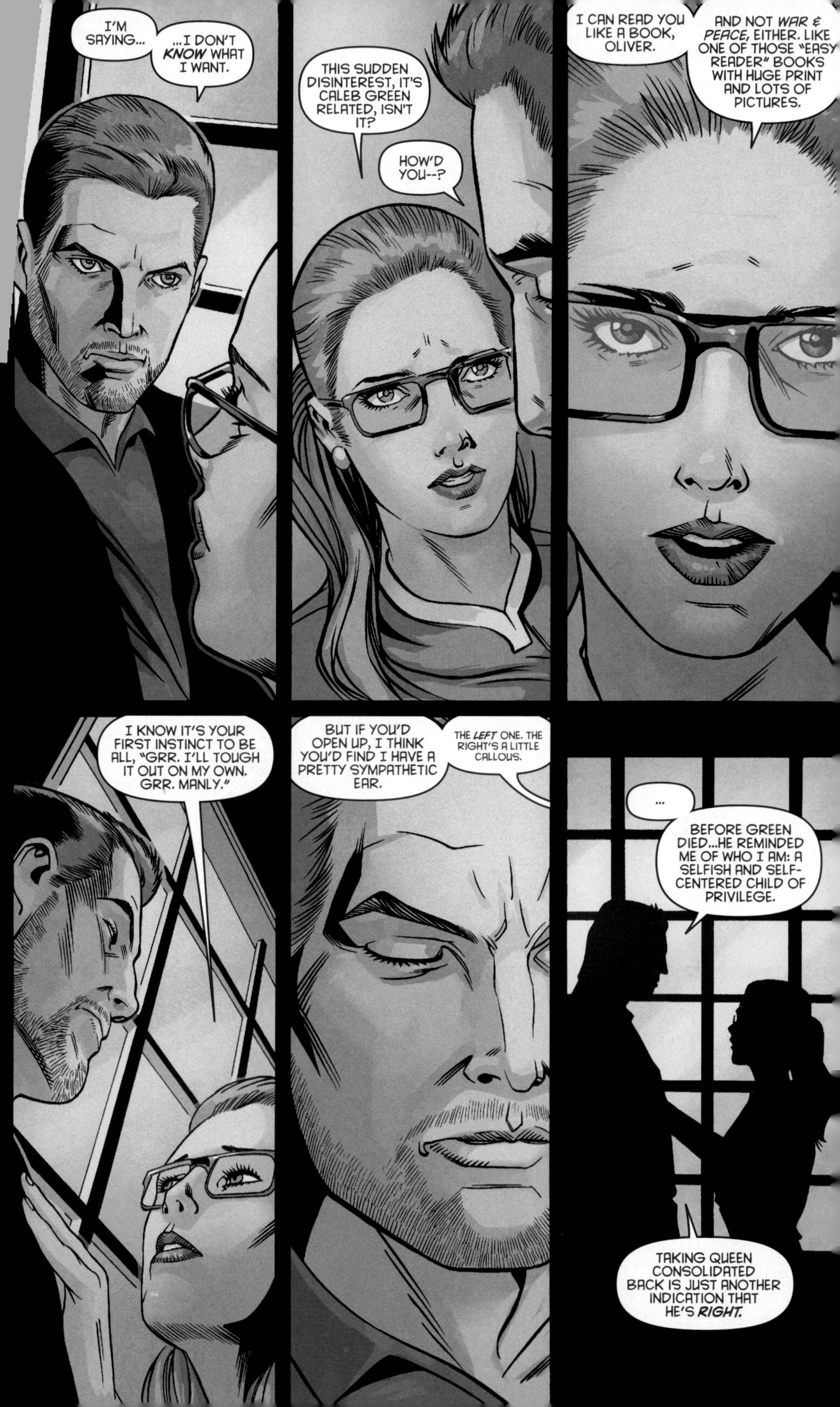
I'M SAYING...
...I DON'T *KNOW* WHAT I WANT.
THIS SUDDEN DISINTEREST, IT'S CALEB GREEN RELATED, ISN'T IT?
HOW'D YOU--?
I CAN READ YOU LIKE A BOOK, OLIVER.
AND NOT *WAR & PEACE*, EITHER. LIKE ONE OF THOSE "EASY READER" BOOKS WITH HUGE PRINT AND LOTS OF PICTURES.
I KNOW IT'S YOUR FIRST INSTINCT TO BE ALL, "GRR. I'LL TOUGH IT OUT ON MY OWN. GRR. MANLY."
BUT IF YOU'D OPEN UP, I THINK YOU'D FIND I HAVE A PRETTY SYMPATHETIC EAR.
THE *LEFT* ONE. THE RIGHT'S A LITTLE CALLOUS.
...
BEFORE GREEN DIED...HE REMINDED ME OF WHO I AM: A SELFISH AND SELF-CENTERED CHILD OF PRIVILEGE.
TAKING QUEEN CONSOLIDATED BACK IS JUST ANOTHER INDICATION THAT HE'S *RIGHT.*

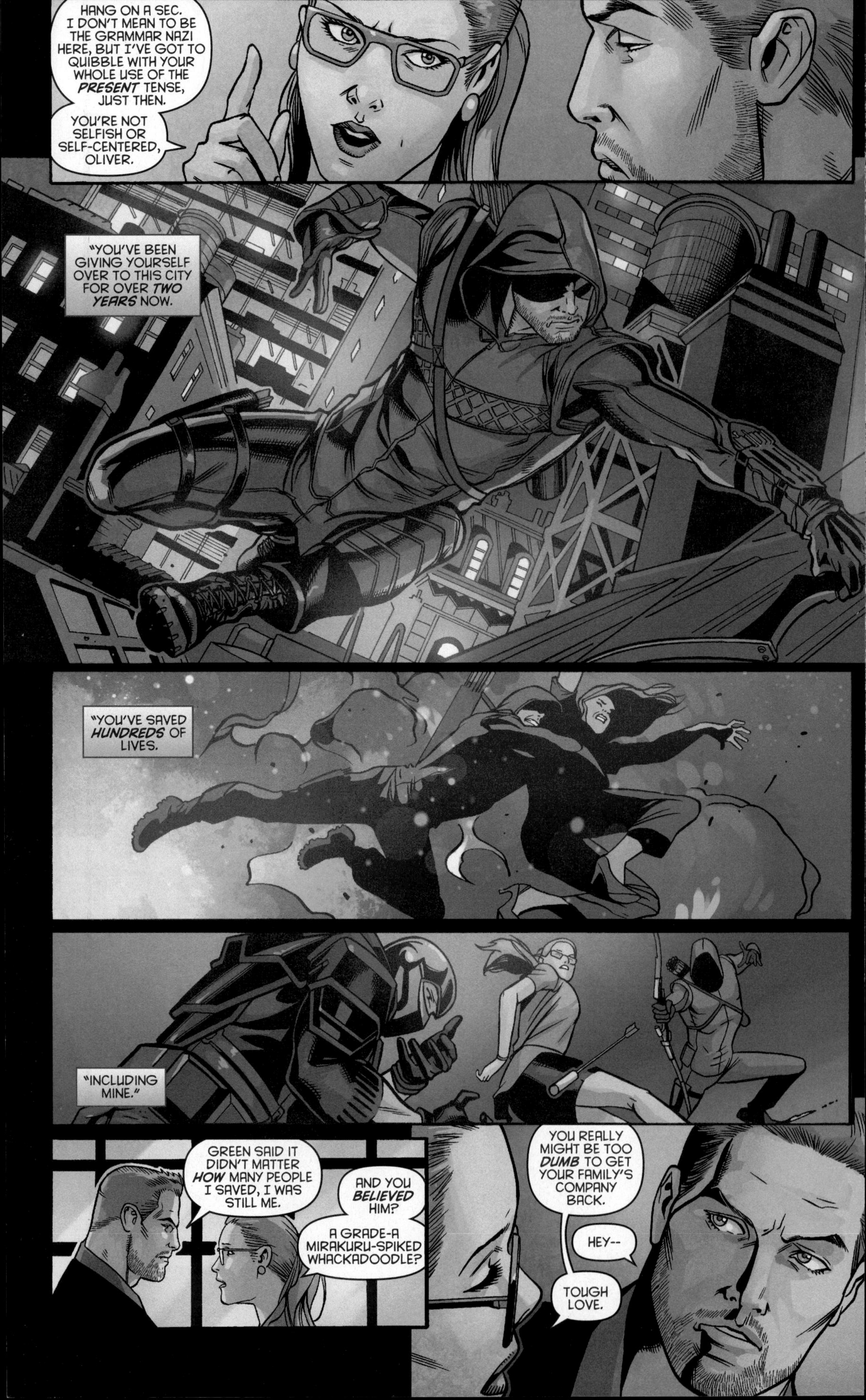
HANG ON A SEC. I DON'T MEAN TO BE THE GRAMMAR NAZI HERE, BUT I'VE GOT TO QUIBBLE WITH YOUR WHOLE USE OF THE *PRESENT* TENSE, JUST THEN.
YOU'RE NOT SELFISH OR SELF-CENTERED, OLIVER.
"YOU'VE BEEN GIVING YOURSELF OVER TO THIS CITY FOR OVER *TWO YEARS* NOW.
"YOU'VE SAVED *HUNDREDS* OF LIVES.
"INCLUDING MINE."
GREEN SAID IT DIDN'T MATTER *HOW* MANY PEOPLE I SAVED, I WAS STILL ME.
AND YOU *BELIEVED* HIM?
A GRADE-A MIRAKURU-SPIKED WHACKADOODLE?
YOU REALLY MIGHT BE TOO *DUMB* TO GET YOUR FAMILY'S COMPANY BACK.
HEY--
TOUGH LOVE.

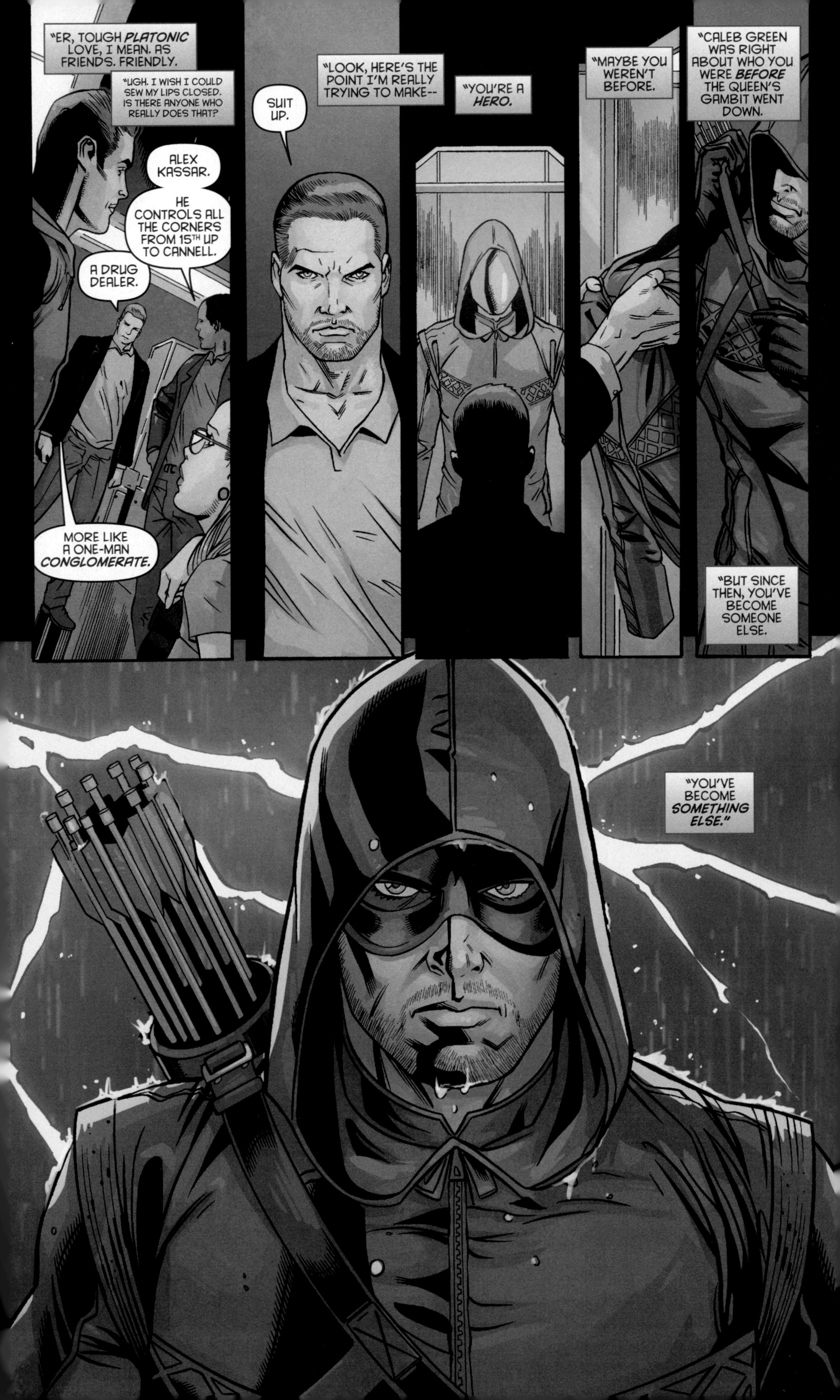
"ER, TOUGH PLATONIC LOVE, I MEAN. AS FRIENDS. FRIENDLY.
"UGH. I WISH I COULD SEW MY LIPS CLOSED. IS THERE ANYONE WHO REALLY DOES THAT?
ALEX KASSAR.
HE CONTROLS ALL THE CORNERS FROM 15TH UP TO CANNELL.
A DRUG DEALER.
MORE LIKE A ONE-MAN CONGLOMERATE.
SUIT UP.
"LOOK, HERE'S THE POINT I'M REALLY TRYING TO MAKE--
"YOU'RE A HERO.
"MAYBE YOU WEREN'T BEFORE.
"CALEB GREEN WAS RIGHT ABOUT WHO YOU WERE BEFORE THE QUEEN'S GAMBIT WENT DOWN.
"BUT SINCE THEN, YOU'VE BECOME SOMEONE ELSE.
"YOU'VE BECOME SOMETHING ELSE."

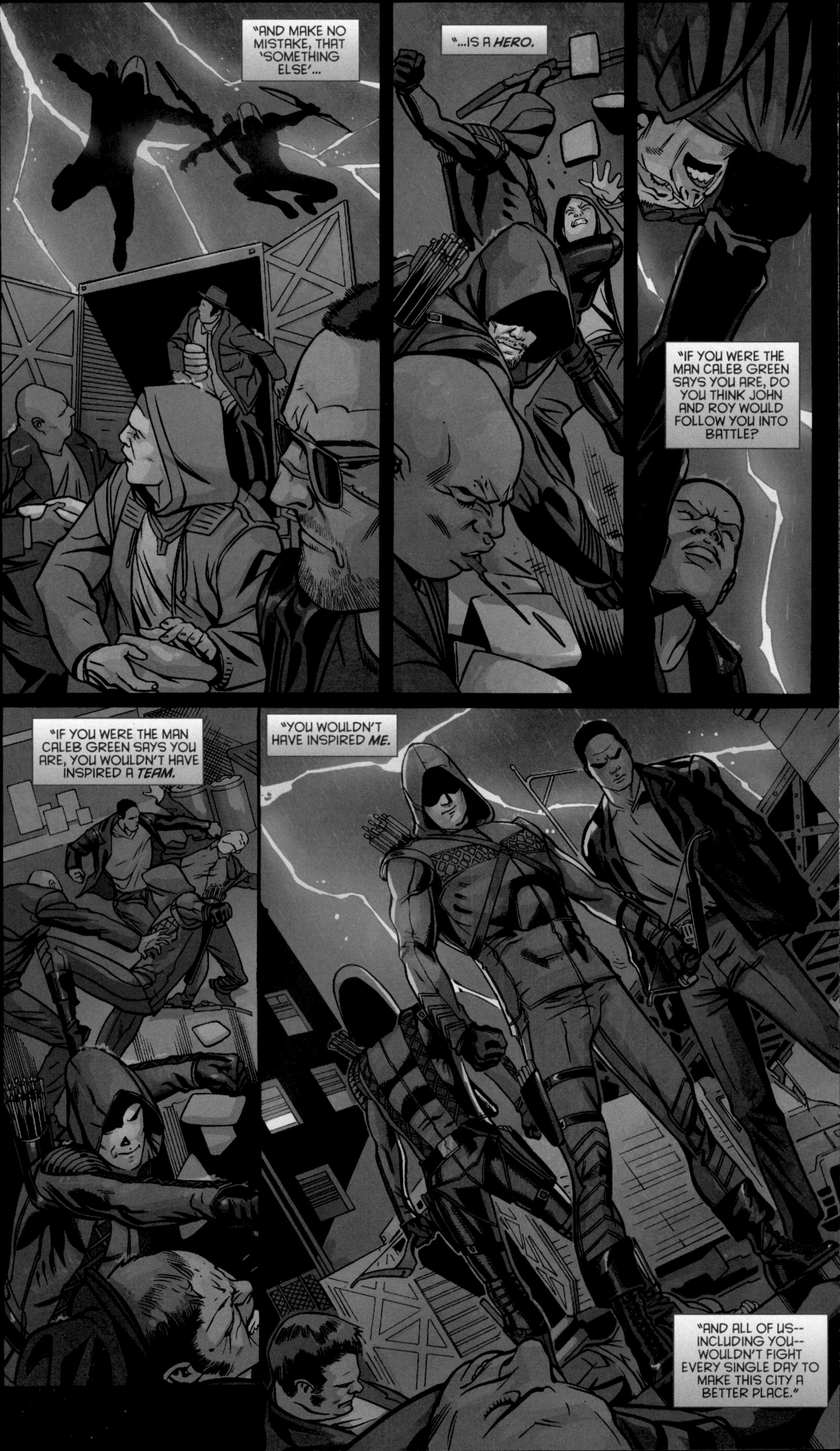
"AND MAKE NO MISTAKE, THAT 'SOMETHING ELSE'...
"...IS A *HERO.*
"IF YOU WERE THE MAN CALEB GREEN SAYS YOU ARE, DO YOU THINK JOHN AND ROY WOULD FOLLOW YOU INTO BATTLE?
"IF YOU WERE THE MAN CALEB GREEN SAYS YOU ARE, YOU WOULDN'T HAVE INSPIRED A *TEAM.*
"YOU WOULDN'T HAVE INSPIRED *ME.*
"AND ALL OF US-- INCLUDING YOU-- WOULDN'T FIGHT EVERY SINGLE DAY TO MAKE THIS CITY A BETTER PLACE."

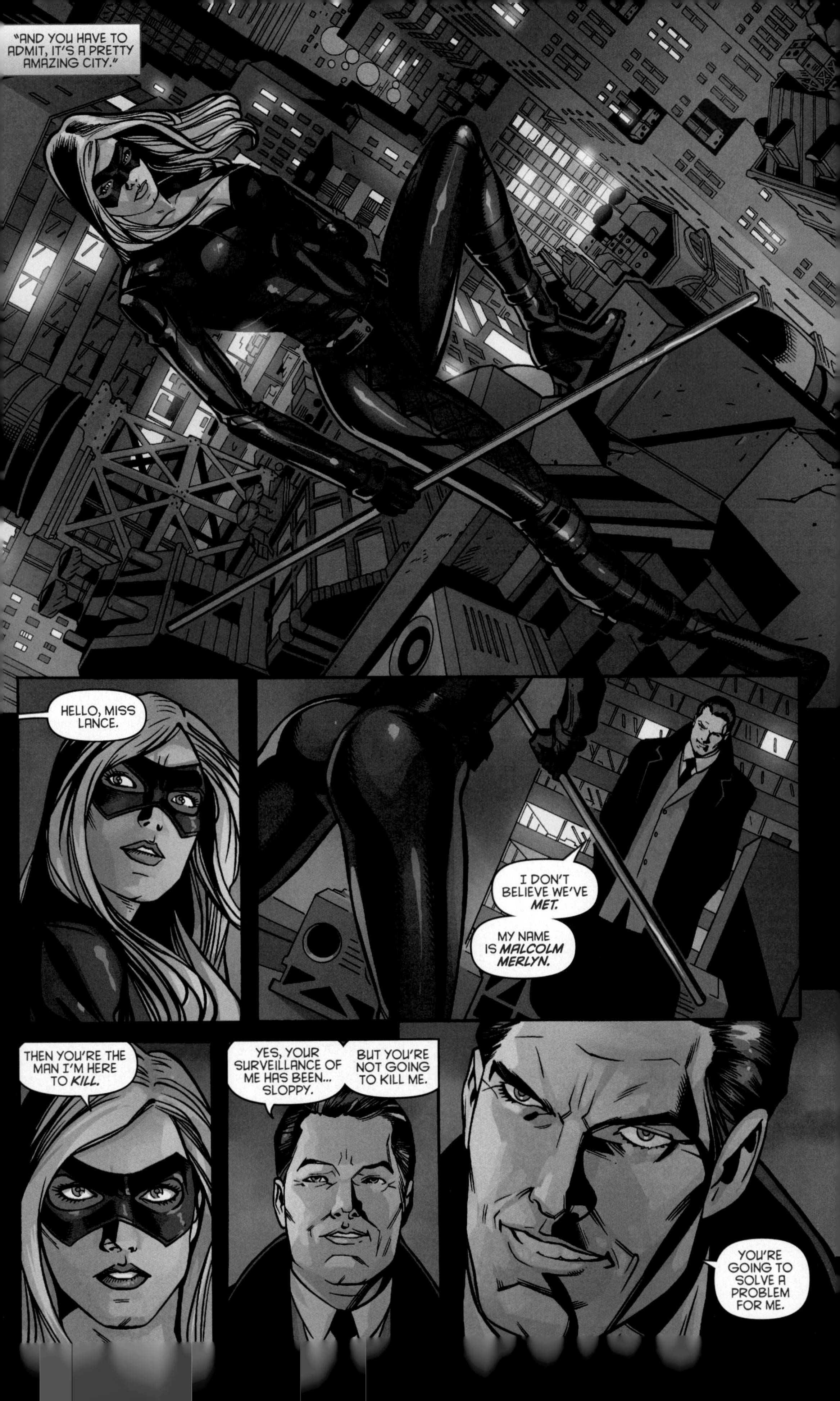
"AND YOU HAVE TO ADMIT, IT'S A PRETTY AMAZING CITY."
HELLO, MISS LANCE.
I DON'T BELIEVE WE'VE *MET.*
MY NAME IS *MALCOLM MERLYN.*
THEN YOU'RE THE MAN I'M HERE TO *KILL.*
YES, YOUR SURVEILLANCE OF ME HAS BEEN... SLOPPY.
BUT YOU'RE NOT GOING TO KILL ME.
YOU'RE GOING TO SOLVE A PROBLEM FOR ME.

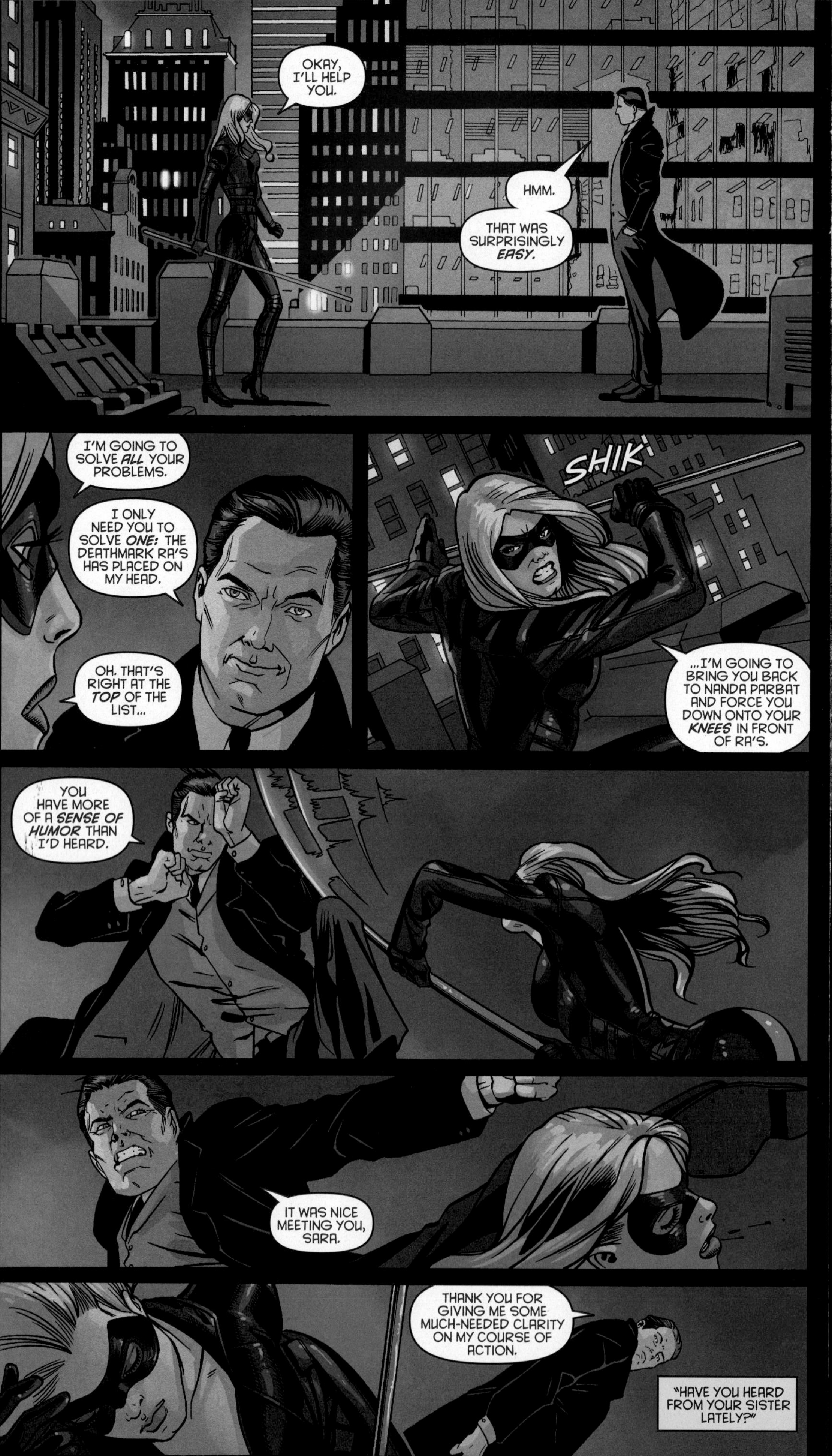
OKAY, I'LL HELP YOU.
HMM.
THAT WAS SURPRISINGLY *EASY.*
I'M GOING TO SOLVE *ALL* YOUR PROBLEMS.
I ONLY NEED YOU TO SOLVE *ONE:* THE DEATHMARK RA'S HAS PLACED ON MY HEAD.
OH. THAT'S RIGHT AT THE *TOP* OF THE LIST...
SHIK
...I'M GOING TO BRING YOU BACK TO NANDA PARBAT AND FORCE YOU DOWN ONTO YOUR *KNEES* IN FRONT OF RA'S.
YOU HAVE MORE OF A *SENSE OF HUMOR* THAN I'D HEARD.
IT WAS NICE MEETING YOU, SARA.
THANK YOU FOR GIVING ME SOME MUCH-NEEDED CLARITY ON MY COURSE OF ACTION.
"HAVE YOU HEARD FROM YOUR SISTER LATELY?"

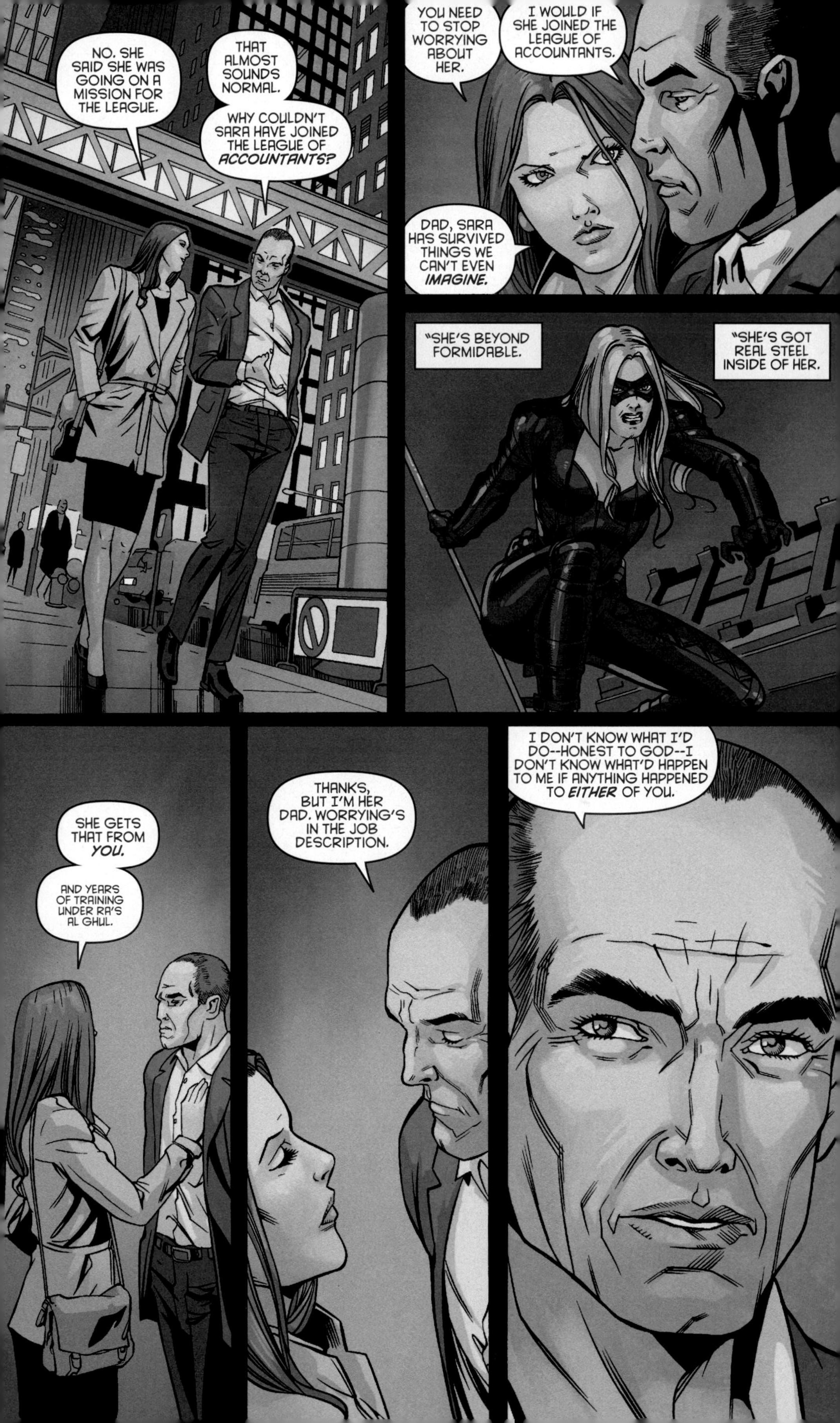
NO. SHE SAID SHE WAS GOING ON A MISSION FOR THE LEAGUE.
THAT ALMOST SOUNDS NORMAL.
WHY COULDN'T SARA HAVE JOINED THE LEAGUE OF ACCOUNTANTS?
YOU NEED TO STOP WORRYING ABOUT HER.
I WOULD IF SHE JOINED THE LEAGUE OF ACCOUNTANTS.
DAD, SARA HAS SURVIVED THINGS WE CAN'T EVEN IMAGINE.
"SHE'S BEYOND FORMIDABLE.
"SHE'S GOT REAL STEEL INSIDE OF HER.
SHE GETS THAT FROM YOU.
AND YEARS OF TRAINING UNDER RA'S AL GHUL.
THANKS, BUT I'M HER DAD. WORRYING'S IN THE JOB DESCRIPTION.
I DON'T KNOW WHAT I'D DO--HONEST TO GOD--I DON'T KNOW WHAT'D HAPPEN TO ME IF ANYTHING HAPPENED TO EITHER OF YOU.

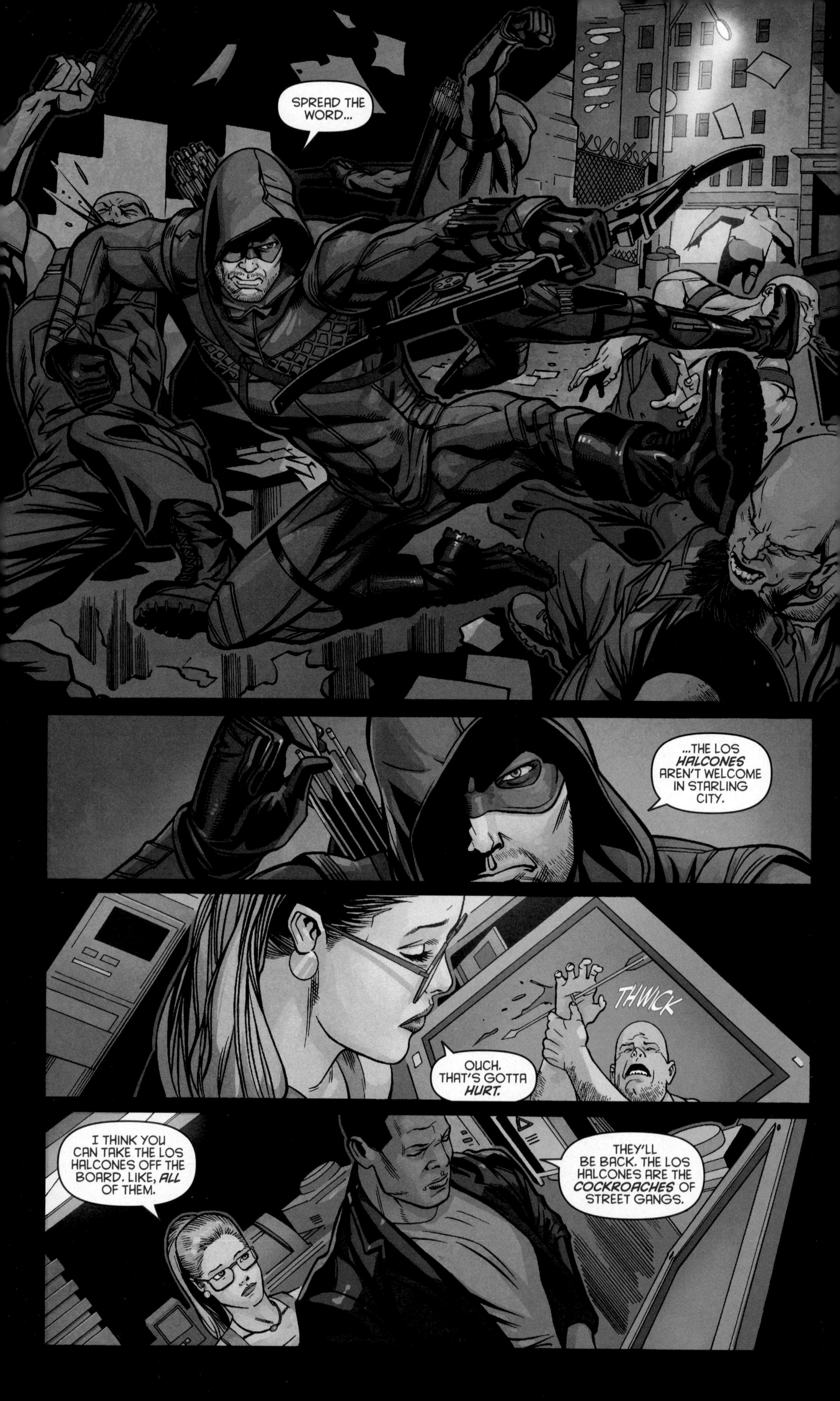
SPREAD THE WORD...
...THE LOS *HALCONES* AREN'T WELCOME IN STARLING CITY.
THWICK
OUCH. THAT'S GOTTA *HURT.*
I THINK YOU CAN TAKE THE LOS HALCONES OFF THE BOARD. LIKE, *ALL* OF THEM.
THEY'LL BE BACK. THE LOS HALCONES ARE THE *COCKROACHES* OF STREET GANGS.

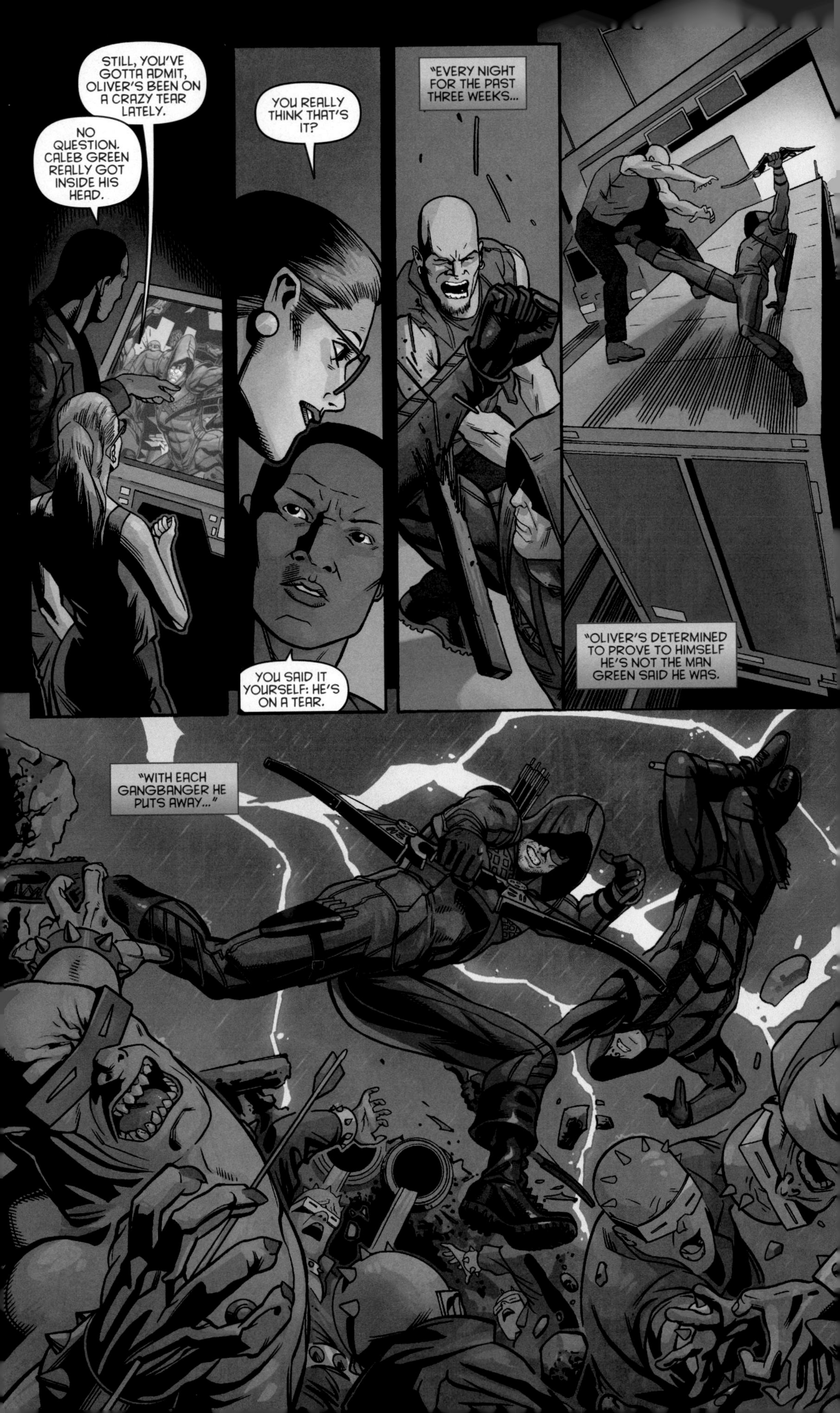
STILL, YOU'VE GOTTA ADMIT, OLIVER'S BEEN ON A CRAZY TEAR LATELY.
NO QUESTION. CALEB GREEN REALLY GOT INSIDE HIS HEAD.
YOU REALLY THINK THAT'S IT?
YOU SAID IT YOURSELF: HE'S ON A TEAR.
"EVERY NIGHT FOR THE PAST THREE WEEKS...
"OLIVER'S DETERMINED TO PROVE TO HIMSELF HE'S NOT THE MAN GREEN SAID HE WAS.
"WITH EACH GANGBANGER HE PUTS AWAY..."

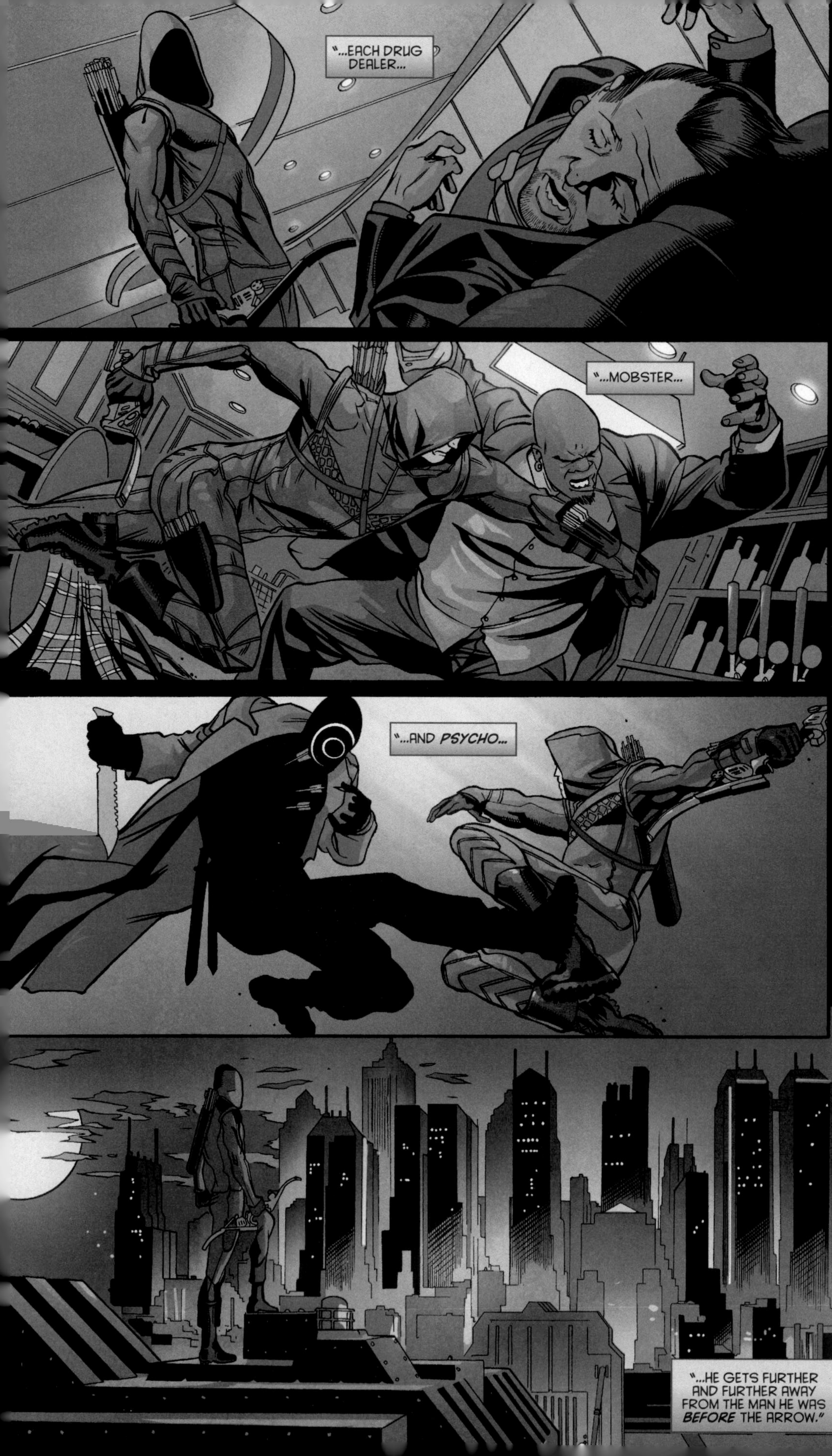
"...EACH DRUG DEALER...
"...MOBSTER...
"...AND *PSYCHO*...
"...HE GETS FURTHER AND FURTHER AWAY FROM THE MAN HE WAS *BEFORE* THE ARROW."

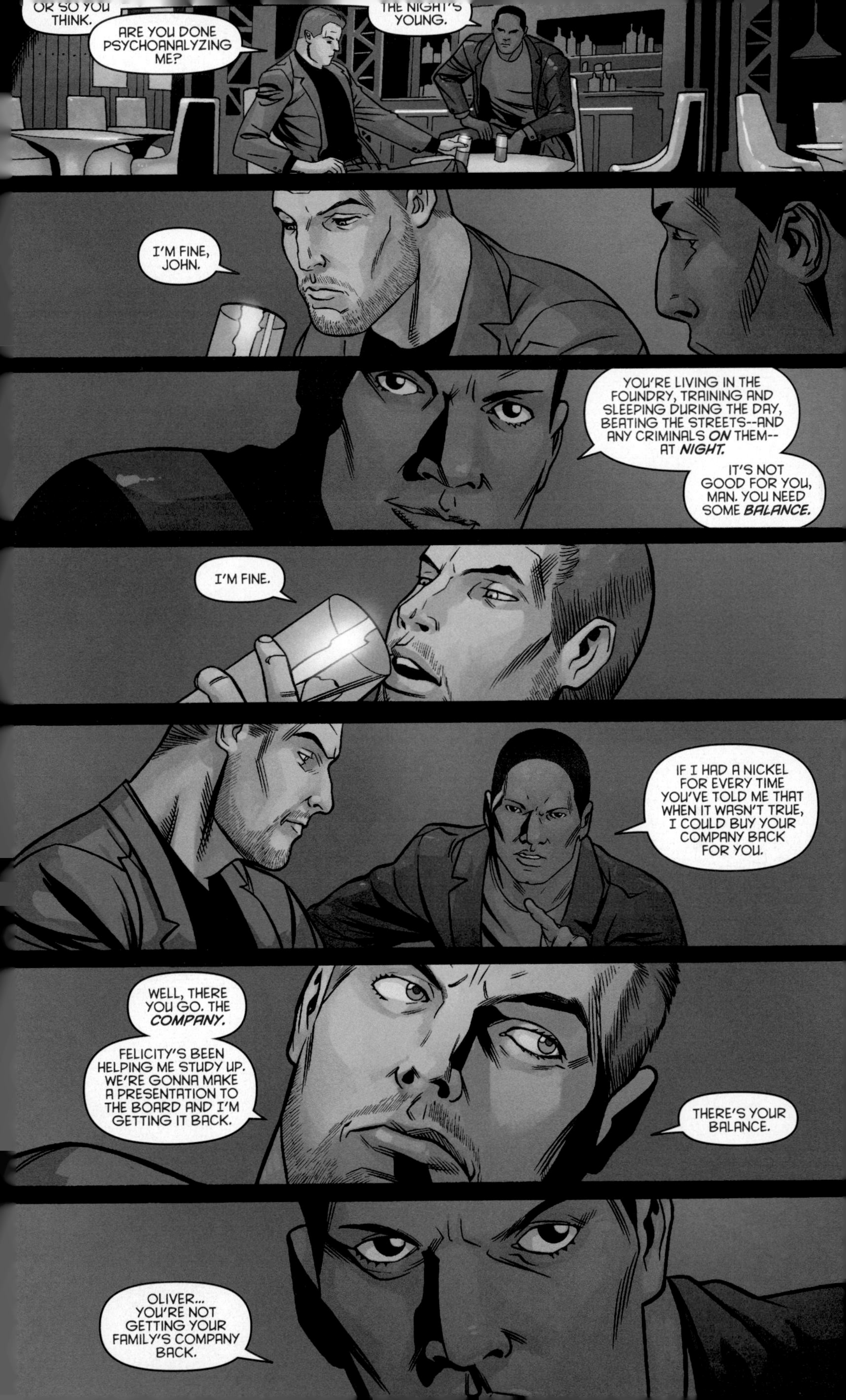
OR SO YOU THINK.
ARE YOU DONE PSYCHOANALYZING ME?
THE NIGHT'S YOUNG.
I'M FINE, JOHN.
YOU'RE LIVING IN THE FOUNDRY, TRAINING AND SLEEPING DURING THE DAY, BEATING THE STREETS--AND ANY CRIMINALS *ON* THEM--AT *NIGHT.*
IT'S NOT GOOD FOR YOU, MAN. YOU NEED SOME ***BALANCE.***
I'M FINE.
IF I HAD A NICKEL FOR EVERY TIME YOU'VE TOLD ME THAT WHEN IT WASN'T TRUE, I COULD BUY YOUR COMPANY BACK FOR YOU.
WELL, THERE YOU GO. THE ***COMPANY.***
FELICITY'S BEEN HELPING ME STUDY UP. WE'RE GONNA MAKE A PRESENTATION TO THE BOARD AND I'M GETTING IT BACK.
THERE'S YOUR BALANCE.
OLIVER... YOU'RE NOT GETTING YOUR FAMILY'S COMPANY BACK.

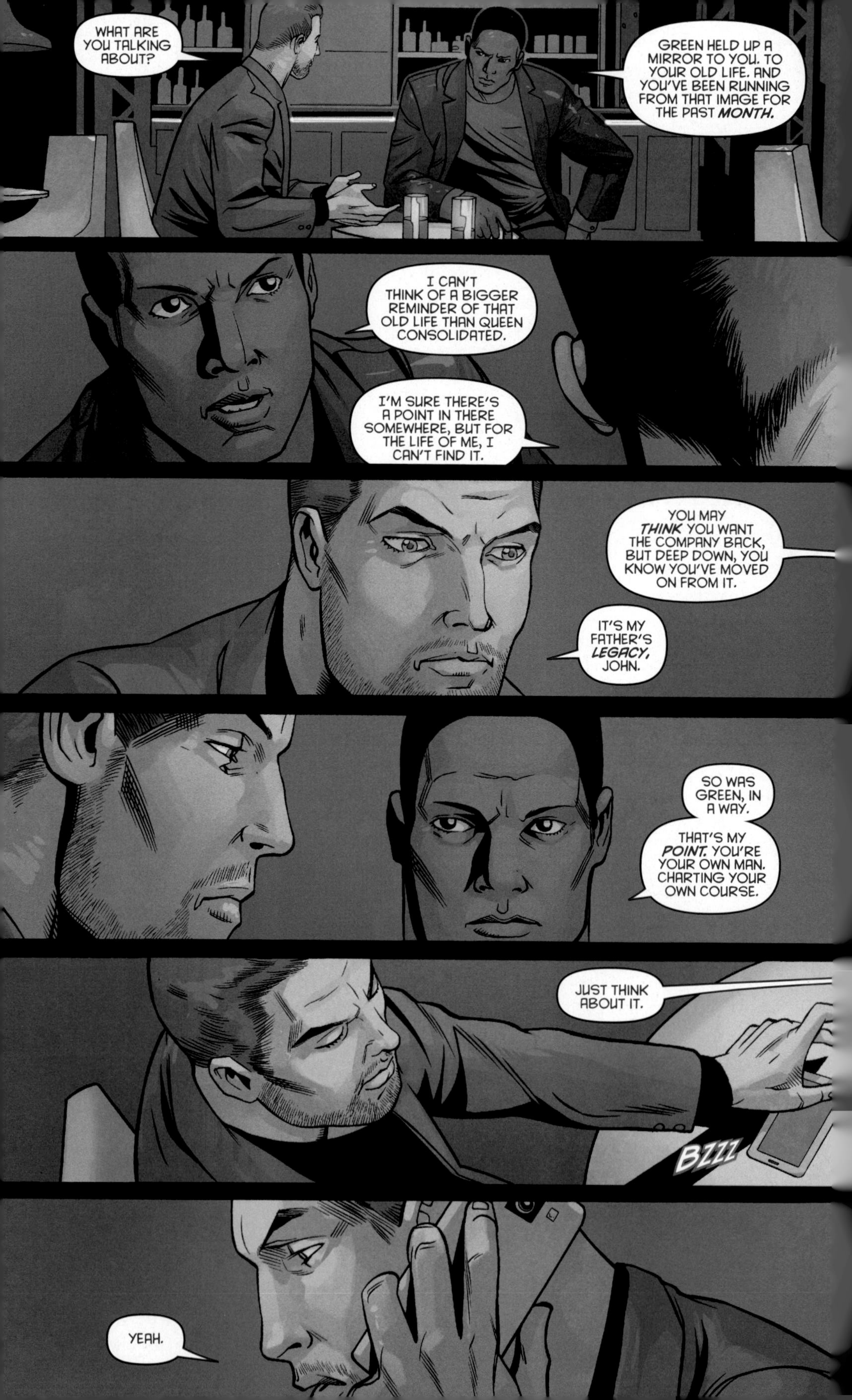
WHAT ARE YOU TALKING ABOUT?
GREEN HELD UP A MIRROR TO YOU. TO YOUR OLD LIFE. AND YOU'VE BEEN RUNNING FROM THAT IMAGE FOR THE PAST MONTH.
I CAN'T THINK OF A BIGGER REMINDER OF THAT OLD LIFE THAN QUEEN CONSOLIDATED.
I'M SURE THERE'S A POINT IN THERE SOMEWHERE, BUT FOR THE LIFE OF ME, I CAN'T FIND IT.
YOU MAY THINK YOU WANT THE COMPANY BACK, BUT DEEP DOWN, YOU KNOW YOU'VE MOVED ON FROM IT.
IT'S MY FATHER'S LEGACY, JOHN.
SO WAS GREEN, IN A WAY.
THAT'S MY POINT. YOU'RE YOUR OWN MAN. CHARTING YOUR OWN COURSE.
JUST THINK ABOUT IT.
BZZZ
YEAH.

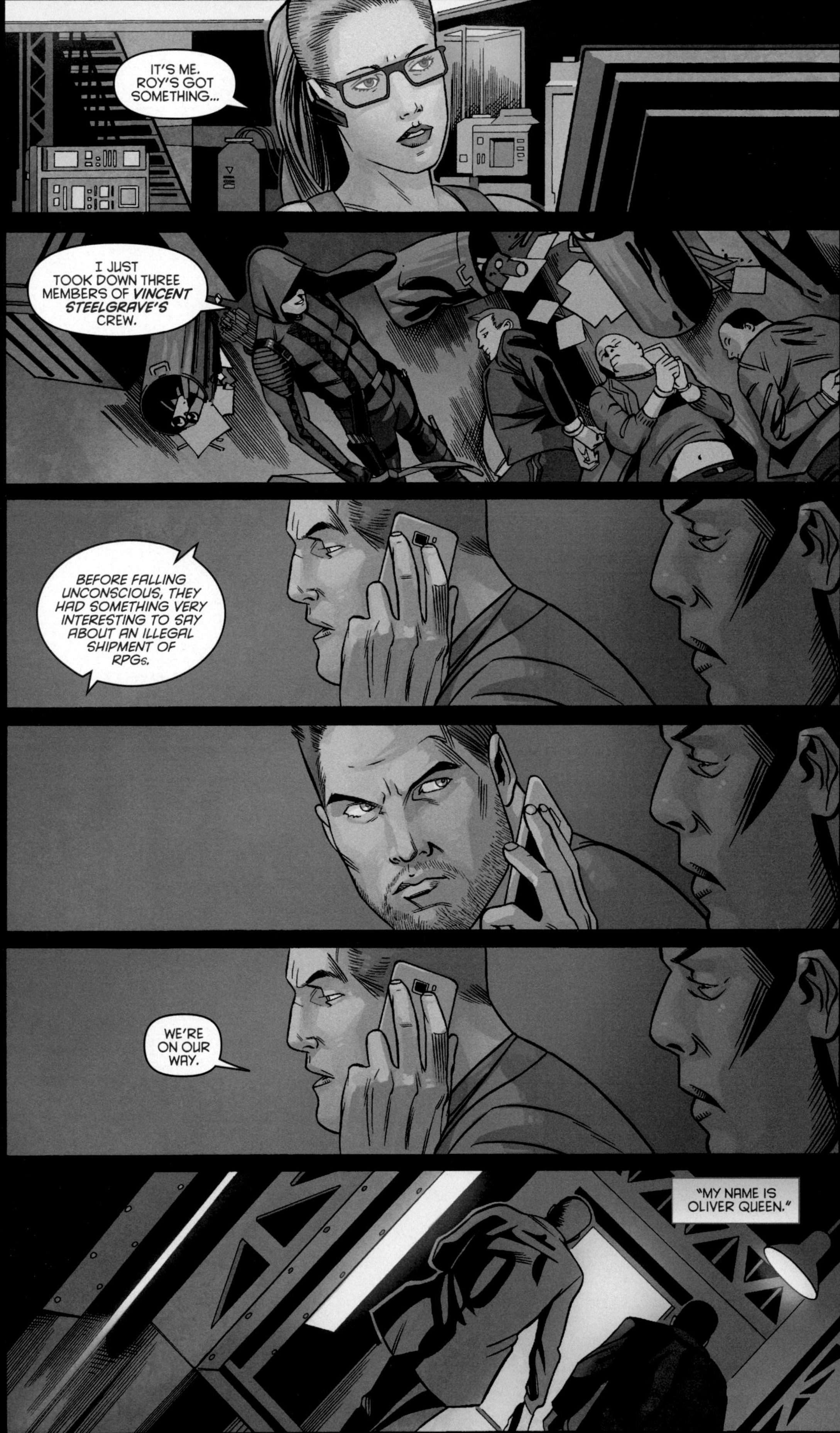
IT'S ME. ROY'S GOT SOMETHING...
I JUST TOOK DOWN THREE MEMBERS OF *VINCENT STEELGRAVE'S* CREW.
BEFORE FALLING UNCONSCIOUS, THEY HAD SOMETHING VERY INTERESTING TO SAY ABOUT AN ILLEGAL SHIPMENT OF RPGs.
WE'RE ON OUR WAY.
"MY NAME IS OLIVER QUEEN."

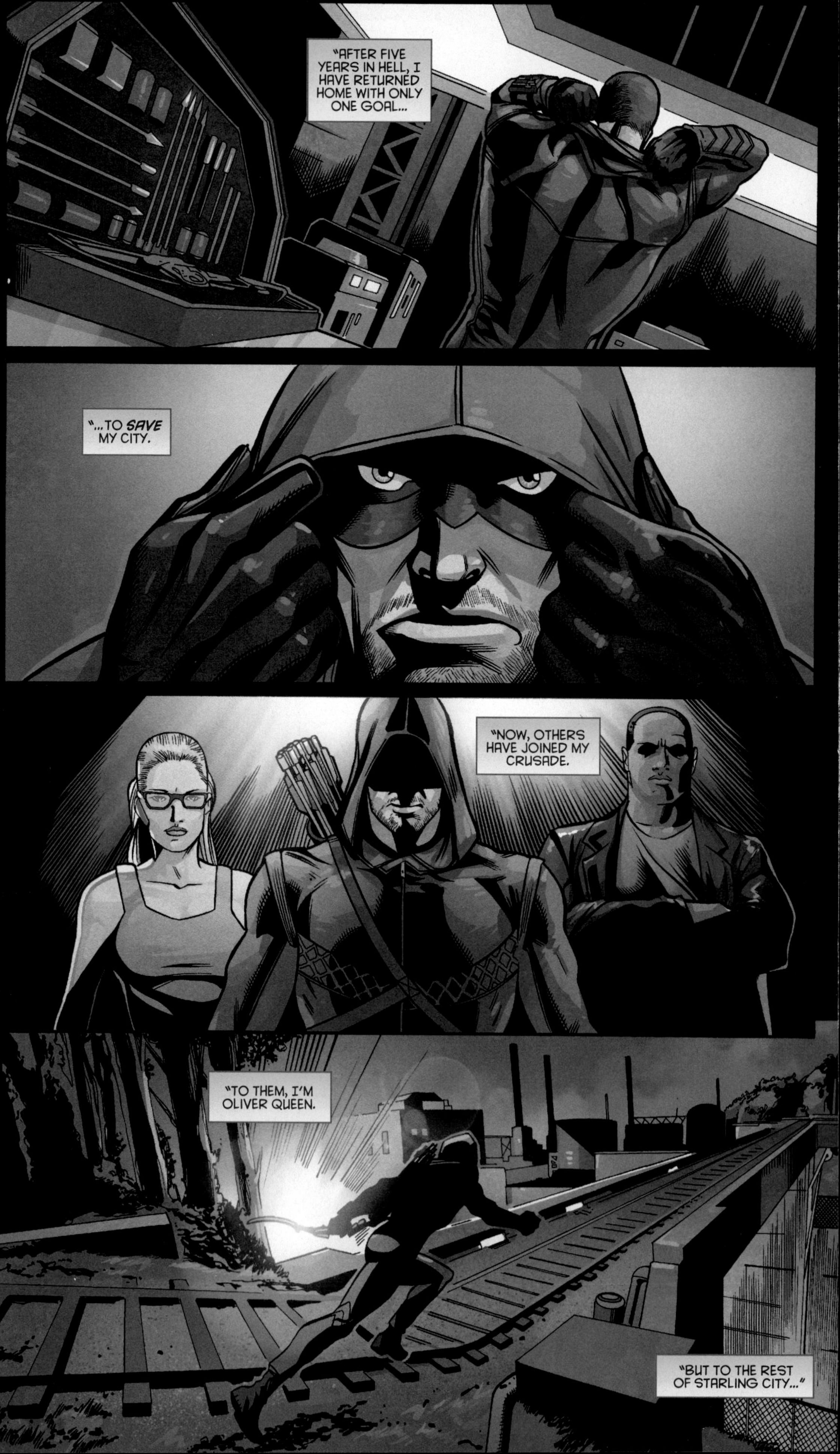
"AFTER FIVE YEARS IN HELL, I HAVE RETURNED HOME WITH ONLY ONE GOAL...
"...TO *SAVE* MY CITY.
"NOW, OTHERS HAVE JOINED MY CRUSADE.
"TO THEM, I'M OLIVER QUEEN.
"BUT TO THE REST OF STARLING CITY..."

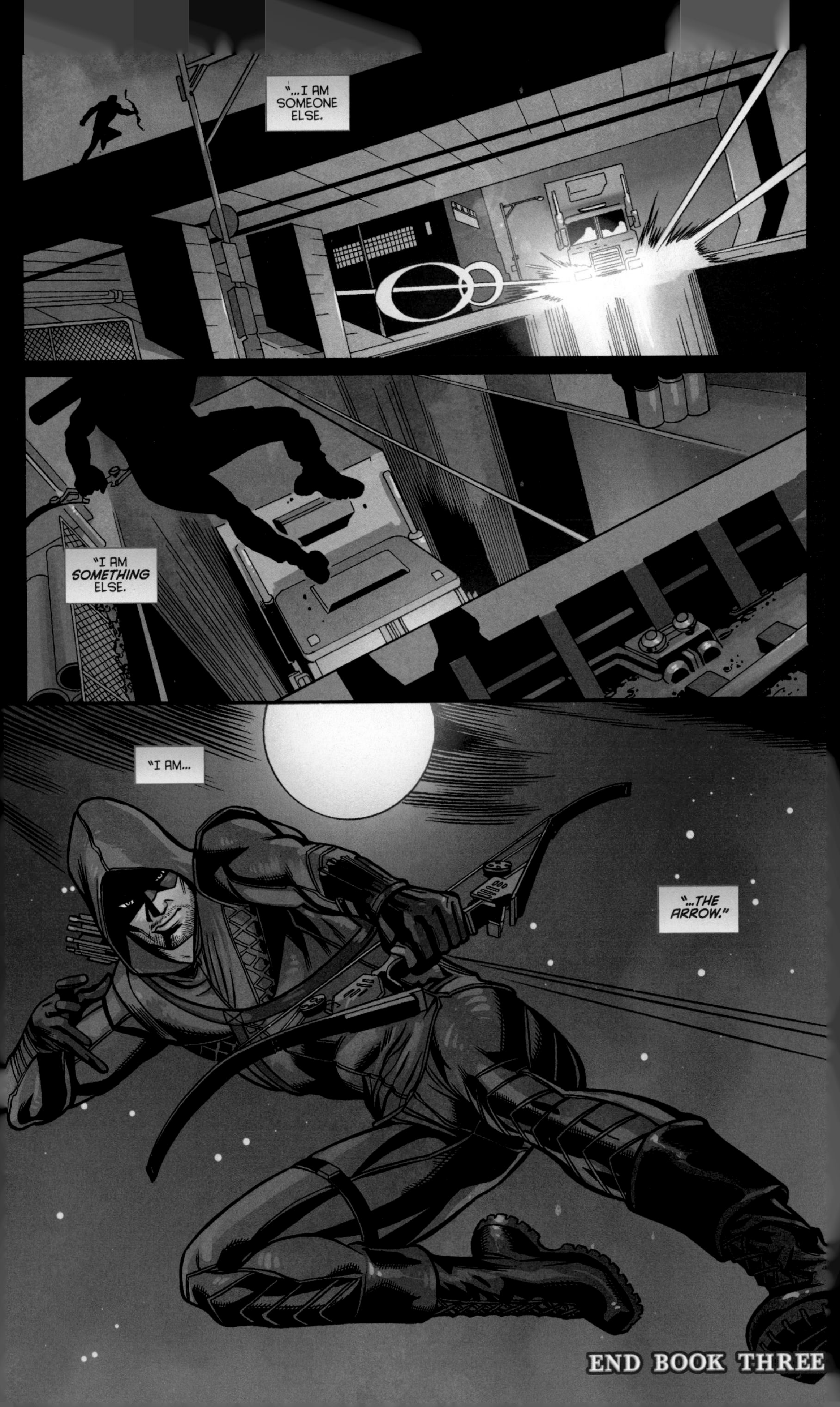
"...I AM SOMEONE ELSE.
"I AM *SOMETHING* ELSE.
"I AM...
"...THE ARROW."
END BOOK THREE

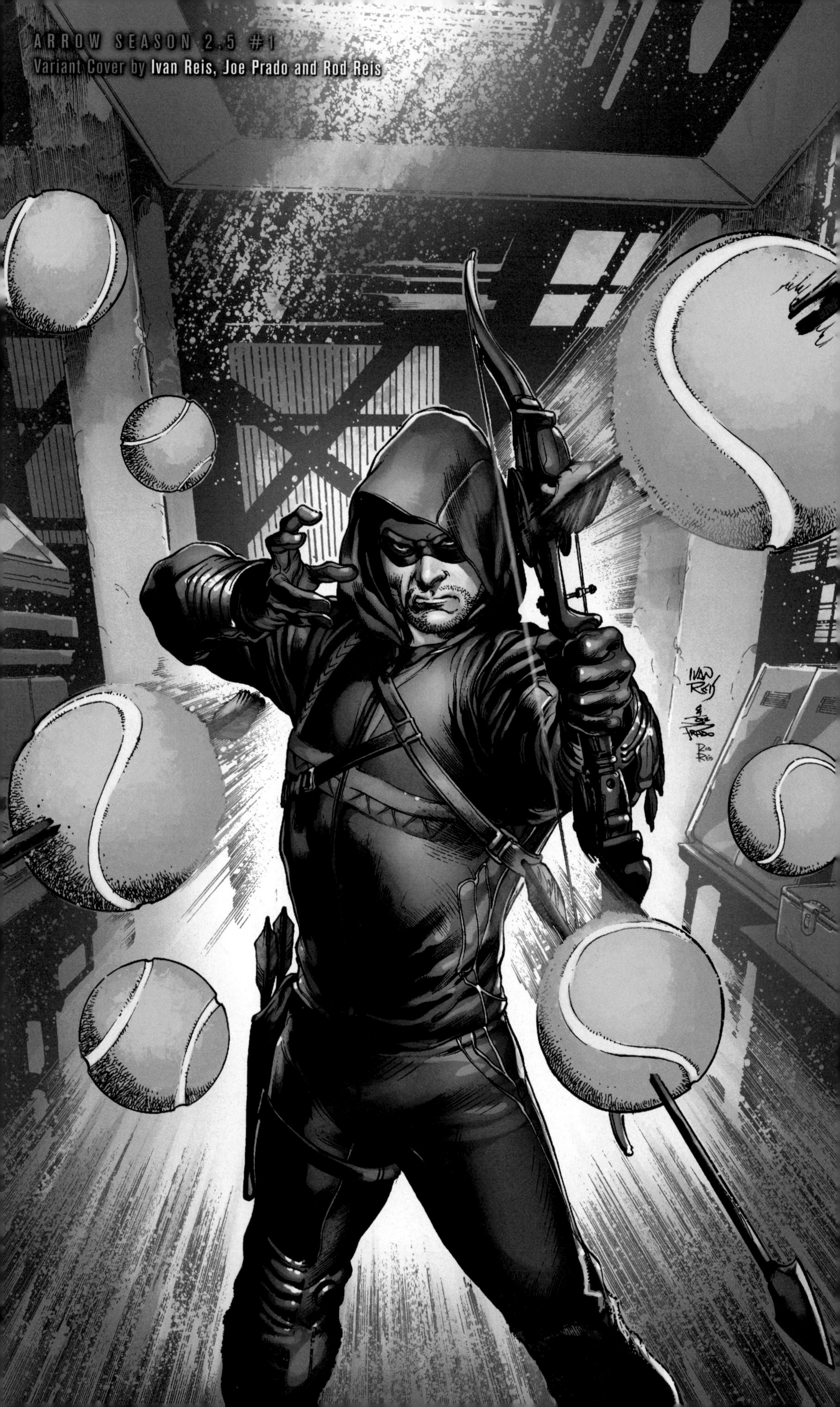

ARROW SEASON 2.5 #1
Variant Cover by Ivan Reis, Joe Prado and Rod Reis

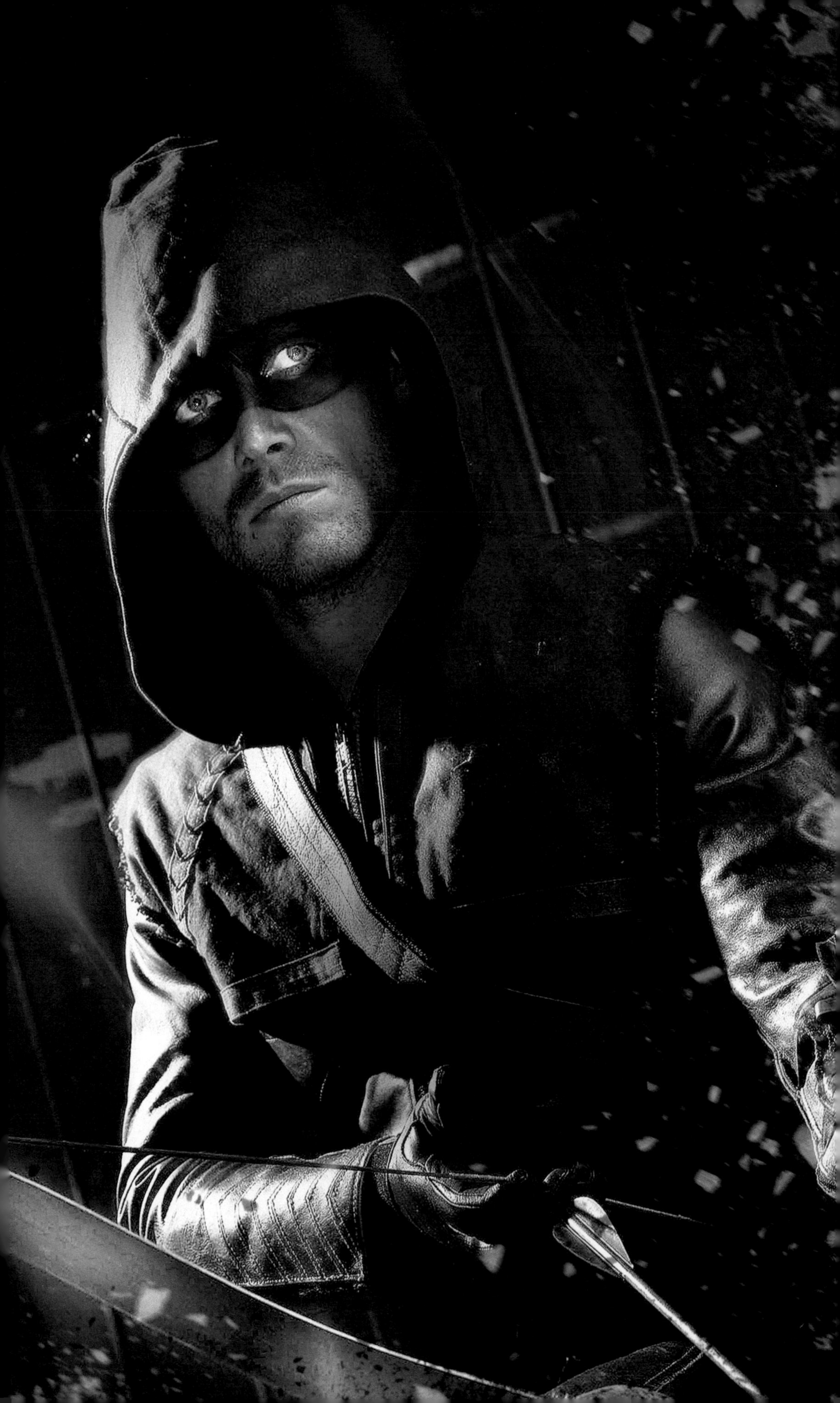

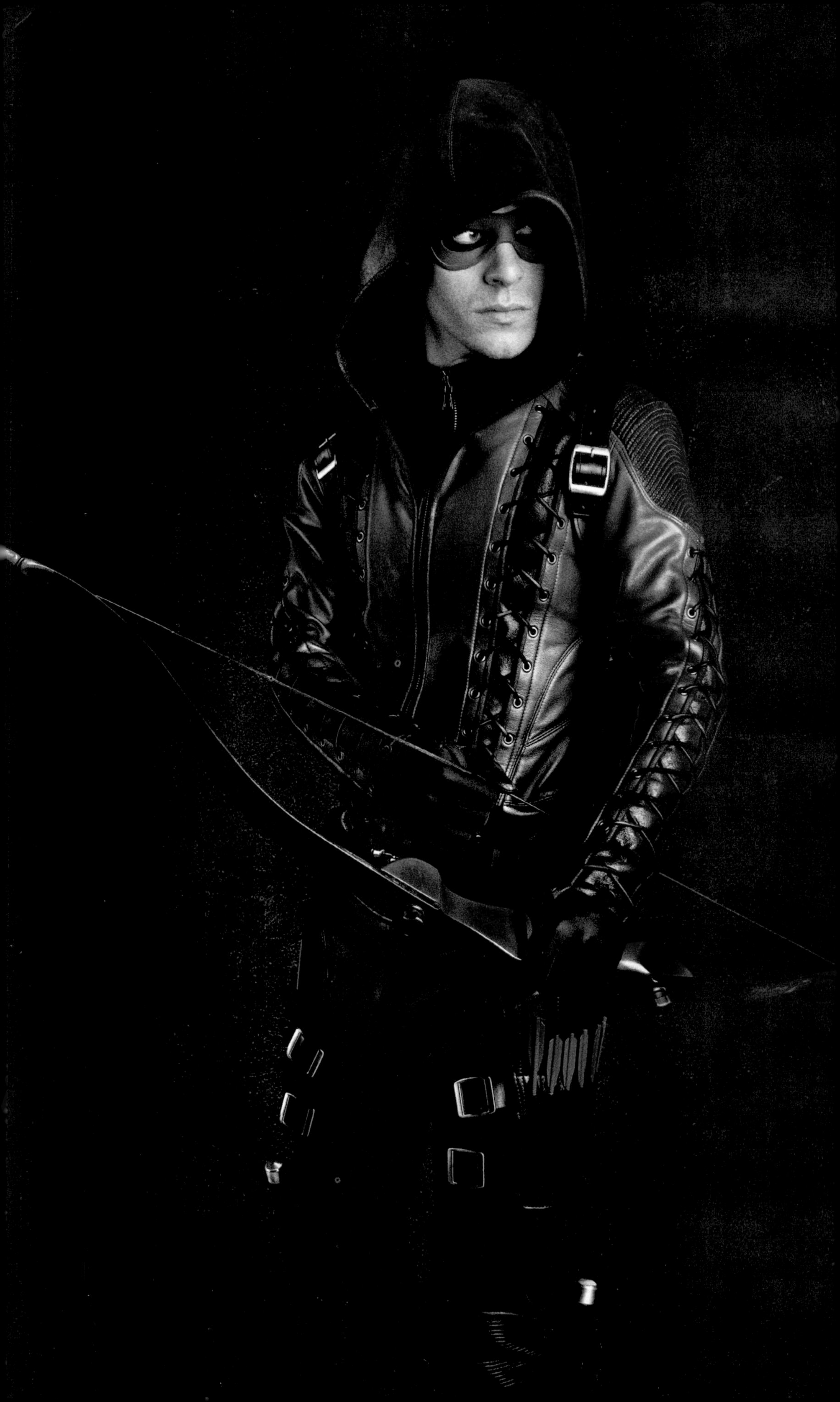

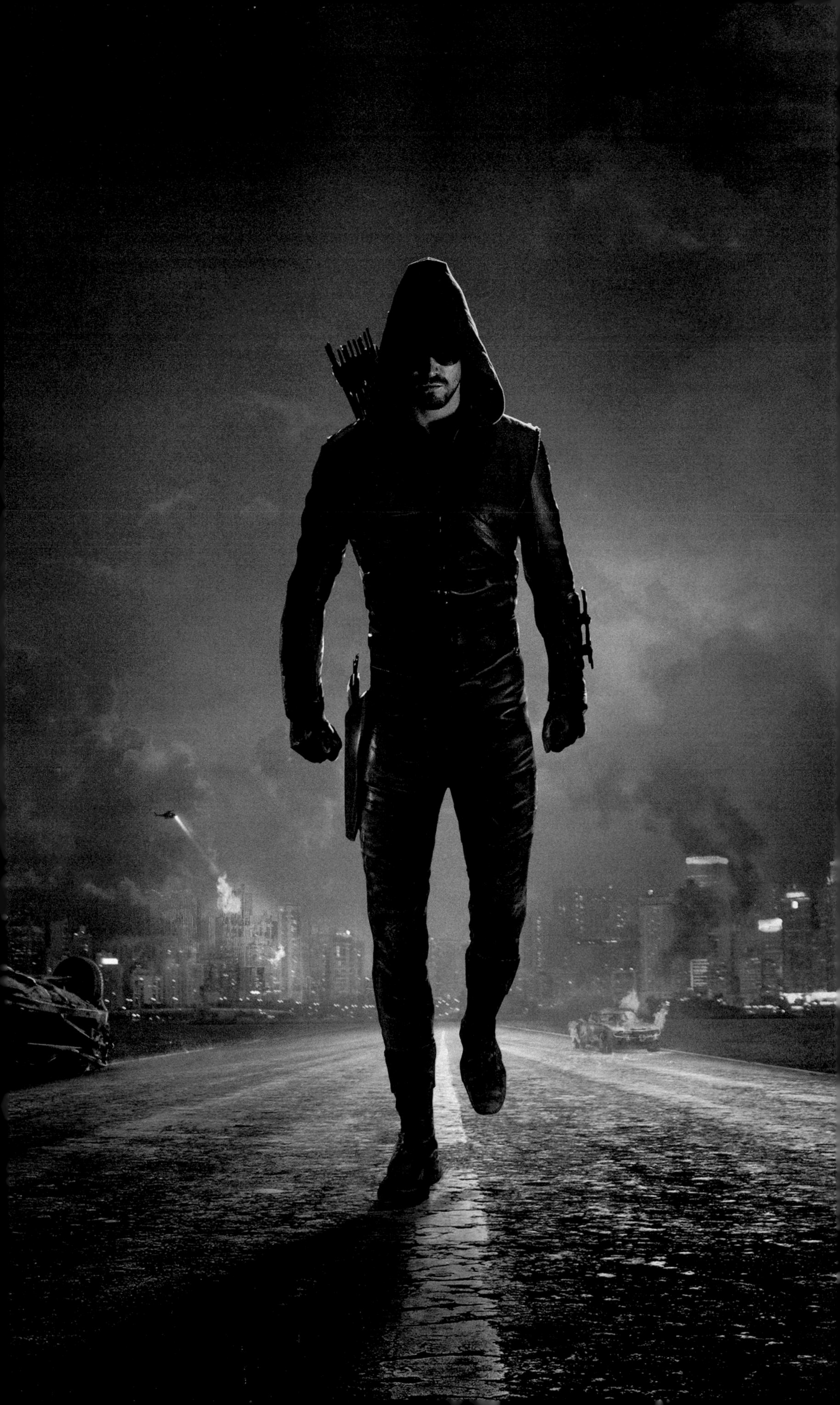

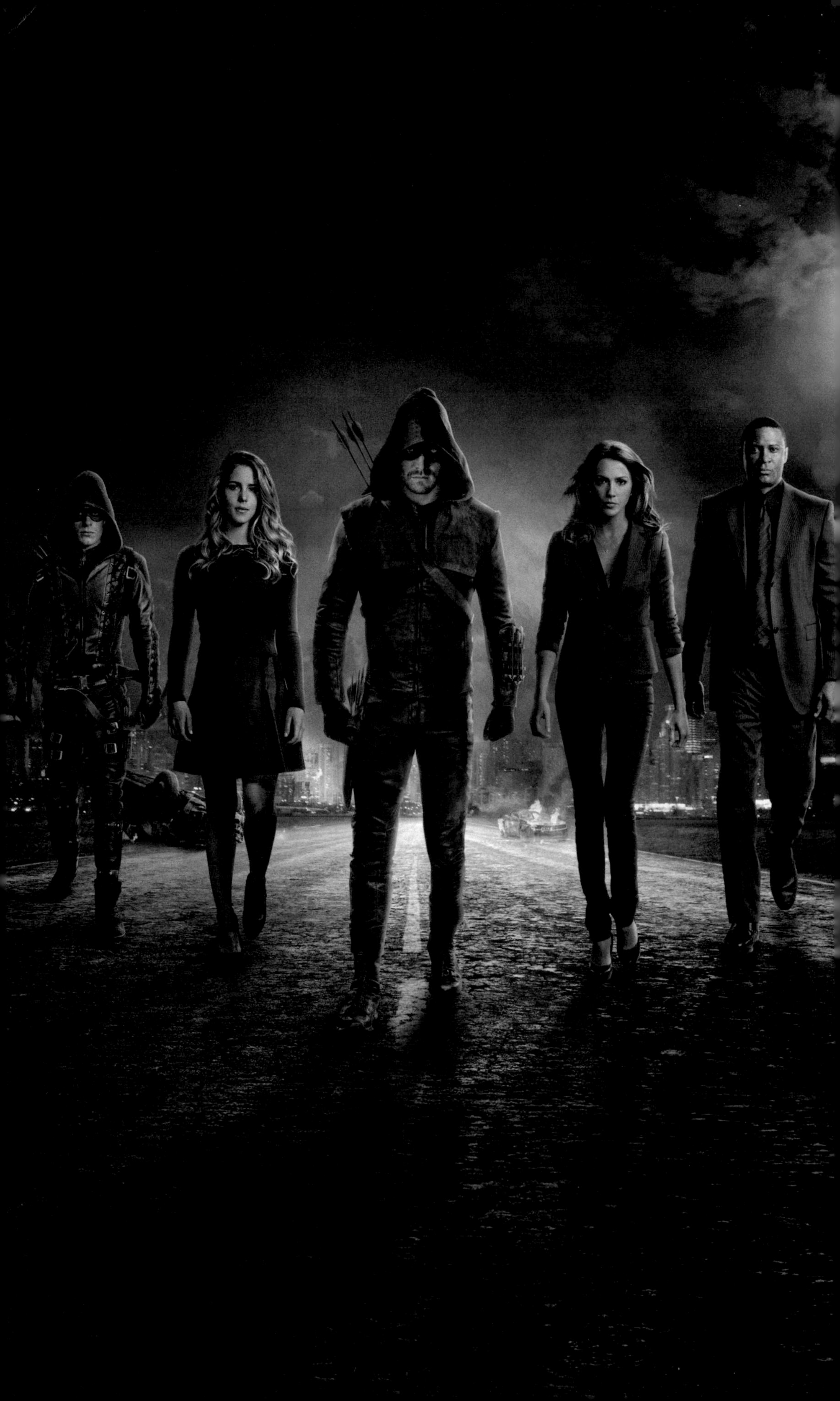

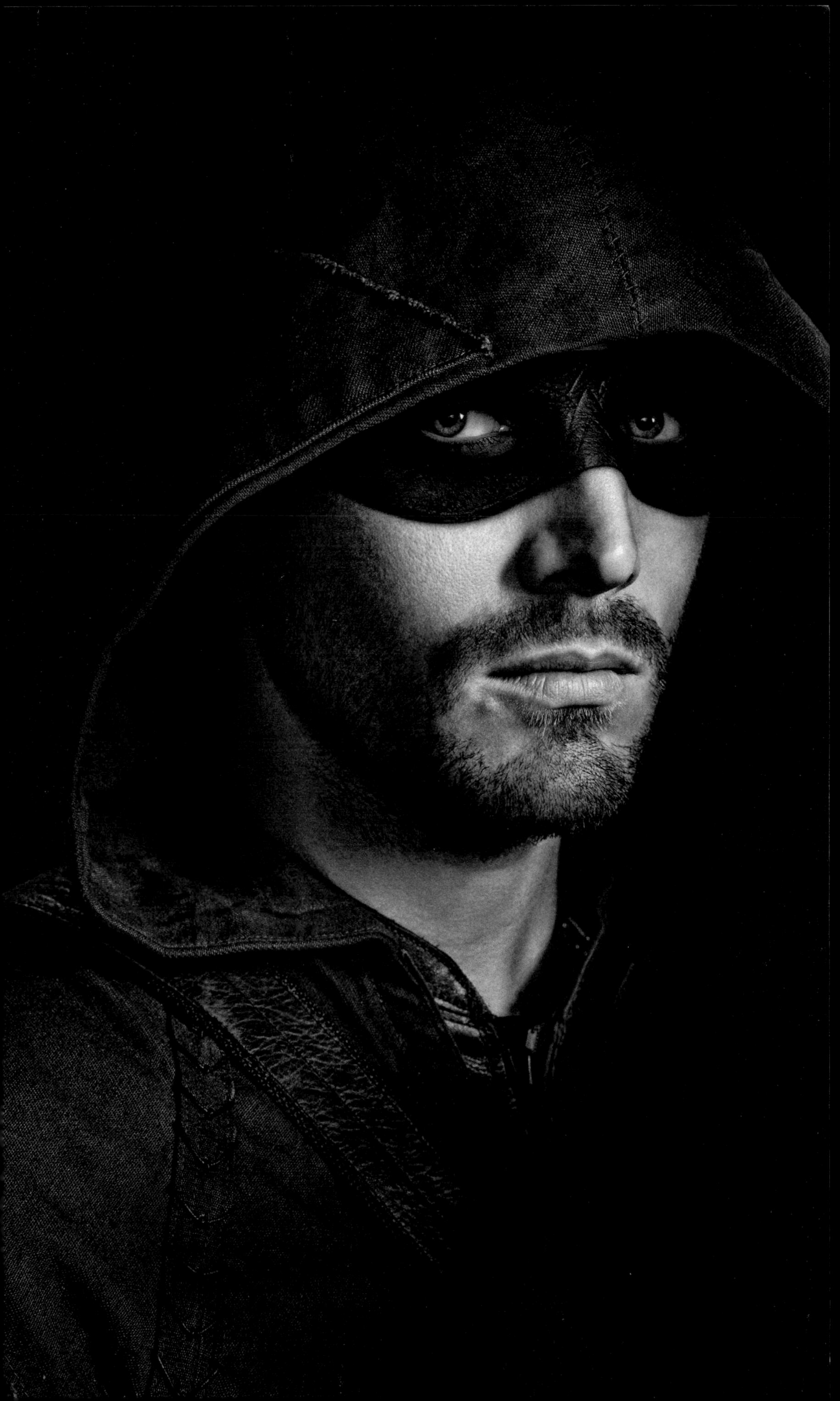

ARROW SEASON 2.5 #9
Cover by **Jason Badower & Annette Kwok**

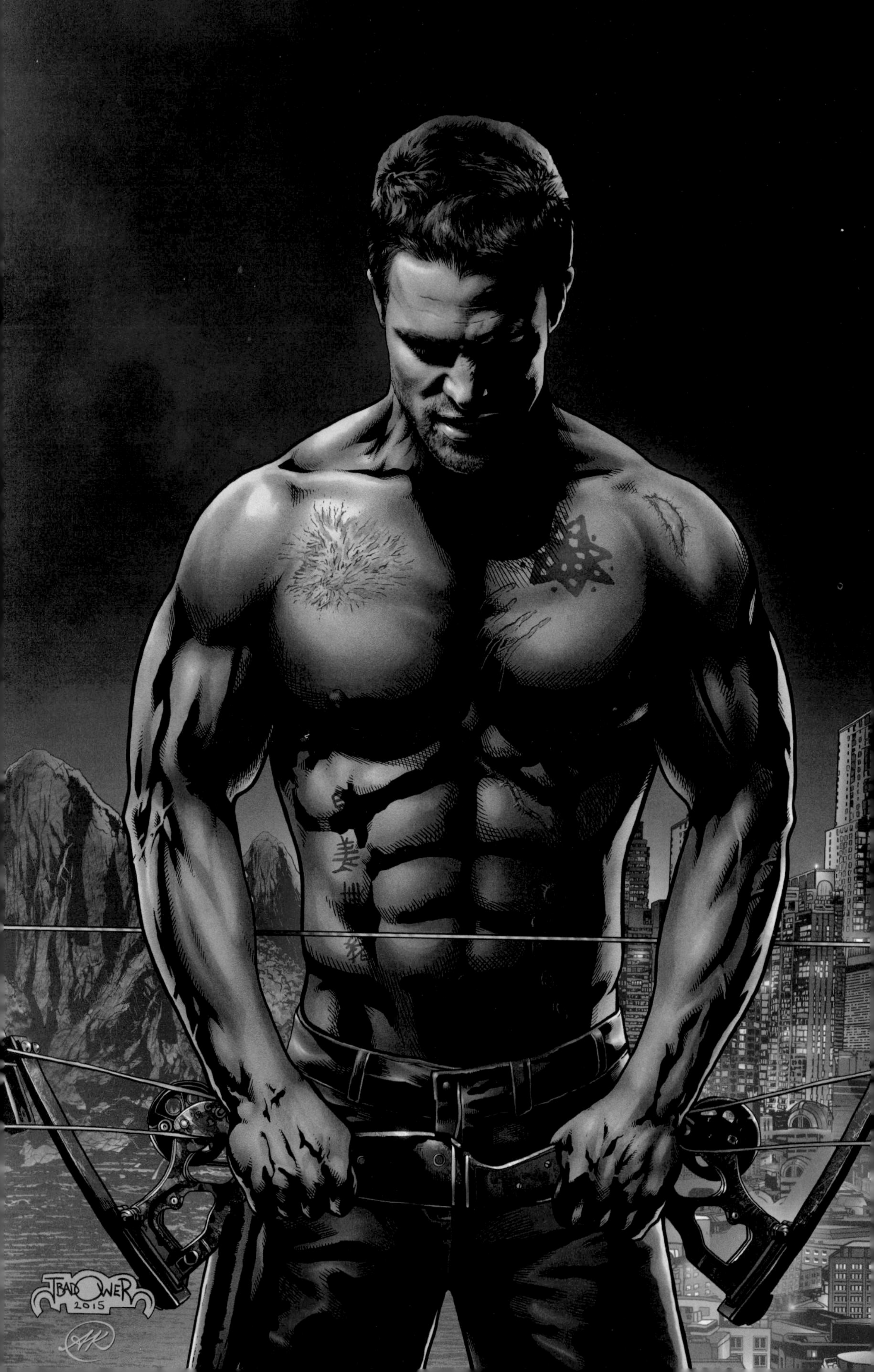

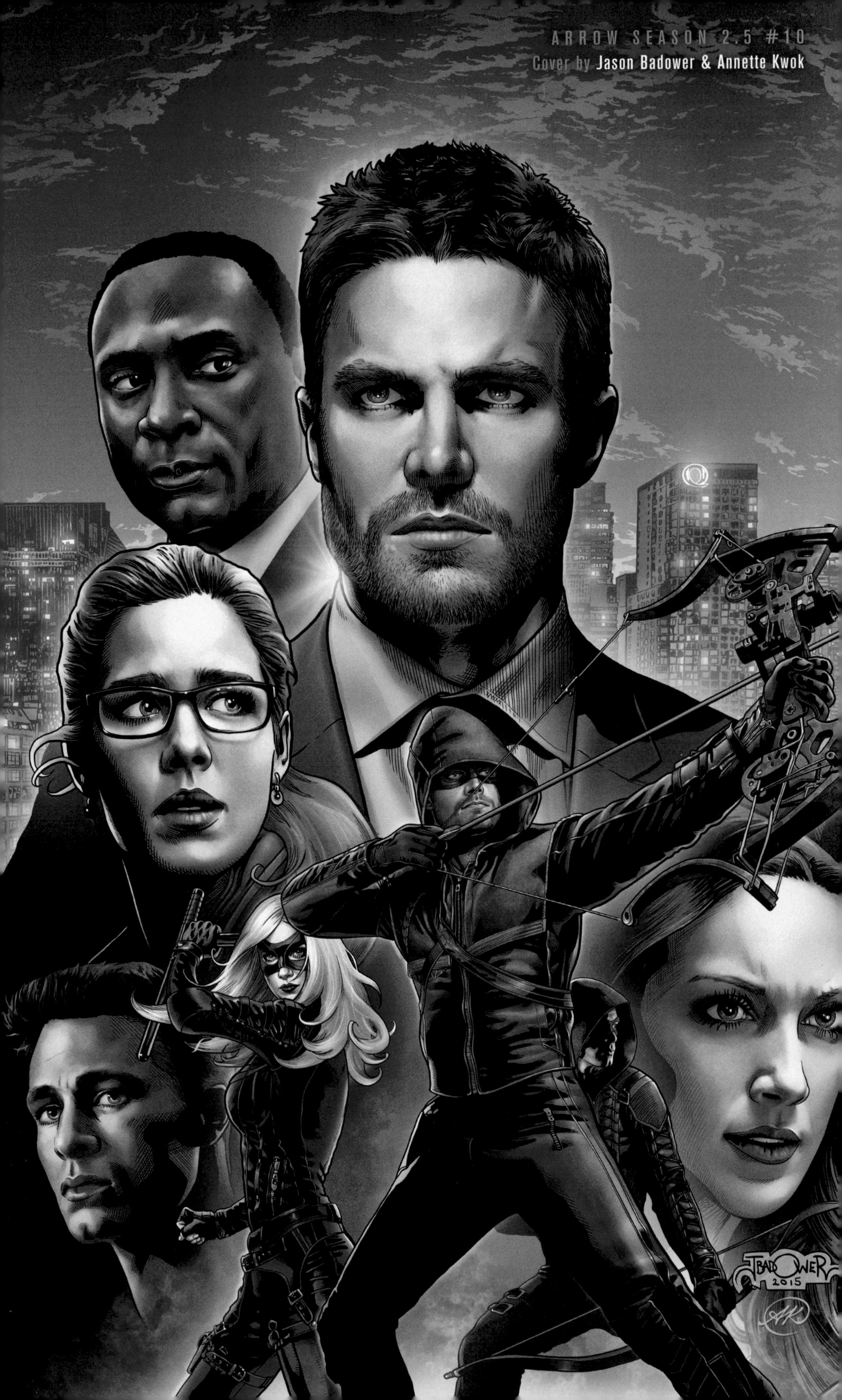
JBADOWER
2015

ARROW SEASON 2.5 #10
Cover by Jason Badower & Annette Kwok

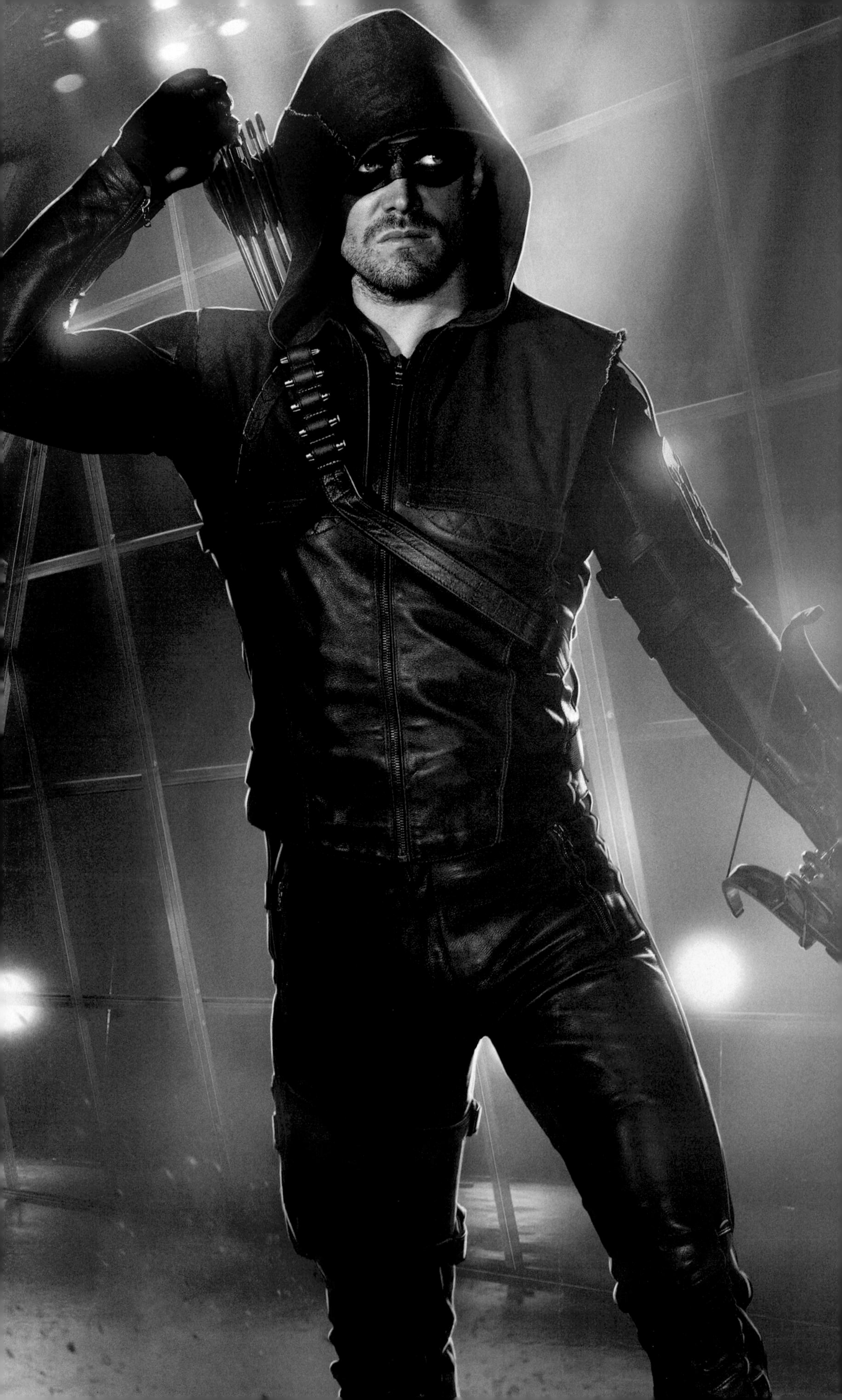

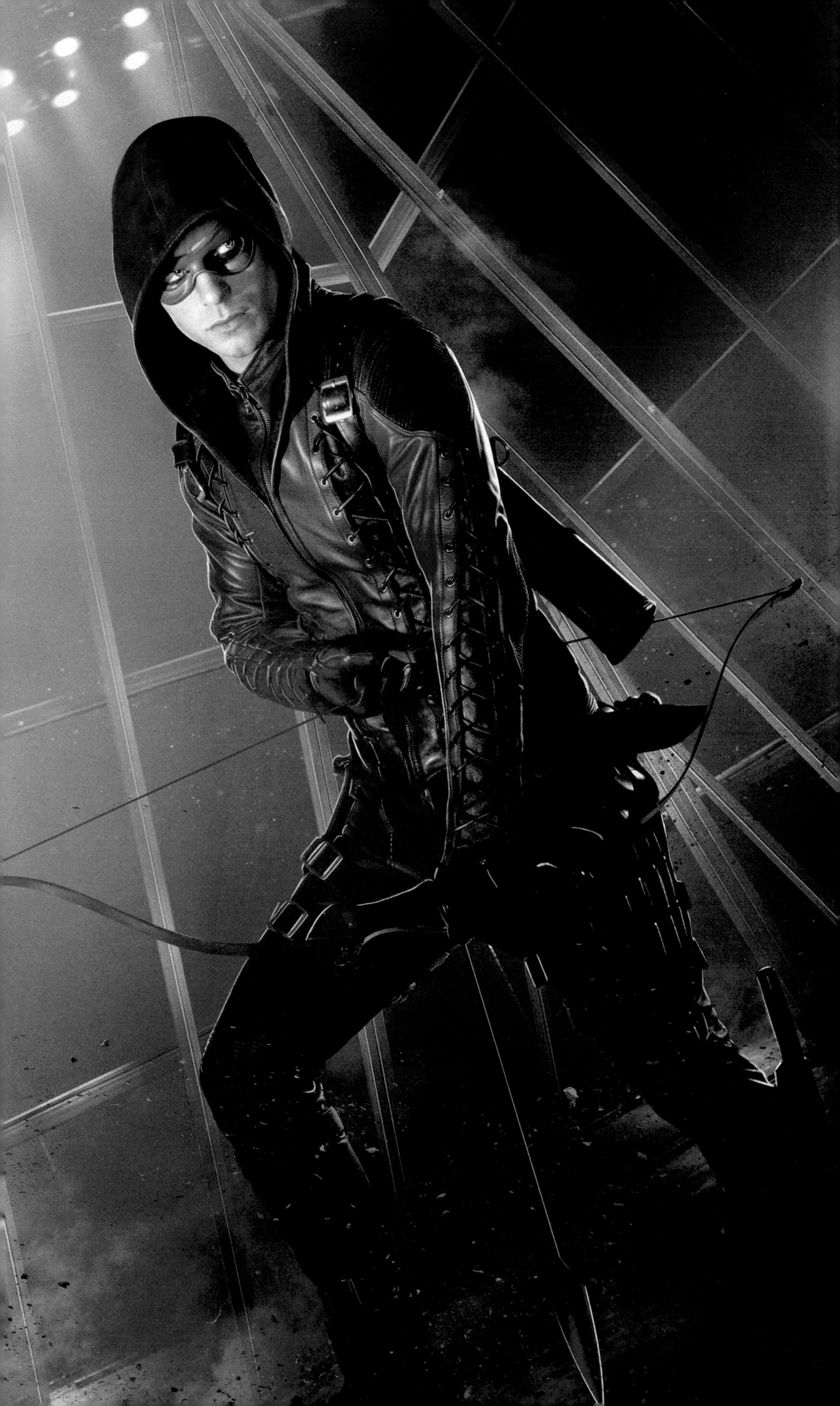

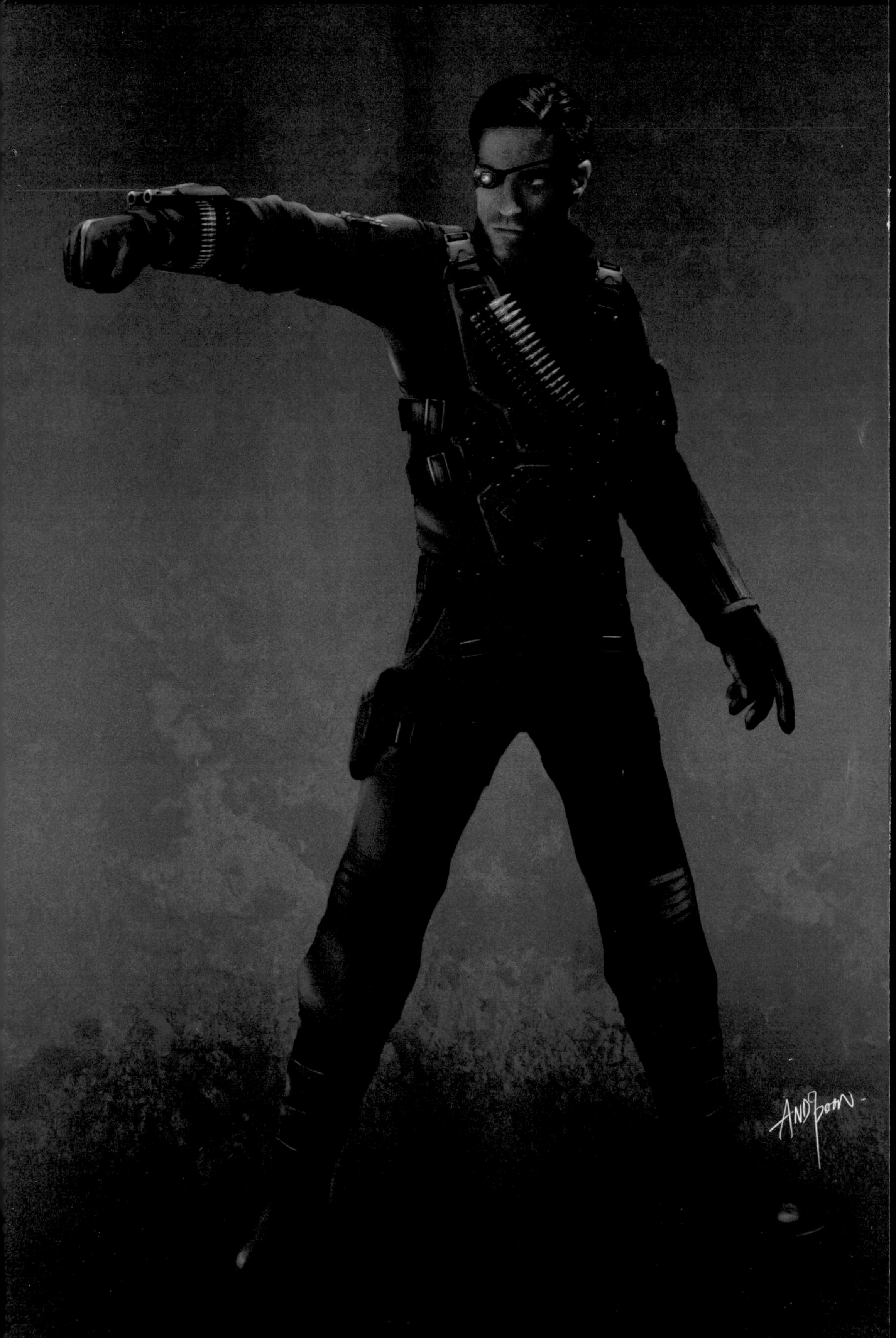

ARROW - season 1

Deadshot 2.0

costume designer - Maya Mani
concept illustration - Andy Poon